Courting Social Justice

JUDICIAL ENFORCEMENT OF SOCIAL AND ECONOMIC RIGHTS IN THE DEVELOPING WORLD

Edited by

Varun Gau

The World Ban

GW00599266

Daniel M. Bri

University of Texas at Austin

CAMBRIDGE
UNIVERSITY PRESS

CAMBRIDGE UNIVERSITY PRESS
Cambridge, New York, Melbourne, Madrid, Cape Town, Singapore,
São Paulo, Delhi, Dubai, Tokyo

Cambridge University Press
32 Avenue of the Americas, New York, NY 10013-2473, USA

www.cambridge.org
Information on this title: www.cambridge.org/9780521145169

First published 2008
Reprinted 2009
First paperback edition 2010

A catalog record for this publication is available from the British Library.

Library of Congress Cataloging in Publication Data

Courting social justice : judicial enforcement of social and economic rights in the
developing world / edited by Varun Gauri, Daniel M. Brinks.
    p.   cm.
Includes bibliographical references and index.
ISBN 978-0-521-87376-5 (hardback)
1. Human rights – Developing countries. 2. Social rights – Developing countries.
3. Law and economic development. 4. Social legislation – Developing countries.
5. Developing countries – Economic policy. I. Gauri, Varun, 1966– II. Brinks,
Daniel M., 1961– III. Title.

K3240.C68 2008
341.4'8 – dc22   2008014565

ISBN   978-0-521-87376-5 Hardback
ISBN   978-0-521-14516-9 Paperback

Contents

Foreword

JUSTICE RICHARD J. GOLDSTONE

I believe it is important for governments and international institutions, including the World Bank, to encourage research into social and economic rights in developing countries, and I welcome this excellent work on the topic. The enforcement of these rights represents a new and controversial area of judicial intervention. Social and economic rights fall into that category of rights, often referred to as *second-generation rights*, that also includes cultural and developmental rights. They are distinguished from *first-generation rights*, which consist of political and civil rights such as equality and the freedom of speech and of assembly.

Second-generation rights were recognized in the 1948 Universal Declaration of Human Rights and given effect in the International Covenant on Economic, Social, and Cultural Rights, which became effective in 1976. However, until comparatively recently, these rights were not taken seriously and were subordinated to civil and political rights. Few states took steps to entrench such rights constitutionally or to adopt legislation or administrative provisions to make such rights enforceable.

A common objection to giving courts jurisdiction over second-generation rights is that judges are ill equipped to adjudicate on the manner in which the legislative and executive branches of government determine how the national budget should be allocated. In countries like the United States of America, there is an additional objection – traditionally only negative rights are enforceable and the courts are regarded as not having jurisdiction to adjudicate positive rights. The latter, so it is argued, should be left exclusively to the domain of the legislative branch of government. It is pointed out that these rights are polycentric and, for example, if more money is spent on defense and education, there will be less to allocate for health and social benefits. How can judges become involved in second-guessing decisions on these issues? They have neither the information nor the training to make such decisions.

On the other side, and especially with regard to new democracies in developing societies, it is persuasively argued that the majority of citizens are not primarily concerned with first-generation rights. They are less interested in the right to freedom of speech or to freedom of assembly and more concerned with having sufficient food to eat, a roof over their heads, and education for their children. If a new constitution is to have credibility and command the respect of the people subject to its provisions, it must take account of these demands and reflect them.

Hence, one finds the inclusion of justiciable social and economic rights in some modern constitutions.

In India, social and economic rights were contained in the Constitution but expressly stated not to be enforceable by the courts. It is telling that in response to popular demands, activist Indian judges carved out enforceable social and economic rights from the right to life that was judicially enforceable. In this way, they have recognized the right to health care, nutrition, clothing, and shelter.[1] The Supreme Court held that a lack of financial resources does not excuse a failure to provide adequate medical services. In this way, the judges of India have imaginatively fused social and economic rights with civil and political rights.

As far as I am aware, this is the first large-scale empirical study that systematically considers the feasibility and advisability of making social and economic rights justiciable. It focuses specifically on two areas: namely, the right to health and the right to education. It contains a structured comparison of five countries: Brazil, India, Indonesia, Nigeria, and South Africa. As such, it provides an indispensable guide for human rights activists, constitutional law practitioners, political scientists, economists, the international development community, and, of course, the judges who are increasingly being called on to enforce these rights.

Each of the country-specific chapters addresses four key steps in the impact of social and economic rights. This is a useful device to bring coherence and structure to the work. The first step is to consider the legal mobilization of demands, whether through negotiation with or without the threat of litigation, and court intervention; the second step relates to the consequences of court intervention, whether this be a negative or positive response or even a decision not to intervene; the third step is the response of the body, usually governmental, to a court intervention; and the fourth step is the reaction of the original claimants who might follow up a court decision by seeking appropriate enforcement of an order made by the court or even by launching a new round of litigation.

Lawyers tend to be primarily concerned with the second step. Their interest typically begins and ends with the outcome of negotiation or litigation, whether the result is positive or negative. However, for the would-be beneficiaries, it is the first, third, and fourth steps that are crucial. They would often prefer a negotiated outcome rather than placing all of their hopes in costly, time-consuming, and often risky litigation. It is the third and fourth steps that will determine whether they have really received any benefit from the enforceability of social and economic rights. They and nongovernmental organizations (NGOs) will wish to know and be advised on the various alternative approaches to realizing these rights. It is in this context that the comparative experience of the five chosen countries becomes so useful and relevant.

---

[1] See, for example, Francis Coralie Mullin v. Administrator, Union Territory of Delhi, (1981) 2 SCR 516 ("The right to life includes the right to live with human dignity and all that goes with it, namely, the bare necessities of life such as adequate nutrition, clothing and shelter and facilities for reading, writing and expressing oneself in diverse forms, freely moving about and mixing and commingling with fellow human beings.").

In some of the chapters there is reference to the "unintended consequences" of litigation. Those consequences might be negative or positive. I recall two South African situations in which there were important and beneficial unintended consequences. The first was during the apartheid era. In 1982, I heard an appeal from a decision in a lower court on a provision of the Group Areas Act, 1950. This was the statute that enforced residential racial segregation. The legislation empowered the government to decree that certain areas of South Africa were to be reserved for the exclusive use of people of one or another color. It was a criminal offense for a person of the "wrong" color to reside or own property in such a group area. The most desirable areas were set aside for whites. Some areas were set aside for Asians. I wrote an appellate opinion in the case of Mrs. Govender, an elderly South African woman of Indian extraction. She faced a criminal charge of residing with her children and grandchildren in a rented house in a part of Johannesburg reserved for whites.

When Mrs. Govender appeared in the trial court, she pleaded guilty and was sentenced to a paltry fine or the alternative of fifteen days in prison, all of which was suspended for three years on condition that she was not convicted of a similar offense during the period of suspension. However, what was most serious for her was an order that she be ejected from her home. Mrs. Govender's counsel had persuaded the judge to suspend the ejectment order for nine months. He did so in light of evidence that established that there were no alternative accommodations for Asians in the Johannesburg area, that Mrs. Govender had been on a waiting list for seven years, and that she might have to wait for another ten years before such accommodations would become available to her. Mrs. Govender appealed to the High Court only on the ground that the judge should have suspended the ejectment order indefinitely or until she was able to find alternative accommodations.

For some thirty years, the lower courts had uniformly and as a matter of course granted ejectment orders in such cases. However, while listening to argument by counsel before the High Court, it struck me that the statute in question did not oblige the judge to grant an ejectment order – it gave him discretion. On the basis of the plain text of the statute, we decided to rule that no such orders could be made without granting the affected party a full hearing and the exercise of judicial discretion. We ruled that in cases where there were no alternative accommodations available, an ejectment order should not be made. We set aside the order made in the case of Mrs. Govender.[2]

The completely unintended consequence of the order was to bring to a perma-nent end all prosecutions under the Group Areas Act. Prosecutors stopped bringing cases because they were unable to establish the availability of alternative accom-modations. Although the government could have amended the statute to make the ejectment orders peremptory, this would have been too embarrassing polit-ically, especially in light of the intense international scrutiny to which apartheid policies were being subjected at that time. In consequence, substantial areas of the

---

[2] R v. Govender, 1986 (3) SA 969 (T).

larger cities in South Africa became "mixed" in the years immediately following
the *Govender* decision.

Another unintended consequence of a positive nature followed the 2000 decision
of the Constitutional Court of South Africa in the *Grootboom* case. Reference is
made to this decision in some of the chapters that follow. It was a decision that
found the housing policy of the South African government, in some respects,
to violate the right to housing contained in the Bill of Rights. In essence, the
Court stated that insufficient attention had been given to the housing needs of
the poorest in our nation and to emergency situations where, through natural
calamities, people were rendered homeless. Less than a year after that decision
was made, a group of residents were rendered homeless by a flash flood in a
poorly resourced black township outside Johannesburg. The national government
immediately established a Cabinet Committee and placed R300 million (South
African rand) at its disposal for emergency relief to be given to the homeless
families. There can be little doubt that that action would not have been taken prior
to the decision in *Grootboom*.

It is rarely appreciated that rights are realized not only when the officials responsible for providing them take appropriate action in consequence of litigation but,
more frequently, when they do so in order to preempt litigation. This is especially
the case with regard to social and economic rights. It follows, I would suggest, that
the instances of court proceedings or even the call for negotiations often reflect
only the tip of the iceberg. The very recognition of these rights induces government officials to modify their behavior and take actions for the protection of needy
people without any outside interventions. This is a much-neglected aspect of the
realization of social and economic rights.

Another neglected issue, usefully canvassed in this book, is that a sustained
litigation policy is often essential for the successful enforcement of these rights.
It is in this context that the involvement of well-resourced and efficient NGOs is
crucial. Too frequently and not unexpectedly, the lawyers involved in a discrete case
consider their work to end with the issue of the court order. That is usually when
the real work begins, if the court's order is to be translated into benefits for a large
number of people. A good illustration of this is provided by the *Treatment Action
Campaign* case, which also came before the South African Constitutional Court
in 2002. This case involved the availability in public hospitals of an antiretroviral
drug – nevirapine – that prevents the transmission of the HIV virus from mothers
to infants at the time of birth. The Court held that the government objections
to the dissemination of the drug were without merit and ordered that the drug
be made immediately available to all mothers who wished to take it. The government complied with the Court's order. Treatment Action Campaign, a most
efficient NGO, used the decision to press, with much success, for more substantial
changes to the regrettable HIV/AIDS policies of the South African government.
The most recent government program aims to provide treatment to 80 percent
of the adults who need it by 2011, increasing the percentage of HIV patients
overseen by professional health-care providers to 70 percent. Equally ambitious
targets have been set for children. The plan calls for an annual review of treatment
guidelines. The major problems are finding the R45 billion (South African rand)

that the South African treasury calculates the program will cost and increasing the capacity of the public health system to deliver the substantially increased health services.

Another much-neglected aspect of litigation based on social and economic rights is the problem faced by judges who are called on to adjudicate claims for the enforcement of those rights. The first problem is the often difficult navigation between the traditional domains of the organs of government – the separation of powers issue. In budgetary matters there is an obvious need for the judiciary to show appropriate deference to the executive and legislative branches. Especially in new democracies, it is important that there is a relationship of respect between the three organs of government. It is a truism that the judiciary is by far the weakest of those branches. The judges have no way, themselves, to enforce their orders. They are entirely reliant on the executive branch in that respect. Their public credibility is also important in ensuring that their orders are respected. If orders made by courts are not conscientiously respected and implemented by the executive branch, judicial credibility will inevitably be prejudiced, with possibly critical consequences for the rule of law.

Judges are frequently criticized by human rights activists for not making stronger orders against government in social and economic rights cases. This was the case with the *Treatment Action Campaign* case, in which our Constitutional Court refused to follow the lower court in issuing a structural order. We said the following:

> The order made by the High Court included a structural interdict requiring the appellants to revise their policy and to submit the revised policy to the court to enable it to satisfy itself that the policy was consistent with the Constitution. In *Pretoria City Council* this Court recognized that the courts have such powers. In appropriate cases they should exercise such a power if it is necessary to secure compliance with a court order. That may be because of a failure to heed declaratory orders or other relief granted by a court in a particular case. We do not consider, however, that orders should be made in those terms unless this is necessary. The government has always respected and executed orders of this Court. There is no reason to believe that it will not do so in the present case.

That belief turned out to be justified, and the government did substantially execute the order made by the Court. However we were also aware that if the government flouted the order, the *Treatment Action Campaign* would have come back to court.

Human rights activists can and should encourage judges to make orders that are likely to yield the most beneficial results for the intended beneficiaries of the litigation and, indeed, also for those who might not be direct parties to such litigation. At the same time, however, human rights activists should be aware of and alert to the complex issues that are at work between the organs of state. In this regard, I emphasize the position of new democracies in which constitutional values might well be subject to stress.

It should also be borne in mind that in new democracies, the legal profession is still in a learning phase. Lawyers too frequently do not prepare their cases adequately at the trial level and expect courts of appeal to come to their relief on inadequate and incomplete records. The *Grootboom* case provides a good illustration.

For the first time on appeal before the Constitutional Court, counsel sought to rely on the approach of the United Nations Committee on Economic, Social, and Cultural Rights that socioeconomic rights contain a "minimum core." (This issue is discussed in some detail in the chapter by Jonathan Berger.) It appears from the reports of the Committee that it considers that every state party to the Convention is bound to fulfill a minimum core obligation by ensuring the satisfaction of a minimum essential level of the socioeconomic rights in question, including the right to housing.

In his opinion on behalf of a unanimous Court, Justice Yacoob said that this minimum core was

> the floor beneath which the conduct of the state must not drop if there is to be compliance with the obligation. Each right has a "minimum essential level" that must be satisfied by states parties. . . . Minimum core obligation is determined generally by having regard to the needs of the most vulnerable group that is entitled to the protection of the right in question. It is in this context that the concept of minimum core obligation must be understood in international law.[3]

There was no evidence at all on the record that would have enabled the Court to begin a consideration of an appropriate minimum core for the provision of housing or access to housing in the South African context. Justice Yacoob went on to say that

> There may be cases where it may be possible and appropriate to have regard to the content of a minimum core obligation to determine whether the measures taken by the state are reasonable. However, even if it were appropriate to do so, it could not be done unless sufficient information is placed before a court to enable it to determine the minimum core in any given context. In this case we do not have sufficient information to determine what would comprise the minimum core obligation in the context of our Constitution.[4]

Many commentators have interpreted this passage as rejecting out of hand the minimum core approach. I do not agree and suggest that future litigants are open to raise the issue on the basis of an adequate factual record in the trial court. This is an issue that highlights the difficulties facing lawyers undertaking constitutional litigation in new democracies. There is a substantial need for learning about what is effectively a new development in the law. The comments of Justice Yacoob should have been seen by the legal profession as a challenge and not as a call to abandon any future reliance on the minimum core approach. South African lawyers, in particular, need to adopt what are, in the United States, often called "Brandeis briefs." These are briefs that contain an analysis of factual data rather than relying solely on legal submissions. It was precisely such a brief that was fundamental to the success of the applicants in *Brown v. Board of Education of Topeka*.[5]

I would also suggest that there is a need in new democracies, and probably in many older ones too, for judicial education in the field of social and economic

---

[3] Government of the Republic of South Africa v. Grootboom, 2001 (1) SA 46 (CC) at para. 31.
[4] *Id.* at par. 33.
[5] 347 U.S. 483 (1954).

rights. This is a topic that few, if any, judges were taught at university. I would refer, in this regard, to the important experience of South African judges who attended conferences during the 1980s and 1990s that were designed to introduce them to domestic and international human rights law. They, too, had never enjoyed formal training in these subjects. Until 1994, human rights law was hardly relevant in a state where human rights were not recognized and violations of them were the order of the day. Those opportunities, enjoyed by a number of South African judges, opened windows and inspired us to use international human rights law norms in our own domestic courts.

I end with a reference to a statement to the Vienna World Conference in 1993 by the UN Committee of Economic, Social, and Cultural Rights. They said that there is

> [t]he shocking reality . . . that States and the international community as a whole continue to tolerate all too often breaches of economic, social and cultural rights which, if they occurred in relation to civil and political rights, would provoke expressions of horror and outrage and would lead to concerted calls for immediate remedial action. . . . Statistical indicators of the extent of deprivation, or breaches, of economic, social and cultural rights have been cited so often that they have tended to lose their impact. The magnitude, severity and constancy of that deprivation have provoked attitudes of resignation, feelings of helplessness and compassion fatigue.[6]

I would suggest that by giving attention to this issue this book will influence governments to pay greater attention to the importance and utility of these rights and will also encourage NGOs to pursue their realization with even greater vigor in the interests of millions of people whose social and economic rights are being neglected.

---

[6] U.N. Doc. E/1993/22, pars. 5 and 7.

Preface

VARUN GAURI AND DANIEL M. BRINKS

This book was conceived as an effort to join three streams of inquiry. First, ever since the mid- to late-1990s, when governance became a development priority, scholars and policy makers have sought institutional reforms to make governments more accountable for failures to provide basic services and alleviate poverty. Second, many of the innovative constitutions that emerged around the time of the "third wave" of democratization, as well as developments in legal and political theory, blurred the once bright-line distinction between negative and positive rights, with the consequence that legal or quasi-legal accountability for social and economic performance became more attractive. And third, studies in judicial politics have elaborated frameworks for assessing the causes and consequences of the legalization of political demands. Simply put, the time had come for a book on the role and impact of courts in fulfilling social and economic rights in the developing world.

A key initial conversation about this project occurred in Bangkok at the Fifteenth International AIDS Conference, where Varun met Jonathan Berger. Over a late-night beer, Jonathan agreed to write a review of social and economic rights court cases in South Africa. Shortly thereafter, Varun had the good fortune to meet Florian Hoffmann and Daniel Brinks, who drafted engaging analyses of health and education rights cases in Brazil. After a handful of conversations, it became clear that Dan and Varun shared research interests and a style of thinking, and that Dan's experiences and skills would contribute enormously to the project, so he became a co-editor. By the summer of 2005, the other key collaborators for this project were also in place – Chidi Odinkalu, Pratap Bhanu Mehta, Bivitri Susanti, and Helen Hershkoff. We all gathered in Washington for two days in September of that year to present our chapter outlines and to propose, debate, repudiate, refine, and then settle on a comparative framework. It was a stimulating and productive meeting that was crucial for the development of a broadly similar methodology across the country studies, a quality that, hopefully, gives this book more argumentative coherence than that of many edited volumes. We also greatly benefited from the participation of Oscar Vilhena Vieira, Siobhan McInerney-Lankford, Caroline Sage, and Mark Tushnet in that workshop.

Well, that was so much fun we decided to do it again and assembled in Washington in the fall of 2006 to present and critique first drafts. Pratap could not attend, but his co-author, Shylashri Shankar, did join us, as did William Forbath and Gretchen Helmke, whose thoughtful comments from outside the project validated, as well

as challenged, aspects of our approach. On the second day, we held a public conference at the World Bank on the book draft and on the general topic of social and
economic rights in developing countries. Speakers at the conference included, in
addition to the contributors to this volume, Ana Palacio, Philip Alston, Shanta
Devarajan, Sanjay Pradhan, William Forbath, Siobhan McInerney-Lankford,
Jacques Baudouy, Chris Beyrer, Jodi Jacobson, Robin Horn, Mara Bustelo, and
Michael Bochenek. A Web cast of that conference can be viewed at http://info.
worldbank.org/etools/BSPAN/EventView.asp?EID=902.

In addition to those who participated in the conference, many others at the World
Bank have given us crucial encouragement, support, and comments, including
Beth King, who has backed and promoted our work throughout, as well as Steve
Commins, Luis Crouch, Nina Cunanan, Adrian Di Giovanni, David Freestone,
Sangeeta Goyal, Imran Hafiz, Susheela Jonnakuty, Steen Lau Jorgensen, Kai Kaiser,
Rosalinda Lema, Rick Messick, Claudio Montenegro, Andy Norton, Oscar Picazo,
Vikram Raghavan, Martin Ravallion, Lars Adam Rehof, Ritva Reinikka, Randi
Ryterman, Hedy Sladovich, Galina Sotorova, Matt Stephens, Doris Voorbraak,
and Alan Winters. To the others who in his ever-increasing forgetfulness Varun is
neglecting to acknowledge here, let him make it up to you with a cup of coffee!

For their comments, insights, and even early advertising of this volume, we are
grateful to many colleagues from the development, human rights, and academic
communities, including Susan Aaronson, Chuck Beitz, Marcia Bento, Mônica
Mendonça Costa, Mac Darrow, Ariel Dulitzsky, Betina Durovni, José Reinaldo
de Lima Lopes, André de Mello e Souza, Carlos Alberto de Salles, Jackie Dugard,
Antonio Gelis Filho, Marty Finnemore, Mariângela Graciano, Fatima Hassan, Larry
Helfer, Jennifer Hochschild, George Hritz, Paul Hunt, Steve Kahanovitz, Sanjeev
Khagram, Juana Kweitel, Malcolm Langford, Sandy Liebenberg, Janet Love, Craig
Mokhiber, Helena Nygren-Krug, Cristina Pimenta, Flávia Piovesan, Thomas
Pogge, Jamie Radner, Usha Ramanathan, Fernando Serec, Veena Siddarth, Judith
Streak, Sérgio Luis Teixeira, Arun Thiruvengadam, Miriam Ventura, Faranaaz Veri-
ava, and Alicia Yamin. To the others out there, please claim your cup of coffee as
well. Kurt Weyland gave us detailed and extremely useful comments on our framework and findings. We also appreciated comments from participants in workshops
held at the World Bank, Princeton University, the University of the Witwatersrand,
the Human Sciences Research Council in Pretoria, the University of Texas at Austin,
Notre Dame University, and Texas A&M University.

The principal sponsors of this research project have been the World Bank's
Research Committee, the World Bank–Netherlands Partnership Program, and the
World Bank Trust Fund for Environmentally and Socially Sustainable Development. Of course, the findings, interpretations, and conclusions expressed in this
volume are entirely of the authors and do not necessarily represent the views of
the World Bank or its executive directors. During the writing phase, Dan also
received the financial support of the Kellogg Institute for International Studies
of the University of Notre Dame, in the form of a one-year Visiting Fellowship,
supplemented by a Faculty Research Assignment from the University of Texas at
Austin. Dan would also like to thank the Government Department at the University of Texas for making possible a one-day workshop to review the nearly final

manuscript. At that workshop we had the good fortune to receive extensive, incisive, and helpful comments from Robert Kaufman and Zach Elkins. Not the least of their contributions was Robert's suggestion for a title, which we have partially adopted. We also thank Cristiano Ravalli for permission to reprint his striking photograph of a scene outside the Madras High Court.

We join the chapter authors in thanking a number of research assistants whose work has been crucial for the country analyses. They are acknowledged by name in the country chapters. In addition, we had terrific research assistants based in the United States who helped with background papers, project coordination, and data analysis, including Leila Chirayath, Mangesh Dhume, Kaushik Krishnan, Brett Stark, Megan Westrum, and Sam Wolfe. John Berger, our editor at Cambridge University Press, has been extremely supportive throughout, and three anonymous reviewers gave us valuable comments at an important stage of the research.

I, Dan, want to especially thank Varun for conceiving and putting together such a great project, for doing all the work of assembling the teams and the funding, and, most crucially, for inviting me to participate. It has truly been a great privilege to work with Varun, both for his intellectual companionship and for his friendship. This book is dedicated to my wife, Sandra, for her patience and support, and especially for moving from sunny Austin to frozen South Bend and back again, just so I could write with fewer distractions.

Finally, I, Varun, dedicate this book to my wife, Ayesha, who has offered comments and insights drawn from her work as a civil rights advocate, and whose support has been my rock during the course of this project, and to my wonderful and lovely children, Yasmeen and Sharif, who show me every day what it means to demand fairness and claim rights.

Contributors

Fernando R. N. M. Bentes is General Coordinator of Legal Studies at Doctum University in Juiz de Fora, Brazil.

Jonathan Berger is Senior Researcher and head of policy and research at the AIDS Law Project in Johannesburg.

Daniel M. Brinks is Assistant Professor of Government at the University of Texas at Austin.

Varun Gauri is Senior Economist in the Development Research Group of the World Bank in Washington, DC.

Richard J. Goldstone, who served as a Justice on the Constitutional Court of South Africa and as Chief Prosecutor at the UN International Criminal Tribunals for Yugoslavia and Rwanda, is Visiting Professor of Law at Harvard Law School.

Helen Hershkoff is Anne and Joel Ehrenkranz Professor of Law at New York University.

Florian F. Hoffmann is Lecturer at the London School of Economics and Political Science and Adjunct Associate Professor at the Catholic University of Rio de Janeiro.

Pratap Bhanu Mehta is President of the Center for Policy Research in New Delhi.

Chidi Anselm Odinkalu is Senior Legal Officer at the Africa Open Society Justice Initiative in Abuja.

Shylashri Shankar is a Fellow at the Center for Policy Research in New Delhi.

Bivitri Susanti has served as Executive Director of the Jakarta-based Center for Indonesian Law and Policy Studies, where she is now a Researcher.

1 Introduction: The Elements of Legalization and the Triangular Shape of Social and Economic Rights

VARUN GAURI AND DANIEL M. BRINKS

A life that achieves the full promise of human dignity requires, among other things, escape from premature death, the resources to withstand debilitating disease, the ability to read and write, and, in general, opportunities and freedoms unavailable in the midst of extreme poverty and deprivation. Over the past few decades, many have adopted the view that commanding some minimal level of social and economic resources not only is constitutive of dignity, but is a basic human right to which someone *must* respond. Yet, one billion people on earth remain extremely poor, and billions of others lack necessities and essential services. The scale of global poverty makes it obvious that no one has assumed the responsibility to respond or that those who have undertaken that responsibility are failing. From the perspective of many human rights activists, then, the challenges become how best to identify those who ought to respond, how best to evaluate those who have attempted a response, and, more generally, how best to assign duties and then hold accountable those who might provide an effective response. And, many believe, it is entirely appropriate to use courts to enforce these rights. Courts are, after all, the paradigmatic institutions for identifying legal duties and responding to claims that rights have been violated.

In many countries, this process is well under way. To begin with, during and since the third wave of democratization around the world, more and more substantive rights have been enshrined in constitutions around the world:

> A review conducted for this paper assessed constitutional rights to education and health care in 187 countries. Of the 165 countries with available written constitutions, 116 made reference to a right to education and 73 to a right to health care. Ninety-five, moreover, stipulated free education and 29 free health care for at least some population subgroups and services. (Gauri 2004:465)

In fact, the right to education has been featured in a majority of the world's constitutions since the beginning of the twentieth century; and more than half have included the right to health starting around mid-century.[1] Some constitutions, such as the recently amended constitutions of Indonesia and Brazil, include judicially reviewable targets for the share of the budget that legislatures should allocate to health, education, or social security.

---

[1] Data supplied by Zach Elkins, from his collaborative project on constitutions with Tom Ginsburg.

Using those formal social and economic rights, courts in many countries have issued a number of prominent decisions. The *Grootboom* ruling of the South African Constitutional Court in 2000, finding a right to housing on behalf of informal settlers, raised the hopes of housing and antipoverty activists around the world. On several occasions, courts in Argentina have required the state to provide or avoid interruptions in the provision of essential medicines, including the 1998 *Vicente* case, in which a court required the state to produce a treatment for hemorrhagic fever and held the Ministers of Health, Economy and Labor, and Public Services personally responsible for doing so (Bergallo 2005). The European Commission for Social Rights ruled in 1998 that Portugal's failure to enforce its child labor legislation constituted a breach of the European Social Charter, a decision that led the country to implement a number of reforms (Arbour 2006). In Costa Rica, a recent newspaper report traced an 80 percent reduction in AIDS mortality rates to a Constitutional Court decision requiring the public health system to make antiretroviral treatment publicly available.[2] The Indian Supreme Court has converted what were once constitutional guiding principles into judicially enforceable rights to housing and education, and against bonded labor (Steiner and Alston 2000). Even in the United States, where the Supreme Court has firmly dismissed social and economic rights claims made on the basis of the federal constitution, rulings on the basis of state constitutions have spurred significant changes in financing for education and social assistance (Forbath 2007; Hershkoff 1999). A recent review analyzes more than two thousand social and economic rights cases from twenty-nine national and international jurisdictions (Langford 2008). Increasingly, then, constitutional rights are supporting demands for social and economic goods and services, often, but not always, through courts or other quasi-legal institutions. And courts are taking an increasingly important role in deciding the extent to which the seemingly nonnegotiable interests embodied in constitutions should be considered and protected in policy making.

With detailed studies of Brazil, India, Indonesia, Nigeria, and South Africa, this book offers empirically grounded answers to many of the questions raised by judicial involvement in the policy-making process. Are courts actually becoming more involved in economic and social policy, or is the "judicialization" phenomenon (Tate and Vallinder 1995) a mirage? Are their interventions meaningful for policy making, as a review of leading case studies suggests (COHRE 2003), and as a comparative account of "rights revolutions" indicates they can be (Epp 2003)? Or are they just so much window dressing, or even a diversion from other potentially more productive policy-making venues, a kind of "flypaper" for would-be social reformers who succumb to the lure of litigation strategies (Rosenberg 1991)? If they are becoming more important, why, and through what channels? And why does judicial intervention on social and economic rights seem so frequent and prominent in some countries and in some issue areas but not in others?

More important, will giving courts a more prominent role in economic and social policy make governments and others more accountable for responding

---

[2] Cantero, M. "Antirretrovirales reducen mortalidad de ticos con SIDA" [Antiretrovirals reduce mortality of Costa Ricans with AIDS]. La Nación, San José, Costa Rica, November 16, 2005.

to extreme poverty and deprivation? Or do legal processes inevitably favor the "haves" so that more judicial involvement will benefit those who are already better off? Hirschl argues that courts represent conservative elite interests, and that they will, in interpreting constitutional rights, advance "a predominantly neo-liberal conception of rights that reflects and promotes the ideological premises of the new 'global economic order' – social atomism, anti-unionism, formal equality, and 'minimal state' policies" (Hirschl 2000: 1063). Is that right? And what of the classical objections to justiciable social and economic rights – that courts will usurp the policy-making power of more representative branches of government and lack requisite skills for policy making on complex topics? What does this new phenomenon mean for academic theories of judicial mobilization, behavior, and impact? Although we do not present definitive answers to all these questions, the case studies and comparative analyses presented in this book shed light on these and other important questions concerning social and economic rights and the place of courts in policy making.

The five countries studied in this book were chosen so as to include common law countries with records of aggressive (India and South Africa) and limited social and economic (SE) rights litigation (Nigeria), and civil law countries with aggressive (Brazil) and incipient (Indonesia) litigation. They include countries with (by global standards) recent and old constitutions, and countries with varying years of democratic experience. Judicial review is abstract and centralized in Indonesia; concrete and diffuse in India, Nigeria, and South Africa; and a blend in Brazil. The countries also vary in levels of national income and state capacity. We draw on this variation to answer questions about the social, economic, political, and institutional conditions that favor judicial involvement in, and judicial impact on, social and economic rights. Wherever possible, the country chapter authors also use within-country variation to measure and then explain the range and impact of litigation on social and economic rights, comparing, for instance, the Northeast with the South and Southeast of Brazil, and the so-called BIMARU states with other states in India.

The focus of this research is on the right to health and health care, and the right to education. These two issue areas provide within-country variation on dependent and independent variables. The country chapter authors compare the extent and nature of litigation in the two policy areas (and, in some cases, in subpolicy areas such as AIDS, medications, and tertiary education), and draw on country-specific and sector-specific characteristics to explain these observed differences. Health and education were chosen because they are almost always considered basic social and economic rights. The two policy areas also exhibit important differences, with a generally larger private sector for health care in most countries, and wider use of public-sector health facilities than of public schools on the part of the middle and upper classes. International mobilization is also higher for health concerns than for education. As much as we would have liked, it was not possible to include all social and economic rights cases in the country sampling strategies. Wherever they considered it important, however, country chapter authors examined, in addition to health care and education, court cases related to other basic rights, such as land, housing, and basic income.

THE MAIN ARGUMENT

To engage the normative question – the desirability of using courts to enforce social and economic rights – we first need an account of what it is that courts actually do when they get involved in policy making. In other words, and as Socrates put it in *Meno*, "If I do not know what something is, how could I know what qualities it has?" A short account explaining judicial involvement in the policy-making process follows. We develop this conceptual framework more fully later in this introduction, and the country chapter authors all use a (suitably adapted) version of it to facilitate our cross-country comparisons in the conclusion.

We argue that one can decompose the life cycle of public-policy litigation into four stages: (a) the placing of cases on the courts' docket (we usually refer to this stage as *legal mobilization*); (b) the judicial decision; (c) a bureaucratic, political, or private-party response; and, in many cases, (d) some follow-up litigation. The product of this four-stage process is what we call the *legalization* of policy in a particular policy area. We understand policy legalization to be the extent to which courts and lawyers, including prosecutors, become relevant actors, and the language and categories of law and rights become relevant concepts, in the design and implementation of public policy. Legalization in this sense is self-evidently a continuous concept and quite often a difficult one to measure with any degree of precision, but this definition is broad enough to capture most of what is interesting about the role of law and courts in the policy arena and yet specific enough to guide our inquiry.

Later in this introduction we characterize these four key "moments" in the legalization process more fully, and we hypothesize that certain features of a country's legal, institutional, and political landscape strongly affect the extent and form of legalization in social and economic policy. Here the crucial point is that each stage of the legalization process involves a choice by one or more strategic actors. Litigants, for instance, move to place cases on the courts' docket (Stage 1) in anticipation of judicial receptivity (Stage 2), eventual state or corporate compliance (Stage 3), and their own capacity to conduct any necessary follow up (Stage 4). States and private parties comply with court decisions in light of the nature of the judicial order (Stage 2) and the prospect that litigants will monitor compliance (Stage 4). Most important, for present purposes, is that courts themselves are deeply implicated in this set of strategic interactions: whereas the prevailing legal superstructure affects court rulings in some important ways, judges also craft their opinions with an eye on the likelihood of compliance (Stage 3), the political reaction and its effect on the standing of the judiciary (Stage 3), and the existence of a strong litigant who can engage in follow up or bring new cases (Stages 1 and 4).

Taking these strategic interactions seriously means that although our definition of legalization continues to include the two dimensions that Tate and Vallinder (1995) identified in their definition of judicialization (i.e., both judicial involvement in policy decision making and legal argumentation in policy discussions outside the courts), it does not depend, as their definition does, on courts making final, all-or-nothing decisions, thereby usurping the functions of more representative institutions. Instead, our definition recognizes the open-ended and interactive

Aggregative/Utilitarian Logic Categorical/Deontological Logic

Figure 1.1. The allocative logic of legislatures and courts.

nature of judicial decision making, suggests that policy-making power is not zero-sum across government branches, and does not smuggle in normative judgments about the proper province of courts. We argue here, and the conclusion will confirm, that courts more often add a relevant actor and relevant considerations than seize decision making power from other actors. Legalization is a continuous phenomenon; but because courts are deeply concerned with the reactions of other actors in the legalization process, and hence with the processes of "normal politics," extreme legalization is the exception, not the rule.

This account of legalization weakens the popular dichotomy between judicial and legislative action. In a common view, courts follow a categorical or deontological logic, particularly when ruling on human rights. The only concerns that enter their decisions are those of the applicants before them, relevant laws and constitutional texts, and their own predispositions – a set of concerns whose narrowness gives rise to charges of judicial imperialism. Legislatures, by contrast, again in this popular view, are able to represent and aggregate the preferences of the voting or relevant public, taking into account the wider interests of the entire polity, including even the interests of future generations, not only of those on whose behalf they presently make law. But if courts are indeed, as we will argue throughout, just one actor in the deeply strategic and iterative process of legalization, they in fact incorporate a wider set of concerns than the popular conception allows. Their decision making, by responding to popular demands, reckoning infrastructural limitations, anticipating legislative and executive priorities, and engaging these other actors in an ongoing dialogue in the process of adjudication, implicitly and explicitly incorporates expenditure trade-offs and other elements of aggregative/utilitarian logic. Moreover, as legalization and rights discourse pushes legislatures toward special solicitude for rights-protected interests, their own decision making edges toward a more categorical/deontological approach.

Figure 1.1 illustrates how the popular account of judicial and legislative logic needs to be corrected. In our view, courts are anchored in more deontological forms of reasoning and valuation, but move to incorporate other logics, especially in social and economic rights adjudication. The diagram also indicates that legislatures, although rooted in an aggregative/utilitarian framework, are, in fact, involved in categorical and deontological decision making far more than the popular account admits. Although we do not make that argument in this book, one needs only to think about the political challenge of reforming entitlements in many Organisation for Economic Co-operation and Development (OECD) countries to see the point.

Legalization does not, however, merely replicate the allocative priorities of the legislative and executive branches. Rather, because legalization differs from the political demand channels in the kinds and amounts of resources needed to stake effective demands, the avenues of access, and the distinct relationships to coercive and persuasive power, it tends to prioritize a somewhat different set of social demands than the political process does. Some of these demands benefit the disempowered and marginalized, as advocates of making social and economic rights justiciable have argued, and as the country chapters demonstrate. On the other hand, legalization might also serve the interests of political and economic elites and the middle classes, who can "dress up" their private interests and claims as social and economic rights, as some have worried when describing public interest litigation (PIL) in India.[3]

In sum, this book takes the view, visible in the country chapters as well as in our introduction and conclusion, that the constitutionalization and legal enforcement of social and economic rights is neither an unalloyed boon nor an outright liability for social justice. Courts can advance social and economic rights under the right conditions precisely because they are never fully independent of political pressures. We will argue that courts can help overcome political blockages, channel important information to political and bureaucratic actors, create spaces of deliberation and compromise between competing interests, and hold states accountable for incomplete commitments. Courts have their greatest impact when policy seems unresponsive to popular demands. On the other hand, although courts can reprioritize claims in a manner that extends access to social and economic goods, the resource intensiveness of litigation sometimes prevents social and economic rights claims from benefiting the neediest, at least at first. This is not inevitable, however, and in some cases social and economic rights litigation may produce significant positive indirect effects for those who do not themselves have the resources to litigate. The final balance will be different from country to country and is open to debate even in the countries we examine. Still, our findings suggest that courts can become important actors in the policy arena while benefiting, or at least without making matters worse for, the underprivileged.

THE SOCIAL AND ECONOMIC RIGHTS TRIANGLE

The scope of this book is somewhat narrower than the account of legalization in the previous section might have suggested. That is because there are many ways in which the legalization of policy can and does affect the availability and quality of social and economic goods, but only some of them involve social and economic rights claims. For example, the ease with which patients can press medical malpractice cases in courts or other forums, which rely on common law or contractual patient–provider relationships that are typically prior to and independent of the constitutional right to health or health care, can significantly affect the quality of

---

[3] Dembowski (2001: 196) repeats some of the rumors and charges, common in India, that environmental PIL is sometimes used to extort money from private industries or to force them to shut down. Indian observers also speak of "PIL inflation" – the cheapening of the procedure as a result of excessive reliance and abuse.

health care in a country.[4] The judicially enforced right to information – not a social or economic right – has been a critical tool in civil society campaigns for health and education around the world, including the mobilization around HIV/AIDS policy in South Africa and the right to food in India, which are studied in this book. Certain first-generation rights, including due process and equality, are often used to widen access to health care and education, as the chapters on South Africa and Nigeria, in this volume, demonstrate. The same is true of the right to a "just administrative procedure," codified in South Africa's Constitution.

By the same token, we do not look at all of the pathways by which social and economic rights can affect the availability and quality of social and economic goods. To begin with, our focus is on *formal rights*. For us, a formal right is a written statement in which a normative claim regarding what one is due has been incorporated into the state's legal framework. This might happen when a treaty or other international instrument is signed or ratified, when a constitutional provision or domestic statute is adopted, or when a court enters a judicial decision. Formal rights are to be contrasted with the broader sense of *rights* as nondiscretionary claims about what one is due. The basis for rights claims in this sense need not be a legal text, but the mere fact that one is a human being (in which case the claim is called a *human right*), one's place in the natural order (a *natural right*), one's membership in a polity of equals (the *rights of citizens*), or something else. Our focus is on formal rights, rather than on rights-based normative claims per se.

We do not, moreover, examine all of the means by which formal rights affect the availability and quality of social and economic goods, but only examine their impacts insofar as they appear in the legalization of policy. We do not systematically assess what happens, for instance, when "rights-based" civil society organizations use constitutional rights or international treaties as mobilizing tools and as vehicles to push for voice, participation, or political accountability. Constitutionally incorporated (and therefore formal) social and economic rights can also lead advocates, courts, and policy makers to reinterpret and give new urgency to certain first-generation rights, such as the right to information or the right to equality. We do not capture that subtle, hermeneutic process in any systematic way.

The present study, then, is neither an exhaustive review of how legal strategies contribute to the attainment of important economic and social goods nor a comprehensive examination of the impact of formal rights; rather, it is an account of the intersection of the two – the extent and the ways in which the use of formal rights in judicial or quasi-judicial contexts contributes to the availability and quality of social and economic goods. Some of the country chapters review the impact of key medical malpractice cases, but they do not claim to have captured all or even most of them in their case sampling strategies. Some alternative legal strategies to make economic or social rights effective, such as the use of the South African constitutional right to just administrative procedure, receive some attention; but others,

---

[4] Some argue, of course, that an increase in cost and a decrease in availability of health care accompany the quality increases associated with malpractice litigation, or that malpractice litigation has on balance a negative effect on health outcomes; we do not address these issues, either.

such as the use of a right to information for framing political and legal strategies to obtain better government services, or the effects of anticorruption cases on expenditures in economic and social areas, are barely addressed for the simple reason that they would make the scope of the study too large. Primarily, then, the country authors focus on the intersection of formal rights and legalization, with a few sidelong glances at other areas where appropriate.

We noted earlier and will subsequently develop the argument that variation in the institutional bases for legalization significantly affects the impact of formal SE rights. We also contend that impacts depend on the ways that these varying institutional bases interact with the kinds of SE rights claims that reach the courts. To elaborate that hypothesis, we need first to develop an empirically useful categorization of SE rights claims, at least insofar as they relate to health and education. To motivate our typology, which we will call the social and economic rights triangle, consider this question. When they apply formal rights, what kinds of legally enforceable duties and liberties do courts create?

Here are some of the claims that have been invoked under the banner of the right to health in countries studied in this book: to receive medical treatment or medication at little or no cost (among many cases in Brazil, Acórdão No. 366.512–5/5–00, São Paulo); gain admission into a hospital emergency room irrespective of ability to pay or medical condition (*Soobramoney v. Minister of Health, KwaZulu-Natal* 1998 (1) SA 765 (CC), South Africa); expand health programs for migrant workers (*Indonesia Citizens Acting for All Indonesian Citizens v. Republic of Indonesia Government* No. 28/Pdt.G/2003/PN.Jkt.pusat, Civil Court, Jakarta, Indonesia); obtain civil damages for negligent substandard care (*Indian Medical Association v. V. P. Shantha* AIR (1995) 6 SC 651, India); prosecute a criminally negligent provider (*Juggankhan v. State of MP* AIR 1965 SC 831, India); be informed regarding and have the power to withhold consent for a medical procedure (*Arunachala Vadivel and Others v. Dr. N. Gopalkrishnan* CPR 548 (1992), India); keep health records confidential (*L. B. Joshi v. T. R. Godbole* SC AIR, India); limit excessive pricing for medications (*New Clicks South Africa (Pty) Limited v. Dr. Manto Tshabalala-Msimang NO* (2004), South Africa); limit the length or extent of patent protection for medications (*Pharmaceutical Manufacturers' Association of South Africa v. President of the Republic of South Africa* 2001); receive reimbursement or financing for a specific procedure under terms of a private insurance contract (among many in Brazil, Acórdão No. 2002.001.26562, Rio de Janeiro); grant bail from prison to receive medical treatment (*Ojuwe v. Federal Government of Nigeria* 3 Nig. Weekly L. Reps. 913, 2005, Nigeria); and limit pollutants in the environment (*Suo Moto v. State of Rajasthan and Others*, Rajasthan High Court 2005, AIR 92[1095], India).

Our country chapter authors also cited a diverse set of cases regarding the right to education: to require local or national government to spend more on education (Judicial Review of the 2006 State Budget Law Case Number: 026/PUU-III/2006, Indonesia); challenge whether a school has sufficient infrastructure to increase enrollment (*Dental Council of India v. Subharti K. K. B. Charitable Trust & Anr.*, 25.04.2001, India); limit the fees that schools can charge at the beginning of the school year (*Ankur Agrawal v. Respondent: State of Madhya Pradesh and Others, 2000*, India); challenge competency testing in a particular language on grounds that it is discriminatory (*Ex parte Gauteng Provincial Legislature: In re Dispute Concerning the Constitutionality of Certain Provisions of the Gauteng School Education Bill of 1995* 1996 (3) SA 165 (CC), April 4, 1996, South Africa); require schools to have functioning water or electricity service (Ação Civil No. 2005.03.00135–0, Fortaleza, Brazil); open a private school that includes a religious affiliation (*Archbishop Okogie v. Attorney General of Lagos State, Nigeria*); disallow corporal punishment in an independent school (*Christian Education South Africa v. Minister of Education* 2000 (4) SA 757 (CC), August 18, 2000, South Africa); and require a public school to accommodate students with disabilities (Ação No. 2002.001.28421, Rio de Janeiro, Brazil).

Reviewing these cases, it is immediately clear that although social and economic rights litigated in courts have included claims for direct state provision of health care or education goods, courts have applied formal social and economic rights to a much wider set of actors, and in so doing have delineated duties and liberties for which a variety of specific actors, and not (or, in some cases, not only) the state, are legally accountable. In fact, as the country chapters in this volume demonstrate, with the exception of Brazil, legal petitions requesting direct state provision form the minority of social and economic rights cases in every country. None of these courts has, to our knowledge, presented a systematic account of the actors, duties, liberties, or relationships potentially subject to formal social and economic rights. Such an account would in any case need to be provisional as emerging technologies and social relationships give rise to new demand channels, new demands, and new rights. What follows is a simple framework for characterizing the duties, liberties, and relationships that are potentially subject to formal rights.

Broadly speaking, there are three kinds of actors involved in the production and distribution of social goods and services – the state, providers, and clients. (Clients are sometimes better described as "citizens" or "recipients.") As analytical terms, the entities "the state" and "clients" are relatively clear in this context, but the term "providers" needs clarification. Generally speaking, providers are the groups of individuals that render essential social goods and services to clients. In health care, this group includes physicians, nurses, pharmacists, and insurers, among others;[5] in education, they include teachers, private school owners, university faculty, and textbook publishers. For other rights, the groups are perhaps less well-defined, but would include groups such as engineers in the case of housing rights, as well as builders, landlords, and the government agency that supervises building and manages public housing.[6]

It is noteworthy that even in cases where services are publicly provided and financed and where the providers are public-sector employees, the providers are,

---

[5] We include industries and other actors whose activities either support or reduce the availability of goods crucial for health, such as clean air and water.

[6] This account of the three types of actors overlaps with and extends the framework in the *World Development Report 2004* (World Bank 2003).

analytically, a distinct set of actors from the state. This is so for three reasons. First, many of the providers are subject to a specific body of private law, whether in the rules of contract or in professional norms and licensing requirements. This means that when courts review an individual's claim to a formal economic or social right and look to define a legal duty to make the right more effective, the expected behaviors and duties of state employees are somewhat distinct from the expected behaviors and duties of the state organs that supervise and employ them. Second, there is almost inevitably a wide latitude of discretion in the provision of economic and social goods. Indeed, in the case of health care and education, it is hard to imagine how those rights could be made effective without granting the professionals that provide them substantial discretion in the performance of their duties (Gauri 1998; Pritchett and Woolcock 2004). That fact means that the performance of professionals in a particular case must be assessed separately from the decisions of the state organs whose task it is to establish the broad policies under which professionals work.[7] Third, responsibility for providing health care and education is substantially decentralized in many countries, including Brazil, India, and Nigeria, and somewhat decentralized in many other countries, such as Indonesia and South Africa, with the result that in most countries the central organs of the state are legally distinguishable from subnational public providers, as well as from, of course, private providers.

Usually, when courts apply formal rights, they modify the set of legally reviewable duties and liberties that extend from one actor toward another; in figurative terms, they work on the connection between two vertices on a triangle, depicted in Figure 1.2, defined by the three key actors – the state, providers, and clients. In this book, we designate the class of legally reviewable duties and liberties that extend between the state and providers *regulation*. Regulation here includes duties on the part of the state to license and set standards for independent schools and private health-care providers, liberties on the part of providers to offer particular medical treatments or import particular medications, requirements that health insurers pay for specific procedures, state restrictions on the power of professional associations to sanction their own members, the state's duty to impose environmental standards on state-licensed or state-owned vehicles, the extent of the liberty of independent schools to set their fees or select students, and the criminal liability of medical practitioners and teachers who commit corporal punishment. Similarly, in this volume we call the legally reviewable duties and liberties extending between the state and clients claims for *provision or financing*. (Later, we will, for convenience, shorten this to *provision* even though these can involve claims for state financing of private provision.) These include the liberties of public schools to collect formal or informal fees; duties to make services more accessible to particular

---

[7] It is worth emphasizing that we do not think that this discretion, whose existence has underlain claims that social and economic rights cannot be enforced by courts, prevents judicial actors from specifying legally reviewable duties and liberties related to SE rights, and holding political, bureaucratic, and private actors accountable to them. Florian Hoffmann and Fernando Bentes examine this issue in Brazil, where courts are divided on the extent to which the doctrine of "administrative discretion" shields public education providers from social and economic rights litigation.

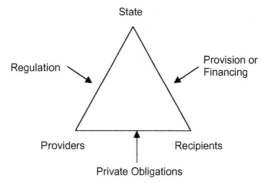

Figure 1.2. Classes of duties and liberties arising in the application of formal social and economic rights.

classes of individuals (children with disabilities, legally resident non-citizens, etc); duties to increase financing for education or health to comply with statutory or constitutional requirements or targets; and duties to provide particular medical treatments or medications.

Finally, we designate the important class of duties and liberties extending between providers and clients, and which clients themselves must enforce, *private obligations*. These cases most often escape analysis in the literature because of the difficult-to-shake background notion that social and economic rights must involve the state. These cases modify the conditions under which independent and public schools can admit, expel, promote, administer tests to, and award degrees to students; the liberties and duties of public and independent schools regarding curriculum; the liberties of classes of students to attend particular schools (e.g., the right of students with disabilities to attend mainstream schools); the conditions under which patients can claim compensation for medical practice under tort or consumer law; requirements that medical providers treat certain classes of patients, such as rape victims; and duties on the part of medical providers to protect medical confidentiality and obtain informed consent prior to treatment. This essentially private law relationship between providers and service recipients turns out to be, in the countries studied in this volume, a significant area of social and economic rights litigation, and one likely to grow as service provision is increasingly privatized.

It is true that every important right requires, for its fulfillment, an assorted collection of duties and liberties. It is also true that some of the duties and liberties arising when courts apply formal social and economic rights are not easily classifiable along a single side of the triangle. For example, cases that limit health-care providers' right to strike are based on the understanding that health-care professionals possess moral duties toward patients; but the actor charged with a newly established duty in this litigation is the state, which is directed to establish new codes regulating the behavior of health-care providers. This could be a regulation or a private obligations case. Because the main issue of concern in the right to strike is the duty of providers, we classify these cases under private obligations, though it could go the other way. Similarly, Indian cases in which civil servants demanded that government-backed benefits schemes reimburse them for hospital expenses, described in Shankar and Mehta's chapter, could be construed as provision cases (because citizens are making claims against the state) or obligations cases (because the state is acting essentially as a private employer). We opt for the latter. Another set of cases that defy simple classification are those that involve balancing conflicting rights. In the *Kyalami Ridge* case in South Africa, described in Jonathan Berger's chapter, the courts weigh the state's duty to provide emergency housing against the right of private homeowners whose property values might suffer as a result of the placement of emergency shelters in their communities. This could be either a provision case or a private obligations case. The large majority of cases, however, address a duty or liberty that extends between two of the key actors – along, in other words, a single side of the triangle. The conclusion to this volume uses this triangle to explain the observed behavior of courts when they apply formal rights.

It is worth noting that this typology of relationships refers to the underlying demand for social and economic goods rather than to the content of the judicial ruling. Particularly in the context of an existing social program that needs clarification or elaboration, a judicial finding might develop rights claims between two vertices of the triangle without explicitly addressing the relationship between the same two actors. This occurs because when courts examine accountability for social and economic rights, they sometimes revise what we will call the *terms of accountability* for social and economic goods. This process involves determining (a) who or which entity is responsible, (b) for what performance standards or benchmarks, and (c) under what threat or potential sanction. A court ruling involving provision, for instance, might adjudicate a federalism question involving the relative balance of central and local government responsibility for certain services. We call this a provision claim even though the citizen/client may not figure prominently, if at all, in the court opinion. An example is the *Mashava* case (described in Jonathan Berger's South Africa chapter), which queried whether the national or provincial government should be responsible for social assistance grants. Similarly, cases that focus on the constitutionality or legality of certain judicially imposed penalties or sanctions can, if they involve constitutionally protected social and economic rights, involve provision or regulation even if the main parties to the case are state officials and a lower court. *Kate v. MEC for the Department of Welfare*, from South Africa, illustrates this point, as does, to a lesser extent, an Indian case that contemplated contempt proceedings against public officials for failure to close down polluting industries – *M. C. Mehta v. Union of India*.

The standard approach to classifying social and economic rights involves a delineation of the nature of the action required to comply with human rights obligations: there are duties to "respect, protect, and fulfill" (see, e.g., Abramovich 2005), or, as in the South African Constitution, duties to "respect, protect, promote, and fulfill." This classification of formal rights is based on the nature of the required duty and is typically applied to states, though there is no reason why it could not be useful for classifying the obligations of providers and other private parties as well. Another approach classifies duties by their purpose: for instance, states should take actions that make health and education services available, accessible, acceptable, and of high quality (see, e.g., UN Committee on Economic, Social, and Cultural

Rights 2000). In a third approach, judicial decisions on rights claims are classified according to the extent of bureaucratic and political discretion they circumscribe (Hershkoff 1999). In all three of these systems of classification, the implicit duty bearer is the state, even though the action, to respect or protect or whatever, often involves private parties as well.

Instead of these classifications, we prefer to use the triangular framework presented earlier for several reasons. First, a scheme based on the relationships affected involves less guesswork than classifications based on identifying the nature of the action involved, discerning the purpose of state action, or assessing the impact of formal rights on bureaucratic and political discretion. Second, the focus on key actors allows us to draw on well-developed literatures regarding the behavior of states, providers, and individuals and then develop more testable hypotheses concerning the impact of court decisions. Third, the three categories separate cases involving different levels of state involvement and financing, with important implications for judicial support and ultimate compliance with judicial orders. Fourth, the triangular classification scheme is more compatible with the large number of cases involving private obligations that we observe in the countries studied, and which we believe will become increasingly important as service delivery is increasingly privatized.

Finally, the focus on the relationships among actors reflects the idea, proposed by Iris Marion Young, that rights are not possessions but "institutionally defined rules specifying what people can do in relation to one another" (Young 1990: 25) By conceptualizing rights as rules that establish an agent's duties and liberties in relation to others, we resist the temptation to conceive of rights, formal or otherwise, as species of property. This is a particularly strong intellectual compulsion in the case of social and economic rights, which are more closely allied to a physical object one might possess (e.g., food, a school, a medicine) than so-called negative rights (e.g., freedom of speech, physical autonomy). Instead, SE rights are here understood as claims to change the rules that govern the production and distribution of basic economic and social goods.

In any case, the literature spends too much energy on debates regarding the classification of the kinds of duties that rights entail. In social life, the legally reviewable duties and liberties that arise from the application of formal rights are always evolving as new technologies interact with new social relationships to create new demands and new rights. As Henry Shue, who first proposed the "avoid, protect, aid" trilogy, puts it:

> Be they dichotomous or trichotomous, typologies are ladders to be climbed and left behind, not monuments to be caressed or polished.... "The very simple tripartite typology of duties," then, was not supposed to become a new frozen abstraction to occupy the same rigid conceptual space previously held by "negative rights" and "positive rights." (Shue 1996: 160)

For purposes of the present study, which focuses on the contributions of judicial and quasi-judicial institutions, it would be particularly constraining to specify completely, and in advance, the kinds of duties and liberties implicit in formal rights because one of the principal functions of courts is to create a political space for the discussion of highly specific, individual cases for which preexisting legal categories are insufficient. Among other things, these examinations of particular needs and demands send information to government about the importance of revising policies, the ways in which policies are implemented, and the means by which entities can be held accountable for them.

HOW INSTITUTIONS AFFECT THE LEVEL, SCOPE, AND FORM OF LEGALIZATION REGARDING SOCIAL AND ECONOMIC RIGHTS

Courts are just one of several demand channels available to actors when they press economic and social claims. Why do they choose courts, rather than other avenues for fulfilling their rights? Under what conditions, in other words, does legalization emerge? As anticipated earlier, the analysis begins with the four potential choke points in the legalization process – the decision to press a claim through the courts (*legal mobilization*), a judicial decision, the response or compliance decision by the target of the claim, and responses by either the original or new claimants to the new policy environment.

While previous accounts attempt to isolate the one principal step or cause that prompts a "rights revolution" (Epp 2003) or produces a significant social change (Rosenberg 1991), the account here views the four decisions as interdependent. They are best understood as decisions made by strategic actors, albeit with limited capabilities and limited information. The decision at each step involves factors that impinge directly on the decision at hand, plus some consideration of what will happen at the next stage. Potential litigants, for example, evaluate their legal capabilities and the likely benefit of going to court against their political resources and the likely benefit of pressing a demand in the political arena instead (or, indeed, of going to the market). The target of the demand responds not only in light of its preferences and the nature of the court order, but also upon consideration of the likelihood of further legal demands. Moreover, the conditions for different types of claims – for service provision, regulation, or private obligations – may well differ.

The most important social prerequisites for the legalization of economic and social demands are the conditions that favor the mobilization of wants and desires into demands. In other words, there must have occurred that transformation of outlook in which, as Hannah Pitkin puts it, "I want" has become "I am entitled to" (Pitkin 1981: 347). This is more likely, of course, after a certain threshold of human development and democratic freedom. The social basis for want is enormous in the countries studied in this volume: infant mortality rates are on average eleven times higher in the selected countries than in the average high-income OECD country and secondary school enrollment rates are on average 30 percent lower (World Bank 2007). But it is also true that in each of the countries modernization, urbanization, at least partial democratization, and economic development have produced historically unprecedented levels of social mobilization, and the widespread translation of the "I want" into the "I am entitled to," certainly in the large urban centers, and in many rural and peri-urban areas as well (see, e.g., McAdam, Tarrow, and Tilly 2001). We may assume, then, that in these countries there exist sufficient levels of need and social mobilization to produce substantial amounts of litigation, should litigation become the preferred channel for presenting demands.

Second, there must exist a minimally autonomous judiciary that can serve as a venue for making demands on state or non-state actors. This, in turn, is in large part a function of the political context. A high quality, multiparty democracy both facilitates the creation of an independent judiciary with the power of judicial review (Bill Chavez 2004; Ginsburg 2003), and makes it less likely that legislative policy makers will easily coordinate to override or stifle judicial intervention (Epstein and Knight 1998; Epstein, Knight, and Martin 2001; Miller and Barnes 2004; Vanberg 2001). One would expect, then, that substantial legalization will more often take place in relatively well-functioning democratic contexts.

In addition, we believe that the level, scope, and form that social and economic rights legalization take is a result of the capabilities and strategic calculations of the key actors involved in the process: individual and collective litigants; judges; and bureaucratic, political, and corporate decision makers. We do not attempt to model legalization as a result of those strategic relationships and varying capabilities. Instead, here we specify a number of social, legal, and political arrangements that affect the calculations all of the key actors in the process and thus the nature of the legalization that emerges. One might think of this as a *reduced form* rather than a structural account. More specifically, the level, scope, and form of legalization is a product of demand-, supply-, and response-side variables.[8] On the demand side are the characteristics of those mobilizing around a particular issue. On the supply side are the features of the legal system with which they must interact if they will press a legal claim, including the likely judicial response. On the response side are the characteristics of the targets of potential demands, including their likely level of resistance, their latent capacity, their organizational development, and the like. Each of these is discussed separately in the following sections.

Demand-Side Factors

Extensive legalization in a policy area, almost by definition, requires significant professional legal assistance. Epp (2003), drawing especially on what was needed in the United States for Supreme Court decisions that substantively expanded individual rights, argues that producing substantial change through the courts requires repetitive and coordinated litigation that is too costly for the ordinary individual litigant. A "rights revolution" will only happen, in his view, if claimants can count on (a) litigation-oriented organizations that can support a prolonged and strategically planned litigation campaign; (b) extensive charitable or state funding, and (c) public interest or rights-oriented lawyers who can do the legal work. Epp argues that the presence of such support structures is not only necessary but nearly sufficient to produce a rights revolution.

---

[8] The supply and demand in this formulation refer to the supply of and demand for judicial services. The response side refers to the target of the demand, to whom a judicial order would be addressed, typically the defendant in a lawsuit.

Although helpful, this account is too closely tied to the U.S. civil rights experience to be applied directly to the countries studied here. It is true that sustained litigation (coordinated or not) that can produce extensive legalization in a policy area requires more than sporadic access to legal professionals. But the quantity and type of legal assistance required depends on the characteristics of the court system as well as on the nature of the claims being brought. To explain legalization in a variety of systems, civil law systems without docket control or centralized constitutional courts of original jurisdiction, for example, and issues, from abstract constitutional challenges of legislation to individual claims for a particular course of treatment, for example, a more general account is necessary. In the most general terms, Epp's research supports the observation that what is needed for legalization is a legal support structure appropriate to the claims being brought, in light of the institutional requirements in each legal system.

Although it is difficult if not impossible to characterize the requisite support structure in the abstract, it is possible to generalize about how some features of the support structure might shape the contours of legalization. A well-developed private bar is likely to be associated with a more extensive individual claims practice, whereas collective claims and claims on behalf of the underprivileged require the presence of well-funded, PIL-oriented organizations. Individual claims addressing the relationship between a provider and a recipient or an individual demand for a particular good or service will not require extensive coordination and are possible even in the absence of litigation organizations. But without these organizations, substantial numbers of these claims will likely arise only among relatively well-off groups in modernized urban settings. Similarly, although a single claim requesting the modification of the regulatory framework can have far-reaching impact and may not require extensive legal support, for such a claim to benefit underprivileged groups primarily it will likely have to come from an organization that represents their interests. The presence of Epp-style public interest organizations, then, will likely be associated not with the number of claims or the scope of their impact, but with the presence of beneficiaries from marginalized classes and groups.

Supply-Side Factors

Epp takes institutional characteristics of the judicial system for granted, but they vary significantly across the cases in this study. The supply of available judicial services depends on logistical, legal, and operational characteristics of the court structure. Examples of logistical variables are the physical availability of judicial facilities – for some communities in Indonesia, for example, the nearest courtroom is at the far end of a three-day trip by ferry and other modes of transportation. The legal characteristics include jurisdictional rules (e.g., the ability to raise constitutional claims in local courts as opposed to centralized bodies), procedural devices (the Brazilian *ação civil pública*, or the Indian PIL), and standing rules (limiting who can sue in Nigeria or expanding standing in India). Operational characteristics refer to the way in which the system in fact operates. Litigants consider, before filing, whether the judge who will decide their case is independent enough to rule against the government or too corrupt to serve as a reliable forum for settling disputes between individual claimants and important drug manufacturers.

A reasonably accessible and functional judicial system is a likely precondition for legalization.

When judges are more supportive of SE claims, legalization is more likely. What explains variance in judicial support for SE claims? Prevailing explanations for judicial behavior fall roughly into three major theoretical strands: legal, attitudinal, and strategic models. All of the models are useful in their own way, and the following account derives some potential explanations from each.

It is possible, indeed likely, that the nature of the legal framework is important. A simplistic, quasi-mechanical account of jurisprudence in which formal rights are uniformly and directly translated into judicial decisions has not sustained critical examination, at least not since the legal realists arrived, and is not plausible. Still, the content of legal rules is an important starting point for two reasons. First, especially in the case of recent constitutions (e.g., South Africa and Brazil), legal texts communicate a sense of dominant political currents – laws are how polities communicate with judges and how judges know what is expected of them. Given that amending constitutions is typically a more difficult enterprise than enacting ordinary legislation, more recent constitutions are more likely than older ones to reflect current majorities.

Moreover, courts incur a cost or risk when they create significant new legal doctrine. To grant a claim to a particular education service in Nigeria, for example, the courts would have to overcome the express constitutional exclusion of economic, social, and cultural rights from their jurisdiction. The Brazilian Constitution, by contrast, offers unconditional support for judicial involvement in determining the adequacy of the health care provided by the state. The less legal doctrine courts have to create in order to offer a legal remedy, the easier it is for them to support a claim and to find political support for their decision. Laws will matter, therefore, even in less mechanistic models of judicial decision making. This suggests that the level and types of legalization depend, at least in part, on the explicit constitutionalization of justiciable SE rights and on more detailed legislative enactments.

The attitudinal and strategic models of judicial behavior, on the other hand, suggest that judges' decisions are driven by their policy preferences, which, in turn, are shaped and constrained by political realities. By virtue of their recruitment and appointment mechanisms and their socialization, judges tend to reflect the attitudes and preferences of dominant political trends (Brinks 2008; Dahl 1957; Segal and Spaeth 2002). If judges are not constrained by political actors, their decisions should reflect these prior preferences. Understanding these preferences requires knowledge concerning what Hoffmann and Bentes in their chapter call the "narrow legal culture," including the composition of the judiciary.

The strategic approach adds that judges are significantly constrained by their political contexts because they depend on political actors for their effectiveness and for their institutional survival (Epstein and Knight 1998; Rosenberg 1991). If this is true, judges will take care that their decisions garner sufficient political support from other branches of government, whatever their own preferences. At a minimum, judges will not adopt positions that are likely to arouse strong opposition from important political actors. Either by influencing judicial preferences or by imposing constraints on judicial decision making, the political context will influence the degree of judicial support litigants can expect and, therefore, their decisions to press legal claims. In short, we would expect more judicial support and, hence, more legalization where there is a greater development of constitutional and legislative frameworks concerning social and economic rights.

Demand- and supply-side variations can interact. Where there is easier access to courts and more judicial support, the professional support structure need not be as strong. For example, a demand originating in the more remote areas of Indonesia and filed in the centralized constitutional court in downtown Jakarta requires a considerably stronger support structure than a demand originating in the city of Rio de Janeiro and filed in the nearest trial court. Moreover, different supply-side characteristics will likely produce different kinds of demands: less politically autonomous courts may still attract demands against private providers but not against the state, whereas highly corruptible courts may not attract any claims against powerful economic actors but serve to process routine demands against lower level bureaucrats. Individual demands require less specialized procedural devices than collective ones, and constitutional challenges often follow different procedures than statutory claims.

To put it in the most general terms, one of the things claimants will take into consideration is the likely payoff of choosing a legal strategy. Unless the objective is something other than winning – something not to be ruled out – judicial support is likely to be essential to the legalization of a particular policy area. If access is difficult and expensive, or if the judiciary is likely to be unsupportive, a rudimentary cost benefit calculation will dissuade many actors from pursuing legal claims.

Response-Side Factors

Since the American statesman Alexander Hamilton penned it, many have repeated the observation that the courts control neither the sword nor the purse, and thus, they rely on the other branches of government to enforce their orders. In the context of SE rights enforcement this implies that the courts rely on the voluntary cooperation of bureaucratic actors in cases against the state and on enforcement action by other state actors in cases against private providers. A review of the literature on court capacity and court enforcement of SE rights suggests that this might be the Achilles' heel of justiciability (see, e.g., Rosenberg 1991 for an extensive analysis of this weakness). But the magnitude of the task involved in carrying out a court-ordered remedy (and thus the extent of bureaucratic cooperation required) depends on the policy area, the nature of the respondent, the nature of the duty sought, and the nature and scope of the relief ordered by the court.

Rosenberg (1991) argues that without the support of elite political actors, judicial decisions cannot produce significant social change, and he concludes that courts are generally superfluous because anything they can accomplish could be done more efficiently by securing the support of political actors in the first instance. One hypothesis is, then, that absent significant political support, courts can have no impact on basic service delivery, and, therefore, strategic litigants will not seek rulings that challenge prominent political decisions. Even with the support of elite actors, determined bureaucratic resistance will be difficult to overcome for courts – especially those courts that, unlike their U.S. counterparts, are not used to exercising supervisory jurisdiction over court-ordered remedial action.

For legalization in the area of social and economic rights, the necessary condition might be yet stronger. For a course of litigation involving service provision to take hold, courts might require not only implicit political support, but also an existing policy infrastructure. To extend access to particular medications in Brazil, for example, the courts need only direct existing clinics, hospitals, and local health secretariats to procure the drugs a litigant demands; but to improve and ensure educational quality the courts may have to invent a new incentive scheme for teachers and an organization to monitor it from the ground up. As the example illustrates, extant policy infrastructure will vary not only across countries, but also by policy area and by the type of claim. If courts are looking ahead to the likelihood of implementation and litigants to the likelihood of judicial support, courts will be more active in those policy areas, claims, and countries where there are preexisting public policy structures. A related matter is the capacity of the target of the demand. If the state is clearly not up to a demand (e.g., world-class health care for all Indians or Nigerians), strategic actors will believe litigation to be futile; similarly, courts will likely be reluctant to impose utopian obligations on the state or bankrupting duties on a private provider. In summary, there will likely be more litigation for provision of services against the state when there is underutilized state capacity and against providers when they are economically strong.

But not all types of claims require the same level of policy infrastructure, latent capacity, and voluntary cooperation; and some are less likely than others to generate determined bureaucratic resistance. Here is where our triangular typology comes most clearly into play. When there are limited state resources to provide services, litigants might still bring claims for greater or different state regulation, rather than direct state provision. When the state is weak, litigants might demand, and courts might impose, additional obligations on private providers or market competition to improve service quality and lower prices. Ministries of finance are less likely to object to rulings that modify regulatory frameworks than to rulings that impose vast new provision obligations. Bureaucrats, on the other hand, might not object at all to rulings that require them to provide more services, if that gives them bigger budgets or allows them to meet client needs that were being frustrated by political decisions. On this account, patterns of legalization will follow the path of least resistance, shifting according to the limits of state and bureaucratic capacity, provider feasibility, and political tolerance. In more concrete terms: in a weak state context, we would expect courts and litigants to emphasize regulation and private obligations; in stronger states, with more infrastructure already in place, we would expect more cases and decisions imposing direct duties on the state to provide services.

Follow Up

The last step in the process of legalization is the response to the compliance decision, the postdecision follow up by initial or new claimants. To the extent the empirical literature addresses this fourth step, it is usually in a discussion of the capabilities of the initial litigants. Partial exceptions to this are Epp (2003), who looks at judicial follow up, but not at implementation, so all we know is that people continued to bring claims on the same issue; and Sabel and Simon (2004), who discuss the iterative nature of public interest litigation in the context of attempts to reform public institutions. This oversight may stem from theoretical or practical reasons – either because the last step appears a reiteration of the first, or because it poses daunting research difficulties, as this project has itself encountered, or both – but it is a crucial determinant of the extent of legalization in a given policy area. Without follow up, individual judicial decisions, no matter how important, remain isolated events with little direct or indirect impact. Moreover, as the following discussion of impact suggests, the follow up does not always involve the initial claimants or even the same demands. Sometimes, the decision opens up opportunities for claimants in other areas altogether, as in South Africa, where the *Grootboom* case on housing rights opened the way to other kinds of SE rights claims.

Follow-up litigation is important for the level and impact of legalization, with or without voluntary compliance with the original judicial decision. In the absence of voluntary compliance on the part of the target of the litigation, the importance of follow up is obvious – no compliance and no enforcement activity means judicial opinions remain parchment victories, suitable for framing and little else. When purely voluntary compliance is unlikely, strategic courts will consider the likelihood that the initial claimants will be willing and able to carry out the necessary monitoring and follow-up litigation. Courts will likely, therefore, be more willing to issue broad rulings that require extensive bureaucratic compliance when the claimants are strong and well organized.

Even decisions that produce some measure of compliance gain in importance from follow-up decisions. For instance, decisions that modify the regulatory framework depend on the presence of a bureaucracy that can undertake requisite monitoring and enforcement, and decisions that impose new duties on providers depend on individuals for enforcement when these duties are violated. Perhaps more important, a first favorable decision will expand the jurisprudential bases for additional claims, the favorable experience of one group might inspire other groups to follow suit, and the fact of voluntary compliance frees resources to press new claims. Under these conditions, we believe, legalization should grow rapidly. As a result, where initial favorable decisions meet with voluntary compliance, there might well be an exponential growth of legalization; where they meet with resistance, there will be either a much lower but steady volume of enforcement litigation (subject to the same claimant resource constraints that limited the initial demand) or, in its absence, very little direct or indirect impact from the initial decisions. But as the volume of demands grows, levels of resistance might also grow, so that once litigation reaches a critical mass, bureaucrats, politicians, or providers might find ways to frustrate the impact of these decisions.

WHAT IS THE IMPACT OF LEGALIZING DEMAND FOR SOCIAL AND ECONOMIC RIGHTS?

Who, if anyone, benefits from the legalization of social and economic rights? Assessing the extent of legalization entails an examination of postdecision implementation and follow up and an evaluation of how many people benefited from the decision. But that accounting does not give a sense of the decision's impact on the overall policy landscape nor its indirect effects. This is what we turn to next. Analytically, one can distinguish kinds of impact beyond that of compliance with individual decisions: the direct effects of decisions on litigants themselves, including their distributional incidence; the direct effect of decisions on nonlitigants; the indirect effect of early decisions on subsequent legal activity (i.e., indirect effects that are *internal* to legal settings and depend on subsequent judicial decisions); and the indirect legislative or regulatory impact of a decision beyond its immediate beneficiaries (i.e., indirect effects that are *external* to legal settings and result from political or bureaucratic/corporate decisions taken in light of or in anticipation of judicial rulings).

Direct Effects and Their Distribution

Measuring the distributive impact of legalization is a challenge because the interesting question is not just who wins but who does not. Each of the country chapters presents at least some information on the characteristics of those who pressed claims in courts. The more difficult problem is inferring who fails to appear in court in order to evaluate whether, when courts begin to allocate SE goods, there is a shift in policy priorities toward the poor, toward the relatively more privileged, or neither. Some of the country authors – Shankar and Mehta in particular – address this problem by comparing the profile of successful litigants to the profile of needs in the country and compare court-ordered remedies to policy priorities identified in the secondary literature. In other cases the comparison is less explicit and depends primarily on identifying who is using the courts.

We have suggested that access to professionals and judicial structures and to a preexisting policy infrastructure is a precondition for extensive legalization. If that is true, and if the benefits of legalization only accrue to privately funded individual litigants who are pursuing individual claims for more state services (along the right leg of the triangle in Figure 1.2), the benefits will be concentrated among those who already have some level of personal resources and access to state services – urban claimants in more modernized contexts with a greater state presence. As legalization becomes more prevalent as a mechanism of public resource allocation, judicial decisions might redirect state resources toward those who are at least minimally wealthy. Trendy middle class concerns – the Brazilian equivalent of the McDonald's hot coffee case[9] is a decision, mentioned in Hoffmann and Bentes's chapter, ordering a penile reconstruction at state expense – would dominate the policy offerings to the exclusion of broader and more important but less "interesting" concerns – child survival in the rural Northeast of Brazil, for example, or the quality of public primary education in Nigeria.

Charitable interventions and state funding for individual claims by indigent litigants, to the extent they are available, can mitigate the potentially regressive cumulative impact of individual claims. On the one hand, legalization will likely have a more egalitarian effect in policy areas or geographical regions that

---

[9] For a discussion of this case and its place in the American popular imaginary, see the discussion of the media's approach to litigation reporting in Haltom and McCann 2004.

somehow produce private- or state-funded free litigation services. On the other hand, the availability of this support will likely reflect political resources. State funding depends on political decisions, and private charitable funding depends on the interest of third parties, often international third parties. An enforcement regime that depends on third parties to identify and fund priorities is likely to produce an enforcement deficit relative to those regimes in which the rights bearers are themselves able to fund enforcement. Thus, these mechanisms are at best remedial and are unlikely to respond directly to the most pressing concerns of the most marginalized populations. In short, it will likely be case that the cumulative *direct* effect of litigation exacerbates existing inequalities in access to goods and services.

An important caveat is in order here. It is crucial not to compare the reality of litigation to an ideal of public-interested-oriented, democratic, legislated policy making. Almost by definition, the elected branches have not solved the economic and social problems that courts are now being asked to address. Removing the courts from a policy-making process that has thus far failed to solve a problem is not a guarantee that legislators and bureaucrats will suddenly make enlightened public policy or aim for the greatest good for the greatest number. Nor is eviscerating the judiciary likely to spark a fit of spontaneous empathy for the poor and marginalized on the part of bureaucrats, legislators, and private providers.

Direct Effects on Nonlitigants

In some cases, either the demand or the remedy is collective in nature, and benefits naturally accrue to nonlitigants. Creating a new school or installing an access ramp on an existing school benefits an entire community, litigants and nonlitigants alike. Direct constitutional challenges of legislation, class actions, and public interest lawsuits by state actors benefit many who would not or could not invest the requisite legal resources to pursue an individual claim on their own. Challenges to the regulatory framework and realignments of the relationship between providers and recipients (the left and bottom legs of the triangle in Figure 1.2) affect all recipients, not just litigants. Collective remedies, then, are the first source of generalized benefits beyond the privileged litigants discussed earlier.

But there is no guarantee that these benefits will accrue to the underprivileged. Improvements to health and education services in response to demands by middle or upper class litigants are likely to benefit the poor only to the extent that those services are jointly consumed by rich and poor alike. The poor, middle, and upper classes all utilize large public hospitals, can potentially consume the same medications when suffering the same illness, and are similarly affected by certain public health threats. They do not often attend the same schools, especially at the lower educational levels, nor do they utilize, generally speaking, the same primary health-care providers. In other words, joint consumption typically occurs more in health care than in education and more for higher-level services (hospitals, universities) than for lower-level ones (primary health care, primary schools).

For benefits to reach poor nonlitigants beyond services involving joint consumption on the part of the rich and the poor, then, it is likely that NGOs and state-supported public interest litigation organizations will have to play a leading role in the litigation process. Epp (2003: 45 et seq.), for example, documents a gradual shift in judicial attention from the concerns of capitalists and corporations to "public interest" concerns as charitable funding and public-interest-oriented litigation organizations became more common in the United States. The risk of outside charitable funding is the introduction of a mediating actor (dependent at least in part on foreign donors or political actors for its funding) between the demands of the poor and the claims made and thus the potential loss of the rights bearers' ability to set priorities. Bivitri Susanti's chapter on Indonesia, for example, documents tensions between poor litigants and their NGO advocates.

This mediated intervention, moreover, requires legal devices that may or may not be available. India's PIL, Brazil's *ação civil pública*, and abstract constitutional challenges to legislation are examples of legal devices that effectively grant standing to civil society or state-sponsored third parties to assert the claims of those who otherwise lack the resources to do so. Nigeria has much more restrictive standing rules that limit the participation of civil society groups, and there seems to be no equivalent to Brazil's Public Prosecutor (*Ministério Público*) in any of the other countries. The degree to which direct effects will favor already privileged groups will depend on the availability of these legal devices and of charitable or state resources to pursue claims. The more that courts act in response to the collective claims of public-interest actors, the more the benefits are likely to extend beyond the middle and upper classes in urban settings.

Indirect Effects Internal to the Legal System

Even in legal systems that do not officially embrace *stare decisis* and binding precedent, high court jurisprudence has a disciplining effect on lower court decision making (for a discussion of the use of precedent in the ostensibly nonprecedential system in France, see Shapiro 1981: 126–156; for a more abstract discussion, see Merryman 1985: 46–47). As a result, in any legal system – though perhaps more openly in common law systems – an initial judicial decision clears the path for subsequent decisions in similar areas. Moreover, decisions can set important substantive or ostensibly procedural principles even in the absence of binding precedents. Rules of standing, like India's PIL and similar causes of action for collective claims in the public interest, often arise first through judicial fiat and are then formalized in legislation or recognized in constitutions. A decision establishing that social and economic rights either can or cannot be enforced by court action has consequences far beyond the policy area directly at issue.

Establishing these entry points in the judicial system is substantially more risky and likely to be more costly than "me too" second-generation litigation. Therefore, even if the first generation of cases is dominated by better-resourced claimants, the second generation may be within the reach of low-income litigants working through storefront or publicly funded lawyers.

Indirect Effects External to the Legal System

These effects are potentially the most important pathway for extending the benefits of judicial intervention beyond the initial litigants. Generally, this occurs when the target of the judicial demand makes a subsequent decision – through legislation, or through corporate or bureaucratic rule making – to extend benefits from the initial demand to all those who are similarly situated. This decision, which we will call *expansive compliance*, is more common than the adversarial model of litigation might predict. Expansive compliance can happen in many ways, of which the following discussion is not an exhaustive catalog but an illustrative selection. The country chapters provide additional examples and details that are unique to each country.

First, perhaps least likely, even utterly unsuccessful litigation campaigns can produce generalized positive policy outcomes if they trigger a political reaction. A well-publicized judicial failure may highlight the inadequacies of the existing legal framework and provoke legal reforms. Media attention to the plight of victims who cannot obtain redress in the courts can galvanize a political response. Alternatively, the courts can provide a venue, focal point, or catalyst for organizing politically to contest governmental policies, even (or especially) if the claimants are unsuccessful.[10] Cases that, because of long delays or interminable appeals, never reach final adjudication can still serve as the locus for negotiations resulting in a consensual remedy. Though probably to a lesser extent than resounding successes in the courts, failed litigation can be one component of a successful political strategy for extending effective rights. Identifying this requires finding settlements and accommodations triggered by unsuccessful litigation and drawing connections between apparently failed legal strategies and political decisions that extend effective rights between lost cases and political mobilization.

Second, the benefits of successful litigation campaigns can diffuse for two reasons. The first involves simple economies of scale. Litigation is expensive for claimants *and* the state. Routine denials to all but those who can afford to litigate can be, on the one hand, an effective rationing device. On the other hand, however, the cost of constantly defending recurring lawsuits that claim extraordinary benefits, plus the cost of providing those benefits on an ad hoc basis to successful litigants, will eventually exceed the cost of simply regularizing their purchase and provision as routine government services. This will require, of course, a sufficiently numerous influx of individual legal claims relative to potential total demand, so that it is not cheaper to limit the benefit to those who can afford to litigate. At that point, it is likely that the government will take the political decision to include the claimed services or goods in the ordinary public-policy offering, so that they become available even for those who cannot afford lawyers.

Another pathway occurs when, once a particular good has been incorporated as a formal right by the courts, potential claimants begin to redefine their notion of what "I am entitled to," raising political demand for that good and thus making

---

[10] See, e.g., Matthew Taylor's forthcoming account of the political uses of courts in Brazil for a description of how the then-opposition Workers' Party used losing cases to win policy objectives (Taylor 2008).

it a matter of urgent public policy. Amartya Sen (1999a: 9–10; 1999b: 153–54), for example, argues that individuals (and societies) identify "needs" from among "the totality of the human predicament" in light of ongoing discussions and redefinitions of what is socially possible and desirable. Litigation campaigns that demonstrate the feasibility of social action can redefine what is socially possible and transform what were utopian aspirations and barely articulated wishes, which could be dismissed or bought off with more tangible short-term benefits, into needs that *must* be met by governments. Alternatively, courts may bring to light unnoticed failings and injustices, place issues on the agenda, redefine priorities, and otherwise raise the visibility of claims that were getting little legislative traction before (see, generally, the discussion of indirect effects in Rosenberg 1991: 25–26).

Similarly, even minimal equal treatment standards require states to offer more generally what they provide individually, so continuing to offer special services to those who sue while denying them to everyone else may become untenable once it becomes public knowledge. A successful litigation campaign, thus, will make it easier to demand that governments cover these needs as a matter of public policy and basic equity.

These three mechanisms for generalizing the benefits of legalization, although conceptually clear and potentially more consequential than direct effects, are empirically difficult to establish. As Rosenberg puts it, "ideas seem to have feet of their own, and tracking their footsteps is an imperfect science" (Rosenberg 1991: 108). This empirical difficulty is probably one of the reasons for the prevailing skepticism of the benefits of legalization. We should not, however, allow skepticism born of methodological rigidity to convert us into the proverbial drunkard who loses his keys at the doorstep but searches under the lamppost where the light is. The country authors indeed do their best to poke around in dark corners and, in a qualitative fashion, trace generalized policy changes that might flow from social and economic rights litigation. In some instances, this pursuit is relatively simple – has a particular medication that was the focus of litigation become part of the official menu of options? In others, it is more difficult – are Brazil's aggressive AIDS policies related to earlier litigation or were they an entirely independent political development? Can one attribute the availability of antiretrovirals for impoverished, remote, rural populations in South Africa – with little or no access to legal and judicial services – to some prominent legal victories won by relatively well-funded groups in major urban centers? To address these questions, the country chapters, among other things, use secondary literature, compare the timing of events, ask claimants and key actors in the policy-making process whether they were influenced by court decisions, and look for explicit references to court actions in the policy-making process.

WHAT DOES LEGALIZATION ADD TO DEMOCRATIC POLITICS?

At every stage of the legalization process, courts are likely to be most effective when they draw on broad-based social and political support. Courts are more likely to be presented with numerous claims if the demands are backed by well-organized and well-funded litigants (Epp 2003); judges are more likely to support claims that fall well within the mainstream of political and legal culture because they are creatures of those cultures (Baum 2000; Dahl 1957; Graber 1993); judges' directives are more likely to be complied with if they have the support of political, bureaucratic, or civil society actors (Epp 2003; Rosenberg 1991); and legalization is most likely to have broad social impact if it is picked up and carried forward through political decisions (Dixon 2007; Rosenberg 1991; Tushnet 2004). Courts are, for dozens of reasons, more effective when working within, rather than against, the dominant currents in the political and policy environments.

Thus, contrary to the image presented in the popular press and despite what some academic accounts have found (see, e.g., Hirschl 2004), courts, even (or especially) when they are strategic actors interested in expanding their effectiveness and power, are not likely to be engaged in imperative monologues, demanding particular policies on behalf of nonrepresentative elites, and frustrating democratic demands for redistributive justice over the long term. Rather, courts are likely to be most effective, and therefore most attractive to strategic litigants, when they resolve obstacles to achieving genuinely popular policies. As a result, their behavior is likely to be more dialogical than monological, drawing on and incorporating the views of a variety of social and political actors.

What, then, is the role of courts in the legalization of SE rights, given that substantial legalization is likely to occur in policy areas that are already popular and in relatively well-functioning democracies? The answer must be that, despite the popularity of the policies, there exist obstacles that prevent their adoption by politicians, bureaucrats, and others. There are potentially three types of obstacles: political blockages, monitoring deficits, and incomplete commitments.[11] These three kinds of obstacles can block the adoption of popular policies in any sector and involve any kind of claim (along any leg of the triangle in Figure 1.2), though there may exist affinities between certain obstacles and the kinds of partners available to courts and thus between certain obstacles and certain kinds of claims.

First, political blockages can impede the government's response to popular demands, creating space for the courts to generate more responsiveness and accountability between voters and their government. This could affect either the direct provision of SE goods or the regulation of providers. One example is when international actors or global market pressures make it too costly for governments to respond to popular demands.[12] Another prominent example is when multiparty democracy edges into the high levels of fragmentation that tend to produce lawmaking deadlocks, as in the case of Brazil (Ames 2001; Mainwaring 1999). Some have attributed the outsized policy relevance of the Israeli Supreme Court, for example, to just this sort of political deadlock (Edelman 1994). Similarly, Graber (1993) and Whittington (2005) argue the U.S. Supreme Court is most consequential when it serves to overcome political obstacles, such as those associated

---

[11] The obstacles we identify overlap with and expand on those identified in Dixon 2007.

[12] In this sense, courts can serve governments as they play Putnam's (1988) well-known "two level game" – domestic constraints can strengthen the hand of governments as they negotiate for concessions from international actors.

with federalism, entrenched political interests, fractious governing coalitions, or other political veto points. These analyses show that even courts whose judges are selected through majoritarian procedures routinely remove political blockages and thereby deliver policies that could not be adopted solely through ordinary democratic processes.

A second category involves monitoring deficits – situations where a government has adopted policies related to service provision or regulation, but where a lack of information, ineffective incentives or toothless sanctions, or bureaucratic incapacity and inertia hinder implementation. Supervising ministries or agencies might be slow to adopt new technologies in health care or might willfully or inadvertently ignore contaminants in the environment. In federal systems and decentralized bureaucracies local officials might resist national policies. Industry actors might "capture" regulators or engage in behavior that, whether or not it responds to market forces, contradicts expressed political commitments. In these instances, the courts correct information deficits or recalibrate performance incentives and sanctions, serving as "fire alarm" monitoring devices (McCubbins and Schwartz 1984).

This function of courts will be especially important when explicit policy mandates outpace bureaucratic development: the delegation of administrative functions to the courts is more likely when policy makers create big policies in a small state (see, e.g., Kagan 2001; Miller and Barnes 2004). It will likely also be visible when monitoring is costly – for example, when the issue is narrow and technical, when the state of the art in an area is rapidly changing, or when the overall regulatory scheme is complex and difficult for policy makers to evaluate. Under those conditions, courts, in response to individual demands presented by the most directly affected, step in on an ad hoc basis to rectify some of the shortcomings of both policy makers and frontline bureaucrats.

Third, incomplete commitments occur where regimes draw substantial legitimacy from an announced project of social transformation and inclusion, broad democratization, or nationalistic development, but fail to deliver material goods on a universalistic basis. In such countries, human rights and related discourses figure prominently in the goals and proposals of most social, political, and even economic actors, including the major political parties. At the same time, policy delivery remains subject to inadequate coverage, clientelistic exchange, and other particularistic mechanisms that detract from the universalization of policy but that are crucial for the maintenance of the extant political order. There arises a certain equilibrium between universal, rights-based, and egalitarian announced policy goals (aspirations) on the one hand and status quo–preserving, particularistic targeted practices (political order) on the other. When this occurs, it might even be said that political and social actors attempt to "free ride" on the legitimating power of the shared, universalistic discourse even as they continue to operate in a discriminatory fashion at their bases.

Under these conditions, social movements excluded from clientelistic networks or policy distributions may arise and mobilize on the basis of the official rights discourse. These groups identify and publicize the inconsistencies between promise and delivery and lean on the official discourse to bring strong demands, particularly highly charged or strongly felt ones. These groups, like the society as a whole, are aware of the prevailing equilibrium between aspirations and order; but for any given claim, these groups may not be able to prove that aspirations can be fulfilled without jeopardizing political order or economic stability. It may indeed be in the interest of political and economic elites to hide information about what is feasible. Legalization is then a process by which information regarding the feasibility of social and economic claims is discovered and debated. In this process, courts respond to demands by appealing to and drawing on the legitimacy of the shared social project. In so doing, constitutional courts may enhance their own prestige and "may be able to lean on the legitimacy of rights themselves to move to the defense of rights" (Shapiro 2004: 13). Kameshni Pillay (2002: 255) discusses the *Grootboom* case in South Africa in these terms. Pillay points out that "one of the ANC's key election promises... was 'homes for all,'" but that the government had failed to deliver on this promise, so that there were 1.3 million informal dwellings in South Africa by 1999 – twice as many as in 1995. Under these conditions, the litigants did not have to search very far to find official (at least rhetorical) support for their demands to adequate housing. The strength of the legitimating discourse itself creates the space for courts to challenge dominant political actors.

In this scenario, courts remain pro-majoritarian actors. Their actions narrow the gap between widely shared social beliefs and incomplete or inchoate policy preferences on the part of the government, or between the behavior of private firms and expressed political commitments. Rights, in this context, function to generate additional uncertainty or "openness" in the political and social system, creating the opportunity to meet deeply felt needs.

We do not mean to argue that courts always get this right or that they are always consciously engaged in one of the three tasks outlined earlier. Our argument is, rather, that courts will be more effective when they act well within the political mainstream and with substantial support from other political actors. More effective courts, in turn, will be more attractive to strategic litigants and will issue more far-reaching decisions under these conditions. Substantial legalization is, therefore, more likely when the courts are (a) engaging in one of these three ideal types of accountability enhancing activities, (b) within a well-functioning democratic context, and (c) acting in response to the demands of relatively developed economies and societies.

THE RESEARCH STRATEGY

Our authors use the four-step account of legalization previously described, modifying it where appropriate. Their measure of legal mobilization focuses primarily on courts, but, where appropriate, chapter authors also include those demands presented in quasi-judicial venues such as national human rights commissions or, as in the case of Nigeria, in regional bodies such as the African Commission on Human and Peoples' Rights. For simplicity, we refer to this activity as litigation, even though in some contexts it may be more akin to mediation or arbitration than to judicial, adversarial litigation.

The country authors measure the extent of legal mobilization on the basis of a representative sample of social and economic rights cases. In the cases of India and South Africa, this included all cases at the High Court level and above; in Brazil, it included all electronically reported cases from the highest courts of four states plus the decisions of the two apex courts; in Indonesia (a unitary country), it included all available cases at any level; and in Nigeria, it included federal court decisions going back to 1979 (when the Nigerian constitution first recognized social and economic rights) and all available cases in three selected states.[13] With this information, it is possible to calculate the number of SE rights cases reaching courts, the likelihood that plaintiffs succeed, whether individual or collective actions predominate, the level of the court rendering the decision, and the rationales typically employed to grant or deny the claim. After that, the chapter authors investigated, as best they could, on-the-ground implementation subsequent to court rulings. Where possible, the authors and their teams interviewed judges, advocates, and others involved in the cases in order to better understand the processes that led to the presentation of a claim in court, the reasons for the judicial decision, and the extent of compliance. In many cases, however, they relied on the secondary literature for data on compliance and on the direct and indirect effects of the litigation. Assessing implementation turned out to be an extremely challenging phase of the research – often court records did not indicate the addresses of the applicants or even the names of their advocates, parties to the cases had moved, lawyers did not remember the selected cases, or confidentiality shielded identifying information from researchers.

Legalization often involves negotiation under the threat of litigation and court intervention (McCann 1994). Therefore, in addition to actual judicial decisions, the country authors included, wherever possible, some discussion of settlements obtained incident to litigation, so long as the threat was formalized in some legal or quasi-legal proceeding. This turned out to be particularly important for the discussion of the Brazilian public prosecutor and for settlements reached by litigants in Indonesia before and sometimes after losing a court battle.

Next, having measured the extent and form of the legalization of social and economic demands, the chapter authors attempt to explain its extent and impact in their countries. To do this, they examine the social, political, and other factors that prompt social actors to go to court, courts to support SE rights claims, and respondents to comply or not comply with court decisions and to do so in either a grudging or an expansive way. To assess indirect effects, they look to see when litigation has extended economic and social goods to individuals who were not parties to the original cases and include some discussion of the distributive impact of the legalization process. For this explanatory part of their chapters, they rely on interviews with key participants, a review of the secondary literature, and their own extensive experiences in the field.

---

[13] The problem of what was (not) "available" turned out to be nontrivial, as the chapter discussions of inadequacies in court reporting systems reveal. Still, we are quite confident that the chapter authors managed, by doing their own searches and by consulting with local experts in social and economic rights, to identify all the relevant decisions that fall within the scope of the project.

A LOOK AHEAD AT THE COUNTRY STUDIES

Each chapter is rich in detail and is, to our knowledge, each country's first systematic empirical examination of health and education rights litigation available in the literature. We describe a few of the central findings from each chapter, in the hope of stimulating your interest in the fascinating historical, political, economic, sociological, and legal investigations that follow.

South Africa

Given the predisposition of the South African courts to enforce social and economic rights, a broad social consensus in support of social transformation and a redress of the social inequities from previous decades, and the significant influence of the South African courts on constitutional theories in other countries, one might have expected the range and impact of South African social and economic rights cases to be more robust. Jonathan Berger's account shows that a few cases have had a significant effect on government policies, particularly those involving the failure of the government to provide antiretroviral treatment to AIDS patients in prison, to pregnant women so as to prevent the transmission of HIV to their children, and to the general population with clinical AIDS. But in other cases – for example, the frequently cited *Grootboom* case involving the right to housing and a series of cases involving the arbitrary suspension of social grants benefits – supportive judicial opinions have had mixed or little impact on government policies. In some cases, they have produced few, if any, benefits for the applicants themselves; most famously, it is reported that Mrs. Grootboom and many of her neighbors still do not have adequate housing. From among the several interesting themes from the chapter, two are noteworthy here. First, the large majority of the cases have used social and economic rights in a defensive manner. Second, despite relatively strong constitutional language, many South African courts have exhibited substantial deference toward the government.

Brazil

Florian F. Hoffmann and Fernando R. N. M. Bentes's chapter finds that since 1996, thousands of Brazilian claimants have filed largely successful court cases involving the rights to health care and education. Most of these have been demands for medications either not regularly provided by governments or provided in theory but not available in practice. There have also been many cases invoking the right to health against private health insurance companies, arguing that a specific procedure should be reimbursable in spite of contractual language. Right-to-education cases at the basic and secondary levels have been far less numerous, but still number in the hundreds. Significant themes in right-to-education cases have been the mainstreaming of children with disabilities, access to preschools, and school repair in rural and urban areas. Among the interesting themes from the chapter are these: medications cases now serve as an informal feedback mechanism for the official government pharmaceutical formulary, providing information to governments when formulary revisions are being demanded; most of the cases have been individual, rather than collective, claims; Brazilian courts have usually relied on a variety of constitutional provisions, particularly the right to life, as well as the existence of legislation implementing the constitutional provisions on the right to health care, when requiring the state to provide medications.

India

Shylashri Shankar and Pratap Bhanu Mehta find that since 1950 there have been 209 cases involving the right to health and 173 involving the right to education at the High Court level and above in India. Cases reached courts in all regions of India, but only 14 percent of those cases originated in the poor and so-called BIMARU states. Nationwide, applicants won 81 percent of the cases. Major areas of litigation included reimbursement for medical expenses on the part of government employees, public health (including industrial pollution, sanitation, and potable water), HIV prevention and AIDS treatment, medical negligence, university admissions and fees, and the establishment of private schools. Indian courts are known for their sweeping judgments, and in many instances it appears that supervision of court orders was difficult and enforcement lax. But in establishing new rules through which patients can claim medical negligence or misconduct, helping create a reliable blood bank, provoking some states to establish midday meals programs in schools, clarifying rules regarding university fees and set-asides for "scheduled castes and tribes" as well as "other backward classes," and limiting air and water pollution, the Indian courts used social and economic rights to change government policies.

Two themes stand out in the Indian cases. First, most cases in India concerned government regulation of health-care facilities or schools, or the relative liberties and obligations of service providers and service recipients; relatively few involved claims for government provision in areas where the government was not already acting. Second, although the majority of cases concerned the interests of the lower-middle or the middle classes, not the interests of the extremely poor, some of the decisions with the broadest implications and the largest number of beneficiaries – the school meals decision, for example – most benefited the least advantaged. Yet other cases, such as decisions promoting clean air and water in large urban areas and clean blood in the blood banks, benefited the rich and the poor alike.

Nigeria

Chidi Anselm Odinkalu finds, in the federal courts and the courts of three Nigerian states since 1979, less than a few dozen cases dealing with the rights to health and education. Almost all of the education cases that reached the courts concerned university education. The Nigerian courts have supported the right to establish and maintain private schools and universities on the basis of the rights to property and free expression, but they have maintained that the state can license and accredit private educational institutions. The majority of health-care cases that reached the Nigerian courts have involved the right to bail for obtaining health care. The African Commission on Human and Peoples' Rights found that hazardous oil field operations in the Niger Delta violated the right to health and clean environment of the Ogoni community, but this opinion was not binding under Nigerian law. Odinkalu argues that judicial attitudes, narrow constructions of standing and judicial procedures, and corruption limit the effectiveness of Nigerian courts in addressing SE rights claims. He concludes that there has been some useful litigation regarding rights *in* education and health care in Nigeria, but little that has expanded the rights *to* health care and education.

Indonesia

The absence of court records makes it extremely difficult to conduct a comprehensive historical review of court cases in Indonesia. Bivitri Susanti identifies seven court cases related to the right to health care from 1995 to 2005, a period that exceeds that of the current constitutional framework. One case, in which a two-year-old boy was paralyzed after allegedly receiving poorly produced polio vaccine during an immunization drive in a rural area, illustrates the stereotypical outcome of cases litigated in the ordinary courts in Indonesia. In a pattern common to many legal disputes in Indonesia, the plaintiff withdrew his claim and negotiated a settlement with the defendant under secret terms. In another case, a group of NGOs sued the government when it failed to provide health care, sanitation, nutrition, and housing to Indonesian migrants forced to return from Malaysia. The court ordered the government to take steps to provide relief to the returning migrants, but it refused to order the government to pass general legislation to protect migrant workers. Nevertheless, the government did pass such a law two years later. The broadest SE claims in Indonesia involved a series of cases challenging the constitutionality of the central government budgets on the grounds that the budgets did not allocate 20 percent to (non-salary) educational expenditures, as required in the constitution and in the basic law organizing the education sector. The Constitutional Court agreed that the budget law was unconstitutional. Although the Court has been extremely reluctant to make any specific directives to the legislature regarding the budget, the central government non-salary education budget has increased significantly in recent years, presumably in response, at least in part, to pressure originating in the Constitutional Court's decisions.[14]

Among the themes from Susanti's chapter are these: legal claims are often settled during the course of (and even more frequently, prior to) litigation; claimants can receive some benefits, and occasionally even a major policy change, despite formally losing the case; and in some instances there appear to be conflicts between the interest of appellants, who seek basic compensation, and their legal representatives, such as NGOs, who seek broader policy changes.

---

[14] Reversing a previous interpretation, the Constitutional Court ruled in 2008 that teachers' salaries should be included in the education budget even though they are considered civil service expenditures. As a result, the government was optimistic that the 2009 budget would comply with the constitutional requirement. *The Jakarta Post*, June 17, 2008.

FINAL THOUGHTS AND CAVEATS

Although Bentham famously criticized human rights as a mere "child of law," Sen emphasizes the inverse relationship, arguing that normative human rights are the "parent of law," in the sense that normative ideals lead governments to establish laws that codify rights (Sen 2004). One could add, and many scholars have, that normative ideals of human rights, including public statements such as the Universal Declaration of Human Rights, have had a direct effect on the language of national constitutions, the structure and contents of international and regional treaties, legal interpretations on the part of domestic courts, domestic legislation, the mobilization of civil society organizations, the emergence of international and national NGOs dedicated to advancing human rights, and even individual and group identities. The present book does not directly examine the rhetorical and inspirational effects of human rights norms and language.

Moreover, the discussion in the empirical chapters does not address in any detail the politics or the direct impact of international human rights treaties. Some of the country chapters describe, in passing, the legal status of, or judicial interpretations regarding, relevant human rights treaties. Full disclosure: one of the goals at the inception of this project was to trace the impact of these international documents. Our initial investigations suggested, however, that in general the direct effect of those treaties is marginal to social and economic rights litigation in the countries examined: courts rarely relied on or even cited international or regional treaty instruments in their written opinions. There may well be other, extrajudicial pathways through which those treaty instruments affect social and economic policies, such as multilateral or bilateral pressure on national governments, or the empowerment of civil society actors. But given our focus on courts, we do not address those pathways in this book.

The role of courts as institutions of democratic accountability receives some important, though sidelong, glances throughout this book. Although courts are in many contexts a crucial element of intrastate or "horizontal" accountability, the chapters make clear that their effectiveness depends on a variety of other actors, including individual plaintiffs, public defenders, private lawyers, executive and legislative committees that make judicial appointments, and civil society organizations. O'Donnell has argued that effective horizontal accountability requires a "whole network of state agencies, culminating in high courts, committed to preserving and eventually enforcing horizontal accountability, if necessary against the highest powers of the state" (O'Donnell 2003: 47). By examining the conditions under which states and private actors have been held legally accountable for the economic and social well-being of citizens, the chapters in this volume begin to map the "whole network" of state agencies and social organizations through which social and economic rights are made concrete. But much more could be done along these lines.

A note on language. Although what one is referring to when using the term *social and economic rights* is clear, some writers prefer the expression *economic and social rights*, or *socioeconomic rights*, or even, drawing on the international covenant, *economic, social, and cultural rights*. The phraseology of choice also tends to vary by country. We did not attempt to impose a rule on the country authors, preferring instead to let their language reflect the flavor of local debates. For the purposes of this book, which is decidedly not a textual analysis of international treaties and national constitutions, the terms are more or less equivalent.

Finally, the debate over whether or not courts can and should enforce social and economic rights has, of course, been the object of an enormous output of scholarly labor.[15] Helen Hershkoff's chapter reviews some of this literature in more detail. Here we will close this introduction with a very brief account that summarizes the arguments in the broadest terms and that may set the stage for some of the discussions that follow.[16] Critics have argued that the judicial enforcement of social and economic rights could be enormously costly and could involve judges in policy questions, such as pharmaceutical research, the benefits of privatization, taxation, and economic productivity, on which they have little expertise. When judges substitute their own judgments on budgetary questions for those of a democratically elected legislature, the branch of government explicitly designed both to represent the policy preferences of citizens and to make the political deals necessary to win public support for policies, moreover, the ensuing policy trajectories could be less legitimate and less politically sustainable. Another group of critics have worried that because judges typically represent elite and business interests, granting courts power over economic and social decision making could only make matters worse for poor people. On the other hand, supporters have responded that judges already enforce civil and political rights, such as rights to physical security and political representation. They note that their rulings on prison systems, law enforcement methods, and voting procedures often lead to significant budgetary outlays, and that courts routinely issue high-stakes and often very technical rulings in the areas of bankruptcy, antitrust, and patents, which have significant economic consequences. To address complex subject areas, courts have already developed a repertoire of procedures and techniques that include the use of expert witnesses and the appointment of special masters or technical organizations to oversee implementation orders. And concerns related to the separation of powers should not be considered in the abstract: the legitimacy of judicial involvement is related to the responsiveness of the other branches of government, which in many instances is demonstrably low.

To repeat, our argument is that the legalization of social and economic rights is neither an unambiguous pathway to social equity nor an illegitimate betrayal of popular democratic processes and outcomes. Precisely because courts need social and political partners to change policy and distribute social and economic goods, the choices and outcomes resulting from legalization will not stray far from

---

[15] An online search of just one database found more than six thousand articles and books with the words "economic" or "social" and the word "rights" in the title. If on average a monograph takes eight weeks to produce, the market value of scholarly labor output on social and economic rights would exceed the annual total income for a medium-size city in a low-income country!

[16] A comprehensive analysis is found in Langford 2008. For reviews from the point of view of advocates, see Scott and Macklem 1992 and Abramovich 2005; for reviews from skeptics, see Dennis and Stewart 2004 and Cross 2001.

dominant national trends. Nevertheless, under certain conditions, the empirical analysis in this book makes it clear that legalization can bring some measure of dignity to those in our world who continue to live in conditions of extreme poverty and deprivation.

BIBLIOGRAPHY

Abramovich, V. E. 2005. Courses of action in economic, social and cultural rights: Instruments and allies. *Sur – International Journal on Human Rights* 2 (English ed.):180–216.

Ames, B. 2001. *The deadlock of democracy in Brazil.* Ann Arbor: University of Michigan Press.

Arbour, L. 2006. Using human rights to reduce poverty. *Development Outreach* 8 (2).

Baum, L. 2000. *The puzzle of judicial behavior.* Ann Arbor: University of Michigan Press.

Bergallo, P. 2005. Justice and experimentalism: Judicial remedies in public law litigation in Argentina. Paper presented at the *Seminario en Latinoamérica de Teoría Constitucional y Política,* Panel 4, June 16–19, Rio de Janeiro. Available from http://www.law.yale.edu/intellectuallife/sela%202005.htm.

Bill Chavez, R. 2004. *The rule of law in nascent democracies: Judicial politics in Argentina.* Palo Alto, CA: Stanford University Press.

Brinks, D. M. 2008. *The judicial response to police killings in Latin America: Inequality and the rule of law.* Cambridge: Cambridge University Press.

COHRE. 2003. Litigating economic, social and cultural rights: Achievements, challenges, and strategies. Geneva, Switzerland: Center on Housing Rights and Evictions.

Cross, F. B. 2001. The error of positive rights. *UCLA Law Review* 48 (4):857–924.

Dahl, R. 1957. Decision-making in a democracy: The supreme court as a national policy-maker. *Journal of Public Law* 6 (2):279–295.

Dembowski, H. 2001. *Taking the state to court: Public interest litigation and the public sphere in metropolitan India.* New Delhi: Oxford University Press.

Dennis, M. J., and D. P. Stewart. 2004. Justiciability of economic, social, and cultural rights: Should there be an international complaints mechanism to adjudicate the rights to food, water, housing, and health? *The American Journal of International Law* 98 (462):462–515.

Dixon, R. 2007. Creating dialogue about socio-economic rights: Strong-form versus weak-form judicial review revisited. *International Journal of Constitutional Law* 5 (3):391–418.

Edelman, M. 1994. The judicialization of politics in Israel. *International Political Science Review* 15:177–86.

Epp, C. 2003. *The rights revolution.* Chicago: University of Chicago Press.

Epstein, L., and J. Knight. 1998. *The choices justices make.* Washington, DC: Congressional Quarterly Press.

Epstein, L., J. Knight, and A. Martin. 2001. The Supreme Court as a strategic national policy maker. *Emory Law Journal* 50 (2):583–611.

Forbath, W. E. 2007. Social rights, courts and constitutional democracy – Poverty and welfare rights in the United States. In *On the state of democracy,* ed. J. Faundez, 101–124. Oxford/New York: Routledge.

Gauri, V. 1998. *School choice in Chile: Two decades of educational reform.* Pittsburgh, PA: University of Pittsburgh Press.

Gauri, V. 2004. Social rights and economics: Claims to health care and education in developing countries. *World Development* 32 (3):465.

Ginsburg, T. 2003. *Judicial review in new democracies: Constitutional courts in Asian cases.* Cambridge: Cambridge University Press.

Graber, M. A. 1993. The non-majoritarian difficulty: Legislative deference to the judiciary. *Studies in American Political Development* 7:35.

Haltom, W., and M. McCann. 2004. *Distorting the law: Politics, media and the litigation crisis.* Chicago: University of Chicago Press.

Hershkoff, H. 1999. Positive rights and state constitutions: The limits of federal rationality review. *Harvard Law Review* 112 (6):1132–1196.

Hirschl, R. 2000. The political origins of judicial empowerment through constitutionalization: Lessons from four constitutional revolutions. *Law and Social Inquiry – Journal of the American Bar Foundation* 25 (1):91–149.

Hirschl, R. 2004. *Towards juristocracy – The origins and consequences of the new constitutionalism.* Cambridge, MA: Harvard University Press.

Kagan, R. A. 2001. *Adversarial legalism: The American way of law.* Cambridge, MA: Harvard University Press.

Langford, M., ed. 2008. *Social rights jurisprudence: Emerging trends in international and comparative law.* Cambridge: Cambridge University Press.

Mainwaring, S. 1999. *Rethinking party systems in the third wave of democratization: The case of Brazil.* Palo Alto, CA: Stanford University Press.

McAdam, D., S. Tarrow, and C. Tilly. 2001. *Dynamics of contention.* Cambridge: Cambridge University Press.

McCann, M. 1994. *Rights at work: Pay equity reform and the politics of legal mobilization.* Chicago: University of Chicago Press.

McCubbins, M., and T. Schwartz. 1984. Congressional oversight overlooked: Police patrols versus fire alarms. *American Journal of Political Science* 28 (1):165–179.

Merryman, J. H. 1985. *The civil law tradition: An introduction to the legal systems of Western Europe and Latin America,* 2nd ed. Palo Alto, CA: Stanford University Press.

Miller, M. C., and J. Barnes, eds. 2004. *Making policy, making law: An interbranch perspective.* Washington, DC: Georgetown University Press.

O'Donnell, G. 2003. Horizontal accountability: The legal institutionalization of mistrust. In *Democratic accountability in Latin America,* ed. S. Mainwaring and C. Welna. Oxford: Oxford University Press.

Pillay, K. 2002. Implementation of *Grootboom:* Implications for the enforcement of socio-economic rights. *Law, Democracy and Development* 6:255.

Pitkin, H. 1981. Justice: On relating public and private. *Political Theory* 9:327–352.

Pritchett, L. and M. Woolcock. 2004. Solutions when the solution is the problem: Arraying the disarray in development. *World Development,* 32 (2):191–212.

Putnam, R. D. 1988. Diplomacy and domestic politics: The logic of two-level games. *International Organization* 42 (Summer):427–460.

Rosenberg, G. N. 1991. *The hollow hope: Can courts bring about social change?* Chicago: University of Chicago Press.

Sabel, C., and W. Simon. 2004. Destabilization rights: How public law litigation succeeds. *Harvard Law Review* 117:1016–1101.

Scott, C., and P. Macklem. 1992. Constitutional ropes of sand or justiciable guarantees? Social rights in a new South African constitution. *University of Pennsylvania Law Review* 141 (1):1–148.

Segal, J., and H. Spaeth. 2002. *The Supreme Court and the attitudinal model revisited.* Cambridge: Cambridge University Press.

Sen, A. 1999a. Democracy as a universal value. *Journal of Democracy* 10 (3):3–17.

Sen, A. 1999b. *Development as freedom.* New York: Random House.

Sen, A. 2004. Elements of a theory of human rights. *Philosophy and Public Affairs* 32.

Shapiro, M. 1981. *Courts: A comparative and political analysis.* Chicago and London: University of Chicago Press.

Shapiro, M. 2004. Judicial review in developed democracies. In *Democratization and the judiciary: The accountability function of courts in new democracies,* ed. S. Gloppen, R. Gargarella, and E. Skaar, 7–26. London: Frank Cross.

Shue, H. 1996. *Basic rights: Subsistence, affluence, and U.S. foreign policy.* Princeton, NJ: Princeton University Press.

Steiner, H. J., and P. Alston. 2000. *International human rights in context: Law, politics, morals.* Oxford: Oxford University Press.

Tate, C. N., and T. Vallinder. 1995. The global expansion of judicial power: The judicialization of politics. In *The global expansion of judicial power,* ed. C. N. Tate and T. Vallinder, 1–12. New York: New York University Press.

Taylor, M. 2008. *Judging policy: Courts and policy reform in democratic Brazil.* Palo Alto, CA: Stanford University Press.

Tushnet, M. 2004. Social welfare rights and forms of judicial review. *Texas Law Review* 82:1895–1919.

United Nations Committee on Economic, Social, and Cultural Rights. 2000. General Comment No. 14: The right to the highest attainable standard of health (Art. 12 of the International Covenant on Economic, Social, and Cultural Rights). Available at http://www.unhchr.ch/tbs/doc.nsf/(symbol)/E.C.12.2004.En.

Vanberg, G. 2001. Legislative–judicial relations: A game-theoretic approach to constitutional review. *American Journal of Political Science* 45 (2):346–361.

Whittington, K. 2005. "Interpose your friendly hand": Political supports for the exercise of judicial review by the United States Supreme Court. *American Political Science Review* 99 (4):583–596.

World Bank. 2003. *World Development Report 2004: Making services work for poor people.* Washington, DC: World Bank. Available from http://go.worldbank.org/ZPTUFPVPG0.

World Bank. 2007. World Development Indicators. Washington, DC: World Bank. Available from http://go.worldbank.org/U0FSM7AQ40.

Young, I. M. 1990. *Justice and the politics of difference.* Princeton, NJ: Princeton University Press.

2 Litigating for Social Justice in Post-Apartheid South Africa: A Focus on Health and Education[1]

JONATHAN BERGER

The socioeconomic (SE) rights protections in the Constitution of the Republic of South Africa, 1996 (*the Constitution*) have been used with varying degrees of success to improve the lives of poor people. Whether enforced directly to advance rights claims or to challenge unjustifiable legislation, or indirectly as part of statutory interpretation, these rights have shown significant potential as tools for the advancement of a pro-poor social justice agenda. But their limits have also been exposed as some judicial officers have struggled to give meaning to competing claims for limited state resources and others have seemingly succumbed – whether consciously or otherwise – to indirect political pressure and problematic arguments regarding the appropriate role for an unelected judiciary.

---

[1] The author of this chapter has been part of – or closely associated with – the legal teams in the majority of health cases discussed in this chapter, which relies heavily on field research conducted by Doron Isaacs and Nick Friedman, then law students at the University of Cape Town (with some assistance from Abigail Marcus, who was then a law student at the University of the Witwatersrand, Johannesburg). In their research, the students met with and interviewed the following people who gave of their time freely: Julian Apollos (attorney, Cape Town); Mark Ayer (attorney, Legal Resources Centre [LRC] Grahamstown); Geoff Budlender (advocate, Cape Bar and formerly attorney, LRC Cape Town); Matthew Chaskalson (advocate, Johannesburg Bar); Pierre de Bruyn (advocate, Port Elizabeth Bar); Francois du Toit (advocate, Pretoria Bar); Hans Fabricius SC (advocate, Pretoria Bar); Gabon Community (affected community, *President of RSA.v Modderklip Boerdery (Pty) Ltd*); S. K. Hassim (advocate, Pretoria Bar); Ismail Jamie SC (advocate, Cape Bar); Rudolph Jansen (advocate, Lawyers for Human Rights Pretoria); H. P. Joubert (advocate, Pretoria Bar); Steven Kahanowitz (attorney, LRC Cape Town); Anton Katz (advocate, Cape Bar); Paul Kennedy SC (advocate, Johannesburg Bar); William Kerfoot (attorney, LRC Cape Town); Julian Knight (attorney, Pretoria); Andre Louw (advocate, Pretoria Bar); Thembeka Majali (former Western Cape provincial coordinator, Treatment Action Campaign); Gilbert Marcus SC (advocate, Johannesburg Bar); Robert Martindale (attorney, Port Elizabeth); Sbu Maseti (attorney, LRC Grahamstown); Mrs. Meltafa (second applicant, *Permanent Secretary, Department of Welfare, Eastern Cape Provincial Government v. Ngxuza*); Candice Mey (advocate, Port Elizabeth Bar); Billy Mothle (advocate, Pretoria Bar); Yasmin Omar (attorney, Springs); Michael Osborne (advocate, Cape Bar); Lorraine Osman (head of public affairs, Pharmaceutical Society of South Africa); Tal Schreier (attorney, University of Cape Town Refugee Law Clinic); Sarah Sephton (attorney, LRC Grahamstown); Tsheliso Thipanyane (Advocate and CEO, South African Human Rights Commission); Wim Trengove SC (advocate, Johannesburg Bar); David Unterhalter SC (advocate, Johannesburg Bar); Faranaaz Veriava (advocate, formerly of the Centre for Applied Legal Studies, University of the Witwatersrand, Johannesburg); and Erhard Wolf (head of Parents' Committee, Mikro Primary School). All their contributions to this chapter are greatly valued and appreciated. Any errors are those of the author alone.

This chapter begins with an introduction to South Africa's legal system, focusing on the supremacy of the Constitution and the manner in and the extent to which it addresses SE rights. In so doing, it starts by briefly tracking the legal and political developments that resulted in a transition from white minority rule to a democratic post-apartheid constitutional state. Thereafter, it contextualizes the SE rights protections in the Constitution, detailing how they relate to each other as well as other key provisions in the Bill of Rights. In particular, the chapter explains that the Constitution's approach to SE rights is – in conceptual terms – largely indistinguishable from the manner in which it addresses civil and political rights.

The chapter then summarizes the cases that form the subject of its main analysis, which is based – in large part – on a systematic implementation study of each of the cases considered. The study involved two key areas of research: qualitative interviews with applicants, respondents, and their legal representatives regarding the cases (with a particular focus on outcome and impact); and desktop research that included a literature review and an analysis of (mostly) reported court decisions. A handful of unreported cases – mostly in the author's and interviewees' areas of expertise – have been considered, with a clear bias toward health rights litigation. Most unreported cases, however, have in all likelihood not been considered.[2] This is primarily because the nature of the study made it difficult – if not impossible – to develop and execute a clear methodology for identifying relevant unreported cases.[3]

The case summaries – eight general "landmark," eleven health, and thirteen education cases – are followed by a section that considers emerging trends and themes in the jurisprudence and is largely based on a review of the relevant literature and court decisions. Thereafter, the chapter focuses on the way in which poor people (and those acting on their behalf) have used two SE rights – access to health care services and education – to greater and lesser effect. In considering the impact of SE rights litigation, the chapter considers the direct impact of cases on litigants and the specific SE rights issues raised. In addition, it addresses the impact of such cases on the broader realization of the relevant rights and SE rights more broadly.

To date, South Africa's Constitutional Court – its highest on constitutional matters – and Supreme Court of Appeal (SCA) – its highest on all other matters – have decided relatively few SE rights cases. For their part, the other superior courts – the various provincial and local divisions of the High Court – have considered many more cases that cover a broader range of SE rights. Collectively, the decisions of the superior courts seem to suggest that a claimant's potential for success may have

---

[2] The author is unable to provide any reliable estimate regarding the numbers of unreported health and education cases.

[3] It is also unclear what can be learned from a study of cases that are not reliant – in any way – on the Bill of Rights for their outcomes, whether an express education or health right or a more overarching right such as the right to just administrative action. In addition, the lower (magistrates) courts, where most of these cases are likely to be heard, have limited constitutional jurisdiction. Further, many public interest bodies are reluctant to litigate in courts where decisions have no value as precedents.

surprisingly little to do with the law itself. Thus, in addition to considerations of impact, this chapter also focuses on those factors that appear to influence successful outcomes. In particular, it considers litigation decisions that influence outcomes, extralegal considerations, and the role of the state in SE rights litigation.

In this chapter we seek to understand what this means for SE rights litigation and those who seek to use and believe in the law as a tool of social change. By considering two very different sets of cases – health and education – in large part from the perspective of those who brought the cases to court,[4] we reach the conclusion that although the jurisprudence of court decisions matters, what matters more is how and in what way individuals and organizations make creative use of the law and the spaces that it is sometimes able to open. Simply put, this chapter documents the centrality of people, passion, organization, and mobilization in litigating for social justice in post-apartheid South Africa.

THE SOUTH AFRICAN CONSTITUTION AND LEGAL SYSTEM

The Constitution is South Africa's supreme law. It is central to developing and implementing law and policy, which it regulates – both directly and indirectly – in at least five important ways.[5]

- It regulates the structure of government.
- It regulates the way in which various branches of government operate.
- It sets out the framework for raising taxes and allocating revenue.
- It guides the content of all laws and policies.
- It regulates the role of government and nonstate actors (such as private corporations) in realizing the entrenched rights.

To a limited extent, this is not new.

The control of public power by the courts through judicial review is and always has been a constitutional matter. Prior to the adoption of the interim Constitution this control was exercised by the courts through the application of common law constitutional principles. . . . The common law principles that previously provided the grounds for judicial review of public power have been subsumed under the Constitution, and in so far as they might continue to be relevant to judicial review, they gain their force from the Constitution.[6]

---

[4] This includes individual and organizational applicants and their legal representatives. Not all potential interviewees were in fact interviewed. Disturbingly, few of the state's legal representatives (in particular employees in the office of the state attorney) were prepared to be interviewed. In addition to the information obtained from one-on-one interviews, this chapter also considers (mostly South African) SE rights literature and the author's personal experience in relation to six of the nine health cases.

[5] For detail on the role of the Constitution in regulating the development and implementation of health law and policy, see generally Hassim, Heywood, and Berger 2007. Also available at http://www. alp.org.za.

[6] Pharmaceutical Manufacturers Association of South Africa: In re Ex parte President of the Republic of South Africa 2000 (2) SA 674 (CC) at Paragraph 33.

Under apartheid, however, South African law recognized the supremacy of Parliament.[7] Opportunities for using the law and legal processes to hold the state to account were few and far between. Not only was the law largely hostile to the dreams, aspirations, and needs of the majority, but so too were most of those tasked with its interpretation and implementation.[8] Democratic South Africa, on the other hand, is fundamentally different. Any law or conduct that is inconsistent with the Constitution is invalid, whether an act or an omission. Constitutional obligations "must be fulfilled"[9] – they "must be performed diligently and without delay."[10] In many respects, therefore, constitutional reform in South Africa was indeed revolutionary.

As a consequence of multiparty negotiations in the early 1990s,[11] the undemocratic apartheid legislature enacted the Constitution of the Republic of South Africa, Act 200 of 1993 (*the interim Constitution*). By the terms of the interim Constitution,[12] the elected representatives of the people were entrusted with drafting a "final Constitution," with the two houses of Parliament (the National Assembly and the Senate[13]) sitting together as the Constitutional Assembly. The Constitution adopted in terms of this process would then be referred to the Constitutional Court – also established in terms of the interim Constitution – for certification on the basis of its compliance with the thirty-four constitutional principles annexed to the interim Constitution.[14]

Despite earlier discussion within the African National Congress (ANC) regarding the need for a new Constitution "to provide for an orderly and fair redistribution by means of the establishment of a minimum floor of rights to a series of carefully defined social and economic goods,"[15] the interim Constitution failed to address SE rights squarely.[16] The text of the Constitution submitted to the Constitutional Court for certification, however, differed markedly – coming under attack from certain circles. During argument in the *First Certification* case,[17] for example,

---

[7] In this regard, see Justice Richard Goldstone's Foreword in this volume.

[8] See Dyzenhaus 2003.

[9] Section 2.

[10] Section 237.

[11] These included participation by parties that were not represented in Parliament and that were unbanned only on February 2, 1990.

[12] The interim Constitution came into force on April 27, 2004, the date of South Africa's first democratic elections.

[13] The Senate of the interim Constitution has been replaced by the National Council of Provinces (NCOP).

[14] For a concise – albeit comprehensive – summary of the certification process, see Ex parte Chairperson of the Constitutional Assembly: In re Certification of the Amended Text of the Constitution of the Republic of South Africa, 1996 1997 (2) SA 97 (CC) at Paragraphs 1–16 ("the *Second Certification* case").

[15] See Davis 2006: 302.

[16] Certain aspects of some SE rights were included. For example, Section 25 of the interim Constitution (dealing with "[d]etained, arrested and accused persons") recognized a right in Subsection 1(b) to "be detained under conditions consonant with human dignity, which shall include at least the provision of adequate nutrition, reading material and medical treatment at state expense."

[17] Ex parte Chairperson of the Constitutional Assembly: In re Certification of the Constitution of the Republic of South Africa, 1996, 1996 (4) SA 744 (CC) ("the *First Certification* case").

some opposed the entrenchment of SE rights on the basis that such rights were alleged to be non-justiciable. The Court disagreed, arguing as follows:

> [T]hese rights are, at least to some extent, justiciable.... [M]any of the civil and political rights entrenched... will give rise to similar budgetary implications without compromising their justiciability. The fact that socio-economic rights will almost inevitably give rise to such implications does not seem to us to be a bar to their justiciability.[18]

In one short paragraph, an end was put to much of the debate of the early- to mid-1990s regarding the appropriateness and practicality of entrenching SE rights in a Bill of Rights.[19] But as many of the cases discussed in this chapter show, the contestation over such rights is far from over. Although their existence and justiciability is both recognized and guaranteed, their true import remains a site of considerable struggle. Nevertheless, in a relatively short period of a single decade – the Constitution has been in force since February 4, 1997 – South Africa's superior courts have developed an SE rights jurisprudence that largely brings with it the ruling ANC's 1994 election promise of "a better life for all."

The SE rights entrenched in the Constitution involve a combination of negative and positive obligations, in essence both requiring the state to act and prohibiting it from acting in particular ways.[20] Thus, although the state is under a general obligation in terms of Section 7(2) of the Constitution to "respect, protect, promote and fulfil" all of these rights, its positive obligations with respect to the SE rights are circumscribed and clarified within the text of each individual provision.[21] These "rights and the obligations they impose go to the heart of the developmental role of the state."[22]

Two further provisions of the Constitution are relevant to the SE rights discussion: Section 39(2), which requires "every court, tribunal or forum" to "promote the spirit, purport and objects of the Bill of Rights" in every matter involving the interpretation of legislation and the development of the common law and customary law; and Section 8(2), which provides that any "provision of the Bill of Rights binds a natural or juristic person if, and to the extent that, it is applicable, taking

---

[18] Paragraph 78.

[19] See Davis 1992; Haysom 1992; Mureinik 1992; Scott and Macklem 1992; Motala 1995; and Liebenberg 1995.

[20] These rights include access to land (Section 25, which also deals more broadly with property rights); access to housing, which expressly includes protection against unjustifiable and arbitrary evictions (Section 26); access to health care services (including reproductive health care) and a guarantee that "[n]o one may be refused emergency medical treatment" (Section 27); access to sufficient food and water (Section 27); access to social security, including "appropriate social assistance" where people are "unable to support themselves and their dependents" (Section 27); and "basic education, including adult basic education" (Section 29). In addition, SE rights are to be found in Sections 23 (fair labor practices), 24 (environment), 28 (children), and 35 (prisoners). For an overview of SE rights in South Africa, see Brand 2005.

[21] For example, the state is obliged in terms of Section 27(2) of the Constitution to "take reasonable legislative and other measures, within its available resources, to achieve the progressive realisation" of the right to have access to health care services.

[22] Davis 2006: 301–302.

into account the nature of the right and the nature of any duty imposed by the right."

The mainstreaming of SE rights – which are now generally understood to be an integral part of a web of "inter-related and mutually supporting" rights[23] – has meant a significant blurring of the distinction between the different "generations" of rights.[24] It is interesting to note that support for such an approach is expressly provided for in a number of key provisions in the constitutional text. Thus, for example, the positive and negative obligations in Section 7(2) apply to all rights. So, too, do the provisions dealing with horizontal application,[25] as well as Section 36(1), which makes provision for the limitation of all rights "in terms of law of general application to the extent that the limitation is reasonable and justifiable in an open and democratic society based on human dignity, equality and freedom."[26]

When looked at closely, the Bill of Rights, thus, seems less concerned with the categorization of rights than with the appropriate location of a particular duty or obligation. Thus, for example, Section 10 of the Constitution simply states that "[e]veryone has inherent dignity and the right to have their dignity respected and protected." As a self-standing justiciable right,[27] Section 10 does not place an express duty on the state – or anyone else for that matter – regarding its promotion or fulfillment. Instead, those aspects of the right appear to be located in the positive obligations with respect to a range of other rights such as access to adequate housing, health care services and social security, which are underpinned by dignity as a foundational constitutional value.

An apparent blurring of the civil/political and socioeconomic "divide" also appears evident with respect to at least two other first-generation rights: equality and the rights of detained persons. Regarding the former, the state is enabled by the Constitution to take "legislative and other measures designed to protect or advance persons, or categories of persons, disadvantaged by unfair discrimination" and to enact national legislation "to prevent or prohibit unfair discrimination."[28]

---

[23] See *Grootboom* at Paragraph 23, where Yacoob held as follows: "Our Constitution entrenches both civil and political rights and social and economic rights. All the rights in our Bill of Rights are inter-related and mutually supporting."

[24] Compare the SE rights cases discussed here with various first-generation rights cases such as Carmichele v. Minister of Safety and Security 2001 (4) SA 938 (CC), Minister of Safety and Security v. Van Duivenboden 2002 (6) SA 431 (SCA) and Van Eeden v. Minister of Safety and Security 2003 (1) SA 389 (SCA). In each of these cases, which deal with the right to freedom and security of the person, the state was held liable for its failure to take specific action that would have averted the rights violations in question. In all three cases, a private third person was directly responsible for the actual violation of the right in question.

[25] Section 8(2) read with Section 8(3), which provides in Subsection (a) for the development of the common law "to the extent that legislation does not give effect to that right."

[26] Further provisions of the Bill of Rights, however, may be read to support – in part – the continued division between first- and second-generation rights. Chief among these are the recurrent references to internally limited SE rights, where the state is generally under an obligation to take "reasonable legislative and other measures." In contrast, the positive obligations with respect to civil and political rights – arising from Section 7(2) – are not ordinarily subject to such an internal limitation.

[27] Human dignity does not only form the focus of an independent constitutional right but is also a foundational constitutional value (Section 1(a) of the Constitution).

[28] Sections 9(2) and 9(4), respectively.

When read together with the entrenched SE rights, an obligation to take remedial action to deal with the inequities of the past and the continued legacy of apartheid on access to and the provision of basic services seems to arise. In other words, the constitutional text suggests that affirmative action measures should primarily benefit those who continue to be disadvantaged by prior unfair discrimination.

With respect to the rights of detained persons in Section 35, two subsections stand out: (2)(c), which accords every person who is detained (including every sentenced prisoner) the right "to have a legal practitioner assigned to the detained person by the state and at state expense, if substantial injustice would otherwise result, and to be informed of this right promptly"; and (2)(e), which guarantees to such persons "the provision, at state expense, of adequate accommodation, nutrition, reading material and medical treatment." In regulating legal representation in such a manner, (2)(c) itself internally limits what has traditionally been regarded as a fundamental civil right. By expressly tying the particular SE rights needs of prisoners to "conditions of detention that are consistent with human dignity," (2)(e) further blurs the categorization divide.

This complexity and nuance appears to be carried through directly into some of the key provisions dealing with SE rights. Thus, the internal limitation that is ordinarily seen as common to all such rights is expressly excluded from the provisions in Section 28 dealing with children's SE rights and those in Section 29(1)(a) entrenching the right to "a basic education, including adult basic education."[29] In other words, the formal structure of these provisions differs in no significant way from that of some civil and political rights. Thus, the right to a basic education appears – at least in form – to be no different from the right to "free, fair and regular elections."[30]

SUMMARY OF THE CASES[31]

All of the thirty-two cases chosen as part of this study – eight general landmark, eleven health, and thirteen education cases – were first decided, finalized, and/or settled on or before June 30, 2006. In each of the chosen cases, at least one party to the litigation invoked an express SE right: health, education, social security, or housing. In some cases, the right was integral to the decision reached by the relevant court; in others, it was only peripheral, if relevant at all. In general, SE rights played the strongest role in the health cases. They played a somewhat lesser role in the general landmark SE rights cases – key legal precedents that consider

---

[29] This does not necessarily mean, however, that such rights are immediately enforceable against the state. Rather, it simply indicates that the primary test for measuring whether the state has discharged its constitutional duties resides outside of an internal limitation, possibly in a Section 36(1) limitations analysis inquiry that is directly applicable to the state's positive obligations arising from Section 7(2).

[30] Section 19(2).

[31] This chapter does not consider the jurisprudence of the Land Claims Court, the Labour Court, or most other specialist courts or tribunals set up in terms of the Constitution. In short, it does not deal with the jurisprudence relating to the right to fair labor practices, environmental rights, and property rights, including access to land (Sections 23, 24, and 25 of the Constitution, respectively).

rights other than health and education but have implications for all SE rights – and ordinarily very little role in the education cases. Nevertheless, all of the cases are primarily concerned with the substantive aspects of the rights in question.

All of the considered cases – with the exception of two health cases – were brought before South Africa's superior courts: the High Court, the SCA and/or the Constitutional Court. Of these cases, judgments in all but one have been published in the official South African Law Reports, with the thirtieth case being settled before any decision could be made (and therefore there is no judgment to report). The two health cases that were not litigated in the superior courts include a complaint that was lodged with the Competition Commission of South Africa and threatened High Court litigation that was settled before papers in the application could be filed.

Within each of the three broad categories, the cases are further divided into sub-categories. In the three parts of this section that follow, these cases are considered chronologically within subcategories (starting with the earliest).

Landmark SE Rights Cases

This category consists of eight key cases that have significant implications for SE rights litigation, including health and education rights litigation.[32] Of the eight, four deal squarely with SE rights protections – two decided on the basis of the express right of access to adequate housing (*Government of the Republic of South Africa v. Grootboom*[33] and *Minister of Public Works v. Kyalami Ridge Environmental Association*[34]) and two on the basis of non-SE rights: equality (*Khosa v. Minister of Social Development; Mahlaule v. Minister of Social Development*[35]) and access to courts (*President of RSA v. Modderklip Boerdery (Pty) Ltd.*[36]). The remaining four cases are all concerned – in substance – with Section 27's guarantee of access to social assistance. Nevertheless, they are landmark in nature because of how they address other concerns: standing, jurisdiction, and holding the state to account.

Decisions on the basis of an express SE right

Grootboom.[37] *Grootboom* represents the first time that the Constitutional Court found the state to be in breach of its obligations with respect to an SE right. Only the second SE rights case to come before the Court,[38] it sets the basic framework for future claims against the state regarding its positive constitutional duties.

In its judgment, the Constitutional Court came to the conclusion that Section 26 of the Constitution does not entitle any person – as of right – to housing

---

[32] The landmark health and education rights cases are dealt with separately in their own categories.
[33] 2001 (1) SA 46 (CC).
[34] 2001 (3) SA 1151 (CC).
[35] 2004 (6) BCLR 569 (CC).
[36] 2005 (8) BCLR 786 (CC).
[37] October 4, 2000.
[38] The first case was Soobramoney v. Minister of Health, KwaZulu-Natal 1998 (1) SA 765 (CC), decided just a month short of three years before Grootboom. Soobramoney is discussed in more detail later.

Table 2.1. *Cases related to socioeconomic rights in South Africa*

Case[a] (year of latest disposition)	Rights claim supported	Brief description	Type of case
		Landmark SE rights cases (excluding health and education)	
Grootboom (2000)	Yes	Requiring the state to create a program for progressive realization of housing rights	Provision (housing)
Kyalami Ridge (2001)	Yes	Constitutional housing right authorizes state action even though the latter impairs private property rights	Obligations (housing)
Ngxuza (2001)	Yes	Procedural case allowing class action to challenge cancellation of social grants	Provision (social grants)
Jayiya (2004)	No	Refuses to hold administrator in contempt for failure to comply with court order	Provision (social grants)
Khosa/Mahlaule (2004)	Yes	State cannot exclude permanent residents from social assistance	Provision (social grants)
Mashavha (2004)	Yes	Requires continued national involvement in social assistance	Provision (social grants)
Modderklip (2005)	Yes	Holds state liable for not providing an appropriate remedy to address land invasions	Obligations (land)
Kate (2006)	Partial	Partial reversal of Jayiya, improving judicial ability to hold administrators to account	Provision (social grants)
		Health cases	
Van Biljon (1997)	Partial	Requires state to provide ARV treatment to two prisoners with AIDS	Provision
Soobramoney (1998)	No	Affirms state criteria for denying access to dialysis	Provision
PMA (2001)	Yes	Pharmaceutical plaintiffs challenge pro-access drug law, but ultimately must drop case	Regulation
Afrox Healthcare (2002)	No	Permits exemption of liability clause in health care contract	Obligations
TAC (2002)	Yes	Orders state to provide ARVs for prevention of mother-to-child transmission of HIV	Provision
Hazel Tau (2003)	Yes	Case challenges drug pricing; settlement opens market to generics	Regulation
Du Plooy (2004)	Yes	Terminally ill prisoner has right to medical treatment (and right to release to die with dignity)	Provision/ Other
Interim Procurement (2004)	Yes	Requires state temporarily to bypass lengthy procurement process to speed access to ARVs	Provision

Case[a] (year of latest disposition)	Rights claim supported	Brief description	Type of case
Affordable Medicines (2005)	Yes	Strikes certain licensing regulations of pharmaceutical services as undue burden on access to medications	Regulation
New Clicks (2005)	Yes	Modifies regulations in part to ensure affordable access to medications	Regulation
Westville (2006)	Yes	Requires state to immediately provide ARVs to prisoners	Provision
		Education cases	
Matukane (1996)	Yes	Prohibits "culture-based" exclusion of black school children	Obligations
Gauteng School Education Bill (1996)	Partial	Establishes right to "own language" education but denies that state must provide it	Provision
Oranje Vrystaatse Vereneging (1996)	Partial	Cannot suspend state subsidies for schools without due process	Provision
Wittmann (1998)	No	Permits state subsidized school to require religious instruction	Obligations
Premier, Mpumalanga (1999)	Partial	Strikes decision to end benefit for needy students in predominantly white schools	Provision
Christian Education (2000)	Partial	Law may prohibit use of corporal punishment in religious schools	Obligations
Harris (2001)	Partial	Cannot exclude six-year-old from school if she is ready	Provision
ED-U-College (2001)	Partial	Dismisses claim that state subsidies to independent schools should not have been reduced	Provision
Bel Porto (2002)	Partial	Dismisses challenges to school reorganization plan	Regulation
Laerskool Middelburg (2003)	Partial	Afrikaans-only school may be required to offer classes in English to needy learners	Obligations
Thukwane (2003)	No	Permits prison to ban educational access to Internet	Provision
Watchenuka (2004)	Yes	Asylum seekers may not be banned from educational opportunities	Provision
Mikro (2005)	Partial	Allows school to continue to offer Afrikaans-only education	Obligations

[a] The case names are presented in abbreviated form in this table. The full name is used the first time each case is discussed in the body of the text.

at state expense. Instead, it held that Section 26(2) "requires the State to devise and implement within its available resources a comprehensive and co-ordinated program progressively to realise the right of access to adequate housing," and that such a program "must include measures . . . to provide relief for people who have no access to land, no roof over their heads, and who are living in intolerable conditions or crisis situations."[39] To the extent that the state's existing housing program did not make provision for such people, it was found to be unconstitutional.

Grootboom sets down a number of key principles relevant to the enforcement of SE rights more broadly. First, it recognizes that although the state has an obligation to create the conditions for access to adequate housing for people at all economic levels of our society, the needs of the poor – who are particularly vulnerable – require special attention. With respect to the rest, particularly those who can afford to pay for adequate housing, the state's primary obligation lies in unlocking the system: ensuring access to housing stock, creating the legislative framework to facilitate self-built houses, and ensuring access to finance.

Second, *Grootboom* mandates the state to develop and implement a reasonable plan to deal with a public problem. In giving some content to the notion of a "reasonable plan," which is by necessity context-specific and dependent on the facts and circumstances of any particular matter, the Court considered the following elements:

- Sufficient flexibility to deal with emergency, short-, medium-, and long-term needs.
- Making appropriate financial and human resources available for the implementation of the plan.
- National government assuming responsibility for ensuring the adequacy of laws, policies, and programs; clearly allocating responsibilities and tasks; and retaining oversight of programs implemented at provincial and local government level.[40]

Kyalami Ridge.[41] *Kyalami Ridge* represents the first reported defensive use of an SE right by the state to insulate a program it had adopted from attack. In this case, the state's constitutional obligations with respect to access to adequate housing were successfully invoked to justify its attempts to provide emergency shelter in the wake of unexpected flooding. In essence, the matter pitted the rights of communities rendered homeless by flooding against those of property owners concerned about "the character of the[ir] neighbourhood" and the potential reduction in "the value of their properties" as a result of the state action.[42]

The case was primarily concerned with the question of whether the government had the legal authority to establish a transit camp – on its own land – to house the

---

[39] At Paragraph 99.
[40] Implicit is a duty to monitor and hold those implementing the plan to account.
[41] May 29, 2001.
[42] Paragraph 93.

survivors of the flood who had been rendered homeless. In its decision, the Court closely addressed Section 26(2):

> The fact that property values may be affected by low cost housing development on neighbouring land is a factor that is relevant to the housing policies of government and to the way in which government discharges its duty to provide everyone with access to housing. But it is only a factor and cannot in the circumstances of the present case stand in the way of the constitutional obligation that government has to address the needs of homeless people, and its decision to use its own property for that purpose.[43]

Decisions on the basis of a non-SE right

Khosa *and* Mahlaule.[44] The first access to social security matters to reach the Constitutional Court, *Khosa* and *Mahlaule* consider the constitutionality of certain provisions of the Social Assistance Act 59 of 1992, which restricted access to various forms of social assistance on the basis of citizenship. They do not consider whether the state's social assistance program is sufficient to discharge its positive constitutional obligations with respect to the right of access to social security. Instead, they consider whether the basis upon which the state had chosen to limit access to its existing social assistance program unreasonably limited another constitutional right – equality (which includes an express prohibition on unfair discrimination).[45]

The Court found that the blanket exclusion of non-citizens "fails to distinguish between those who have become part of our society and have made their homes in South Africa, and those who have not . . . [and] between those who are being supported by sponsors who arranged their immigration and those who acquired permanent residence status without having sponsors to whom they could turn in case of need."[46] In so doing, it rejected the argument that the extension of the benefits in question would "impose an impermissibly high financial burden on the State,"[47] also noting that the state failed to provide "clear evidence to show what the additional cost of providing social grants to aged and disabled permanent residents would be."[48]

Modderklip.[49] In *Modderklip*, the SCA had to balance the property rights of a landowner whose farm had been unlawfully occupied – and who had obtained an eviction order that had proved too costly to implement – with the housing rights of people who would be rendered homeless if evicted from the informal settlement

---

[43] Paragraph 107.
[44] March 4, 2004.
[45] For a discussion on substantive equality and SE rights, see Fredman 2005. For further analysis of *Khosa*, see Sloth-Nielsen 2004.
[46] Paragraph 58.
[47] Paragraph 60.
[48] Paragraph 62.
[49] May 13, 2005 (upholding the decision of the SCA – albeit for different reasons – in Modder East Squatters v. Modderklip Boerdery (Pty) Ltd.; President of the RSA v. Modderklip Boerdery (Pty) Ltd. 2004 (8) BCLR 821 (SCA) – 27 May 2004).

on the landowner's property. The SCA held that "by failing to provide land for occupation by the residents of the . . . Informal Settlement, [the state] infringed the rights of the landowner . . . and also the [Section 26(1)] rights of the residents."[50] It, therefore, permitted the residents to remain in their homes until the state made alternative land available, awarding "constitutional damages" to the landowner "to be calculated in terms of . . . the Expropriation Act."

On appeal, the essence of the SCA decision remained intact, effectively permitting the occupiers' continued settlement on the land and ensuring financial compensation for the landowner. In short, the Constitutional Court held that "the state, by failing to provide an appropriate mechanism to give effect to the . . . [original] eviction order . . . infringed the right of Modderklip Boerdery (Pty) Ltd which is entrenched in Section 34 read with Section 1(c) of the Constitution."[51] In so doing, it effectively reinforced the principle that the state cannot sit back when rights are being violated. In particular, the state has a vested interest in and responsibility to ensure that the rule of law is maintained.

Social assistance cases

Permanent Secretary, Department of Welfare, Eastern Cape Provincial Government v. Ngxuza.[52] Ngxuza was the first right to social assistance case to be decided by the SCA, coming some two and a half years before the Constitutional Court decision in Khosa and Mahlaule. As in a number of other social assistance cases,[53] it, too, considered a provincial government's attempts to deal with fraudulent beneficiaries of social grants. To root out corruption, the provincial government of the Eastern Cape had suspended the payment of all social grants (in the case of the applicants, disability grants), failing "to differentiate between the fraudulent and undeserving and unentitled on the one hand, and on the other the truly disabled." Welfare benefits were revoked "unilaterally and without notice to those concerned."[54]

Unfortunately, the substantive social assistance issues were only to be addressed much later. Instead, the state's defense in the High Court – and the subject of the appeal to the SCA – focused on two key questions of law:

- First, were the applicants entitled to proceed with a class action? In addition to seeking relief for themselves, the applicants persisted in their relief on behalf of "many tens of thousands of Eastern Cape disability grantees they alleged were in a similar predicament to themselves, in that they, too, had had their grants unfairly and unlawfully terminated."[55]
- Second, could the class action – if appropriate – also include members of the class who, for reasons of history, did not fall within the jurisdiction of the

---

[50] Paragraph 52.
[51] Paragraph 68. Section 34 of the Constitution deals with the right of access to courts, with Section 1(c) entrenching the rule of law as one of the Constitution's foundational values.
[52] 2001 (4) SA 1184 (SCA) – 31 August 2001.
[53] See, e.g., Maluleke v. Member of the Executive Council, Health and Welfare, Northern Province 1999 (4) SA 367 (T) and Rangani v. Superintendent-General, Department of Health and Welfare, Northern Province 1999 (4) SA 385 (T).
[54] Paragraph 7.
[55] Paragraph 1.

Grahamstown High Court (where the case was originally filed) but rather within the jurisdiction of the Bhisho and/or Mthatha High Courts?[56]

The SCA answered both questions in the affirmative, effectively allowing the substantive issues to be addressed thereafter by the High Court.

Jayiya v. Member of the Executive Council for Welfare, Eastern Cape.[57] The facts that gave rise to *Jayiya* are all too familiar for those seeking to claim social assistance benefits in provinces such as the Eastern Cape: an application for a permanent disability grant remaining unprocessed for nineteen months; a High Court application to compel the state to do its job; and a subsequent order mandating the state to process the grant application and commence payment within thirty days if granted (or provide "adequate reasons" if not granted) and to pay the costs of the application. Unfortunately, such relief had generally proven insufficient, with grants remaining unprocessed or unpaid, resulting in some creative decision making by other Eastern Cape benches. This was not, however, the case in *Jayiya*. The appeal before the SCA was limited to the lower court's refusal to call "upon the second respondent to explain, first, why she had not complied with an order of court . . . second, how she intended to comply with it and, last, why she should not be imprisoned for her contemptuous failure to have done so."[58] On this central issue, the SCA held that the common law "cannot evolve in such a way as to (retrospectively) create a new crime or extend the limits of an existing one." In other words, the court was not prepared to contemplate civil imprisonment of a state official for failure to pay a money debt. Implicit in *Jayiya* is that the problem lies not in the common law but rather in Section 3 of the State Liability Act 20 of 1957, which "outlaws the 'attachment' of the nominal defendant or respondent in proceedings against a government department."[59]

Mashavha v. President of the RSA.[60] Another social security case, *Mashavha* appears to consider only legal technicalities and not substance. But in considering the constitutional validity of a 1996 presidential proclamation seeking "to assign the administration of almost the whole of the Social Assistance Act . . . to provincial governments," it brings into clear focus the many real problems that this assignment caused in the lives of poor people. It is arguable that but for the assignment, many of the enforcement cases such as *Ngxuza* and *Jayiya* would not have arisen.

Mashavha did not make any reference to the right of access to social security – which includes social assistance – in declaring the assignment of the legislation

---

[56] In addition to the South Eastern Cape Local Division based in Port Elizabeth, the Eastern Cape is made up of three provincial divisions of the High Court: the Eastern Cape Provincial Division (Grahamstown), the Ciskei Provincial Division (Bhisho), and the Transkei Provincial Division (Mthatha). The demise of apartheid and the reincorporation of Ciskei and Transkei into South Africa have not yet been accompanied by a rationalization of the court structure.

[57] 2004 (2) SA 611 (SCA) – 31 March 2003.

[58] Paragraph 1.

[59] Paragraph 18. For further information on this statutory provision, see the text following Note 143.

[60] 2004 (12) BCLR 1243 (CC) – 6 September 2004.

unconstitutional. But by removing the weak provinces' control of the statute's administration, it has resulted in ensuring the greater involvement of national government in the implementation and administration of the state's social assistance program, as well as greater national oversight in this regard. It is hoped that this will improve access to social assistance in the poorer and administratively weaker provinces such as Limpopo and the Eastern Cape, and greater accountability and compliance with orders of court in the likelihood that some of the problems survive the new system.

MEC, Department of Welfare, Eastern Cape v. Kate.[61] Although the facts in *Kate* are important – particularly for the applicant who was successful in securing her social grant, with back pay and interest – the case will be remembered for another reason. In an angry judgment that is deeply concerned about the "chilling effect" of *Jayiya*,[62] the Port Elizabeth High Court attempted to undo much of the damage that appears to have followed in *Jayiya*'s wake.

Despite the focus of *Jayiya* being on the issue of contempt of court proceedings following noncompliance with a money order,[63] the SCA's unnecessary pronouncements on numerous issues had apparently resulted in the state adopting the position "that an applicant is not entitled to claim . . . arrears and interest in the High Court by way of application and that, if a valid claim for such payments exists, it should be sought by way of delictual or contractual action in the Magistrates' Court."[64]

In what seems like a particularly unprecedented move, *Kate* (in the High Court) attempted to deal with *Jayiya* (in the SCA) in a manner that removed much of its sting and allowed the Eastern Cape courts to get back to their core business – holding the state to account so that people can exercise their right of access to social security. Although not going as far as the High Court, the SCA in *Kate* effectively undid much of *Jayiya*'s damage, limiting its reach significantly.

The SCA also characterized the relationship between the provincial government and the High Court in interesting terms, noting as follows:

> The judgment of the [High] court . . . is mainly a riposte to this court's judgment in *Jayiya* and traverses issues that did not arise in the case that was before it, which the learned judge freely acknowledged. He said that he felt compelled to traverse those issues because, he said, this court itself went beyond the issues that were before it in *Jayiya*, with the result that doubt and confusion has been thrown on what until then had been incremental and cautious progress by the High Court in what he described as 'a kind of dialogue' between it and the provincial government to find a way out of the impasse.[65]

---

[61] 2006 (4) SA 478 (SCA) – 30 March 2006 (effectively upholding the essence of the High Court decision in Kate v. MEC for the Department of Welfare, Eastern Cape 2005 (1) SA 141 (SECLD) – 1 September 2004).

[62] Paragraph 1.

[63] The judgment in *Kate* asserts that the "issues of back pay and interest were not directly relevant to the ultimate issue for decision in *Jayiya*" (Paragraph 13).

[64] High Court decision at Paragraph 5.

[65] At Paragraph 19, footnote omitted.

However, the key issue – holding government officials properly to account – remained somewhat unresolved.

Health Cases[66]

This category consists of eleven health cases: nine that span three distinct categories; one (*Afrox Healthcare Bpk v. Strydom*[67]) that sits within its own category; and one (*Du Plooy v. Minister of Correctional Services*[68]) that seemingly defies categorization.[69] Of the first ten, half are concerned with the provision of health services – either through the development of new or the implementation of existing policy. Of the remaining cases, four deal with the state's role – directly and indirectly – as a regulator of health goods and services, with the final case dealing with the common law relationship between (private) service providers and users of those services. It is interesting to note that the Treatment Action Campaign (TAC)[70] – arguably South Africa's most prominent and effective civil society organization active in the HIV/AIDS and health care fields – has been involved in a majority of these cases: as an applicant in four and amicus curiae (friend of the court) in a further two cases.

Provision of health services: Development of new policy

Van Biljon v. Minister of Correctional Services.[71] The first reported decision on access to health care is surprisingly not based on the right of access to health-care services, but rather on the Section 35(2)(e) right of detained persons to "the provision, at state expense, of adequate ... medical treatment." *Van Biljon* saw four sentenced prisoners living with HIV/AIDS approach the Cape High Court for an order compelling the relevant authorities to provide them – at state expense – with antiretroviral (ARV) treatment.[72]

It was common cause that ARV treatment, recognized as "'state of the art' medical treatment" for HIV infection,[73] was generally unavailable in the public health system.[74] Nevertheless, the Court directed the state "to supply first and second applicants with the ... [ARV] medication which had been prescribed for them ... for as long as this medication is prescribed for them on medical grounds."

---

[66] For an overview of the right to health in South Africa, see Ngwena and Cook 2005: 107.

[67] 2002 (6) SA 21 (SCA) – 31 May 2002.

[68] [2004] 3 All SA 613 (T).

[69] For ease of convenience, the last two cases are dealt with together under a generic "other" category.

[70] See http://www.tac.org.za.

[71] 1997 (4) SA 441 (C) – 17 April 1997.

[72] Of the four applicants, only the first two were already in possession of prescriptions for ARV medicines. It is unclear from the judgment whether ARV treatment was medically indicated for the third and fourth applicants, although this does seem likely.

[73] Paragraph 59.

[74] On November 19, 2003, more than six years after *van Biljon* was decided, South Africa's Cabinet finally adopted the *Operational Plan on Comprehensive Care and Treatment for HIV and AIDS* ("the Operational Plan"), which identifies ARV treatment as one of the key interventions to be made available in the public health system to persons who comply with relevant clinical assessment. The Operational Plan is available at http://www.info.gov.za/otherdocs/2003/aidsplan.pdf.

It made no general order regarding the provision of ARV treatment to other similarly situated prisoners.

Two considerations underpin the decision. First, the Court rejected the argument that "adequate medical treatment" is defined by what is ordinarily available in the public health system,[75] recognizing that prisoners with HIV are more exposed to opportunistic infections than people with HIV outside of prison and may therefore require better treatment. Second, much emphasis was placed on the finding that the state had not been able to prove that it was unable to afford to provide the required treatment.

Soobramoney v. Minister of Health, KwaZulu-Natal.[76] *Soobramoney* involves access to renal dialysis – at state expense – in the public sector, where it is limited to those who satisfy strict medical criteria. The "primary requirement for admission . . . to the dialysis programme . . . [is] that the patient must be [medically] eligible for a kidney transplant."[77] It was common cause that the applicant had been denied access on the basis that he did not satisfy the medical criteria.

After his unsuccessful application to the Durban High Court, the applicant appealed directly to the Constitutional Court, challenging the denial of access on the basis of two constitutional rights: life (Section 11) and the guarantee that "[n]o one may be refused emergency medical treatment" (Section 27(3)). In its judgment, however, the Constitutional Court adjudicated the claim on the basis of the state's positive obligations with respect to health care access arising from Section 27(2), holding that the guidelines according to which access to renal dialysis had been denied are reasonable and had been applied "fairly and rationally."[78] In the result, the state had complied with its Section 27(2) constitutional obligations. Mr. Soobramoney's appeal was dismissed. He died a week later.

Soobramoney recognizes that the right of access to health care services does not impose an obligation on the state to provide everything to everyone and that "[t]here will be times when . . . [managing limited resources] requires . . . [the state] to adopt a holistic approach to the larger needs of society rather than to focus on the specific needs of particular individuals within society."[79] In other words, the broad need for a particular service in a context of limited resources constitutionally may justify a governmental decision to allocate funds to such services even in the face of demonstrable harm to a particular individual. Considered differently, the decision seems to suggest that the broad need for a particular service would render any decision of the state to focus instead on lesser threats to public health, in general, to be unreasonable and therefore actionable.

Minister of Health v. Treatment Action Campaign (No 2) [TAC].[80] *TAC* pitted South Africa's most vocal critic of government's response to HIV/AIDS against

---

[75] Paragraph 43.
[76] 1998 (1) SA 765 (CC) – 27 November 1997.
[77] Paragraph 3.
[78] Paragraph 25.
[79] Paragraph 31.
[80] 2002 (5) SA 721 (CC) – 5 July 2002.

the Minister of Health, the program's most ardent supporter. At issue was the national Department of Health (DoH) policy on the prevention of mother-to-child transmission (MTCT) of HIV infection and the use of ARV medicines in this regard. In a context informed by the President's public questioning of the link between HIV and AIDS and the associated campaign of misinformation against the use of ARVs, the stakes could not be any higher. The Constitutional Court was faced with two key issues. First, was the state entitled to limit the provision of nevirapine for the purposes of preventing MTCT to eighteen identified sites, "even where it was medically indicated and adequate facilities existed for the testing and counseling of the pregnant women concerned"? Second, had the state "devise[d] and implement[ed] within its available resources a comprehensive and co-ordinated programme to realise progressively the rights of pregnant women and their newborn children to have access to health services to combat . . . [MTCT]"?[81] On both issues, the Court held in favor of the TAC and against the impugned state policy.[82]

Provision of health services: Implementation of existing policy

Interim Procurement.[83] A key obstacle standing in the way of provincial implementation of the public-sector ARV treatment program in early 2004 was the failure of the DoH to procure an interim supply of ARV medicines pending the finalization of the formal tender. Funds had already been allocated to the provinces for the purchase of ARV medicines, with many public health facilities at that stage being in a position to begin providing treatment immediately. But treatment could not be provided until ARV medicines had been procured by the DoH on behalf of the provinces.

Initially, the DoH would only commit itself to procuring ARV medicines on behalf of the provinces in terms of a formal tender process that was not expected to deliver ARV medicines until late 2004 (and in fact was only completed in May 2005). Of concern was the fact that the DoH chose not to make use of a legislative framework that permits it to procure goods and services in the interim pending the finalization of a formal tender process. In this case, the delay in procuring ARV medicines was costing lives.

The TAC's legal representatives began taking the necessary legal steps to compel the DoH to use its interim procurement procedures. Litigation was averted – at the eleventh hour – when the health MinMEC[84] decided on March 23, 2004, to procure ARV medicines in the interim through a national price-quotation system. This decision was communicated to the TAC's legal representatives on March 24, 2004, a day before an urgent application was to be filed in the Pretoria High Court and a day after draft papers had been couriered to the Minister's office. As a result

---

[81] Paragraph 135.

[82] For further discussion of *TAC*, see Heywood 2003a and 2003b.

[83] This case – which once more pitted the TAC against the Minister of Health – was not filed, as the demands were met at the end of March 2004.

[84] The health MinMEC was a committee comprised of the Minister and her provincial counterparts (the nine provincial members of the executive councils [MECs]). MinMEC has subsequently been replaced by an expanded National Health Council, which largely plays the same role.

of the MinMEC decision, provinces such as Gauteng were able to begin providing ARV treatment on April 1, 2004.[85]

N v. Government of Republic of South Africa (No 1); N v. Government of Republic of South Africa (No 2); N v. Government of Republic of South Africa (No 3) (Westville).[86] In the first major challenge to the implementation of the Operational Plan – the public-sector ARV treatment program – to go to court,[87] fifteen prisoners at Westville Correctional Centre (WCC) and the TAC filed papers in the Durban High Court alleging that state authorities were unreasonably restricting access to ARV treatment. In particular, they sought an order compelling the state "with immediate effect to provide antiretroviral treatment, in accordance with the . . . Operational Plan, to the First to Fifteenth Applicants, and any and all other similarly situated prisoners at Westville Correctional Centre."[88]

On June 22, 2006, the state was ordered immediately to remove all restrictions to ARV treatment at WCC. It was also ordered to file an affidavit within two weeks setting out the steps it intended to take to make ARV treatment available to all prisoners at WCC who wanted and needed it. This did not happen. Instead, the state applied for leave to appeal, resulting in the applicants filing an application to compel. When the court eventually granted leave to appeal on the merits, it also compelled the state to implement the original orders without delay.

Regrettably, it required a further court order for the state to start complying with the initial judgment. In a strongly worded judgment handed down on August 28, 2006, the respondents were ordered to implement the original orders "unless and until" set aside on appeal. This included the obligation to file an affidavit "setting out the manner in which it . . . [would] comply with . . . [the] order" by September 8, 2006. The state's affidavit, which was indeed filed on this date, was found to be wanting in several respects.[89] At the time of writing, the matter remained unresolved. Lengthy negotiations with the state, which began at the instance of the Deputy President, had yet to result in a final settlement.

Regulation
Pharmaceutical Manufacturers' Association of South Africa v. President of the Republic of South Africa [PMA].[90] One of the first steps taken to give effect to the National Drug Policy of 1996 – and thereby increase access to medicines – was the enactment of the Medicines and Related Substances Control Amendment Act 90 of

---

[85] See Treatment Action Campaign 2004.

[86] 2006 (6) SA 543 (D); 2006 (6) SA 568 (D); and 2006 (6) SA 575 (D) – 22 June, 25 July, and 28 August 2006 (as yet unresolved).

[87] The first major challenge – Interim Procurement – was settled before papers were to be filed in court.

[88] The court papers are available at http://www.alp.org.za/modules.php?op=modload&name=News&file=article&sid=297.

[89] For further discussion on the deficiencies in the plan, see Hassim and Berger 2006: 18–19. For further discussion of Westville, see Muntingh and Mbazira 2006 and Hassim 2006.

[90] Case No. 4183/98, High Court of South Africa (Transvaal Provincial Division) – case withdrawn on April 18, 2001.

1997. But before it could be brought into force, the Pharmaceutical Manufacturers' Association of South Africa (PMA) and most of its members sought an interdict to prevent its promulgation. Surprisingly, the PMA did not restrict its challenge to those provisions of the amendment that could be read to amend the Patents Act 57 of 1978 by stealth. Instead, it opposed all the mechanisms introduced to increase access to medicines, including the abolition of perverse incentives designed unduly to influence dispensing practices, mandatory generic substitution of off-patent medicines, and the introduction of a mechanism to ensure transparent pricing.

It remains unclear why the PMA sought to challenge these provisions, given that they are common to many developed countries and undeniably permitted in a constitutional system that recognizes a right of access to medicines and imposes positive obligations on the state regarding the right's progressive realization. Although the promulgation of such provisions were indeed likely to have a negative impact on the profit levels of the PMA's members, South African–based subsidiaries of multinational pharmaceutical companies, any attempt to block their passage in a developing country would have run the risk of a public relations disaster. Perhaps the PMA viewed the South African activist landscape in early 1998 as relatively benign. But that changed in December 1998 with the birth of the TAC.

As the matter only came before the High Court in early 2001, as a result of delays on all sides, the statute was effectively put on ice for a number of years. When it finally came to court in March 2001, the TAC sought – and obtained – permission to intervene in the proceedings as amicus curiae. Six weeks later and following worldwide protests against the pharmaceutical industry, the lawsuit was withdrawn, apparently in exchange for an agreement that government would comply with its obligations in terms of international trade law. It would take a further three years before the amended Medicines and Related Substances Act 101 of 1965 ("the Medicines Act") would become operational, on May 2, 2004.[91]

Hazel Tau v. GlaxoSmithKline South Africa (Pty) Ltd and Boehringer Ingelheim (Proprietary) Limited.[92] Alleging that GlaxoSmithKline (GSK) and Boehringer Ingelheim (BI) were acting in violation of Section 8(a) of the Competition Act 89 of 1998 by charging excessive prices for certain of their ARV medicines to the detriment of consumers, Hazel Tau and others argued – in a formal complaint lodged with the Competition Commission – that the prices charged by the two groups of pharmaceutical companies for their essential and life-saving medicines were directly responsible for the premature, predictable, and avoidable deaths of women, men, and children living with HIV/AIDS.

The complaint – which assembled the testimonies of people living with HIV/AIDS and health care workers who treat people living with HIV/AIDS, as well as the expert evidence of leading HIV clinicians, nurses, scientists, economists, and actuaries – attempted to show that even when allowance was made for the costs of research and development, higher profits, licensing fees, and the incentive to

---

[91] For further analysis of *PMA*, see Heywood 2001 and Cameron and Berger 2005.
[92] Complaint before the Competition Commission of South Africa, Case No. 2002Sep226 – settled on December 9, 2003.

develop new drugs, the prices of these ARV medicines could not objectively be justified.[93] The Competition Commission – the body entrusted by law to investigate
alleged infringements of the Competition Act – concurred.[94]

In October 2003, just over a year after the complaint was lodged, the Commission
announced that it had decided to refer the complaint to the Competition Tribunal
for adjudication.[95] As a result of its investigation, it had found sufficient evidence
to support the referral on the basis of prohibited excessive pricing as well as
two additional grounds, both of which dealt with the failure of GSK and BI to
license generic manufacturers in the circumstances. By December 2003, within two
months of the Commission's announcement, GSK and BI entered into separate
settlement agreements with the complainants and the Commission respectively,[96]
in terms of which the two groups of companies effectively agreed to open up the
market for these drugs to generic competitors.[97]

Affordable Medicines Trust v. Minister of Health.[98] In the Pretoria High Court,
a challenge to various regulations issued in terms of the Medicines Act was dismissed with costs. At issue was the manner in which the regulations gave effect
to the well-established public health principle that seeks to ensure that those who
prescribe medicines ordinarily do not dispense them as well. However, where pharmaceutical services are in short supply, such a principle should not prevent medical
practitioners other than pharmacists from dispensing medicines. Yet in trying to
give effect to this principle, the regulations went too far – making it particularly
difficult, if not impossible, for such practitioners to prove that their dispensing
services were indeed required and that they were worthy of being licensed.

On appeal, the Constitutional Court upheld most of the regulations – with the
exception of those dealing with various factors to be considered in licensing applications: the existence of other licensed facilities in the relevant area; a description of
the relevant area; the estimated number of health care users in the area; and demographic considerations such as disease patterns and health status of users.[99] Given
the difficulties in obtaining such information, which the state is ordinarily not able

---

[93] See Beresford 2003.
[94] The South African Competition Authority is comprised of the Competition Commission (which
investigates and "prosecutes"), the Competition Tribunal (which adjudicates) and the Competition
Appeal Court (which hears appeals from the Competition Tribunal and is comprised of High Court
judges). Decisions of the appeal court may, in appropriate cases, be taken on appeal to the SCA
and/or the Constitutional Court.
[95] See Competition Commission (2003).
[96] The agreements with the Commission were subsequently declared to be null and void in the
(as yet unreported) Competition Appeal Court decision in GlaxoSmithKline South Africa (Pty)
Ltd. v. David Lewis N.O. and Others [2006] ZACAC 6 (6 December 2006). The agreements with
the complainants, which remain valid, are available at http://www.alp.org.za/modules.php?op=
modload&name=News&file=article&sid=225. For further clarification on this issue, see AIDS
Law Project 2006.
[97] For further discussion of *Hazel Tau*, see Berger 2005 and Avafia, Berger, and Hartzenberg 2006.
[98] 2005 (6) BCLR 529 (CC) – 11 March 2005.
[99] As already indicated, the rationale behind these provisions was to ensure that licenses are only issued
where needed – where pharmacists are not able to provide the required services, as recommended
by the World Health Organization.

to provide, the regulations placed an undue burden on prospective licensees to adduce the required evidence.

In its judgment, which struck the provisions down on the basis that the empowering statute did not give the Minister the power to pass them, the Court did not consider the right to have access to health services at all. In the hearing, however, numerous judges were noted to be deeply concerned about the implications of the regulations for ordinary people reliant on the services of "dispensing doctors" and other non-pharmacists. Although the case was pursued primarily because a failure to be licensed would serve to cut off a significant revenue stream from many health care practitioners, in particular dispensing doctors, it was generally understood that access to such services is essential where pharmaceutical services are ordinarily in short supply.

Minister of Health v. New Clicks South Africa (Pty) Ltd.[100] *New Clicks* considers the validity of the medicine pricing regulations, a second set of regulations promulgated in terms of the Medicines Act that address pricing concerns at all points in the medicines supply chain – from manufacturers through to retail pharmacists. In particular, the regulations sought to give effect to many of the access-friendly provisions in the empowering statute by introducing – among others – the following: a transparent pricing mechanism to ensure that add-ons (such as pharmacists' dispensing fees) are expressly identified; the concept of international benchmarking of ex-manufacturer medicine prices; processes for determining permissible annual increases in medicine prices; and a mechanism for the submission of information on the basis of which the DoH would be able to determine the reasonableness or otherwise of medicine prices. Although attacked in their entirety, those regulations dealing with an "appropriate dispensing fee" to be charged by pharmacists were singled out as particularly egregious.

The Cape High Court, which upheld the regulations in their entirety, did not consider the right to have access to health care services. On appeal before the SCA, the right featured more prominently, in large part because of TAC's amicus curiae intervention that sought to draw a direct connection between overregulation and access to pharmaceutical services. However, although the SCA's decision dealt with particular aspects of the right, it was nevertheless largely based on statutory interpretation and the constitutional principle of legality. Simply put, did the Medicines Act authorize the Minister to regulate in such a fashion? It is important to note that in evaluating the appropriateness of the dispensing fee for pharmacists, the SCA considered its impact on the viability of pharmacies. In particular, it drew attention to the need for an appropriate balance to be struck between the interest of the public in being able to purchase affordable medicines and the interests of dispensers as suppliers of medicines. In essence, it held that access requires both affordability and availability.

---

[100] 2006 (2) SA 311 (CC) – 30 September 2005 (overturning in large part the decision of the SCA in Pharmaceutical Society of South Africa v. Minister of Health; New Clicks South Africa (Pty) Limited v. Dr. Manto Tshabalala-Msimang NO [2005] 1 All SA 326 (SCA) – 20 December 2004).

The state's appeal to the Constitutional Court was upheld in part. Instead of striking down the regulations as a whole, the Court altered a number of them directly through the reading in and/or excision of certain words. But on the central issue – the dispensing fee – the essential reasoning of the SCA was upheld. The fee was struck down and the government was sent back to the drawing board. Despite TAC's amicus curiae intervention arguing for a remedy that mandated an interim dispensing fee pending the state's finalization of the process, the Constitutional Court disagreed. Instead, it suggested that unreasonably high dispensing fees may well be actionable in terms of other legislation. At the time of writing, the newly published dispensing fee – which was to have come into effect on January 1, 2007 – had been placed on ice as it was the subject once again of legal action. It remains unclear when and how the quantum of the dispensing fee will be finalized. In the meantime, dispensing fees remain largely unregulated – in many cases, the dispensing fees remain high, notwithstanding the Court's suggestion that this may not be lawful.

Private obligations

Afrox Healthcare. *Afrox Healthcare* represents the discomfort of many judges in applying SE rights to the conduct of the private sector. In that case, a patient had suffered damages as a result of the negligent conduct of a nurse employed in a private hospital. The hospital had sought to avoid liability by invoking the provisions of an exemption clause that "absolved the hospital and/or its employees and/or agents from all liability and indemnified them from any claim . . . for damages or loss of whatever nature."[101] Unsuccessful in its defence, the hospital took the matter on appeal to the SCA.

In considering whether a particular contractual term was contrary to public policy and therefore invalid, the SCA was urged to consider the impact of the right of access to health care services on the development of the common law, as required by Section 39(2) of the Constitution.[102] Despite holding that specific exclusionary clauses could be declared contrary to public policy and as such unenforceable, the SCA found that it was also in the public interest that contracts entered into freely by parties with the requisite capacity to contract should be enforced. It, therefore, found in favor of the hospital.

In its view, the applicant should have expected to find such an exemption clause in the contract, a person who signs a written agreement without reading it does so at his or her own risk and there is no reason – in principle – to differentiate between private hospitals and other service providers. In addition, there was no obligation on the hospital admissions clerk to draw the applicant's attention to the clause. The fact that most – if not all – private hospitals include similar clauses in their contracts did not seem to have any impact on the decision.[103]

In a more recent decision dealing with the constitutionality of a time limitation clause in a short-term insurance policy, the Constitutional Court focused attention

---

[101] The exemption clause did not extend to "intentional omission by the hospital, its employees or agents."

[102] Unfortunately, this argument was only raised for the first time on appeal and not in the High Court.

[103] For further discussion of *Afrox Healthcare*, see Brand 2002.

on the right to approach a court for redress, as entrenched by Section 34 of the Constitution. In *Barkhuizen v. Napier*,[104] the majority reasoned as follows:

> Ordinarily, constitutional challenges to contractual terms will give rise to the question of whether the disputed provision is contrary to public policy. . . . What public policy is and whether a term in a contract is contrary to public policy must now be determined by reference to the values that underlie our constitutional democracy as given expression by the provisions of the Bill of Rights. Thus, a term in a contract that is inimical to the values enshrined in our Constitution is contrary to public policy and is, therefore, unenforceable.[105]

When read in the light of this case, *Afrox Healthcare* may well be bad law.

Provision/other

Du Plooy.[106] This case concerns the refusal to grant medical parole to a prisoner with a terminal illness (leukemia). The Pretoria High Court found the refusal to be an infringement of the relevant statutory provision[107] as well as various constitutional rights, including the right of a sentenced prisoner "to conditions of detention that are consistent with human dignity including. . . the provision at state expense of adequate . . . medical treatment" and the right to have access to health-care services.

The judgment, which was handed down only days after oral argument, merely makes these claims without saying anything further. As such, it is not possible to understand why the High Court was of the view that this was an access case, given that the applicant did not argue that access to health care services had been denied or that his release was necessary to ensure access. Instead, the case was solely about the applicant being released to die with dignity – at home and not while incarcerated. According to lawyers involved in the matter, the right of access to health care services was not central to its resolution. Instead, the Bill of Rights as a whole – in particular the right to dignity – was decisive.

Education Cases[108]

There are thirteen education cases that cover the three categories: provision or financing, obligations and choice of schooling, and regulation. Of the thirteen cases, in seven the underlying demand is for state provision or financing, with three cases addressing access to education and four involving the eligibility of privileged (ordinarily white) schools for state support. Five cases involve obligations, particularly "choice of schooling," which concerned either positive choices to be taught in a particular language or according to the dictates of a particular religion, or the claim of autonomy to exclude on the basis of language (ordinarily translating into racial exclusion). One case involves the regulation of a school reorganization plan.

---

[104] 2007 (5) SA 323 (CC).
[105] At Paragraphs 28–30.
[106] March 15, 2004.
[107] Section 69 of the Correctional Services Act 8 of 1959.
[108] For an overview of the right to education in South Africa, see Veriava and Coomans 2005: 57.

Provision (Access to Education and State Financing)
Ex parte Gauteng Provincial Legislature: In re Dispute Concerning the Constitutionality of Certain Provisions of the Gauteng School Education Bill of 1995.[109]
Gauteng School Education Bill concerns the referral to the Constitutional Court by
some members of the Gauteng provincial legislature – acting in terms of the provisions of the interim Constitution – of certain allegedly unconstitutional provisions
of the Bill. In essence, the Court's decision concerned Section 32(c) of the interim
Constitution and whether it created "a positive obligation on the State to accord
to every person the right to have established, where practicable, schools based on
a common culture, language or religion subject only to the qualification that it is
practicable and that there is no discrimination on the grounds of race."
      The Court held that the language of the subsection does not support the sub-
mission that "every person can demand from the State the right to have established
schools based on a common culture, language or religion." Instead, it simply allows
people to establish such schools. Although Subsection (a) was held to have created
a positive right with respect to basic education and Subsection (b) a positive right
regarding instruction in the language of one's choice where reasonably practicable,
Subsection (c) was characterized only as a freedom – as a defensive right. As a
result, the relevant provisions of the Bill were upheld.

Oranje Vrystaatse Vereneging vir Staatsondersteunde Skole v. Premier van die
Provinsie Vrystaat.[110] *Oranje Vrystaatse Vereneging* deals with a challenge to the
suspension of subsidies for state-aided schools (which prior to the introduction
of a 1988 education statute had been public schools). Holding that the schools
had a legitimate expectation that the subsidies would continue, the Bloemfontein
High Court set the suspension decision aside. The right to education was not
considered, the decision being based largely on the basis of the right to procedurally
fair administrative action.

Premier, Mpumalanga v. Executive Committee, Association of State-aided Schools,
Eastern Transvaal.[111] *Premier, Mpumalanga* concerns a challenge to an executive
decision to discontinue the payment of scholarships for certain needy students
in state-aided schools in the province. In the main, such schools educated white
students. The challenge to the executive decision was therefore understood by
many commentators as an attempt to block transformation of apartheid's legacy
in education.
      As the case only concerned the manner of the scholarships' termination, edu-
cation rights were not invoked. Instead, an application was brought before the
Pretoria High Court in terms of Section 24 of the interim Constitution – alleging
a breach of the right regarding just administrative action. The ruling was upheld
on appeal to the Constitutional Court, which held that the termination of the
scholarships was procedurally unfair, thereby dismissing the appeal.

---

[109] 1996 (3) SA 165 (CC) – 4 April 1996.
[110] 1996 (2) BCLR 248 (O) – 30 November 1995.
[111] 1999 (2) SA 91 (CC) – 2 December 1998.

Minister of Education v. Harris.[112] *Harris* concerns a challenge to a notice issued by the Minister of Education stating that a learner at an independent school could not be enrolled in the first grade unless he or she reached the age of seven in the same calendar year. The daughter of the applicant, who only turned six in January of the relevant year, was deemed ready for school, but because of the Minister's notice she would have to wait an entire year before starting school.

In the High Court, the Minister's notice was declared unconstitutional on a number of grounds, including unfair discrimination on the basis of age, incompatibility with Section 28(2) of the Constitution (dealing with the best interests of the child) and the Minister's lack of legal authority – in the empowering statute – to do so. The Constitutional Court appeal was decided on the narrowest of bases – that the Minister exceeded the powers conferred on him by the relevant legislation and thereby infringed the constitutional principle of legality. In neither court was there any analysis of the right to education.

Permanent Secretary, Department of Education and Welfare, Eastern Cape v. ED-U-College (PE) (Section 21) Inc.[113] *ED-U-College* concerns the reduction of state subsidies to independent schools, raising "questions about the extent to which Courts may review budgetary allocations" and being based on Section 33 of the Constitution (which recognizes a right to just administrative action). The government attempted to justify the reduction on the basis that the funds allocated to the provincial education department by the provincial legislature had themselves been reduced. Predictably, the Constitutional Court's decision was silent about education rights. It held that the determination of a subsidy formula and its implementation in terms of the relevant statutory provision do not constitute administrative action and therefore fall outside of the purview of Section 33. The case was therefore dismissed.

Thukwane v. Minister of Correctional Services.[114] Among other grounds, *Thukwane* was based on the right to further education in Section 29(1)(b) of the Constitution. Concerning a challenge to prison policy regarding the utilization of computers and restrictions with respect to certain fields of study, *Thukwane* considered the absolute ban on fields of study that require anything to be done outside of prison, such as attendance at lectures. In particular, the applicant was denied access to the Internet, which he alleged was necessary for his studies. The limitation of his education right was considered to be reasonable and justifiable and therefore in accordance with Section 36(1) of the Constitution.

Minister of Home Affairs v. Watchenuka.[115] *Watchenuka* concerns the rights of asylum seekers to seek employment and to study while waiting to be recognized as refugees. In terms of Section 11(h) of the Refugees Act 130 of 1998, the Standing

---

[112] 2001 (4) SA 1297 (CC) – 5 October 2001.
[113] 2001 (2) 1 (CC) – 29 November 2000.
[114] 2003 (1) SA 51 (T) – 19 June 2002.
[115] 2004 (4) SA 326 (SCA) – 28 November 2003.

Committee for Refugee Affairs has the power to "determine the conditions relating to study or work ... under which an asylum seeker permit may be issued." However, the effect of the relevant regulation promulgated by the Minister of Home Affairs, when read together with the prescribed form, prohibited asylum seekers from undertaking any employment and studying. This was therefore struck down on the narrow basis that the minister had no power to impose the prohibition. In addition, the Standing Committee's general prohibition of employment and study for the first 180 days after a permit had been issued was also held to be in conflict with the Bill of Rights.

The SCA's decision addresses the freedom to study, which is seen as an inherent part of human dignity and is recognized as being expressly protected by Section 29(1) of the Constitution. That provision, the court held, was not concerned with the obligation of the state to provide social or economic goods. Although this right may indeed be limited, the court held that a general prohibition for asylum seekers is not constitutionally valid. The matter was therefore referred back to the Standing Committee to consider the matter afresh.

Private obligations (choice of schooling)
Matukane v. Laerskool Potgietersrus.[116] Matukane and two others unsuccessfully applied to have their (black) children admitted to the English stream of a state-aided dual-medium (English and Afrikaans) public (and largely white) school. They alleged – as did the provincial minister for education representing the interests of similarly placed parents and the broader public interest – that admission was refused on the basis of race. The school replied that it was entitled to refuse admission on the grounds of culture, a position the applicants viewed as a poor disguise for a racist – and therefore unlawful – exclusion policy.[117]

Although a number of constitutional grounds – including the education right in the interim Constitution – were invoked, the matter was largely decided on the basis of unfair racial discrimination. Nevertheless, the decision does provide a useful discussion of the relationship between Section 32(c), dealing with the right "to establish, where practicable, educational institutions based on a common culture, language or religion, provided that there shall be no discrimination on the ground of race" and Section 32(b), dealing with the right "to instruction in the language of his or her choice where this is reasonably practicable."

Wittmann v. Deutscher Schulverein, Pretoria.[118] *Wittmann* concerns an attempt to declare as unconstitutional the compelling of a school learner to attend religious instruction classes and school prayers at a private school run by the Evangelical Lutheran Church. According to Section 14(2) of the interim Constitution, "religious observances may be conducted at State or State-aided institutions under

---

[116] 1996 (3) SA 223 (T) – 16 February 1996.
[117] It was common cause that there were only two public schools in the town offering English-medium education – one that was overcrowded and the respondent, Laerskool Potgietersrus.
[118] 1998 (4) SA 423 (T) – 4 May 1998.

rules established by an appropriate authority for that purpose, provided that such religious observances are conducted on an equitable basis and attendance at them is free and voluntary." Section 15(2) of the final Constitution is strikingly similar.[119]

It was common cause that the school received state subsidies. Nevertheless, based on a narrow view regarding the interim Constitution being restricted to vertical application, the section was deemed not to be applicable.[120] The Pretoria High Court controversially held that even if the section is indeed applicable, a right of nonattendance can be waived. This, it held, was what happened when the learner subjected herself to the school's regulations.

Christian Education South Africa v. Minister of Education.[121] *Christian Education* considers a challenge to a provision of a statute prohibiting corporal punishment in schools, asking whether – in the context of freedom of religion – this violates the rights of parents in private religious schools. The relevant provision was challenged on a number of grounds, including Section 29(3) of the Constitution that guarantees everyone "the right to establish and maintain, at their own expense, independent educational institutions."

The Constitutional Court's decision, however, is limited to Sections 15 and 31 of the Constitution, which collectively deal with various aspects of the right to freedom of religion – there is no analysis whatsoever of the education right in question. The judgment simply assumes that the law limits both freedom of religion provisions of the Constitution, but finds that it does so in a way consistent with the limitations test in Section 36(1) and is therefore constitutional.

Laerskool Middelburg v. Departementshoof, Mpumalanga Departement van Onderwys.[122] The only public school in the Middelburg area with Afrikaans-only instruction was instructed by the provincial education minister to enroll twenty learners who were to be taught in English. After it refused, its power to admit learners was withdrawn. English-speaking children were thereafter enrolled once the school had been declared to be dual-medium. The application, which sought to set this aside, was unsuccessful. In its decision, which addresses the content of Section 29(2) of the Constitution regarding a rights claim to a public single-medium school, the court held that this is clearly subordinate to the right of every South African to education and is necessarily linked to the practicability thereof.

The court further held that there had indeed been noncompliance with the regulations that require schools offering tuition in the desired language to be at capacity before any single-medium school could be declared to be dual-medium.

---

[119] Both Constitutions may be applicable – the interim Constitution with respect to the decision to compel attendance and the final Constitution with respect to any ongoing compulsion.

[120] The horizontal application of the final Constitution may result in a somewhat different interpretation. As the court did not consider any continuing conduct, it left the issue unresolved.

[121] 2000 (4) SA 757 (CC) – 18 August 2000.

[122] 2003 (4) SA 160 (T) – 14 November 2002.

The capacity requirement had not been met in this case. Nevertheless, the application was dismissed because – on the basis of the best interests of the child as entrenched by Section 28(2) of the Constitution – the interests of learners were best served by allowing an English course to be created at the school. This was despite the court's finding that administrative justice rights had indeed been limited.

Western Cape Minister of Education v. Governing Body of Mikro Primary School.[123] *Mikro* concerns an unsuccessful appeal against a High Court decision that set aside the decision of the Western Cape provincial education minister to enroll English-speaking children at an Afrikaans-medium school. Despite attempts to convince it otherwise, the school had been unwilling to change its language policy, adopted by the governing body in accordance with its constitution and relevant legislation giving such powers to the body.

Although not really decided on the basis of the right to education in Section 29 – it was decided on the basis that the minister did not have the power to do what he did and that he had other legal avenues open to him to deal with the school's language policy (which he had not taken) – the SCA did make a number of findings regarding the right. In particular, it challenged the assertion that Section 29(2) "should be interpreted to mean that everyone had the right to receive education in the official language of his or her choice at each and every public educational institution where this was reasonably practicable."

Instead, it held that the right "to receive education in the official language or languages of . . . choice in public educational institutions where that education is reasonably practicable is a right against the State." As such, "the 40 learners in question had a constitutional right to receive education in English in a public educational institution provided by the State if reasonably practicable but, even if it was reasonably practicable to provide such education at . . . [Mikro Primary School], they did not have a constitutional right to receive education in English at . . . [Mikro Primary School]."

Regulation
Bel Porto School Governing Body v. Premier, Western Cape.[124] Another education case that did not explicitly address education rights, *Bel Porto* concerns the employment of general assistants who had been employed at schools that – under apartheid – fell under the "white" department of education catering for white disabled children. After the consolidation of the previously segregated education departments following the democratic transition in 1994, the policy to employ general assistants had been reviewed. Although initially argued on the basis of a number of SE rights (including Section 26 [housing] and Section 27 [health care]), the case was only really pursued on the basis of the right to equality (Section 9) and just administrative action (Section 33). A majority of the Constitutional Court dismissed the application, whereas a minority found that Section 33 rights had indeed been violated.

---

[123] 2005 (10) BCLR 973 (SCA) – 27 June 2005.
[124] 2002 (3) SA 265 (CC) – 21 February 2002.

EMERGING TRENDS AND THEMES IN THE CASE LAW

Despite the relative dearth of SE rights jurisprudence, a review of the case law and literature – including cases that consider health, education, social security, housing, and other basic service claims (such as access to water) – nevertheless shows that various trends and themes have started to emerge. This section of the chapter, thus, begins by considering four emerging trends, followed thereafter by a consideration of two key emerging themes: enforcement and prioritization. In general, the trends and themes reinforce the positive–negative rights divide and reassert what has long been common cause among public interest lawyers – that the existence of constitutional protection is a necessary albeit insufficient condition for the full realization of rights. In other words, although the law may be used effectively as a tool of social change, litigation and other forms of legal action are incapable – in and of themselves – of bringing about sustainable change and fundamental transformation.

Emerging Trends

In particular, the following four trends stand out. First, in common with most civil and political rights cases, SE rights cases have largely been defensive in nature, being somewhat indistinguishable from other forms of rights litigation. Even in such cases where the claims have been positive in nature, litigants have generally asserted their rights only when their rights have been threatened, not simply unrealized. With the notable exception of health-related claims (and to a significantly lesser extent certain social security matters), the reported cases reflect that litigation has ordinarily sought to resolve particular claims to a good or service rather than be used to address systemic problems.

It is unclear why this has been the case. Very active in the struggle against apartheid, many civil society organizations that one would have expected to be at the forefront of such legal challenges have instead preferred to work for change within the newly democratized – but as yet untransformed – system. Other parts of civil society, such as many of the so-called new social movements focusing on a range of issues from lack of access to land to electricity cutoffs,[125] have perhaps been unwilling to make active use of a Constitution perceived to be "liberal." Although their demands have been framed in the language of rights, they have generally been unwilling to claim such rights through proactive legal action.

Second, each case has ultimately turned on its own facts. Ever mindful of and guarding against deciding issues in advance, courts have been slow to answer important constitutional questions in the absence of disputes that cannot be resolved in any other way. Their decisions have gone to great lengths to draw a clear distinction between an overarching framework and its application to the specific facts of any particular dispute. Nevertheless, they have – to some extent – been

---

[125] Such organizations include the Landless People's Movement (LPM), the Soweto Electricity Crisis Committee (SECC) and the Anti-privatisation Forum (APF). For a brief discussion of these organizations, see Gumede 2005: 280–283.

willing (where necessary) to sketch the broad parameters within which SE rights claims are to be adjudicated. This is most evident in their focus on the development and application of the *reasonableness review standard* mandated by the Constitution itself,[126] instead of placing much reliance on the more concrete – but rather blunt – *minimum core* approach proposed by certain litigants and recognized in international law.[127]

Third, courts are not yet fully comfortable in adjudicating and resolving claims that involve the failure of the state to take positive measures to promote and fulfill SE rights. Once the state has decided on policies and/or legislation that purport to give effect to its positive constitutional obligations, courts seem quite confident in their ability to assess the reasonableness or otherwise of such state action. Where rights have been entrenched in statute, courts have generally been steadfast in ensuring their realization. But where claims have been largely based on a simple failure to act, courts appear less likely and/or able to provide a comprehensive solution. This reluctance and/or inability to act is mostly evident in the gap between the creative forms of relief granted following negative infringement (for example, in a case such as *Modderklip*) and the less inspiring types of orders in matters involving express positive claims (such as in *Grootboom*, for example).[128]

Finally, the practice of SE rights litigation takes place within a context informed not only by the constitutionalization of both first- and second-generation rights but also by the entrenchment of fundamental guarantees that are not ordinarily found in bills of rights: access to information, just administrative action, and access to courts. Increasingly, SE rights claims are being developed and formulated on the basis of these novel guarantees. Obtaining written reasons for administrative decisions and accessing state held and privately held documents, for example, has the potential both to facilitate and enrich the litigation process. Such actions are likely to provide valuable evidence without which an SE rights claim may remain unsubstantiated.

Before exploring the key themes of enforcement and prioritization, one additional issue requires consideration: the manner in and the extent to which SE rights claims can and should be used to hold the private sector to account. As

---

[126] The Constitution itself expressly recognizes various standards of review. Reasonableness review is expressly recognized with respect to the state's positive obligations regarding various SE rights (see, e.g., Sections 26(2) and 27(2)), as well as in the right to just administrative action (Section 33) and the general limitations clause (Section 36(1)).

[127] The "minimum core" approach to SE rights claims recognizes that the state ordinarily has an obligation to ensure certain minimum levels of service provision. Regarding the Constitutional Court's approach to minimum core entitlements, see Pieterse 2006: 479–488. For more discussion about the concept of minimum core, see generally Bilchitz 2002; Bilchitz 2003, 2006; Liebenberg 2004.

[128] However, courts are now generally less concerned with legal technicalities and more likely to seek just and fair solutions. In many ways, Section 38 of the Constitution has made this possible: It allows courts to "grant appropriate relief" when rights have been "infringed or threatened"; and it broadens standing requirements, allowing a wide range of persons to approach courts for relief. See, in particular, Campus Law Clinic (University of KwaZulu-Natal (Durban)) v. Standard Bank of South Africa Ltd. 2006 (6) BCLR 669 (CC), where the Constitutional Court recognized – in principle – that nonparties to a particular dispute may be able to take matters on appeal.

already mentioned, Section 8(2) of the Constitution provides for some degree of horizontal application. But the Constitution does not provide much guidance in this respect. Although the jurisprudence is developing well with respect to the state's obligations to regulate the private sector so as to increase access to certain basic goods and services, the same cannot be said for those cases dealing directly with the impact of SE rights on the conduct and activities of the private sector.

A few cases – such as *Kyalami Ridge, New Clicks, Modderklip,* and *Afrox Healthcare* – highlight the extreme variance in the emerging jurisprudence in this regard. The interpretation and development of the common and statutory law – insofar as the private sector is concerned – have become the new sites of struggle. Given the manner in which the common law in particular has developed to entrench and protect certain vested interests, this is perhaps unavoidable in the context of a Constitution that mandates "every court, tribunal or forum . . . [to] promote the spirit, purport and objects of the Bill of Rights" in "interpreting any legislation, and when developing the common law or customary law."

Although perhaps predictable, this particular aspect of the constitutional enterprise is nevertheless cause for concern. The same Constitution has resulted in jurisprudence ranging from the progressive pro-poor decision in *Kyalami Ridge* to the conservative pro–big business opinion in *Afrox Healthcare.* What the emerging case law perhaps suggests is that the private sector should be challenged indirectly, with the state being held to account for its failure to regulate appropriately.

Emerging Themes

Enforcement

In a range of cases, the Constitutional Court has recognized that it not only has broad powers to grant "appropriate relief,"[129] but that it has the discretion to make "any order that is just and equitable."[130] In particular, it held in *Fose v. Minister of Safety and Security* that appropriate relief "will in essence be relief that is required to protect and enforce the Constitution," recognizing that "the courts may even have to fashion new remedies to secure the protection and enforcement of . . . all-important rights."[131] Yet whereas the Court has been willing to acknowledge the breadth of its powers, it has – at times – been relatively conservative in the exercise of its remedial discretion.

Nevertheless, a broad range of remedial tools have been developed. In *National Coalition for Gay and Lesbian Equality v. Minister of Home Affairs,*[132] for example, the Court had to consider what to do with a statutory provision that had been declared unconstitutional on the basis of its being underinclusive. It was clear that the only way in which the unconstitutionality could be cured was by extending to the class of persons the statutory benefit that had been unfairly denied

---

[129] Section 38.
[130] Section 172(1)(b).
[131] 1997(3) SA 786(CC) at Paragraph 19 (footnote omitted).
[132] 2000 (2) SA 1 (CC).

them.[133] Despite being requested by the state to refer the matter back to Parliament for consideration, the Court chose instead to read certain words into the impugned provision so as to extend the benefit in accordance with the requirements of the Constitution.

In *August v. Electoral Commission*,[134] the Court had to consider how best to ensure that all prisoners had the opportunity to register to vote in the 1999 general elections. It had found that the Independent Electoral Commission's disenfranchisement of prisoners, purportedly in accordance with the provisions of the relevant electoral legislation, was not permitted by the Constitution. Handing down its judgment just a few weeks before the elections, it not only ordered the Commission to register all prisoners, but also to lodge a detailed plan of how the Commission planned to implement the order. That plan would be available for public scrutiny. In this respect, *August* is but one step away from the retention of supervisory jurisdiction.

Yet, the Constitutional Court's creativity with respect to relief in civil and political rights cases has largely not been matched in SE rights cases. Declarations of constitutional invalidity have, in the main, been accompanied by orders that many consider to be too weak and/or reliant on the bona fides of government. To be fair, the Court has seen few such cases, affording it very little opportunity to develop its jurisprudence in this regard. Further, its orders must be understood within a context informed by the need for an appropriate balance to be struck between antagonists in a new site of political struggle. A case such as *TAC*, for example, is both deferential in some respects ("government has always respected and executed orders of this Court") and prescriptive in others ("Government is ordered, without delay").[135]

South African courts have limited political capital, an important point to note in a country where the ruling party has such a majority of electoral support. For strategic reasons, they might be wise to use their firepower sparingly – only for the most crucial issues. This runs the risk, however, of judges being perceived as sitting in ivory towers, from where they are unable to see the problems of court judgments not being enforced. At the other extreme, they may be accused of being unaware of their appropriate boundaries and how far they can go. In such cases, they should probably guard against pushing government to be openly contemptuous of orders.

Deference is often spoken about in the context of respect for the elected branches of government. Implicit in this discourse is the concern about antimajoritarianism and a negative impact on democracy. What is not often considered is the ability of court decisions to stimulate participatory democracy – enabling people to act, entrenching their ability to speak to government and requiring government to respond to them. In some cases, court processes can give people power that they otherwise would not have – allowing them to counter vested rights and compelling

---

[133] In addition to married persons, persons in permanent same-sex life partnerships were thereafter able to benefit from certain statutory immigration rights.

[134] 1999 (3) SA 1 (CC).

[135] *TAC* at Paragraph 129.

courts to engage in a process of balancing interests. Thus, the legal process, where it effectively compels the state to subject its decisions to rigorous public debate, potentially underpins and strengthens the democratic process.

How then should rights claimed be vindicated? Kent Roach and Geoff Budlender argue that,

> while declarations and requirements that governments report to the public will often be sufficient in those cases in which governments are merely inattentive to rights, stronger remedies involving mandatory relief and requirements of governmental reporting to the courts may be necessary in some cases, and particularly where governments are incompetent or intransigent with respect to the implementation of rights.[136]

This framework, which recognizes that remedies have to match the reason for noncompliance with constitutional duties, provides an appropriate backdrop against which to discuss courts' retention of supervisory jurisdiction and another hotly contested form of relief: using coercion against state officials.[137] These two issues are now addressed in turn.

Supervisory Jurisdiction. The most appropriate way to vindicate SE rights may indeed be to require government to say what it is going to do, provide a timetable and report on implementation continually. Such a remedy, also known as a structural or a supervisory interdict, allows courts to test government's plans for constitutionality and to hold the state to its own undertakings – detailed court orders are therefore seen only as matter of last resort. It also provides civil society with a tangible basis for mobilization, particularly at the local level, where close interaction with those affected is required. This requires both sets of lawyers to interact – whether directly or indirectly – with affected communities.

The debate regarding supervisory jurisdiction has unfortunately been a zero-sum game, with the structural interdict being seen as the Holy Grail – the clearest indication of the ability of the judiciary to remain independent and hold the state to account. Although recognizing the value of such orders in appropriate cases, it is perhaps more important to understand what considerations should be taken on board in evaluating whether – and in what form – supervision (by a court or any other institution) is necessary. In addition, it is important to strike a balance between granting immediate relief and sending the state back to the drawing board so that systemic failures may be addressed on a more sustainable basis.

So when would it be appropriate for a supervisory order and what should such an order be capable of achieving? The limited case law to date suggests that central to the analysis is whether there is evidence to suggest that the state is unwilling to comply with an order of court. In *TAC*, for example, the Constitutional Court

---

[136] Roach and Budlender 2005: 327. Roach and Budlender distinguish between three "escalating levels of remedies": "Level 1: General declarations with possible reporting to the public for inattentive governments; Level 2: Mandatory relief with reporting to the court for incompetent governments; and Level 3: detailed mandatory interdicts enforced by contempt proceedings for intransigent governments" (pp. 346, 348, and 349 respectively).

[137] See also Swart 2005.

decided to abandon the supervisory order originally issued by the Pretoria High Court largely on the basis that changed circumstances did not justify such an order, that "government has always respected and executed orders of this Court . . . [and that there] is no reason to believe that it will not do so in the present case."[138] In the Court's view, the state had already shown the requisite political will to implement such a program without compulsion.

These changed circumstances included – but were not limited to – a Cabinet commitment to implement a comprehensive MTCT prevention program made public on April 17, 2002, a fortnight before the Constitutional Court hearing on the matter and some two and a half months before judgment was handed down. Although developments that occurred subsequent to the December 14, 2001, decision of the Pretoria High Court – coupled with the very prescriptive nature of the Constitutional Court – may have obviated the need for a supervisory order along the lines of that originally issued, subsequent developments have shown that the final order did not achieve compliance. Thus, it was only in response to the initiation of contempt of court proceedings that Mpumalanga, one of the most recalcitrant provinces, was prepared to commit to a comprehensive program and to set out the details thereof on oath.[139]

The experiences of those working to monitor the implementation of both court-ordered and government-initiated programs suggest that the *TAC* approach to supervisory orders both undermines their true value and fails to recognize the practical difficulties faced by civil society and other stakeholders in holding government to account. Supervisory orders have the potential to ensure the availability of regular flows of information on the basis of which implementation may be monitored and evaluated. Without some form of court-ordered supervision, even if limited to ensuring the availability of certain documents or information on a regular basis, it is often difficult to evaluate whether the state has indeed complied with a court order.

Recognizing the need for a supervisory order does not necessarily mean court supervision or even court involvement. It is arguable that courts should only be involved on an ongoing basis where this is strictly necessary, such as in the most egregious of cases where there is sufficient evidence to doubt the state's bona fides or where time is of the essence, such as in cases where irreparable damage would be done if implementation were to be delayed or in matters where delays would render the order academic. But in many other cases, a supervisory order may not require ongoing court involvement. Instead, constitutional and statutory bodies could be tasked with monitoring the state's compliance with a court order.[140]

A further argument in support of supervisory orders notes that even where aggrieved litigants (or potential beneficiaries of a court order) are able to establish a failure on the part of government to comply with an order of court, it is often difficult for them to enforce their rights by way of contempt proceedings. In

---

[138] Treatment Action Campaign 2004, Paragraph 129.

[139] See Heywood 2003a.

[140] See Vumazonke v. Member of the Executive Council for Social Development, Eastern Cape Province, unreported decision of the Port Elizabeth High Court in Case No. 2004/050 (25 November 2004).

some cases, limited resources may restrict their ability to approach a competent court for appropriate relief. In others, certain political considerations may further complicate matters, making it virtually impossible to litigate even when there is a clear cause of action and resources are available. In the case of the contempt of court proceedings regarding Mpumalanga, for example, those seeking to investigate compliance with the order in *TAC* found that many public-sector health care providers were unwilling to blow the whistle. Simply put, the political climate had created a context within which health care providers feared intimidation if they were seen to be assisting the TAC in any way.

In such a case, a supervisory order may well have assisted in drawing an independent commission or other statutory institution properly on board, whether as a party to enforcement proceedings or as a court-appointed rapporteur. Without such an order, a body such as the South African Human Rights Commission (SAHRC) may be under significant political pressure not to investigate and report on noncompliance with court orders, despite being requested by civil society to do so.[141] In the case of Mpumalanga, for example, a TAC-initiated complaint to the SAHRC was followed by an investigation that – to date – has yet to result in any official report or recommendation.[142]

Using Coercion Against State Officials. Many of the Eastern Cape social assistance cases indicate a lack of political will to implement court orders. This begs the question: how does one "create" political will – through moral persuasion or by coercion? Many SE rights litigators prefer the latter: civil imprisonment for contempt of court; attachment of the personal property of state officials; and *de bonis propriis* (adverse personal) costs orders against state officials. By far, adverse personal costs orders appear to be the most sought after. However, although this may ensure compliance in a particular case, it is questionable whether it will have the effect of creating a culture of compliance within the civil service.

Despite a somewhat valiant attempt to undo much of the damage apparently caused by the SCA in *Jayiya*, *Kate* nevertheless concludes that South African law does not allow for the committal of a state official to prison following a finding of contempt of court with respect to an order sounding in money. Despite limiting the reach of *Jayiya*, it still left untouched a key source of the problem, Section 3 of the State Liability Act 20 of 1957. That provision precludes a successful litigant from executing against state assets or the private assets of a state official. Given the limited options available, it seemed appropriate that Section 3 – which removes the only real enforcement mechanism in relation to an order against the state sounding in money – be challenged directly.

This is indeed what happened in the case of *Nyathi v. Member of the Executive Council for the Department of Health Gauteng*.[143] In the Pretoria High Court, a

---

[141] For discussion of the role of the SAHRC in relation to SE rights, see Newman 2003 and McClain 2002. See also Groenewald and Bangerezako 2006.

[142] See, e.g., AIDS Law Project, *Submission to the Ad Hoc Committee on the Review of State Institutions Supporting Constitutional Democracy* (in particular Annexure 1).

[143] [2008] ZACC 8.

portion of Section 3 was declared inconsistent with the Constitution and therefore invalid. In that case, the applicant had claimed damages after a central venous line was incorrectly inserted by a public hospital, resulting in a stroke and paralysis on one side. Although the case was not opposed by the state and the full quantum of damages had yet to be determined, the High Court ordered the state to make an interim payment to cover medical expenses. The challenge to Section 3 arose following nonpayment. Confirmation proceedings before the Constitutional Court – which automatically follow whenever a court declares a statutory provision or conduct of the President to be unconstitutional – took place on August 30, 2007. On June 2, 2008, a majority of the Court confirmed the High Court's finding that the provision is indeed in conflict with the Constitution. The declaration of invalidity was suspended for twelve months to give Parliament sufficient time to correct the defect in the law.[144]

Prioritization

How have South African courts addressed the question of prioritization, and what – if any – trade-offs have been made? Perhaps the starting point in any discussion on prioritization is *Grootboom*, which recognizes that, whereas the state has an obligation to create the conditions so that people at all economic levels of our society are able to realize their SE rights, the needs of the poor – who are particularly vulnerable – require special attention. Whereas the needs of others must also be addressed, the fulfillment of their social and economic rights does not necessarily involve the allocation of state resources; for them, the state may only be required to establish an appropriate policy framework.

Grootboom can and must be read together with *Soobramoney*, which recognizes that the right of access to health care services does not impose an obligation on the state to provide everything to everyone at once. Instead, it mandates the state to use its limited resources – wherever necessary – in a manner that works toward the "larger needs of society rather than . . . the specific needs of particular individuals within society."[145] This does not mean, however, that the state should only address the health care needs of the majority of the population, but rather that it must manage its resources in a manner that achieves maximum societal benefit.

The notion of prioritization brings with it two interrelated areas of contestation. First, it requires the judiciary to involve itself in the allocation of limited resources. Consider the "available resources" argument, ordinarily understood as potentially providing government with an excuse not to provide services. Implicit in *Soobramoney* – a case in which the state was able to justify the restricted provision of health services on the basis of limited resources – is that the concept may rather be used to challenge the state's allocation of a disproportionate share of the budget

---

[144] The state has at least two options at its disposal. First, it could allow for execution against the assets of the state and/or those of the responsible political head. Second, it could legislate a new crime of contempt of court – with prospective effect – that applies to state officials who intentionally disregard court orders sounding in money. If Parliament fails to act within twelve months, the state and/or its officials will be treated in the same way as any other unsuccessful defendant in a matter sounding in money.

[145] At Paragraph 31.

to a relatively insignificant need if this has the effect of undermining its ability to address priority needs.

But instead of directing the reallocation of resources from one aspect of state policy to another, which may very well involve an unconstitutional breach of the separation of powers doctrine, courts can generally be expected to place the state in the difficult position of having to explain why it cannot afford to expend resources on a particular public priority. Instead of simply being allowed to plead poverty, the state is expected to justify its actions and come up with plausible explanations for budgetary allocations. This may require the state to justify expenditures on nonpriority areas. If this were to be the case, it would effectively allow courts to redirect resource allocation by default.[146]

Second, it necessarily involves courts identifying what matters are worthy of prioritization. On this issue, the jurisprudence suggests – at least at first glance – that courts do not decide such matters themselves. Instead, the courts appear at times to go to great lengths to show that the state itself considers a particular issue as a priority. Once having identified that a particular priority need is already recognized in existing government policy, courts have been able to focus on the means chosen by the state to address that particular need. Thus, in *Grootboom*, despite the lack of "measures . . . to provide relief for people who have no access to land, no roof over their heads, and who are living in intolerable conditions or crisis situations,"[147] the Court's starting point is the identification of the state's "comprehensive and co-ordinated" housing program.

In *TAC*, the Court's point of departure was the government's "formidable array of responses to the pandemic," which included a government-devised "programme to deal with mother-to-child transmission of HIV at birth."[148] Yet, despite a well-documented history of state inaction and reluctant acceptance of the need to implement a public-sector program to prevent MTCT, the Court nevertheless portrayed the program as one that was freely chosen by the state. Once having identified the program as a government initiative, the Court is in a better position to address its unreasonableness and inadequacy.

The emerging jurisprudence of the Constitutional Court places little reliance on the concept of minimum core entitlements as articulated in international human rights law. This appears to limit – if not largely eliminate – the ability of individual litigants to advance SE rights claims,[149] and, at first glance, seems to be at odds with any focus on prioritization. But when seen in the context of the judiciary's preference for basing decisions on policy choices already taken by the state, the Court's understanding of minimum core – potentially relevant only as part of a

---

[146] In *Khosa*, for example, the state was forced to justify why the provision of certain social assistance benefits to permanent residents would be unaffordable, as it claimed was indeed the case. In particular, the state argued that the extension of the benefits in question to all eligible permanent residents would be too expensive. But the Constitutional Court remained unconvinced, noting in its judgment that the state failed to provide clear evidence to support this assertion.

[147] At Paragraph 99.

[148] At Paragraph 4.

[149] This has significant implications for and may result in reliance on the work of strong organs of civil society.

general reasonableness test – is not only consistent but may be particularly strategic. In this way, the possibility for minimum core arguments to enter through the back door – as and when necessary – still exists.[150]

QUANTIFYING IMPACT

How does one assess impact? In assessing the influence of SE rights cases, one cannot but consider their impact on a wide range of different levels. First, one must consider whether a particular decision resolved the dispute at hand (using this terminology from the Introduction to this volume, this would be *direct effects on litigants or others*). Second, one needs to look at the broader impact of the case on the realization of the right in question (which the Introduction calls *indirect effects* outside the legal system). Finally, one needs to consider the extent to which the matter has provided a basis for other rights claims or has contributed to the development of SE rights jurisprudence (indirect effects through the legal system).

But before considering these three levels, it is important to recognize that impact is not easily measured. Many cases are settled. Others never make it to court – or even to the attention of the authorities – because of extremely limited access to lawyers and legal services.[151] Perhaps more important, the express recognition of SE rights in the Constitution – being accompanied by duties on the state regarding their realization – has the potential to work within the state to the direct benefit of poor people, influencing policies, departmental agendas, and government spending priorities. Knowing that courts are both empowered and mandated to demand that government justify its resource allocations, bureaucrats may indeed feel compelled to conduct themselves reasonably and accountably.

Direct Impact on Litigants and Others

In the majority of cases that are considered in this chapter, poor litigants were largely successful in vindicating their SE rights, managing to secure orders suggestive of some sort of personal relief. A case such as *Modderklip* perhaps represents a high point: not only has the threat of the community's eviction been removed, but basic services – including fresh water and weekly refuse removal – have been provided by the local municipality. In addition, residents are able to make use of a school

---

[150] In this regard, see *Grootboom*, which regards the idea of minimum core as potentially relevant "in determining whether measures adopted by the State are reasonable" (at Paragraph 33). See also Pieterse 2005: 500, where the author argues that "the Constitutional Court's rejection of a minimum core approach to the interpretation and enforcement of socio-economic rights need not be seen as altogether precluding an entitlement-orientated approach to these rights." He continues: "Overall, there appears to be sufficient textual backing and institutional leeway for courts directly to remedy infringements of particular socio-economic rights in appropriate circumstances, whether or not such remedies flow from endorsement of the minimum core standard as enunciated in international law" (pp. 501–502). Further, see Mazibuko v. City of Johannesburg, as yet unreported decision of the Johannesburg High Court in Case No. 06/13865 (30 April 2008). That decision, which expands on the concept of minimum core obligations within reasonableness review, is widely expected to be taken on appeal.

[151] See Langa, "Keynote Address: HIV and Access to Legal Services Conference"; and AIDS Law Project, "Consensus Statement on Improving Access to Legal Services for People Living with HIV/AIDS."

and clinic in the nearby formal township of Daveyton. Simply put, security of tenure for the so-called Gabon community of Modderklip has translated directly into access to water, education, and health care services.

In general, however, court victories – on their own – appear seldom to bring sufficient relief to rights claimants. Instead, they simply provide the basis on which further action – whether legal or otherwise – may be based. Such action, however, requires resources, staying power, and the political space provided by a range of civil and political rights. Consider, for example, the monitoring role assigned to the SAHRC by the Constitutional Court in *Grootboom*. Although the Court suggested that the SAHRC should monitor implementation of the order as a whole,[152] the latter chose only to monitor the implementation of an agreement entered into between the applicants and the state.[153] This agreement, which was first breached by the state shortly after it had been concluded,[154] has never been properly implemented.[155]

It does not appear that the SAHRC has ever held the state to account for its failure to deliver to Irene Grootboom and the Wallacedene community in Cape Town. More disturbing, no one has taken the SAHRC to task for its failure to do the limited role it ascribed to itself. No one has questioned why it failed, at the very outset, to take on board the broader role defined by the Constitutional Court.[156] In contrast, persistent follow up and skillful media and legal work has resulted in significant – albeit insufficient – compliance in *Westville*.[157]

> According to the evidence put forward by the State [in further court papers in September 2006], the vast majority of prisoners at the Medium B section of... [Westville] who know their HIV status and need ARV treatment are in fact now accessing such treatment. In addition, the prison hospital has been accredited by the Department of Health to provide ARV treatment onsite. It also appears that there is improved co-ordination between the Departments of Health and Correctional Services with regard to the delivery of HIV-related health care services to prisoners.[158]

---

[152] In its intervention, the SAHRC had indicated that it "had the duty and was prepared to monitor and report on the compliance by the State of its S[ection] 26 obligations." With this in mind, the Court noted that the SAHRC "will monitor and, if necessary, report in terms of these powers on the efforts made by the State to comply with its S[ection] 26 obligations in accordance with... [the] judgment" (at Paragraph 97).

[153] The SAHRC reported back to the Court but unfortunately only focused on the narrow order of court relating to the circumstances of the respondents themselves rather than the broader mandate expressly authorized by the Constitutional Court. See Pillay 2002.

[154] This necessitated a further application to make the agreement an order of court. In this regard, see Grootboom v. Government of the Republic of South Africa (unreported order in Case No. CCT 38/00 (21 September 2000)), available at http://www.constitutionalcourt.org.za/Archimages/2874.PDF.

[155] Although the applicants initially got some relief (being moved to a community hall as an interim remedy before the main case was initially argued in the High Court), more than seven years down the line, little appears to have changed.

[156] For further discussion on the appropriate role to be played by the SAHRC, which has yet to be a primary litigator in any SE rights matter, see AIDS Law Project, "Submission to the Ad Hoc Committee." According to a senior employee, at least two factors prevent the SAHRC from giving full effect to its SE rights mandate – an inadequate budget and insufficient pressure from civil society.

[157] This has only been possible because of the significant resources invested in the case by the applicants' pro bono legal representatives.

[158] Hassim and Berger 2006: 18–19.

Westville raises another concern. In that case (as in *TAC*), court processes them-selves were used – in bad faith – to frustrate the implementation of court orders. In both cases, the state sought (unsuccessfully) to appeal implementation orders that had been sought – and indeed obtained – pending the resolution of further appeal processes on the substantive issues. In its August 28, 2006, judgment, the Durban High Court noted as follows:

> The authorities do not view with particular favour appeals from implementation orders. These have taken place – I gather – on extremely rare occasions. It is somewhat ironic and sad that both occasions relate to the government seeking to avoid the effect of court orders for the provision of ARVs. See *Minister of Health v. Treatment Action Campaign (1)* 2002(5) SA 703 (CC).[159]

Unfortunately, problems with implementation are somewhat widespread. *Watchenuka*, for example, required a series of legal interventions for substan-tive progress to be made. Technically, the judgment was implemented, meaning that asylum seekers now have the right to work and study in South Africa.[160] Yet, securing a Section 22 form, which sets out the basis upon which an asylum seeker may reside in South Africa and confirms this right, may take up to six months.[161] Severe delays in issuing Section 22 permits have lead to further litigation.[162]

Similarly, *Ngxuza* required at least four further court hearings to ensure substan-tial compliance. Following the SCA's decision, the parties negotiated a settlement, which in essence recognized that whereas each and every cancellation of the social grant of a member of the relevant class of persons on whose behalf the class action had been brought was unlawful, the state would not have to reinstate a person if it was found that he or she should never have received the grant in the first place. This would occur in those cases where the person was not disabled or unemployed or did not qualify for the relevant grant on the basis of a lawful exclusion criterion. On perusal of the relevant records, those whose grants had been wrongly canceled would be reinstated as beneficiaries and would receive back pay.

Many beneficiaries were reinstated immediately. But those members of the class who had only received temporary disability grants were not given back pay. Instead, they were simply reinstated for a temporary period after which they were removed from the system again. In terms of an order of court dated March 20, 2002, the

---

[159] *Westville* (second implementation order) at Paragraph 15

[160] The word "prohibited" (referring to work and study) apparently still appears on the Section 22 forms – it has to be crossed out each time a form is filled out.

[161] Those with access to the right legal advice and assistance can, nevertheless, overcome these problems. Consider, for example, the proactive role played by legal advice officers at the University of Cape Town's Refugee Law Clinic. They issue letters to clients explaining about the rights of asylum seekers. Even though these have no legal status, they are generally taken seriously by the police. In addition, the clinic ensures that clients get interviews with the department, provides letters to tertiary institutions explaining the backlogs at the department and the rights of their clients to study, deals with appeals before the Refugee Appeals Board, and works closely with the United Nations High Commission for Refugees on repatriation applications.

[162] These forms are not given when an asylum seeker first presents at a border post or a Department of Home Affairs office. When first presenting, an asylum seeker is given a slip to come back for an appointment to get a Section 22 form to begin the application process.

state was obliged to provide reasons why persons were either not reinstated as beneficiaries or were classified as temporary beneficiaries only. It failed to do so properly, resulting in further legal action being prepared on behalf of certain members of the class. According to the applicants' lawyers, the matter was only finally resolved in mid-2006, some five years after the SCA's landmark decision in the matter.

A "conciliatory" judgment in *New Clicks*, which saw all parties claim victory, initially appeared to have allowed for a solid working relationship to develop between parties that were previously engaged in acrimonious litigation. Some stakeholders believed that the Pricing Committee – primarily tasked with running the process to revise the dispensing fee – had finally taken its job seriously. This was perhaps to be expected, as the credibility of the statutory body – composed in large part of individuals from academia and the private sector – had been severely dented by the judgment.

But the manner in which the Pricing Committee addressed the revision of the dispensing fee is nevertheless cause for concern. In its judgment of September 30, 2005, the full Court held "that given the great public interest in resolving this matter, it would be desirable for... [the process of determining the appropriate dispensing fee] to be complete within 60 days."[163] This did not happen. Instead, a draft revised dispensing fee was published for comment five months later,[164] with the final revised dispensing fee – then set to come into effect on January 1, 2007 – only published fourteen months after the judgment on December 1, 2006.[165] At the time of writing, the revised fee had not yet come into effect – the matter having yet again landed in court.

Response to the lack of regulation has been varied.[166] New Clicks, a retail pharmacy chain and one of the key applicants, continued to charge the (low) dispensing fee declared by the Constitutional Court to be inappropriate. Some smaller pharmacies continued to charge significantly higher dispensing fees, arguably in contravention of Section 42 of the Pharmacy Act 53 of 1974.[167] At least one of the three main private hospital groups no longer charges any dispensing fee on medicines. Lost profits on dispensing fees are suspected to have simply been built into "costs"

---

[163] At Paragraph 20.

[164] See National Department of Health, "Announcement of a draft dispensing fee and release of a revised HR Plan" (9 March 2006), available at http://www.doh.gov.za/docs/pr/2006/pr0309.html.

[165] Regulations Relating to a Transparent Pricing System for Medicines and Schedules Substances: Amendment, Government Notice No. R. 1210 (*Government Gazette* No. 29443, December 2006).

[166] The Court dealt with the unregulated dispensing fee as follows: "It would not be just and equitable for pharmacists not to be entitled to charge a dispensing fee in the interim before the appropriate fee is determined by regulation. There is no reason to believe that pharmacists, who are members of an ethical profession, will seek to exploit the situation by charging excessive dispensing fees. Should any pharmacist attempt to do so, that would constitute misconduct in terms of Section 42 of the Pharmacy Act, 53 of 1974" (at Paragraph 19).

[167] On June 9, 2006, I accompanied a friend to a small pharmacy in Johannesburg where he purchased ARV medicines to treat his HIV infection. In the case of Aspen Nevirapine, he was charged an uncapped 38.5 percent of the regulated price. In the case of Aspen Lamzid, he was charged an uncapped 30.5 percent dispensing fee. These dispensing fees were significantly in excess of the draft revised fee published for public comment on March 31, 2006, as well as the revised fee that was – at that point – to come into force on January 1, 2007.

elsewhere. This is precisely what is to be expected from that part of the private sector – the hospital groups – that remains largely unregulated and relatively free from price competition.[168] The complexity of court orders might also affect impact. The relief in *Mikro*, for example, was clear. The judgment required the school to accept the twenty-one black children – who wished to be taught there in English – until the end of 2005, whereupon they would be transferred to the dual-medium (English and Afrikaans) school some 1.2 kilometers down the road. This happened. In this case, significant pressure was placed on government by the parents of both sets of learners – the Afrikaans-speaking black and white children enrolled at Mikro and the twenty-one English-speaking would-be Mikro learners. Perhaps the pressure was such that, in the wake of a court decision highly critical of the state's conduct, the children's interests had to be given effect.

Broader Impact on the Specific SE Rights Issue Raised

Grootboom is a classic example of delayed – and flawed – implementation, a case of too little, too late. The "crisis relief program" that took government four years to produce has been described as inadequate; its implementation slow. Contrast this with *TAC*, which saw substantially better compliance from the state, despite some initial foot-dragging that led to contempt of court proceedings in the province of Mpumalanga. Continued monitoring by civil society was – and clearly remains – of the utmost importance.

Perhaps because of its high-profile work regarding the implementation of the public-sector ARV treatment program – which owes its existence in large part to the court victory – many people believe that the TAC has continually monitored the implementation of *TAC*, putting pressure on government to comply with the order. Given the detail of the order granted by the Constitutional Court, in some ways perhaps dispensing with the need for a structural interdict, it should have been possible for an organization of TAC's size and strength to do what is clearly required to ensure effective implementation. But this did not happen. Despite recognizing the importance of the issue in the case, the organization's focus was largely on the bigger picture, seeing *TAC* as an entry point to develop the right to health in general and access to ARV treatment in particular. The TAC admits that it was a mistake to take its eye off the ball. Its current plan of action thus focuses attention on improving the state's MTCT prevention program.[169] *Mikro* seems to have had a significant impact on the school's conduct after the litigation, as well as providing a clear basis for future provincial education department intervention in language policy implementation. The school appears

---

[168] But see the National Health Amendment Bill, 2008, Government Notice No. 611, *Government Gazette* No. 31114 (2 June 2008), which seeks to introduce some level of private sector price regulation. No one, including civil society, is happy with the bill. The private medical industry seems resistant to regulation of any sort, whereas civil society has raised rule-of-law concerns (among others) regarding the manner in which the regulation is proposed.

[169] Had this work happened earlier, coverage, uptake, and its linkages with the ARV treatment program would in all likelihood have been better.

to have become acutely aware of the need to counter any perceptions of racism – the case involved allegations of linguistic rights in education as a cover for racism – and has taken steps to reach out to black people in the broader community. For example, it has recently enrolled poor black children from a local wine farm. The children's laborer parents, who cannot afford school fees, are happy for their children to learn in Afrikaans. In terms of broader policy, *Mikro* now requires provincial governments seriously to consider maintaining single-language schools, with the test for dual-medium schools being one of practicality.

But with respect to a range of other cases, such as *van Biljon, Jayiya,* and *Ngxuza,* the broader impact on the specific SE rights issue raised has been somewhat different – either minimal or in fact damaging:

- Too little seems to have changed in the Department of Correctional Services' policy on ARV treatment following *van Biljon,* as is evident in *Westville.*
- *Jayiya* represented a significant setback, apparently having resulted in a more lax response to the implementation of court orders by the Eastern Cape Department of Welfare. Most disturbingly, it had the potential to reach beyond the issue of social security, as it went to the very heart of the enforcement of court orders against the state.
- Since *Ngxuza,* many people have been advised to seek legal advice regarding the problems they have with accessing social grants. Many, however, don't approach organizations like the Legal Resources Centre (LRC) – the applicants' legal representatives – because of political reasons. It appears that some organizations dissuade people from approaching the LRC, channeling them to African National Congress (ANC) party structures instead.

Impact on the Other Rights Claims and SE Rights Jurisprudence

The irony – and perhaps the tragedy – of *Grootboom* is that although it is widely and extensively quoted, setting the basis for the enforcement of the right to housing and other SE rights, it has meant very little for the Wallacedene community other than its fifteen minutes of fame. In the housing rights arena, broadly speaking, *Grootboom* has underperformed. It has, however, made a significant impact on evictions and local government housing policy. Not only do poor people now have some degree of bargaining power to fight evictions, but courts also appear less willing to grant evictions. In short, *Grootboom* appears to have established a strong defensive right that prohibits evictions in the absence of alternative accommodation being made available.[170]

---

[170] See, e.g., City of Cape Town v. Rudolph 2004 (5) SA 39 (C), Port Elizabeth Municipality v. Various Occupiers 2005 (1) SA 217 (CC), City of Johannesburg v. Rand Properties 2006 (6) BCLR 728 (W), Ritama Investments v. Unlawful Occupiers of Erf 62 Wynberg [2007] JOL 18960 (T); and *Modderklip,* all of which build on the strong foundation set by *Grootboom.* The broader impact of *Modderklip* is discussed elsewhere in this chapter. See also Mahomed 2003. It is interesting to note, however, that it took more than a year for any reference to *Rudolph* to appear in the council minutes of the City of Cape Town.

But *Grootboom* has yet to be used to ensure the creation of that alternative accommodation. It may have registered strongly with courts and government, but the latter has not known what to do in the face of an overly broad and nondirective Constitutional Court order, made in the absence of any follow-up mechanism such as a supervisory order. In contrast, although *TAC* also failed to secure a supervisory interdict, it did result in a detailed order that left little room for doubt as to what was required of the state.

Compared to *Grootboom*, the impact of social assistance litigation has perhaps been much broader – both positively and negatively. On the upside, the welfare department in East London – a medium-size port city in the impoverished and largely rural Eastern Cape province – has been consolidated and reconstituted and appears to be improving. According to lawyers who have been litigating on this particular issue in that city, grant cancellations in the absence of reasons are now quite rare. At the national level, the cumulative effect of the long list of orders against the state is apparent in the formation of the South African Social Security Agency (SASSA),[171] which is tasked with "act[ing], eventually, as the sole agent that will ensure the efficient and effective management, administration and payment of social assistance."[172]

Sometimes litigation is welcomed by officials who understand how it helps them to do their jobs properly – by removing political obstacles or by helping to identify and hone in on the relevant issues and assist officials in thinking through solutions. Consider *Westville*, where the state's attempts to comply with an interim execution order have started to be characterized by some degree of creative thinking. To deal with a shortage of health care providers in the prison hospital, for example, officials eventually followed the applicants' suggestion and secured the services of sessional doctors.[173]

But then there is the damaging effect of cases such as *Jayiya*, in whose wake courts in the Eastern Cape have largely been powerless to enforce their orders. Somewhat akin to *Jayiya* in terms of its effect is *Soobramoney*, which shows what can happen when the "wrong" cases are litigated.[174] *Soobramoney*, which came after *van Biljon*, appears to have prevented anyone – at least until *Westville* – from bringing a more universal, *van Biljon*–like case. Given the Constitutional Court's decision in *Grootboom*, with its focus on programatic rather than individual relief in SE rights cases, *Soobramoney* was understood as a red light insofar as individual access to an SE right was concerned.

Westville has shown that this need not be the case. In the right circumstances, the nondelivery of goods and services to a defined group – in this case the individual prisoner-applicants and all those at the same prison who were similarly situated – may be determined to be unreasonable and therefore actionable. It is important

---

[171] See http://www.sassa.gov.za.

[172] Section 3(a) of the South African Social Security Agency Act 9 of 2004. SASSA's officials appear to acknowledge the problems in the delivery of social grants and are aware of the string of judgments. But they will still have to deal with significant problems at provincial government level. Regardless of how efficient SASSA may be, it will still have to operate within a context characterized by underperforming – and in many cases failing – provincial administrations.

[173] Private practitioners employed on part-time contracts.

[174] In his defense, Soobramoney had no choice but to bring his application.

to understand, however, that *Westville* was only litigated after the context had been radically altered: a more advanced SE rights jurisprudence and fundamental shifts in state policy, such as the adoption of the Operational Plan to provide ARV treatment in public health facilities.

In looking at broader impact, however, it is important to consider the issue from another perspective – that of the rights claimants' understanding of the role of the law (the Constitution in general and SE rights in particular) and their rights claims beyond the particular case in question. *Grootboom* appears not to have empowered Wallacedene as a community, with significant tensions on the ground between individual claims to houses and the general well-being of the community as a whole. This seems to suggest that the litigation process has failed to instill in the applicants any understanding of the nature and reach of SE rights and their realization.

Perhaps the best example of how a decisive legal victory has been used in support of a popular struggle is that of the adoption, development, and implementation of a comprehensive public-sector HIV/AIDS treatment program that includes the use of ARV treatment where medically indicated. The benefit was not simply accidental – preparation for and the manner in which *TAC* was litigated saw the case being conceptualized as an integral part of the broader campaign for access to treatment.[175] In addition to the direct impact of the order in *TAC* on the state's MTCT prevention program, the case arguably provided the kick start that was needed to shift the state into action.

The first breakthrough came in the Cabinet statement of April 17, 2002. There, in addition to a commitment to implement a comprehensive MTCT prevention program and other necessary interventions,[176] the government for the first time publicly recognized the importance of ARV treatment as part of a comprehensive approach to dealing with the HIV/AIDS epidemic, acknowledging that ARV drugs "can improve the quality of life of People Living with AIDS, if administered at certain stages in the progression of the condition and in accordance with international guidelines and protocols."

Shortly after the Constitutional Court handed down its decision in *TAC* in July 2002, the government established a Joint Health and Treasury Task Team "charged with examining treatment options to supplement comprehensive care for HIV and AIDS in the public health sector."[177] In its *Update on Cabinet's Statement of 17 April 2002 on fighting HIV/AIDS* issued three months later on October 9, 2002, the government stated that its "ultimate objective is to ensure that South Africans living with AIDS can have access to the treatment they need under conditions that will benefit them," and that it was working "to create the conditions that would make it feasible and effective to use antiretrovirals in the public health sector."

Following an intensification of the TAC's programme of action, including a march of twenty thousand people on the opening of Parliament on February 14,

---

[175] Unfortunately, this example of public interest lawyering in the arena of SE rights appears to be the exception rather than the rule.

[176] These include post-exposure prophylaxis using ARV medicines to prevent HIV transmission following rape and other forms of sexual assault.

[177] Operational Plan at p.13.

2003, and a campaign of civil disobedience that began on the eve of Human Rights Day in 2003,[178] the Cabinet "convened a special meeting [on August 8, 2003] to consider the Report of the Joint Health and Treasury Task Team." At that meeting, it recognized the need to act with urgency and decided "the Department of Health should, as a matter of urgency, develop a detailed operational plan on an antiretroviral treatment programme."[179] On November 19, 2003, the Cabinet adopted the Operational Plan, with ARV treatment as one of its core components.[180]

We will most likely never know with certainty the extent to which *TAC* was responsible for these momentous developments regarding HIV/AIDS treatment. One can only reflect on the strong evidence that undoubtedly points in the direction of significant influence. But even if one were to recognize the decision as a watershed, what is also clear is that – in and of itself – the judgment did not result directly in a sustainable policy shift. Although it certainly helped to strengthen the organizational profile of the TAC as a key role player of substance, it simply laid the foundation for further advocacy, campaign work, mobilization, and litigation.[181]

For example, the emerging health rights jurisprudence has been used successfully by the TAC in at least three further matters relating to access to treatment for HIV/AIDS: *Hazel Tau, Interim Procurement,* and *Westville.* The settlements in the first case, in which the TAC and others sought to use the emerging case law in a head-on challenge to the pricing practices of two multinational pharmaceutical companies, have directly resulted in increasing access to sustainable supplies of affordable ARV medicines. In the second matter, the TAC's success in compelling the Minister of Health to procure an interim supply of ARV medicines (pending the finalization of the formal tender process) gave provinces with existing capacity the space to implement the Operational Plan with urgency. For example, Gauteng province began to provide ARV treatment only days after the Minister's capitulation on the issue. Others followed shortly thereafter. This would not have been possible if they had waited for the finalization of the tender, which took more than a year. And as a result of *Westville,* speedier implementation of the Operational Plan in prisons – while still bedeviled with problems – is now firmly on the agenda.

FACTORS INFLUENCING SUCCESSFUL OUTCOMES

In the previous section, we considered the impact of SE rights litigation. What was not considered – and what this section now addresses – are the factors that appear to support successful SE rights litigation. At the outset, it is important to note that many of the legal techniques adopted by human rights lawyers under apartheid

---

[178] The civil disobedience campaign was suspended later at the request of the former Deputy President. A decision to resume the campaign was taken at the TAC's biannual congress in early August 2003. Only days later, the Cabinet instructed the DoH to develop the Operational Plan.

[179] Statement on Special Cabinet Meeting: Enhanced Programme against HIV and AIDS (8 August 2003), available at http://www.info.gov.za/speeches/2003/03081109461001.htm.

[180] Operational Plan at p. 246.

[181] Developments in HIV/AIDS law, policy, and public-sector program implementation are ongoing. In this regard, see generally http://www.tac.org.za. The relatively slow pace of implementation (of the Operational Plan), however, suggests that much of this work has only begun.

remain applicable – and in use – today.[182] However, express recognition of rights to equality and dignity – not to mention SE rights – provides the activist lawyer with a much-improved legal toolbox.

A useful starting point in analyzing the factors that influence successful outcomes is to understand how SE rights claims are understood, framed, and pursued. Thus, a belief among some litigators that judges will rule on technical, administrative grounds if at all possible has resulted – to some degree – in a tendency toward placing SE rights litigation within an administrative law model, which sees the SE right playing the role of a tiebreaker only where there is ambiguity in the administrative rules. This ambivalence toward SE rights is reflected, for example, in the *Ngxuza* legal team choosing deliberately to avoid invoking the right to social security, apparently out of a fear that judges would be unsympathetic and that the rights issues would delay the case. This is to be contrasted with those who see the express constitutional recognition of SE rights as allowing judges to be less deferent and concerned about breaching the separation of powers.[183]

Two distinct models of litigation strategies, thus, seem to be emerging. On the one hand, many of the social assistance and education cases have followed an administrative law model of judicial review. On the other, many of the health cases have relied directly on express constitutional protections to make sense of (or transform, where necessary) the particular provision of law – whether common, statutory, or constitutional – that forms the basis for the rights claim in question.[184] It is important to note that the approach taken is not merely of intellectual interest. Instead, it seems to be at the heart of decisions regarding what gets litigated, how cases are fought in the court of public opinion, and who ultimately benefits. As Mureinik so eloquently argued in his seminal piece "Beyond a Charter of Luxuries: Economic Rights in the Constitution,"[185] the power of all SE rights is their ability to compel the state publicly to justify its conduct. Only by holding the state to account can people's basic needs – to housing, health care, education, social security – be realized.[186]

---

[182] For further information about human rights lawyering under apartheid, see Abel 1995.

[183] Another view sees SE rights giving particular focus to administrative review, with rational government decision making being directed toward achieving certain SE goals. For further discussion on the relationship between SE rights and administrative justice, see de Villiers 2002 and Plasket 2003.

[184] This approach is not simply one adopted by litigators. Davis 2006: 304 notes that "the record of adjudicating these [SE] rights over the first decade since the advent of democracy in South Africa reveals both a judicial and academic retreat into administrative law." He continues (at 319): "Deference . . . is inextricably linked to the administrative law model which is presently hegemonic in this area of South African law."

[185] Mureinik 1992.

[186] In this regard, see *Ritama Investments* (see Note 170) where Bertelsmann held as follows: "Having heard argument by counsel I informed the parties that I intended to order the fourth and fifth respondents [the Metropolitan Municipality of Johannesburg and the relevant provincial minister of housing respectively] to attend court in person at a date to be arranged in the near future, together with those officials that might be needed to assist them, to explain their failure to assist the court so far and to inform the court and the other parties of the present state of affairs in Alexandra. They should be prepared to subject themselves to examination and cross examination" (p. 16 of the typed judgment). The judgment includes a list of nineteen questions for the twelve witnesses to be called.

Ultimately, perhaps, the approach taken by many lawyers in any given case may have less to do with underlying philosophy than with what is perceived to be the most secure legal route in the circumstances of a particular conflict. If this is true, then the marginal or central role played by SE rights may appear to be decided on a basis that fails to consider the relevance of extralegal factors in rights litigation. This may help explain the differential impact of "successful" cases – *Hazel Tau*, for example, being settled on a basis substantially better than what had been sought in the papers.

Before addressing the factors that influence successful outcomes, two final points are worth noting. Very few of the cases analyzed reflect a proactive use of SE rights. Instead, most involve reaction to negative infringements of rights. Similarly, few of the cases are truly landmark by nature – most battle to move beyond their narrow facts. Thus, the sample of cases analyzed tends largely to reflect nothing more than a seemingly endless collection of cases concerning disputes about the state's authority to deny assistance to individuals for substantive reasons. For the true potential of SE rights – as entrenched in the Constitution – to be unleashed, serious thought must be given more regularly to moving beyond the individual, or even class action, suit for relief.

Litigation Decisions That Influence Outcomes

To understand successful SE rights litigation, it is important to explore certain decisions taken by litigants and/or their legal representatives. In particular, this section considers decisions regarding the characterization and timing of cases. As it is also vital to understand who takes these decisions, this part of the chapter also considers the roles played by clients and their legal representatives.

Characterization

The reported education cases are particularly instructive on the issue of characterization of a claim, given the ways in which they may be differently understood. On the one hand, they may be perceived to be a clash between the retention of (largely white) privilege and a bona fide attempt by government to ensure quality education for all. On the other, they may be better characterized as the reliance of constitutionally entrenched rights to ward off an ever-encroaching and arrogant disrespect for diversity and minority rights. Or the reality may lie somewhere between.

Two rights claims have ordinarily been advanced in education cases: the first, based on the margins of the right to education, deals primarily with linguistic rights; the second, based completely outside the right to education, focuses on just administrative action. None of them involves a positive claim to education.

Characterized by some as an attack on a minority language by the hegemony of English, *Mikro* focused on the linguistic right in Section 29(2) of the Constitution. This right, which appears to straddle the border between SE rights on the one hand and civil and political rights on the other, owes its very existence to political compromise during the constitutional drafting process. It is, therefore, not surprising that any reliance thereupon is viewed with suspicion. To their credit (and possibly their disadvantage), the parents of the excluded children did not play the race card, relying instead on the best interests of the child directive in Section 28 of the Constitution.

With respect to numerous health and anti-eviction cases, litigators have sought – without much difficulty – to bring the dire circumstances of their clients to the judiciary's attention. Judges are made to feel the pain – by way of on-site inspections,[187] photographs, and emotional affidavits. Consider Nontsikelelo Patricia Zwedala's affidavit in *Hazel Tau*, in which she explained how she was made aware of her HIV infection:

> In March 1998 I was diagnosed HIV positive. I was not given proper counselling. I was told by a doctor at the Nyanga clinic that I "should wait for my death."[188]

In that case, the complainants had sought – from the very outset – to make it literally a matter of life and death. To this end, their statement of complaint alleged that the GlaxoSmithKline and Boehringer Ingelheim groups of companies had "engaged in excessive pricing of [antiretroviral medicines] . . . to the detriment of consumers" and that this was "directly responsible for premature, predictable and avoidable deaths of people living with HIV/AIDS."[189]

Timing

Timing played a crucial factor in *TAC*, which was launched only after a long four-year history of engagement on the specific issue. In addition, it built on the organization's previous work to reduce ARV medicine prices, as well as scientific developments regarding the proven efficacy of a simple and affordable MTCT prevention intervention. Equally important, the TAC did not act until it had given the state a reasonable opportunity to explain why – in the face of the available evidence – it continued to refuse to permit the use of ARV medicines for MTCT prevention outside of a limited number of pilot sites, let alone to provide the medicines at state expense. Simply put, litigation came onto the agenda when all other options had been exhausted.

By its nature, proactive litigation provides the time and space for carefully coordinated legal action. Consider also the example of *Ngxuza*, launched deliberately to escape the reach of the Promotion of Administrative Justice Act 3 of 2000 (PAJA). Lawyers initiating this class action were concerned that PAJA might hamper their case. As it turns out, the state was quick to invoke every possible legal technicality, incurring the wrath of the SCA and vindicating the lawyers' concerns:

> [W]hen an organ of government invokes legal processes to impede the rightful claims of its citizens, it not only defies the Constitution . . . [but] also misuses the mechanisms of the law, which it is the responsibility of the courts to safeguard. The

---

[187] This happened, for example, in *Grootboom* (High Court) and *Ritama Investments* (see Note 170).

[188] The affidavit is available at http://www.tac.org.za/Documents/DrugCompaniesCC/Tau_v_GSK–Zwedala_affidavit.doc.

[189] See Paragraph 17 of the original statement of complaint, available at http://www.tac.org.za/Documents/DrugCompaniesCC/HazelTauAndOthersVGlaxoSmithKlineAndOthersStatementOf Complaint.doc.

province's approach to these proceedings was contradictory, cynical, expedient and obstructionist. It conducted the case as though it was at war with its own citizens, the more shamefully because those it was combatting were in terms of secular hierarchies and affluence and power the least in its sphere.[190]

Had the litigation been initiated in the PAJA era, the state may very well have frustrated the prosecution of the case even further, possibly even seeking a further appeal to the Constitutional Court.

Clients' and legal representatives' roles

Many claims for SE benefits at state expense are the domain of the poor and the marginalized. As such, it is not surprising that much of the litigation conducted on behalf of rights claimants is conducted with little of their input insofar as lawyering is concerned. Although a few notable exceptions – such as *TAC* – may exist, the bulk of cases analyzed follow this trend to a greater or lesser extent. Consider, for example, *Grootboom, Ngxuza,* and *Jayiya*:

- Once the legal representative of the Wallacedene community was appointed in *Grootboom*, he made all the key strategic decisions, including getting the initial judge assigned to the case to conduct an inspection *in loco*.[191] But although the community is said to have understood the proceedings well, they nevertheless appear to have been wholly reliant on their lawyers.
- Although the *Ngxuza* clients were advised throughout the proceedings, they nevertheless played little role in making decisions.[192]
- In *Jayiya*, direct consultations with clients provided their legal counsel with insight into the problem to be addressed and provided the clients with a sense of personal involvement. Nevertheless, firm control over the case remained with the lawyers.

A notable exception is *TAC*, which saw the organization largely running its own case – although making all strategic decisions on the advice from legal counsel. This meant that *TAC* was not run simply as a litigation matter. Communities were mobilized through workshops; general public support was sought through a petition; activists engaged with health care providers at public health facilities; and active use of the media was sought and obtained. But *TAC* is not the norm.

So who litigates SE rights claims on behalf of poor people? In general, such litigation is run by relatively well-resourced nonprofit organizations (NPOs) and a handful of private practitioners.[193] Whereas at least one such practitioner believes

---

[190] *Ngxuza* at Paragraph 15 (footnotes omitted).

[191] His instinct proved correct – seeing the material conditions in which the applicants found themselves, the judge ordered interim relief.

[192] The second applicant admitted that she had no prior knowledge of a social security right. Although she knew that it was simply wrong for her disability grant to be cancelled, she had no idea of the source of the right upon which her claim was adjudicated.

[193] The legal profession in South Africa, as in the United Kingdom, is structured along the lines of a split bar – being comprised of attorneys (who act directly on behalf of clients, seldom argue matters in court, and are represented by the Law Society of South Africa [http://www.lssa.org.za]) and advocates (who are briefed by attorneys, specialize in court work, and are represented by the

that private attorneys make better public interest lawyers, questioning the independence and agenda of certain NPOs, the evidence seems to suggest otherwise. The outcomes in *TAC, Ngxuza,* and *Westville* are certainly preferable to those in *Grootboom* and *Jayiya*.[194]

But consider *Modderklip,* an interesting example of how a small firm – led by a larger-than-life, tenacious attorney – collaborated with the residents of the informal settlement: the disciplined Gabon community. It confirms what many litigators understand – that large groups of people cannot be well represented unless they are well organized, able to take decisive action, and resilient to undue pressure.[195] Making use of an outdoor "community office" where meetings were held, the community made decisions on the basis of consensus-building and inclusivity. For their part, the lawyers provided free legal services all the way to the Constitutional Court. To date, they continue to assist as the community successfully asserts its claims to free basic municipal services.[196]

What then about the unrepresented? Limited financial resources limit access to legal remedies.[197] The general unwillingness of the legal profession to give freely of its time and expertise raises concerns about appropriate state regulation, particularly given the right of access to courts in Section 34 of the Constitution and the state's positive obligations to "respect, protect, promote and fulfil"[198] this right.[199] Simply put, the state has a duty to take reasonable measures to ensure that Section 34 is given practical meaning.

Extralegal Considerations

So far, this section has touched on various litigation-related issues associated with success or failure in SE rights litigation. Next, we move beyond the narrow confines of the legal process and address certain extralegal considerations – the awareness of rights; mobilization and the role and nature of civil society; and public opinion, public relations, and the role of the media – which make it plain that the

General Council of the Bar of South Africa [http://www.sabar.co.za]). The reference to private practitioners in the text is a reference to private attorneys. Private advocates are invariably briefed by attorneys in NPOs to argue their matters in court. In many cases, the brief is accepted pro bono, at significantly reduced rates, or on a contingency basis (accepting payment only if and when the matter is won and the opposing side is ordered to pay costs).

[194] One central problem with reliance on the good will of private practitioners is that, given their clients' inability to pay, pro bono work has to be carefully balanced with other (paying) work. In addition, there is the problem of private attorneys ordinarily operating in a vacuum, often cut off from civil society and community-based organizations.

[195] Given lawyers' responsibilities to their clients, the broader public interest often has to be abandoned when litigating on behalf of individuals or weak communities. Organizational clients – such as the TAC – provide greater room for public impact lawyering.

[196] It is unclear whether the residents sought their attorneys out, or the attorneys "discovered" them.

[197] Langa, "Keynote Address: HIV and Access to Legal Services Conference"; AIDS Law Project," Consensus Statement on Improving Access to Legal Services for People Living with HIV/AIDS."

[198] Section 7(2) of the Constitution.

[199] There is a concern relating to the capacity of public interest law firms and groups to litigate sufficient numbers of SE rights cases that are very labor and resource intensive. In addition, the very small number of advocates who ordinarily act in such matters raises similar concerns.

merits of any case are not necessarily predictive of success. As is the case with the previous section, which discussed litigation decisions that influence outcomes, a close analysis of the particular circumstances and facts of each matter would be required to determine which of the factors may be most important in securing a successful outcome.

Awareness of rights

Simply put, knowledgeable clients – who are aware of their rights and legal processes – assist in securing favorable outcomes. The reality of SE rights litigation in South Africa – with limited exceptions – is unfortunately the opposite. For example, the Eastern Cape social grants cases are characterized by a limited understanding of rights,[200] tempered, however, by some understanding that court processes might assist claimants in receiving their grants. Of further – perhaps greater – concern is the limited understanding and appreciation in civil society of how SE rights litigation may be used to advance social justice.

The lack of rights awareness raises the question of who bears the responsibility to ensure widespread understanding of rights and how they may be used to improve people's lives. Some point directly toward the SAHRC. Given its express constitutional mandate to "promote respect for human rights and a culture of human rights" and "promote the protection, development and attainment of human rights,"[201] it appears to be the central body tasked with educating people about their rights.[202] But it has not done this with any real measure of success.[203]

Mobilization and the role and nature of civil society

Lawyers working in the field of SE rights are unanimous on the relationship between social mobilization and the successful use of the Constitution. *TAC* shows that people can be mobilized well on an issue that affects them personally and their communities directly. But it also raises more questions than it provides answers. How, for example, can the TAC's example be replicated in different settings?[204] Asked differently, why do we not see an expansion of education rights in the same way that we have seen in relation to health rights?

A common response is that it is easier to mobilize on AIDS. Although there may be some merit to the argument that the nature and impact of the HIV/AIDS epidemic makes social mobilization easier, given that people may literally be fighting for their lives, it does not explain why the TAC has – to some extent – been able

---

[200] By definition, those who are eligible for social assistance must – as a result of their age (being too young or too old) or disability – be unable to work. For information on education levels and unemployment rates in South Africa, see Bhorat 2004.

[201] Section 184(1) of the Constitution.

[202] See Section 184(2)(d) of the Constitution, which expressly empowers the SAHRC "to educate" in the performance of its functions. The Constitution, thus, recognizes the need for public education – conducted by the SAHRC – as an integral part of developing a rights culture and ensuring that rights are claimed.

[203] See Newman 2003; McClain 2002; Groenewald and Bangerezako 2006.

[204] For example, what is the relevance of the TAC's example for rural and other communities where large civil society structures may not exist and seem unlikely to exist in the foreseeable future?

to mobilize across class lines on an issue that still remains heavily stigmatized and disproportionately affects poor people. Perhaps it is not the issue per se but rather the impact of the issue on society – well understood and explained by the TAC – that matters.[205]

Public opinion, public relations, and the role of the media

The importance of public opinion was well understood in *Mikro*. Much time was spent by the litigants trying to win the media over, with a key spokesperson deliberately making himself available for more than just answering questions. This approach seems to have borne fruit – an initially hostile mainstream media warmed to the school's position over time. This was crucial given the perception that the school's conduct was racially motivated – a big and powerful white school refusing to admit small and weak black children.

Publicly, cases and/or demands are often framed in the broader public interest so as to attract sympathy and understanding. Thus, an opinion piece on *Westville* argues as follows:

> The Westville prisoners' judgment will help us to put more pressure on the minister of health to do her job and is likely to lead to the restoration of health and dignity for many of their fellow human beings.[206]

A concern that often rises relates to unholy alliances and the frequent jumping on of bandwagons. Take *Mikro*, once again, as an example. Despite its limited funding for the case (appeals on radio and in the press for support yielded little), the school rejected offers by certain organizations whose right-wing ideological agendas it does not share. It was also quick to reject overt party-political support, although it did accept behind-the-scenes advice.

The Role of the State in SE Rights Litigation

Whereas there is often a direct correlation between poor conduct on the part of the state in defending its actions against SE rights claims and a poor legal outcome for the state,[207] it is unclear whether there is any causal link between the two.[208] *TAC*, however, provides strong evidence that there is indeed such a link. In that case, the state – for dogmatic reasons effected through direct political interference with departmental employees – made no concessions and thereby prevented any sound legal strategy from developing. Had it been willing to concede to certain of

---

[205] However, the TAC's experiences in organizing and mobilizing show that urgent crises lend themselves more easily to urgent action. Ongoing headaches lead to fatigue.

[206] Geffen, Berger, and Golembeski 2006.

[207] Not only is this bad for the state, but it is also potentially bad for the broader public interest and the development of SE rights jurisprudence. But more important, it may have a chilling effect on others claiming their rights. Those without deep pockets cannot withstand long, drawn-out legal proceedings, even if the prospects of ultimate success are great.

[208] Consider *Ngxuza* as an example. The second applicant was saddened by the state treating her and her daughter as fraudsters. It is unclear if she would still have taken action had her claim to social security been dealt with in a different manner.

the TAC's demands early on, it may well have avoided the devastating judgment ultimately delivered by the Constitutional Court.[209]

But even where there is no direct causative effect, the way in which the state defends itself against – or in the case of matters such as *Mikro*, purports to advance – SE rights claims, is cause for concern in a democratic society where government is constitutionally required to conduct itself openly and accountably. Its response ordinarily seems unrelated to the merits of any particular case. This raises key questions that find no easy answers.

Why are cases litigated?

Contrary to what the state may believe, many in civil society regret the time and energy that must be spent in litigating matters that should be easily resolved. Compared to the various settlements reached in health rights cases dealing with the private sector, there is a dearth of settlements in litigation between civil society and the state.[210] In two key cases concerning the private sector – *PMA* and *Hazel Tau* – not a single argument on the merits was ever advanced in court. In both cases (although significantly less so in *PMA*), the private sector players recognized the political imperative to settle when faced with an ongoing public relations disaster but nevertheless armed with somewhat arguable legal cases. For its part, the state has actively defended cases with significantly lower prospects of success.

Consider *Mikro* as an example. There is a widespread perception that *Mikro* was pursued – with vigor – to please political masters, unchecked by sound legal advice. The school apparently made conscious attempts to resolve the case without going to court but had no option but to act when all other options had been exhausted. In this regard, the provincial department of education appears not to have considered the negotiations seriously. Instead, its conduct has been described by one of the key actors – whose identity shall remain protected – as bombastic, demanding, and unconsultative.

Other attempts to settle matters with the state on reasonable bases have been similarly rebuffed. *Ngxuza* and *Westville* come to mind. It is interesting to note that the same senior counsel represented the state in both cases. Whether such a correlation indicates a causal effect is discussed in further detail in the following section dealing with the role of the state's lawyers. What is beyond dispute is a consistent pattern of rejecting reasonable offers of settlement.[211]

The particular circumstances of *van Biljon*, however, seem to suggest that the state's decision to defend in that case may indeed be justifiable. In that case, the alternative outcome sought was early release. In addition, at the time the case was

---

[209] When it did effectively concede – by announcing its decision on April 17, 2002, to implement the universal rollout of an MTCT prevention program – it was rewarded by not having to suffer the indignity of a supervisory order. However, it was still unwilling to concede that it had ever been wrong, going on to defend the matter with great vigor and misguided zeal.

[210] Interventions by South Africa's new deputy president in late 2006 brought significant potential for change, and the possibility of settlement, in certain cases. In this regard, see Mlambo-Ngcuka 2006.

[211] Some SE rights litigators, when acting on behalf of the state, have been able to convince their clients to settle weak cases.

brought, ARV treatment was not available in the public health sector at all – nor would it become available for another seven years. The state was rightly concerned to provide prisoners with medical treatment that was significantly better than that being provided to non-incarcerated South Africans.

Similarly, there are other difficult legal matters with respect to which the state should be able to – and in fact does – seek guidance from the courts. A few justifiable decisions, however, are not enough to break what appears to be a particularly bad pattern of wasting limited resources to defend cases that are unlikely to yield positive results for the state.[212] The question that arises, however, is whether there is a conscious decision to litigate in such circumstances. Simply put, the ability to identify which cases to pursue or settle presupposes capacity on the part of the state to deal appropriately with rights claims.[213] In this regard, it is disturbing to note the widespread perception that key government decision makers lack the requisite legal capacity.[214] Of concern is that the state also appears to lack the flexibility to settle cases, suggesting that perhaps what is needed is an ombudsperson to decide whether the state should settle, mediate, or litigate.

What is the role of the state's lawyers?

There is a concern among some litigators that advocates acting on behalf of the state are often not conducting themselves as officers of the court. In his judgment in the second interim execution application in *Westville*, Justice Nicholson drew attention to the state's failure to learn from its previous unsuccessful attempt in *TAC* to appeal an interim execution order.[215] Perhaps not surprising, the same senior counsel represented the state in both *TAC* and *Westville*. He should have known better.[216]

The role of the state's lawyers remains unclear. There is a perception among some litigators that government abdicates too many decisions to its lawyers. Others appear to have been deliberately prevented from doing their jobs properly. In *van*

---

[212] A notable exception is *Interim Procurement*, which was effectively settled a month before the third democratic national and provincial elections in 2004. This allowed for the public-sector provision of ARV treatment to begin in the immediate run-up to the elections. Many opposition parties cried foul. For civil society, this was an important lesson in how litigation, mobilization, and political processes can be exploited to great benefit. But it also raises the concern regarding the state's motivation behind defending other claims.

[213] This, in turn, is based on the assumption that the state is able to understand when it acts unconstitutionally. This is not necessarily the case. *New Clicks* seems to suggest that, at least insofar as the DoH is concerned, it has very limited capacity to oversee regulation and other law-making processes.

[214] When it does settle (ordinarily late), it usually does so on terms significantly worse than would have been the case has it settled earlier.

[215] See the text referenced by Note 159.

[216] Concerns regarding his conduct are considerably widespread. Some litigators do not believe that his approach, which is based on the courts and judges "knowing their place" necessarily reflects that of senior officials and cabinet ministers who are perceived to have a better and more nuanced understanding of the appropriate role and function of the judiciary in a constitutional democracy. In particular, he appears to have played a particularly divisive role in attempts to reach a settlement in *Westville*. Despite an express instruction from the deputy president to settle the matter, with the text of a substantive agreement between the parties having been reached, the case remains unresolved.

Biljon, for example, repeated requests for budgets in order to make a credible resource constraint argument came to nothing. Instead, the state's legal counsel was given limited information and access only to low-level officials.

Two further concerns arise. The first is the allegation that the office of the state attorney lacks independence from government departments – it being argued that it is rare for the state attorney to advise the state that there is no legal defense, even in clearly indefensible cases. The second is the increasing reliance (in certain weaker provinces) on private law firms to defend the state. Such firms have no interest in settling cases – ticking clocks generate fees.

Does the state learn from SE rights cases?

Whereas certain high-ranking individuals in government are at times perceived to be deliberately obstructing progress, several litigators note that litigation may be welcomed by particular government officials as it allows them to do what may be politically unpopular. This implies both reluctance and willingness within the same state to learn from SE rights cases. Unfortunately, individuals do seem to matter greatly.

If the state's approach in *Westville* is anything to go by, it appears to have learned little.[217] Many of the same blunders committed in *TAC* appear to have been repeated – the resistance to implementing interim execution orders standing out as a classic example.[218] Although much of the AIDS denialist language that characterized *TAC* appears to have gone, with the safety and efficacy of ARV medicines no longer taking center stage, the state's penchant for refusing to concede any point and to fight regardless of the merits remains as strong as ever.

With respect to the Eastern Cape social assistance cases, matters appear to have gotten worse. Applications were initially unopposed, with court orders rarely enforced. An instruction to oppose all applications has now resulted in significant delays and the clogging of court dockets, resulting in a directive being issued by the Judge President of the Eastern Cape High Court that only eight social grant applications are to be set down each week. This is clearly insufficient,[219] leading one lawyer to recommend setting up a special court to hear such applications.

CONCLUSION

It took more than four years for government to formulate and adopt – and even longer to implement – a plan to address the particular gap in the state's housing program identified in *Grootboom*.[220] Prior to that, it had only publicly admitted

---

[217] To its credit, the state is more than just one or two of its departments. Some departments are reputed to deal with litigation very seriously and professionally. This is well documented in many of the non-SE rights cases.

[218] Not all of the state's response in *TAC* was a blunder. See, e.g., Note 209.

[219] The SCA in *Kate* explains why: "An affidavit deposed to by the attorney for the Black Sash . . . records that in a period of six weeks during the latter part of 2005 there were almost 2000 such cases on the roll of the High Court. On one occasion Plasket J noted that there were 102 cases relating to social assistance on his motion court roll for that week" (at Paragraph 5).

[220] However, as is suggested in Note 168, the adopted crisis relief program remains inadequate.

sometime in 2001 – and only following the widely publicized and highly politicized occupation of land at Bredell in Gauteng[221] – that such a gap had to be remedied. But for Irene Grootboom and her community, it has been an even longer wait. She may have had much more than her fifteen minutes of fame, but she still does not have access to housing as promised by the Constitution. This simply begs the question: Why is she not back in court?

From Irene Grootboom's perspective, *Grootboom* is a failure, the type of which Davis – the author of the High Court decision in the matter – cautions against:

> A failure by successful litigants to benefit from constitutional litigation of this kind can only contribute to the long term illegitimacy of the very constitutional enterprise with which South Africa engaged in 1994. A right asserted successfully by litigants who then wait in vain for any tangible benefit to flow from the costly process of litigation, is rapidly transformed into an illusory right and hardly represents the kind of conclusion designed to construct a practice of constitutional rights so essential to the long-term success of the constitutional project.[222]

If we look at the largely successful health cases – two-thirds of which have involved the TAC – and compare them to the relatively weak education cases, we understand why Irene Grootboom's rights have yet to be realized. It appears necessary – alongside civil and political rights – to grant constitutional recognition to SE rights and to make them justiciable. The same can be said for progressive jurisprudence that develops the right, either assisting or compelling the state to act.

But without ensuring that litigation is informed and supported by civil society mobilization, organization, and advocacy, the state cannot – and will not – be held to account. Although litigation remains an indispensable tool, without which the inertia of a flawed political process may never be broken, it becomes most effective when its use is limited and targeted. Simply put, broad social change will not be won in the courts alone. This is well known and recognized by groups such as the TAC, which have relied on the existence of an express right to health in South Africa's Constitution to save hundreds of thousands of lives.

But the existence of a right to education – arguably a stronger right in as much as the Constitution does not expressly refer to its progressive realization – appears to have done little. Although the state apportions the largest portion of its social spending budget to education,[223] it has yet to be compelled to prioritize its resources in a manner that fundamentally addresses the country's key educational challenges. Instead, we see the right being invoked in attempts to exclude (black) children from (white) schools, or simply to retain privilege. A right to education may indeed be more difficult to invoke than a right to health. But unless and until we see an education rights movement somewhat akin to what we see in health,[224]

---

[221] See James 2002.

[222] See Davis 2006: 314.

[223] For an analysis of state spending on education, see Wildeman 2006.

[224] An interesting development was the establishment in mid-2007 of the nonprofit organization Equal Education. Zackie Achmat, until recently the TAC's chairperson, was one of Equal Education's founding members.

we will never know just how powerful Section 29 of the Constitution – a seemingly unqualified right – may in fact be.

REFERENCES

Abel, R. 1995. *Politics by other means: Law in the struggle against apartheid.* Routledge: New York.

AIDS Law Project. n.d. *Consensus statement on improving access to legal services for people living with HIV/AIDS.* Available at http://www.alp.org.za/modules.php?op=modload& name=News&file=article&sid=280.

AIDS Law Project. n.d. *Submission to the Ad Hoc committee on the review of state institutions supporting constitutional democracy* (in particular Annexure 1). Available at http://www.alp.org.za/modules.php?op=modload&name=News&file=article&sid=340& DC100SID=fa0b1f56a4e20c2c2a14132e1d5440d4.

AIDS Law Project. 2006, December 8. "TAC agreements with GlaxoSmithKline and Boehringer Ingelheim remain in force," press release. Available at http://www.alp.org.za/ modules.php?op=modload&name=News&file=article&sid=331

Avafia, T., J. Berger, and T. Hartzenberg. 2006. The ability of select sub-Saharan African countries to utilise TRIPs flexibilities and competition law to ensure a sustainable supply of essential medicines: A study of producing and importing countries. Tralac Working Paper No. 12, University of Stellenbosch Printers, Stellenbosch, South Africa. Available at http://www.tralac.org/pdf/20061002_Avafia_TRIPsandCompetitionLaw.pdf.

Beresford, B. 2003. *The price of life – Hazel Tau and Others v. GlaxoSmithKline and Boehringer Ingelheim: A report on the excessive pricing complaint to South Africa's Competition Commission.* Available at http://www.alp.org.za/modules.php?op=modload&name= News&file=article&sid=222.

Berger, J. 2005. Advancing public health by other means: Using competition policy. In P. Roffe, G. Tansey, D. Vivas- Eugui et al (eds.), *Negotiating health: Intellectual property and access to medicines.* London: Earthscan: 181–204.

Bhorat, H. 2004. The development challenge in post-apartheid South African education. In L. Chisholm (ed.), *Changing class: Education and social change in post-apartheid South Africa.* Pretoria: Human Sciences Research Council Press: 31–55.

Bilchitz, D. 2002. Giving socio-economic rights teeth: The minimum core and its importance. *South African Law Journal* 119: 484–501.

Bilchitz, D. 2003. Towards a reasonable approach to the minimum core: Laying the foundations for future socio-economic rights jurisprudence. *South African Journal on Human Rights,* 19: 1–26.

Bilchitz, D. 2006. The right to health care services and the minimum core: Disentangling the principled and pragmatic strands. *ESR Review* 7(2): 2–6.

Brand, D. 2002. *Afrox Healthcare v. Strydom:* Supreme Court of Appeals, Case No. 172/2001, 31 May 2002(unreported at date of writing). *ESR Review* 3(2): 17–18.

Brand, D. 2005. Introduction to socio-economic rights in the South African Constitution. In D. Brand and C. Heyns (eds.), *Socio-economic rights in South Africa.* Pretoria: Pretoria University Law Press: 1–56.

Cameron, E., and J. Berger. 2005. Patents and public health: Principle, politics and paradox. *Proceedings of the British Academy* 131: 331–369. Also published in D. Vaver (ed.). 2005. *Intellectual property rights.* London: Routledge.

Competition Commission. 2003. October. Media Release No. 29 of 2003: *Competition Commission finds pharmaceutical firms in contravention of the Competition Act.* Available at http://www.compcom.co.za/resources/Media%20Releases/MediaReleases%202003/Jul/ Med%20Rel%2030%200f%2016%20Oct%202003.asp.

Davis, D. M. 2006. Adjudicating the socio-economic rights in the South African constitution: Towards "deference lite"? *South African Journal on Human Rights* 22: 301–327.

Davis, D. M. 1992. The case against the inclusion of socio-economic rights demands in a bill of rights except as directive principles. *South African Journal on Human Rights* 8: 475–490.

Department of Health. 2003, November 19. *Operational plan on comprehensive care and treatment for HIV and AIDS*. Available at: http://www.info.gov.za/issues/hiv/careplan. htm.

Department of Health. 2006, March 9. *Announcement of a draft dispensing fee and release of a revised HR plan*. Available at http://www.doh.gov.za/docs/pr/2006/pr0309.html.

De Villiers, N. 2002. Social grants and the promotion of administrative justice act. *South African Journal on Human Right*, 18: 320–349.

Dyzenhaus, D. 1995. *Judging the judges, judging ourselves: Truth, reconciliation and the apartheid legal order*. Oxford: Hart.

Fredman, S. 2005. Providing equality: Substantive equality and the positive duty to provide. *South African Journal on Human Rights*, 21: 163–190.

Geffen, N., J. Berger, and C. Golembeski. 2006. ARV ruling for prison spotlights access to health for all. *Cape Argus*, June 29. Available at http://www.capeargus.co.za/index.php? fSectionid=498&fArticleId=3316390.

Government of the Republic of South Africa. 2003, August 8. *Statement on special cabinet meeting: Enhanced programme against HIV and AIDS*. Available at http://www. info.gov.za/speeches/2003/03081109461001.htm

Groenewald, Y., and H. Bangerezako. 2006. A fresh look at our watchdogs. *Mail & Guardian*, November 21. Available at http://www.mg.co.za/articlePage.aspx?articleid=290663& area=/insight/insight_national.

Gumede, W. M. 2005. *Thabo Mbeki and the battle for the soul of the ANC*. Cape Town, South Africa: Zebra Press.

Hassim, A. 2006. The "5 star" prison hotel? The right of access to ARV treatment for HIV positive prisoners in South Africa. *International Journal of Prisoner Health*, 2: 157–171.

Hassim, A., and J. Berger. 2006. Case review: Prisoners' right of access to anti-retroviral treatment. *ESR Review*, 7(4): 18–21.

Hassim, A., M. Heywood, and J. Berger (eds.). 2007. *Health & democracy: A guide to human rights, health law and policy in post-apartheid South Africa*. Cape Town, South Africa: SiberInk.

Haysom, N. 1992. Constitutionalism, majoritarian democracy and socio-economic rights. *South African Journal on Human Rights*, 8: 451–463.

Heywood, M. 2001. Debunking conglomo-talk: A case study of the amicus curiae as an instrument for advocacy, investigation and mobilisation. *Law, Democracy and Development*, 5: 133–162.

Heywood, M. 2003a. Contempt or compliance? The TAC case after the Constitutional Court judgment. *ESR Review*, 4(1): 7–10.

Heywood, M. 2003b. Preventing mother-to-child HIV transmission in South Africa: Background, strategies and outcomes of the Treatment Action Campaign case against the Minister of Health. *South African Journal on Human Rights*, 19: 278–315.

James, D. 2002. Tenure reformed: Policy and practice in the case of South Africa's landless people (seminar, Wits Interdisciplinary Research Seminar, October 28). Available at http://wiserweb.wits.ac.za/events%20-%20wirs.htm.

Jones, P., and K. Stokke (eds.). 2005. *Democratising development: The politics of socio-economic rights in South Africa*. Leiden, The Netherlands: Martinus Nijhoff.

Langa, P. 2006. Keynote Address. Presented at the HIV and Access to Legal Services Conference, February 17–18. Available at http://www.alp.org.za/modules.php?op=modload&name=News&file=article&sid=280.

Liebenberg, S. 1995. The international covenant on economic, social and cultural rights and its implications for South Africa. *South African Journal on Human Rights*, 11: 359–378.

Liebenberg, S. 2004. Basic rights claims: How responsive is "reasonableness review"? *ESR Review* 5(5): 7–11.

Mahomed, A. 2003. *Grootboom* and its impact on evictions: *Neville Rudolph and Others v. City of Cape Town*. *ESR Review* 4(3): 2–4.

McClain, C. 2002. The SA Human Rights Commission and socio-economic rights. *ESR Review* 3(1): 8–9.

Mlambo-Ngcuka, P. 2006. Stop HIV and AIDS – Keep the promise. Address delivered by the Deputy President at the World AIDS Day event, KaNyamazane, Nelspruit, Mpumalanga, December 1, 2006. Available at http://www.info.gov.za/speeches/2006/06120112451001.htm

Motala, Z. 1995. Socio-economic rights, federalism and the courts: Comparative lessons for South Africa. *South African Law Journal* 112: 61–87.

Muntingh, L., and C. Mbazira. 2006. Prisoners' right of access to anti-retroviral treatment. *ESR Review* 7(2): 14–16.

Mureinik, E. 1992. Beyond a charter of luxuries: Economic rights in the constitution. *South African Journal on Human Rights* 8: 464–474.

Newman, D. G., 2003. Institutional monitoring of social and economic rights: A South African case study and a new research agenda. *South African Journal on Human Rights*, 19: 189–216.

Ngwena, C., and R. Cook. 2005. Rights concerning health. In D. Brand and C. Heyns (eds.), *Socio-economic rights in South Africa*. Pretoria, South Africa: Pretoria University Law Press: 107–152.

Pieterse, M. 2006. Resuscitating socio-economic rights: Constitutional entitlements to health care services. *South African Journal on Human Rights*, 22: 473–502.

Pillay, K. 2002. "Implementing *Grootboom*: Supervision Needed" *ESR Review*, 3(1): 13–14.

Plasket, C. 2003. Administrative justice and social assistance. *South African Law Journal*, 120: 494–524.

Roach, K., and G. Budlender. 2005. Mandatory relief and supervisory jurisdiction: When is it appropriate, just and equitable? *South African Law Journal* 122: 325–351.

Scott, C., and P. Macklem. 1992. Constitutional ropes of sand or justiciable guarantees: Social rights in a new South African constitution. *University of Pennsylvania Law Review* 141: 1–148.

Sloth-Nielsen, J. 2004. Case review 1: Extending access to social assistance to permanent residents. *ESR Review* 5(3): 9–11.

Swart, M. 2005. Left out in the cold? Crafting constitutional remedies for the poorest of the poor. *South African Journal on Human Rights* 21: 215–240.

Treatment Action Campaign. 2004. MinMEC agrees to interim procurement of antiretroviral medicines: Court action averted at last moment. Available at http://www.tac.org.za/newsletter/2004/ns25_03_2004.htm.

Veriava, F., and F. Coomans. 2005. The right to education. In D. Brand and C. Heyns (eds.), *Socio-economic rights in South Africa*. Pretoria, South Africa: Pretoria University Law Press: 57–84.

Wildeman, R. A. 2006, June 28. A review of national and provincial education budgets 2006, IDASA Occasional Paper. Available at http://www.idasa.org.za/index.asp?page= output_details.asp%3FRID%3D997%26OTID%3D16%26PID%3D40.

3 Accountability for Social and Economic Rights in Brazil

FLORIAN F. HOFFMANN AND
FERNANDO R. N. M. BENTES

The Brazilian AIDS movement has succeeded in extracting the judiciary's transformative potential, giving momentum to widespread structural reforms on the
basis of the strategic use of domestic legislation within a wider human rights
perspective.

Miriam Ventura[1]

It is not within the competence of the judicial branch [. . .] to act as a legislator
of positive law, whereby it would impose its own criteria upon matters which can
only be legitimately defined by the legislature . . .

Justice Celso de Mello[2]

This chapter examines the origins and impact of litigation for health and education
rights in Brazil. The first section examines the demand- and supply-side factors
that are related to the decision to legalize demands. The second section analyzes
the reasons for judicial support, or denial, of these claims. A third section studies
the bureaucratic and political response to court-ordered remedies for violations of
constitutional rights to health care and education. Finally, a conclusion summarizes
the discussion and presents four models of litigation for health and education rights
in Brazil.

[1] See Relatório Consultoria Projeto 914BRA59 (PNDST/AIDS) 2003. *Proposta de um plano de trabalho
para as assesorias jurídicas das ONG/AIDS*, March (revised version), p. 12; also cited in Mário Scheffer,
Andrea Lazzarini Salazar, and Karina Bozola Grou, 2005. *O remédio via justiça: Um estudo sobre o
acesso a novos medicamentos e exames em HIV/AIDS no Brasil por meio de ações judiciais*. Brasília:
Ministério da Saúde.
[2] *In re* 322348 AgR/SC.

The research team included, during different periods, Guilherme Peres de Oliveira, Gustavo Proença,
Mariana Fittipaldi, Pedro Henrique Batista Barbosa, Priscila Madalozzo Pivato, Renata Monteiro,
and Teresa Robichez; in addition, Teresa Robichez and Renata Monteiro worked on the qualitative
follow-up study, and Teresa Robichez and Ivanilda Figueredo provided overviews of the secondary
literature and newspaper reports; Helen C. C. Ferreira helped with the consolidation of the quantitative
data, and Ediomar Fernandes Estock with footnotes. Finally, Márcia N. Bernardes provided valuable
input and logistical assistance in the early phase of the project. And, of course, the editors of the present
volume, Varun Gauri and Daniel Brinks, were at all times present in the back – and occasionally in the
foreground. This study would, evidently, not have been possible without these collaborators, and we
are profoundly grateful to them for having joined us in this effort; no responsibility for any defects in
this study falls, however, on them.

The overall conclusion from the information presented is that Brazil has experienced exponential growth in the rate of litigation over health rights, with a much more modest increase in education rights litigation. Most of the demands are individual demands, for specific health-care-related goods and services and are concentrated in the more developed states, such as Rio de Janeiro and Rio Grande do Sul. The courts have been very open to these individual claims and much less willing to accept collective claims. As a result, the prosecutor's office, which is the primary user of collective causes of action in Brazil, has come increasingly to rely on negotiation under the threat of litigation to shape and motivate policy development in rights-protected areas in Brazil. We conclude that litigation is having a strong impact, with mixed consequences for democracy and distributive justice in Brazil, and that a backlash on the part of policy makers and bureaucrats may be on the midterm horizon.

The chapter is based on a quantitative and qualitative survey of health and education rights litigation in five Brazilian states, namely, Bahia (BA), Goiás (GO), Pernambuco (PE), Rio de Janeiro (RJ), and Rio Grande do Sul (RS), and the two superior tribunals, namely, the Federal Supreme Court (*Supremo Tribunal Federal*– STF) and Superior Court of Justice (*Superior Tribunal de Justiça* – STJ). On the state level, only the state appellate courts (*Tribunais de Justiças* – TJs) were examined, as case records at lower level courts are not electronically searchable. Inferior federal courts were not included in the survey, as they only account for a small number of the relevant jurisprudence, though some federal cases came up in the literature and press review, especially in relation to access to HIV/AIDS drugs cases, over which federal courts exercise partial jurisdiction.[3]

THE MOMENT OF LEGALIZATION: SUPPLY- AND DEMAND-SIDE FACTORS OF SOCIAL RIGHTS LITIGATION

The Supply Side: Legal System and Social Rights Infrastructure

The Brazilian legal system is a hybrid of the (North) American and the continental European (Roman-Germanic civil) legal systems. Whereas Brazilian constitutional law and, to some extent, its judicial institutions show considerable American influence, private law, as well as the general judicial mentalité are firmly grounded in the civil law tradition.[4] The main reference point is the 1988 Federal Constitution (*Constituição Federal*), which is the seventh constitution since Brazil became an independent country in 1822. It marks the transition to democracy after twenty-one years of military rule. The transition was gradual, running from the institution of the first civilian president in 1984 to the first free and direct presidential election in 1989, with the apex being the promulgation of the new Constitution in 1988.[5] Drafted by a Federal Congress that doubled as Constituent Assembly – an arrangement imposed by the remnants of the outgoing regime and, hence, typical

---

[3] Insofar as the HIV/AIDS program is federally co-administered.
[4] Eduardo C. B. Bittar, 2003. *História do direito brasileiro*. São Paulo: Editora Atlas.
[5] José Afonso da Silva, 2007. *Comentário contextual à Constituição*. São Paulo: Malheiros.

for the top-down nature of the transition – it took two years, from 1985 to 1987, to be elaborated.[6] It is a lengthy and heterodox document, strongly reflective of different corporate interests, and more of a grand compromise than a master plan for a newly democratic Brazil. Yet, it is the most democratic basic law Brazil has ever had, and it has given rise to a vibrant constitutional culture that has been playing an important part in subsequent social and political developments.

The system of government established by the Constitution is presidentialist, though with parliamentarist undertones, notably in the form of the executive's need to rely on more or less stable multiparty coalitions in Congress. The judiciary is entirely independent and fiercely safeguards its supervisory competences over governmental conduct. Being a federation, Brazil is comprised of three administrative levels, notably, the Union (*União*), the States (*Estados*), and Municipalities (*Municípios*). Although in some issue areas, such as education, each federal entity's competences are clearly set out in the Constitution, in others, such as health care, the so-called principle of federal solidarity prevails,[7] giving the three entities concurrent and competing competences and obligations. The courts, as guardians of the Constitution, exercise supervisory jurisdiction over these competences, but they have traditionally refrained from meddling with the administrative division of labor that has emerged among the three levels.[8]

Judicial review is mixed, combining the American-inspired diffuse-concrete form with the continental European centralized-abstract one. The former allows all ordinary tribunals to pronounce on the constitutionality of legislation in concrete cases and is applicable only *inter partes* (between the parties) whereas the latter is reserved to specialized constitutional tribunals adjudging the constitutionality of laws in the abstract, and has an *erga omnes* (toward all) effect.[9] Within this mixed scheme of constitutional judicial review, the STF is both the equivalent of the U.S. Supreme Court, that is, the highest court of appeal in constitutional matters, and a specialized constitutional court for abstract review of legislation, actionable by a clearly delimited range of public actors, such as the president, the House and Senate, and a number of other entities.[10] Diffuse-concrete control of constitutionality remains the more common form of judicial review, especially as STF decisions within this ambit are not binding beyond the decision in question. Hence, in theory at least, there are no precedent-setting cases, and each judge is free to interpret the law afresh even for very similar factual situations. Indeed, the absence of formal binding precedent (stare decisis) means that case loads are very

---

[6] Luiz Roberto Barroso, 1999. "Dez anos da Constituição de 1988." In Ingo Sarlet (ed.), *O direito público em tempos de crise: Estudos em homenagem a Ruy Ruben Ruschel* (pp. 190–196). Porto Alegre: Livraria do Advogado.

[7] José Afonso da Silva, 2007. *Curso de direito constitucional positivo*, 28th ed. São Paulo: Malheiros.

[8] Gilberto Bercovici, 2003. *Desigualdades regionais, estado e constituição*. São Paulo: Max Limonad, pp. 156–7.

[9] José Adércio Leite Sampaio, 2002. *A constituição reinventada pela jurisdição constitucional*. Belo Horizonte: Del Rey, pp. 41–43.

[10] See Art. 103, which specifies the direct action of unconstitutionality (*ação direta de inconstitucionalidade*) and the direct action of constitutionality (*ação direta de constitucionalidade*).

high.[11] Moreover, with the exception of a few lead cases,[12] jurisprudence will not be cited. These formal rules, are, however, tempered in practice. As we observe in the cases we examine, the spectrum of arguments used by plaintiffs, defendants, and judges will, over time, consolidate into a fairly fixed list of standard arguments for similar factual situations, and the limited and widely recognized set of reasons on which claims or decisions can be based, as well as informed intuition about the decision habits of the courts, will, de facto, create a considerable degree of legal certainty.

Below the STF are the four federal superior courts, with the *Superior Tribunal de Justiça* (STJ) being the most important.[13] The STJ is the final court of appeals for all infra-constitutional matters, whether on the federal or the state level. Then there are the ordinary courts on the federal and state level: the Federal Courts of Justice (*Justiça Federal* – JF) of the first instance, and the Regional Federal Tribunals (*Tribunais Regionais Federais* – TRFs) of the second instance, the jurisdiction of which comprises federal legislation. On the state level, there are the *Tribunais de Justiça* (TJs), which are divided into single judge first-instance chambers and second-instance appellate chambers comprised of three to five senior judges (*desembragadores*). Although the Brazilian legal system contains specialized courts for labor, military, and electoral matters, there are, unlike in most European civil law systems, no separate administrative tribunals, with most disputes concerning public administration being dealt with in the ordinary tribunals. That said, the TJs, as well as the JF, are organizationally divided into thematically specialized benches; most health rights actions are, thus, dealt with by the TJ's public administration bench (*Fazenda Pública*), whereas most education cases fall within the ambit of the children and adolescents division (*Criança e Juventude*).

In addition to the tribunals, there are a number of other relevant judicial actors, namely, the (State and Federal) Prosecutor's Office (*Ministério Público*), the Public Defender's Office (*Defensoria Pública*), and the (Municipal, State, or Federal) Solicitor's Office (*Procuradoria do Município* [PM]/*Procuradoria do Estado* [PE]/*Advocacia Geral da União* [AGU]). The *Ministério Público* (MP) is an independent judicial body present at both the state and the federal level and charged, in the text of Article 127 of the Constitution, with the general "guardianship of the legal order, the democratic system of government, and inviolable social or

---

[11] The STF alone decided more than 110,000 cases in 2006 only; see http://www.stf.gov.br/portal/cms/verTexto.asp?servico=estatistica&pagina=movimentoProcessual. In 2004, however, a constitutional amendment created the *súmula vinculante* by which the STF, by a two-thirds majority of its judges, can declare the bindingness of a certain precedent – a competence it has, so far, only used sparingly and the ultimate effect of which is not yet discernible; see Alfredo Canellas, 2006. *Constituição interpretada pelo STF*. Rio de Janeiro: Freitas Bastos. Available at http://www.stf.gov.br/institucional/regimento/p2t1c4.asp (accessed on December 8, 2007).

[12] See Gilmar Ferreira Mendes, "O efeito vinculante das decisões do Supremo Tribunal Federal nos processos de controle abstrato de normas." *Jus Navigandi*, 43. Available at http://www1.jus.com.br/doutrina/texto.asp?id=108 (accessed on December 17, 2007); and Carlos Aurélio Mota de Souza, 1996. *Segurança jurídica e jurisprudência: Um enfoque filosófico jurídico*. São Paulo: LTr.

[13] The others are the Superior Electoral Court (*Tribunal Superior Eleitoral*), the Superior Military Court (*Tribunal Superior Militar*), and the Superior Labor Court (*Tribunal Superior de Trabalho*).

individual interests." It has a wide range of competences, enumerated in Article 129, that include the supervision of compliance by public authorities on all levels with the rights guaranteed in the Constitution and the initiation of a particular type of (abstract-collective) suit, the so-called public class action, or, literally, "civil public action" (*ação civil pública*) on virtually all issues of public interest.[14] Similarly, the MP enjoys a number of administrative control competences, the two most relevant of which are the administrative inquest (*inquérito administrativo*) and the adjustment of conduct injunction (*termo de compromisso de ajustamento de conduta*).[15] Moreover, it has wide-ranging investigatory powers, and, most important, may act entirely on its own initiative, though it may receive and consider complaints from the general public. The *Defensoria Pública*, in turn, is, like the MP, a public body of civil servant lawyers. These lawyers work as defense counsel in criminal matters, but, it is important to note, also as general counsel in certain civil actions for indigent defendants or plaintiffs. For the purposes of the Defensoria Pública, indigence is determined via a means test, the nature of which varies across states – in some it is strictly tied to specific income limits, in others it is assessed relative to the value of the claim brought.[16] Last, the PM/PE and the AGU are roughly equivalent to government solicitors in the United States, and argue their respective public authority's case before the courts.

With regard to legal process, the overwhelming majority of health and education rights cases are comprised of just two types of civil action: individual and public. Individual actions (*ações individuais*) are brought by individual plaintiffs represented by private attorneys or the Defensoria Pública against public authorities claiming the provision of a specific good or service *inter partes*. Public class actions, in turn, belong, as was seen, mainly to the tool kit of the MP. They concern the "structural" noncompliance by public authorities with their legal obligations, such as the constitutional minimum spending threshold for health and education. Public class actions apply *erga omnes* (toward all) and have, thus, a much more far reaching impact than individual ones. They are, however, not to be confused with class actions under U.S. law, which involve an aggregate of individual plaintiffs; the equivalent action in Brazilian legal process, the so-called collective action (*ação coletiva*) is virtually absent from the kinds of cases examined in this study.[17]

When sued in health or education matters, public authorities often avail themselves of a vouching in procedure (*denúncia da lide*) to bring any other potentially responsible entities – usually on a different federal level – into the trial as co-defendants. In addition, most public authorities are legally obliged to appeal adverse first-instance decisions at least once. Remedies usually consist of the provision of the good or service claimed, though the latter may, occasionally, be

---

[14] The MP is not formally the only judicial organ competent to propose *ações civis públicas*, but it is the most prolific user. See Art. 5 of *Lei 7347/85*.

[15] See Eduardo Appio, 2006. *Controle judicial das políticas públicas no Brasil.* Curitiba: Editora Juruá; Hely Lopes Meirelles, 1998. *Direito administrativo brasileiro.* São Paulo: Malheiros Editores; and Marcos Maselli Gouvêa, 2003. *O controle judicial das omissões administrativas.* Rio de Janeiro: Editora Forense.

[16] See *infra* n. 46.

[17] See Sandra Lengruber da Silva, 2004. *Elementos das ações coletivas.* São Paulo: Editora Método.

converted into a monetary value to be paid out to the claimant where this is considered more effective or viable.[18] On some occasions, courts have also accorded compensatory damages, such as when the impugned authority is found to have withheld medicines previously provided to the claimant on a regular basis.[19]

Finally, to understand the dynamic of social rights litigation in Brazil, general legal culture needs to be taken into account: the Brazilian legal profession is, on the whole, still deeply imbued in the formalist tradition it absorbed from the continental European systems.[20] As such it is marked by legal positivism and professional corporatism.[21] It perceives itself as a closely knit elite community with strict entry criteria (notably the bar exam, as well as the difficult entrance exams to all first-level public legal offices) and fiercely guards its independence.[22] Political and social attitudes range from conservative and paternalistic among the older and more senior legal actors to progressive and human rights–oriented among the younger ones. Because law, as in most late-modern societies, has become the predominant mode of public interaction, the legal profession has been elevated to a central (perhaps the most central role in public matters) vanguard position of which it is keenly aware.[23] Perceptions by the general public of the law and the legal profession, in turn, are, as would be expected, stratified: knowledge of legal remedies and awareness of constitutional rights are highly dependent on social class, and most important on the level of education, even if the work of a well-organized civil society is beginning to diminish the class gap in legal and rights consciousness.[24] However, there remains a widespread lack of confidence in the integrity of the legal profession and the efficacy of fundamental rights, which is only slowly dispelled as younger and more progressive individuals are joining the profession.[25]

[18] See interview with Mauro Luís Silva de Souza, Promotor de Justiça and Coordenador do Centro de Apoio dos Direitos Humanos of the Ministério Público of Rio Grande do Sul, June 9, 2005.

[19] See, e.g., Civil Action No. 2001.001.09980 (TJ Rio de Janeiro).

[20] See, inter alia, Antonio Caros Wolkmer, 2000. História do direito no basil, 2nd ed. Rio de Janeiro: Forense; Giselle Cardoso Andrade, 2006. Formação do Bacharel em direito no século XIX. Available at http://www.direitonet.com.br/artigos/x/29/67/2967/ (accessed on February 24, 2007); see also the separate (concurring) opinion by Judge Antonio Cançado-Trindade in the first-ever case against Brazil before the Inter-American Court of Human Rights, Ximenes-Lopes v. Brazil, available at http://www.corteidh.or.cr/docs/casos/articulos/Seriec_149_esp.pdf (accessed on December 4, 2007).

[21] See, in particular, Eliane Botelho Junqueira, 1999. Faculdades de direito ou fábricas de ilusões? Rio de Janeiro: Letra Capital/IDES; and Eliane Botelho Junqueira, Josè Ribas Vieira, and M. G. P. Fonseca, Juízes: Retrato em preto e branco. Rio de Janeiro: Editora Letra Capital.

[22] Américo Bedê Freire Jr., 2005. O controle judicial de políticas públicas. São Paulo: Revista dos Tribunais, pp. 51–53.

[23] Luiz Werneck Viana et al., 1999. A judicialiazação da política e das relações sociais no Brasil. Rio de Janeiro: Revan, pp. 21–23.

[24] See Eliane Botelho Junqueira, 2003. Brazil: The road of conflict bound for total justice. In Lawrence M. Friedman and Rogelio Pérez-Perdomo (eds.), Legal culture in the age of globalization: Latin America and Latin Europe (pp. 64–107). Palo Alto, CA: Stanford University Press.

[25] See Centro de Pesquisa de Opinão Pública (DATAUnB), Consultoria para Construrçao do Sistema Integrado de Informações do Poder Judiciário, "14. Relatório: A imagem do judiciário junto à população brasileira." Available at http://pyxis.cnj.gov.br/pages/downloads.jsp (accessed on December 4, 2007).

As far as legal doctrine is concerned, the overall consensus on (constitutional) social rights is that they are non-derogable and inviolable, that is, that nothing relieves public authorities of their duty to provide for the object of the rights in question. This strong statement requires some qualification, however, and two distinct strands are observable in Brazilian rights jurisprudence. One strand, the traditional one dominant among the older judiciary, is more cautious. These judges make a strong distinction between directly justiciable rights and so-called program-matic rights. The latter are considered too abstract to be directly justiciable[26] and are taken merely to set general policy objectives. In this view, rights are understood to give rise to negative claims regarding nonfulfillment but not to positive ones regarding the particular way in which the policy in question should be shaped. This jurisprudentially conservative view has increasingly given way among a new generation of judges and commentators to the idea that even programmatic norms impose a duty on the government to take affirmative public policy steps toward their implementation. This is perhaps the product of an increasing sense of social responsibility among judges, exemplified in the statute of the São Paulo–based Association of Judges for Democracy, which speaks of the judiciary's role in "the defense of the rights of children, the poor, and minorities, from the perspective of the general emancipation of the disadvantaged."[27] Moreover, some courts have made use of a remedy akin to a preliminary injunction, the *mandado de segurança*, to allow individuals to claim for the positive fulfillment of a right even in the absence of governmental policy or regulation.

In general, however, the courts are most willing to grant claims that look most like traditional forms of action: individual claims for specific violations of clear rights, which prompt individual remedies. Indeed, the STF has ruled that the judi-ciary is not competent to decide on the shape of public policy,[28] and in many of the decisions we see explicit references to the separation of powers. In collective cases and higher courts in particular, we find the claim that the courts will not presume to craft public policy, and in almost all cases only such norms as have a clearly defined object will be considered directly justiciable.[29] Although some have argued that the lack of a serious effort on the part of the government to pro-duce such implementing legislation might itself amount to actionable negligence, most programmatic norms are considered to require implementing legislation.[30] Judicial enforcement of social and economic rights is further tempered by the Brazilian equivalent of what in international social rights discourse is known as

---

[26] Jorge Miranda, 1990. *Manual de direito constitucional*, 4th ed. Coimbra: Coimbra Editora, p. 218.

[27] See Estatuto da Associação Juízes para a Democracia, Arts. 2 & 4; Lúcia Barros Freitas de Alvarenga, 1998. *Direitos humanos, dignidade e erradicação da pobreza: Uma dimensão hermenêutica para a realização constitucional*. Brasília: Brasília Jurídica, p. 194f.

[28] Arno Arnoldo Keller, 2001. *O descumprimento dos direitos sociais: Razões políticas, econômicas e jurídicas*. São Paulo: LTr, p. 108.

[29] Luís Roberto Barroso, 2003. *Interpretação e aplicação da constituição: Fundamentos de uma dogmática constitucional transformadora*. São Paulo: Saraiva; and Mauro Cappelletti, 1999. *Juízes legisladores?* Porto Alegre: Fabris: p. 96.

[30] Barroso (2003), *passim*.

the *progressive realization precept*:[31] the courts apply a viability reservation (*reserva do possível*), which holds that the applicability of fundamental rights must be seen in the context of existing economic and political realities.[32] This reservation has little purchase at the trial court level on the thousands of individual claims to medication, but plays a stronger restraining role at the appellate and apex court level and in collective cases. The judicial context is, therefore, cautiously propitious to claims grounded in economic and social rights, especially those that seek individual remedies. We will return to the specifics of judicial pronouncements and litigant argumentation later.

The constitutional and legislative framework is, if anything, even more positive. Both of the rights studied here, the right to health and education, are first identified as "social rights" in Article 6 of the Constitution. In relation to health, both the fundamental right to health, as well as the organization of health care are elaborated in Articles 196 and 200. The main constitutional instrument of the health-care regime is the Unified Health System (*Sistema Único de Saúde – SUS*), the cornerstones of which are the universalization of health care, the pluralization of health-care financing, and the decentralization of health-care provision based on the already mentioned principle of federal solidarity. Municipalities are responsible for primary care delivery in the country, with higher levels of health-care facilities primarily under the management of states, though the federal government and the more well-endowed municipalities do manage a number of hospitals and other centers. The pooled federal, state, and municipal financing is used to reimburse public and privately contracted providers through more than seventy different payment modalities. This staggering number testifies to the extreme complexity of the SUS's internal governance regime that is taken to be one of the main causes for its suboptimal performance.[33] Hence, as is shown in the present study, the system is frequently unable to react to unforeseen deficits in the health infrastructure, so that affected patients are driven either to seek private substitutes for the service in question or to turn to the courts in order to force the system to accommodate a particular demand. This confusion about who is responsible for delivering goods and dissatisfaction with actual service delivery and with the range of options offered are what drive the overwhelming majority of cases filed.

The constitutional provision that health care is a "right of all and a duty of the state" has been interpreted to mean that SUS services must be provided free of charge to the entire population. Constitutional Amendment 29, passed in 2000, sets the minimum percentages of budget resources the federal, state, and municipal

---

[31] This concept plays, of course, a central, if much discussed, role in the International Covenant on Economic, Social, and Cultural Rights; see Philip Alston and James Heenan, 2007. *Economic, social and cultural rights: A bibliography.* Leiden, The Netherlands: Martinus Nijhoff.

[32] *Id.,* p. 107. See decision by Judge-Rapporteur Celso Mello in Recurso Especial No. 271286 of September 12, 2000.

[33] See, *inter alia,* Governance in Brazil's unified health care system. World Bank Report No. 36601-BR, February 15, 2007. Available at http://www-wds.worldbank.org/external/default/WDSContentServer/WDSP/IB/2007/03/06/000090341_20070306085417/Rendered/PDF/36601OBR.pdf (accessed on December 10, 2007).

governments are required to spend on health. Nevertheless, some 25 percent of the Brazilian population purchases private health insurance or receives it as a benefit from their employers. Most use this insurance to obtain care from private providers not affiliated with SUS. Still, many private insurance plans do not cover a variety of expensive medications and procedures or do not cover certain patients, with the result that even wealthy patients seek care in the public sector for certain conditions. These exceptions to coverage by private insurers are the second most important subject of litigation based on the right to health care.

Like health care, the general cornerstones of education policy are also constitutionally mandated, including a determination that 25 percent of state and municipal budgets, and 18 percent of the federal budget, must be earmarked for education. Of the states' and municipalities' 25 percent, 15 percent is specifically to be allocated to primary education. Historically, primary and, to some extent, secondary education have been marred by comparatively low enrollment rates and poor student performance, with the system generally having tended to disproportionately favor tertiary education.[34] States and municipalities are primarily responsible for the management of primary and secondary education, which is the focus of the present analysis. Nevertheless, federal involvement increased in the 1990s, primarily in efforts to mitigate disparities in municipal and state resources for education.[35]

The main such reform was implemented in 1996, when the Fund for the Maintenance and Development of Primary Education (*Fundo de Manutenção e Desenvolvimento do Ensino Fundamental* [FUNDEF]) was created. The objective was to bring primary education closer to the particular needs of different communities and to, thereby, increase school attendance and decrease dropout rates. The Federal Education Ministry retains, however, a crucial role in the definition of overall standards. In general, civil society had little involvement in negotiations regarding the FUNDEF, which was primarily conceived of by the bureaucracy of the (Federal) Ministry of Education, in conjunction with state and municipal governments. As of 2007 the FUNDEF was being replaced by the Fund for the Maintenance and Development of Basic Education and for the Valorization of Education Professionals (*Fundo de Manutenção e Desenvolvimento da Educação Básica e de Valorização dos Profissionais da Educação* [FUNDEB]). The latter is meant to build on the experience – and critiques – of FUNDEF, first by broadening its range to include, in addition to primary education, child care and secondary education; second, by adjusting state and municipal tax revenue and the allocation formula; and, third, by significantly increasing federal top-up spending, from

---

[34] Louis de Mello and Mompert Hoppe, 2005. Education attainment in Brazil: The experience with the FUNDEF. Economics Department Working Paper No. 424, OECD ECO/WKP(2005)11, of April 4, 2005. The authors of this report point out that tertiary education consists of no more than one-fifth of total education spending, but that per capita spending on each student as a percentage of GDP in tertiary education is more than three times the average of countries in the Organisation for Economic Co-operation and Development (OECD).

[35] Ação Educativa, 2006. "Quadro comparativo das mudanças na Constituição federal promovidas pela Emenda n° 53/2006/." Available at http://nsae.acaoeducativa.org.br/portal/index.php?option=com_ultimas&task=category&id=1&Itemid=216 (accessed on December 4, 2007).

FUNDEF's around 400 million reals to nearly five billion reals over a fourteen-year period.

Both health and education administrative regimes are complemented by Federal, State, and Municipal Health and Education Councils (*Conselhos de Saúde/ Conselhos de Educação*) in which government administrators, professionals, patients, and parents are represented. These have formal supervisory functions within the SUS and the FUNDEF/FUNDEB, with the state and municipal councils, in particular, monitoring local policy implementation.[36]

In summary, health policy is administered by a complex, intricate network of entities, spanning all three levels of government. The policy structure and coverage is comprehensive and complex, though it frequently suffers from mismanagement and inefficiency. Patients sometimes have a difficult time securing what the policy promises and navigating the various layers of bureaucracy. Educational policy, in contrast, although similarly comprehensive, is not as complex. Responsibility across levels of government is more clear cut, and the location and source of services, although not necessarily of optimum quality, is at least clearly identifiable. In both cases, there has been some provision for local community involvement, through Health and Education Councils, in monitoring local policy implementation. Litigation, as we will see next, tends to concentrate on the more complex policy areas.

The Demand Side: Socioeconomic Makeup and Litigiousness

Even if the supply side of social and economic rights in large part structures the demand for litigation, there are, nonetheless, factors exogenous to this (legal) supply that need to be considered in order to understand the impact of such litigation in Brazil. The most relevant of these is clearly the overall socioeconomic makeup of the examined states and, as a derivative of that, the levels of litigiousness present in them. These data appear especially important to explain the considerable regional differences in litigation patterns, although we cannot control for the more difficult to measure supply side factors, such as the institutional infrastructure or the local legal culture. In general, the five states have been chosen as more or less representative of the different regional development patterns in Brazil, so that some general inferences as to the factors that positively or negatively contribute to both litigiousness and to the impact of litigation may be (cautiously) drawn.

In relation to basic social indicators, the pattern that emerges reveals Rio de Janeiro and Rio Grande do Sul at the top end and clearly above the Brazilian average, Goiás somewhat in between, and Pernambuco and Bahia on the lower end and below average.

As far as litigation rates are concerned, a recent study by the University of Brasília[37] shows that the rates of first-instance state court cases per one hundred

---

[36] See Lei 9424/96.

[37] See *Relatório Final* and *Annexes* of the World Bank–funded study by DataUnB on the establishment of an integrated judicial information system; available at http://www.stf.gov.br/seminario/ (accessed on March 24, 2008).

Table 3.1. *Basic social indicators, 2000*

	Brazil	Pernambuco	Bahia	Rio de Janeiro	Rio Grande do Sul	Goiás
Population* (absolute and percentage of national)	169,799,170	7,918,344 (2.2%)	13,070,250 (7.7%)	14,391,282 (8.5%)	10,187,798 (6.0%)	5,003,228 (2.9%)
GDP/per capita (R$)*	5.740	3.279	3.206	7.946	7.389	3.603
Income Inequality (ratio of income of top 20% over bottom 20%)*	26.2	24.4	20.7	18.2	21.0	18.5
Poverty Rate* (population with household below half of minimum salary [about US$ 84])*	25.6%	40.9%	45.5%	11.8%	16.6%	22.9%
Illiteracy Rate* (for population above age 15)	13.6%	24.5%	23.2%	6.6%	6.7%	11.9%
Infant mortality rate**	31.8	58.2	45.4	21.3	15.1	25

* Source: Instituto Brasileiro de Geografia e Estatística.
** Source: Ministério de Saúde/Fundação Nacional de Saúde.

thousand inhabitants follow the same pattern as general socioeconomic makeup: Rio Grande do Sul leads by a high margin over Rio de Janeiro, which is followed by Goiás, and then by Pernambuco and Bahia. Indeed, Rio Grande do Sul's population resorts to the courts more than three times as often as that of Pernambuco or Bahia, and just under that multiplier in relation to Rio de Janeiro. Generally speaking, there seems to be a strong correlation between overall affluence, levels of education, and litigiousness. To be sure, many other factors impact education levels, and these, in turn, do not automatically translate into higher levels of litigation but would require complementary factors such as adequate access to justice. But given the relative institutional uniformity across Brazil and the fact that access to justice is generally positively correlated with wealth, regional variation is, as would be expected, clearly explainable by differentials in wealth and education. The wealthier and more educated populations generate more litigation. The mere existence of a legal framework, or, conversely, the inadequacy of basic services, is not enough to bring about a social rights–litigation revolution.

The Intersection of Supply and Demand: Access to Justice and the Role of Organized Civil Society

Formally, access to justice is, to a significant degree, dependent on the specific judicial regime in place in each state. Generally, where there is a Defensoria Pública attending to the indigent population, the MP is likely to focus on its original functions of attending to larger, public class action–type issues. Middle-class claimants, in turn, will, by and large, resort to private lawyers. Where no Defensoria Pública is in place, the MP or sometimes state-specific legal aid bodies, such as the *Procuradorias de Assistência Jurídica* (PAJs), tend to assume the former's functions as much as their jurisdiction permits. Whereas that jurisdiction is all-encompassing with regard to the MP, it is limited with regard to PAJs, which, for instance, are precluded from bringing actions against state governments or are not procedurally competent to request required information from respondent public authorities.[38] The result of these formal limitations is the informal transfer of jurisdiction to the MP, which, in effect, comes to assume the functions of the Defensoria Pública where the latter is absent or weak.

This is problematic from an access to justice perspective, because the MP is not formally actionable by individual plaintiffs but exclusively acts on its own initiative. This means that its decision to take up individual actions is discretionary and will vary across states, issues, and social class of the beneficiaries, as well as according to the specific narrow legal culture of its members. The general impression is that the *Ministério Público* tends to especially pick up headline-grabbing cases that are amply reflected in the media.[39] However, media attention is more frequently obtained by those claimants who voice their complaints loudly and eloquently, which, in turn, is more often the case with well-represented middle class claimants than with indigent ones. Hence, the MP's "aura of efficacy," and its self-assumed

[38] See Lei Complementar n° 51 do Estado de Goiás, April 19, 2005.
[39] José Reinaldo de Lima Lopes, 2006. *Direitos sociais – Teoria e prática*. São Paulo: Editora Método.

role as a (progressive) judicial vanguard have created a centripetal effect by which cases normally outside of its functional jurisdiction are drawn toward it. This drawing force may be the result of an expansive MP deliberately pulling in cases, as happens in Rio Grande do Sul, or other judicial or nonjudicial actors pushing cases toward it. In São Paulo, for example, the MP has complained that many nongovernmental organizations (NGOs) prefer to lobby the MP to take up certain causes than to provide legal assistance and litigation services themselves.[40] Thus, although, on the one hand, the MP may be crucial in putting previously underexposed issues onto the judicial and, potentially, also the political agenda, it may, on the other hand, inadvertently weaken judicial empowerment of individual claimants and the bottom-up mechanisms designed to attend to them.

Another factor that affects access to justice is the relative scarcity of public or private providers of such access. Pro bono services, university legal clinics, and clinically oriented NGOs are still comparatively underdeveloped.[41] Likewise, in Pernambuco, the TJPE itself has established a statewide network of Integrated Citizenship Centers (*Centros Integrados de Cidadania* – CIC) that offer a wide range of basic judicial and pre-judicial services, including dispute mediation and rights education.[42] The overall number of lawyers working within these contexts, however, is small and insufficient to fill the gap between costly private attorneys and either nonexistent or institutionally weakened or overburdened Defensorias Públicas.

Another way to think about access to justice is to ask whether those most in need of basic services enjoy preferential access to courts. This would be substantive, rather than formal, equality in access to courts, and would involve some form of means-testing in the provision of pro bono legal services. Here the picture in the sampled states is mixed. In Rio Grande do Sul and Goiás, a relatively stringent means test is applied by the Defensoria Pública and the PAJ, respectively, whereas in the other states the idea of relative indigence prevails, according to which indigence has to be judged by the Defensoria Pública – or, eventually, the courts – on a case-by-case basis and in relation to what percentage of income is or would be spent on the realization of the right in question.[43] There is, hence, neither a uniform policy

---

[40] See interview with Westey Conde y Martin Júnior, Promotor de Justiça, Coordenador do Centro de Apoio Operacional às Promotorias de Justiça de Defesa da Cidadania, of the *Ministério Público* of Pernambuco, August, 25, 2005.

[41] Unlike in the United States, pro bono work has not traditionally been promoted by the profession, with pro bono initiatives having, in fact, encountered initially fierce opposition from the Brazilian Bar Association; see, e.g., Raquel Souza, 2002. OAB cria polêmica sobre prestação de advocacia gratuita. In *Folha de São Paulo* (Tempo Real) of January 9, 2002. Also available at http://www1.folha.uol.com.br/folha/dimenstein/temporeal/gd090102.htm (accessed on December 4, 2007); see, however, the pioneering work of the Instituto ProBono in São Paulo, at http://www.institutoprobono.org.br/ (accessed on December 4, 2007).

[42] See interview with Westey Conde y Martin Júnior (n. 40).

[43] In Goiás, the Defensoria tends to reject middle class plaintiffs, except in cases of high-cost medicines not covered by private insrance; interview with Carla Queiroz, Procuradora do Estado, Coordenadora da Área Cível da Procuradoria de Assistência Judiciária do Estado de Goiás, June 6, 2005; in Rio Grande do Sul, in turn, an "objective" means test is applied in that only plaintiffs earning up to three minimum salaries may avail themselves of the Defensoria, although this criterion is adjusted by the number of dependents, augmenting the threshold by half a minimum salary for

on means-testing across states, nor is there a common attitude by judicial actors on class differentiation.

Whether this has a negative impact on access to justice by indigent plaintiffs is difficult to measure because there is no clear evidence for a crowding out of the latter by middle class claimants.[44] The latter do not generally turn to the Defensoria Pública or equivalents anyway, but rather will engage a private attorney. For as long as the budgetary impact of granting individual actions is, by and large, not taken into account by the judiciary, no overall litigation limit is in place, and no action, regardless of where it originates, is a priori refused. Rather, what constrains access to justice by the indigent population seems to be a general lack of rights consciousness and trust in the judiciary, combined with institutional deficiencies on the part of the Defensoria Pública or its respective substitutes, such as insufficient staff, lack of in loco presence, or the perception of inefficacy on part of potential plaintiffs.

In Salvador (BA), for instance, the Defensoria Pública is located in a middle-class borough not serviced by public transport.[45] In Pernambuco, in turn, the relatively scarce use of the Defensoria Pública by the indigent population was taken to be a reason for why the latter also attended to (lower) middle-class claimants.[46] Similarly, in Goiás, the PAJ has been used by lower-middle-class claimants to obtain court orders for the admission or retention of their children to private schools.[47] Another take on this has been offered by a Rio Grande do Sul prosecutor who argued that the judiciary, by tending to grant individual (private) actions but not MP-brought public class actions, discriminated against indigent plaintiffs, depriving them of the indirect access to justice they are accorded through MP action.[48]

In relation to organized civil society a distinction has to be drawn among general civil society, organized civil society (notably NGOs), and other nonstate actors, such as pharmaceutical companies. NGO activism on health issues originated in Brazil's highly influential and highly successful HIV/AIDS policy mobilization.[49] HIV/AIDS NGOs often became partners of public authorities in the implementation of basic health services, and even today, they receive significant financing

each dependent, as well as overall costs, including rent payments; interview with Adriana Burger, Coordenadora da Área Cível da Defensoria Pública do Rio Grande do Sul.

[44] See for this thesis, inter alia, interview with Antonio Gelis Filho, Fundação Getúlio Vargas (São Paulo), May 9, 2005; as well as ibid. 2004, O poder judiciário e as políticas públicas de saúde: Uma análise empírica de decisões do Supremo Tribunal Federal e do Superior Tribunal de Justiça in I EnAPG, Resumo dos Trabalhos – I EnAPG. Rio de Janeiro: ANPAD.

[45] Collective interview with Paulo Emílio Nadier Lisbôa, Procurador do Estado, Antônio Moisés, Assessor do Secretário Estadual de Saúde, and Roberto Lima Figuêredo, Procurador do Estado. September 1, 2005.

[46] Interview with Leônidas Siqueira Filho, Procurador do Estado, Chefe-Adjunto do Setor Contencioso, August 26, 2005.

[47] Collective interview with Carla Queiroz (Coordenadora da Área Cível da Procuradoria de Assistência Judiciária do Estado de Goiás), and with two (non-examined) PAJ procuradores, Antônio Carlos Ferreira Braga and Darcy Gomes, June 6, 2005.

[48] See supra n. 21.

[49] See Richard Parker, 2003. Construindo os alicerces para a resposta ao HIV/AIDS no Brasil: O desenvolvimento de políticas sobre o HIV/AIDS, 1982–1996. Divulgação em Saúde Para Debate, 27 (August), pp. 8–49.

from all three federal levels of government.[50] They have, thus, assumed the double roles of social service providers and interest groups, with legal action frequently representing a point of convergence between the two. Evidence suggests that NGO litigation strategies will focus on the federal level closest to the locality of the plaintiff as well as the one with which the best relations are enjoyed. There is a widespread conviction that individual actions are by far the most successful way to proceed, as public class actions, which could, in theory, be initiated by a registered civil society organization, receive much higher judicial scrutiny, are less likely to be successful, and may even risk a backlash from a judiciary otherwise sympathetic to individual actions.[51] Although most HIV/AIDS NGOs do not exclude middle class clients, many end up primarily representing indigent claimants, which gives them an additional important "access to justice" function. Often, NGOs have a semi-institutionalized relationship with the MP that includes information sharing and mutual "litigation encouragement."

The question that arises is, of course, why this NGO litigiousness is absent in virtually all other health and education areas. To be sure, there are now a number of civil society organizations linked to specific chronic diseases and conditions that attempt to emulate the example of HIV/AIDS NGOs, yet, by and large, all other access to medicines and treatment, as well as education rights cases, are brought either by private attorneys, by the Defensoria Pública, or by the MP, with NGOs playing an altogether minor role. One way to answer the question is to see the present period as one of transition from a legislation-oriented to a litigation-oriented strategy that will eventually lead to the widespread recognition in civil society that the courts may be the more effective way to implement social rights.[52] Another possible response lies in the combination of institutional setting and legal culture that could be taken to favor the MP, rather than NGOs, as the principal agent of society's interests. This "crowding out" thesis, already touched on earlier, is not without plausibility. Yet, if one combines the first with the second answer, the future may yet see the ascent of a large-scale, NGO-driven litigation wave that may, once again, change the legal–political landscape.

With regard to other nonstate actors, the most relevant are, of course, private corporations, that is, pharmaceutical companies. These are certainly implicated in the generation of health rights litigation, though their influence is, as would be expected, mostly indirect. It is direct only in those relatively rare cases where a lawyer with ties to the industry encourages potential patients to sue for a specific medicine.[53] Indirectly, however, pharmaceutical companies are able to push litigation for medicines in their portfolio via their ordinary relationship with physicians who prescribe their products or confirm such prescriptions as expert witnesses, as well as via induced media coverage.[54] Even NGOs are not always immune to

---

[50] See Scheffer et al., *supra* n. 1, p. 71ff.

[51] See interview with Karina Gueiros, GESTOS (Pernambuco), August 26, 2005; and collective interview with Juliana Paiva Costa, Carolina Rezendo, Juliane Messias, and Jucarlos Alves, all of *Gapa – Grupo de Apoio e Prevenção da Aids* (Bahia).

[52] See n.1.

[53] See Scheffer et al. (2005), n. 1.

[54] *Id.*

overtures from the pharmaceutical industry, and some openly admit that they are co-sponsored by private sector health companies.[55]

In short, then, state-funded legal services are problematic for many underprivileged communities, especially in Bahia, or in rural areas. NGOs have, by and large, not undertaken direct public class action litigation, except in the area of HIV/AIDS and on behalf of a few other rather narrowly drawn categories of medical patients. Much of the slack is taken up by the Ministério Público, which does not, however, have a clear mechanism for public input or accountability. Middle class groups, however, have ready access to legal professionals to pursue individual claims.

Survey Method and Challenges of Data Collection

The quantitative survey consisted of an internet search and the coding of thirty-five variables in a standard template. In all, more than ten thousand cases were examined. The qualitative survey consisted of *in loco* interviews with judicial and other relevant actors in each of the five states, as well as in São Paulo; a review of relevant literature and press cuttings; and an in-depth examination of a number of illustrative cases, with a view to gauge both the context and the enforcement dimension of the litigation in question. In terms of the types of action examined, only the two most common types were looked at in the qualitative study: notably, individual actions brought both by individual plaintiffs through private counsel or the Defensoria Pública on behalf of indigent plaintiffs and public class actions brought by the MP. Substantively, the main health rights litigated were access to medicines and treatment, and the main education rights were access to school places and school fee issues. There are two issue areas that were considered only tangentially, namely, civil actions against private health insurance companies and cases concerning affirmative action. The former has been appreciated to some extent in the both quantitative and qualitative study on account of the causal link that exists between health rights actions against public authorities emanating from privately insured, that is, middle class, plaintiffs and deficiencies in private health insurance coverage, which is ultimately regulated by the public sector. With regard to affirmative action, it is currently one of the most keenly debated issues in Brazilian public discourse, in particular because mandatory affirmative action policies have been introduced in several public educational facilities.[56] However, cases concerning affirmative action have not been considered in the survey, as they, arguably, primarily concern a classic civil, rather than a social, right and thus have to be seen in a different context.

---

[55] *Id.*, at 61ff.

[56] The issue has, however, generated so much controversy that legislation concerning federal institutions has been stalled in Congress; several state governments have implemented university quota systems for Afro-Brazilian and public school candidates, though several of these have been legally challenged. See, *inter alia*, A.S.A. Guimarães, 2000. *Tirando as máscaras: Ensaios sobre racismo no Brasil.* São Paulo: Paz e Terra; for a recent and controversial statement against certain types of affirmative action policies, see Peter Fry, Yvonne Maggie, Marcos Chor Maio, Simone Monteiro, and Ricardo Ventura Santod, 2007. *Divisões perigosas: Políticas raciais no Brasil contemporâneo.* São Paulo: Editora Civilização Brasileira.

However, the mentioned characteristics of the legal system – orientation toward legislation, not cases; absence of binding precedent; diffuse control of constitutionality – and the large caseloads it generates represent a considerable challenge to any quantitative appreciation of social rights litigation in Brazil. The main difficulty has been in data gathering: first, completeness of data varies across states because of decentralized data processing and different standards of archiving, so that not all the required information could be obtained in some of the states. Second, because of the very large number of cases in Rio Grande do Sul and Rio de Janeiro, and because only brief summaries of the opinions (*ementas*) and not full judgments (*acordões*) are searchable, a shortened template was applied to these two states, narrowing the range of data available. In addition, neither the Defensoria Pública nor the MP maintain case files open after the decision, unless specific enforcement (legal) action is taken. Individual defensores may, in many cases, be involved in de facto enforcement, but this largely remains beneath the radar and can only be gauged through anecdotal evidence from the actors involved. Similarly, data on the fate of formally successful (private) individual actions can only be obtained directly from the plaintiffs or their lawyers. In many instances, no contact information for plaintiffs is provided in case files, and where contact can be established, information is not always volunteered. Likewise, many private attorneys refuse to give out information on cases or plaintiffs.

The quantitative analysis covers the period of 1994 to 2004 and includes only state tribunals (TJs). At the federal level, the focus was limited to the apex courts – the STJ and the STF.

It should be emphasized that focusing on this level likely excludes the large majority of cases from the quantitative analysis because they occur and are resolved at lower-level courts of first instance. There are anecdotal reports, for instance, that a middle-sized municipality in the state of Rio of Janeiro can receive two or three dozen cases related to the right to medication in a single month. Summed over all municipalities in Rio, this rate of litigation would easily exceed the three thousand cases identified in this study for the entire state from the period 1994 to 2004.

Although these limitations somewhat diminish the study's comprehensiveness, they do not, arguably, distort the overall findings and the conclusions drawn from them. The reason is that, as was pointed out earlier, despite the large number of cases, the portfolio of legal argument is limited, judicial attitudes are well known, and case outcomes are relatively predictable.

Statistical Patterns, Legal Argument, and Illustrative Cases

The patterns that emerge across the five states and the two apex tribunals reveal two overall trends. The first is a striking asymmetry between a large number of health and a comparatively small number of education rights cases: our database includes more than 7,400 health cases and just less than 300 education cases. The second, conversely, suggests that the fewer education cases might have greater impact, as there is a predominance of individual actions in health rights and of public class actions in education rights cases. Only 2 percent of the health cases are collective cases, whereas 81 percent of the education cases make collective claims.

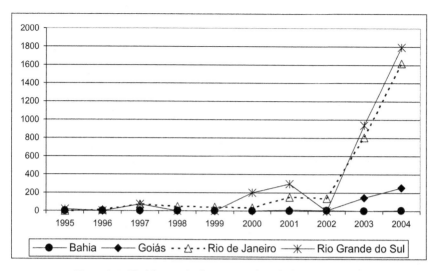

Figure 3.1. Health cases in four state tribunals, by year of filing.

With regard to health rights cases, Rio Grande do Sul is, as would be expected given that state's socioeconomic profile and its overall litigiousness, the champion of health-rights litigation, closely followed by Rio de Janeiro. The Rio Grande do Sul data is even more impressive when calculated per capita, which shows that, within the examined period, there has been an average of one legal health rights action for every 2,848 inhabitants, compared to Rio de Janeiro, where this figure is 5,298 inhabitants per each such action. The figures for Goiás, in turn, have to be qualified by the specificities of that state: as was already explained, the MP there essentially holds a monopoly on filing social rights cases in general and health rights cases in particular. According to interview data, the rise in health rights cases between 2003 and 2004 is coincidental with one particular *promotor* (prosecutor), Issac Benchimol, at the *Promotoria da Saúde do Centro de Apoio Operacional dos Direitos do Cidadão*, responsible for health rights litigation within the Goiás MP. Bahia, in turn, is, in many ways, the odd state out in the examined sample because, in contrast to all other states, it does not have any expressive litigation figures at all.

The predominant type of action is direct provision claims by individuals against the state. These cases account for 85 percent of all cases. Obligation claims, mostly by individuals against private health insurance companies, represent another 13 percent, leaving less than 1 percent for regulation cases. At the apex court level, the STF (the primary constitutional court) has decided very few cases in this area, although it has modestly increased its health rights jurisprudence since 1998. The STJ (the highest ordinary court of appeals), in turn, seems to better reflect the general trend of a steep rise in health rights cases since 1998 (see Figure 3.2).

In education, no clear trend is discernible apart from the lack of individual cases, and the prevalence of public class actions. Education rights litigation oscillates across time in Rio de Janeiro and Rio Grande do Sul, with clear and larger spikes

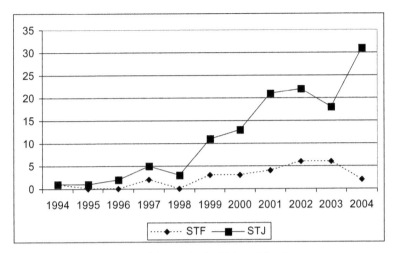

Figure 3.2. Health cases in the highest federal courts.

later in the period but without establishing a consistent trend (see Figure 3.3). In Bahia and Goiás during this period we find fourteen and ninety-two education cases, respectively, but the reports do not include date-of-filing information, so we cannot say what the trend has been.

As noted, there are a great deal more collective cases in the education arena than in health. Provision cases still dominate, comprising 64 percent of the total, but regulation and obligation cases comprise 26 and 11 percent, respectively, compared to 0.07 percent and 13 percent in the health area.

A claim frequently, if informally, articulated by both academics and practitioners is that the lower courts were more supportive of these claims than the apex courts. To test this claim, we tracked the fate of all the cases in our data set that were

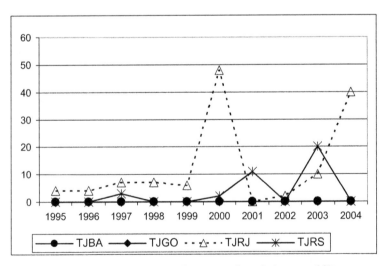

Figure 3.3. Education cases in four state tribunals, by year of filing.

Table 3.2. *Plaintiffs' success rates across three judicial levels*

	All trial court decisions	Decisions that initially favor plaintiffs		Decisions that initially favor defendants		Decisions that partially favor plaintiffs	
	84	54		25		5	
	100%	64%		30%		6%	
All appellate court decisions		For P	For D	For P	For D	For P	For D
for P: 51 (61%)	for D: 33 (39%)	41	13	8	17	2	3
		76%	24%	32%	68%	40%	60%
All apex court decisions — for plantiff TOTAL: 69 (82%)		36	12	4	12	2	3
		88%	92%	50%	71%	100%	100%
for defendant TOTAL: 15 (18%)		5	1	4	5	0	0
		12%	8%	50%	29%	0%	0%

Note: Each column tracks the progress of a set of cases from the trial courts to the apex courts, noting the percentage that favors plaintiffs or defendants at each stage.

considered by all three levels of the judicial system – from trial courts, through the intermediate appellate courts, to the highest courts. What we found, presented in Table 3.2, was surprising. Plaintiffs begin, as expected, with a success rate of about 70 percent, if we count partial successes. At the appellate level, the conventional wisdom holds, though without as much force as one might imagine: the courts of appeals reverse 24 percent of the cases that favored the plaintiffs, but they also reverse 32 percent of the cases that favored the defendants, and give the defendants three of the partial wins, so that the overall plaintiffs' success rate drops to just more than 60 percent (fifty-one out of eighty-four cases) at the intermediate appellate level. But the apex courts reverse this trend. Of the twenty-five cases that initially favored the defendants, sixteen are reversed in favor of the plaintiffs, and all the partial cases go back to the plaintiffs. Perhaps most telling is the fate of the cases in which the courts of appeal reversed a pro-plaintiff decision – in twelve of these thirteen cases the apex courts returned the case to the plaintiffs' ledger. The result is that, at the end of the day, the plaintiffs end up with an 82 percent success rate, higher than even their initial rate in the trial courts.

THE MOMENT OF DECISION: JUDICIAL SUPPORT FOR HEALTH AND EDUCATION RIGHTS CLAIMS

In terms of the specific legal arguments used by plaintiffs, respondents, and courts, the following picture emerges for individual health rights cases, which, as was seen, represent an overwhelming majority of the examined caseload: plaintiffs tend to rely alternatively on the right to health care, as guaranteed in Articles 6 and 196, or the right to life, as enshrined in Article 5 of the Constitution, in conjunction with a showing of their inability to pay for the requested good (e.g., medicines or school places) or service (e.g., medical treatment or school logistics). HIV/AIDS patients additionally rely on Law No. 9.313 of 1996 that sets out the free distribution of the HAART (Art. 1) and establishes the principle of federal solidarity as to cost sharing and provision of the medicines in question.

Public authorities, in turn, attempt to rebut plaintiffs' claims by pointing to the lack of budgeted funds, in conjunction with a reference to Article 315 of the Penal Code (*Código Penal*) that makes the "irregular use of public funds," including expenditures with no prior legal basis, an offense punishable with one to three months imprisonment and a fine; Article 167 of the Constitution, prohibiting the commencement of programs or projects not included in the annual budget law; and Article 37 of the Constitution, obliging public authorities to comply with good administrative practices, which would not be the case if, for example, lengthy public bidding procedures, such as for the purchase of specific medicines, were not observed.[57] On a more general level, public authority defendants often allege that a court order against them constitutes a violation of the separation of powers, as enshrined in Article 2 of the Constitution, as well as an infringement of the principle of equality, as set out in Article 5 of the Constitution, on account of the differrential treatment afforded to successful plaintiffs.

The courts, in turn, tend to decide health-rights cases on the basis of the right to life (Art. 5 CF88) or, less frequently, the right to health (Arts. 6 and 196 CF88), as well as the guarantee of personal dignity as set out in Article 1, Section III, of the Constitution. In addition, courts have founded their decisions, inter alia, on a range of complementary arguments, such as that fundamental rights and human dignity prevail over administrative or budgetary norms, that certain fundamental social rights are an essential part of the "humane democracy" (*democracia humanizada*) that the constitution establishes, that fundamental social rights are both justiciable in ordinary tribunals, and their realization by means of legal action does not infringe the separation of powers.

Legal argument in education rights actions has a less clearly delimited portfolio, though a few broad lines can be discerned: in particular, in the more numerous public class actions, the MP has tended to argue on the basis of the constitutional right to education as a plainly justiciable claim, coupled with the affirmation that it – the MP – has a legitimate and, in principle, enforceable interest in monitoring public authorities' fulfillment of their corresponding duty. This line of argument has to be seen in the context of the two main objections education-related public class actions have faced from both the impugned public authorities, as well as from the majority of courts: notably, that education rights are programmatic and that public authorities enjoy administrative discretion in their implementation.[58] Indeed, the frequent use of the programmatic norm argument to justify nonfulfillment of a particular education rights claim might be taken to imply that education

---

[57] Penal Code Art. 315 Decreto-Lei No. 2.848, December 7, 1940.
[58] See Romualdo P. de Oliveira, Theresa Adrião (eds.) 2001. *Gestão, financiamento e direito à educação: Análise da LDB e da constituição federal*. São Paulo: Xamã.

rights, in general, are considered by the courts as less directly justiciable than health rights. However, that conclusion has to be qualified by the difference in judicial attitude with regard to individual and public class actions. As was seen, the former dominate in health rights litigation, whereas the latter do so in education rights actions.

In addition to these two (counter) arguments, public authorities have also attempted to differentiate their obligations according to education level. They have contended that alleged failures to provide preschool (*creche*) places do not constitute a present injury to any unenrolled child, only an abstract obligation to provide in the future.[59] This defense has generally been accepted by the courts, even in cases where the latter have admitted that a *creche* place shortage is "public and notorious." One way the MP has devised to circumvent this procedural blockage is to collaborate with an area's Legal Guardianship Council (*Conselho Tutelar*), an independent supervisory body that often has access to precise figures of children waiting for creche or preschool places.[60] Although most judges have considered the MP's request to be generic and, hence, unsubstantiated, a minority has gone as far as conceding that social rights actions must, by their very nature, be generic. This group of judges has also tended to disallow the administrative discretion defense, holding that discretion did not apply to the provision, as such, of a service related to a fundamental right, but merely to the way it was provided. Similarly, courts following this line of argument have held that budgetary limitations could not be used as a defense for nonfulfillment of a fundamental right when it was demonstrable that the public authority's overall budget exceeded the amount required. In one decision, the court additionally contended that a lower degree of administrative discretion applied to rights related to children and adolescents.[61] In another, the court came close to positivizing the right to education by declaring that public authorities had to organize themselves in such way as to aid the educational progress of its citizens.[62] In yet another noteworthy decision on an individual claim, the court explicitly compared education – here concerning creche places – to health rights when it declared that "the normative substance of the present question is the same as in access to medicines actions – what is sought is the preservation and concretization of values dear to society, such as that of life, which implicates human dignity and, consequently, health and education."[63]

In general, the courts' reasoning in the examined cases can be divided into four distinct perspectives. The first sees health and education rights as essentially

[59] See Ação Educativa, Ação na justica, obstáculos e possibilidades de acesso, No. 10, June 16–29, 2005. Also available at http://www.acaoeducativa.org.br/base.php?t=nger_0275&y=base&x=lnger_0001&z=03 (accessed December 17, 2007).

[60] Created, in each state, by the Statute for Children and Adolescents (*Estatuto da Criança e Adolescente*), see Title V.

[61] See Ação Educativa, Ação na justica, obstáculos e possibilidades de acesso, No. 18, October 6–19, 2005 & No. 20, November 3–16, 2005. Also available at http://www.acaoeducativa.org.br/base. php?t=nger_0275&y=base&x=lnger_0001&z=03 (accessed December 17, 2007).

[62] See Ação Educativa, Ação na justica, obstáculos e possibilidades de acesso, No. 20, November 3–16, 2005. Also available at http://www.acaoeducativa.org.br/base.php?t=nger_0275&y=base&x=lnger_0001&z=03 (accessed December 17, 2007).

[63] See Ação Educativa, *supra*.

derivative of a set of individual civil rights. The second sees them as collective social rights that are largely programmatic in nature, though they may still be negatively actionable in case of nonfulfillment. The third sees them as concretized within regulatory frameworks such as the SUS or the FUNDEF that are based on principles of good administration such as budgetary propriety and public procurement. The fourth, in turn, sees them as public goods subject to scarce economic resources to be allocated by democratically legitimated decision makers and not by unelected judges. The first two perspectives can be broadly categorized as rights-granting, the latter as rights-restrictive, with the first pair prevailing in winning and the second pair in losing individual and public class actions.

With regard to the social rights case typology that structures the empirical studies in the present volume, the great majority of health cases in Brazil concern individual provision or financing claims, notably access to medicines and, less frequently, access to treatment. These concern, in the older social rights terminology, essentially fulfillment obligations.[64] On an abstract level, the nature of the fulfillment of social rights by governmental actors has been dealt with in "grand" decisions such as the notorious declaration of unconstitutionality of the provisional act adjusting the minimum wage, in which the STF declared that by providing for an amount that was objectively not sufficient for subsistence, the federal government had committed an act of omission by not attending to its obligations under Article 7 of the Constitution – setting out the purposes of the minimum wage.[65] On a more concrete level, the great majority of actions have concerned governmental failure to fulfill specific demands for medicines and treatment. The pioneer cases here were, of course, on access to HIV/AIDS drugs, with the first such action brought in 1996.[66] Since then, access to medicines cases have skyrocketed and have become a real concern for public authorities, not least as the claimed medicines now range from diapers to Viagra and include many high-cost items for rare diseases. A recent study by Ana Márcia Messeder, Claudia G. S. Osorio-de-Castro and Vera Lucia Luíza[67] that examined 389 (qualitatively weighed) individual actions against the state of Rio de Janeiro in the period from 1991 to 2001 showed that, up to 1998, HIV/AIDS-related drugs amounted to more than 90 percent of actions, a figure that had dropped to just less than 15 percent by 2000. The reason was the slow start that the universal free HAART-drug dispersion program had in Rio de Janeiro. From 2000 onward, the picture of claims for medicines diversifies but still clusters around a number of medicines classified as exceptional by the SUS and linked to

---

[64] George Marmelstein Lima, *Efetivação do direito fundamental à saúde pelo poder judiciário*, unpublished master's thesis submitted at the Department of Law at the Universidade de Brasília. Available at http://www.georgemlima.hpg.ig.com.br/saude.htm.

[65] Art. 7(1) stipulates that "[workers have the right to a] minimum wage nationwide, established by law, capable of satisfying their basic living needs and those of their families with housing, food, education, health, leisure, clothing, hygiene, transportation, and social security"; for an English version of the Brazilian Constitution, see the International Constitutional Law (ICL) site at http://www.oefre.unibe.ch/law/icl/br00000_.html (last visited on February 24, 2007).

[66] Scheffer et al. 2005, supra n. 1.

[67] Ana Márcia Messeder, Claudia Garcia Serpa Osorio-de-Castro, and Vera Lucia Luiza, 2005. "Mandados judiciais como ferramenta para garantia do acesso a medicamentos no setor público: A experiência do estado de Rio de Janeiro." *Cadernos de Saúde Pública*, 21(2), pp. 525–534.

chronic conditions such as Crohn's disease, chronic viral hepatitis C, severe kidney disease, hypertension, and heart disease.[68] The authors also point out that the medical foundations of at least 10 percent of the prescriptions underlying the examined actions were doubtful, a fact that, despite the (theoretical) availability of expert witnesses, is generally not considered by the courts.[69] Treatments claimed in the courts, in turn, have included hearing aids, ultrasound and encephalogram examinations, prostheses, publicly funded hospitalization in a private facility because of lack of room or lack of required equipment in the public system, psychological or psychiatric treatment of indigent adolescents, bone-marrow transplants, pacemakers, and transport to medical facilities, to name but a few.

Although many access-to-medicines cases involve relatively inexpensive drugs, there are some hard cases of rare diseases requiring very costly medication. In a recent preliminary injunction granted by the TJ-Bahia, the state was ordered to supply four doses of *Erbitux* (*Cetuximab*) per week to a cancer patient, with each dose of the imported medicine costing approximately US$1,500.[70] In another recent case, the TJ–Rio de Janeiro granted a public class action by the MP mandating the state to supply more than one hundred medicines for such diseases as Alzheimer's, gastric ulcer, inflammatory intestinal disease, diabetes, asthma, severe bronchitis, lung emphysema, or epilepsy. In this case, the MP had decided to act after more than 2,800 individual actions for medicines for any of these conditions had been brought between January and July of 2006 only.[71]

Yet, not all cases are granted, in part because some are genuinely hard cases that involve rare diseases and high-cost medicines. In one such case, four children with Gaucher disease claimed lifelong provision with the only currently available medicine, *cerezyne*, which, at the time, cost roughly one million U.S. dollars per annum for the four children.[72] The (state of) *Distrito Federal* alleged that it had only roughly one-third of that sum available, and that the legal requirement of budgetary propriety prohibited it from making unapproved ad hoc expenditures. It also argued that the medication in question was not, in fact, therapeutic, but merely mitigated the symptoms, and that this kind of expense on four individuals, even if children, would put at risk the provision of a host of other medicines and treatments. The claimants won in the first instance, but lost on appeal, with the presiding judge balancing the individual's irreducible right to life with the legal requirements of good administration. Similarly, in a case involving a new type of interferon for treatment of hepatitis C, at the time up to thirty times more costly than the regular interferon commonly used, the STJ reversed an earlier decision by the TJ–São Paulo mandating the state to provide the medicine, arguing that there was as yet no medical consensus on its efficacy.[73] It is interesting to note that the STJ, however, left the door open for patients with a different form of

[68] *Id.*, p. 528.
[69] *Id.*, p. 531.
[70] See Luiz Francisco, 2006. "Justiça obriga Bahia a fornecer remédio a paciente com câncer." *Folha de São Paulo* (May 11).
[71] See O Globo Online (August 18, 2006).
[72] As related in Marmelstein Lima, *supra* n. 64, p. 30.
[73] *Id.*, p. 32.

hepatitis C for which the new interferon was thought to be effective. Federal tribunals have decided in a similar way in treatment cases, for example, in relation to experimental treatment of retinitis pigmentosa in Cuba,[74] HIV/AIDS therapy in the United States, or even gender-reassignment surgery of a transsexual, the refusal of which was considered by the court not to amount to irreparable damage.[75] Yet, in São Paulo, an action on prosthetic penis surgery abroad was, nonetheless, granted.[76] Closely related to the access of medicines and treatment cases are those concerning allegations of the nonfullfillment of health rights in the maintenance of public hospitals. Here, the courts have generally held that although there is no positive right to a particular infrastructure, there is a negative one with regard to maintenance.[77]

The other two duty classes are much less frequent. Regulatory issues are occasionally taken up in individual or public class actions, such as a case brought by a middle class patient asking the authorities for changes in the regulation of fees charged by private health facilities cooperating with the public health system. This case eventually reached the STF, which emphasized the equality before the law clause and granted the claim.[78] Similarly, there are several cases in which health regulation was considered to be insufficiently protective of the right to health, such as when when tax regulation or social security legislation insufficiently differentiated categories of especially vulnerable persons, such as the handicapped, the elderly, or children.[79] There also exist a number of cases primarily involving private obligations; the large majority of these entail claims against private insurers.[80]

Education rights, in turn, by and large concern the provision by the responsible public authority of basic infrastructural elements, such as an adequate number of student places and teachers, school endowment, student transportation, or, indeed, special schemes for handicapped or otherwise disadvantaged students. Frequently, these issues are linked up with broader claims as to public authority compliance with minimum education spending requirements. The majority of these claims are, by their very nature, public class actions brought by the MP, and they frequently concern highly technical administrative disputes. As in health rights claims, the state or municipality would rarely dispute the existence or applicability of the right as such, but rather the particular obligations pertaining to its realization. Hence, in São Paulo, for instance, the MP has been actively monitoring education spending by the state and municipal governments, using preliminary injunctions to require

---

[74] Id., p. 124.
[75] Acão Civil Pública, 2001. 71.00.026279-9, São Paulo.
[76] Several interviewees described this case, which has acquired a legendary quality.
[77] Id., p. 27.
[78] RE 226.835, of December 14, 1999; see also, Flávia Piovesan, 2006. "Justiciabilidade dos direitos sociais e econômicos no Brasil: Desafios e perspectivas." *Araucaria – Revista Iberoamericana de Filosofia Política y Humanidades*, 15(April): 128–146.
[79] For a list of specific infra-constitutional regulation of these categories, see Marmelstein Lima, *supra* n. 64, p. 22.
[80] See Antonio Joaquim Fernandes Neto, 2002. *Plano de saúde e o direito do consumidor.* Belo Horizonte: Del Rey.

either authority to provide a detailed spending balance to enable supervision of its compliance with the minimum spending floor.[81] Similarly, it initiated proceedings as to the unconstitutionality of a municipal bylaw allowing for the incremental payment of the required sum. In other cases, the MP has directly requested state or municipal governments to contract more teachers to ensure adequate provision and quality of education.[82] In Rio de Janeiro, for example, it successfully challenged the state government to contract mathematics, geography, and history teachers for schools in the Duque de Caxias municipality, where teachers in these disciplines were entirely lacking. The success of this public class action was probably also due to the aggravating fact that a public entrance examination (*concurso público*) for teaching staff in these disciplines had been implemented, but no incumbents were subsequently nominated by the state government. Here, a daily fine of approximately $280 was imposed on the state, pending the nomination and contracting in of the required teachers.[83] One problem with this type of action has been that in order to minimize the fines incurred, public authorities will simply hire temporary teaching staff without setting up a public entrance examination. Besides causing potential concern about teaching quality, this form of remedying the lack of teaching staff is, of course, hardly sustainable in the long term. Another frequent object of MP action is student transport, both for general students and for those with special needs. There are a number of successful public class actions requiring state or municipal governments to provide free transportation to primary and secondary schools[84] or to set up specific transportation schemes for individual special needs students.[85] Similarly, it has been through public class actions that particular schools have been required to install special access facilities for students with handicaps.[86] It is interesting to note that in these special needs students' cases the MP has, de facto, acted on behalf of individual plaintiffs on the assumption that only a public class action will result in the required remedy. Claims concerning the provider–recipient relationship, such as tuition and matriculation fee disputes, or state–provider regulatory issues concerning entrance exams, teaching quality, or different forms of discrimination, are altogether much rarer and apply to a much greater degree to private educational establishments with a predominantly middle class clientele.

Especially with regard to health rights, the current situation has to be seen in light of the significant precedent set by the successful campaign for the

---

[81] See Ação Educativa, Ação na Justica, 2005. Obstáculos e possibilidades de acesso, 18(October): 6–19. Also available at http://www.acaoeducativa.org.br/base.php?t=nger_0275&y=base&x=lnger_0001&z=03 (acccessed December 17, 2007).

[82] *Id.*

[83] Processo 200300217751, TJRJ, Ação Civil Pública.

[84] Processo 70000676015, TJRS, Ação Civil Pública.

[85] See, *inter alia,* cases examined in Ela Wiecko Volkmer de Castilho, "Direito à Educação e o Ministério Público," (conference presentation at the I. Congresso Interamericano de Educação e Direitos Humanos, Brasília, 2006). Available at http://www.acaoeducativa.org.br/downloads/EST1.pdf (accessed December 17, 2007).

[86] *Id.*

universalization of the provision of HAART drugs in the 1990s. It is generally agreed that civil society, and especially NGOs working with HIV/AIDS patients and high-risk communities are primarily responsible for educating the general public and governmental actors to move from a view of the infection as a "gay cancer" when the first cases were reported in Brazil in the early 1980s toward an aggressive stance on combating the epidemic in the 1990s.

Because of the delimited subject matter, the existence of a well-functioning public policy as well as, and unusually, the high-profile involvement of NGOs, the case of HIV/AIDS almost functions like a controlled laboratory experience of health rights litigation in Brazil. Consequently, it has received a much higher degree of analytical scrutiny than any other area within social and economic rights, with the possible exception of issues related to affirmative action in education.[87] Two recent studies, in particular, provide some valuable insights on the HIV/AIDS litigation universe. In a 2005 Ministry of Health survey, *Remédio via Justiça*,[88] undertaken by Mário Scheffer, Andrea Lazzarini Salazar, and Karina Boyola Grou, the authors examined judicial argument in more than four hundred cases stemming from the STF, STJ, the five federal tribunals, and state courts in Rio Grande do Sul, Santa Catarina, São Paulo, Rio de Janeiro, Ceará, and the Distrito Federal. Their findings are complemented by a more or less contemporaneous study by Camila Duran Ferreira, published, so far, in two separate pieces, *O judiciário e as políticas de saúde no Brasil: O caso de AIDS* and *A atuação do judiciário na concretização dos direitos sociais*.[89] This survey is based on a quantitative and qualitative analysis of 144 HIV/AIDS-related cases of access to medicines and treatment in the TJ-São Paulo. The overall picture that emerges from these studies is one in which judges will, by an overwhelming majority, look at the right to health from a purely individual civil rights perspective, with economic or social impact considered secondary and subordinate. Likewise, insofar as the right to health is considered to be collective, rather than individual, economic and social impact arguments are used to justify nonconcession. Furthermore, in medicine-granting cases, procedural arguments by public authority defendants based on the negative impact of ad hoc judicial concessions on administrative due process were generally discarded as being of lesser importance than fundamental civil rights. Hence, the courts are broadly favorable to the concession of medicines to HIV/AIDS patients, but of financial impact or correlative (due process) rights. Without attempting, in the majority of cases, to appreciate the medical arguments provided by public authorities, judges tend to consider the prescribing physician to be the relevant authority to determine objective need. Indeed, the authors include a number of decisions in which judges interpreted Lei 9.313, the 1996 law that directed the Ministry

---

[87] As stated earlier, affirmative action was not examined in the present survey.

[88] Scheffer et al. (2005), *supra, n. 1.*

[89] Camila Duran Ferreira et al., 2004. "Atuação do judiciário da concretização dos direitos sociais: Um estudo empírico do reconhecimento do direito à saúde como direito fundamental", unpublished manuscript based on "O judiciário e as políticas de saúde no Brasil: A caso AIDS," Prêmio IPEA 40 anos, IPEA-Caixa.

of Health to provide HIV/AIDS patients free access to "all medication necessary for their treatment," as granting universal free access to any medication or treatment that a competent physician prescribes.[90] The *Consenso*, or list of approved medications and procedures, is here (re)interpreted as merely an administrative guideline aimed at facilitating the dispensing of the most common medicines.[91] As is the case with virtually all access-to-medicines decisions, no appreciation of the merit of the prescription is undertaken, as long as the prescribing physician is duly accredited. Similarly, with regard to the very frequent intragovernmental quarrel as to which level of government would be responsible for paying for the requested medicine, the authors find that the courts have generally abstained from analyzing relevant SUS or state- and municipal-level implementation legislation to determine objective responsibility. Instead, they generally emphasize the principle of federal solidarity in their reasoning, but nonetheless decide against the public authority impugned in each particular case, which tends to be states and municipalities.

The Role of the Different Judicial Actors in Social Rights Litigation

As for the courts, there are, as discussed earlier, essentially two competing views on administrative judicial review: a rights-granting and a rights-restrictive one. The former is prevalent in individual actions, the latter in collective actions. In neither case, however, will courts engage in substantive review of public policy, as can, inter alia, be derived from the relative difficulty the MP has in winning high-impact collective action suits. Within the rights-granting perspective, two basic attitudes can be discerned: one essentially aims to "civilize" constitutional social rights by substituting the right to health with the right to life, human dignity, and so forth; the other sees (individual) health rights litigation in the context of a more proactive judicial role in the implementation of (human) rights. In this latter case, however, the emphasis is on judicial activism and the judicialization of rights, rather than on a substantive theory of social rights. In individual actions, courts will usually not seek to establish individual culpability or negligence on the part of a public authority, but will tend to concede the right based on the authority's "objective responsibility," which is in line with the overall tendency toward formal and not substantive review. The rights-restrictive perspective, in turn, is, as was already seen, pervasive in public class actions. It is, hence, much rarer, and arguments are not as settled as in the rights-granting perspective. Its basic notion is simply that courts ought not to force the executive branch to do things it cannot responsibly do. Its underlying premise is, of course, the separation of powers and the implied assumption that neither branch of government should unduly encroach on the other. This line of argument still finds a wide echo among the judiciary who

---

[90] Scheffer et al., 2005, *supra* n. 1, p. 99ff. The text of Lei 9.313 is available at http://bvsms.saude. gov.br/bvs/aids/legis/leg_fed/lein9313.html.

[91] See, e.g., Acórdão 20000110749342APC, or Acórdão 2001.02.01.028752–8/Rio de Janeiro (Tribunal Regional da 2ª Região).

continue to be wary of being seen as political, or as encroaching on policy makers. A similar take on this "viability reservation" has been the argument, first articulated by the STF, that public authorities are merely required to do what is administratively possible, and that it is not the judiciary's task to engage in cost–benefit analysis, but merely to enforce the constitution.[92] Another factor that potentially influences judicial attitudes to social rights is the enormous heterogeneity of age and experience among the judiciary. Judges can be in their early twenties or nearing seventy, with experience levels ranging from none to premilitary rule. In a fast-changing social environment such as Brazil, these age differentials necessarily account for very different types of judicial logics among the relevant actors. Judges are also exposed to significant social pressure, as in Brazil's still largely personalistic culture, no real distinction is made between the judge as officeholder and as private person.[93]

As far as the MP is concerned, its role varies considerably across states. Whereas in Goiás the courts have accepted the MP's action on behalf of individual claimants by means of public class actions as a substitute for individual actions sponsored by the Defensoria Pública, their counterparts in Rio Grande do Sul have tended to strictly limit the MP's role. As a result, the Rio Grande do Sul MP has focused much more on its pre-judicial, investigative competences and has directly interacted with state and municipal administrations. It has, thereby, been both bypassing formal court proceedings and acting as a de facto co-administrator. An example is a recent family-planning scheme implemented in primary schools that the MP developed together with the Porto Alegre municipality.[94] This initiative came about as a result of the MP's concern over the high pregnancy rate and related medical problems of indigent minors, and it was brought about by purely administrative action. A similar "joint" MP–municipality project, the school flight (vôo escolar) program, was developed for children with handicaps in order to enable them to go to regular schools.[95] This prosecutorial activism does not go unchallenged, though, with many public authorities alleging that the MP is neither competent nor qualified to design public policy. They, nonetheless, tend to comply with the terms set by the prosecutors rather than challenge them in court. In part, this tension may simply be due to the common aversion policy makers and administrators have to robust judicial checks and balances. However, as will be taken up again later, the proactive role the MP has been playing in some states is ambivalent. After all, an unelected organ with far-reaching prerogatives purporting to act in the public interest, and

---

[92] See, inter alia, José Eduardo Farias, 2005. Direitos humanos, direitos sociais e justiça. São Paulo: Catavento.

[93] Junqueira et al., 1995, supra n. 21.

[94] See supra n. 21.

[95] See Lei de Diretrizes e Bases da Educação Nacional – Lei n° 9.394/1996, art. 4°; and Estatuto da Criança e do Adolescente – Lei do Adolescente n° 8.069/90, Art. 54, which establish the obligation to provide complementary transportation, on the basis of which the "school flight" scheme was established; see collective interview with Joyce Pernigoiástti (Secretária de Educação Adjunta), Roberto Adornes (Gestor Administrativo-Financeiro), Ramiro Tarragô (Assessor Financeiro da Secretaria de Educação), and Letícia Albuquerque (Assessora Jurídica da Secretaria de Educação), all of the Porto Alegre Municipality, June 10, 2005.

especially on behalf of the disenfranchised and excluded, fits well with the partly paternalistic, partly authoritarian tradition that has played such a dominant role in Brazilian history.[96]

The Defensoria Pública, in turn, plays a significant role in places like Rio de Janeiro, though in others, like Pernambuco, the *defensores* are underpaid and not publicly examined (*concursados*); here, most are recycled *Procuradores da Assistência Judiciária Estadual*, an equivalent of the PAJ that preceded the establishment of a Defensoria Pública proper. In Rio Grande do Sul, in turn, the Defensoria Pública disposes of functional, but not of budgetary autonomy vis-à-vis the state government, which has limited its size and, hence, effectiveness. In Goiás, for its part, the Defensoria Pública was formally created by State Law 9785/85, but has not been established yet. In its absence, the State Attorney's Office created a PAJ that attends citizens in the capital Goiânia, but that is considered highly ineffectual. With the exception of the PAJ's area coordinators, who are civil servants proper, the majority of PAJ staff are merely underpaid and under-endowed appointees of the state government.[97] However, where, like in Rio de Janeiro, the Defensoria Pública is fully functional, it may come to play a crucial role not just in bringing (and winning) individual actions on behalf of indigent plaintiffs, but, perhaps even more important, as an enforcement agency. Interview data suggests that compliance by public authorities can be a considerable problem in Rio de Janeiro.[98] With regard to indigent plaintiffs, for instance, it is essentially left to the individual *defensores* to bring a case to supervise compliance. Frequently, the latter does not merely consist in bringing enforcement action in cases of noncompliance, but in organizing compliance from the moment of the judicial decision onward. However, the more active a role the Defensoria plays, the more obstacles it will face from public authorities. Indeed, anecdotal evidence suggests that in some cases, public authorities will directly attempt to hinder the Defensoria's work. Hence, in one municipality in Rio de Janeiro, for instance, the mayor withdrew municipal office space and logistics originally ceded to the Defensoria on account of it bringing too many access-to-medicines actions against it.[99]

Last, with regard to the public authorities and their respective legal divisions, their overall attitude seems, by and large, to be pragmatic. By law, most are obliged to appeal negative first-instance decisions, but depending on the particular claim, they may pursue appeals only pro forma and only up to the second instance, though in some cases an appeal is launched simply to buy time and adjourn any payments to be made. More important, in many case types, such as access to medicines or school infrastructure, only a judicial determination can dispense a

---

[96] See interview with Raul Martins, Coordenador de Planejamento da Secretaria Municipal de Saúde do Município de Porto Alegre, June 10, 2005.

[97] See, again, collective interview with Carla Queiroz (Coordenadora da Área Cível da Procuradoria de Assistência Judiciária do Estado de Goiás), and with two (non-examined) PAJ *procuradores*, Antônio Carlos Ferreira Braga and Darcy Gomes, of June 6, 2005, *supra* n. 48.

[98] See interview with Denis de Oliveira Praça, Director-General of the Rio de Janeiro Association of Public Defenders, October 11, 2007.

[99] *Id.*

public authority from the normally required public bidding process.[100] Hence, already in individual actions, but especially in public class action suits, it is plainly in the public authority's interest to litigate, and thereby win the right to purchase the goods in question for the cheapest market price. Evidence from Rio de Janeiro and Pernambuco suggests that in health rights cases, a distinction is usually made between medicines included in the union's or states' official buying list,[101] and those not on any list, as well as access to treatment and any public class action suit brought by the MP. In the first case, the PM/PEs will generally only appeal once, whereas in the second case, a proper defense, potentially up to the STF, is mounted. Despite these overall trends, most PEs do not seem to have an explicit litigation strategy in place but, rather, will act on the basis of experience and a certain cost–benefit assessment. Moreover, and as was already pointed out, in most cases, the PM/PE will not dispute the applicability of the particular right in question; instead, they tend to challenge any determination of their particular compliance responsibility on good administration grounds and attempt to shift the onus of compliance onto a different federal level. In some states, such as Rio Grande do Sul, collaboration among the different judicial actors is encouraged through joint technical committees, though the judiciary has, so far, not cooperated enthusiastically with these.[102] However, ad hoc collaboration between the judge, the MP, the impugned public authority, and sometimes also the Defensoria Pública does occur.[103]

The logic of that collaboration has been shown in a recent study by Luiz Werneck Vianna and Marcelo Baumann Burgos,[104] in which the authors reconstruct in detail the way four public class actions and one pre-judicial settlement were brought, decided, and implemented. One of these concerned access to medicines in the state of Rio de Janeiro. The authors show how the initial momentum for the *ação* emerged through a dialogue among a number of concerned actors: notably, several NGOs representing patients suffering from chronic diseases such as kidney failure, the Defensoria Pública, and the state health council, as well as the MP's own intuition that individual actions for access to certain medicines were on the surge. As a result of this pooling of information, the MP felt on firm enough ground to initiate formal proceedings against the state and the municipality by means of a public class action, in order to remedy the problem structurally and, therefore, eliminate the cause of the mounting number of individual actions.

The MP grounded its case in the typical fashion, relying on the fundamental character of the right to health, its association to human dignity, and its status

---

[100] Lei 8.666 of June 21, 1993, Art. 24.

[101] These lists are, of course, in part the product of earlier litigation, by which a particular medicine came to be included. The general procedure is for the state health authority to react to large-scale litigation on a particular medicine by, within the SUS, negotiating with the union on which level of government will bear the cost of providing it. It will then eventually be included on a buying list.

[102] See *supra* n. 21.

[103] See interview with Adriana Burio Grande do Suler (Defensora Pública – Coordenadora da Área Cível da Defensoria Pública), June 9, 2005.

[104] L. Werneck Vianna, and M. Baumann Burgos. 2005. Entre princípios e regras: Cinco estudos de caso da ação civil pública (Between principles and rules: A study of five public class actions). *DADOS – Revista de Ciências Sociais* 48(4), pp. 777–843.

as self-executing. It cited a previous STF decision holding that the programmatic character of the right to health only refers to the organization of the public health system, but not to the right's core content, which is derivative of the right to life and, hence, non-derogable.[105]

The trial judge thereupon convened the MP, the Defensoria Pública, and the municipal and state health secretariats to negotiate an amicable solution. This resulted in a blueprint for a new institution, a unified medicines dispensation counter that was aimed at raising efficiency in the dispensation of medications and, thus, reducing the need for litigation on this count. Several of the actors who participated in the negotiation later affirmed that no party had brought along a ready blueprint, but that the idea of the unified counter actually emerged in the discussion. Moreover, the judge stated that during the entire process, he was continuously beleaguered by individuals in need of particular medicines, as well as by some specialized NGOs; he admitted to feeling personally pressured, a fact that contributed to his decision to admit the *ação* and to invite the parties to construct from it a real and viable solution of the problem.

In the end, however, although the counter was subsequently created and all parties declared themselves satisfied with the process, its stocking with medicines was delayed and insufficient. The consequence of this was, in turn, the massive concession of (individual) preliminary injunctions granting access to medicines supposedly available at the counter. As a result, the new counter became entirely absorbed by the administration of injunctions, and was unable to provide the general efficiency-enhancing service for which it was created.

This exemplary case demonstrates well the logic behind social rights litigation in Brazil. Although it deals with the relatively rare instance of a successful public class action on access to medicines, it nonetheless contains the typical features of such litigation in general: formalistic rights-oriented legal argument, the individualization of the legal issue through the presence of the victims in the trial and the personalization of the decision in relation to the judge, the absence of any viability or cost–benefit analysis, or, indeed, of medical expert evidence, a rights-conceding decision, and compliance problems in the aftermath. What is, of course, different from the standard (successful) individual access-to-medicines decision is the joint judicial–administrative decision-making process that aims to create a real remedy to the problem at hand. Yet, its spirit is, arguably, no different from the judicial paternalism that informs most of the standard decisions, nor has it been able to overcome the compliance problem any more effectively.

Finally, a recurrent issue raised by public authorities is the nonappreciation of technical evidence and, generally, the lack of technical expertise on the part of the judiciary. Although expert witness services (*peritos técnicos*) are available in the tribunals and within the MP, they are frequently not used to evaluate the sustainability of technical argument brought by the claimants. As early as 2001, the national HIV/AIDS program, overwhelmed by the large number of actions for

---

[105] See decision of Justice Moreira Alves, in RE No. 264.269–0/24/11/2000.

access to Kaletra urged patients and judges to refrain from claiming and conceding such actions, respectively, without evaluating the prescription and the patient's particular diagnosis.[106] It further pointed to a consensus in the international medical community that the initiation or substitution of HAART medications did not constitute a medical emergency, as claimed in most of the actions requesting, inter alia, *Kaletra*.[107] Uninformed judges facing inadequate prescriptions couched in the rhetoric of a life and death emergency would, in the view of the federal HIV/AIDS administrator, all too easily fall prey to scientifically (and economically) unsound "fashion prescriptions."[108] A somewhat extreme case on the same line concerned a United States–based Chinese physiologist, Peter Law, offering, in partnership with three renowned São Paulo physicians, so-called myoplast transfer treatment against Duchenne's muscular dystrophy. Controversial from the beginning, and eventually disqualified by the U.S. Food and Drug Administration (FDA) in 2000 and by the Brazilian Federal Medical Council (*Conselho Federal de Medicina*) in 2002, Law and his partners nonetheless had set up shop in São Paulo in 1996 and attracted several Brazilian children and adolescents suffering from the disease, as well as a number of patients from abroad, to submit themselves to the US$150,000 treatment. In nine cases the (Brazilian) patients won full or partial financing for the treatment from the TJs in São Paulo and Santa Catarina, as well as in one federal court, amounting to a total of approximately $220 million. Indeed, as was later shown by an investigative journalist, Law's Brazilian partners encouraged potential patients to sue for access to the treatment and even directed the children's parents to a lawyer of their confidence.[109] Once the scam was uncovered, the São Paulo and Santa Catarina PEs affirmed that they were looking into ways to recoup the money potentially through proceedings in the United States. Although probably an extreme case, it nonetheless shows the potential precariousness of decisions based merely on formal, rights-fulfillment-oriented argument and not on a substantive appreciation of the merits of each action.

THE MOMENT OF COMPLIANCE: EFFECT AND ENFORCEMENT OF JUDICIAL DECISIONS ON HEALTH AND EDUCATION RIGHTS

Aggregate Direct and Third-Party Effects

The direct impact of litigation on the provision of health and education goods and services is influenced by two factors: success of litigation and compliance

---

[106] Document issued by the Programa Nacional de DST/AIDS on 14/08/2001; see also Scheffer et al., 2005, *supra* n. 1, p. 28.

[107] Medical emergency and AIDS medicines; on December 1, 2005, however, the Federal MP and a number of HIV/AIDS NGOs initiated a public (class) action against the Federal Health Ministry in order to oblige it to initiate compulsory licensing proceedings against Kaletra's patent-holder, Abbott Laboratories; see press clipping, available at http://www.cptech.org/ip/health/c/brazil/abia11302005.html (accessed on February 25, 2007).

[108] See a letter to the editor by Paulo Roberto Teixeira, in the "Painel do Leitor," *Folha de São Paulo*, April 2, 2003; cited also in Scheffer et al., 2005, *supra* n. 1, p. 30.

[109] Conceição Lemes, 2002. "Médicos tornam doença em caso de polícia." *No Mínimo*. Also available at http://www.distrofiamuscular.net/mioblastos.htm.

with the (successful) decisions. As for the former, the picture that has emerged in the previous section clearly shows the great majority of individual health rights actions to be successful, followed by public class actions in education with a much lower absolute frequency but reasonably high success rates, and public class actions on health rights with low frequency and success rates. Hence, in all, individuals pursuing the most common health-rights claims to access to medicines and to treatment, and regardless of whether they are brought by private attorneys or the Defensoria Pública, currently stand a high chance of obtaining a formal judicial remedy. By contrast, "structural" remedies, whether related to education or health, are less frequent, less sucessful, and, generally, less predictable. However, if litigation success is a necessary condition for direct effect, it is only through compliance with judicial remedies that this effect becomes, in fact, effective by providing the claimant with the good or service claimed. Yet, as was already variously hinted at, in some states such as Rio de Janeiro (but much less so in others, such as Rio Grande do Sul), there is a considerable compliance problem. One reason is the formalistic style of rights-conceding decisions, which, by and large, do not contain specific implementation instructions to the public authority in question. This essentially leaves it up to the plaintiff or to the Defensoria Pública to see to the implementation of decisions and to take enforcement action if necessary. The Defensoria, however, will usually only gain cognizance of compliance problems if the indigent plaintiffs report these, which, interview data suggests is often not the case. Indeed, there appears to be considerable attrition on the part of plaintiffs who are continuously told that some or all of the required and judicially ordered medicines are not available. The usual pattern is not that the public pharmacy in question will deny outright the provision of the medicine, but that it will either promise delivery in the future or dispense the medicine but later discontinue dispensation; in both cases, logistical difficulties will be cited. As a result, many indigent plaintiffs become persuaded that even enforcement action through the Defensoria Pública is not going to make any difference.[110]

Indeed, enforcement action brought by the claimant or the Defensoria Pública, and ocasionally also by the MP, is not always effective. Even daily fines of approximately US$550 to $1,100 – in individual access-to-medicine cases – for non-compliance with a preliminary injunction (*mandado de segurança*) are often not enough to induce compliance, nor is the issue of a prison mandate for a state or municipal health secretary for criminal contempt, which is hardly ever enforced, although there are cases where, for instance, a school director has been temporarily detained at a police station for not having complied with court orders mandating the admission of pupils. This is, however, an exception, so that enforcement action frequently takes an informal route by, for example, personalizing their case vis-à-vis the public authority in question. Hence, in one exemplary case, the claimant stated she eventually succeeded in obtaining her medicine only because she personally knew a civil servant in the state health secretariat who sped up her

---

[110] See, e.g., the proceedings of a recent seminar in Rio Grande do Sul, Seminário medicamentos: Políticas públicas e medicamentos, available at http://www.ajuris.org.br/sem_med/sem_med.htm (accessed December 17, 2007).

process.[111] Alternatively, *defensores públicos* often end up being the only enforcement agents of their cases, despite being insufficienty equipped for this task. One
interviewed *defensora*, for instance, recounted a case in which she brought and
won an action concerning the setting up of a home care unit for a cancer patient
and subsequently had to organize its installation herself, as no other organ was
formally charged with acting on the decision.[112] Significantly, the perception that
compliance was, in effect, left to a nonexpert acting out of goodwill led her to
resolve not to bring similar actions in the future. This state of affairs is additionally
aggravated by the general lack of compliance with enforcement action, that is, of
secondary compliance action. As was already noted, the Defensoria Pública may
formally bring compliance actions that may result in personal fines or even prison
mandates for the responsible public administrator, most commonly the municipal
or state health or education secretary. However, such prison mandates are virtually
never enforced, and the fines frequently end up being discounted later on. It is
only through being extraordinarily insistent that a *defensor* will be able to force
compliance, a stance he or she will not be able to take with most cases. For this
reason, the Defensoria has, like the MP, taken to work directly with public health
providers and general civil society on the extrajudicial settlement of potential
disputes.

Yet another alternative form of ensuring implementation pursued in some cases
in Rio de Janeiro has been for the courts to order the public authority in question
to deposit the cost of the required medicine into the plaintiff's account, rather than
to have the former provide it directly to the plaintiff. This is used, for instance, in
cases where state or municipal pharmacies do not stock the medicine and allege
that obtaining it would not be doable; the plaintiff can then demand that the sum
be transferred to him directly. This has, however, attracted criticism from the MP
that alleges that the courts do not exercise any supervisory jurisdiction over the
actual use of such funds.

In summary, it is difficult to specify the magnitude of the real impact of litigation.
Insofar as compliance with decisions is at least partial or temporary, resort to the
courts will certainly have made a difference to the plaintiffs in question. In addition,
the fact that the judiciary is, increasingly, an intermediary in the provision of basic
health and education services in itself conditions the conduct of public authorities
and improves their compliance record. Yet, the way judicial access to health and
education works precludes it from functioning as a straightforward distribution
mechanism generating an output symmetric to its input.

Indirect Effects Internal to the Legal System: The Impact
of Threatened and of Settled Litigation

With regard to the impact of threatened litigation, the two types of action examined
so far have to be distinguished. As for individual actions, with the exception of the

---

[111] Information taken from qualitative (interview-based) data on sample cases.
[112] Interview with Denis de Oliveira Praça, Director-General of the Rio de Janeiro Association of Public
Defenders, October 11, 2007.

very few formally precedent-setting (*súmula*) decisions, no individual case would be able to exert any influence beyond its immediate object. However, informally, judicial actors will, of course, tend to develop a hunch about the decision habit of specific tribunals or, indeed, sometimes of individual judges, in relation to specific types of action, and they may base their litigation behavior on this informal knowledge. This judicial hunch may, in turn, lead to attempts to reach a friendly settlement rather than to initiate formal proceedings, and certainly the Defensoria Pública may use this tool in relation to common types of actions, but it is difficult to measure the absolute importance of this practice, as it usually lies below the radar of case and judicial news reporting, and can, if at all, only be traced through anecdotal evidence by the involved actors. Nevertheless, given the well-known problems with compliance in some states, the Defensoria is increasingly engaged in the attempt to construct enforceable solutions in conjunction with public authorities in lieu of legal action. This, however, would work mostly with common types of medicines where distribution is impaired by purely logistical problems and not where new types of medicines requiring extra budgetary allocations are concerned.

The situation is very different, however, with regard to the MP and public class actions. As explained earlier, formal public class actions face a much higher degree of judicial scrutiny and are less successful than individual actions, largely on account of the judiciary's reticence to underwrite what often amounts to fairly detailed public policy proposals on part of the MP. Hence, in some states, the MP has taken to avoiding direct judicial confrontation with public authorities, and has, instead, taken an administrative legal route by means of the threat to initiate an administrative inquest against a public authority with a view to forcing it to agree to terms of settlement without going to court. This practice is, however, similarly under the radar, because it only enters the screen if either side resolves to take the judicial road, for example in case of contestation by or noncompliance with the settlement (*termo*) by the public authority. Yet, its impact cannot be underestimated, because it is probably the most direct form in which a branch of the judiciary influences public administration. There are innumerable schemes in which the MP de facto acts as a partner of public authorities, proposing and supervising the implementation of specific policies. This partnership is, of course, not always voluntary on the part of public authorities, and the latter tend to see it as undue intervention, but frequently they still prefer to comply with it rather than face court proceedings. Indeed, because the terms of the agreement are negotiated with the MP, the degree of influence the public authority has over the outcome, including the budgetary impact, is significantly higher than in a court decision.[113]

The indirect legal impact of settled litigation, in turn, appears to be largely insignificant because of the absence of any precedent. Although, as was already pointed out, the STF now has a procedural means to make some of its decisions

---

[113] Luciana Aboim Machado Gonçalves da Silva, 2004. *Termo de ajuste de conduta.* São Paulo: LTr; Ricardo Augusto Soares Leite, 2003. "Reflexões acerca do termo de compromisso de ajustamento de Conduta." Available at http://www.escola.agu.gov.br/revista/Ano_III_junho_2003/Ricardo-Descumprimento%20do%20Termo%20de%20Compromisso.PDF (accessed on December 10, 2007).

effectively binding in the form of the *súmula vinculante*, it still only covers a small minority of subject matters. That said, the aggregate of similar decisions on standard cases does generate a degree of predictability of which all judicial actors will be aware, and which, de facto, functions as a form of judicial common wisdom or, indeed, informal stare decisis.

Indirect Effects External to the Legal System: The Impact on Policy Creation, Administration, and Budget

Apart from the direct and the indirect internal effects litigation has on the distribution of basic health and education services, the crucial question is, of course, whether and to what extent judicial output generates repercussions in the political system, notably in the form of new or changed policies. An answer to this question must, in the Brazilian case, distinguish between the impact litigation has on policy creation or policy change, on the one hand, and on policy administration, on the other. With regard to the former, there has been a significant time lag between the clamor produced by the steep increase in litigation since at least 2002 and the political echo it has occasioned. Indeed, in education, there is no measurable direct policy impact to speak of, though the turn to litigation has, arguably, begun much more recently than with regard to health rights. In the latter's case, HIV/AIDS litigation is, again, the area in which litigation has had the most impact, though its main impact has, arguably, been on policy administration, rather than on policy creation.

There is no evidence that the 1996 law that extends HIV/AIDS treatment and services to all who need it was brought about by litigation. Rather, it was an NGO-led media campaign and congressional and state governmental lobbying,[114] driven by the worldwide introduction of HAART at that time and the immediate demand by the Brazilian HIV/AIDS community for it to be made available publicly, that led to the policy's creation.[115] In fact, as the study by Scheffer, Salazar, and Grou shows, access to HAART-drugs litigation began more or less parallel to the creation of the policy, and only reached its numerical apex as of 1999, as a result of initially inefficient distribution patterns and also on account of concerns that governmental attitudes vis-à-vis universal access might be changing. If access to HAART litigation is, as will be discussed later, still the main driving force of health rights litigation, it has grown to be so only in close relation to an already existing legislated policy. The same goes, a fortiori, for other types of access-to-medicines litigation as it will necessarily concern the SUS, which is itself a preexisting policy framework that has not significantly changed through litigation.

However, the political system is beginning to respond to this increasing judicial input. Discontent with the growing budgetary impact of health rights litigation, as well as the de facto judicial administration of a number of health and education policies has been mounting among executive agencies on all federal levels for some time. This has crystallized into some initial steps aimed at curbing litigation and its

---

[114] Scheffer et al., 2005, *supra* n. 1, pp. 22ff.
[115] *Id.*, pp. 81ff.

effects. Hence, in March 2007, the Federal Health Ministry created a Commission for the Rational Use of Medicines (*Comissão para o Uso Racional de Medicamentos*) comprised of different public health administrators and aimed at elaborating guidelines for the use of SUS-included medicines, to be used, among others, by public authorities in access-to-medicines cases. In parallel, the Federal Health Minister has openly criticized the "indiscriminate" judicial concession of medicines sometimes not even certified in Brazil, alleging that Brazil was, with help from the judiciary, becoming a "luxury guinea pig."[116] Among others, the health minister recently met with the govenors of the most (health) litigious states – Rio Grande do Sul, Paraná, Santa Catarina and Mato Grosso do Sul – to discuss strategies to curb excessive litigation and has called for new legislation to that end. It is important to note, however, that these measures do not expand on the content or distribution of basic services, but, on the contrary, aim to limit the judicial concession of such services in the context of existing policies. Significantly, this political push back received initial support from the highest judiciary when the current president of the STF, in a recent decision, declared that only medicines included in Health Ministry administrative guidelines were to be considered justiciable.[117] However, important as that declaration is, it does not formally set binding precedent and is, so far, only an indication of a potential change in judicial attitudes. The extent to which courts down the line will follow this reasoning or will be effectively disciplined by new legislation remains to be seen.

The picture is different, however, when it comes to policy administration or implementation. Here the pioneering HAART cases show that litigation can work as a signaling mechanism for demand in new medicines, and, hence, for the expansion of an existing public policy. Once a certain litigation density has been reached, public authorities tend to seek cover by including the medicine in the SUS list or the *consenso terapêutico*. An example from Rio de Janeiro concerns four leukemia cases brought by a private attorney on behalf of three paying (i.e., middle class) and one pro bono indigent patient in relation to unlisted leukemia medication.[118] All plaintiffs won their cases, and medicines were initially distributed, though, in one case, distribution was subsequently discontinued. Renewed legal action then resulted in a prison mandate for the municipal health secretary in the case of continued noncompliance. Eventually, the medicine was included in the SUS list and distribution regularized. In this context, administration and implementation have to be distinguished. The former relates to the administrative decision to include a new item in the list of medicines to be distributed by public pharmacies. Implementation relates to the de facto carrying out of that policy so that the medicine is actually available in the public pharmacy in sufficient quantity. The early "access to HAART drugs" actions clearly fall into this latter category

---

[116] See Rudolfo Lago, interview with Federal Health Minister José Gomes Temporão, "Médicos não devem fazer greve", *Isto É*, June 21, 2007. Available at http://www.terra.com.br/istoe/edicoes/1965/artigo53460–1.htm (accessed on December 8, 2007).

[117] See Suspensão de Tutela Antecipada nr. 91, Judge Rapporteur Ellen Gracie.

[118] See collective interview with Renan Aguiar (FIOCRUZ) and Edson Schueler (Ivan Nunes Ferreira Advogados), May 11, 2005.

because, despite legislation requiring it, it took considerable time for ART cocktails to be made widely available. The same is true for most other medicines. In part the reasons for non- or insufficient implementation are legitimately linked to time-consuming public procurement, price negotiation, and registration issues. Hence, in one case, for example, the state of Rio Grande do Sul had, after the contract with the provider of an antidepressant (Topiramato) drug had expired, initiated a competitive bidding process that resulted in the award of a new contract to the same provider; the state was then successfully sued by a competitor, which resulted in the annulation of the bidding process, with the collateral effect being the temporary non-provision of the medicine.[119] Yet, in other circumstances, various forms of maladministration, including inertia, incompetence, haggling between authorities, or political impasse are the reason for the failure to distribute medications. In this latter case, litigation serves as a corrective for negligence on the part of public authorities. Although this can be said to have a positive effect on policy implementation, it may also have the flip side of making public authorities more or less deliberately wait for judicial mandates until they implement the policy in an incremental way. Given the overall scarcity of resources and lack of consensus on how to best spend them among policy makers, the latter attitude may be quite frequent.

Indeed, some public authorities allege that current judicial practice leads to administration by judicial order, rather than by a democratically legitimate executive.[120] The state of Pernambuco, for instance, has felt obliged to open a representation in Brasília for the sole task of appealing state or federal court decisions to the STF and STJ.[121] In Goiás, in turn, most citizen complaints concerning the Goiánia municipality – which shoulders the largest share of public health provision – are settled prior to judicial decision by means of negotiations between the MP's Promotoria da Saúde and the Municipal Health Secretariat.[122] In Rio Grande do Sul, for its part, there are two distinct and, indeed, starkly contrasting views on the interface between judicial institutions and public health administration. The first is held by the MP, which has considered it its task to enforce proactively the constitutionally mandated minimum spending on health.[123] To that end it has recently proposed a scheme whereby the state would be obliged to use any leftovers from the previous budget, as well as projections on the subsequent budget to fill any gaps; in relation to municipalities, the MP has established terms of settlement including mandatory deadlines (*termos de ajustamento*) to compel the

---

[119] *Zero Hora*, September 19, 2006. Available at http://zerohora.clicrbs.com.br/zerohora/jsp/default.jsp? uf=1&local=1&section=capa_online.

[120] See *supra* n. 98.

[121] See interview with Leônidas Siqueira Filho, Chefe-adjunto do Setor Contencioso, August 26, 2005.

[122] See interview with Antônio Guise (Diretor do Departamento de Conrole e Avaliação da Secretaria Municipal de Saúde), June 7, 2005.

[123] The precise legal provisions are as follows: municipalities need, according to Art. 198, Para. 20 of the Constitution, and art. 77 of the Transitional Constitutional Provisions Act (*Ato das Disposições Constitucionais Transitórias*), to spend 15 percent of their annual budget on health; according to the same provisions, states need to spend a minimum of 12 percent; both states and municipalities must spend a minimum of 25 percent on education, as mandated in Art. 212 of the Constitution.

required minimum spending.[124] One of the problems of such relatively advanced programs is that their costs often exceed the mandated minimum spending, leading to intra-administration disputes over allocation of extra funds. Projects such as the *vôo escolar* show that with a well-functioning inter-institutional partnership between the relevant public authority and the MP, potential problems can be administratively preempted, so that formal judicial process is limited to cases of extreme noncompliance with constitutional and infraconstitutional norms. Such public-policy partnerships represent, in the MP's view, a real step toward social inclusion.[125]

The contrasting view, in turn, is held by the relevant public authorities. A case in point is the Porto Alegre municipality, where, in the view of municipal officials there is now a continuous attempt on part of the MP to "invade" the health-related competences of the municipality. The MP's actions, they claim, are highly prejudicial to public finances and to the quality of health care, require three reports to the Ministério Público daily, and require the Health Secretary to operate under (as yet unenforced) arrest warrants.[126] A recent example were twenty-five separate individual judicial orders requiring the municipality to provide free transport for plaintiffs with special needs, even if the provision of transport clearly fell outside the health brief, and even if a transportation scheme organized rationally by the municipality might have required fewer vehicles.[127] In the Secretariat's view, this undesirable state of affairs could be remedied if the MP took steps to incorporate the technical – in this case medical – expertise necessary to assess health rights cases. Indeed, this would help to resolve unnecessary lawsuits before they even started.[128]

In all this, the core point of controversy is, as would be expected, the budgetary impact the aggregate of litigation is beginning to have. Yet, for all its importance, precise figures on the impact of decisions are difficult to come by, as there is no central monitoring of litigation costs by public authorities, and the legal-administrative process is complex, especially when it comes to the frequent ad hoc deals between different federal levels in relation to the shifting of funds from one to another.[129] In addition, as was already seen, judges by and large do not engage in any form of substantive cost or economic impact analysis of their decisions, and, in fact, frequently counter cost-based arguments by public authority defendants with references to the absolute character of the fundamental right in question. Data are, hence, largely anecdotal, but may, nonetheless, be indicative of the general trend. In health, the driving force of judicially enforced health rights continues to be the HIV/AIDS program; indeed, as will be discussed in greater detail in the following, litigation for inclusion of new HAART drugs and also for the often unlisted

---

[124] Whether on account of MP actions or of other factors, the numbers on the municipal level are impressive: in 2003, of 497 municipalities, only 8 did not comply with the mandated minimum spending; in 2004, this figure rose to 45, prompting the MP to supervise health spending even more vigorously.
[125] See *supra* n. 18.
[126] See *supra* n. 21.
[127] See *supra* n. 98.
[128] See interview with Raul Martins, *supra* n. 98.
[129] See again, Governance in Brazil's unified health care system, *supra* n. 33.

drugs against opportunistic infections has become a semi-institutionalized form of expanding and refining the universal access scheme adopted by the government. This, together with the increasing cost of individual medications, has been increasing the cost of the HIV/AIDS program to more than R$1 billion per annum in 2006. In all, the Federal Health Ministry's extra spending on judicially granted medicines for all types of disease rose from R$188,000 in 2003 to around R$26 million in the first half of 2007 alone.[130] This trend is also reflected on the state level. In Paraná, for example, the extra cost for judicially granted medicines skyrocketed from roughly R$200,000 in 2002 to R$14 million during the first half of 2007 only. In São Paulo, in turn, the state spent R$48 million on litigated medication in 2004, out of a total medical budget of R$480 million – or roughly 10 percent of the medication budget.[131] The Federal Health Ministry estimates that in all states, litigation-related extra spending will amount to R$1 billion in 2007 alone.[132]

Moreover, it is not just the quantitative rise of litigation costs that is considered to be problematic, but also the particular quality of the granted medicines or treatments. A good part of the latter fall into the high-cost category of exceptional medicines concerning rare diseases and long-term treatment of the chronically ill. According to Ministry of Health data, the total cost for this category of medicines had already risen from R$680 million in 2002 to R$1.7 billion in 2005, with a tendency to grow even further. It could, hence, be argued that the increasing share litigated medicines and treatments have of the overall health budget favors individualized high-cost medicines and treatments over low-cost collective benefits such as vaccines or primary care medicines.

The overall data clearly suggest that the exponentially mounting litigation costs have put public health administrators on a collision course with current judicial practice concerning health and education rights. That said, overall costs are not fully reflective (yet) of litigation numbers because of the already-mentioned compliance problem in some of the examined states. However, although it is true that permanent or temporary noncompliance is a way for public authorities to (illegally) control costs, the number of litigants eventually successful not only in winning their cases but also in then obtaining the required medicines is still higher than the number of those who fail to concretize their judicial mandates.

CONCLUSION: FOUR MODELS OF LITIGATION

What, then, can be concluded from the complex multicolored and multitextured picture of social rights litigation in Brazil that has emerged in the preceding sections? Has a "rights revolution" occurred at least within the ambit of health and education? Has litigation caused these basic services to be distributed more widely, especially among the poorer layers of society? Have the courts empowered

---

[130] See data of Federal Ministry of Health – HIV/AIDS Program, at http://www.aids.gov.br/data/Pages/ LUMIS16BA7E58PTBRIE.htm (accessed on December 17, 2007).
[131] Interview with Oscar Vilhena Vieira, Conectas/SUR and Fundação Getulio Vargas, May 10, 2005.
[132] *Supra* n. 133

Brazilians and made good on the constitutional promise to make them true stakeholders in the health and education system? The first part of an ultimately inconclusive answer has to point to the sheer numbers: on the basis of the new constitution, a revamped health and education system, and progressive legislation such as Lei 9.313, there clearly has been an explosive aggregate increase of health and education cases as of around 2002. Hence, if Brazilians initially staked their hopes for a (social) rights revolution essentially on lobbying, namely, in the form of crafting a rights-heavy constitution and pushing for implementing legislation, the focus has, in the past five years or so, shifted from Congress to the courts. It is here that citizens have found formal remedies to the inefficiencies of the health and education system, and they have started using these remedies at a breathtaking rate. This, of course, testifies to an overall increase in rights consciousness and litigiousness, and, thus, to a greater de facto accountability of public health and education authorities. Indeed, the fact that judicial actors are playing an increasing role in the administration of health and education policies has led to a slow but perceptible change in the attitudes and practices of public administrators, more oriented toward preventing litigation in the first place by generating effective outputs.

However, the follow-up question about whether these changes have also led to a wider and more even distribution of health and education goods is more difficult to answer and not immediately apparent from the numbers. What is still clearly shown in the quantitative study is the great numerical divide between both individual and public class actions, and between health and education rights litigation. Hence, by a vast margin, individual health rights actions, most notably access-to-medicine and access-to-treatment cases, account for the observed litigation explosion; whereas public class actions, which are the main instrument of litigation in education, linger on at a low level. To be sure, one successful public class action may, because of its collective effect, count for many hundreds or thousands of individual actions on the same subject matter. Yet, as is also still evident from the quantitative study, the courts have applied two levels of scrutiny for either type of action. Whereas in individual (access to medicine and treatment) actions the mere showing of prima facie evidence of medical need is usually accepted as sufficient for a claim to stand, courts are very reticent to appear to directly influence executive policy administration by conceding *erga omnes* claims. As a result, the litigation "success story" really only applies to individual access to medicines and treatment, and, thus, largely bypasses education. That said, there is a slight difference between health and education public class actions, with the latter being granted at a higher rate than the former. Yet, even in successful individual access to medicines and health actions, the number of claimants who actually obtain the granted remedy for the required period is lower than the winning case count implies. In some of the sampled states, such as Rio de Janeiro, there is a considerable compliance problem, and enforcement action tends to depend on the personal initiative either of the individual claimant or a particular *defensor público* who is then transformed into a compliance agent. And even enforcement action does not always lead to the remedy actually being provided. In this sense, the de facto hurdles for obtaining medication or treatment through the courts are relatively high and require a considerable investment of time and money, even for nominally indigent claimants.

In addition, the judicialization of public health generates a number of collateral effects that qualify the direct benefits obtained from successful litigation. The main one consists of the queue-jumping phenomenon that results from the massive concession of preliminary injunctions granting medicines or treatment on pain of heavy daily fines for noncompliance. This evidently scrambles established priorities, such as for specially vulnerable groups, and undermines legitimate policy objectives. Given overall scarcity of funds and stringent administrative rules on extra-budgetary expenditure, the effect of this injunction flood is generally not any fundamental change in health policy, but rather the ad hoc shifting of funds toward litigant patients. This phenomenon is aggravated by the prevailing judicial formalism and the resulting reticence on the part of the courts to engage in substantive determinations of need, adequacy, or proportionality. In this sense, the relation between the judge's and the administrator's logic is scant, with there not being, as yet, any institutional mechanism or cultural construct to bring both logics together. Another side effect of the current judicial decision practice relates to public class actions and the MP. In response to the reticence on the part of the courts to grant these structural remedies, the MP has, in at least some of the examined states, shifted from litigation to pre-judicial administrative control. The MP thereby assumes the role of co-administrator or, indeed, policy maker, a role as potentially beneficent for the categories of individuals contemplated by a particular measure as it is problematic in relation to democratic legitimacy and rational public administration.

Two other factors further complicate a straightforward conclusion with regard to the impact of litigation on the availability of health and education goods. First is the question of the distribution of litigation benefits across social class. Here, a clear picture is difficult to draw, for the main indicator of legal indigence, notably cases filed by the Defensoria Pública, is skewed by the divergent definitions of indigence applied by different Defensorias in the sampled states. Although the majority of Defensoria clients certainly belong to the poorer layers of society, middle class claimants are also increasingly driven to the Defensoria on account of their growing relative indigence in relation to medicine prices and insufficient coverage from private health insurers. What is clear, though, is that individual actions filed by private attorneys emanate from middle class plaintiffs who tend to turn to the courts immediately after being rejected at a public health authority and will, consequently, have a comparatively speedy trial. By contrast, indigent plaintiff's cases usually only come to court after an odyssey in public health institutions, the Defensoria Pública, and possibly the MP, all of which imply considerable waiting periods. Even if the end result may be the same, namely, the concession of the requested medicine or treatment, the indigent plaintiff is much less in control of his or her process and usually has to wait considerably longer for a positive outcome. There is, hence, an appreciable difference in access to justice between middle class and indigent plaintiffs.

Whether this implies that health rights are being "captured" by the middle class is a different question. If the capture thesis is to imply that middle class plaintiffs are effectively taking away social rights from indigent plaintiffs, then the figures are inconclusive. There is no evidence whatsoever that the courts are favoring middle class over indigent plaintiffs. Nor is the greater difficulty of indigent plaintiffs to bring a case in itself evidence for a transfer of health services to the middle class and away from indigent plaintiffs. For as long as courts show little interest in the aggregate impact their individual decisions are having on municipal and state budgets, there is no overall cap on how much is being spent on court-ordered compliance with rights and, therefore, no a priori limitation on how many plaintiffs are granted their rights. Where the middle class capture thesis may have some currency is, of course, in relation to the injunction flood mentioned earlier. Here, the queue-jumping of litigant patients, many of whom are middle class, at public pharmacies does have a direct impact on nonlitigant patients, the majority of whom are, quite likely, indigent.[133]

The second complicating factor concerns the considerable regional differences in litigation behavior. As is evident from the quantitative study, the number of people treading the judicial road differs starkly, with, as a general trend, litigiousness decreasing from south to north, from comparatively wealthier to poorer regions. Yet, it is not merely relative affluence and its expected impact on such factors as education and rights consciousness, but also differences of local cultures, legal and political, and the resulting institutional framework that account for this difference. It is only where the MP is vibrant, where the Defensoria Pública is empowered, and where judges are reasonably rights-oriented that litigation numbers skyrocket. Nevertheless, it should be noted that with the exception of Bahia, all other states within the sample display a similar overall trend, even if in different magnitudes.

What, then, explains the seemingly ambivalent outcomes of health and education litigation? The present study could only so much as scratch at the surface of an answer to this question, which would require a much deeper analysis of the life of the law in Brazil. Preliminarily, the reasons that can be derived from this analysis have to do with a certain Janus-like quality of the different judicial actors that makes their role and influence on litigation outcomes ambivalent. Judges, for their part, see themselves as guardians of the constitutional order and the fundamental rights implied in it, but their formalist style and corporativist disposition distances their decision practice, regardless of whether in successful individual or unsuccessful public class actions, from the realities of health and education administration.

The MP, in turn, acts as a powerful vanguard of judicial transformation and, in health and education, effectively fulfills the functions of a citizens' ombudsperson. Its institutional setup, however, makes it not fully accountable in relation to which causes it adopts and how widespread its impact will be, and its proactive stance may crowd out more representative civil society actors. The Defensoria Pública, for its part, is the key to access to justice for indigent claimants, unmatched by any civil society alternative such as legal clinics or legal aid NGOs, but it still suffers from considerable logistical limitations and is overburdened by its double role as public litigant and de facto enforcement agent. Last, civil society and, indeed, individual claimants are not unambivalent either. On the one hand, more and more people are aware of their constitutional rights and unafraid of entering the judicial

---

[133] This statement derives from informed intuition, as the survey data does not directly reveal the social class of nonlitigant users of public pharmacies.

process to make good on them. On the other hand, there are clearly distorting effects that work on (some) claimants, notably the pharmaceutical lobby in health rights which, with physicians and, to a certain degree, organized civil society as intermediaries, stimulates and, thus, inflates certain types of access to medicines or treatment litigation. In addition, the extent to which organized civil society has adopted a judicial strategy in relation to health rights varies greatly, with HIV/AIDS still by far the most litigation-oriented movement, even though, as noted, more and more NGOs are beginning to look to the courts as a crucial field of action.

In all, four distinct models of social rights litigation can be identified in the Brazilian context. The first model is the individual action for access to medicines and treatment, in which individuals, both middle class and indigent, success-fully litigate for health services, though they may subsequently face compliance problems that tend to be overcome to a greater degree by attorney-aided middle class claimants. Because of its numerical importance and success rate, this model has the largest financial and, therefore, potentially, policy-changing impact. The second is the public class action model in both health and education, in which demands for structural remedies[134] brought by the MP are frequently rejected by courts unwilling to interfere with executive competences, even though there is a greater willingness to concede structural education actions than their health equiv-alents. The third is the HAART litigation model, in which the organized HIV/AIDS movement acts as a semi-institutionalized feedback mechanism into the HAART therapeutic consensus by filing demands for new HAART drugs as soon as they are released anywhere and sometimes even before they are certified in Brazil. As this model is based on individual actions, it is highly successful, with litigants not only winning but also generally not facing the compliance problems other litigant classes face because of the federalized and extraordinary nature of the Brazilian HIV/AIDS program. Although in that sense, sui generis, this model is at least in part adaptable to other causes, including in relation to education.

The fourth is the emerging negotiated settlement model in which primarily the MP, but also increasingly the Defensoria Pública and the courts themselves, will seek to avoid formal judicial proceedings and will directly negotiate solutions with public authorities and the other involved judicial actors. This model, when successful, effectively introduces *erga omnes* solutions through the back door and, being joint judicial–executive action, has the greatest direct and immediate impact on policy formation. It may still not always generate the desired results, but it clearly marks a break with what could be termed the *responsibility gap*, which normally stands between the judiciary and the executive and that obfuscates the attribution of responsibility for tangible end results. This last model, which to some extent must be backed by the credible threat of litigation, also comes closest to what Charles Sabel and William Simon have recently described as the judicial experimentalist model,[135] in contrast to the traditional command and control model of judicial control of administrative practice. It is clear that with regard to social rights

---

[134] See Charles F. Sabel and William H. Simon, 2004. Destabilization rights: How public law litigation succeeds. *Harvard Law Review* 117: 1015.
[135] *Id.*

litigation in Brazil, that traditional model is, at least in part, dysfunctional, even if it may still generate aggregate effects that will over time affect policy. However, it is as yet too early to tell whether judicial–executive co-administration is capable of making an overall difference in relation to health and education policies and, more important, on the number of people effectively benefited by them.

In all, social rights litigation is currently in a process of transition and may change considerably over the next couple of years. The reasons are that, on the one hand, the litigation explosion is likely to continue and further increase, with HAART litigation serving as the model; and on the other hand, there are the first signs of a concerted executive backlash against this litigation explosion on account of the growing financial burden it is causing. The mentioned initial measures now taken at the federal level are likely to be broadened, and it is even conceivable that an STF motivated by concerns expressed by the executive will begin to more pro-actively roll back the current decision practice. In the best of cases, this backlash will be accompanied by a lessons learned exercise by which health and education policies are gradually adapted and budgeted to avoid litigation in the first place, but this is by no means a certain outcome. Conversely, however, any legislation or even an STF-driven curb on litigation cannot in itself hold back demand. Certainly, experimentalist "friendly settlement" practice is going to be further encouraged by formal limitations to litigating, and, perhaps, there will be a shift away from individual and toward public class actions as the more rational way of administrative control. In any case, even facing a transitional moment, social rights litigation will continue to play an at once transformative and destabilizing role, true to the syncretism that characterizes so much of Brazil.

4 Courts and Socioeconomic Rights in India

SHYLASHRI SHANKAR AND
PRATAP BHANU MEHTA

"Compelling action by authorities of the states through the power of mandamus is an inherent power vested in the judiciary," said India's Prime Minister, but warned that "substituting mandamus with a takeover of the functions of another organ may, at times, become a case of over-reach . . . these are all delicate issues which need to be addressed cautiously."[1] Manmohan Singh was speaking at a conference of regional chief ministers and high court chief justices in April 2007. A similar point was made by a former Chief Justice of the Supreme Court in March 2007 who cautioned the courts on legitimate and illegitimate intervention; and also by the Speaker of the legislature who said, "I will be failing in my duty if I do not point out that there has been an encroachment in the legislative arena." These cautionary words from the heads of the legislature, executive, and the judiciary imply that the Indian courts have not just been activist, but over-activist. Is that true?

In the last two decades, the higher judiciary in India transformed non-justiciable economic and social rights such as basic education, health, food, shelter, speedy trial, privacy, anti–child labor, and equal wages for equal work into legally enforceable rights.[2] In a famous judgment on the right to education, the judges even said that a right could be treated as fundamental even if it was not present in the fundamental rights section of the constitution.[3] Subsequent judgments established the rights to a healthy environment, nutrition food, shelter for the poor, and the primacy of the right to health and privacy for an HIV-positive employee who was fired after taking the company physical.[4]

These judgments have triggered a view that the interpreters of the law became lawmakers in India.[5] Some scholars and parliamentarians agree, but others argue that the judiciary did not encroach into legislative or executive space.[6] Drawing on

---

[1] Line dividing activism and over-reach is a thin one: PM's caution to bench. *Indian Express*, 2007. April 7.
[2] Sathe 2002.
[3] Unnikrishnan v. State of AP, 1 SCC 645 (1993).
[4] M. C. Mehta v. Union of India, 3 SCC 756 (2001); Murli S. Deora v. Union of India, 8 SCC 765 (2001); MX v. Hospital ZY, 8 SCC 296 (1998); Common Cause, AIR 1996 S.C. at 935; P. G. Gupta v. State of Gujarat, Supp (2) SCC 182 (1995); U. P. Avas Evam Vikas Parishad v. Friends Coop Housing Society Ltd., 3 SCC 456 (1995).
[5] Dam 2005; Sathe 2002.
[6] Desai and Muralidhar 2000; Muralidhar 2002.

evidence from litigation on the rights to health and education, we argue that Indian judges have not become lawmakers (contrary to the judicialization arguments of Tate and Vallinder 1995) or have even been activist in these two spheres if activism is defined quantitatively in terms of the number of decisions that find government actions unconstitutional (Choudhry and Hunter 2003). In fact, the judges were reluctant to strongly penalize the government even when the state failed to fulfill its statutory obligations. Instead, courts adopted what Tushnet (2004) calls weak remedies, such as setting up committees and negotiation channels. We discuss the probable reasons for such behavior within theories of institutionalism and civil society activism. Our evidence questions whether the judicial arena provides the right avenue for improving the realization of social rights to health and education.[7]

The first section addresses the constitutional framework of social and economic rights and the power of the courts. The second and third sections focus on the nature and extent of legalization of health and education rights, highlighting the argument that courts have, at best, played an indirect role in influencing policy. The fourth section assesses the impact of the courts for the effective delivery of these rights. In the conclusion, we return to the implications for the debates on the court's role in delivering social goods.

THE CONSTITUTION, THE COURTS, AND SOCIAL AND ECONOMIC RIGHTS

Rights, which are guaranteed by the state and enumerated in the constitution, are enforceable claims on the delivery of goods, services or protections by specific others.[8] Social rights are at systemic risk in legislative democracies because those who would benefit from them lack political power. As Tushnet (2004) points out, there are three ways in which a constitution can recognize social and economic rights: (a) by enumerating them but making them non-justiciable; (b) by making them justiciable but allowing courts to find a violation only when the legislature dramatically departs from the constitutional requirements; or (c) by making them enforceable to the same extent as civil and political rights. Tushnet argues that in the long run it would be better to opt for non-justiciable social rights because enforceable rights would force courts to adopt strong remedies that could spark political opposition and even noncompliance.

> Constitutional provisions dealing with rights – of whatever generation – involve trade-offs between norm articulation, the availability of individual remedies, and the strength and credibility of the institutions created to enforce those rights. . . . Coupling strong rights with weak remedies, particularly when those remedies are rarely deployed because of resource constraints on plaintiffs, may be a formula for producing cynicism about the constitution. (Tushnet 2004: 1913, 1915)

---

[7] Those who argue that the courts are not capable of delivering social rights include Rosenberg (1998) and Scheingold (1989).

[8] Sunstein 1995: 727.

Drawing on the Irish experience, the Indian constitution distinguished between enforceable fundamental rights, which were to be protected from incursions by the state, and non-enforceable directive principles, which were goals and duties of the state and included social and cultural rights highlighted in the Universal Declaration of Human Rights; the International Covenant on Civil and Political Rights; and the International Covenant on Social, Economic and Cultural Rights. It was "the intention of the Assembly that in future both the legislature and the executive should not merely pay lip-service to these principles enacted in this part but that they should be made the basis of all executive and legislative action that may be taken thereafter in the matter of governance of the country," said B. R. Ambedkar, the chairman of the constitution drafting committee.[9] The framers made the fulfillment of the rights to food, health, and basic education contingent on the state's economic capacity.

The people, rather than the courts, were supposed to prod the state to provide these goods.

India is a federal republic with a Westminster-style parliamentary system, a strong central government and a unified judiciary under an apex court. The Supreme Court, assisted by twenty-one high courts and numerous lower courts, is often described as the most powerful court in the world.[10] The Supreme Court has original, appellate, and advisory jurisdiction on any dispute between the central and state governments, and between state governments. Apart from a brief hiatus during an emergency regime (1975–77), the Supreme Court has rebuffed every legislative amendment aimed at curtailing judicial review and even increased its power to interpret the constitution through a basic structure doctrine.[11] Judicial independence increased in the early 1990s when the apex court appropriated the power to appoint itself and lower court judges.[12]

But this power is offset by the high case load because the apex court, unlike its American counterpart, has no control over its docket. As one serving judge pointed out, the government (a litigant in more than 70 percent of the cases) is responsible for the high caseload because it appeals automatically when it loses in a lower

---

[9] Constituent Assembly Debates. Also see Austin 1996.

[10] The decision of the Supreme Court is binding on all courts in India (Article 141) and noncompliance invites contempt of court (Articles 129, 142, and 215). The Supreme Court possesses advisory jurisdiction in matters referred to it by the president of India under Article 143. The court possesses some structural judicial independence from the executive – the president appoints judges to the Supreme Court (who then retire at the age of sixty-five) after consultation with the chief justice (CJ) and members of the government. At the intermediate appellate level, the high court stands at the head of a state's judicial administration. The high court CJ is appointed by the president, in consultation with the CJ of India and the governor of the state. Other high court judges are appointed after consultations with the high court CJ. Apart from writ jurisdiction and legal and fundamental rights, the high court has jurisdiction over all lower courts in its territory. District-level courts are at the bottom of the integrated judiciary. Trial work occurs at the bottommost level, whereas the other two have trial and appellate jurisdiction. Unlike in the United States, these levels administer state and federal laws. In addition to the formal legal apparatus, a parallel informal system of *lok adalat* (people's courts) exists to resolve disputes in a conciliatory manner.

[11] Kesavananda Bharati v. State of Kerala, 4 SCC 225 (1973); Muralidhar 2002.

[12] Supreme Court Advocates on Record Case (MANU 1994).

court.[13] Epp (1998) highlights the incoherence in the Supreme Court's agenda caused by overload in cases, fragmentation of the twenty-six supreme court justices into small panels that allows inconsistency to creep into decision making, and the short terms served by the justices (one to six years). Of approximately 100,000 cases (admitted and pending) in 2006, the court disposed of 56,540 cases, which means that each judge dealt with 3,846 cases that year.[14] A high court judge deals with seventy to one hundred cases a day. These institutional obstacles raise questions about whether judges even have the time to be activist on non-enforceable social and economic rights.

In the initial decades after independence in 1947, the Supreme Court endorsed the distinction between fundamental rights and directive principles citing the economic incapacity of the state.[15] By the 1970s, the court (nudged by the executive) shifted toward the view that one of the basic features of the constitution was harmony and balance between the directive principles and fundamental rights.[16] The judges began incorporating rights to health, food, education, shelter, and so forth into the fundamental rights to equality (Article 14) and life and liberty (Article 21).

Why the shift? Scholars attribute the transformation to the post-emergency attempt by judges to recoup legitimacy after their capitulation to an authoritarian executive from 1975 to 1977. According to legal scholar Upendra Baxi, "Judicial populism was partly an aspect of post-emergency catharsis. . . . Partly, it was an attempt to refurbish the image of the court tarnished by a few emergency decisions and also an attempt to seek new, historical bases of legitimation of judicial power."[17] Judicial activism of the post-emergency period, according to Sathe (2002), involved a liberal interpretation of constitutional provisions like Articles 21 and 14 and the reconceptualization of the judicial process by making it more accessible and partici-patory. There is some basis to this claim because the judges who were tarred by their acquiescence to the executive during the emergency era were also among those who championed the court's orientation toward social rights. Supreme Court judges like Krishna Iyer and P. N. Bhagwati liberalized rules of locus standi (the right to bring an action) and simplified the appeals process through the introduction of public interest litigation (PIL).[18] Common law systems permit only those persons whose rights are directly affected to approach the court. The PIL system allows any member of the public (individuals or NGOs) to espouse public interest causes by sending a letter or petition to the Supreme Court (and now also to the high

---

[13] The observation was reiterated in other studies on the judiciary. See Galanter and Krishnan 2004 and Sathe 2002.

[14] Hazra and Debroy (2006) point out that if a case takes more than three years to be decided, then chances are that it will take more than ten years to get a judgment.

[15] Rao, Justice K. Subba. 1970. Human rights. *SCC (Jour)* 1(56). State of Madras v. Champakam Dorairajan, 1951.

[16] Minerva Mills v. Union of India, 6 SCC 325 (1980).

[17] Baxi 1985.

[18] See Vandenhole 2002 on the difference between public interest litigation (PIL) and social action litigation. In this chapter we use the term *PIL* because it is the term used by the Indian courts.

courts). Since the mid-1980s, the court has heard PILs on environment, women's rights, and poverty issues, among others, brought by public-spirited individuals and organizations.[19] The Right to Information Act, 2005, provided a new tool for NGOs to litigate on some socioeconomic rights. For instance, NGOs spearheading the right-to-food campaign decided to approach the Supreme Court after the Right to Information Act allowed them to see letters between the central and state government on food stocks.[20]

Some analysts charge that the courts used PILs as a tool to creatively read rights into the constitution, later becoming law makers, and even super-executives.[21] Is the observation valid? Let us examine the behavior of the higher courts in health and education.

DEFINING A RIGHT TO HEALTH AND EDUCATION

In 1992, a minority opinion of Justice K. Ramaswamy in a three judge panel (which included the Chief Justice) argued:

> The term health implies more than an absence of sickness. Medical care and health facilities not only protect against sickness but also ensure stable manpower for economic development. Facilities of health and medical care generate devotion and dedication to give the workers' best, physically as well as mentally, in productivity... In the light of Articles 22 to 25 of the Universal Declaration of Human Rights, International Convention on Economic, Social and Cultural Rights, and in the light of socio-economic justice assured in our constitution, right to health is a fundamental human right to workmen.[22]

Although commending Ramaswamy for his concern, the majority opinion, however, held that in the absence of legislation, one could not talk of a right to health. Health and education rights of citizens including securing the health and strength of workers (Article 39e), effective provision within the limits of the state's economic capacity for rights to work, education and public assistance in event of unemployment, old age, and sickness (Article 41), and raising the level of nutrition and standard of living and public health (Article 47) belonged to non-enforceable directive principles.

By 1997, the minority ruling had become settled law that "right to health is integral to right to life" and the government had a "constitutional obligation to provide the health facilities" for its employees, which later expanded to cover all citizens by the turn of the century.[23]

---

[19] The case of Hussainara Khatoon v. Home Secy, State of Bihar, 1 SCC 108 (1980), was one of the first PILs to be tried by the Supreme Court. However, the PIL system has increased the workload of an already overworked apex court. To prevent misuse, a committee reviews the PIL petitions and sends legitimate ones to the justices, but even this is not sufficient.

[20] Interview with Mr. Anup Srivastava, Human Rights Law Network, New Delhi, January 30, 2006.

[21] Dam 2005; Andhyarujina 1992.

[22] CESC v. Subhash Chandra Bose and Others (AIR 1992 SC 573).

[23] State of Punjab v. Mohinder Singh Chawala (AIR 1997 SC 1225).

In 1992, the court declared that all citizens had a right to education.

Every child of this country has the right to free education until he completes the age of 14 years. Thereafter his right to education is subject to the limits of economic capacity . . . the effect of holding that the right to education is implicit in the right to life is that the state cannot deprive the citizen of his right to education except in accordance with the procedure prescribed by law.[24]

Did judges address the main problems in the sectors? Did these judgments have any impact on the government's health or education policies? A big problem with linking judgments to policies is the following: How does one determine whether the court was responsible for a policy? For instance, ten years after *Unnikrishnan*, the Parliament passed the eighty-sixth constitutional amendment providing for free and compulsory education for all children between six to fourteen years as a fundamental right under Article 21A. But interviews with government officials and other experts suggest that the amendment was induced by political motives (it was piloted as part of an election promise by a political party) rather than the court's ruling.[25] The fate of the Right to Education Bill in 2005, slated for debate in parliament in 2006, and then shelved indefinitely by the government on grounds of a budgetary crunch, confirms their contention. In this study, the court would have an impact on policy if the government or the relevant institution cites the judgment as the reason for formulating it. To assess the impact on policy, we must examine the extent and impact of legalization of health and education rights.

THE LEGALIZATION OF ECONOMIC AND SOCIAL DEMANDS

The extent of legalization depends on three factors: demands made for these rights in court, ease of litigation, and the enforcement of a decision. We collected cases in the higher courts where the judges or litigants explicitly used the right to health or education to justify their arguments. Our analysis captures only a fraction of the total litigation on health and education, but we deliberately limited our scope to assess the impact of courts on policy because a court's use of a right to health or education would have greater legal and policy influence. We focused on the higher judiciary because they establish the final interpretations of the law and were most likely to influence policy.

---

[24] Appellants: Unni Krishnan, J. P. and Others v. Respondent: State of Andhra Pradesh and Others (MANU 04.02.1993). It clarified the position in Mohini Jain v. State of Karnataka and Others (MANU 30.07.1992) that gave all citizens at all levels a right to education. A high court judgment, Smt. Ranjanben Rambhai Patel, President v. State of Gujarat (MANU 24.09.2001), expanded it to include pre-primary education in Gujarat.

[25] An education ministry official said that the amendment was due to political and economic considerations such as the need to develop an indigenous skill base to meet the demands of economic liberalization (interview with Amit Choudhary, MoHRD, New Delhi, January 31, 2006). Others in the NGO sector point to a link between the judgment and the amendment. The answer seems somewhere in between – the judgment provided a rationale when the government was ready to undertake the legislation.

Table 4.1. *Health and education cases profile*

Category of states	Total cases	Impact favors citizen	Impact does not favor citizen	Private obligation	Government obligation	PIL	Writ petition	Other
BIMARU	64	49	15	25	35	8	15	41
Non-BIMARU	318	248	70	118	180	39	110	169

From 1950 to 2006, the Supreme Court alone disposed of 1,158,303 cases, and the twenty-one high courts disposed of hundreds of thousands of cases each, of which cases dealing with a right to health or education (HE) composed only 382 cases.[26] Using the classification of socioeconomic rights that Gauri and Brinks develop in the introduction to this volume, almost half the caseload on HE rights dealt with enforcing the obligations of providers and clients, whereas a third focused on regulation.[27] Only 15 percent involved provision and financing of health care or education. The impact of the decision in more than 80 percent of the cases favored a citizen's right to health and education.

Table 4.1 shows that the impact of the judgments overwhelmingly favored the citizen rather than the violator, who could be the plaintiff or defendant; poor (BIMARU) states had significantly lower rates of litigation on HE, and PILs were used in only a third of the cases.[28] Only eight PILs were registered from poor states and were successful in 75 percent of the cases. The state/government was the defendant in 77 percent of the cases, whereas individuals (43 percent),

[26] Supreme Court Registrar, March 2007. These cases were collected using a keyword search on an online Web site of high court and Supreme Court cases (Manupatra.com). Supreme Court cases are of two types: those that were appealed from the lower high court and those that were sent directly as a PIL (e.g., the right-to-food cases). Not all cases decided in the courts are reported, and not all reported cases are published in the Supreme Court Recorder or the All India Reporter (for high courts). It was hard to get an accurate estimate of the percentage of cases that are reported – the Supreme Court Registrar said it did not have the figure. Manupatra reports 80 to 90 percent of the cases where judgments were reported; our sample captured 80 to 90 percent of the Manupatra cases. We used a keyword search including combinations such as "health/education and fundamental rights," "right to health/education," articles in the directive principles dealing with health and education, "public health," "medical negligence," "HIV/AIDS," "medicines," "drug policy," "blood banks," "primary schools," "PILs," and so forth. The sample is not comprehensive. Please note that the cases do not include ongoing petitions nor environmental cases (except insofar as the latter include references to the "right to health"). Moreover, we do not examine the tens of thousands of cases in the lower courts, medical councils, consumer courts, lok adalats, national human rights commissions, and a number of tribunals. We also do not examine out-of-court settlements or cases that are negotiated outside with the threat of a court ruling.

[27] Regulatory issues included duties outlined by state for providers (environmental cases on clean air, regulation of private schools); provision or financing included legally reviewable duties between state and clients (duties to make services more accessible to new clients like nonresident Indians (NRIs) and duties to increase financing for education to comply with statutory requirements); and provider–recipient obligations included state providers' and private providers' obligations to citizens, and vice versa.

[28] Bihar, Madhya Pradesh, Rajasthan, and Uttar Pradesh are referred to as BIMARU states. These states typically have lower incomes and literacy rates than other states of India.

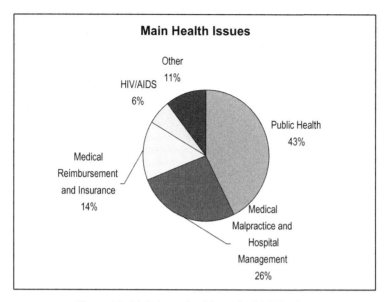

Main Health Issues

Figure 4.1. Main issues in right-to-health litigation.

NGOs/public-spirited citizens (19 percent) private institutions (16 percent), and unions (12 percent) were the main plaintiffs.

THE EXTENT OF LEGALIZATION IN HEALTH

Of the 209 right-to-health cases, only a quarter were decided in the Supreme Court. The rest were in the high courts, with 70 percent of the cases litigated in Delhi, Bombay, Allahabad, and the southern states. Regulation accounted for the bulk (44%) of the cases, followed by provider/client obligations (35%) and provision/financing (18%). The state was the defendant in 86 percent of the cases, but was likely to win only around 30 percent of the time. Figure 4.1 illustrates the kinds of issues that right-to-health cases address.

Despite the high (80 percent) success rate of PILs, only a fifth of the health cases were PILs. These cases focused on the absence rather than the quality of facilities promised by the government.[29] These low rates of litigation by NGOs confirm the contention that the rights-based approach to social needs in India was judge-led rather than NGO-led (Epp, 1998).[30] It corroborates other research on the negligible emphasis by NGOs on litigation as a public action strategy owing to the time-consuming and costly nature of approaching courts and the poor

---

[29] India does not have a system of class action suits. We classified cases registered by NGOs as collective cases to enable cross-country comparisons.

[30] The low representation of PILs in our caseload may also be because most PILs are ongoing and involve a series of interim orders passed by the court, which were not included in our sample. Even so, a review of ongoing petitions does not significantly increase the number of PILs relative to a total caseload that incorporated ongoing non-PIL petitions.

Table 4.2. *Winners in right to health litigation*

Issues	Individual v. state	Individual v. private institutions	NGO v. state	Private institutions v. state	Unions v. state	Total
Public health	7 (14)	1 (1)	34 (40)	4 (16)	2 (8)	48 (79)
Med negligence	12 (18)	5 (6)	5 (7)	0	1 (2)	23 (33)
Med reimbursement	23 (25)	0	0	0	1 (2)	24 (27)
HIV	4 (6)	1 (2)	3 (3)	1 (1)	0	9 (12)
Other	5 (6)	1 (1)	4 (5)	0 (1)	0	10 (13)
TOTAL	51 (69)	8 (10)	46 (55)	5 (18)	4 (12)	114 (164)

Note: Numbers denote winning cases; total cases are in parentheses.

enforcement of decisions.[31] Although more than half the cases were filed after 1997 and 70 percent of the cases were decided within two years of being registered in the relevant court, a case could take more than five years if it was appealed in the Supreme Court.[32]

The higher levels of litigation in urban areas and richer states reflect the importance of income and access to courts in facilitating litigation. Poor people rarely approached courts, and when they did, it was through NGOs.[33] For instance, several cases dealt with the reimbursement of hospital expenses incurred by middle class government employees. Public health concerns were reflected predominantly by NGOs or public-spirited persons who were plaintiffs in more than 50 percent of these cases and won more than 80 percent of the time (Table 4.2).

Using the notion of a right to life with dignity, judges expanded the ambit of health to include physical, social, and mental well-being and aimed at the policy goals of a healthy environment, nutrition, and socioeconomic justice. Table 4.2 shows that against the state, individuals won 73 percent of the time, doing so overwhelmingly in medical reimbursement and HIV cases, and less so in medical negligence cases, and had only a 50 percent chance of winning in public health cases. NGOs won 80 percent of their cases against the state, whereas private institutions and unions were less likely to win against the state.

The pro-citizen trend of judgments was uniform across health issues. But what do the judgments imply for the effective enjoyment of these rights by the citizens? Did judges address the main issues plaguing the health sector and deliver effective rights to citizens? Effective rights means that individuals are likely to get the social good they ought to receive. The next section examines that issue.

[31] Krishnan 2006.
[32] Note that the length of time was calculated using the date filed and date decided in a particular court. The time does not include time spent in lower courts before the appeal to the higher judiciary. Galanter and Krishnan (2004) point out that there were 23 million pending cases in India as of 2001, of which about 20,000 were in the Supreme Court, 3.2 million in the High Courts, and 20 million in lower/subordinate courts. Seventy percent of the backlog dealt with criminal cases. In the high courts, more than half the cases were more than three years old, 37 percent were more than five years old, 14 percent were more than ten years old; more than 60 percent had the government as a party to the case.
[33] Bandhua Mukti Morcha v. Union of India and Others (SC, PIL 1983).

THE IMPACT OF LEGALIZATION IN HEALTH

The impact of legalization depends on the enforcement of the decision in conjunction with the relevance to the broader needs of the health sector.[34] India accounts for a third of global tuberculosis (TB) incidence and the largest number of active TB patients, 20 to 30 million episodes of malaria per year, and the largest number of HIV-positive persons in the world, though proportionately prevalence is low compared to many developing countries.[35] The health-care system in India favors those who can pay. In India, the richest fifth receives three times the curative health-care subsidy of the poorest fifth.[36] A World Health Organization (WHO) report revealed that public health subsidies disproportionately benefit higher quintiles, though such imbalance was lower in southern states.[37] Southern and western states performed well on health indicators, but BIMARU states did poorly. In India's federal setup, health is a shared subject between the center and states.[38] Despite the availability of free medical treatment in government hospitals, poor people prefer private providers because of the inefficiency of the state-run services.[39] Medical care is now the second most common cause of rural family debt. The number of people not taking any treatment in the mid-1990s because they could not afford it was double what it was a decade earlier, composing nearly one in every four rural Indians and one in five urban Indians.[40] This stemmed from a mismatch between stated goals and low levels of public expenditure, 0.9 percent of the gross domestic product (GDP) on medical services (versus 2.2 percent by lower-middle income countries).[41]

The urgent requirements were the reform of the public delivery of curative services (more doctors, equipment, and medicines), the provision of municipal services for a disease-free existence, and the regulation of private health care, particularly the complaints mechanism.[42] How does the litigation address these

---

[34] The main legislation in public health are Public Health Acts (which have not been updated since the colonial era) and Prevention of Food Adulteration Act, 1954 (which focuses more on punishing offenders rather than educating businesses on hygiene). The food sector is governed by multiple laws in different ministries.

[35] More than 5.1 million Indians, mostly from Maharashtra, Goa, Karnataka, Manipur, Mizoram, and Nagaland, are infected with HIV, with World Health Organization estimates projecting 35 million by 2015 (UNAIDS 2003).

[36] *World Development Report 2004*, p.3.

[37] Misra, R., R. Chatterjee, and S. Rao. 2003.

[38] Although the Central Council for Health and Family Welfare sets the goals and strategies for the public sector in health care after consultations with all levels, states are primarily accountable for service delivery through a network of primary health care centers. Both the center and the states have a joint responsibility for programs listed under the concurrent list, including social security, social insurance, medical professions, and prevention of epidemics.

[39] The government provides publicly financed and managed curative and preventive health services from primary to tertiary level, accounting for about 18 percent of the overall health spending. The private sector, which mainly provides primary health care, plays a dominant role in the provision of individual curative care through ambulatory services and accounts for about 82 percent of the overall health expenditure and 4.2 percent of the GDP. Private profit-oriented curative services account for 80 percent of medical services in India.

[40] Sainath 2006.

[41] *Id.*

[42] World Health Organization, *The India health report*. Available from http://www.who.int/countries/ind/en/.

issues? The attitude of courts varied depending on whether the issue was a tussle between an employer and employee, state and citizen, provider and client, or regulation of providers.

Provider–Client Claims: Medical Negligence and Medical Reimbursement

Courts had a direct influence on making doctors legally accountable for negligence, and an indirect influence on facilitating a complaints redressal mechanism. Medical malpractice suits favored the patient's rights a majority of the time even though the burden of proof to demonstrate negligence rested on the patient. More than half of the thirty-three cases were brought by individuals (patients) against state-run hospitals and doctors, 66 percent of the rulings favored patients, and the enforcement mechanism was clearly specified with damages and time limits (see Table 4.2). Doctors were defendants in a third of the cases, and only one case was registered in a poor state. In *Jacob Mathew*, the apex court framed guidelines under which a doctor could be tried in criminal courts for negligence. "Negligence is the breach of a duty caused by omission to do something which a reasonable man guided by those considerations which ordinarily regulate the conduct of human affairs would do, or doing something which a prudent and reasonable man would not do."[43] Intention and lack of proper care and caution were key in determining negligence. A doctor would have "no absolute or total immunity . . . from liability for his negligence."[44] In *Cosmopolitan Hospitals*, the court allowed patients to get remedies through the consumer redressal forum.[45] Consequently, except primary health centers and hospitals that offered free treatment to all patients, all doctors and hospitals are now liable under the Consumer Protection Act.[46]

The court favored the patient when a delay in operating and providing oxygen led to brain damage, an abdominal pack was left in the body, death was caused by failure to perform an appendicitis surgery, and the state's failure to maintain electric lines led to amputation and death.[47] The court said,

> If people go to such Government Hospitals and Public Health Centres for improvement of their health but instead return with further damage to their health on account of infection at such Government Hospital or Public Health Centre,

---

[43] Jacob Mathew v. State of Punjab and Another (MANU SC0457/2005).
[44] Dr. C. S. Subramanian and Others v. Kumarasamy and Others (MANU 1994); Naseema Firdous and Others v. State of Jammu & Kashmir and Others (MANU 2001).
[45] Cosmopolitan Hospitals and Another v. Vasantha P. Nair and v. V. P. Santha and Others; Dr. A. Indira Narayanan v. Government of India and Others (MANU 1993), Saroj Iyer and Another v. Maharashtra Medical of Indian Medicine, Bombay and Another (MANU 2001); T. T. Thomas v. Eliza (MANU 1986); Gurukutty v. Rajkaran (MANU 1991).
[46] Redressal forums have been established at the district, state, and national levels.
[47] Mr. Sakil Mohammed Vakil Khan v. Dr. Miss Perin Irani and Others (1999 (4) Bom CR65); Jasbir Kaur and Another v. State of Punjab and Others (MANU 1995); Arun Balakrishnan Iyer and Another v. Soni Hospital and Others (MANU 2003), Mrs. Arpana Dutta v. Apollo Hospitals Enterprises and Others (MANU 2000); Miss Haneefa Bano v. State of J&K and Others (MANU 1997); Joginder Kour and Another v. State and Others (MANU 2004); State of Tripura and Another v. Amrita Bala Sen and Others (MANU 2004).

their fundamental right to life under Article 21 of the Constitution would stand infringed.[48]

But judges were aware of the limits of their expertise. In complex operations or where the technical equipment did not reveal complications, the court gave the benefit of doubt to the doctor/institution.[49]

Medical reimbursement cases constituting 16 percent of the health cases were primarily about the obligations of the state to its primarily middle class employees. In nearly 90 percent of the cases, the court favored full reimbursement of medical expenses of the employee-patient, arguing that a welfare state had a constitutional obligation under Article 21 and Article 47 to provide health facilities to its employees. The remedies were straightforward – judges fixed the amount of damages to be paid within a time limit, with monetary penalties for noncompliance. The court's intervention had a larger policy impact, albeit for a small and already favored fraction of the population (about 10 percent of the population consists of formal sector workers and their families) – eligibility requirements were relaxed to include new entitlements and new classes of persons, and even overturned existing policies. At the high court level, the judges extended the coverage to new groups such as wives, pensioners, and municipal pensioners.[50] The judgments also expanded the entitlement package to cover emergency treatment in private hospitals, specialized equipment, and expensive treatment.[51]

State–Private Provider Regulation

Judges backed the state's regulation of the private sector, which had only a 28 percent chance of victory when bringing cases against the state.[52] Manufacturers challenged government orders regulating the manufacture and sale of alcoholic and addictive substances. The court ruled that because the state was bound to uphold the right to life and health (Articles 21 and 45), it could limit the sale of *gutka* and *pan masala,* ban the supply of country liquor in polyethylene sachets and abolish country liquor shops. The right to work (Article 19) was not absolute and would be subservient to public health. "Adulterated foodstuff have a direct bearing on public health... well settled principles relating to the matters pertaining to

---

[48] Haripada Saha and Another v. State of Tripura (MANU 2000).

[49] Prabha G. Nair v. Mohanan (MANU 2001); Philips India Ltd. v. Kunju Punnu and Another (MANU 1974); Venkatesh Iyer v. Bombay Hospital Trust and Others (MANU 1998); Rukmani v. State of Tamilnadu, rep. by its Secretary, Health Department and The Dean, Government Hospital (MANU 2003); Dr. Smt. Beena Yadu v. State (MANU 2003); Dr. J. N. Shrivastava v. Rambiharilal and Others (MANU 1980); Ismat Sara v. State of Karnataka (MANU 1980).

[50] S. K. Sharma v. Union of India and Another (Delhi HC); Kamlesh Sharma v. Municipal Corporation of Delhi and Another (Delhi HC); 2002; Keshav Kishore Sharma v. Municipal Corp. of Delhi (Delhi HC).

[51] K. S. Mathew v. Union of India, (Delhi HC, 2002–05); Narendra Pal Singh v. Union of India and Others. (Delhi HC 1998–99); P. R. Kanwar through Indra Kumar v. Union of India and Another (Delhi HC: 1999–2003); Prithvi Nath Chopra v. Union of India and Another (Delhi HC: 2003–4); R.D. Gupta v. DDA and Others (Delhi HC: 2003–5); V. K.Gupta v. Union of India and Another (Delhi HC: 2001–2).

[52] Of the twenty-five cases where private companies were plaintiffs, the court upheld only seven cases.

public health should be kept in mind by the Court while approaching such matters. Attending to public health is of the highest priority perhaps the one at the top," said the court.[53]

In cases where the government had failed to comply with existing rules on medicines, the judges asked the government to follow its guidelines on the manufacture and procurement of oral polio vaccine, the associations of drugs and pharmaceuticals to follow new rules issued by the government in line with WHO guidelines, and the government to pass legislation mandating severe punishment to those involved in the manufacture of spurious drugs.[54] The court was more effective with specific types of noncompliance; it imposed fines on a chemist for selling spurious drugs and reprimanded the government for not prosecuting the accused, and found a hospital guilty of purchasing contaminated IV fluids at exorbitant prices.[55] Few cases dealt with poor access to medicines by the vulnerable groups. Only three high court cases dealt with drug policies, of which only one dealt with the culpability of the chemist in selling spurious drugs. One reason for the low caseload on access to medicines could be that generic medicines in India are relatively inexpensive. However, with the Trade Related Aspects of Intellectual Property Rights (TRIPS) compliance by India in 2005 (as compared to Brazil, which adopted the patents regime in 1995), we may see an increase in litigation on access to medicines in the next decade.[56]

Some judgments were more contentious, drawing criticism that the legal rulings could be hijacked by vested interests. For instance, the judges did not recognize practitioners of alternative medicine as doctors because they had not been certified by the Indian Medical Council.[57] This and other rulings on environmental cases raise questions about the capacity of judges to grapple with complicated public policy issues, which will be addressed in the final section. The high caseload coupled with the short stints of judges at the apex court did not allow sustained scrutiny of compliance. High court judges have a longer tenure (twelve to eighteen years) but their high caseload (eighty to one hundred cases a day) does not give them time to

---

[53] Dhariwal Industries Ltd. and Another v. Union of India and Others (Bom HC 1982–2002); Shivashakti Agency v. State of AP and Others (AP HC 2002).

[54] PUCL v. Union of India and Others (Del HC, PIL, 1996–2003) – "The Ministry of Health and the Director General of Health Services and other concerned agencies without further loss of time must ensure [within three months] that the drug manufacturers should not be permitted to market their drugs unless the quality of the drug is approved by a high level committee or body consisting of doctors and other experts of impeccable integrity and eminence."

[55] Sahil Society for the Welfare of Aged Poor and Homeless, v. UoI and Another (Al HC, PIL 1998); Association of Drugs and Pharmaceuticals v. AP Health and Infrastructure (MANU 2001); State of Maharashtra v. Jethmal Himatmal Jain and Another (MANU 1994).

[56] The TRIPS Agreement prescribes universal minimum standards for seven types of intellectual property rights including patents. The implication of conforming to patents is that pharmaceutical companies can no longer manufacture generic drugs until the expiry of twenty years of the patented life of the medicine. The TRIPS regime would cut off the current supply of generic drugs by Indian companies at affordable prices to many parts of the world, reducing access to new and affordable medicines.

[57] Rajesh Kumar Srivastava v. A.P. Verma and Others (MANU 2005); Charan Singh and Others v. State of U.P. and Others (MANU 2004); Electro Homoeopathic Practitioners Association of India and Another v. A. P. Verma, Chief Secretary, Government of U.P. and Others (MANU 2004).

monitor compliance. Evidence from the judgments indicates that once the court's scrutiny lapsed, the situation reverted to status quo ante – and judges were aware of it.[58]

State–Citizen Obligations: Public Health and Medical Services

Public health and medical services posed the most complex and urgent problems in the health sector. The court had a direct policy impact on legally increasing the access of citizens to medical services and free antiretrovirals for HIV patients. One judgment said:

> This is a welfare State, and the people have a right to get proper medical treatment. In this connection, it may be mentioned that in U.S.A. and Canada there is a law that no hospital can refuse medical treatment of a person on the ground of his poverty or inability to pay. In our opinion, Article 21 of the Constitution, as interpreted in a series of judgments of the Supreme Court, has the same legal effect.[59]

However, as we shall see shortly, when it came to enforcement, it was a different story. The judges, who turned a deaf ear to the government's pleas about a resource crunch, said that the state was constitutionally responsible for providing citizens with potable water, clean environment, and sanitation as part of the right to life.[60] "By affirmative action, the court could compel a statutory body to carry out its duties to the community including creation of sanitary conditions," said the court in a *suo moto* (on its own motion) case on the degradation of Jaipur city.[61] Similarly, in environmental disasters such as the leakage of poisonous gas in Bhopal from a Union Carbide plant, which caused the deaths of more than 2,500 persons and damaged the health of thousands, the higher judiciary gave compensation to the victims and directed and monitored compliance by the state in establishing a specialized hospital. The court favored the maintenance of ecology and pollution-free air in urban and residential areas and asked industries like stone crushing units, rice mills, and brick kilns to shift.[62] But in activities beneficial to the public such as hospitals in residential areas, the courts dismissed petitions from the residents.

---

[58] See Koolwal v. State of Rajasthan (1986).

[59] CVL Narasimha Rao v. Principal Secretary, Medical and Health Dept. (PIL, MANU 2001).

[60] Constitutional Article 243W read with Schedule XII (entries 5, 6, and 12) states that it is the duty of Municipal Authorities to provide clean drinking water. Siromani Mittasala, Chairman, Paryavarana Parirakshaka Parishad v. President, Brindavanam Colony, Welfare Association (AP HC, PIL, 2001); S. K Garg v. Respondent: State of U P. and Others (Al HC, PIL, 1998); Dr. K.C. Malhotra v. State of MP and Others (MP HC, PIL, 1992–93); Prasanta Kumar Rout, Orissa Law Reviews v. Respondent: Government of Orissa, Represented by Secretary, Urban Development Department and Others (Or HC PIL, 1994).

[61] Suo Moto v. State of Rajasthan (Raj HC, 2004).

[62] T. RamaKrishna Rao v. Chairman, Hyderabad Urban Development Authority, Hyd. and Others (AP HC, 1998–2001); Kamlawati v. Kotwal and Others (Allahabad HC PIL, 2000); Obayya Pujary and Others v. The Member Secretary, Karnataka State Pollution Control Board, Bangalore and Others (Kar HC, PIL); Rural Litigation and Entitlement Kendra, Dehradun and Others v. State of U.P. and Others (SC, PIL); Research Foundation for Science, Technology and Natural Resources Policy v. Union of India (UOI) and Others (SC); Vivek Srivastava son of Late Sri J. P. Srivastava v. Respondent: Union of India (UOI) through its Secretary, Ministry of Defence and Others (Al HC

Several judgments increased the access and availability of medical treatment to citizens. The court issued guidelines to hospitals on providing medical facilities to accident victims, banned strikes by doctors in tertiary referral hospitals because it would infringe the right to medical treatment, and quashed a notification appointing doctors on contract saying that the right to life demanded proper treatment, which could be ensured only through fair selection and regularized appointments.[63]

However, the court was more circumspect on the issue of quality of services provided by the state. Relatively few cases dealt with the quality and provision of medical services in rural areas, including the pitiable conditions of government hospitals, health centers, and doctors.[64] The court opted to apply indirect pressure on the government through weak remedies such as committees to improve and fill vacancies in primary health care centers and address the concerns of doctors.[65]

Prevention and Treatment of Key Public Health Concerns

As noted earlier, India is poised to become the world capital of HIV-infected persons by 2015. The major problems in HIV are the regulation and removal of unsafe practices (e.g., blood-screening practices), enforcing provider–client treatment and employment obligations, and allocation of adequate funds for public education and treatment.[66] A handful of cases dealt with provision and financing of medicines for HIV/AIDS, and 75 percent of HIV rulings favored "public health." The low use of litigation (only twelve cases) by patients, NGOs and the court itself is striking, and reflects the importance of prior legislation and civil society litigation for the court's intervention.

The high courts expanded the access to free medical treatment to AIDS patients including armed personnel and prostitutes, asked the state to start public education on safe sex practices for prostitutes, provided maintenance for a wife suffering from HIV contracted through blood transfusion during pregnancy, said that the right of a fiancée to a healthy existence (Article 21) overrode the HIV-positive man's right to privacy,[67] gave back wages to a casual laborer who had been deleted from the selection panel because of his HIV-positive state, lowered the cost of diagnostic

---

2004–5); C. Kenchappa and Others v. State of Karnataka and Others (Kar HC, PIL); K. Muniswamy Gowda and Another v. State of Karnataka and Others (Kar HC).

[63] Chander Prakash v. Ministry of Health, Nirman Bhavan. (Del HC, treated as PIL, 2001); Court on Its Own Motion v. All India Institute of Medical Sciences (Del HC, 2001–2); Junior Doctor Association v. State of Jharkhand and Others (Jhar HC, 2003–4).

[64] C. V. L. Narasimha Rao v. Respondent: Principal Secretary, Medical and Health Dept. and Others (AP HC, PIL, W.P. No. 11542 of 2001); S. K. Garg, advocate v. State of U.P. and Others (AL HC, PIL,1998); Siddha Raj Dhadda v. State of Rajasthan (MANU PIL 1989).

[65] Salekh Chand Jain v. Union of India and Others (Del HC, PIL, 2002); Supreme Court Young Advocates Forum v. Union of India and Others (Del HC, 1997–02).

[66] The center is supposed to provide funds to states so that they can deal with treatment of opportunistic infections like tuberculosis. Of the 600 INR ($15) that the government spends annually per person on health care, per capita expenditure on HIV/AIDS is less than a dollar. Contrast this with estimates by a Delhi-based NGO, the Lawyers Collective, of US $1,000 needed per annum for antiretrovirals and care. Source: http://www.indiatogether.org/2003/oct/hlt-aidsmed.htm

[67] Dr. Tokugha Yepthomi v. Apollo Hospital Enterprises Ltd. (AIR 1999 SC 495).

kits,[68] instituted free medical treatment to HIV-positive prisoners, and deleted a clause from an insurance policy because it excluded poor people.[69]

High court judgments had a direct legal effect in two key areas: they reduced the cost of antiretroviral (ARV) kits and facilitated a government policy to provide free ARVs. The Human Rights Law Network along with the Punjab Voluntary Health Association (VHA) filed a petition in the Supreme Court in 2003, asking for free and equitable access to ARV treatment.[70] The court issued notices to the government National AIDS Control Organisation (NACO) and the state governments. The Delhi Network of Positive People, an NGO formed by persons living with AIDS, dashed off a similar petition to the Delhi High Court asking for free access to medicines, treatment, and care. Earlier petitions by the VHA dealt with equitable treatment of AIDS patients by health-care workers and the right to a safe working environment for health-care workers and doctors.[71] In response to the Punjab petition and pressure from domestic and international actors, the Indian government announced a new policy in 2003 of providing free ARVs to one hundred thousand patients in six high incidence states by 2005.[72] From March 2006, three ARV drugs (which cost 3,000 INR [Indian rupees] or approximately US$75) were available free of cost to patients below the poverty line at all Delhi hospitals. However, none of the twenty-six hospitals had kits to detect the extent of HIV infection and calculate the dosage of ARVs.[73] But the legal effect did not translate into effective rights for 770,000 (WHO estimate) AIDS patients who are too poor to afford even the reduced cost ARV kits, while their access to free ARVs was stymied by poor compliance by the government. Only 10,255 patients had enrolled in the program by July 2005.[74]

AN OVERALL ASSESSMENT OF THE COURT'S IMPACT ON HEALTH POLICY AND THE EFFECTIVE DELIVERY OF RIGHTS

The evidence shows that the judiciary directly facilitated policies that increased legal access to medical services, environmentally friendly areas, and regulatory mechanisms. First, the court's rulings expanded access of some services (like

---

[68] Merind Ltd. v. State of Maharashtra (6/5/2004 Bombay HC).

[69] L.I.C. of India and Another v. Consumer Education and Research Centre and Others (SC Civil Appeal No. 7711 of 1994). The plaintiff, an NGO, asked for a declaration from the court that the insurance policy confining benefits only to the salaried class from government, semi-government, or reputed commercial firms was discriminatory and offended Article 14. Denial thereof to larger segments, including the poor, violates their constitutional rights. The judges agreed with the plaintiff.

[70] Voluntary Health Association of Punjab v. Union of India (Writ Petition Civil, 311/2003).

[71] http://www.globalpolicy.org/socecon/develop/aids/2003/0913indiaarv.htm

[72] Nick Robinson, Courting the last option, *Hard News*, http://www.hardnewsmedia.com/portal/2005/10/157

[73] Teena Thacker 2006. From March, HIV drugs free at govt hospitals, *Indian Express*, February 19.

[74] The irony is that Indian pharmaceutical companies (one of the largest exporters of ARVs) have been instrumental in reducing the price to US$350, but it is the poor in other countries like Brazil who have benefited. At present, only public schemes such as the Employees State Insurance Scheme, Central Government Health Scheme, and the railways give free ARVs, medicines, and care to their effected employees, who compose a fraction of the 5.1 million HIV afflicted.

medical reimbursement, access to ARVs, food, use of consumer courts to complain about doctors) to new classes of beneficiaries. The judges were instrumental in expanding the ambit of the right to food to all states even though the initial case was registered in Rajasthan. The court's receptiveness to the petition prompted the original plaintiff (an NGO) to file PILs on the right to food in a number of regional high courts. Although the introduction of cooked midday meals in primary schools "would not have happened without the Supreme Court cracking the whip,"[75] the court's effectiveness in mandating enforcement of its directives has been low. In an attempt to cope with the ramifications of the court's rulings on the right to food, the government introduced an education levy to finance a midday meal scheme in schools.

Second, the court also influenced new policies on health-related issues such as a ban on smoking in public places in Kerala, a switch to clean fuels in Delhi and Mumbai, and oversight of the pesticide content in soft drinks such as Pepsi and Coke.[76] Citing the obligation of the government to improve public nutrition (Article 47), the court struck down a new method of distributing sugar, which allotted more quantity to persons with higher income, saying it would result in inequitable distribution and nutrition.[77]

A 1996 apex court judgment, which came in response to a PIL on the malpractices and malfunctioning of blood banks, directed the government to set up a national council and state councils of blood transfusion and to consider legislation on regulating blood banks.[78] An analysis of the court's role in the eventual regulation of blood banks illustrates the promise and the inadequacy of court interventions. The councils were established in most states by 2004 with budgets allotted by NACO, and a national blood policy was evolved in 2000 to finance, regulate, and provide safe and adequate quantity of blood, blood components, and blood products.[79] Government officials claimed that "the blood transfusion service has sufficiently been cleaned up based upon the Supreme Court order . . . the percentage of HIV infection occurring through blood has come down from 8 percent to 3.4 percent in the last four years."[80] However, experts point out that the transfusion of infected blood continues to be responsible for around 6 percent of AIDS and hepatitis cases in the country.[81] Drug controllers were ill-equipped to

---

[75] Dreze 2003.

[76] K. Ramakrishnan and Another v. State of Kerala and Others (Ker HC, 1998–99); Smoke Affected Residents Forum v. Municipal Corporation of Greater Mumbai and Others (Bom HC 2002); Karnataka Lorry Malikara Okkuta (R), by its General Secretary and Others v. The State of Karnataka, by its Chief Secretary and Others (Kar HC); M. C. Mehta v. Union of India and Others (SC, Writ Petition (C) No. 13029 of 1985); Santhosh Mittal v. State of Rajastahan and Others (SC PIL).

[77] R. Ramanujam Chettiar v. The Commissioner and Secretary to the Government of Tamil Nadu, Food and Co-operative Dept., Madras (Mad HC, 1981).

[78] Common Cause v. Union of India and Others, PIL, 1996. See the NACO Web site (http://www. nacoonline.org/program.htm) for a summary of government actions on Supreme Court directives.

[79] http://bloodbanksdelhi.com/content/NationalBloodPolicy2002.htm.

[80] J V. R. Prasad Rao, additional secretary, Health, quoted by Nidhi Srivastav: "Experts call for a national blood policy," Express Healthcare Management, http://www.expresshealthcaremgmt.com/20020131/transfusion1.shtml.

[81] http://www.hinduonnet.com/fline/fl2214/stories/20050715001008500.htm.

handle the task of monitoring blood banks because of the multiplicity of agencies involved, whereas advisory councils lacked the authority to punish erring blood banks. These inefficiencies generated a gap between growing demand and reduced supply of clean blood, leading to noncompliance by commercial blood banks who do not always conduct the prescribed tests and the illegal reentry of professional blood donors, who had been banned in 1998.

The judiciary had an indirect impact on facilitating regulatory mechanisms of nongovernmental agencies. The Supreme Court prodded the Medical Council of India to institute a formalized mechanism for hearing complaints on medical negligence. "The decision to formulate guidelines has been taken in view of the Supreme Court directive in the Malay Ganguly Case, which was a PIL filed in the year 2000 [decided in 2003] alleging lack of transparency and lack of proper mechanism on the part of MCI in dealing with cases of medical negligence."[82]

Thus, despite the expansive nature of the judgments, selective impact on some policies, and the expansion of selected social goods to new classes of beneficiaries, the courts had a limited and indirect impact on increasing the efficacy and access of citizens to better health. The courts avoided grappling with core issues of poor management of the public health and medical services by the government. And NGOs and others did not challenge these gaps in court. Only one PIL dealt with the poor functioning of a state AIDS Control Program and the judgment said that "the funds released by the Government of India shall not be diverted to any other Heads of Account except for the purpose of implementation of the programme as per guidelines and strategies formulated by the NACO and the funds withheld so far shall be released for the Programme."[83] The poor enforcement of these directives, addressed in the final section, highlights the question of the court's effectiveness in generating policy and delivering health rights to citizens. But first, let us examine the situation of education rights.

THE EXTENT OF LEGALIZATION IN EDUCATION

Forty-five years after independence, the court transformed education into a fundamental right for children ages six to fourteen years. We looked at all cases where either the litigant or the court expressly relied on the right to education to argue its position. The constitution promises the right only to children in primary and elementary education, but in our cases we included secondary school cases within "schools" and university-level cases in "university." Let us examine the patterns in court.

Only 47 percent of cases focused on primary (the focus of the right) and secondary education, whereas the rest (including most Supreme Court rulings) related to university-level concerns. At the high court level, of the 149 cases, Allahabad, Bombay, and the four southern states accounted for half the litigation. Despite

---

[82] See Jayshree Padmini, MCI drafts investigation guidelines for professional misconduct, available at http://www.expresshealthcaremgmt.com/20030228/policy.shtml. Malay Ganguly v. Respondent: Medical Council of India and Others, Writ Petition (C) No. 317 of 2000.
[83] Subodh Sarma and Another v. State of Assam and Others (PIL) (1996–2000).

Table 4.3. *Winners in right to education litigation*

Issues	Individuals v. state	Individuals v. private	NGOs v. state	Private v. State	Unions v. State	Total
Students	34 (51)	2 (5)	4 (5)	0 (2)	4 (5)	44 (68)
Teachers	4 (8)	2 (2)	2 (3)	1 (1)	10 (15)	19 (29)
Private Sector/ Minority Institution	2 (3)	1 (3)	1 (2)	15 (33)	0 (1)	19 (42)
Government	0 (1)			1 (1)	1 (2)	
Other	1 (1)		1 (1)		0 (1)	2 (3)
TOTAL	41 (64)	5 (10)	8 (11)	16 (36)	15 (23)	85 (144)

Note: Numbers denote winning cases; total cases are in parentheses.

experiencing much greater need in this area, the poorer BIMARU states accounted for only 28 percent of primary and secondary school-level cases (mainly teacher, student, and private-sector issues) and 18 percent of university-level cases. Figure 4.2 shows the distribution of education cases across courts of different jurisdictions.

As figure 4.3 shows, individuals, private institutions, and unions (mainly student and teacher) – the more literate, urban, and well-off sections – were most likely to come to court. The negligible use of courts by NGOs (7 percent of plaintiffs) is evident from the fact that PILs accounted for only 4 percent of the cases. The Supreme Court dealt mainly with university-level issues relating to the autonomy of private and minority institutions to admit students, charge capitation fees, charge differential fees, and general administration. These cases mainly focused on the access of well-off students to higher education rather than the access and quality of education for the poorer sections. A handful of cases dealt with the poor quality of rural schools and teacher absence. Admissions, exams, and activities of students accounted for 45 percent of the caseload, whereas 32 percent of cases were brought by private institutions on issues relating to autonomy, permission to start new schools/universities, and affirmative action. Obligations (62 percent) between the providers and citizens were more frequently litigated than were regulation (25 percent) and provision/financing (13 percent).

COURTS' JUDGMENTS

An overwhelming majority of judgments favored a citizen's right to education. About 77 percent of the cases were decided within two years in the high court, and if appealed, within four years from start to finish; so judges seemed to be aware of the time constraints imposed by the academic system.

The state, which was the defendant in 80 percent of the cases, lost more often than it won. NGOs had a high success rate, followed by individuals and unions, who won 65 percent of the time, whereas the private sector had a 44 percent chance of victory against the state. Individual plaintiffs arguing for student-related issues had a 67 percent chance of winning in court against the state, while teacher salary and tenure issues had a 66 percent chance of success. Individuals had only a 50 percent

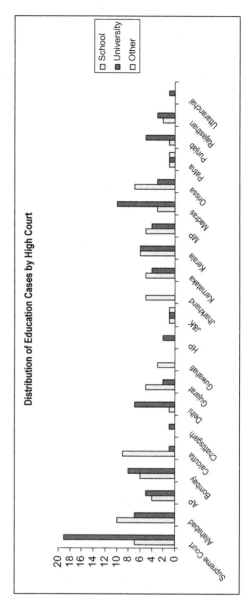

Figure 4.2. Number and kinds of right-to-education cases, by court.

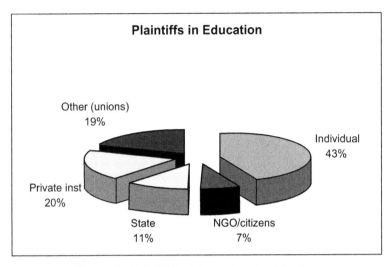

Figure 4.3. Plaintiffs in right-to-education litigation.

chance of winning against private and minority institutions. If one were to loosely group NGOs and unions into collective cases and compare them to noncollective cases, both had approximately similar chances of victory (65 percent).[84] The courts commonly used the fundamental right to education and public safety arguments to favor education rights. A second-rung rationale involved the "duty of the state" argument. So, for instance, the courts said student safety included physical and mental safety, which meant that they deserved access to better-quality education. Does this mean that judges had a great impact on policies and an effective right to education?

THE IMPACT OF LEGALIZATION ON EDUCATION

The litigation patterns did not reflect the main sectoral concerns: high dropout rates, poor teaching record evident from the low functional literacy and numeracy of students, rampant teacher absence, and poor quality of school infrastructure.[85] Most cases dealt with access rather than quality. The caseload in court reflects the malaise affecting the education sector in India, where the emphasis is on access, often at the expense of quality and learning outcomes. India has one of the largest education systems in the world. At the elementary level, of the 931,471 schools in twenty-five states, 80 percent were located in rural areas. The government ran 65 percent of the schools and the rest were managed by private (government

[84] Note that India does not have class action suits. For purposes of comparison with Brazil, we grouped NGO-led cases and cases registered by unions (teachers, doctors, students) as collective cases.

[85] Issues relating to student admissions and exam policies were found in Calcutta, Gujarat, Kerala, MP, Bombay, and Delhi; teachers appointments, and salaries were among the main issues in Jharkhand, AP, Gujarat, Rajashtan, and Allahabad; autonomy, clearances, and functioning of private institutions were litigated in Calcutta, AP, Bombay, Jharkhand, Kerala, and Karnataka; at the Supreme Court, the issue of distribution was fairly equal among teachers, government policies, and private institutions.

Table 4.4. *Main issues and impact in right-to-education cases*

Issues	Total cases	Primary and secondary (77 total cases)		University (87 total cases)	
		Alleged rights violator wins	Citizen wins	Alleged rights violator wins	Citizen wins
Access, Admissions, fees	54	5	7	5	29
Teacher presence (salaries, selection, tenure)	29	0	23	0	5
Infrastructure (facilities, new institute approvals, etc.)	41	3	17	1	19
Quality (exams, teaching)	25	3	5	2	10
Autonomy of private/minority institutions	15	2	7	0	4
TOTAL	164	13	59	8	67

aided and unaided) organizations.[86] The government launched the Sarva Shiksha Abhiyan (SSA) program to achieve universal primary education by 2007, but the results were mixed. School infrastructure was poor: only 42 percent of schools had common toilets, and not all schools had drinking water facilities. Boys outnumbered girls in enrollment, with the poorer BIMARU states showing the lowest enrollment for girls; there were low Scheduled Caste (20.84 percent) and Scheduled Tribe (9.71 percent) enrollments in government-run schools. Surveys by the National Institute for Education Planning and Administration (NIEPA) show that about 42 percent of children drop out of school before reaching Grade V. The average pupil–teacher ratio was 39 to 1. Almost forty-four thousand schools were getting by with para-teachers rather than regular appointees.

Table 4.4 shows that access and quality issues at the primary school level – a key area of concern for the state – took a backseat to litigation on teacher-related issues of salary and tenure. The judgments overwhelmingly favored teachers when they challenged the state on appointments, parity of pay, and other issues discussed in the next section, but there were almost no cases on teacher absence and quality of teaching. Private institutions managed by religious minorities and others often came to court and won their cases against the state's intervention in their institutions. Very few cases focused on the functioning of government schools. In a case in Meghalaya, the courts said that public schools established and maintained by the government and providing quality education with better

---

[86] *NIEPA 2004 report*, available at http://educationforallinindia.com/anlayticalreport2004summary.pdf.

facilities than those of government primary and upper primary schools could not be made beyond the reach of weaker sections of the society by fixing higher fees for the students.[87] At the university level, admissions- and fee-related issues followed by new institute approvals and facilities and conduct of exams were the main areas of litigation. Let us examine the main issues fought out in court.

Students (Access and Quality of Education)

Admissions (access to education) were among the most frequently litigated issues in primary education. The judges supported students when the authorities acted in an arbitrary fashion in admission, expulsion, and exam policies;[88] banned corporal punishment on grounds that it affected attendance and increased the dropout rate;[89] and included the right to study in a language medium of one's choice in the right to education.[90] Very few cases focused on the quality of education. The courts increased the facilities for children by mandating that the government provide free textbooks until Grade IV.

> In view of the fact that a large amount of rupees 827.39 crores is available for primary education, it cannot be said that the financial position of the state is such that it is not possible for the state government to provide for free text-books to students below the age of 14 and studying standards I to IV. The financial requirements as envisaged in article 41 of the constitution is thus met with.[91]

Courts held the government in contempt for not complying with the court's directions in granting courses; allowed the state to make policy decisions to improve the quality of education by mandating that school children pass a middle standard exam within fourteen years, and study English/Hindi before taking the matriculation exam, and fulfill attendance requirements; allowed students who were unable to take exams because of riots to retake them;[92] and provided state financial aid

---

[87] Meghalaya Parents and Guardian Association v. State of Meghalaya and Others (MANU 2001); M. Meenakshi and Another v. Respondent: Principal, Kendriya Vidyalaya, NTPC (R) and Others (MANU 2003).

[88] Miss Lumbini Baruah v. Respondent: Cotton College, Guwahati and Others (MANU 20.08.1996); Harishankar Vishwakarma v. Respondent: Board of Secondary Education and Others (MANU 2003); Sweety Khandelwal and Others v. Respondent: Divisional Secretary, Board of Secondary Education, Indore and Others (MANU, 1994); Amarjeet Jena v. Respondent: Council of Higher Secondary Education, Orissa and Others (MANU 21.09.1998); Abu Zaid (minor) and Another v. Principal, Madrasa-Tul-Islah Saraimir, Azamgarh and Others (MANU 28.07.1998); Jaisree Pal and Others v. Respondent: State of West Bengal and Others (MANU, 1989).

[89] Parents Forum for Meaningful Education v. Union of India (MANU). In September 2006, in a *suo moto* case, the Himachal Pradesh High Court directed the police to investigate charges of corporal punishment in a school. See *Times of India*, September 12, 2006.

[90] Tamil Nadu Tamil and English Schools Association rep. by its General Secretary, Mr. B. T. Kumar v.The State of Tamil Nadu rep. by its Secretary to Government School Education Department (MANU 2004).

[91] Ganesh s/o Madhavrao Jadhav v. Respondent: The Maharashtra State Board of Secondary and Higher Secondary Education and Others (MANU14.08.1992).

[92] Shenaz Bannu and Mehboob Miya v. Respondent: State of Gujarat (MANU 05.07.2002).

to a school for students with handicaps, dismissing the government's excuses of a budgetary crunch and their contention that the deaf and hard of hearing were more capable than the blind.[93] The judges also tried to curtail misuse of the right by noting that no student could insist that a school of his choice should provide him with education in the manner he wanted or could get his exam papers reevaluated.[94]

Teachers (Selection, Salaries, and Quality)

Teacher absence and appointments are major concerns in education policy. Teacher absence ranged from 17 percent in Maharashtra to 30 percent in Bihar. From 2001 to 2004, of the 535,203 approved teacher positions at the all-India elementary level, only 310,506 positions had been filled.[95] The court cases did not reflect teacher absence, but did focus on the selection, salaries, and to a lesser extent on the quality of teachers. On selection criteria, the court upheld the parity of bachelor of education degrees with teacher training certificates and asked the state to appoint these teachers to the twenty-one thousand posts vacant in the primary school program.[96] The court rejected the government's decision to reserve seats for women and for science subjects in teacher appointments and prevented the state from unlawfully terminating a teacher appointed under a welfare scheme.[97]

A handful of cases touched on the quality of teachers. The court agreed with a PIL that only qualified teachers should be appointed to provide quality education to children and that criminals could not be presidents of educational institutions; and it dismissed petitions from teachers who were unqualified or who challenged universally applicable policy decisions of the state.[98] The judgments obliquely addressed teacher quality by instituting regular payment of salaries and parity of pay for teachers and nonteaching staff of private (government-aided) and public institutions. The judges said that irregular payments and inequality would result in disgruntled teachers and would negatively affect the quality of education.[99] The standard of teaching should not suffer because of nonpayment of salaries resulting from a budgetary crunch, said the court, pointing out that

---

[93] Annakutty Robert v. State of Kerala (MANU 2000); Devinder Kumar v. Punjab State and Others (MANU 1991); Miss Debopriya Ganguly v. Respondent: State of West Bengal and Others 2004; Ramchandra Tandi and 30 Others v. Respondent: State of Orissa and Others (MANU 17.03.1994).
[94] Midhun Murali (minor) v. Fertilizers and Chemicals, Travancore 1998; Sujit Kumar Banerjee and Others v. State of West Bengal; Kumud Singh v. Union of India (MANU 04.02.2005).
[95] Source: Indiastat.com.
[96] Ved Prakash Tiwari and Others v. State of U.P. (MANU 2003).
[97] Anand Kumar Tiwari v. State of U.P. and Others (MANU 2001); Kishanlal Kushwaha v. State of MP (MANU 2000).
[98] Binod Vikash Manch and Another v. Respondent: State of Jharkhand and Others (MANU PIL 2003); Padmanav Dehury v. State of Orissa (MANU 1998); Devendra Singh and Others v. State of U.P. (MANU 14.05.2004); Tahira and Others v. State and Others (MANU 2003).
[99] Smt Susheela Srivastava v. State of U.P. (MANU 1998); Sebastien v. State of Kerala (MANU 2001); Suresh Kumar Dwivedi v. State of MP (MANU 1993); SR Higher Secondary School v. State of Rajasthan (MANU 2002); Sirijit Chandra Singh v. Mr. J. R. Kalia, President, WWA Cossipore English School Managing Committee and Others (MANU 1.2.1999).

by denying primary school teachers proper salaries and allowances the state violated Articles 21, 14, and 19(1)(a) of the Constitution. The claim of the teachers
of the primary classes to get proper salaries and the fundamental right of children to get education were two sides to the same coin, said the court.[100] However, the court held, teachers had no right to strike despite nonpayment of their
salaries.[101]

> Since right to education is a fundamental right, and right to uninterrupted edu-
> cation in School or College is also a fundamental right, and that Articles 39, 41, 45
> and 46 have also highlighted the importance attached to children, this judgment
> [denying the teachers the right to strike] is made applicable not only to Govern-
> ment schools, Government aided schools, but – also to similar other schools and
> other institutions which impart education.[102]

Private Institutions: Regulation and Provider–Client Obligations

Private institutions frequently challenged access-related regulations of the government, such as the refusal of permission to establish new schools. In response, the
court said that the right to establish and administer an educational institution was
a fundamental right available to all, as was the right to impart education.[103] However, none had a right to get state recognition without satisfying the validly imposed
requirements of infrastructure, teacher recruitment, and so forth.[104] Poor quality,
particularly of private schools, was immediately penalized by the court. Unrecognized schools "with little or no infrastructure and with a lack of qualified teaching
staff cannot be permitted and the State would be justified in dealing with such
institutions with strictness."[105] Where government-aided schools lacked teachers
and other facilities because of a budgetary crunch, the court directed the state to
rectify the situation by supplying teachers.[106] The private sector also challenged

---

[100] Ramji Tiwari and Others v. District Inspector of Schools and Others (MANU 1997); Sonalben
Vasudev Prasad Jani v. Municipal Girls High School (MANU 2001); Sabita Swain and Others v.
Respondent: The State of Orissa and Others (MANU 2000).
[101] Ravindra Kumar, Advocate v. State of U.P. (MANU 1998). In response to teacher demands, the court
instead directed the state to increase its budgetary allocation for education.
[102] Sathyavan Kottarkkara v. State of Kerala (MANU 1996).
[103] For a contrary ruling, see Dwarika Prasad Pandey, Manager, Junior High School, Known as Shri
Chandra Shekhar Azad Poorv Madhyamik Vidyalay v. State of U.P. through its Principal Secretary,
Primary Education and Others, 2005.
[104] State of Karnataka v. Noble Saint Education Society (MANU 16.02.1993); St. Marina's Social
Welfare Association (Regd.) v. Respondent: Commissioner for Public Instruction (MANU 11.3.96);
West Bengal Board of Secondary Education v. Respondent: Dakhiruddin Khan and Others (MANU
2002); West Bengal Madrasah Education Board v. Respondent: Shaikh Sahajamal and Others. WITH
Appellants: Secretary W.B.B.S.E. and Others v. Respondent: Sadhana Banerjee and Others (MANU
2004); Kendua Rakshakali Vidyamandir and Others v. Respondent: West Bengal Board of Secondary
Education and Others (MANU 1999); In Re: Shri Jhalu Roy and Others v. Respondent: State of West
Bengal and Others (MANU 1999).
[105] Gramvikas Shikshan Prasarak Mandal, Sondoli, through its Chairman v. Respondent: The State of
Maharashtra and Others (MANU 11.4.2000); Joan of Arc v. Respondent: The Managing Trustees of
Thiruvalluvar Manram's Charitable Trust and Others (MANU 06.09.2000).
[106] Government Aided School Yaruingam v. State of Manipur (MANU 2000).

the government's incursions into its autonomy, to which the court replied that there was no right to impart education[107] and no right to government grants,[108] that government-funded private schools could not refuse to implement the government's reservation policies,[109] and that the state could regulate admissions and make reservation policies applicable to private unaided schools.[110]

Judges accepted budget shortfalls as a sufficient reason to close private schools because the private companies were not obliged to open schools when they could not afford to.[111] Neither was the government duty bound to pay salaries of teachers in aided higher secondary schools if it could not afford to do so.[112]

The court's impact on policy was primarily indirect – it upheld state policies on educational standards rather than force the government to formulate new policies. The court's rulings upheld quotas for "backward classes" in private schools, and policies on curriculum. In a few cases like *Ravindra Kumar, Advocate v. State of UP*, the court directed the state to increase budgetary allocation for education. It also expanded salary benefits to new classes of teachers and access to better-quality schools for poor people. However, the court's response fell short of addressing the key concerns in the sector – remedies focused on improving access rather than quality, and they penalized private rather than government providers for failing in their obligations.

If we assessed the court's impact vis-à-vis constitutional rights, then we would have to give judges a poor grade because a majority of the right-to-education cases were at the university level. In the next section, we ignore the constitutional extent of the right and focus more broadly on the court's impact on higher education.

University

The constitutional right to education was not meant for higher education, which suffered from lack of quality rather than access. However, litigants who came to court from educated, middle class, and urban areas used the right to argue for a host of issues ranging from a right to strike to a right to get government aid.

University-level students used a right to education to argue for admissions to professional courses, political activities on campus, and fees. The Supreme Court disagreed with a Delhi court decision and agreed with a Kerala court ruling that

---

[107] Dwarika Prasad Pandey, Manager, Junior High School, Known as Shri Chandra Shekhar Azad Poorv Madhyamik Vidyalay v. State of U.P. through its Principal Secretary, Primary Education and Others, 2005; Christ Church College v. State of U.P. (MANU 2004).

[108] Sri Ramanjaneyaswami Vidya Saunsthe, Kumbaloor, Honnali Taluk, Shimoga District v. Respondent: State of Karnataka and Others (MANU 9.12.99); Laxmidhar Pati and Others v. Respondent: State of Orissa and Others (MANU 1995); Keraleeya Samajam and Others v. Respondent: State of Maharashtra and Others (MANU).

[109] Diddi Rambabu v. Respondent: Principal, Hyderabad Public School, Ramanthapur and Others (MANU 1998); The Proprietary High School, Trust, Ahmedabad, and Others v. State of Gujarat and Another (MANU.1984).

[110] Gnyana Mandir Trust and Others v. State of Karnataka and Another (MANU 1.3.1996).

[111] Chatradhar Mahto and Others v. State of Jharkhand and Others (MANU 2003); Ranchi Zila Nagrick Unayan Parisad, H.E.C. Ltd. v. State of Jharkhand and Others (PIL MANU 2003).

[112] State of Kerala v. Manager, St Rochs (MANU 2002).

the right to participate in elections was a statutory right, not a fundamental one.[113] The high courts upheld the right of students to higher education and professional courses; rejected quotas for nonresident Indians (NRIs) but upheld reservations for Delhi city students in professional colleges; rejected an upper-age limit, a merit limit, and a time limit for applying to a course; and chastised the Calcutta government for "criminal" delay in publishing examination results. The court was more lenient when students and women were involved. It asked the college to admit a woman who had not received the relevant information by mail saying that the right to education of weaker sections, especially women, was important.[114] But powerful groups also benefited from the court's leniency; candidates admitted because of political influence were allowed to continue the course because it would affect their future. Some high courts had a more expansive interpretation of the state's obligations on education – a college had to resume teaching a course despite lack of funds.

Teachers got a favorable response from the court because of the need for "good quality teachers." On the issue of parity of pay for teachers of recognized, aided private schools with their counterparts in government schools and the subsequent obligation of the state to bear the expenditure, the judges argued that the state was obliged to treat both sets of teachers equally and should "endeavour to review and increase the budget allocation" for education.[115] The judges chastised the state government for ad hoc–ism in regularizing teacher appointments;[116] instructed the state to reappoint a librarian who had been fired because of withdrawal of government funding; and upheld a district-based selection of teachers in Himachal Pradesh on grounds that locals would know the culture better.[117]

Private institutions used the right to education to challenge nonrecognition by the government, but the court rejected these petitions on grounds of quality. The court held that the right to education did not include the right to conduct courses without government approval. "We cannot convert the University into an orphanage for these students," said the court in a judgment denying permission to an unrecognized college for veterinarians on grounds that these courses were specialized subjects needing course work and training.[118] The court objected to the policy of giving guest lecturers in Chennai preference during hiring, saying that

---

[113] University of Delhi and Another v. Shri Anand Vardhan Chandal (MANU 09.07.1996); Maharashtra State Board of Secondary and Higher Secondary Education v. Respondent: K. S. Gandhi and Others (MANU 12.03.1991); Anand Vardhan Chandel v. Univ. of Delhi (MANU 1978); Kerala Students Union v. Sojan Francis (MANU 2003–4); Vijaykumar v. State of Kerala (MANU 2003); Committee of Mgt SM College and Others v. State of U.P. (MANU 2004).

[114] Pratibha Singh v. Respondent: Dean, Lakshmi Bai National College of Physical Education, Gwalior, M.P. (MANU 1990).

[115] State of HP v. HP State Recognised and Aided Schools Managing Committtes and Others (MANU 10.05.1995).

[116] Sri Rabinarayan Mohapartra v. State of Orissa and Others (MANU 02.04.1991).

[117] Prafulla Kumar Sahoo v. Respondent: State of Orissa and Another (MANU 2002); Ms. Lalima Gupta and Another v. State of H.P. and Another (AIR 1993 HP 11; MANU/HP/0003/1993).

[118] Bharatiya Veterinary Educational Society, Bangalore and Others v. Respondent: State of Karnataka and Another etc. (MANU 29.9.85).

their quality was questionable.[119] Thus, courts acted as quality controllers, vetting the entry and operation of new institutions.

Government regulation was challenged on the issue of the extent of affirmative action in minority institutions and quotas in government and private colleges. In *Inamdar* the court clarified that private, minority, and nonminority self-financed institutions had the autonomy to fix fee structure and admissions policy, subject to reasonable restrictions of public interest.[120] Aided minority institutions would have to submit to some amount of regulation as a condition of receiving aid or recognition. The courts struck down 100 percent reservations for in-state students, saying that it contravened the right to education;[121] allowed quotas for candidates from hill areas because the beneficiaries were socially and educationally "backward" classes but deemed reservations for rural areas as unconstitutional because the classification was based on residence.[122] The courts said that the state had "the legal duty, subject to availability of the seats in the institutions, to make the right to medical education available to every eligible person";[123] but then chastised a southern state government for permitting medical colleges to overfill their seats.[124] One case even held that the state had a constitutional mandate (Articles 39 and 21) to grant legal aid to society and ought to permit a private entity to open a law college.[125] In one case, the apex court said that the government could be forced to provide grant in aid to government-recognized private law colleges, despite the government's argument that the judiciary was interfering in a policy decision. "It is open to the Court to direct the executive to carry out the directive principles of the Constitution, when there is inaction or slow action by the state."[126]

Overall, it appears that the courts have done little to secure the right of students to a decent primary and secondary education. The higher level of activity on private school and university education might be the result of more legal resources available to private providers, who can contest the state's accreditation decisions. Courts had a direct impact on quality by enforcing mechanisms to ensure that only good-quality private institutes were given approvals to run schools and universities. However, they could do little about the 65 percent of schools that were government run, which educated 73 percent of all enrolled students. Overall, the judiciary

---

[119] M. Saravanakumar v. Secy to Govt Edn Dept (MANU 2005).

[120] P.A. Inamdar and Others v. Respondent: State of Maharashtra and Others (MANU 12.08.2005); The Ahmedabad St Xavier's College Society and Another v. State of Gujarat (MANU 26.04.1974); Islamic Academy of Education and Another v. Respondent: State of Karnataka and Others (MANU 14.08.2003); Appellants: T.M.A. Pai Foundation and Others v. Respondent: State of Karnataka and Others (MANU 31.10.2002); and for the impact of the Pai judgment, see Sapthagiri Educational Trust v. Government of Pondicherry (MANU).

[121] Dr. Vipul Gupta v. State of U.P. through Secretary, Medical Education and Training and Others (MANU 2004).

[122] State of Uttar Pradesh and Others v. Respondent: Pradip Tandon and Others (MANU 19.11.1974).

[123] Samir Kumar Das v. State of Bihar and Others (MANU 1981).

[124] A citizen of India v. State of Karnataka and Others (MANU 20.09.1996).

[125] Bharati Vidyapeet v. State of Maharashtra and Others, AIR 2004 SC 1943 (2004), 11 SCC 755 MANU/SC/0251/2004.

[126] State of Maharashtra v. Manubhai Pragaji Vashi and Others (MANU 16.08.1995).

focused more on client–provider obligations and less on regulation and financing. The reason for this may well be that Indian courts, as courts elsewhere, see issues related to state provision and financing as a legislative or executive prerogative.

Let us now turn to the compliance with court orders. Our argument was that the judiciary was aware of its inability to elicit executive branch compliance because of its overloaded dockets, panel-style treatment of cases, rules regarding judicial tenure, and other institutional constraints. Therefore, it adopted weak remedies.

COMPLIANCE

More than half the cases in education and more than 60 percent in health were claims for government provision or regulation. According to Mark Tushnet (2004: 1906):

> Constitutional provisions allowing governments to adopt reasonable programs to achieve social welfare rights, a willingness to find some programs unreasonable and a remedial system that does not guarantee that any particular plaintiff will receive individualized relief: these are the characteristics of weak substantive social rights.

Tushnet outlines several types of weak remedies: declarations that identify the strength of the right rather than the remedies; or a requirement that the government develop plans (through committees or other means) within a reasonably short but unspecified time to eliminate constitutional violations. Indian judges used both types of weak remedies to deal with cases of government failures to meet statutory obligations. The court typically used two types of supervision for weak remedies:[127] (a) A supervising ministry or authority had to report to the court from time to time, following which the court would issue new directions;[128] and (b) in some cases, the court itself monitored implementation, leaving open the window for petitioners to come back to court if the directives were not implemented (as in the clean-air cases in Delhi).

In Table 4.5 the type of enforcement preferred by judges in cases involving the government shows that judges were more likely to favor a committee-style approach for public health issues where complexity was high and the judge's own grasp of the myriad interlocking policies was low. In medical reimbursement, a relatively less complex issue, we see more emphasis on time-bound actions with penalties for delays imposed on the states. In education, on the other hand, judges favored strong enforcement of government and private provider obligations. Of the seventy-eight cases where the government was a defendant, the court favored

---

[127] See Vandenhole 2002, which outlines ten categories of social action litigation in India and the limited impact of such litigation on the actual access to the rights.

[128] Bandhua Mukti Morcha; Rakesh Chand v. State of Bihar, Rural Litigation and Environment Kentra v. State of Uttar Pradesh; Saarthak Registered Society and Another v. Union of India (SC PIL 2001–2). The judges said that a board of visitors must be formed by the state mental health authority in every State within a time bound period and a compliance report be filed to the apex Court. Also see B. R. Kapoor and Another v. Union of India (UOI) and Others (SC PIL).

Table 4.5. *Enforcement mechanism in right-to-health cases involving government*

Issues	No enforcement mechanism	Committees	Strong enforcement	Status Quo	Other
Public health	0	28	6	8	3
Medical malpractice	3	3	12	8	5
Medical reimbursement	0	1	24	5	0
HIV/AIDS	0	3	4	0	0
Other	1	4	7	0	0

strong enforcement and the status quo a third of the time, and weak and no enforcement 10 percent of the time.

Judicial directions were usually couched in the language of suggestions and recommendations generated through committees. For instance, although agreeing with a PIL petitioner that authorities should not provide groundwater with a high fluoride content, the court *asked* the state to consider evacuating the affected villagers. The Calcutta high court judges *asked* the government to investigate charges that groundwater was contaminated because of overuse by soft drink companies, and *recommended* that the state make rainwater harvesting mandatory for these companies. It directed a committee to *examine* ways to improve services in government hospitals, and *asked* the government to pass legislation banning the use of carcinogenic insecticides and color additives.[129] The judges rarely issued strong remedies for government providers. In a Jharkhand case, the judge issued detailed instructions to local officials to certify within two months that the meals (served in a mandatory midday meal scheme) were fit for human consumption after an NGO filed a PIL alleging adulteration of the food.

Compare this to the compliance mechanism favored in education cases (Table 4.6). Judges opted for strong enforcement (with time limits and penalties) in 27 percent of the school and university cases, and weak enforcement in only 11 percent of the cases. Evidence from the follow up on enforcement of Delhi High Court education decisions suggests that the authorities complied with court directives. This could be because of the nature of these cases – follow up by the affected individuals and the relative noncomplexity of the solutions as compared to public health or medical negligence. Even here, the unwillingness of the court to penalize the government is evident in their satisfactory rating of the government's efforts to strengthen the standard of education despite criticism in a PIL on the government's inept implementation of compulsory elementary education.[130]

It is doubtful whether the reliance on intermediate mechanisms has helped in the effective delivery of social and economic rights. Judges were aware of the disconnect between their directives and the government's propensity for

---

[129] Dr. Ashok v. Union of India and Others (SC, PIL); Paschim Banga Khet Mazdoor Samity v. State of West Bengal and Another (SC PIL).
[130] Satya Pal Anand v. State of Gujarat (MANU 07.08.2000).

Table 4.6. *Enforcement mechanisms in right-to-education cases*

Enforcement mechanism	Student issues	Teacher issues	Private sector issues	Government sector issues	Other	Total
None	10	5	6	0	0	21
Committee	7	5	7	1	0	20
Strong enforcement	23	11	10	1	3	48
Status quo	32	9	27	1	3	72
Other	5	1	6	0	0	12
TOTAL	77	31	56	3	6	173

noncompliance but could do little about it.[131] The problem with weak remedies is the greater possibility that the rights remain unenforced – in several cases the government shelved committee reports citing budgetary shortfalls. Even when the court instituted time limits, enforcement depended more on monitoring by the litigant. The right-to-food and right-to-education campaigns demonstrate the importance of NGOs in monitoring progress.[132] Even when NGOs supervised progress, the results did not match the promise contained in the judgment. For instance, despite a Supreme Court judgment in 2001 giving each enrolled child up to Grade V, at least 300 kilocalories of a cooked meal, several glitches, including slow implementation in Bihar, Jharkhand, and Uttar Pradesh; poor quality of meals; and cost cutting by panchayats because of lack of separate earmarked funds for midday meals, undercut effectiveness. Despite judicial support, even the right-to-food campaign is looking beyond legal tools to carry out and sustain its work. Some of the problems of litigation included the access, time, funding, and efficacy of court judgments.[133] A survey of the court's orders shows that the state governments have been quite reluctant to enforce the directives. As Jean Dreze points out, the basic food policy remained unchanged even while committed civil servants did commendable work in specific areas, such as the Baran district in Rajasthan (Dreze 2003).

CONCLUSION

Critics and our opening quotes point to the recent spate of judgments on school admissions, affirmative action in elite institutions, and environmental policies

[131] See Koolwal v. State of Rajasthan (1986).

[132] In April 2001, a human rights NGO, the People's Union for Civil Liberties, filed a PIL with the Supreme Court saying that the central government and six state governments should be held responsible for mass malnutrition in their states. This was in the wake of several hundred starvation deaths in Orissa despite the fact that the granaries were full of rotting stocks. In one of its interim orders passed on November 28, 2001, the Supreme Court said that where people were unable to feed themselves adequately, the state had the obligation to provide for them. The order directed all state and central governments to ensure public awareness and transparency of these programs and introduce cooked midday meals in primary schools within six months. The order thus had the effect of converting the benefits of nutrition-related programs into legal entitlements. School authorities say that although enrollments have not improved, school attendance has gone up by 10 to 12 percent because of the scheme. (http://www.indiatogether.org/2006/dec/edu-midday.html).

[133] The campaign has seen thirty-two hearings over four years, with the Supreme Court allotting an hour every two to three months to hear each petition.

as an instance of larger involvement by the judiciary in policy making. They would be correct in the environmental arena, perhaps because of the greater NGO activity and interest of judges in the issues.[134] But in health and education, the patterns show low impact of courts on policies, the reluctance of judges to penalize government providers as compared to private providers, and the corresponding lack of emphasis by NGOs and others on litigation as a strategy to obtain social goods.

Judges could get involved if one of three conditions exists: (a) no law on the issue (judgments in the 1980s and 1990s transforming social rights into justiciable rights); (b) the legal framework exists but is not implemented (judgments on municipal failures to provide potable water); or (c) the legal framework is inadequate to meet new challenges (judgments on intellectual property rights and drug policies). Our evidence shows that the court's role in health and education policies was indirect and minimal at best, focusing more on (b) and less so on (a) and (c). Even here, the courts can only intervene if cases are brought before it. The low rates of litigation by NGOs and the minimal use of PILs confirm Epp's (1998) argument that social rights litigation (except environmental) lacks the support structures for a full-fledged rights revolution. Interviews with the right-to-food campaigners suggest that litigation has been time consuming, costly, and relatively ineffective as compared to traditional mobilization strategies. Social Jurist, a civil rights group consisting of lawyers and activists, filed several petitions in the Delhi High Court on health and education issues, but progress is slow.[135]

This can be explained by the fact that judges are members of an institution whose rules emphasize restraint rather than activism. The allocation of cases by the Chief Justice, lack of enforcement capacity, and the emphasis on collaboration rather than dissent in the two- or three-judge panels encourage conformity and status quo behavior. Judges realize that their decisions may not be enforced, and they will not be there long enough to ensure compliance. Hence, they only pick battles that they can win – less complex issues that pit the court against private providers rather than the government.

The behavior of the Indian courts belies theories about the conditions for activism. There are two sets of theories about the conditions for activism. "Juristocracy" theories focus on the motives underlying the creation or empowerment of the judiciary by legislators or other elites.[136] The argument is that political elites transfer power to judges in hopes that they will be conservative and/or protective of rights.[137] In India, the Supreme Court seized some elements of independence (the power to appoint itself) through its own judgments; political elites did not transfer power to judges. The second set of theories attributes such empowerment to legal choices of judges rather than to the short-term self-interest of elected power holders (Tate and Vallinder, 1995). In fact, Gillman (2002) points out that these scholars

---

[134] Some benches in the court are self-styled as "green" benches, and judges like former Supreme Court Justice Kuldip Singh proudly refer to themselves as green judges.

[135] PIL on deficiency of Delhi authorities in providing electricity, potable water, and decent toilets in schools (All India Lawyers Union v. Municipal Corporation of Delhi, C.W. No. 5329 of 1997 and C.W. No. 33 of 1998).

[136] See Voigt and Salzberger 2002 for an overview.

[137] Gillman 2002; Hirschl 2004.

saw activism as being inconsistent with the preferences of legislators. Within this tradition, one sees theories about fractured governments generating more room for expansion of judicial power or post-crisis judges engaging in activism (Tate, 1993). The transformation of unjusticiable social rights into legal ones in the post-emergency era confirms a post-crisis behavior, but the results from our analysis show that the position of judges on social rights was consistent with and not opposed to the promises of successive governments. Take the example of a right to education. The constitutional amendment was piloted in 1996 by a minister from a political party who had made it an election promise, and it finally passed during a different party's rule in 2002.

But it is not a completely pessimistic story. Court interventions did extend benefits to larger groups of beneficiaries and included poorer and backward classes. In health, the judgments expanded the concept of access, but not actual access to ARVs for the large number of AIDS patients. But the same example shows that the effective delivery of these rights depends on the government. Some findings from the Delhi High Court suggest that the court's scrutiny, in conjunction with NGO and media attention, may force the government to implement directives.[138]

The evidence raises concerns about whether the court is the right arena to ensure the provision of social goods like education and health. Are judges qualified to assess the implications of their judgments? For instance, a recent interim ruling by the Supreme Court permitting the implementation of a 2002 pharmaceutical policy that sought to put in place a mechanism that would allow the government to intervene when prices of essential drugs behaved abnormally was interpreted by the government as allowing a drug price-control policy. In education, it is debatable whether the court's ruling in *Unnikrishnan* has been beneficial or detrimental to the quality of learning. Preliminary evaluations of the government's SSA shows that the emphasis is on putting children in schools (i.e., the targets are met) rather than ensuring learning outcomes.[139] Even PILs have come under a huge strain. The Prime Minister warned that

> PILs have great utility in initiating corrective action, [but] PILs cannot become vehicles for settling political or other scores. We need standards and benchmarks for screening PILs so that only genuine PILs with a justiciable cause of action based on judicially manageable standards are taken up. This will also ensure consistency in judicial pronouncements ... the Supreme Court could take the lead in framing rules in this regard.[140]

Courts have at best provided temporary solutions to complex problems of public health and primary education, but they were more effective in addressing simpler issues dealing with government regulation of private providers and obligations of

---

[138] Our study tried to follow up on enforcement, but it was very difficult to track down the lawyers in regional courts because the bar associations did not keep record of the thousands of lawyers practicing in a high court.

[139] Bhandari 2006.

[140] Line dividing activism and over-reach is a thin one: PM's caution to bench, *Indian Express*, April 7, 2007.

private providers to citizens. The declaratory language of the judgments focused on the strength of the right rather than the remedies. Perhaps that is all overburdened and understaffed courts in countries like India can do.

BIBLIOGRAPHY

Andhyrarujina, T. R. 1992. *Judicial activism and constitutional democracy in India.* New Delhi: M. N. Tripathi Private Ltd.

Austin, G. 2000. The Supreme Court and custody of the constitution. In B. N. Kirpal et al (eds.). *Supreme but not infallible: Essays in honour of the Supreme Court of India* (pp.1–15). New Delhi: Oxford University Press.

Austin, G. 1996. *The Indian constitution: Cornerstone of a nation.* Oxford: Clarendon Press.

Barak, A. 2002. A judge on judging – The role of a supreme court in a democracy. *Harvard Law Review* 116: 16–162.

Baruka, G. C. 2007. Contemporary views on access to justice in India. In A. K. Hazra and B. Debroy (eds.), *Judicial reforms in India - Issues and aspects* (pp. 101–18). New Delhi: Academic Foundation.

Baxi, U. 1980. *Indian supreme court and politics.* Delhi: Eastern Book Company.

Baxi, U. 1985. Taking suffering seriously: Social action litigation in the Supreme Court of India. In R. S. R. Dhavan and S. Khurshid (eds.), *Judges and the judicial power* (pp. 289–315). Bombay: Tripathi.

Baxi, U. 2002. The (im)possibility of constitutional justice: Seismographic notes on Indian constitutionalism. In E. S. Z. Hasan and R. Sudarshan (eds.), *India's living constitution – Ideas, practices, and controversies* (pp. 31–63). New Delhi: Permanent Black.

Baxi, U. 2007. The rule of law in India. *SUR* 6: 7–27.

Bhandari, L. 2006. Class monitor needed. *Indian Express,* October 20, http://www.indianexpress.com/story/14984-2.html.

Cameron, C. M. 2002. Judicial independence: How can you tell it when you see it? And, who cares? In S. B. Burbank and B. Friedman (eds.), *Judicial independence at the crossroads: An interdisciplinary approach* (pp. 134–147). Thousand Oaks, CA: Sage.

Choudhry, S., and C. E. Hunter. 2003. Measuring judicial activism on the Supreme Court of Canada: A comment on *Newfoundland (Treasury Board) v. Nape. McGill Law Journal* 48: 525–562.

Clayton, C. W., and H. Gillman, eds. 1999. *The Supreme Court in American politics: New institutionalist interpretations.* Chicago: University of Chicago Press.

Cover, R. 1983. Nomos and narrative. *Harvard Law Review* 97: 4–68.

Dahl, R. 1957. Decision-making in a democracy: The Supreme Court as a national policy-maker. *Journal of Public Law* VI,(2): 279–95.

Dam, S. 2005. Lawmaking beyond lawmakers: Understanding the little right and the great wrong. *Tulane Journal of International and Comparative Law* 13: 109.

Das, G. 1987. *Supreme court in quest of identity.* Lucknow, India: Eastern Book Company.

Davis, D. (1992). The case against inclusion of socio-economic rights in a bill of rights except as directive principles. *South African Journal on Human Rights* 8: 475.

Desai, A. and S. Muralidhar. 2000. Public interest litigation: Potential and problems. In B. N. Kirpal et al (eds.). *Supreme but not infallible: Essays in honour of the Supreme Court of India.* New Delhi: Oxford University Press.

Dhavan, R. 1977. *The Supreme Court of India: A socio-legal analysis of its juristic techniques.* Bombay: N. M. Tripathi.

Dhavan, R. 1980. *Justice on trial: The Supreme Court today.* Allahabad, India: A. H. Wheeler & Co.

Dreze, J. 2003. Hunger admidst plenty. *India Together,* December 2003, http://www.indiatogether.org/2003/dec/pov-foodsec.htm

Dua, B. D. 1983. A study in executive-judicial conflict: The Indian case. *Asian Survey* 23(4): 463–483.

Dworkin, R. 1986. *Law's empire.* Cambridge, MA: Belknap Press.

Dworkin, R. 1999. *Taking rights seriously.* Delhi: Universal Law.

Epp, C. 1998. *The rights revolution.* Chicago: University of Chicago Press.

Epstein, L., ed. 1995. *Contemplating courts.* Washington, DC: Congressional Quarterly Press.

Epstein, L., and J. Knight. 1998. *The choices justices make.* Washington, DC: Congressional Quarterly Press.

Feeley, M., and E. Rubin. 1998. *Judicial policy making and the modern state: How the courts reformed America's prisons.* Cambridge: Cambridge University Press.

Ferejohn, J. 1999. Independent judges, dependent judiciary: Explaining judicial independence. *Southern California Law Review* 72(2–3): 353–84.

Forbath, W. E. 1994. Why is this rights talk different from all other rights talk? Demoting the court and reimagining the constitution. *Stanford Law Review* 46: 1771.

Gadbois, G. H. 1968. Indian Supreme Court judges – A portrait. *Law & Society Review* 3: 317–36.

Gadbois, G. H. 1977. Indian judicial behaviour. *Economic and Political Weekly,* 149–66.

Gadbois, G. H. 1985. The Supreme Court of India as a political institution. In *Judges and the judicial power,* R. Sudarshan Rajeev Dhavan and Salman Khurshid (eds.). Bombay: Sweet and Maxwell.

Gajendragadkar, P. B. 1965. *Law, liberty and social justice.* Bombay: New Age Printing Press.

Galanter, M. 1997. *Law and society in modern India.* Delhi: Oxford University Press.

Galanter, M., and J. K. Krishnan. 2004. Bread for the poor: Access to justice and the rights of the needy in India. *Hastings Law Journal* 55: 789–834.

Gillman, H. 2002. How political parties can use the courts to advance their agendas: Federal courts in the United States, 1875–1891. *American Political Science Review* 96: 511–524.

Goldstein, L. F. 2004. From democracy to juristocracy. *Law and Society Review* 38: 611.

Hazra, A. and B. Debroy, editors. 2006. *Judicial reforms in India: Issues and aspects.* New Delhi: Academic Foundation.

Helmke, G. 2002. The logic of strategic defection: Court-executive relations in Argentina under dictatorship and democracy. *American Political Science Review* 96(2): 291–303.

Hirschl, R. 2000. The political origins of judicial empowerment through constitutionalization: Lessons from four constitutional revolutions. *Law and Social Inquiry* 25(1): 91–149.

Hirschl, R. 2004. *Towards juristocracy – The origins and consequences of the new constitutionalism.* Cambridge, MA: Harvard University Press.

Hirschl, R., N. Tate, and T. Ginsburg. 2003. *Judicial review in new democracies – Constitutional courts in Asian cases.* Cambridge: Cambridge University Press.

Iyer, K. 1992. *Justice at crossroads.* New Delhi: Deep and Deep.

Iyer, K. 1987. *Our courts on trial.* New Delhi: B. R. Publishing.

Kashyap, S. 1994. *Our constitution.* Delh: National Book Trust.

Krishnan, J. 2006. Lawyering for a cause and experiences from abroad. *California Law Review* (March) 574–615.

Levi, E. H. 1949. *An introduction to legal reasoning.* Chicago: University of Chicago Press.

Llewellyn, K. 1931. Some realism about realism – Responding to Dean Pound. *Harvard Law Review* 44: 122–1264.

McCann, M. W., and G. L. Houseman, eds. 1989. *Judging the constitution – Critical essays on judicial lawmaking*. London: Scott, Foreman/Little, Brown Series in Political Science.

Mehta, P. B. 2005. India's judiciary: The promise of uncertainty. In D. Kapur and P. B. Mehta (eds.), *Public institutions in India*. New Delhi: Oxford University Press.

Misra, R., R. Chatterjee, and S. Rao. 2003. *India health report*. New Delhi: Oxford University Press.

Muralidhar, S. 2002. Implementation of court orders in the area of economic, social and cultural rights: An overview of the experience of the Indian judiciary. Paper presented at the First South Asian Regional Judicial Colloquium on Access to Justice, New Delhi, November 1–3.

Rao, K. S. 1974. *Social justice and law. First Shyama Prasad Mookerjee memorial lectures*. New Delhi: National Publishing House.

Rau, B. N. 1960. *India's constitution in the making*. Edited by B. Shiva Rao. Bombay: Orient Longmans.

Rosenberg, G. N. 1991. *The hollow hope: Can courts bring about social change?* Chicago: University of Chicago Press.

Rosenberg, G. N. 1992. Judicial independence and the reality of political power. *Review of Politics* 54: 369–398.

Rosenberg, G. N. 1998. Knowledge and desire: Thinking about courts and social change. In D. Schultz, *Leveraging the law – Using the courts to achieve social change*. New York: Peter Lang

Rosencranz, A., and M. Jackson. 2003. The Delhi pollution case: The Supreme Court of India and the limits of judicial power. *Columbia Journal of Environmental Law* 28: 223.

Sainath, P. 2006. The health of nations. *India Together*, February 18, http://www.indiatogether.org/2006/jan/psa-health.htm.

Sathe, S. P. 2002a. *Judicial activism in India*. Delhi: Oxford University Press.

Sathe, S. P. 2002b. Judicial enforcement of socio-economic and cultural rights. Paper presented at the First South Asian Regional Judicial Colloquium on Access to Justice, New Delhi, November 1–3.

Scheingold, S. 1989. Constitutional rights and social change: Civil rights in perspective. In M. W. McCann and G. L. Houseman (eds.), *Judging the constitution – Critical essays on judicial lawmaking*. London: Scott, Foreman/Little, Brown Series in Political Science.

Seervai, H. M. 1983. *Constitutional law of India* (3rd ed.). New Delhi: N.M. Tripathy.

Segal, J., and H. Spaeth. 2002. *The Supreme Court and the attitudinal model revisited*. Cambridge: Cambridge University Press.

Sen, A., and J. Dreze. 1995. *India: Development and participation*. New Delhi: Oxford University Press.

Setalvad, A. M. 2000. The Supreme Court on human rights and social justice: Changing perspectives. In B. N. Kirpal et al (eds.). *Supreme but not infallible: Essays in honour of the Supreme Court of India* (pp. 232–255). New Delhi: Oxford University Press.

Shapiro, M., and A. S. Sweet. 2002. *On law, politics and judicialization*. Oxford: Oxford University Press.

Shue, H. 1980. *Basic rights: Subsistence, affluence, and U.S. foreign policy* (2nd ed.). Princeton, NJ: Princeton University Press.

Sousa, M. 2006. Judicial roles in the policy making process and public policy in Latin America. Paper presented at the American Political Science Association, Philadelphia, August 31.

Sunstein, C. R. 1995. Propter honoris respectum: Rights and their critics. *Notre Dame Law Review* 70: 727.

Tate, C. N. 1993. Courts and crisis regimes – A theory sketch with Asian case studies. *Political Research Quarterly* 46(2): 311–38.

Tate, C. N., and T. Vallinder. 1995. The global expansion of judicial power: The judicialization of politics. In C. N. Tate and T. Vallinder (eds.), *The global expansion of judicial power* (pp. 1–24). New York: New York University Press.

Tushnet, M. 2004. Symposium: Constitutional courts in the field of power politics: Social welfare rights and the forms of judicial review. *Texas Law Review* 82: 1895.

UNAIDS. 2003. *AIDS Epidemic Update*. Available from: data.unaids.org/Publications/IRC-pub06/JC943-EpiUpdate2003_en.pdf.

Verma, J. S. 2007. The Indian polity: Separation of powers. Pandit Kunji Lal Dubey Memorial Lecture. April 26, 2007. Available here: http://speakerloksabha.nic.in/speech/SpeechDetails.asp?SpeechId=212.

Vandenhole, W. 2002. Human rights law, development and social action litigation in India. *Asia Pacific Journal on Human Rights and the Law* 2:136–210.

Voigt, S., and E. M. Salzberger. 2002. Choosing not to choose: When politicians choose to delegate powers. *Kyklos* 55(2): 289–310.

5 The Impact of Economic and Social Rights in Nigeria: An Assessment of the Legal Framework for Implementing Education and Health as Human Rights

CHIDI ANSELM ODINKALU[1]

A lot of falsehood has been published over the years in newspapers about my government and I never lose sleep over them because less than five per cent of Borno people can read and understand what is written in newspapers.[2]

INTRODUCTION

Development requires open and accountable government, which, in turn, needs a healthy and educated population. Conversely, a population that is destitute in both health and awareness is more likely than not to suffer bad government gladly. Public-policy making, especially in developing contexts such as Nigeria, involves the allocation of public resources for the realization and advancement of development as a public good. As a public good, development – or what African leaders in the New Partnerships for Africa's development have called "people-centered development,"[3] extends to the all-round betterment of human well-being and is guaranteed by the strength, legitimacy, and effectiveness of public institutions, including the judiciary and administrative machinery of government. Irrespective of how the public interest in these outcomes is framed in law or the constitution, it remains true that the governance context largely frames its realization or

---

[1] Senior Legal Officer, Open Society Justice Initiative. The views expressed here are those of the author and do not represent the views and opinions of the Open Society Institute, the Open Society Justice Initiative, or any of the associated foundations of the Open Society Network. The author acknowledges the invaluable research assistance of Saka Azimazi, Legal Officer with the Nigerian National Human Rights Commission; Tony Nwapa, Justice Initiative Fellow and Co-Director of the Rights Enforcement and Public Law Centre (REPLACE) in Abuja, Nigeria; and Hope Krukru, LL.M. Class of 2007, Faculty of Law, Department of Law with International Relations, University of Kent, Canterbury, United Kingdom. Responsibility for any errors or inaccuracies in the text that follows remains entirely attributable to the author alone.

[2] Alhaji Ali Modu Sherrif, Governor of Borno State (in northeastern Nigeria), justifying why the high rate of illiteracy in his state has enured him against criticism and negative press, as quoted in the newspaper *Thisday*, Thursday, December 14, 2006, 97 (backpage).

[3] NEPAD Base Document, adopted in Abuja, Nigeria, October 23, 2001, para. 7.

frustration. This context, in turn, is a function of "a political environment which guarantees human rights and the rule of law, [which is] popular-based."[4]

Good government is founded on a tripod of three values: credibility, accountability, and capacity. The credibility of the government is essential for and reinforces its service delivery. *Credibility* is a function of the nature of government's electoral legitimacy or mandate, its fidelity to the norms of political behavior and attention to guaranteeing essential public goods. *Accountability* has both political and institutional dimensions. Politically, it speaks to the ability of people to participate in their government, and if necessary, to change it through transparent electoral processes; institutionally, it refers to how far the institutions and mechanisms of government are able to play their roles in ensuring that government operates properly within the law. Implicit in the political, institutional, and service delivery dimensions of government is the assumption that there is the institutional *capacity* to fulfill these functions. This institutional capacity is to be found in the independence and capacities of the judiciary, civil service, and bureaucracies of government.

Theoretically at least, the dispersal of power within the institutions and processes of elective government should constrain possibilities for official venality. The accompanying protection of civil liberties and human rights should make for open and transparent government and provide a check on abuse of power. Competitive politics underpinned by periodic renewal through elections of the mandate to govern should reward politicians with a credible record of protecting the public resources and manifest interest in promoting people-centered development. Together, these three occurrences – dispersal of power, kinetizing the institutions of accountable government, and competitive electoral politics for periodic renewal of government's mandate – should keep government focused on the public good.

With this theoretical infrastructure, it is difficult to understand how, as in the example of Borno State of Nigeria – replicated in many other states in Nigeria – cited at the beginning of this chapter, a government can trumpet the illiteracy of its people to buttress its unwillingness to protect public welfare or as a strategy for precluding public accountability of any sort. This level of executive malevolence places additional oversight responsibilities on the judiciary and undermines traditional objections to the judicial protection of economic, social, and cultural rights, based as they are on the twin notions of judicial restraint and the overwhelming political legitimacy of the elected arms of government.[5] As explained by Anthony Lester and Colm O'Cinneide:

---

[4] Declaration on the Political and Socio-Economic Situation in Africa and the Fundamental Changes Taking Place in the World, AHG/Decl.1 (XXVI), 1990, para 10.

[5] These arguments are well articulated by Lord Lester of Herne Hill QC and Colm O'Cinneide as follows:

> For reasons of democratic legitimacy, crucial resource allocation decisions are better left in the hands of the legislature and the executive, rather than being determined by an unelected judiciary, whose membership is usually comprised of individuals from national socio-economic elites. If unaccountable judges are taking the place of elected administrators then this will leave the judiciary open to charges of judicial Caesarism.

See, Lord Lester of Herne Hill QC & Colm O'Cinneide, 2004, The effective protection of socio-economic rights, in Yash Ghai and Jill Cottrell (eds.). *Economic, social and cultural rights in practice: The role of judges in implementing economic, social and cultural rights*, (pp. 19, 20).

The Judiciary has an important role to play where there exists a sufficiently gross failure to uphold basic socio-economic rights. Where the other two branches have comprehensively failed to fulfil their responsibilities, then, "the least dangerous branch" has a duty to intervene.[6]

In the face of this considerable public-policy responsibility of the judiciary in a context such as Nigeria's, a 2004 report on the housing rights in West Africa by the Centre on Housing Rights and Evictions, concluded: "[I]n Nigeria... it is difficult to make the Constitutional provisions on economic, social and cultural rights a basis for legal complaints before a court of law."[7] The report summarized the Centre's assessment of the constitutional status of economic and social rights as well as institutional attitudes to and policy impact of their implementation in Nigeria in three main conclusions. First, the legal enforcement of constitutionally recognized economic and social rights in Nigeria is difficult. Second, the courts are, at best, reluctant to entertain complaints based on these rights. Third, Nigeria lacks the bureaucratic and institutional capacities to implement these rights. The report continued:

> ... the situation with ratified international legislation is even worse. The Nigerian courts are reluctant to hear cases on the above-mentioned grounds, and even in cases of admissibility the judges have been unfavourable.... It appears that the government makes policies and establishes funds it cannot strategically implement for good governance and the benefit of the people.[8]

If true, these premises would limit any meaningful judicial role in the implementation of economic and social rights in Nigeria. The present study investigates whether this is indeed the case.

As tempting as it is to accept these assertions on face value, it is prudent nevertheless to subject them to some interrogation. For these conclusions to be significant, it is necessary to ascertain whether they reveal a bias against enforcement of economic and social rights that does not apply to other forms or categories of human rights in Nigeria. If such bias is established, is it a zero-sum trade-off of one category of rights for another or is it a doctrinal or ideological rejection of the relevance or utility of judicial and legal enforcement mechanisms to economic and social rights? For instance, is the judicial and other institutional capacity for the implementation of civil and political rights substantially more efficient or adequate than that for economic, social, and cultural rights? Are the courts more effective in protecting the former category of rights than the latter? Does the constitutional regime of human rights in its provisions, as in its operations, favor one category of rights over another? These questions go beyond the mechanistic application of legal rules by courts and judges or administrative rules by the bureaucracy. They address the normative foundations on which a state is founded, the state of respect for these norms, and the efficacy of the institutions that govern the civic space.

---

[6] Id., 19, 21.
[7] Centre on Housing Rights and Evictions (COHRE), 2004. *Housing rights in West Africa: Report of four fact-finding missions*, 21.
[8] Id.

This chapter examines how the Nigerian judiciary has executed its notionally enhanced role to protect economic and social rights and investigates the extent to which the formal guarantees of the rights to education and health are recognized in Nigeria as controlling factors in public-policy making. The underlying assumption is that Nigeria is one of those contexts where, in the words of Lester and O'Cinneide, "the other two branches have comprehensively failed to fulfil their responsibilities." The chapter begins with a brief introduction to the universe of both economic, social, and cultural rights generally and of legal, constitutional, and institutional infrastructure for the protection of human rights in Nigeria. In addition to provisions of Nigeria's 1999 Constitution, this section also considers other legislative instruments applicable to education and health. Thereafter, it examines the extent of recognition of these rights in judicial decision making and in the work of the National Human Rights Commission. Following this is an analysis of trends and tendencies in judicial decision making concerning economic and social rights in Nigeria and of the impact of such decisions where ascertainable.

NORMATIVE FOUNDATIONS OF ECONOMIC AND SOCIAL RIGHTS IN INTERNATIONAL AND NIGERIAN LAW

Two areas of public good that are central to people-centered development and governance are health and education. Education and health care are also economic and social rights guaranteed in international and regional human rights treaties. The Universal Declaration of Human Rights entitles everyone to a standard of living adequate for the health and well-being of themselves and their families, including "housing and medical care."[9] The same Declaration also contains a guarantee of education as a human right, which shall be "free, at least in the elementary and fundamental stages."[10] The Universal Declaration does not indicate what fundamental education means, especially whether it is the same or different from elementary education.

States Parties to the International Covenant on Economic, Social, and Cultural Rights undertake to guarantee the rights of everyone to the "enjoyment of the highest attainable standards of physical and mental health."[11] They equally recognize the rights of everyone to education that shall be directed at the full development of human personality and the sense of its dignity. The Covenant requires primary education to be free and available to all, secondary education to be generally available and accessible to all, and higher education to be equally accessible to all on the basis of capacity.[12] Far from being peremptory, however, the rights guaranteed in the Covenant are programmatic – that is, to be realized incrementally over time – and the Parties to the Covenant merely undertake to

take steps, individually and collectively and through international assistance and co-operation, especially economic and technical, to the maximum of available

[9] Universal Declaration of Human Rights, Article 25(1).
[10] *Id.*, Article 26(1)
[11] International Covenant on Economic, Social, and Cultural Rights, Article 12(1).
[12] *Id.*, Article 13(1)–(2).

resources, with a view to achieving progressively the full realization of the rights recognized in the present Covenant by all appropriate means, including particularly the adoption of legislative measures.[13]

In addition to the Covenant, the African Charter on Human and Peoples' Rights, which is the principal regional human rights instrument for Africa, guarantees a right to the best attainable state of physical and mental health,[14] and to education.[15] The Charter additionally provides for the rights of the aged and persons with disability to special protection, prohibition of discrimination, and the rights of peoples to economic, social, and cultural development.[16] The Charter is domestic law in Nigeria.[17] In terms of the hierarchy of laws within Nigeria, it is subordinate only to Nigeria's Constitution and above other legislation applicable within the country.[18] In addition to the African Charter itself, the African Charter on the Rights and Welfare of the Child and the Protocol to the African Charter on Human and Peoples' Rights on the Rights of Women in Africa also contain additional guarantees on health and education for children and women on the continent, respectively. Unlike the African Charter, neither the Protocol nor the child rights Charter has been rendered into domestic law in Nigeria.

Far from the popular misconception that economic and social rights are future rights dependent on the availability of optimal resources to underwrite their fulfillment, the best authorities in international law now accept that these rights comprise a composite of both negative and positive obligations on the part of the State. As explained by the African Commission on Human and Peoples' Rights, economic and social rights entail three sets of corresponding obligations on the part of the State: to respect, protect, and fulfill. The obligation to respect requires the State to refrain from interfering with the enjoyment of the rights and to respect rights holders, including their freedoms, autonomy, resources, and liberty of action. The obligation to protect asks the State to protect right-holders against other subjects by legislation and provision of effective remedies. The obligation to fulfill is the "positive expectation on the part of the State to move its machinery towards the actual realisation of the rights."[19] In practice, this means that economic and social rights to health and education entail positive duties on the part of the State to guarantee access to these social goods and to refrain from constraining the public in their provision, access or enjoyment of these rights. This jurisprudence provides a framework for public–private partnership in the provision of both health and education as economic and social rights.

The tendency to classify rights as economic, social, cultural, civil, or political, although intellectually convenient, is not entirely sustainable in either practice or

---

[13] Id., Article 2(1).

[14] African Charter on Human and Peoples' Rights, Article 16(1)

[15] Id., Article 17.

[16] Id., Articles 18, 22.

[17] African Charter on Human and Peoples' Rights (Ratification and Enforcement) Act, Cap 10, Laws of the Federation of Nigeria, 1990.

[18] Peter Nemi v. Attorney-General of Lagos State [1996] *Nig. Weekly L. Reps.*, (Part 452), 42.

[19] Communication 155/96, Social and Economic Rights Action Centre (SERAC) & Another v. Nigeria (2001) *African. Hum Rts. L. Reps*, 60 66–67, paras. 44–47.

enforcement.[20] There are different routes to enforcing economic and social rights. Law courts and the legal process are one route, but not the only one. Legislative and administrative interventions are equally important options. Lawyers and litigants everywhere, including in Nigeria, have also proved quite adept at extending the reach of due process rights to the protection of economic and social rights. The scope of economic and social rights in this study, and of the materials examined in preparing it, is therefore operationally elastic.

A NOTE ON LEGAL TRADITIONS AND METHODOLOGY

This study has relied on legislative and judicial source materials available in Nigeria up to May 2007. The controlling legal instruments for this purpose are the 1999 Constitution of the Federal Republic of Nigeria and the African Charter on Human and Peoples' Rights (Ratification and Enforcement) Act, which domesticates the African Charter on Human and Peoples' Rights in Nigeria, and with it, the economic and social rights guarantees contained in that treaty. Applicable statutes creating rights, obligations, or institutional procedures in education and health were also examined.

With regard to the scope and selection of jurisprudence and court decisions considered or reflected in this chapter, an explanation of Nigeria's culture of public law litigation and enforcement is necessary. Four essential features of this culture are noteworthy for our purposes. First, as a matter of law and procedure, Nigeria's courts consider contests over the trial jurisdiction of a court in any particular case and over the standing of parties to sue so fundamental to litigation that these are treated as priority interlocutory or preliminary issues to "be determined first before the Court can take any further step in the proceedings."[21]

Second, a party to legal proceedings who is dissatisfied with the ruling of a court on a legal issue – such as jurisdiction or standing to sue – is entitled under Nigeria's 1999 Constitution to appeal against that ruling to the Supreme Court.[22] The standard reflex of the government in nearly all human rights litigation in Nigeria is to challenge the jurisdiction of the court or the standing of the claimant to initiate the proceedings. These interlocutory contests and appeals against judicial decisions invariably suspend, delay, and redefine the substantive legal issues in dispute in these proceedings. This creates considerable uncertainty in litigation for the enforcement of human rights in Nigerian courts. Writing on the jurisdiction of Nigerian courts, Lawal Pedro complains about "the frequency with which counsel raise objections to the jurisdiction of court or tribunal on being served with an

---

[20] As Shylashri Shankar and Pratap Bhanu Mehta show in this volume, Indian courts have built up a formidable body of jurisprudence to demonstrate this in their interpretation of Section 21 of the Indian Constitution, extending the scope of the right to life to livelihood and related protections. Maneka Gandhi v. Union of India, AIR 1978 SC 597, 623–624; Mehta v. Union of India, (1991) SC 420; Olga Tellis v. Bombay Municipal Corporation, AIR 1986 SC 180.

[21] Lawal Pedro, 2006. *Jurisdiction of courts in Nigeria: Materials and cases*, Lagos State Ministry of Justice Law Review Series, 1. See Jeric (Nigeria) Ltd. v. UBN Plc., [2000] 12 *Sup. Crt.* (Part II) 133.

[22] Constitution of the Federal Republic of Nigeria, 1999, secs. 233(2)(a) & (b) & 241(1)(b)&(c).

originating process and without any attempt to meet the case of the plaintiff or prosecution on the merit" and laments that:

> this has often worked injustice and great hardship on the plaintiff or complainant who, hoping to get justice within a reasonable time, has submitted a dispute or grievance against a defendant for determination. The defendant promptly challenges the jurisdiction of the Court and thus deprives it [of] the power to come expeditiously to the rescue of the Court. Thus, several cases were delayed beyond reasonable time due to interlocutory appeals on the issue of jurisdiction of the Court.[23]

Third, in consequence of these two factors, public law litigation can encounter considerable delay, often lasting beyond one decade, where there have been interlocutory appeals up to the Supreme Court.[24] Lawal Pedro points out that "the appeal process may take between five to ten years before the preliminary issue of jurisdiction is finally resolved one way or the other."[25] A classic example of how delay unfolds in the enforcement of human rights in Nigerian courts is the case of *Alhaji Mudashiru Kokoro-Owo & 6 Others v. Lagos State Government and 6 Others.*[26] The appellants in this case, plaintiffs in the court of first instance, were representatives of a squatter population, numbering in the hundreds of thousands, who were forcibly evacuated in July 1990 from 3,100 acres of land known as Maroko, adjacent to the high-brow Victoria Island in Lagos. The Lagos State government had compulsorily acquired the land in question from the original owners, the Oniru Chieftaincy family, in August 1972, formally gazetted the acquisition in the same year, and compensated the family. However, they re-allocated part of the land compulsorily acquired to the Oniru Chieftaincy family under a scheme of adjustment in 1977.

Following their forced eviction, the appellants on July 11, 1990, filed a claim before the Lagos High Court seeking enforcement of their fundamental rights together with an application for an interlocutory injunction to restrain the Lagos State government from continuing with the demolition of the buildings and other facilities in Maroko or reallocating the land. Five days later, the High Court refused the application for interlocutory injunction, holding that the application did not involve the claimants' fundamental human rights. On appeal, the Court of Appeal granted their application in part by restraining the Lagos State government from reallocating the land pending the final determination of the case.

While the case was pending, the Oniru Chieftaincy family applied for and was granted a Certificate of Statutory Right of Occupancy over the land that had

---

[23] Pedro, *supra*, at 5.

[24] See Tunde I. Ogowewo, 2005. Self-inflicted constraints on judicial government in Nigeria, *Journal of African Law* 49(1): 39, 46–53.

[25] Pedro, *supra*, at 1. In Amadi v. NNPC [2000] 10 *Nig. Weekly L. Reps.* (Pt. 675) 76, the interlocutory appeal to the Supreme Court took thirteen years to resolve, at the end of which the case was remitted back to the High Court for trial. In Mojekwu v. Mojekwu [1997] 7 *Nig. Weekly L. Reps.* 512, a claim over a widow's inheritance rights took thirty-one years to come to a final decision before the Nigerian Court of Appeal. A survey by the Lagos State Ministry of Justice in 2006 suggested that most public law claims took an average of twelve years with interlocutory appeals to come to a decision.

[26] [2001] 11 *Nig. Weekly L. Reps.* 237.

been reallocated to them in 1977. The appellants then sought to bring contempt proceedings against the Lagos State government for breach of the Court of Appeal's interlocutory injunction against allocation of the land in dispute. On May 4, 1995, the Court of Appeal dismissed their application, holding that there had been no allocation in breach of the order. On May 18, 2001, nearly eleven years after the case began in the Lagos High Court, the Supreme Court upheld the decision of the Court of Appeal on the interlocutory point of whether or not the Lagos State government was in breach of the order against allocation of the land. The original human rights claim concerning the forced eviction of the Maroko inhabitants remained pending in the High Court and, with the reallocation of the land, had been overtaken by events.

Fourth, even after a final decision in cases involving government or public authority as defendant – typical in human rights cases – there is no guarantee of enforcement or compliance, especially in cases where the decision affects the assets of government. This is because under the Sheriffs and Civil Process Act, court orders against the assets of government, such as money or other property, can be enforced only with the consent of the Attorney-General at the federal or state level, depending on which government agency is affected.[27] Attorneys-General routinely decline such consent. Thus, it has been said with reference to public law, and especially human rights, claims against the government in Nigeria that "there seems to be no value in maintaining suits against a party whose own consent must be sought before the benefits of the judgment can be enjoyed."[28]

Each of these features constitutes a filter limiting the number and scope of human rights cases that reach Nigeria's court system. Together, they produce two consequences of significance to this study. They contribute significantly to "eroding public confidence in the judicial process."[29] Follow up to public law decisions leads nowhere. Compliance trails do not exist, and many court decisions do not seem to produce desired or, indeed, any policy consequences. The effect of this erosion is most felt in the enforcement of human rights claims generally, especially in economic and social rights. Even with the most robust operationalization of these rights, relevant cases remain sparse and hard to come by. As is shown in the following, by refusing to enforce economic and social rights, the Nigerian courts have, through restrictive doctrine, discouraged litigation on economic and social rights.

These features of the Nigerian legal culture also make it impossible to develop any coherent analytical framework – quantitative or qualitative – for human rights litigation in general and economic and social rights jurisprudence in particular. This is because most cases get redefined through interlocutory appellate processes and restrictive rules of standing away from substantive challenges of economic and social rights violations to technical legal disputes over jurisdiction, ripeness of the suit, or standing of the claimants to initiate the case. Although it is useful to acknowledge the original dispute in terms of economic and social rights claims, the

---

[27] Sheriffs and Civil Process Act, Cap. 407, Laws of the Federation, 1990, sec. 84(1)–(3).
[28] Mmuozoba, C. U. 2007. Quest for justice beyond fair trial: Provisions of the Sheriffs and Civil Process Act as metaphor for injustice, *Nig. Bar Journal* 5(1): 79, 90.
[29] *Id.* at 91.

jurisprudence that results often bears no relation to the original issues formulated for judicial resolution and, when it does, mostly has the effect of foreclosing or stopping the litigation. As a mechanism for policy reform or action for implementation of economic and social rights, therefore, this chapter will show that the judicial process in Nigeria, owing mostly to self-inflicted doctrinal constraints, has so far proved to be timid, self-limiting, and quite inadequate.

This study is based on a review of case law from the federal court system and a representative sampling of the state courts. At the federal level, we reviewed reported decisions of federal courts dating back to 1979, when economic and social rights first entered the lexicon of constitutional rights in Nigeria. In the absence of electronic or online source materials, this had to be done manually using the indexes of existing law reports. Additional examination of case and law reports were also undertaken in Lagos and Rivers states – two of the states with the most sophisticated litigation markets in Nigeria. We similarly undertook a survey of decisions from the courts of Kaduna State in northwestern Nigeria, which, however, did not reveal any relevant decisions. This involved travel to Kaduna, and research assistance was provided by lawyers active in Lagos and Rivers states. We have also relied on some unreported decisions of both federal and state courts, discovered in the course of interviews of court users and their counsel. Every effort has been made to reflect reported jurisprudence irrespective of the state from which it originates.

In addition to legislative and judicial source materials, we have also reviewed and relied on the petitions received and considered by the Nigerian National Human Rights Commission, a national human rights institution operational in Nigeria since 1996. Again, in the absence of an electronically organized and accessible database of the Commission's casework, this was also done manually.

These source materials have been supplemented by interviews with counsel, advocacy and public institutions, such as Nigeria's Civil Liberties Organization (CLO), Social and Economic Rights Action Centre (SERAC), the Social and Economic Rights Initiative (SERI), and the National Human Rights Commission (NHRC), and petitioners involved in three of the cases considered.[30]

NIGERIA: POLITICAL, INSTITUTIONAL, AND CONSTITUTIONAL CONTEXT

Nigeria is a federation comprised of thirty-six states and a federal capital territory (Abuja). It won independence from the United Kingdom in October 1960. For most of its post-independence history, Nigeria has been politically unstable. The story of governance instability in Nigeria began in January 1966, when the post-independence government was overthrown in a bloody military coup. In forty-eight years as an independent country, Nigeria has had twelve presidents and heads of government, eight of whom ruled in twenty-nine years of military

---

[30] Feedback from the public officials has, by prior arrangement with them, been used with circumspection. The institutional culture, governed by the Nigerian Official Secrets Act, warrants concern for their anonymity.

rule. It has experienced eight military rulers, seven military-inspired changes of government, five of which have been successful military coups, six constitutions (including one that was never used),[31] four constitution-drafting processes, four programs of transition from military to civilian government,[32] at least three unsuccessful coup attempts,[33] three civilian regimes, two constituent assemblies, two transition programs from military to elective government and one civil war.[34] Nigeria returned to civilian government at the end of fifteen unbroken years of military rule under a Constitution that entered into force on May 29, 1999.[35]

Nigeria is Africa's most populous country with a population estimated to be somewhere between 120 and 140 million, and an annual population growth rate of 3.2 percent.[36] Male life expectancy is an estimated 46.8 years, whereas female life expectancy is 48.1 years. According to 2003 estimates, the male adult literacy rate in Nigeria is about 75 percent, whereas female adult literacy is about 60 percent. The Nigerian government estimates that about 57 percent of the population lives below the poverty line, but the World Bank's estimate is closer to 70 percent. Nigeria is comprised of about 389 ethnic and language groups.[37] A majority of Nigeria's population lives in rural areas on subsistence land tenure. Petroleum accounts for about 90 percent of its documented annual national revenue.[38]

A Bill of Rights was adopted in Nigeria in 1959, on the eve of independence, on the recommendation of the Willink Commission, constituted by the departing colonial government to allay the fears of minority nationalities of domination in

---

[31] The 1989 Constitution drafted under the auspices of the Babangida regime was abrogated before it was formally promulgated following the annulment of the presidential elections of June 1993. See Attorney-General of Anambra State & Others v. Attorney-General of the Federation & Others, [1993] *Nig. Weekly L. Rep.* (Part 302) 692.

[32] With the notable exception of the regime of Major-General Mohammadu Buhari (December 1983– August 1985), every military regime in Nigeria has evinced an intention to design and implement a program of transition to elected civilian government. See Awa U. Kalu 1994, The democratization of Nigeria: More bullet(s) or ballot?" *Lawyers Biannual* 1(1): 40.

[33] It is widely believed that the claim (in early 1995) by the regime of the late General Sani Abacha to have foiled a coup attempt against it by a group allegedly comprised of middle-ranking army officers without command positions, retired generals, civilian pro-democracy activists, and journalists was not credible. *Africa Confidential*, for instance, reported that "[t]here is new concern that human rights activists . . . and independent journalists . . . will be roped into a secret treason trial held under military rules. Such reports confirm that the tribunal is purging dissidents rather than trying plotters." See Nigeria: Widening the net, 1995. In *Africa Confidential* 36(14): 8.

[34] The Nigerian civil war began in 1967 and formally ended on January 15, 1970.

[35] Chapter II of the 1999 Constitution of the Federal Republic of Nigeria provides for economic, social, and cultural rights, whereas Chapter IV provides essentially for civil and political rights. The distinction may well be a hangover from the 1979 Constitution that was enacted at the height of the Cold War. It is arguable that the present constitution does not comply with the United Nations Resolution 48/134 of December 1993, to the extent that all human rights are equal, universal, indivisible, interrelated, interdependent, and inalienable.

[36] The UN Statistics Division estimated Nigeria's population in 2002 to be 120,046,000. A national population census published in October 2006 put Nigeria's population at 140,003,542 with an annual growth rate of 3.2 percent since 1991. See "Legal notice on the publication of the 2006 Census," *Federal Republic of Nigeria Official Gazette*, B50, January 19, 2007. www.population.gov.ng/pop_figure.pdf.

[37] http://en.wikipedia.org/wiki/Category:Ethnic_groups_in_Nigeria (accessed June 9, 2007).

[38] See https://www.cia.gov/cia/publications/factbook/geos/ni.html (accessed January 19, 2007).

a post-independence Nigeria. The Commission recommended the incorporation into Nigeria's Independence Constitution of the basic human rights guarantees in the European Convention of Human Rights. This became Nigeria's Bill of Rights at independence in 1960.[39] This situation remained unchanged until the adoption of Nigeria's 1979 Constitution.

Economic and Social Rights in Nigeria's Constitution

Human rights were incorporated into Nigeria's Independence Constitution in 1960, following the Report of the Commission appointed to inquire into the fears of minorities and the means of allaying them.[40] The Bill of Rights mostly imported the rights provisions contained in the European Convention of Human Rights and excluded economic and social rights guarantees. It took Nigeria's 1979 Constitution to accord social and economic rights constitutional recognition for the first time. Even then, they were mostly recognized as non-justiciable Fundamental Objectives and Directive Principles of State Policy in Chapter II of the Constitution. This arrangement was repeated in Nigeria's current 1999 Constitution. Chapter II of Nigeria's Constitution contains provisions relating to economic and political equity, rights to economic activity, adequate shelter, welfare rights, access to health and medical care, social justice, access to education, and the environment.[41]

In addition, Chapter IV of Nigeria's Constitution contains an enforceable Bill of Rights. The rights guaranteed in this chapter fall into the category generally described as civil and political rights, including the rights to life, liberty, dignity, fair trial, free expression, association, assembly, freedom from discrimination, and the prohibition of torture.

Nigerian courts have held that they are precluded by Section 6(6)(c) of the Constitution from enforcing the provisions of Chapter II, including economic and social rights.[42] This section provides that the judicial powers of Nigerian courts shall not

> except as otherwise provided by this Constitution, extend to any issue or question as to whether any act or omission by any authority or person or as to whether any law or any judicial decision is in conformity with the Fundamental Objectives and Directive Principles of State Policy set out in Chapter II of this Constitution.

However, Section 13 of the same Constitution requires that "it shall be the duty and responsibility of all organs of government, and of all authorities and persons

---

[39] Chinonye Obiagwu & Chidi Anselm Odinkalu, 2002. Nigeria: Combating legacies of colonialism and militarism. In Abdullahi An-Na'im (ed), *Human rights under African constitutions: Realizing the promise for ourselves* (p. 211).

[40] The Commission was chaired by Sir Henry Willink, a colonial officer, and its report is better known as the *Willink Commission Report* [1959].

[41] Sections 15–18 & 20, Constitution of the Federal Republic of Nigeria 1999.

[42] Archbishop Anthony Olubunmi Okogie & 6 Others v. Attorney-General of Lagos State, [1981] *Nig. Const. L. Reps.* 337.

exercising legislative, executive or judicial powers, to conform to, observe and apply the provisions" of Chapter II.

It is noteworthy that Section 6(6)(c) is made subject to other provisions of the Constitution, including Section 13, which is clearly applicable to the judiciary. It is arguable, therefore, that the structure of the Constitution obliges the courts to apply and enforce the Chapter II rights. However, Nigerian courts have held that Section 6(6)(c) controls the application of Section 13 to the end that the provisions of Chapter II are not justiciable, claiming that,

> While section 13 of the Constitution makes it a duty and responsibility of the judiciary, among other organs of government, to conform to and apply the provisions of Chapter II, Section 6(6)(c) of the same Constitution makes it clear that no court has jurisdiction to pronounce any decision as to whether any organ of government has acted or is acting in conformity with the Fundamental Objectives and Directive Principles of State Policy. It is therefore clear that Section 13 has not made Chapter II of the Constitution enforceable.[43]

The results of this are threefold. First, Chapter II makes economic and social rights programmatic in Nigeria. The Federal Government has exclusive competence to legislate for the application or realization of items in Chapter II.[44] Second, reflecting the dominant judicial doctrine, very few cases are filed explicitly to enforce economic and social rights. However, third, advocates nevertheless seek enforcement of what would be regarded as social and economic rights through other envelopes of constitutional rights guarantees, including the prohibition against discrimination and due process guarantees.

The Status of the African Charter on Human and Peoples' Rights and Other International Instruments in Nigeria

Nigeria has ratified the African Charter on Human and Peoples' Rights, the Protocol Establishing the African Court on Human and Peoples' Rights, the International Covenant on Economic, Social, and Cultural Rights, the International Covenant on Civil and Political Rights, and the Convention on the Elimination of All Forms of Discrimination against Women. Section 12(1) of the 1999 Constitution, however, provides that "no treaty between the Federation and any other country shall have the force of law except to the extent to which such treaty has been enacted into law by the National Assembly."

The only treaty that has been so enacted is the African Charter on Human and Peoples' Rights.[45] The Charter is the principal regional human rights treaty for Africa. It contains an integrated regime of rights including economic, social,

---

[43] *Id.* at 339. For a contrary view, see Justice C. A. Oputa, 2007, Towards justiciability of the fundamental objectives and directive principles of state policy in Nigeria. In Chris Okeke (ed.), *Towards functional justice: Seminar papers of Justice Chukwudifu Oputa* (pp. 1–11). Ibadan, Nigeria: Gold Press Limited.
[44] Item 60(a), Exclusive Legislative List.
[45] African Charter on Human and Peoples' Rights (Ratification & Enforcement Act), Chapter 10, Laws of the Federation of Nigeria, 1990.

cultural, civil, and political rights.[46] As explained earlier, the Charter guarantees the rights to health and education. Nigeria's Supreme Court has held that these Charter rights are enforceable through court process deploying the rules of procedure of Nigerian courts.[47] However, the same court has also held that in the scheme of obligations and entitlements, the African Charter is below the Nigerian Constitution, and conflicts between the two instruments must be resolved in favor of the Constitution.[48] This, it has been argued, means that

> the Charter, even though it has been domesticated, cannot introduce justiciable rights that the Constitution has declared non-justiciable.... However, it can be argued that the Charter, being a statute of its own, stands on its own legs, and its provisions can be enforced without the ouster provision of section 6(6)(c) of the Constitution.[49]

The African Charter establishes a regional Commission on Human and Peoples' Rights, which receives and adjudicates on complaints alleging violations of any Charter rights against member States of the African Charter system. In the leading case of *SERAC & Another v. Nigeria* the Commission elaborated its competence to adjudicate complaints of violations of economic and social rights in the Charter, affirming that "international law and human rights must be responsive to African circumstances."[50] Decisions of the Commission, a significant number of which have been reached in cases against Nigeria, contribute to a growing regional jurisprudence on economic and social rights.[51] However, they are generally treated as nonbinding by African States, fueling the view that "non-compliance with its recommendations by the States concerned was one of the main reasons for the erosion of its [the Commission's] credibility."[52] The African Court on Human and Peoples' Rights, which is currently in the process of being established, will have jurisdiction to issue binding decisions on these rights.[53]

Federalism and Division of Powers

Nigeria is a federal territory comprising thirty-six states and one federal territory. As with all federal territories, the division of powers between the federation and the states is one between enumerated and residual powers. Nigeria's 1999 Constitution contains two lists of enumerated powers in the Second Schedule. The Exclusive Legislative List contains items on which the federal government alone can legislate,

[46] Chidi Anselm Odinkalu, 2002. Implementing economic, social and cultural rights under the African Charter on Human and Peoples' Rights. In Malcolm Evans & Rachel Murray, *The African Charter on Human and Peoples' Rights: The system in practice 1986–2000* (p. 178).
[47] Ogugu v. State, [1996] 6 *Nig. Weekly L. Reps.* (Pt. 316) 1, 30–31.
[48] Chief Gani Fawehinmi v. Sani Abacha [2000] *Nig. Weekly L. Reps.* (Pt. 660) 228.
[49] Chinonye Obiagwu & Chidi Anselm Odinkalu, *supra* n. 39 at 227.
[50] *SERAC*, para. 68.
[51] For a discussion of this jurisprudence, see Chidi Anselm Odinkalu, *supra* n. 46.
[52] Fatsah Ouguergouz, *The African Charter on Human and Peoples' Rights: A comprehensive agenda for human dignity and sustainable democracy in Africa*, 657 (2003).
[53] For information on the African Court, visit www.africancourtcoalition.org (accessed January 10, 2007).

whereas the Concurrent Legislative List contains items on which both the federation and states can legislate subject to the doctrine of covering the field.[54] The effect of this doctrine is essentially that a federal legislation will prevail in case of conflict with state legislation that covers the same field as the federal legislation. Items of economic and social rights – health, housing, the environment, education, water – are all within the concurrent legislative list.

Courts and Recourse Systems

Section 6 of the 1999 Constitution vests the judicial powers of the Nigerian State in the courts established thereby. The federation and state have different systems of trial courts, whereas the appellate court system is essentially federal. These courts are the

- Supreme Court
- Court of Appeal
- Federal and/or State High Courts
- Sharia and/or Customary Courts of Appeal (these are of coordinate jurisdiction with the High Courts)
- Customary, Magistrates, Area, and other lower courts and tribunals.

The Supreme Court is the Apex Court. It receives appeals from the Court of Appeal. The Supreme Court also has original jurisdiction in all disputes between the federation and any state or between two or more states of the federation. The Court of Appeal has original jurisdiction in determining electoral disputes for election to the Presidency of Nigeria. Otherwise its jurisdiction is entirely appellate. The federal and state High Courts have primary or first instance jurisdiction for trying all cases alleging violation of Constitutional rights. Each state has its own High Court. There is also a federal High Court. State and federal High Courts can sit in different divisions. Each division may comprise a cluster of two or more courts/judges.

Most states in northern Nigeria have Sharia Courts of Appeal for application of Muslim personal law. Since 1999, most of the states with Sharia Courts of Appeal have extended the jurisdiction of those courts to cover *Huddud* crimes or crimes of morality founded on Islamic law, such as adultery. Most states of southern Nigeria, by contrast, establish Customary Courts of Appeal for resolution of disputes over application of ethnic customary law. The Sharia and Customary Courts of Appeal receive appeals from the Area, Magistrates, and Customary Courts.

The Chief Justice, the President of the Court of Appeal, and Justices of the Supreme Court (twenty plus the Chief Justice) and Court of Appeal, as well as judges of the Federal High Court and the High Court of the Federal Capital Territory (Abuja), are appointed by the President upon nomination by the National Judicial Council and are subject to confirmation by the Upper Chamber (Senate) of the National Assembly. This procedure is adapted for the State High Courts,

---

[54] See Attorney General of Bendel State v. Attorney General of the Federation & 22 Others, [1982] 3 *Nig. Const. L. Reps.* 1; Parts 1 & II, 2nd Schedule, Constitution of the Federal Republic of Nigeria, 1999.

Customary Courts, and Sharia Courts of Appeal, with the modification that the state legislatures, unlike the federal legislature, are unicameral. State governments, upon recommendation of State Judicial Service Commissions, appoint magistrates and Area Court judges. In addition to the courts, there is also a statutory National Human Rights Commission, which monitors and advises the government and its departments on the implementation of human rights.[55]

Judicial Procedure for Enforcement of Human Rights

Section 46(1) of Nigeria's 1999 Constitution entitles any person alleging the violation or threat of violation of their constitutionally enforceable rights to apply to "a High Court in the State for redress."[56] Such an application may be made to the High Court of the State or, if it exists, a Federal High Court sitting in the state.

Broadly, there are three possible forms of judicial procedure by which human rights claims could be initiated in Nigeria. The constitutional chapter containing the Bill of Rights (Chapter IV) provides for an expedited process under special rules made under Section 46(3) by the Chief Justice of Nigeria to regulate claims for enforcement of constitutional rights. These rules, known as the *Fundamental Rights (Enforcement Procedure) Rules*,[57] provide for a two-stage process. Claimants first have to apply to the High Court (state or federal) for permission (leave) ex parte and, if this permission is granted, must then initiate the substantive claim within eight days of such permission being granted. Relatively few – if any – claims of economic and social rights are commenced this way, except those cases seeking interlocutory or interim injunctive reliefs against the invasion of existing rights of an economic or social nature,[58] or those framed as claims to enforce the constitutional right to freedom from discrimination.[59]

It is also possible to seek the enforcement of rights by the procedure of judicial review recognized in the rules of the various High Courts of Nigeria. Alternatively, a claimant could proceed by way of an ordinary writ. The downside to this last option is that such cases could easily get ensnared in the notoriously tardy court processes described earlier in this chapter.

Besides judicial recourse, a complainant or victims may also petition the National Human Rights Commission. The Commission offers an administrative recourse of a non-adversarial nature. It may investigate the complaint, mediate between the complainant and respondent, and make recommendations as it deems appropriate. However, the decisions of the Commission are nonbinding unless backed by a judicial order. In addition, a Public Complaints Commission (Ombudsman) exists to investigate and redress administrative violations.[60]

---

[55] Chapter N46, Laws of the Federation of Nigeria, 2004.

[56] Constitution of the Federal Republic of Nigeria, 1979, Section 46(1).

[57] These rules were made and published in January 1980, see Vol. 11, *Laws of the Federation of Nigeria*, 2004, C23–165.

[58] Such as to prevent forced eviction, e.g., Kokoro-Owo v. Lagos State [1995] *Nig. Weekly L. Reps.* 760.

[59] See, Badejo v. Federal Minister of Education & 2 Others, discussed under "Access to Educational Institutions" later.

[60] Public Complaints Commission Act, Cap P37, *Laws of the Federation*, 2004.

Access to Courts and to Government

A major hurdle for all processes of enforcement of rights in Nigeria is standing to initiate or undertake legal proceedings. The dominant doctrinal position of the Nigerian courts is that a litigant must disclose "personal interest" in the subject matter of the proceedings.[61] This is a major obstacle to the enforcement of all rights in Nigeria. It precludes the pursuit of impact litigation for the public interest.[62] In addition, "individual victims who are required to disclose personal interest in the matter rarely succeed because, personal interest, defined as interest over and above that of the general public, is difficult to prove where the alleged violation (or governmental failure) also affects other members of the public."[63] This further diminishes the number of cases of economic and social rights that percolate into the court system.

Quite apart from these, courts are mostly located in urban areas. Since 1888 when the first Nigerian lawyer was enrolled to practice in the colonial court system, more than sixty thousand lawyers have been registered to practice in Nigeria. Legal services are located mostly in urban areas and are arguably beyond the reach of a majority of the population.[64] The 1999 Constitution mandates the federal legislature to "make provisions for the rendering of financial assistance to any indigent citizen of Nigeria where his right under this Chapter (Bill of Rights) has been infringed or with a view to enabling him to engage the services of a legal practitioner to prosecute his claims, and for ensuring that allegations of infringement of such rights are substantial and that the requirement or need for financial or legal aid is real."[65] A Legal Aid Council established under the Legal Aid Act of 1976 exists and is empowered to provide legal aid to accused persons and suspects in criminal proceedings subject to a means test.[66] In June 2005, Nigeria's Justice Ministry published draft proposals for the reform of this Act to accommodate legal assistance for human rights violations.

Access to government and government records, which is essential for the effective protection of economic and social rights, is difficult. Bureaucratic tradition and policy in Nigeria is dictated by the Official Secrets Act. The Act prohibits public disclosure of all "classified matter" defined as

> any information or thing which, under any system of security classification, from time to time, in use by any branch of the government, is not to be disclosed to the public and of which the disclosure to the public would be prejudicial to the security of Nigeria.[67]

---

[61] Adesanya v. President, [1982] 1 NCLR, 231.

[62] Tunde Ogowewo, 1995. The problem with standing to sue in Nigeria, *Journal of African Law* 9:39; also, Tunde Ogowewo 2000, Wrecking the law: How Article III of the Constitution of the United States led to the discovery of a law of standing to sue in Nigeria, *Brooklyn Journal of International Law 26:* 527.

[63] Chinonye Obiagwu & Chidi Anselm Odinkalu, 2002. *supra* n. 39 at 233.

[64] *Id.* at 240.

[65] Sections 46(4)(a)–(b), Constitution of the Federal Republic of Nigeria, 1999.

[66] Legal Aid Act, Section 7, Chapter L19, *Laws of the Federation of Nigeria,* 2004.

[67] Official Secrets Act, Sections 1(1) & 9, *Laws of the Federation of Nigeria,* 2004.

The National Security Agencies Act establishes a State Security Service (SSS) to, among other things, protect and preserve all non-military classified matters concerning the internal security of Nigeria.[68]

In practice, every governmental record is part of a system of security classification. Thus, these Acts have the combined effect of precluding from disclosure every governmental record except those required in judicial proceedings under the provisions of the Evidence Act relating to evidence of public records.[69] It is not uncommon to see pieces of legislation marked "Secret" or "Confidential." Nigeria's bicameral federal legislature passed a Freedom of Information Bill sponsored by a coalition of civil society and media advocacy groups in February 2007. However, in April 2007, Nigeria's then President, Olusegun Obasanjo, refused to assent to the Bill which thus lapsed with the end of the legislative term at the end of May 2007.[70]

Customary Law and Discrimination

One complicating factor that blurs any notional lines between categories of rights in Nigeria is the coexistence of traditional and civic societies beside, but with minimal interaction with, one another. Customary law remains a major source of law affecting an overwhelming majority of Nigeria's people who subsist in rural economies.

In addition to issues posed in the context of enforcing constitutional protections, economic and social rights also arise in the context of resolving the conflicts between customary/traditional society and the civic guarantees of constitutional rights.[71] For instance, in deference to deeply entrenched patriarchal mores, unmarried, female students or pupils who get pregnant are routinely taken out of school by their families (to save face and family honor) or suspended by school authorities, in situations in which the agency of the male partners in the pregnancy is not even acknowledged. Although these situations clearly implicate economic and social rights and affect the rights to both education and health of the pregnant young mother, deeply ingrained notions of family shame and honor usually preclude such cases from ever creating a paper trail of judicial or administrative precedent.

---

[68] *National Security Agencies Act,* Section 2(3)(b), Chapter N74, *Laws of the Federation of Nigeria,* 2004.

[69] Nigeria's Evidence Act defines public documents as "(a) documents forming the acts or records of the acts (i) of the sovereign authority; (ii) of official bodies and tribunals; and (iii) of public officers, legislative, judicial and executive, whether of Nigeria or elsewhere; or (b) public records kept in Nigeria of private documents." See Evidence Act, Section 109, *Laws of the Federation of Nigeria,* 2004.

[70] See President Obasanjo refuses to sign the Freedom of Information Bill, http://www.mediarightsagenda.org/obasanjorefuses.html (accessed June 10, 2007). Also, Edetaen Ojo 2006, "Nigerian Freedom of Information bill: History and current status" (on file with the author).

[71] See Uzoukwu v. Ezeonu II, [1991] 6 *Nig. Weekly L. Reps.* (Pt. 200) 760, where the Nigerian Court of Appeal implemented economic and social rights in the context of eliminating traditional slavery practices. Similarly, in Muojekwu v. Muojekwu [1997] 7 *Nig. Weekly L. Reps.* (Pt 152) 283, the same court applied economic and social rights in protecting a widow from being disinherited by her surviving brother-in-law in customary law.

Land Tenure and Natural Resources Exploitation and the Environment

Land tenure is relevant to understanding the application of economic and social rights in a predominantly rural economy like Nigeria. For the most part, the major institution of landholding in Nigeria was the family. Family members received allocations for subsistence and use. The family council or elders agreed to alienation or sale of land. In northern Nigeria, the Emirate Council or authority played the same role.

In 1978, the military regime then in power promulgated a Land Use Decree (now Act), No. 6, which vested legal title in lands in any part of the country in the governors of the states where land is located in trust for the people (except for lands already vested in the federal government). Similar powers were vested in relation to rural lands in the local (government) authorities. Under this Act no person in an urban area shall, without the consent of the government of a State, erect any building, walls, fence, or other structures, cultivate, enclose, or do any act in respect of any land without a prior certificate of occupancy or license.[72] State governments are empowered to grant Statutory Rights of Occupancy, whereas local governments grant Customary Rights of Occupancy, for a maximum duration of ninety-nine years. The Act unnecessarily bureaucratized landholding and use. Far from discouraging speculation as it was intended to, it rapidly institutionalized it, dislocating many families from their ancestral lands and leading to many cases of unlawful and forced evictions and consequential impoverishment.[73]

The Minerals and Petroleum Acts vest ownership of all minerals, including solid minerals, fossil fuels, and hydrocarbons, and all lands bearing such minerals in Nigeria, in the federal government. Government may, additionally, acquire lands for public purpose. In all these cases, there is an obligation to compensate affected owners and users of the land but the standards of compensation are unclear and the processes unduly bureaucratic and corrupt.

The federal government exclusively licenses and regulates the operations of oil companies and other natural resource extractors. These operations take place mostly in the ecologically rich but fragile ecosystem of the Niger Delta region in southern Nigeria. The regulatory environment is quite weak and inadequately policed. Over the years, this has allowed the oil companies to develop abysmal oil-field practices characterized by, among other things, hazardous seismographic operations, poor installation and maintenance of pipelines, twenty-four-hour gas flaring within range of human habitation, and regular blowouts. During the same period, most host communities have suffered irreparable damage to their environment and subsistence and experienced infrastructural degradation. Hazardous petroleum exploitation operations have also created twin crises of public health and educational attainment for host communities.[74]

---

[72] Section 43 (1)(a)–(b), Land Use Act.
[73] See, Ike Okonta and Oronto Douglas, 2003. *Where vultures feast: Shell, human rights and oil*, London: Verso.
[74] See SERAC & Another v. Nigeria.

LEGAL IMPLEMENTATION OF THE RIGHT TO EDUCATION
IN NIGERIA: APPLICABLE STANDARDS AND JURISPRUDENCE

The broad policy approach, discernible from the limited jurisprudence on the right to education in existence in Nigeria, encourages private enterprise in the provision or supply of education. There have been no successful challenges on the question of access to education. There is a considerable body of jurisprudence on the protection and regulation of the rights of students in tertiary education but not to other levels of education, especially basic, primary, or secondary. Regulatory standards are mostly statutorily defined and have not been elaborated in jurisprudence. The picture that emerges is that the courts have, through legitimizing private provision, broadened the supply of educational places without consciously adverting to access rights, stimulating demand, or prescribing or guaranteeing standards among the various providers, both public and private.

Chapter II of Nigeria's 1999 Constitution recognizes education as a social good and an economic and social right. Under its social objectives, it declares that the Nigerian social order shall be founded on the ideals of freedom, equality, and justice, including respect for equality of rights, obligations, and opportunities; sanctity of the human person and respect for human dignity; humane governmental policy making; harm reduction; and independence and impartiality of the courts.[75] The Constitution contains a provision on educational objectives in Section 18 as follows:

(1) Government shall direct its policy towards ensuring that there are equal and adequate educational opportunities at all levels.
(2) Government shall promote science and technology.
(3) Government shall strive to eradicate illiteracy; and to this end, government shall as and when practicable provide –
    (a) free, compulsory and universal primary education;
    (b) free secondary education;
    (c) free university education; and
    (d) free adult literacy programme.

It has been shown earlier how Nigerian courts have held the rights in this Chapter of the Nigerian Constitution to be non-justiciable. Quite clearly, Section 18 makes the realization of the right to education incremental, through the use of the expressions "as and when practicable" and "strive to eradicate." Under the division of powers in the Constitution, the federal legislature has exclusive competence to legislate for the realization of Chapter II rights.[76] Similarly, the regulation of minimum standards of education at all levels is also on the exclusive legislative list.[77] Education is, otherwise, on the concurrent legislative list and, therefore, within the zone of shared competence of both federal and state authorities.[78]

---

[75] Constitution of the Federal Republic of Nigeria, 1999, Article 17(1).
[76] Id., Second Schedule, Part I, Item 60(a).
[77] Id., Item 60(e).
[78] Id., Part II, Item L27–30.

The right to education is also protected by the African Charter on Human and Peoples' Rights (Ratification and Enforcement) Act as an enforceable right. Notwithstanding this, the Nigerian courts studied in this research have, to date, received no reported case framed in terms of this provision. However, the Constitution also guarantees in Section 39(1) an enforceable right to "freedom of information, including freedom to hold opinions and to receive and impart ideas and information without interference" and to establish and operate a medium for that purpose.[79]

The basic structure of Nigeria's educational system and the responsibilities of government with respect to education are mostly governed by statutes, some of which are now examined in the following.

Compulsory, Free Universal Basic Education Act

In 2004, Nigeria's Federal government enacted a Compulsory, Free Universal Basic Education Act (UBE Act).[80] The Act requires "every government in Nigeria" to provide free, compulsory, and universal basic education.[81] It defines basic education as "early childhood care and education and nine years of formal schooling."[82] This provision is wide enough to include both childhood education and adult education to remedy the educational disadvantage suffered by members of historically deprived communities who have not had access to education. However, the Act itself only provides for free and compulsory basic education for every child up to the end of junior secondary education,[83] excluding remedial basic education for adults. It creates a duty punishable with criminal sanction on all parents to ensure that their children or wards attend and complete basic education.[84]

To implement its provisions, the Act creates a Universal Basic Education Act Commission to be funded by a block grant of not less than 2 percent of the Consolidated Revenue Fund of the federal government, contributions from state and local governments, or from donor funds.[85] The functions of the Commission extend to policy development on basic education, provision of adequate basic education facilities, and governance of the basic national curricula and syllabi and other necessary instructional materials in use in early childhood care and basic education.

---

[79] *Id.*, Section 39(1)–(2).
[80] Federal Republic of Nigeria 2004, *Official Gazette*, 91(66), Govt. Notice No. 142, Lagos, Nigeria: Federal Government Press.
[81] *Id.*, Section 2(1).
[82] *Id.*, Section 15(1).
[83] *Id.*, Sections 2(1) & 3(1).
[84] *Id.*, Sections 2(2) & 4.
[85] *Id.*, Section 11(1). In Nigeria, there is a distinction between the Federation Account and the Consolidated Revenue Fund. All revenue accruable to the Federation and its constituent units is paid into a Federation Account. The Federal government and each of the States are then required to maintain a Consolidated Revenue Fund into which incomes and revenue accruable to them are paid. See *Id.*, Sections 162(1) & 80(1).

Provision of Adult, Primary, and Vocational Education

Under Nigeria's Constitution, state and local authorities are responsible for providing primary education. In this respect, the Fourth Schedule to the Constitution provides that "the functions of a local government council shall include participation of each council in the government of a State as respects . . . the provision and maintenance of primary, adult and vocational education."[86] Nigeria's Supreme Court decided in 2002 that "so far as primary education is concerned, a local government council only participates with the State government in its provision and maintenance. The function obviously remains with the State government."[87]

Three additional points may be made here. First, the federal government does not have a constitutional responsibility to provide primary, adult, and vocational education but has exclusive responsibilities to regulate standards and curriculum at all levels of education, including these. It has, however, voluntarily undertaken under the UBE Act to contribute toward the costs of primary education under the terms of the Act. Second, the Constitution appears silent on pre-primary and nursery education. Third, there is nothing in the Constitution that precludes private providers from participating in these levels of education. Indeed, this issue has been the subject of litigation in two separate cases.

In *Adewole & Others v. Alhaji Jakande & Others*,[88] the plaintiffs challenged the legality of proposals by the Lagos State government to abolish private schools. The Lagos State High Court held, among other things, that the proposal to abolish private schools violated the applicants' property rights under Section 40 of the 1979 Constitution.[89] The Court further affirmed the freedom of parents to direct the upbringing and education of their children by having a choice of schools where they are to attend.

Similarly, in *Archbishop Okogie & Other v. Attorney General of Lagos State*,[90] the proprietors of private primary schools in Lagos State relied on a provision in Section 36(1) of the 1979 Constitution to challenge a circular of the then Lagos State government issued on March 26, 1980, purporting to abolish private primary education in the State. In their claim, the plaintiffs, led by the Catholic Church, which had an interest in protecting its network of mission primary schools around the State, argued that the circular was a violation of their constitutional rights.

The Court held that it was precluded by Section 6(6)(c) of the Constitution from enforcing any rights founded on the Chapter II provisions concerning Fundamental Objectives and Directive Principles of State Policy in the Nigerian Constitution. However, it concluded that "the establishment and running of primary and secondary schools, if undertaken by government, is a social service but, if undertaken

---

[86] *Id.*, 4th Schedule, para. 2

[87] Attorney General of the Federation v. Attorney General of Abia State & 36 Others, [2002] 6 *Nig. Weekly L. Reps.* 673.

[88] (1981) 1 *Nig. Const. L. Reps.* 262 at 279.

[89] Section 44 of the 1999 Constitution.

[90] Archbishop Okogie & 6 Others v. Attorney General of Lagos State [1981] *Nig. Const. L. Reps.* 337.

by a private citizen could be an economic activity" and, thus, deserving of legal protection. It affirmed also that the educational objectives in the constitutional Fundamental Objectives "are a directive to government and not to private citizens."[91]

Interpreting the right to freedom of expression, opinion, and information in Section 36(1) and (2) of the 1979 Constitution, the Court of Appeal held that the State has no right to interfere with the freedom or any constitutional right of the citizen except as allowed by the Constitution itself. It found that "a school must be accepted as a medium for the dissemination of knowledge and ideas,"[92] a medium that could not be minimized or abrogated by the broad declaration of education objectives in Section 18. In so doing, the Court established that the categorization of rights between civil and political and economic, social, and cultural rights is permeable.

Generally speaking, the Court of Appeal grounded the private proprietorship and provision of primary schools in the right to freedom of expression and information under the Constitution. However, in its view, State governments may license private providers and may revoke such licenses in accordance with law and due process. Both property and free expression are enforceable as civil and political rights under Chapter IV of Nigeria's 1999 Constitution.

With respect to basic adult education for historically excluded persons and communities, Nigeria's federal Ministry of Education supervises two important parastatals – the National Commission for Nomadic Education and the National Commission for Adult Education, Mass Literacy and Non-Formal Education, both established to provide on a continuing basis access to educational instruction for deprived communities, especially nonsedentary communities.[93]

Secondary and Tertiary Education and Minimum Educational Standards

There are also a National Secondary Education Commission[94] and a National Universities Commission (NUC).[95] The former Commission regulates minimum standards in secondary schools, whereas the latter does the same in universities. Respectively, these Acts govern federal funding of secondary and university education through the establishment of a National Secondary Education Fund and a National Universities Commission Fund. The powers of both Commissions to regulate minimum standards are subject to the overriding powers of the Federal Education Minister to regulate minimum standards in education under the Education (National Minimum Standards and Establishment of Institutions) Act, including pre-primary, primary, secondary, technical, higher, and special education.[96]

---

[91] Archbishop Okogie & Others v. Attorney General of Lagos State, at 340.
[92] Id.
[93] Federal Ministry of Education 2006. The restructuring of the Federal Ministry of Education: The emergence of a new FME, Ref. ME/FME/42/XIV/13, 8–9.
[94] National Secondary Education Etc. Act, Chapter N73, Laws of the Federation, 2004.
[95] National Universities Commission Act, Chapter N81, Laws of the Federation, 2004.
[96] Education (National Minimum Standards and Establishment of Institutions) Act, Chapter E3, Laws of the Federation 2004.

The federal government is also a provider of secondary education. In particular, it operates the Federal government colleges that exist in each state and enroll about 120,718 people, or 3 percent of the population of 6.4 million secondary school students in the country.[97] The management of these schools has been transferred to private operators.[98] Each publicly owned and funded university is established under a separate law adopted by the federal or state government.

Private Universities

In *Dr. Basil Ukaegbu v. Attorney-General of Imo State*,[99] a state government instituted proceedings challenging the right of the appellant, a private operator, to establish a private university. The Supreme Court of Nigeria upheld the rights of private individuals to establish and operate tertiary and post-primary institutions. The Court also affirmed the need to balance this entitlement with the right of every member of the community to what it called freedom from unsavory and diabolical institutions and teachings, a right to freedom from dissemination of information that could lead to public disorder, or that is "morally wrong." Thus, private proprietorship of universities remains subject to regulation by public authorities. The National Universities Commission determines eligibility for licensing and regulates academic standards in all universities, both public and private.

Access to Educational Institutions

The right to education should encompass a right of access on the basis of equal opportunities to publicly funded educational institutions. The enforcement of this right may, however, be denied through narrow technical rules on access to judicial remedies. The leading case on this is *Miss Adeyinka A. Badejo v. Federal Minister for Education & 2 Others*.[100] In this case the plaintiff, a child, sued through her friend and father, Dr. Babafemi Badejo, claiming that she was denied an opportunity to be called up for an interview for admission into the Federal government college on the basis of a "quota system," a policy of the government that discriminated against her on the basis of her state of origin. She initiated proceedings before the Lagos State High Court praying, among other things, for an injunction restraining the Minister from carrying out the interview for admission into the schools pending the determination of her case and a declaration that the quota policy adopted by the respondents in the selection of candidates for interview for admission into Federal government colleges in 1989 was discriminatory to the applicant and, therefore, unconstitutional and void. The Court refused the application for injunction, holding that the applicant did not have standing to initiate the case.

Dissatisfied with this decision, Miss Badejo appealed to the Court of Appeal, which decided that she had standing, but held, nevertheless, that because the

---

[97] Federal Ministry of Education 2006, p. 6.
[98] *Id.*
[99] [1983] *Nig. Sup. Crt. Cases*, 160.
[100] [1996] 8 *Nig. Weekly L. Reps.* (Part 464)15.

interview complained of had already been completed about fifteen months earlier, the matter had been overtaken by events and, therefore, there was nothing to be remitted to the lower court for further action. The Court also held that the interest of the State in the sustenance of the educational system prevailed over the rights of the applicant to access the Court or the educational system. The Court of Appeal struck out the case. On further appeal, a three-to-two majority of the Nigerian Supreme Court upheld the decision of the Court of Appeal. Access to education was therefore denied on the grounds of technical rules of standing to sue and a polarization of individual against State interests. It is noteworthy that by the time the interlocutory appeal to the Supreme Court was disposed of in 1996, Miss Badejo had left secondary school and her underlying suit had become moot.

Educational institutions are also precluded from arbitrarily altering their entry requirements to the detriment of students seeking admission. In *Ogunmadeji & Others v. Moshood Abiola Polytechnic*,[101] plaintiffs gained admission to study mass communications at the defendant institution. At the time of applying for the course, the entry requirement was an ordinary pass in mathematics. However, after admission but before registration, the defendants altered the course require-ments, requiring a credit pass in mathematics. Plaintiffs did not possess this new qualification and brought this action challenging the right of the university to alter the course requirement after they had been admitted based on the earlier advertised minimum entry requirement. The Court found in favor of the students, holding that the applicants acquired the right to registration as students on sat-isfying advertised and stated entry qualifications. This right could not be denied through a retrospective change in the entry standards. The Court concluded that the polytechnic was bound to respect the rights of plaintiffs and register the Plain-tiffs as students of their institution. The decision of the Court in this case could easily also have been grounded in the administrative law doctrines of legitimate expectation or in the prohibition of arbitrariness.

Protection of Rights in Education – University Due Process Cases

In *Garba v. University of Maiduguri*,[102] the appellants before the Supreme Court challenged the decisions of the Disciplinary Board of the Senate of the Univer-sity of Maiduguri in suspending them from the university for crimes allegedly committed during a demonstration, during which students destroyed university property, including burning down the residence of the Deputy Vice-Chancellor. The appellants, alleged members of a campus gang, were charged with responsibil-ity for various criminal acts, including looting, arson, destruction of property and indecent assault punishable under the penal code applicable in Northern Nigeria. The panel established by the university to investigate these allegations included the Deputy Vice-Chancellor whose residence was destroyed by the acts alleged against the appellants. On the recommendation of the investigation panel, the Disciplinary Board of the university's senate expelled the appellants from the university.

---

[101] [2001] 1 CHR, 372.
[102] [1986] 1 *Nig. Weekly L. Reps.* (Pt.18) 550.

The appellants challenged the expulsion in court, arguing that the process denied them a fair hearing to defend themselves before a competent tribunal with jurisdiction to adjudicate on the crimes for which they were charged by the university. They further contended that the decision of the university expelling them was taken without giving them an opportunity to clear themselves on an allegation of crime before a competent court. In its decision, the Supreme Court declared the expulsion of the appellants unlawful as neither the investigation panel nor the Disciplinary Board of the Senate of the university was competent to adjudicate on a crime. The decision expelling them from the university was therefore declared invalid.[103] However, the Courts will respect the decisions of universities where students have been given a fair hearing before disciplinary decisions and will decline to assume jurisdiction until the remedies available within the university system have been exhausted.[104]

Examinations and Certification

The right to education includes rights against providers of education (the Introduction to this volume calls these rights involving private obligations). One of such claims imposes an obligation on providers to examine and certify students or receivers of education. The organization of examinations and certification of completion of secondary education is the responsibility of the West African Examinations Council (WAEC)[105] and the National Examinations Council (NECO).[106]

The Nigerian Court of Appeal has held that the relationship between a student or candidate and these statutory examination certifying bodies is regulated by administrative not contract law, and that once certified, a secondary school certificate or result may not be decertified by the examinations regulating bodies, except in compliance with administrative law requirements, including respect for due process requirements of fair hearing.[107] In *Omodolapo Adeyanju v. West African Examinations Council*, the applicant sat and passed her final secondary school graduation examination conducted by the respondents. The Council subsequently withdrew and canceled the applicant's certificate for alleged examination misconduct without giving her the opportunity to be heard before the decision to withdraw and cancel her results was taken. She successfully challenged the decision in the High Court but the Council refused to release her certificate. On appeal, the Court of Appeal decided that under the West African Examinations Council Act, the withdrawal of a certificate or the cancellation of a candidate's result obtained in an examination conducted by the Council is a punishment that could not be

---

[103] See also In Akintemi v. Onwumechili, (1985). *1 Nig. Weekly L. Reps.* (Pt. 1) 68.

[104] Marshall I. Gil Amadi v. Rivers State University of Science and Technology & 2 Others, SUIT No. PHC/404/90, Judgment of the Honorable Justice S. E. Charles Granville, High Court of Rivers State, January 31, 2002.

[105] West African Examinations Council Act, Chapter W4, Laws of the Federation, 2004.

[106] National Examinations Council Act, Chapter N36, Laws of the Federation, 2004.

[107] Omodolapo Adeyanju v. West African Examinations Council, [2002] 13 *Nig. Weekly L. Reps.* (Pt. 785) 479.

meted out administratively without fair hearing. In ordering the release of the certificate, the Court observed:

> WAEC is an administrative body specifically established by statute to conduct examinations and award certificates. Its relationship with the candidates for it examination has statutory flavour. Consequently, it cannot punish any of its candidates without compliance with the due process of the law. In the instant case, the respondent cannot punish the appellant for purportedly engaging in examination malpractice without giving the appellant the opportunity of being heard.[108]

Generally, universities derive their powers to certify their own graduates from the laws or license establishing them. Nigeria's Supreme Court has held that it will generally respect the autonomy of the university to govern itself and will not interfere with the exercise of the powers of certification of graduates by a university because "a university is a place of great learning and research" and that it views "with trepidation, the day the court would immerse itself into the cauldron of (an) academic issue which is an area it is not equipped to handle. It will indeed be alarming for any court worth its salt to enter into the arena of questioning why a university has refused to award a degree to any student."[109]

In the earlier case of *Esiaga v. University of Calabar*,[110] the university had suspended the appellant, a final year student and Speaker of the Student Union Parliament of the respondent university, after allegedly discovering material in his room associated with a banned student gang or cult. The student initiated the proceedings to enforce his fundamental rights, seeking orders to nullify his suspension from the university and for the release of his results. The Supreme Court held that "in so far as examinations are conducted according to the university rules and regulations and duly approved and ratified by the University Senate, the courts have no jurisdiction in the matter."[111]

It is now well settled in Nigerian law that

> disputes involving the setting, sitting, marking of examination papers and publishing the results as well as the conferment and award of degrees, diplomas and certificates to deserving students are matters within the domestic forum of a university, [so that] any resort to a court action would be premature.[112]

This body of jurisprudence has firmly established the scope of a zone of domestic jurisdiction for universities within which they can exercise powers of administrative discipline and punishment after due observance of the rules of fair hearing. However, the considerable volume of litigation on the exercise of the universities' powers of discipline and administration tends to suggest that there remain

---

[108] *Id.* at 499.
[109] Patrick Magit v. University of Agriculture Makurdi & Others [2005] 19 *Nig. Weekly L. Reps.*, 211, 250.
[110] [2004] All F.W.L.R. (Pt. 206) 381.
[111] *Id.* at 404.
[112] Fetuga v. University of Ibadan, [2000] *Nig. Weekly L. Reps.* (Pt. 683) 118; University of Ilorin v. Oluwadare, [2003] All F.W.L.R. (Part 338) 747.

considerable areas of dispute about the capacities of the universities to respect the rules of fair hearing in their internal administration.

LEGAL IMPLEMENTATION OF THE RIGHT TO HEALTH IN NIGERIA: APPLICABLE STANDARDS AND JURISPRUDENCE

The right to health is even less extensively litigated in Nigeria than the right to education. Aspects of health care-related rights that have so far received judicial attention include access to medical care for HIV-positive prisoners and access to appropriate health care as a consideration for granting bail. As in education, private provision is very much permitted, subject to licensing, but service standards are again not adequately institutionalized or policed. Access issues remain outside the purview of available jurisprudence and constitutional provisions. The law has failed so far to be an instrument for stimulating demand for health care or ensuring accountability for nonavailability of health-care services.

Like the right to education, the only explicit health care-related provisions in Nigeria's Constitution are contained in the chapter on Fundamental Objectives and Directive Principles of State Policy (Chapter II). Specifically, Section 17(1) of the Constitution requires that the State social order shall be founded on the ideals of freedom, equality, and justice. In pursuit of these ideals, "governmental actions shall be humane."[113] In particular, the government is required to direct its policy toward ensuring that "the health, safety, and welfare of all persons in employment are safeguarded and not endangered or abused,"[114] and that "there are adequate medical and health facilities for all persons."[115] The Constitution also makes additional provisions for prevention and protection of child abuse and neglect,[116] and for "public assistance in deserving cases or other conditions of need."[117] As has been shown earlier, Nigerian courts have generally been reluctant to enforce Chapter II rights. In Nigeria's federal structure, health is a subject in the concurrent legislative list in which states and the federal government share responsibilities.

Apart from these provisions, Article 16 of the African Charter on Human and Peoples' Rights, which is domestic law in Nigeria, guarantees the rights of every individual to enjoy the best attainable state of physical and mental health and the responsibility of governments to take the necessary measures to protect health. The provisions of the African Charter, unlike those in Chapter II of Nigeria's Constitution, are judicially enforceable.

The National Health Insurance Scheme Act

One of the earliest legislative measures adopted by the civilian government that assumed power in Nigeria in 1999 was the National Health Insurance Scheme

---

[113] Constitution of the Federal Republic of Nigeria, 1999, Section 17(2)(c).
[114] *Id.*, Section 17(3)(c).
[115] *Id.*, Section 17(3)(d).
[116] *Id.*, Section 17(3)(f).
[117] *Id.*, Section 17(3)(g).

Act.[118] The Act establishes the National Health Insurance Scheme to ensure access to good quality and cost-effective health-care services to insured persons and their dependents.[119] The objectives of the scheme include ensuring equitable distribution of health-care costs among different income groups, ensuring adequate distribution of health facilities within the federation, and ensuring the availability of funds to the health sector for improved services.[120]

The Act establishes a Governing Council for the National Health Insurance Scheme for determining the overall policy and ensuring the effective implementation of policies and procedures of the scheme. The Council licenses and registers health maintenance organizations (HMOs) and health-care providers that provide medical services to insured persons and their dependents.[121] Defined elements of curative care include prescribed drugs and diagnostic tests; maternity care for up to four live births for every insured person; preventive care, including immunization, family planning, and prenatal and postnatal care; consultation with a defined range of specialists; hospital care in a public or private hospital in a standard ward during a stated duration of stay for physical or mental disorders; eye examination and care, excluding testing and the actual provision of eyeglasses and a range of prosthesis and dental care as defined.[122]

The HMOs are responsible for collection of contributions from eligible employers, employees, and voluntary contributors as well as rendering to the scheme returns on their activities as required by the Council. Contributions to the scheme include contributions from employers, employees, voluntary individual contributors and organizations, and local and state governments. The Council determines contributions from employers and employees toward the scheme from time to time. Under the Act an employer is not allowed to reduce the remuneration or allowances of the employee for the purposes of offsetting their responsibilities under the scheme. The Act is applicable to all employers with a minimum of ten employees.[123] Contributions under the Act are tax deductible for income tax computation purposes.[124]

Health and the Right to Bail

Although not part of the fundamental rights guaranteed under Chapter IV of the Nigerian Constitution, Nigerian courts have occasionally drawn on the constitutional recognition of health-care entitlements in translating and applying constitutionally enforceable rights. One such right is the right to personal liberty and its intersection with the right to life. The right to personal liberty is a human right that may be restricted in enforcement of police and criminal justice powers of arrest. However, arrested persons are entitled to bail except in the most heinous

---

[118] National Health Insurance Scheme Act, Chapter N42, Laws of the Federation of Nigeria, 2004.
[119] Id., Section 1(1).
[120] Id., Section 5.
[121] Id., Section 6.
[122] Id., Section 18(1).
[123] Id., Section 16(1).
[124] Id., Section 40.

offenses, or if there is evidence to suggest that they will interfere with the criminal process or will avoid trial. Ill health and the need for specialized medical attention are also recognized grounds for granting of bail.[125] In the case of *Gani Fawehinmi v. The State*, the Court of Appeal held:

> The fact that an applicant is a hypertensive patient who sees a special Cardiologist every other day for medical examination for the purpose of dosage control of the use of his prescribed drugs and that the medical equipment being used for his check-up are not normally movable is a special circumstance warranting the grant of his application for bail pending the determination of his appeal.[126]

The prevailing judicial position in Nigeria is that although not precluded from doing so, it is unusual to grant bail in capital cases, such as murder.[127] In the case of *Mohammed Abacha v. The State*, the Supreme Court of Nigeria held, however, that "whatever the stage at which bail is sought by an accused person, ill-health of the accused is a consideration weighty enough to be reckoned as special circumstances; however, mere allegation will not be sufficient as a special circumstance."[128] Such special circumstances may be made out by showing that:

(a) the ill-health of the accused is infectious or contagious or poses a real hazard to other occupants of the detention facility or prison;
(b) the prison or government authorities do not have access to medical facilities required to treat the accused or suspect;
(c) the allegations of ill-health are supported by positive, cogent, and convincing medical report issued by an expert in the field of medicine in which the accused suffering from the ill-health is referable.[129]

In the case of *Federal Republic of Nigeria v. Danjuma Ibrahim & 5 Others*,[130] two senior police officers accused of murder in the extrajudicial execution of six innocent youths applied for bail on health grounds. One of them was diagnosed with pelvic ulcer, diabetes, and cardiomyopathy, whereas another was diagnosed with HIV/AIDS. The Court granted bail to the two applicants on these grounds, holding that "the deplorable conditions in the prison today has since been taken judicial notice of by the Court of Appeal ... the prison authority is incapable of managing the conditions of health of the two applicants."[131]

In *Chukwunyere v. Commissioner of Police*,[132] the High Court of Nigeria's now defunct East Central State held that it would grant bail on liberal grounds to

---

[125] Chinemelu v. Commissioner of Police [1995] *Nig. Weekly L. Reps.* (Pt. 390) 467.
[126] [1990] 1 *Nig. Weekly L. Reps.* (Pt. 127) 486, 496–497. See also Chukwunyere v. Commissioner of Police [1975] 5 *East Central State L. Reps.* 44.
[127] Abacha v. The State [2002] 5 *Nig. Weekly L. Reps.* 761; State v. Bamaiyi, [2001] 8 *Nig. Weekly L. Reps.*, 715.
[128] *Id.*
[129] Ojuwe v. Federal Government of Nigeria [2005] 3 *Nig. Weekly L. Reps.* 913.
[130] Federal Republic of Nigeria v. Danjuma Ibrahim & 5 Others, Federal High Court, Charge No. FCT/HC/CR/79/2005, In re: Motion No. M/4717/2005, Unreported Ruling of Hon. Justice 1. U. Bello, of August 2, 2006.
[131] *Id.* at 20.
[132] Chukwunyere v. Commissioner of Police [1975] 5 *East Central State L. Reps.* 44.

an accused person suffering from diabetes, hypertension, or similar ill health "characterized by sudden or severe attacks and crises." However, the High Court of Rivers State has held that general ill-health not characterized by such sudden or severe attacks is not of its own a special ground to justify the granting of bail on health grounds.[133]

Right to Health and the African Charter

The case of *Social and Economic Rights Action Centre (SERAC) & Another v. Nigeria*[134] was a communication before the African Commission on Human and Peoples' Rights involving alleged violations resulting from the oil-field operations of the state-owned Nigerian National Petroleum Corporation (NNPC) and its joint-venture partner, the Shell Petroleum Development Corporation (SPDC). Specifically, the communication alleged that the NNPC and SPDC joint venture undertook hazardous oil field operations that contaminated the air, water, and soil of the Ogoni community in the Niger Delta, thereby violating the rights to health and clean environment under Articles 16 and 24 of the African Charter on Human and Peoples' Rights. In addition, the communication alleged that these companies, on behalf of the Nigerian State, failed to provide or permit studies of potential or actual environmental and health risks caused by these hazardous operations.

In reaching its decision, the Commission relied on the decision of the European Court of Human Rights in *X and Y v. Netherlands,*[135] where the Court held that government must take action to uphold, protect, and promote human rights as part of a domestic, rights-based development process. The European Court went further, holding that government must ensure an environment conducive to the fulfillment of human rights commitments by regulating the activities of private parties that affect the enjoyment of these rights in order to ensure the rights-based development of society.

Applying these principles to *SERAC's* case, the Commission found that the Nigerian government was responsible for the violations caused by the activities of SPDC and NNPC because it failed to fulfill its obligations guaranteed under the African Charter, which entail creating an enabling environment and regulating the activities of private parties to ensure the enjoyment of the rights guaranteed by the Charter. The Commission found that oil-field activities complained of, including pollution, blowouts, gas-flaring, and destruction of human habitation and associated agricultural resources violated, among other rights, the rights to nondiscrimination, life, property, and health in Articles 2, 4, 14, and 16, respectively, of the African Charter as well as the right to a general satisfactory environment in Article 24 of the Charter. As with the right to education, this

---

[133] State v. Donald Jaja, Charge no. PHC/IC/97, Ruling of Honorable Justice Acho Ogbonna, of February 4, 1988.

[134] (2001) *African Hum. Rts. L. Reps.* 60.

[135] 91 *Eur. Court. Hum. Rts.* (1985) (Ser. A) 32.

case demonstrates considerable permeability between the recognized categories of rights.

HIV/AIDS, Mental Illness, and Access to Remedies

In *Festus Odafe & 3 Others vs. AG Federation & 3 Others*, the Nigerian Federal High Court relied on the African Charter on Human and Peoples' Rights rather than Nigeria's Constitution to protect the right to health.[136] The applicants in this case were HIV-positive detainees in prison custody. They complained that they were denied requisite medical attention by the prison administration in a manner that unlawfully discriminated against them on grounds of their HIV-positive status and denied them their inherent dignity as human beings. Upholding their case, the Court ruled:

> Article 16 (2) [of the African Charter] places a duty on the state to take necessary measures to protect the health of their people and to ensure that they receive medical attention when they are sick. All the respondents are federal agents of this country and are under a duty to provide medical treatment for the applicants. . . . I therefore hold that the state having failed to provide medical treatment for the applicants who are diagnosed as HIV/AIDS carriers, their continuous detention without medical treatment amounts to torture.[137]

Concerning the appropriate remedy and argument that affording redress to violations of the right to health as a positive right entails high incidence of cost that would be unduly burdensome to government and the public purse, the trial judge further ruled:

> A dispute concerning socio-economic right such as right to medical attention requires a court to evaluate state policy and give judgment once it is consistent with the Constitution. I therefore appreciate the fact that the economic cost of embarking on medical provision is quite high. However, the statutes have to be complied with too and the state has a responsibility to all the inmates in prison regardless of offence involved, as in the instant case where the state has wronged the applicants by not arraigning them for trial before a competent court within a reasonable time and they have been in custody for not less than two years suffering from an illness.[138]

The trial judge in this case ordered the authorities to relocate the applicants to a medical hospital and also awarded costs in their favor.

This enlightened approach to both HIV/AIDS and the right to health is not shared by all Nigerian courts. The Court of Appeal has indeed barred HIV-positive persons from attending court proceedings in which they are party.

---

[136] Unreported, Suit No. FHC/PH/CS/680/2003, Judgment of Honorable Justice R. O. Nwodo, of February 23, 2004.
[137] *Id.* at 11.
[138] *Id.* at 13.

In *Georgina Ahamefule v. Imperial Medical Centre & Dr. Alex Molokwu*,[139] the applicant, an auxiliary nurse, sued the defendants, her employers, challenging her dismissal from employment on the grounds that she was HIV-positive. At the hearing, counsel for the defendants bizarrely objected to the applicant's presence in court, arguing that she could infect others in court. He requested the Court to take expert medical evidence to convince itself of the nonexistence of such risk before admitting the applicant into court to testify. The judge, even more bizarrely, ruled:

> Having listened to the arguments of both Counsel on the issue of the risk of an HIV patient-plaintiff giving evidence in Court, I am of the opinion [that] the view of the learned Counsel for the Defendants should be respected in view of the fact that life has no duplicate and must be guarded jealously. It is hereby ordered that an expert opinion be heard on the subject-matter either from an expert in Nigeria or from any other part of the world where research has been fully carried out.[140]

Dissatisfied with this ruling, the applicant appealed to the Court of Appeal, which, in a judgment delivered in April 2004, held that an appeal of this kind of ruling could only be brought with permission of the lower court, which had not given such permission in this case.[141]

The scope of protection of the right to health extends to mental health. The case of *Ishmael Azubuike & 3 Others v. Attorney General of the Federation & 3 Others*,[142] was instituted on behalf of mentally ill prisoners at the Maximum Security Prison in Kirikiri, Lagos, asking the Court to find their continued detention unconstitutional and to move them to a suitable psychiatric unit for treatment. The Court held that their confinement in prison without treatment violated their constitutional entitlement to personal dignity. The Court continued:

> I hold and declare that the convicted Applicants who are diagnosed as mentally retarded though not certified in compliance with S. 7 of the Prisons Act, have rights to proper medical treatment while in prison custody, sequel to the Prison Act, in particular, S. 7 and 8, and the Prisons Regulations, and the United Nations Standard Minimum Rules for the Treatment of Prisoners. I hold and declare that the failure of the . . . Respondents to give the Applicants proper medical attention while awaiting death row amounts to inhuman treatment but does not amount to degrading treatment.[143]

Through these decisions, the courts appear to have sought to reconcile the different constitutional and legal texts on health in upholding the responsibility of the state to respect, protect, promote, and fulfill the enjoyment of the right.

---

[139] Unreported, Suit No. ID/1627/2000, ruling of Honorable Justice Olufawo of the High Court of Lagos, Ikeja Division, 5 February, 2001.

[140] *Id.* at 3.

[141] Georgina Ahamefule v. Imperial Medical Centre & Dr. Alex Molokwu, CA/L/514/2001 & CA/L/225/2001, judgment of the Court of Appeal, Lagos Division, of April 21, 2004 (unreported).

[142] Unreported, Suit No. FHC/PH/CS/679/2003, Judgment of Honorable Justice R. O. Nwodo, Federal High Court, Port Harcourt Division, of February 23, 2004.

[143] *Id.* at 19.

HEALTH AND EDUCATION IN THE WORK OF THE NIGERIAN NATIONAL HUMAN RIGHTS COMMISSION

The National Human Rights Commission (NHRC or the Commission) was established by the National Human Rights Commission Act of 1995.[144] The Commission has a sixteen-member Governing Council including a chairman and an executive secretary. The council members who all serve on a part-time basis represent a variety of interests, including women and civil society. The Commission presently operates from five zonal offices: Lagos (southwest), Port Harcourt (south-south), Kano (northwest), Maiduguri (northeast), and Enugu (southeast) of Nigeria, in addition to a headquarters office located in Abuja.[145] It has staff strength of about three hundred divided among the zonal offices and four broad departments.

Mandate and Functions of the Commission

The mandate of the NHRC is set out under Section 5 of the Enabling Act that provides that the Commission shall

a. deal with all matters relating to the protection of human rights as guaranteed by the Constitution of the Federal Republic of Nigeria, the African Charter, the United Nations Charter and the Universal Declaration on Human Rights and other international treaties on human rights to which Nigeria is a signatory;

b. monitor and investigate all alleged cases of human rights violation in Nigeria and make appropriate recommendations to the Federal Government for the prosecution and such other actions as it may deem expedient in each circumstance;

c. assist victims of human rights violations and seek appropriate redress and remedies on their behalf;

d. undertake studies on all matters relating to human rights and assist the Federal Government in the formulation of appropriate policies on the guarantee of human rights;

e. publish regularly reports on the state of human rights protection in Nigeria;

f. organize local and international seminars, workshops, and conferences on human rights issues for public enlightenment;

g. liaise and cooperate with local and international organizations on human rights for the purpose of advancing the promotion and protection of human rights;

h. participate in all international activities relating to the promotion and protecion of human rights;

i. maintain a library, collect data, and disseminate information and materials on human rights generally; and

---

[144] It was originally enacted as the National Human Rights Commission Decree No. 22 of 1995. By virtue of S. 315(1)(a) of the 1999 Constitution, it became an Act of the National Assembly.

[145] A sixth zonal office for the North Central zone in Jos (north-central) was to become functional in the first half of 2006.

j. carry out all such other functions as are necessary or expedient for the
    performance of these functions under the Act.

The Commission employs a variety of methods in actualizing its protective
mandate. It uses:

*   *Litigation:* This involves either institution of judicial proceedings *suo motu* (on
    its own motion) or assisting in the prosecution or holding watching briefs in
    criminal proceedings. The Commission also appears as amicus curiae (friend
    of the court) in certain landmark cases.
*   *Mediation and Conciliation:*[146] This is usually done by a small panel of two
    or three officers of the Commission to avoid the lengthy and sometimes
    protracted course of litigation. A large majority of complaints have been
    settled amicably through this method.
*   *Public Hearing:* The Commission holds Human Rights Forum monthly in var-
    ious locations in the country. Sometimes, it invites alleged violators within
    such locations to answer to the allegations made against them by com-
    plainants. This method usually acts as a public-awareness strategy and as
    a means of holding public officers accountable, though in a small way.
*   *Advisory Services:* This involves offering professional advice to potential or
    actual human rights violators. The police in particular have been a benefi-
    ciary of this method. The dismantling of or reduction in road blocks across
    the country comes from this. As a matter of statutory requirement,[147] the
    Commission also gives advice to government and its agencies on matters
    concerning respect for human rights and the fulfillment of international and
    constitutional obligations. To be able to give such advice, the Commission
    engages in research. In 2004, the Commission embarked on a prison audit
    throughout the country. The report of that exercise was submitted to govern-
    ment and has formed the basis for massive prison reform in Nigeria.

The method to be adopted in any case depends largely on the nature of the
complaint and sometimes on the remedy requested by the complainant. But more
often than not the Commission decides on the best method to achieve the best
result in the circumstances. Again, the Commission receives complaints cutting
across all human rights. It has interpreted its mandate to include all human rights
without the usual distinction between civil and political rights on the one hand
and economic, social, and cultural rights on the other.

Admissibility

Cases and complaints taken to the National Human Rights Commission should
comply with its rules of admissibility. The admissibility rules of the Commission
are not stringent. Noncompliance with them does not necessarily signify automatic

[146] See the preambles to the NHRC Act.
[147] Section 5(b) of NHRC Act.

Table 5.1. *Number of cases concerning livelihood rights taken to the National Human Rights Commission*

	1996	1997	1998	1999	2000	2001	2002	2003	2004	2005
Number of complaints	41	114	221	343	572	593	421	432	287	300
TOTAL 3324										

a These figures were valid up to September 2005.

rejection of the complaint. This is to ensure that no one is shut out of a possible remedy for human rights violations. Complaints may be lodged by

(i)   Any person(s) acting on his/her/their own behalf;
(ii) Any person(s) acting on behalf of another person(s) who cannot or is unable to act in his/her/their own behalf;
(iii) Any person acting as a member of or in the interest of a group or class of persons; and
(iv) Any association acting in the interest of its members.

The Commission will reject a complaint if

(i)   the content or nature of the complaint does not fall within the mandate of the Commission;
(ii) the complaint is unwarranted or unfounded in law or is based on hearsay or rumor;
(iii) the language of expression is couched in abusive, insulting, or disparaging manner;
(iv) the subject matter of the complaint is already before a court of law or another statutory body; or
(v)   the complaint is anonymous.

In view of the perceived non-justiciability of economic, social, and cultural rights in Chapter II of the Constitution, most victims do not themselves bring complaints of the violation of such rights to the Commission. The majority of complaints received by the Commission allege violations of civil and political rights. There is, however, a large number of cases concerning violation of livelihood rights.[148] Categorizing these cases has involved making judgment calls. But on all categories, the number of complaints keeps increasing steadily over the years. The summary statistics of the cases are in Table 5.1.

Table 5.2 disaggregates the activities of the Commission in a sample of cases that could be conceivably classified as raising the rights to health or education (the table includes only those cases for which the complete file was accessible). There

---

[148] This category includes cases alleging the following: wrongful termination of employment; nonpayment of entitlement/compensation; medical or right to health; right to education; and seizure of land or demolition of homes.

Table 5.2. *Number of health and education cases taken to the National Human Rights Commission*

	1996	1997	1998	1999	2000	2001	2002	2003	2004	2005
Right to health	2	3	7	12	30	40	29	36	33	15
Right to education	–	1	–	2	5	7	6	1	1	3
TOTAL	2	4	7	14	35	47	35	37	34	18
GRAND TOTAL										
233										

were a total of 1,378 complaints received by the Commission under this broad classification. Of this number, 1,370 had been resolved one way or the other by the end of 2005, and only 8 remain pending. At the end of 2006, the pending complaints were three from 2004 and five from 2005.

The number of complaints dealt with by the Commission within the category of rights to health and education are few but significant for two main reasons. First, they signify that the Commission has interpreted its mandate widely to include all rights including economic, social, and cultural rights. Second, they also imply that economic, social, and cultural rights can be implemented administratively. It is noteworthy that while all the complainants are private persons or individuals, the alleged violators of these rights are mostly government and its agencies or corporate bodies.

As stated earlier, which method is adopted for the resolution of any complaint depends largely on the circumstances. In Table 5.2 most of the complaints were resolved through mediation or conciliation. Specifically, on the rights being considered here, only three have gone through litigation. In the each of those three cases, the Commission joined the matter as a third party and not as the initiator of the judicial proceedings. This helped to hasten the determination of the case or led to amicable settlement and then consent judgment.

CONCLUSIONS: PHILOSOPHY AND IMPACT OF JUDICIAL ENFORCEMENT OF EDUCATION AND HEALTH AS HUMAN RIGHTS

In Nigeria, the implicit interinstitutional bargain that underwrites the posited judicial restraint in the enforcement of economic and social rights does not exist or, if it did, has long broken down. The elected arms of government appear disinterested in effectively guaranteeing nondiscriminatory access to education and health. Far from picking up the slack, the judiciary has disabled itself from intervening through a combination of both judicial timidity and self-imposed constraints. These constraints include the doctrinal exclusion of economic and social rights from the scope of judicial powers, narrow and exclusionary rules of standing to sue, a crippling epidemic of interlocutory appeals, and prolonged delays in court proceedings.

With the exception of the doctrinal exclusion, all these constraints are applicable, with some adaptation, to the enforcement of civil and political rights. However, unlike economic and social rights, Nigerian courts suffer no doctrinal inhibitions in the enforcement of civil and political rights. As shown earlier in this chapter, most successful cases of judicial enforcement of health and education as human rights have been achieved through the route of civil and political rights. Through restrictive rules of standing to sue, Nigerian courts manifest a general discomfort with broadening access to judicial redress in public law cases generally. However, these rules are easier to overcome in the enforcement of civil and political rights than in economic and social rights cases. It is, thus, the case that to a great extent, Nigerian courts are more favorably disposed to the enforcement of civil and political rights than to economic and social rights.

Not surprising, Nigerian jurisprudence on economic and social rights is at best episodic, sparse, and incoherent. There is inadequate material for any serious quantitative analysis and the jurisprudence, apart perhaps from that concerning the domestic jurisdiction of universities, hardly profits rigorous analysis.[149] To the extent that any general observations may be made, it could be said that judicial philosophy, in a somewhat inarticulate manner, has favored the protection of rights *in* education and health although appearing rather helpless to protect or uphold rights *to* education or health.

To use the template developed by the African Commission on Human and Peoples' Rights in the *SERAC* case, Nigerian courts have felt comfortable recognizing the obligation of the State to respect and protect, including an obligation "to refrain from interfering in the enjoyment of" education,[150] and "to take measures to protect beneficiaries . . . against political, economic and social interferences,"[151] but failed to recognize an enforceable legal obligation on the part of the State to positively promote access to education as an entitlement of the citizen.

This conclusion is easily evident as the jurisprudential foundation or attitude of the major decisions concerning education as an economic and social right in Nigerian courts. The Court of Appeal said so expressly in upholding the rights of existing private proprietors of primary schools against expropriation by the State in *Archbishop Okogie & Others v. Attorney-General of Lagos State*, where it observed: "in our system, the State has no right to interfere with the freedom or any other constitutional right of the citizen save as allowed by the Constitution itself."[152] Taking this approach, the courts are able to uphold the rights to private proprietorship of educational institutions at all levels, affirming this on the bases of a mixture of entitlements to economic activity,[153] rights to freedom of expression and information,[154] and the right to property.[155] In all these cases, the courts were asked and were primarily involved in protecting the interests and profits of the proprietors (suppliers and providers) rather than the claims of students, their

---

[149] See E. S. Nwauche 2007, Rethinking the exclusive jurisdiction of Nigerian universities in academic matters, *Nig. Bar Journal* 5:1.

[150] *SERAC*, para. 45.

[151] *Id.* at para. 46.

[152] Archbishop Okogie & 6 Others v. Attorney General of Lagos State, [1981] *Nig. Const. L. Reps.* 337, 340.

[153] *Id.*

[154] *Id.*

[155] Adewole & Others v. Alhaji L. K. Jakande, [1981] 1 *Nig. Const. L. Reps.* 262, 279.

parents, or other consumers. These cases have firmly established the roles of private education providers, but there is limited jurisprudential guidance on the extent of state obligations to provide or guarantee access to or standards in education, except the affirmation by the Supreme Court in *Nnanna Ukaegbu's* case of the power of the State to regulate private providers of tertiary education.

Similarly, in the examination and expulsion cases, the courts have used due process arguments to protect students from arbitrary deprivation of already existing educational places and admissions. However, in the *Badejo* case, which asserted a right of access to an educational place or institution, the courts did not hesitate in relying on technical rules of access and standing to preclude substantive consideration of a right of access on a nondiscriminatory basis to secondary education.

The consequences flowing from this are at best mixed. Fundamentally, it remains doubtful whether Nigerian courts are prepared to recognize and protect a human right to education with a constitutional basis.[156] There has emerged from the jurisprudence, however, a consequential recognition of education-related entitlements in the interstices of other constitutional rights rather than as a right in itself. The pragmatic protection of private proprietorship or supply of education from pre-primary to tertiary has had the consequence of increasing educational places at all levels. In reality, what Nigerian courts achieve here is recognition of a right to economic activity extending to the supply of education to those who can pay the prices charged by the providers. Consequently, the jurisprudence has broadened access to education simply by making more places available to those with the means. Access to basic education has been partly addressed through the Universal Basic Education Act. The question of standards and quality of the available education has not yet attracted judicial attention.

Similarly, the insistence of the courts on rigorous due process standards in student discipline protects students in their educational places without extending rights of access to educational institutions. In terms of constitutional fundamentals, the Nigerian Court of Appeal has merely recognized a responsibility on the part of the government to provide education as a social service,[157] rather than as a legal obligation. There has been no judicial elaboration of state obligations in the provision of access or other legal guarantees to this social service.

This interstitial approach to judicial protection has been replicated in relation to the right to health. Essentially, the jurisprudence suggests that Nigerian courts have felt able to take an infection-control or harm-reduction view of health in the cases, and will afford remedies to reduce the risks of spread of infectious or contagious diseases, such as HIV/AIDS or tuberculosis in confined spaces, especially in a prison or in places of detention. They will also, in exceptional cases, as shown in the bail cases, recognize and uphold a duty on their part to take steps to ensure that an applicant in the care or control of the State does not die from the inability of the State to provide them with adequate conditions of health care, deploying due process and penal policy arguments.

---

[156] Our research did not turn up any litigation seeking enforcement of education-related rights in the African Charter.

[157] Archbishop Okogie & 6 Others v. Attorney General of Lagos State, *supra* n. 42.

In practice, given the overwhelming prevalence of poverty and the poor state of health facilities, this relief is available only to relatively comfortable or famous detainees who can afford upmarket medical care for serious ailments. It is no accident that the major cases on this point concern a famous lawyer (Gani Fawehinmi), the exceptionally wealthy son of an ex-military dictator (Mohammed Abacha), and two well-connected senior police officers accused of rather heinous human rights violations (in *Danjuma Ibrahim*). The effect again is a judicial privatization of access issues. This is far from a firm or genuine recognition of health as a human right or a judicial elaboration of the elements of the constitutional obligations of the State to facilitate access to health care or service to citizens. The case of *Georgina Ahamefula* dramatizes in an extreme way a general judicial tendency against access rights either directly or in association with economic and social rights.

In effect, Nigerian courts implicitly recognize an obligation on the part of the State in some cases to respect or protect rights related to health and education but not an obligation to promote or fulfill these rights. To use a rough and ready metaphor, Nigerian courts may protect entitlements in health and education only as a shield against arbitrariness, a real and present risk of untimely death or spread of contagion, but not as a ladder that promotes access to greater well-being for all. Viewed in this context, the courts have only felt able to consider cases in which the remedies are negative or cost-neutral to the State, such as cases seeking injunctions or declarations. Compliance in these cases has been mostly easy to achieve. By contrast, there are no reported cases upholding access rights or awarding cost-sensitive remedies, such as damages or affirmative policy measures.

As a practical matter, only in the cases of *Odafe* and *Azubuike*, discussed under the right to health, were efforts made on the part of government to comply with the judicial orders. In both cases the government, through the prison authorities, made efforts to provide access to medical care to the prisoners/ plaintiffs, but has not yet developed a systemwide policy response to implement the decisions in these cases. In most other cases considered, the outcomes were favorable to government or, in any case, against the petitioner/plaintiff mostly on technical grounds.

The practical result of the cases has been to promote private provision of these essential services in health and education, and, concomitantly, a diminution of the role of the State in guaranteeing both as essential social goods. This has widened the access gap between those who can and those who cannot afford these services without in any way improving the quality assurance or standards of service provision by either the public or private sector. Put another way, the growth of private participation in and provision of health and education services has not been matched by growth in the regulatory capacity of the State or its administration.

In terms of their jurisprudential value, the decision of the Court of Appeal in the case of *Archbishop Okogie v. Attorney-General of Lagos State* continues to govern judicial attitudes regarding the enforcement of economic and social rights, excluding such rights from the purview of judicial enforcement as constitutional entitlements.

The effect of the widely cited decision of the African Commission on Human and Peoples' Rights in the *SERAC* case, is yet to be seen in judicial reasoning and attitudes, or in the communities of the Niger Delta. The few improvements to the communities' well-being have accrued from a combination of local initiatives involving both political engagement with and escalation against government and private oil interests alike, rather than from any single legal intervention. However, the *SERAC* case has certainly inspired and opened up new possibilities for an articulate and growing body of advocates for the legal protection of economic and social rights who are, through legislative and courtroom advocacy, indirectly translating the promise of the case into medium- to long-term public-policy agendas. One of the consequences is the growth of civil society advocacy initiatives for the protection of economic and social rights such as the Social and Economic Rights Initiative (SERI) and Alliances for Africa (AfA), which focus on training and developing civil society advocacy skills for economic and social rights.

One other constraint that limits the utility of judicial implementation of these rights is the duration of litigation. To take a few examples, the case of the prisoners with HIV/AIDS, *Festus Odafe & Others v. Attorney-General of the Federal,* initiated on November 25, 2002, took about fifteen months to come to judgment, in February 2004, on the question of whether the prison had a responsibility to provide them with care and treatment. In the case of *Georgina Ahamefula v. Imperial Medical Centre,* the interlocutory question whether an HIV-positive person could testify in court in her case was first raised in January 2001, and was decided upon by the Court of Appeal in February 2004. It was still pending in the Supreme Court at the time of writing, more than six years after it first arose. The case of access to education involving *Miss Adeyinka Badejo v. Federal Minister of Education* was first initiated in September 1988 but came to judgment in the Supreme Court on the interlocutory question of whether or not she had standing to sue more than eight years later, on October 21, 1996, by which time Badejo had completed her secondary education elsewhere and was in the final year of her undergraduate studies! In all these examples, the Nigerian judicial process appears inadequate to provide both specific remedies to the plaintiffs and more generalized policy response to the violations. In all but the first of these three examples, interlocutory applications unduly delayed a consideration of the substantive claims to an extent that irreparably damaged the utility of judicial remedies.

A close examination of the relevant caseload of the National Human Rights Commission indicates that it has considered cases against mostly individuals and corporate entities and institutions, without being constrained by any state-actor requirement. It is not clear whether this is the result of a clear notion of the horizontal applicability of these rights between or against non-state actors. From the point of view of staff and members of the Council of the Commission, it seems that their approach has been determined by two things. First, their nonadversarial procedures focus on mediation without necessarily producing a legally binding decision in the same way that a court decision does. Second, to the extent that the Commission's procedures entail a consideration of legal points, those are confined to statutory rather than constitutional arguments that can only be resolved by Superior Courts of Record, to which category the Commission does not belong. There is, thus, nothing that precludes the Commission from hearing or considering cases in which the statutory, contractual or common law obligations of the parties are at issue. The National Human Rights Commission has the facility of providing a comparatively cost-effective administrative venue for the implementation of economic and social rights. The effectiveness of this process, however, remains at best unproven.

On the whole, evidence of a systemwide impact of the legal and judicial system remains, like the jurisprudence, quite sparse. However, there is significant but yet only minimally explored capacity for civil society advocacy initiatives to influence policy and encourage the administrative and legislative implementation of these rights. Whether or not this potential is fully optimized will depend in part on the future political and institutional evolution of Nigeria.

6 The Implementation of the Rights to Health Care and Education in Indonesia[1]

BIVITRI SUSANTI

SOCIAL RIGHTS AND CORRUPTION

There is a well-known saying in Indonesia: "When your rooster is stolen, do not go to the law enforcers, because you will then lose your goat." Although it is unclear precisely when this phrase became popular, corruption in the Indonesian judiciary can be traced back to the 1945 to 1966 period – the years of the Soekarno presidency and the first presidency of the newly independent Indonesia.[2]

In the years following Indonesian independence, judges were increasingly seen as "instruments of the revolution."[3] In line with this conception of the role of the judiciary, the president was formally granted far-reaching powers and influence over the judicial system.[4] According to scholars of the Indonesian judiciary, this cooptation of the judiciary by the Soekarno administration began what would become a tradition of corruption within the Indonesian judiciary.[5] Despite hailing itself as the "New Order" administration, the Soeharto government that directly followed the Soekarno administration did nothing to alleviate the lack of independence of the Indonesian court. During both the Soekarno and Soeharto administrations, lower court judges were frequently put under the jurisdiction of the executive. Lacking the legitimacy of a truly independent judiciary, a corrupt, bureaucratic

---

[1] This chapter is based on the author's own expertise in Indonesian litigation, reviews of available cases and media reports, and interviews with key actors. Dimas Prasidi and Agus Ramdani participated in the interviews and conducted field research. Interviews were held with A. Irman Putra Sidin, Constitutional Court; Anwar Stirman Rasyid Rahmat, plaintiff in *Buyat* case; Cecep Kosaih, Cidabak First Court; Choirul Anam, former public defender at Jakarta Legal Aid; Dadang Trisasongko, former public defender at Jakarta Legal Aid; Frans Hendra Winata, private lawyer; Habib Chirzin, National Commission of Human Rights; Ines Thioren Situmorang, Jakarta Legal Aid; Iskandar Sitorus, Health Legal Aid; Jajang, Sukabumi First Court; Jevelina Punuh, JATAM; Lambok Gultom, APHI; Luhut MP Pangaribuan, private lawyer; Manik, Ministry of Health; Nurlela, Teacher; Opik, plaintiff in *Cibadak Polio* case; Philippa Venning, Peri Umar Farouk, World Bank; Rex Richard Panambunan, State Electricity Company; Royke Bagalatu, Health Legal Aid; Sebastiaan Pompe; Siti Maemunah; JATAM; Suratno, South Jakarta First Court; and Umar Suyudi, Ministry of Environment.
[2] See Daniel S. Lev 2000, p. 161.
[3] Official explanation to Law No. 13 of 1965 regarding judicial power. This law was changed in 1970 and in 1999.
[4] There was, for example, Law No. 14 of 1964 regarding the Supreme Court allowing direct government interference in cases before the court.
[5] S. Pompe 2005, p. 53.

culture emerged within the Indonesian judicial system.[6] This culture of corruption has been studied in depth, and the lack of a functioning bar association until 2005, the absence of a promotion and placement system for judges, and the lack of a true judicial oversight system are frequently cited as being the most significant contributing factors.[7]

In line with these analyses, there is evidence that this culture of corruption has not abated. In a United Nation's Special Rapporteur on Civil and Political Rights in Indonesia report in 2002, the researchers found that,

> During the Special Rapporteur's mission, a number of reports were issued by various Indonesian organizations alleging widespread and systemic corruption within the administration of justice system.[8]

In Transparency International's 2006 Corruption Perceptions Index, Indonesia ranks 130 out of 163 countries listed.[9] The public-perception survey conducted by Transparency International Indonesia also reveals that the judiciary is perceived as one of the most corrupt state institutions, together with the parliament, the police, and public prosecutors.[10]

These strongly negative perceptions of the judiciary have important consequences for citizen behavior. In 2001, an Asia Foundation survey showed that 62 percent of citizens said that they would avoid going to the courts at all costs.[11] This raises the question: If not the judicial system, what, then, is the preferred way to resolve disputes among citizens and between citizens and the state? In the face of a dysfunctional formal system for dispute resolution, informal institutions have become a more popular alternative. In particular, the process known in Indonesia as *musyawarah untuk mufakat* or *musyawarah*, which literally means "consensus through deliberation," plays a crucial role in the lives of Indonesian citizens.

Though popular, the informal institution of musyawarah remains an imperfect alternative to the formal judicial system. On one hand, musyawarah's origins in traditional Indonesian negotiations make it a familiar means for dispute resolution. On the other hand, the concept of musyawarah also has strong negative connotations and is used by many Indonesians to describe dealings with the often corrupt judges and court clerks of the Indonesian judicial system. Despite these varied meanings of the term, the Asia Foundation survey found that 86 percent of Indonesians believe that, compared to litigation and other formal procedures, musyawarah is the more trusted option for dispute resolution.[12]

---

[6] On the "culture of corruption," see Gary Goodpaster 2002. Reflections on corruption in Indonesia, In Tim Lindsey and Howard Dick (eds.), *Corruption in Asia: Rethinking the governance paradigm,* 87.

[7] See among others: Lev, *supra*, Pompe, *supra*, and the Supreme Court of Indonesia 2003.

[8] D. P. Cumaraswamy 2002.

[9] http://www.transparency.org/content/download/10825/92857/version/1/file/CPI_2006_presskit_eng.pdf (accessed March 10, 2007).

[10] http://www.ti.or.id/banner/go/52/ (accessed March 10, 2007).

[11] The Asia Foundation 2001.

[12] *Id.*

The deeply rooted corruption in Indonesia undoubtedly has a significant impact on the fulfillment of social rights. As a World Bank report points out:

Corruption weakens the ability of the state to deliver basic public goods: essential services and the rules that allow societies to function effectively. As such it taxes most the poor and the vulnerable, Indonesia's silent majority, creates high macro-economic risks, jeopardizes financial stability, compromises public safety and law and order, and above all, it undermines the legitimacy and credibility of the state in the eyes of the people.[13]

Although corruption has been the main obstacle in the quest for human rights, an awareness of basic human rights issues is itself lacking. According to the Asia Foundation survey, 56 percent of all respondents were unable to provide a single example of a right to which they were legally entitled. Furthermore, of respondents with no formal education, 97 percent were unable to provide a single example. Among those few examples provided by respondents, the majority cited the very examples contained in the question itself, essentially reiterating a right of which they were only recently informed. Among these examples, the ones most frequently cited by respondents included the right to fair treatment under the law, the right to a secure living environment, and the right to legal protection.[14]

The lack of awareness of basic fundamental rights is at least partly due to the fact that discussions of such rights are generally absent from Indonesian political discourse. Discussions on human rights issues have predominantly focused on past human rights violations, especially those violations occurring during the Soeharto administration. Though the nature of human rights violations committed during the Soeharto government may have been gross, this emphasis on the past has effectively removed discussion of current human rights from the public sphere.

In contrast to the condition of the state of civil and political rights during the Soeharto administration, standards for health care and education under Soeharto were relatively high, at least in part because the main task, given the prevailing level of state capacity, was the simple provision of basic services. The relative successes of the Soeharto administration stemmed from the aggressive development agenda pursued by his government. As Soeharto took over the government from the "socialist-oriented" president Sukarno in 1966, he implemented radical economic reforms. Foreign aid and investment were encouraged with the intention of reviving the Indonesian economy. Soeharto's New Order government also implemented the Development Paradigm, in which virtually every effort undertaken by the government was to be directed at development needs, with an emphasis on inflation, economic growth, and economic stability.[15]

In large part, these innovations brought about positive developments for the Indonesian economy. They were to be short-lived, however, as the macro economic policies of Soeharto failed to build a strong foundation for economic sustainability,

---

[13] The World Bank 2003. *Combating corruption in Indonesia, enhancing accountability for development* (accessed January 2, 2007).

[14] The Asia Foundation, *supra.*

[15] Because of this paradigm, too, in the early 1990s, Soeharto was called *Bapak Pembangunan* ("the Father of Development") by the state-controlled media.

Q5. As a citizen, you have many rights, including the right to take legal action in case of theft, violence, or injury to person or property. Can you give other examples of such rights?

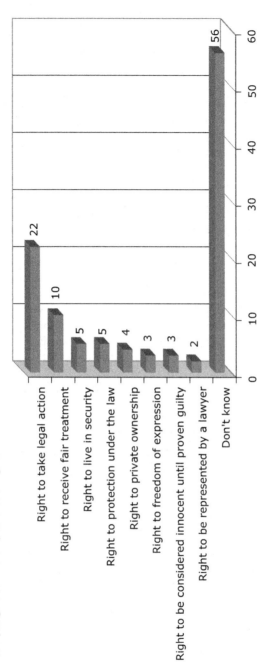

Figure 6.1. Citizens' knowledge of fundamental rights. *Source:* The Asia Foundation 2001. *Citizens' perception of the Indonesian justice sector.*

and the Indonesian economy fell victim to an economic crisis in mid-1997.[16] The looming crisis, however, was largely unforeseen at the time; because of the repressive nature of the administration, the facts and details of economic management were not revealed.

The fall of Soeharto, indeed, was a turning point in Indonesian history. Indonesia's economic difficulties exposed the more pervasive flaws of the Indonesian political system, while also creating an environment more conducive to political reform. Going beyond a mere change of leadership, the end of the Soeharto administration was accompanied by fundamental changes to the Indonesian political system, and the Constitution was amended in 1999, 2000, 2001, and 2002. Although political considerations precluded more sweeping reforms, and the government refused the demand advocated by nongovernmental organizations (NGOs) for an entirely new constitution, only a relatively few provisions remained from the original 1945 Constitution. Ultimately, the revamped constitution contained 166 new provisions (including sections), and only 29 of the provisions stayed intact.

One effect of these drastic changes to the Constitution was an extensive emphasis on human rights. Provisions regarding economic, social, and cultural rights, as well as civil and political rights, were inserted into the Constitution, and the enactment of human rights laws regulating these provisions soon followed. In addition, many of the human rights covenants previously ratified by Indonesia became national laws in 2005, including the International Covenant on Economic, Social, and Cultural Rights (ICESCR) and the International Covenant on Civil and Political Rights (ICCPR).

Despite these constitutional reforms, social policy in the country as a whole continues to struggle in several crucial aspects. According to the United Nations Development Programme's *2006 Human Development Report*, Indonesia's Human Development Index (HDI) is a middling 0.71 and is ranked 108 out of 177 countries.[17] The Director General for Elementary Education at the Ministry of Education, Indradjati Sidi, has stated that more than 30 percent of elementary schools are either ruined or in a state of irreversible decay. A large percentage of state elementary schools can no longer be used safely. As a result, all activities in these schools are conducted outside because the government has failed to allocate the necessary funds to rebuild them.[18]

The juxtaposition of Indonesia's progressive constitutional reforms with its utter inability to meet the basic needs of its citizens symbolizes, for many, the problems of modern Indonesia. Critics blame the gap between Indonesia's high aspirations and its grim realities on the lack of adequate legal protections, as A. Patra M. Zen explains: "[Economic and social] rights in principle have become constitutional rights, but they have not become rights. That is to say, they cannot be enforced using the domestic legal framework."[19] The question of the justiciability of the

---

[16] R. Tanter 1991.
[17] UNDP, Human Development Report 2006. Data tables available at http://hdr.undp.org/en/media/ hdr_2006_tables.pdf.
[18] *The Jakarta Post*, March 2, 2004.
[19] A. P. M. Zen 2005, p. 71.

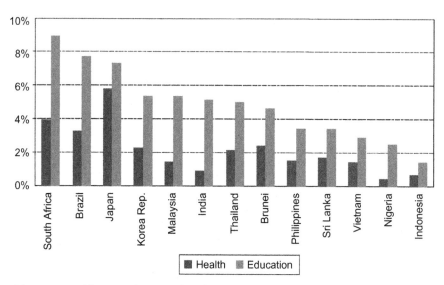

Figure 6.2. Public expenditure on health and education, average 1996–2000 (% GDP). *Source:* World Development Indicators 2004. *UNDP Indonesia Human Development Report,* 2004.

rights to health care and education has become a central issue. This again raises a fundamental question about Indonesians' distrust of the legal system: How often have courts been utilized as a means of enforcing the state's obligation to fulfill these rights?

The research conducted here suggests that, given the size and population of Indonesia, the number of cases on the rights to health care and education is startlingly small. This chapter, which examines Indonesian court decisions issued during the period of 1995 to 2005, finds only seven cases on the right to health care and five cases concerning the right to education. In light of the poor condition of health care and education in Indonesia, the paucity of cases brought before the court is unexpected and demands further analysis.

This chapter examines the above mentioned twelve cases addressing health care and education in Indonesia and will be presented in six parts. This section put the discussion within the context of Indonesian political history, corruption in the Indonesian judiciary, and the state of social rights in Indonesia. The second section elaborates the constitutional and legislative framework for the right to health care and the right to education in Indonesia. The third section explores the legislative framework and the structure of the judiciary as well as the National Human Rights Commission, as the institutions most directly related to the cases studied. Next, the fourth and fifth sections examine cases on the rights to health care and education in narrative. Facts obtained from legal briefs and interviews serve as case studies, allowing us to assess the impact that the relatively few cases have had on Indonesian policy. Finally, the analyses from the preceding sections are constructed into several conclusions to answer the essential question this book's introductory chapter poses: How, if at all, is the Indonesian court becoming involved in the creation of economic and social policy?

METHODOLOGY

Decisions from 1995 to 2005 by both apex courts in Indonesia, the Supreme Court and the Constitutional Court, are the subject of this study. However, relevant cases that have not been final and binding are also examined to enrich the findings. The period of 1995 to 2005 is chosen because it represents a turning point for Indonesians vis-à-vis the legal system: It has only been since 1995 that NGOs and legal aid institutions began to actively support the economic and social claims of marginalized people in Indonesia. It is widely understood that before this point, Indonesian citizens were grossly unaware of their social and economic rights, and that NGOs have played a vital role in recent public empowerment.

The cases considered in this study were restricted to those heard at the national level. The reasons for this are pragmatic because Indonesia is a unitary state with one structure of the judiciary (there is no state–federal court system). All cases in all high courts (appellate court) have the final appeal process (cassation) in the Supreme Court. Also, the Kelsenian Constitutional Court of Indonesia is centralized. The decisions of the Constitutional Court are final and binding. Thus, it is believed that judicial opinions and political situations throughout the Indonesian judicial system will be virtually the same.

A major obstacle for this research has been the limited sources of information and data on the decisions of the Supreme Court. Whereas the newly established Constitutional Court has a reliable database accessible on its Web site,[20] it is difficult to gain access to the decisions of the lower courts, let alone to identify the lower court cases most relevant to this study.

Until recently, only selected decisions were printed in a jurisprudence series, *Yurisprudensi Indonesia*.[21] Sebastiaan Pompe, an expert on the Indonesian judiciary, has highlighted the limitations of these sources. Pompe found that although the Supreme Court decided close to eight thousand cases in 1990, only fifty-eight of them were published in *Yurisprudensi Indonesia* (0.6 percent).[22] Another striking fact is that in the early 1990s (1991–1995), there was not any jurisprudence published by the Court.[23]

To deal with these obstacles, the initial stages of the research focused on exploring media coverage of those court cases concerning the rights to health care and education. Other sources that have proved valuable for this study are the National

---

[20] Information on the Constitutional Court is available at www.mahkamahkonstitusi.go.id

[21] Research was conducted in 2005–2006, when it was difficult to find decisions. It is important to note that there is now a Decree of the Chief Justice of the Supreme Court No. 144/KMA/SK/VIII/2007 regarding Transparency Information in the Court. This decree is the work of the Supreme Court Reform Team Task Force on Judicial Transparency that consists of judges, court clerks, and individuals outside the Court. Another output of the team are the web sites www.mahkamahagung.go.id and www.putusan.net, which have been online since 2007.

[22] Pompe, *supra* at 436. See also G. Churchill 1992.

[23] Pompe, *supra* at 436.

Human Rights Commission, NGOs working in the field of social and economic rights, and legal aid institutions.

Although NGOs may be an alternative source for data, the databases of the NGOs are also often poor. Interviews, therefore, provided an important means of seeking data and gathering information.

THE CONSTITUTIONAL AND LEGISLATIVE FRAMEWORK FOR THE RIGHTS TO HEALTH CARE AND EDUCATION

Given its economic difficulties and vast and diverse population, the Indonesian case presents an especially great challenge for the effective extension of formal constitutional rights. It is a unitary state of thirty-three provinces with a population of 240 million, but one that is geographically divided. As a large archipelagic country consisting of more than 13,600 islands, Indonesia faces distinct problems of enforcement, review, and oversight.

The narrative of constitutional rights in Indonesia began during the preparation of the declaration of independence, which was announced on August 17, 1945. On August 18, Soekarno, one of the declarers, became the first president of Indonesia, and the first Constitution of the Republic of Indonesia (*Undang Undang Dasar 1945*) was enacted. The preparation of the constitution had been ongoing since early 1945. The 1945 Constitution, however, was generally concise to a fault and overly vague. Articles regarding human rights issues were very few, though the rights to education and health care were included.[24]

On the right to education and to health care, the 1945 Constitution reads:

Article 31
1. Every citizen has the right to education.
2. The government shall establish and conduct a national educational system which shall be regulated by law.

Article 34
The poor and destitute children shall be cared for by the State.

Only four years after the 1945 Constitution was enacted, a new constitution, establishing a new system of government, was elaborated. In 1949 the Indonesian and Dutch governments came to an agreement, as the Dutch, backed by the Allied forces, claimed that Indonesian independence was unacceptable. Under the 1949 Constitution, Indonesia became a federalist government set up as the United States

---

[24] The discussion regarding human rights provision during the drafting of the Constitution is noteworthy. There were supporters of the "integralistic state," in which the state does not have the obligation to provide the citizens' rights, as well as opponents, who wanted to insert human rights provisions into the Constitution. See the minutes of BPUPKI meeting in Sekretariat Negara RI, *Risalah Sidang Badan Penyelidik Usaha-Usaha Persiapan Kemerdekaan Indonesia (BPUPKI) – Panitia Persiapan Kemerdekaan Indonesia (PPKI) 28 Mei 1945 – 22 Agustus 1945* (Jakarta: Sekretariat Negara RI, 1995), at pp. 262, 275–278, and 321. For discussion regarding the integralistic principle, see M. Simanjuntak 1997. *Pandangan Negara Integralistik.* Jakarta: PT Pustaka Utama Grafiti; and K. Jayasuriya 1999, p. 173.

of Indonesia. In the 1949 Constitution, the right to health care and the right to education were once again included.

One year after the enactment of the 1949 Constitution, the Indonesian government enacted its third constitution in its short history. The 1950 Constitution, or "Temporary Constitution of 1950," set up a unitary state and a parliamentary system of government. The Temporary Constitution of 1950 also mandated the establishment of a *Konstituante* or Constitutional Assembly, a legislature charged with the task of drafting a new and definitive constitution to replace the temporary constitution. The Konstituante attempted to complete this task from 1956 to 1959, until, in July 1959, the project was declared a failure. As a result, the government reverted to a reenactment of the 1945 Constitution by Presidential Decree, issued on July 5, 1959, and known as *Dekrit Presiden 5 Juli 1959.*[25]

The 1945 Constitution was ambiguous and elliptical as it was considered a temporary constitution drafted in a short period of time and only intended to ease the transition to independence. In part because of its vagueness, Soekarno was able to use constitutional justifications for staying in power for twenty-one years, followed by Soeharto's term of thirty-two years. During these two administrations, the 1945 Constitution was repeatedly used as a pretense for justifying authoritarian rule, despite the fact that the 1945 Constitution was never intended to last beyond the country's earliest years.

After the fall of Soeharto in 1998, the 1945 Constitution was finally challenged and accused of being a tool for authoritarian leaders. The amendment to the 1945 Constitution made significant changes in Indonesia's legal and political system, and of the approximately 166 new provisions in the amended Constitution, only 29 provisions stay unchanged. New articles on human rights are among the most important changes.

The amended Constitution of 1945 establishes a presidential system. The parliament is comprised of the House of Representatives (*Dewan Perwakilan Rakyat,* or DPR) with 550 members and the Regional Representatives Council (*Dewan Perwakilan Daerah,* or DPD) that has 128 members. Although there are two chambers of parliament, Indonesian laws are made only by the House of Representatives. The Regional Representative Council does not have authority in the legislative process, apart from providing recommendations to the House.

The fall of Soeharto brought about significant changes in the country. Being a unitary state, Indonesia now has thirty-three provinces, whereas it used to have twenty-seven provinces that included East Timor. The Soeharto administration applied a very strong control over the region, but since 1999 Indonesia has applied a new concept of regional autonomy. It is now stipulated by the law on regional governments that all implementation of public services is under the authority of the regional governments, with the exception of foreign policy, defense, security, judicial matters, monetary and fiscal policy, and religious affairs.

The health-care and education systems work within this context of decentralization. As this section will show, the new decentralization concept, together with other factors, significantly affects the state of health care and education.

---

[25] See A. B. Nasution 1992.

The Indonesian legal system is a complex mixture of civil, Islamic, and traditional law. Islamic family law, which deals with divorce, guardianship, and inheritance cases, is applicable to Muslim citizens. There are designated religious courts for Islamic family law cases. The structure of the religious court follows the structure of the court in general from the district level to the Supreme Court. In addition, because of a long-term conflict in Aceh, an area in Sumatera Island, Islamic law is applied in that province based on Law No. 11 of 2006 regarding the Aceh Government.[26]

INDONESIAN CONSTITUTIONAL CHANGE (1999–2002) AND THE RIGHTS TO HEALTH AND EDUCATION

The second amendment to the Constitution in 2000 introduced Chapter XA on Human Rights. Many of the new provisions mirror the rights contained in international human rights covenants. These rights include civil and political rights (Article 28A), equal treatment before the law (Article 28D), economic, social, and cultural rights (Article 28C), the right to a healthy environment (Article 28H, Section 1), and the right to receive medical care (Article 28H, Section 1) and social security (Article 28H, Section 3). The state is obligated to protect, advance, and fulfill these rights (Article 28I, Section 4).

The insertion of human rights concerns in the Constitution continued through the fourth (and last) amendment to the Constitution in 2002. The fourth amendment resulted in even more stringent requirements on the state to fulfill economic, social, and cultural rights. Article 31, Section 4, states that "the state shall prioritize the budget for education to a minimum of 20 percent of the State Budget." This article goes further than other human rights considerations in the Constitution because it specifically regulates a number of positive duties that the state is required to fulfill: take care of impoverished people (Section 1), develop a system of social security and empower the underprivileged (Section 2), and provide public services including medical facilities (Section 3). Furthermore, the state is also obligated to advance science, technology, and the national culture (Article 31, Section 5, and Article 32, Section 1) and to preserve local languages (Article 32, Section 2).

Following the amendments, two new laws concerning human rights were enacted, namely, Law No. 39 of 1999 regarding Human Rights and Law No. 26 of 2000 regarding the Human Rights Court. Law No. 39 further regulates the provisions in the Constitution. Law No. 39 also establishes the National Commission of Human Rights and the Human Rights Court. The Human Rights Court, under the jurisdiction of the court of criminal cases, hears cases that pertain to the gross

---

[26] This law was enacted in 2006 as a result of the Helsinki Agreement between the Indonesian government and the Free Aceh movement. The application of Islamic law was initiated in the Abdurrahman Wahid Administration in 1999, and then it was strengthened by this new law. The unique form of special autonomy established by this law will certainly create complexity in providing health care and education. The law does contain a set of excellent provisions of human rights, but the accommodation of certain schemes, such as Islamic-based curriculum, will require further advancement in the legal environment.

violation of human rights.[27] Thus, it is not relevant to the rights to health care and education discussed in this chapter and is not discussed at length.

Apart from the Bill of Rights in the Constitution and the new laws concerning human rights, Indonesia has ratified important international human rights treaties, including the newly enacted law concerning the ratification of the International Covenant on Economic, Social, and Cultural Rights (Law No. 11 of 2005).

THE LEGISLATIVE FRAMEWORK FOR EDUCATION

Education in Indonesia is under the control of the Ministry of Education. The Ministry provides general guidelines and standards on education and manages the educational system throughout the country. Direct services, however, are delivered by the regional government.

Schools are divided into three stages: (a) primary education of six years; (b) secondary education, which is divided into a three-year junior high school period and a three-year senior high school period; and (c) university.

The government directly provides education through subsidized state schools, especially in remote areas. State schools are made available in every *Kelurahan*, the lowest level of administration in the region. There is one state university in almost all provinces in Indonesia. The government also provides (inadequate) salaries for teachers of state schools and universities.

The Law on National Education System regulates basic compulsory education, which typically covers nine years of schooling. In principle, this means that the government is obligated to ensure that education is readily available for the first nine years of one's education. In reality, however, the measures have often not been successful. As mentioned earlier, more than 30 percent of elementary schools are either ruined or in a state of irreversible decay. The lack of funds in the budget is often cited as the main obstacle for providing basic compulsory education.[28]

There is political will to improve education in Indonesia, at least in principle. The constitutional provision regarding the 20 percent allocation of the state budget for education has been reinforced by Article 49 of Law No. 20 of 2003, concerning the National Education System. The provision states that the 20 percent budget allocation must exclude the salaries of teachers and of regional government training funds, thereby requiring that more money be delegated overall. In addition, the 20 percent obligation is also applicable for the budget at the provincial and district levels. However, based on a study conducted by the Ministry of Finance, the 20 percent ratio can only be achieved after 2009, and even then only on the assumption of 5 percent economic growth and 8 percent growth on education spending per year.[29]

---

[27] The Human Rights Court is the only one of its kind in the world. Usually courts for gross violation of human rights are in regional or international tribunals. It is said that the Indonesian Human Rights Court was established to protect General Wiranto, who is allegedly responsible for gross violations of human rights in East Timor, from being taken to an international tribunal.

[28] *The Jakarta Post*, March 2, 2004.

[29] *Media Indonesia*, January 27, 2004, Pendidikan paling cepat 2009 anggaran pendidikan capai 20% APBN.

The criticisms toward the government's efforts to increase the quality of education were answered by applying "The Reduction of Government Subsidy on Oil Program" of 2005. The Program covers the areas of education, health care, village infrastructure, and the "Direct Cash Subsidy." On education, the government uses a scheme called "School Operational Fund Support" (*Bantuan Operasional Sekolah*) to support the nine-year period of compulsory schooling. In particular, it provides operational budgets for state schools as well as scholarships for poor students.

THE LEGISLATIVE FRAMEWORK FOR HEALTH CARE

Health care in Indonesia is organized by the Ministry of Health, based in Jakarta, which provides direct services as well as standards of health care for private health-care providers. As in the case of education, the health services are delivered by regional governments. The central government, for the most part, merely provides the regulatory framework, health-care standards, and standards for the medical profession.

Direct services by the government are provided through state hospitals and Centers for Public Health Care (known in Indonesia as *Pusat Kesehatan Masyarakat* or *Puskesmas*) in many areas. In addition, the Ministry of Health also helps regional governments to set up and organize Integrated Health Care Service Posts (*Pos Pelayanan Terpadu or Posyandu*) in the villages. By law, there must be a minimum of one Center for Public Health Care in every *Kecamatan*, the lower level of administration under the district level.

In 2003 the Ministry of Health reported that there were 7,237 Centers for Public Health Care, 21,267 Assisting Centers, and 6,392 Mobile Centers.[30] These numbers, however, do not properly reflect the poor quality of health care in Indonesia. In a 2000 report by the World Health Organization (WHO) on the Health System Improving Performance, Indonesia ranked 106th on a list of 191 country members in terms of achievement. In other health-related categories Indonesia does not fare much better, ranking 92nd out of the 191 country members.[31]

To improve the quality of health, "The Reduction of Government Subsidy on Oil Program" 2005 was made applicable to health care. On health care, the government uses the scheme of free health services in the Centers for Public Health Care as well as in the state hospitals. Free health care services are given when individuals present the Health Card for Poor Families (*Kartu Kesehatan Keluarga Miskin*), a scheme organized by PT. Askes, a state-owned health insurance company. A reimbursement is given to the state hospitals based on the number of patients who present a card to obtain services.

It is important to note that the implementation of this program remains highly criticized and controversial. Most criticisms center around two issues: flaws in the

---

[30] Indonesian Ministry of Health 2003. Draf Sistem Kesehatan Nasional. http://www.depkes.go.id/index.php?option=com_downloads&Itemid=50&func=fileinfo&parent=category&filecatid=60 (accessed June 5, 2006).

[31] Indonesian Ministry of Health 2003. Sistem Kesehatan Nasional, p. 5.

system of distribution of the cards and inconsistencies in who qualifies as a poor family.[32] The card is issued by the local *Puskesmas* after a complicated procedure. An applicant has to obtain an identification card as well as letters from the *Kelurahan,* the lowest government administration dealing with the citizens' registration, and the Ministry of Social Affairs stating his/her level of poverty. This process typically takes a minimum of four months.[33] The problem is that the identification card is issued by the Kelurahan office only for those living in the Kelurahan area. The poor in urban areas, on the other hand, are not aware of the importance of the identification card, and Kelurahan officials have failed to be effective in registering these residents.[34]

THE JUDICIARY AND THE NATIONAL HUMAN RIGHTS COMMISSION

To examine how the rights to health care and education are enforced, it is important to understand the judiciary as it pertains to economic and social rights. The constitutional basis for the judiciary in Indonesia is laid out in Articles 24, 24A, 24B, and 24C of the Constitution, as amended in 2001. The Indonesian judicial power is implemented by a Supreme Court and judicial bodies underneath it in the form of public courts, religious affairs courts, military tribunals, and state administrative courts, and by a newly created Constitutional Court (Article 24).

The Constitutional Court's authorities and responsibilities include reviewing laws against the Constitution, determining disputes over the authorities of state institutions whose powers are given by the Constitution, overseeing the dissolution of political parties, and hearing disputes regarding the results of a general election (Article 24C, Section 1). Also, the judiciary has the authority to impeach the president and/or the vice-president (Article 24C, Section 2). Side by side with the Supreme Court and the Constitutional Court, the Judicial Commission (as detailed in Article 24B) has the authority to propose candidates for appointment as justices of the Supreme Court and possesses further authority to maintain and ensure the honor, dignity and behavior of judges. Table 6.1 compares Indonesia's Supreme Court to its Constitutional Court.

There is also a National Commission of Human Rights, whose role, though minimal for actually resolving human rights cases (because it is not part of the judicial system per se), is vital for the advancement of justice in Indonesia. One of the most important tasks of the Commission is to provide human rights reports to the police and the Attorney General's Office for further investigation and to the parliament in public hearings. The Commission does have the authority to examine human rights cases, but the examination report is then presented only as

---

[32] See the study conducted by Indonesian Consumer Association Foundation 2005 and see E. Rachmawati 2005. Kompensasi BBM untuk Kesehatan: Barang Mewah Bagi Mereka Yang Papa. *Kompas Daily,* September 13.

[33] *Media Indonesia Daily,* March 2, 2005.

[34] See the report of Urban Poor Consortium, an NGO based in Jakarta, http://www.urbanpoor.or. id/content/view/56/48/ (accessed March 10, 2007).

Table 6.1. *Comparing the Supreme Court to the Constitutional Court of Indonesia*

	Supreme Court	Constitutional Court
	A court system inherited from the Dutch colonial administration (since 1920s), established in the Constitution of independence in 1945.	European model of constitutional court, established in 2003 after the amendments to the Constitution in 1999–2002. A European model: decisions of the Court are binding and are not subject to appeal.
Jurisdiction	• General Criminal, Civil, Family Law, State Administration, Military Courts • Judicial review of government regulations, presidential regulations, and regional regulations • Disputes regarding the results of local (provincial and regency levels) parliamentary and executive elections	• Judicial review of laws • Disputes regarding the results of the national parliamentary election and presidential election • Disputes between state agencies • Impeachment of the President/ Vice President
Structure	Courts under the Supreme Court are: • The General Courts of Justice (for civil and criminal cases). There are specialized courts under the general court (e.g., Anti-Corruption Court, Commercial Court, Human Rights Court) • The courts of religious affairs (for Islamic family law only) • The courts of state administration • The courts of military affairs These courts are divided into District Courts at the district/county level and Courts of Appeal at the provincial level. Each of the four judicial branches has its own Appellate Courts.	There is no lower level court for the Constitutional Court. All decisions of the Constitutional Court are binding and are not subject to appeal.

(continued)

Table 6.1 *(continued)*

	Supreme Court	Constitutional Court
Legal Standing	• Citizens Law Suit (with no standing requirement) is acknowledged based on a landmark decision on the "Nunukan case" (examined in this research). • Legal standing for NGOs is acknowledged based on a landmark decision regarding environmental case (*WALHI v. Five Government Bodies and PT. Inti Indorayon Utama*, 1988). • Class Action is acknowledged under the Supreme Court regulation No. 1 of 2002, which was issued based on landmark decisions regarding environmental cases.	• No specific legal standing required: Indonesian individuals, community groups espousing customary law, public or private legal entities, and state institutions may file a judicial review petition to the Constitutional Court so long as they are able to confirm that their constitutional rights are injured by the enactment of a law.
Judges	• At all levels of court the verdicts are made by a tribunal of three judges. • There is a career system for judges, starting at the level of the District Court. • The judges of the Supreme Court are nominated by the Judicial Commission, selected by the parliament, and administratively appointed by the president. Those from outside the Court (legal scholars, lawyers, prosecutors) can be candidates. • There is no term of office, but judges must retire at age 65. • There are 5,842 judges, including 49 Supreme Court Judges.[35]	• Comprised of nine judges. The nine judges hear and decide in full bench. • The judges are selected by the parliament (DPR) from the candidates nominated by the government, the parliament (DPR), and the Supreme Court. The term of office of a constitutional judge is five years, and he/she may be reelected for another term.

[35] Supreme Court of the Republic of Indonesia, Annual Report 2005.

a recommendation for further investigation by the police and the public prosecutors, and cases cannot be resolved on the authority of the Commission alone.

The Supreme Court

The Indonesian Supreme Court (*Mahkamah Agung*) is the highest court in the Indonesian judicial system, according to Article 24 of the Constitution. Beneath the Supreme Court there are four branches of the judicature: (a) the General Courts of Justice, which have jurisdiction to try civil and criminal cases (Law No. 2/1986 of March 8, 1986 amended by Law No 8/2004 of March 29, 2004); (b) the courts of religious affairs (Law No. 7/1989 of December 29, 1989); (c) the courts of state administration (Law No. 5/1986 of December 29, 1986 amended by Law No. 9/2004 of March 29, 2004); and (d) the courts of military affairs (Law No. 31/1997 of October 15, 1997).

Under the Supreme Court, there are District Courts at the district/regency level and Courts of Appeal at the provincial level. Of the four areas of court, each has its own Appellate Courts. Law No. 4/2004 regarding Basic Provisions on Judicial Power of January 15, 2004, contains the basic provisions pertaining to the lower courts. Cases at all levels are tried by a tribunal of three judges. Law No. 35/1999, amending Law No. 14/1970, provided for the judicial institutions to be under the authority of the Supreme Court. In March 2004, the general and administrative courts, in June 2004 the religious courts, and in September of that year the military courts (regulated by Presidential Decree No. 56/2004 of July 9, 2004 for the military courts) were each placed under the Supreme Court for administrative, organizational, and financial matters.

The Supreme Court is the court of final appeal or cassation (*kasasi*). Law No. 14/1985 on the Supreme Court of December 30, 1985, as amended by Law No. 5/2004 of January 15, 2004, regulates the authorities and procedures for the Supreme Court. The Court has discretion to determine whether it will reexamine a case or only examine the decision of the respective Courts of Appeal (decisions made by general, special, administrative, and military Courts of Appeal may be appealed to the Supreme Court). Much like the United States Supreme Court, the Indonesian Supreme Court does not review findings of fact made in lower courts but, instead, only hears appeals on questions of law. It is also empowered by statute to review the conformity of government regulation, presidential regulation, and regional regulation.

The Court system under the jurisdiction of the Supreme Court has been under severe scrutiny since the fall of Soeharto in 1998. As described at the outset, corruption is widespread. As Rifqi S. Assegaf puts it, the problems of the Court are myriad:

The pervasive influence of corruption, collusion and nepotism in the Supreme Court, intervention by the other branches of government in decisions of the Supreme Court, the long delays in the hearing of appeals, a lack of legal certainty arising out of judgments that are at odds with each other, the low quality of many Supreme Court decisions, the rigid, excessively legalistic interpretation of the law by some Supreme Court justices, and the handing down of decisions that are unenforceable are only some of the major issues that have eroded the prestige of the Supreme Court and become of serious concern to the public at large.[36]

The Supreme Court has acknowledged many of these problems and even initiated reforms starting in 2003, when it issued the *Blueprint for the Reform of the Supreme Court of Indonesia*. Institutional changes have been launched, but there is no evidence to suggest that fixing the deeply rooted and endemic corruption will occur in the near future. Figure 6.3 illustrates the jurisdiction of the Indonesian Supreme Court over various kinds of inferior courts.

Constitutional Adjudication

The opportunity for constitutional adjudication was made available for the first time in 2003, when the Indonesian Constitutional Court was first established. Before 2003, there were only two legal procedures that could be used to review regulations: first, judicial review of government regulations based on statutes (parliamentary acts) in the Supreme Court; and second, challenges to government policy in the Administrative Court.

Indonesian individuals, community groups espousing customary law, public or private legal entities, and state institutions may file judicial review petitions to the Constitutional Court, but only on the condition that they are able to confirm that their constitutional rights are injured by the enactment of a law.

The Constitutional Court is composed of nine constitutional judges. The nine judges hear and make decisions only when all nine, or a full bench, are present. The judges are selected by the parliament (DPR) from among candidates nominated by the government, the parliament (DPR), and the Supreme Court. The parliament selects three judges from names submitted by the government, three judges from those submitted by the Supreme Court, and three judges from a list prepared by the parliament (DPR) itself. The selected judges are then formally appointed by presidential decree. The term of office of a constitutional judge is five years. After the term, he/she may be reelected for only one subsequent term.

The National Human Rights Commission

The National Human Rights Commission was established during the Soeharto administration as a result of international pressure. It was established by a presidential regulation (No. 50 of 1993) and put under the control of the president. It has since, however, developed some independence vis-à-vis the government. Enacted as the authoritarian government of Soeharto fell, Law No. 39 of 1999 regarding Human Rights provided a new basis for the National Human Rights Commission.

The Human Rights Commission consists of a maximum of thirty-five members appointed by the president based on the selection process conducted by the House

---

[36] R. S. Assegaf 2004.

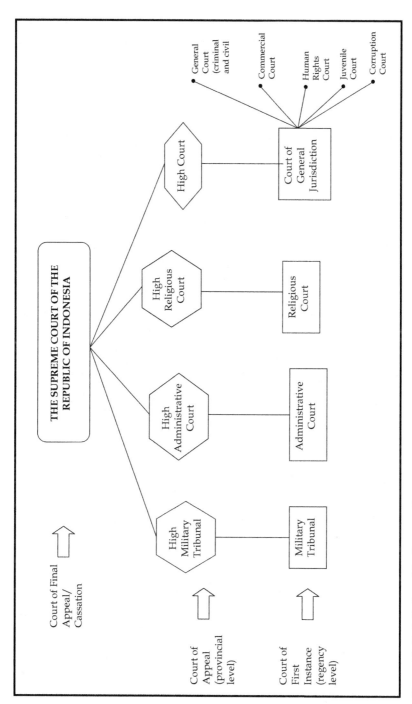

Figure 6.3. Jurisdiction of the Supreme Court.

of Representatives. In fact, the number of members has always been less than thirty-five, which has limited the effectiveness of the Commission. There were, for example, twenty members for the period of 2002 to 2007, and only eleven have been selected for 2007 to 2012. The members' term of office is five years, and members may serve for a maximum of two terms.

The responsibilities of the Commission are outlined in Indonesian law, and include conducting research, monitoring, educating the public, and mediating in human rights cases. The Commission provides consultation, negotiation, mediation, and reconciliation and refers the parties to court when necessary. The Commission also provides the government and the House of Representatives with recommendations regarding settlements in human rights cases.

The primary roles played by the Commission are to educate both the government and the public on human rights issues, to establish a network of human rights defenders, and to receive complaints concerning human rights violations. In this last respect, receiving complaints concerning human rights issues, the Commission has had mixed success. Commissioner Habib Chirzin (2002–2007) has stated that not many people are aware of the Commission's role in receiving human rights complaints.[37] In an interview given as part of this research, Chirzin explained that after receiving a complaint, the Commission conducts a mediation procedure. If the mediation fails to resolve the issue to the satisfaction of both parties, the Commission then recommends that the parties go to court. This occurs rarely, however, because most cases are settled through the relative efficiency of the mediation process and its tendency to provide both parties with satisfactory outcomes.

In June 2004, the Commission decided to structure its internal organization according to the internationally recognized human rights categories. There are now subcommissions on economic, social, and cultural rights, as well as on civil and political rights and the protection of special groups.

THE IMPLEMENTATION OF THE RIGHT TO HEALTH CARE AND ITS IMPACT ON POLICY

As mentioned earlier, research for this project found only a few cases within the 1995 to 2005 period that are directly related to health care in Indonesia. In total there are seven cases, consisting of three cases of medical malpractice, one case on the judicial review of the law concerning the national security system, and three cases concerning the environment. These seven cases are listed and briefly summarized in the following paragraphs.

Each of the three medical malpractice suits are cases that establish the relative obligations of patients and providers, especially on the issue of compensation when patients have suffered negligent or substandard care. There are three cases that can be categorized as regulatory cases. The first is the judicial review of the National Social Security System Law in the Constitutional Court by the East Java Legislative Council, a case concerning the state regulation of providers and insurers. The other

---

[37] Interview with Habib Chirzin, Commissioner at the National Commission of Human Rights, January 17, 2006.

two regulatory cases are cases concerning the establishment of state regulation of industrial, commercial, or governmental emissions. Finally, the last case, involving provision of health services to excluded groups, concerns a citizen lawsuit on the question of deportation of illegal immigrants from Malaysia to Nunukan.

These seven cases are grouped according to the typology of the cases as explained in the introductory chapter of this book. The descriptions of the cases will specifically address the case position, the situation which led to the case, the socioeconomic condition of the plaintiff, the legal representative of the plaintiffs in the case, and the impact of the case on policy. The cases will then be analyzed to identify the patterns regarding the use of litigation in respect to policy.

Cases Establishing the Relative Obligations of Patients and Providers with Regard to Medical Malpractice

Opik v. Republic of Indonesia Government (Civil Court, Cibadak, West Java), Case No. 13/Pdt.G/2005/Pn.Cbd.

This case involves a civil action brought by Opik, a resident of Cidadap RT 02 RW 02, Girijaya Subdistrict, Cidahu District, Sukabumi Regency. Ismail, two years of age, the son of Opik, participated in the polio immunization drive on April 24, 2005, which was being held at the time in Cidadap. After being immunized, the child developed a fever and paralysis. The Cidahu District, where Opik lives, was (and is) primarily inhabited by poor residents. Cidahu is approximately a one-hour drive by car. The place where Opik lived was quite isolated and only accessible by means of a badly damaged narrow road that only allowed for the passage of one vehicle at a time. The house he lived in lacked a title certificate. The plaintiff had only graduated from elementary school and worked in the informal sector, doing some trading and some farm work. In this case, the plaintiff was suing through the Health Legal Aid Bureau, which provided legal services to him free of charge.[38]

Opik sued the regent of Sukabumi through the head of the Sukabumi District Health Agency (1st defendant), the Governor of West Java through the head of the West Java Health Agency (2nd defendant), the government of the Republic of Indonesia through the Republic of Indonesia Minister of Health (3rd defendant), and PT Bio Farma Indonesia (4th defendant) on the grounds that they were guilty of committing an unlawful act.[39]

The plaintiff argued that the defendants had been negligent in producing and administering the polio vaccine and failed to do so in accordance with the prevailing regulations regarding the quality of services and medical actions. In particular, the argument was that the polio vaccine produced by the 4th defendant was not in line

---

[38] Health Legal Aid Bureau is a NGO based in Jakarta specializing in advocating for poor people and dealing with health cases concerning the victims of contaminated natural environments. It has been especially active in medical malpractice cases and is frequently a vocal critic of the government's actions in the health-care sector.

[39] The term *unlawful act*, in Indonesian *Perbuatan Melawan Hukum*, taken from the Dutch civil law term *onrechtmatige daad,* is a concept similar to tort in common law.

with the recommendations of WHO, and failed to comply with the standards set by WHO.

The trial commenced on July 13, 2005, with the examination of the evidence. However, during the second court session, the plaintiff decided, against the advice of his legal advisers, to enter into negotiations toward reaching an out-of-court settlement. Following these negotiations, Opik decided to drop his lawsuit, and he withdrew his letters of appointment from his counsel. In the third court session, the president of the Cibadak District Court read out the decision of the court to accept Opik's decision to drop his action.

As this case concluded with the withdrawal of the action by the plaintiff, the Court was unable to respond to the original claim or award damages to the plaintiff. For its part, the only documentation that the Court produced was an order accepting the motion on the part of the plaintiff to be allowed to drop his case. Because negotiations took place out of court, it is quite likely that monetary compensation was paid by the defendants to the plaintiff, though the exact amount of this compensation is unclear. The Health Legal Aid Bureau is also unaware of how much Opik received as he withdrew his letters of representation from the Health Legal Aid Bureau prior to the dropping of his action.

Because this case was resolved without a court decision, no lasting improvements in health services resulted from the case itself. For the government's part, new posts were set up for the vaccination of children who had been missed in the previous round of vaccination. Nothing, however, was done for the children who had been left paralyzed as a result of the previous round of vaccinations.

Not long after the incident occurred, the government announced an epidemic emergency in the area. The announcement, however, was not a result of lessons learned from the Opik case, but was intended to provide special treatment for the polio outbreak in the area. Polio victims were forbidden from leaving the area to seek treatment and instead were treated by the government and put in isolation as required in an epidemic emergency. Yet, the ineffectual nature of this policy was evident in the large numbers of people moving in and out of the area, even though isolation was technically being enforced.[40]

Manteb Mulyono v. Dr. Amir Toyib, Cipto Mangunkusumo Hospital, and the Republic of Indonesia Government (Civil Court, Jakarta); Case No. 42/Pdt.G/2005/PN.JKT.PST

This case began when Wulan Yulianti, eight years of age, the daughter of Manteb Mulyono, who lives in Bojong Koneng Village in Bekasi, was declared to have a tumor and needed immediate surgery. On November 11, 2003, Wulan was referred to the state-owned hospital of Cipto Mangunkusumo in Jakarta. After a series of medical checkups, on December 8, 2003, the doctors conducted surgery to remove the tumor. However, it was later found that the tumor was not removed. The doctor only conducted the surgery to take liquid to determine whether or not the tumor had reached a dangerous state. The examination showed that the tumor was not yet

---

[40] Interview with Opik on May 5, 2006, in Cibadak.

dangerous and the doctor recommended that Wulan be released from the hospital, although there was still an unhealed wound caused by the surgery.

Two and a half months after the surgery, Wulan's condition was deteriorating, and Mulyono took her daughter back to the hospital to receive a second surgery. The same procedure was conducted by the same doctor, again without completing it. Additionally, a wound in her abdomen was left open for purposes of a scheduled third surgery. However, according to the operational procedure of the hospital, there were to be no surgeries on Friday, Saturday, or Sunday, thus postponing Wulan's third surgery until Monday, even while her condition worsened. On Sunday, April 25, 2004, Wulan passed away as a consequence of the open wound.

Manteb Mulyono lives in the outskirts of Jakarta. Mulyono is a laborer with a daily wage of less than 30.000 IDR (Indonesian rupiahs), equivalent to US$3.30. The plaintiff was suing through the Health Legal Aid Bureau and was provided legal services free of charge.

On February 7, 2005, Mulyono filed a civil case against Dr. Amir Toyib, SP.BA (1st defendant), Cipto Mangunkusumo Hospital (2nd defendant), and the Government of the Republic of Indonesia through the Ministry of Health through the Director General of Medical Services of The Ministry of Health (3rd defendant) on the grounds that they were guilty of committing an unlawful act. The plaintiff argued that the defendants had conducted medical malpractice, which led directly to the death of his daughter.

On August 10, 2005, the District Court of Central Jakarta declared a provisional decision that the case had been rejected as an error in persona because the records showed that the 1st defendant was not listed as a doctor at the hospital.

Because the case was rejected from the outset by the Court, this case did not have any policy impact.

*Iwan Pahriwan v. Dr. Ottman Nasution, Karya Medika Hospital,
and the Republic of Indonesia Government (Civil Court, Bekasi);*
Case No. 41/Pdt.G/2005/PN.Bekasi

This was a civil case regarding medical malpractice occurring in the Karya Medika Hospital in Cibitung. The plaintiff was Iwan Pahriwan, the father of Felina, who died because of an open wound after an abdominal surgery. At that time, Dr. Ottman Nasution, who treated Felina, said that the surgery was successful and that the wound would naturally repair as the tissue healed. Felina underwent surgery on January 11, 2004, but the open wound continued to fester until her death in September 2004. A month prior, on August 20, 2004, Iwan Pahriwan took his daughter to the Cipto Mangunkusumo Hospital to treat the wound. The hospital declared that her condition was already critical, but Felina died soon after, on September 6, 2004.

Iwan Pahriwan is a small trader living in Bekasi, an urban area near Jakarta. His legal complaint was argued through free services provided by the Health Legal Aid Bureau.

The plaintiff argued that the death of Felina was caused by the negligent acts of the defendants in treating the wound. Pahriwan attempted to claim damages on the grounds of medical malpractice, namely, negligence in conducting a medical procedure and failure to comply with the prevailing regulations regarding the quality of services and medical procedures. This claim was based on the argument that health-service providers must inform the patient or her parents or her relatives about the potential impact of a medical procedure.

During the trial, the defendants successfully argued that they had conducted all the necessary actions and treatments according to official medical professional standards. The decision was ultimately decided in favor of the defendant.

The same case was also brought to the criminal court but was then withdrawn by the plaintiff. There were no direct implications for policy.

Regulatory Cases: State Regulation of Providers and Insurers

Judicial Review of the National Social Security System Law in the Constitutional Court by East Java Legislative Council; Case No. 007/PUU-III/2005
In this case, the Constitutional Court used the provisions of the Constitution to test Article 5 of the National Social Security System Law (No. 40 of 2004). Article 5, in essence, provided for the vesting of the power to provide social security solely in JAMSOSTEK, TASPEN, ASABRI, and ASKES, all of which are state-owned companies. The petitioners argued that this contravened Article 18, Section 5, of the Constitution on the granting of wide-ranging local government autonomy, save in those areas of administration that were reserved by law to the national government. The definition of "State" given in Article 18 of the Constitution covered both the central and local governments. The question of providing social security was not something that had been reserved exclusively to the central government under Article 13 of the Local Government Law (No. 32 of 2004). The Constitutional Court indeed held that the provision of social security schemes was one of the social functions of the State (made up of both the central and local governments). This was clear from Article 18, Section 5, of the Constitution, as further spelled out by Article 22(h) of the Local Government Law. Thus, it was not only the central government that had the power to provide social security schemes, but also local governments. Accordingly, the central government, through the National Social Security System Law, had no right to prohibit local governments from providing social security to its citizens.

Consequently, the Constitutional Court allowed the petition striking down Articles 5(2), (3) and (4) of the National Social Security System Law. Following this decision of the Constitutional Court, local governments are now empowered to establish and operate their own social security plans, even though the overall system remains centralized.

Regulatory Cases: State Regulation of Industrial, Commercial, or Governmental Emissions

The People of Buyat v. the Republic of Indonesia Government (Civil Court, Jakarta); Case No. 406.PdtG/2004/PN.Jaksel
This case was based more directly on the right to health. In particular, the right to health was being compromised in the case of the Buyat people because of the poor

quality of the water in Buyat Bay, on which they depended for their livelihoods. It was alleged that the poor quality of the water in the bay was the result of pollution caused by a mining concern, PT Newmont Minahasa Raya. The Minister of Health, as the party responsible for establishing and administering public health policy, had an obligation to maintain and improve the health of people throughout Indonesia, including environmental health, as provided for by Article 9 and Article 22 of the National Health Law (No. 23 of 1992). The plaintiffs argued that the Minister of Health had been negligent in discharging this duty through his insufficient response to the pollution of Buyat Bay and the ensuing health problems suffered by its residents. In fact, it was alleged that some people had already died as a result of the pollution in the bay. It was argued that the Minister of Health had not fulfilled his obligation to prevent the pollution of Buyat Bay by his failure to ensure the safe handling of liquid, solid, and gaseous waste, as well as of radiation. His failure to control noise pollution and the illnesses afflicting the people of Buyat Bay as a result of the alleged pollution were also factors. The residents of Buyat Bay were seeking damages for the injuries they suffered as a result of these negligent government acts, and in this case the Minister of Health was the party primarily responsible.

The plaintiffs were three residents living around Buyat Bay, Bolaang Mongondow, a rural area in North Sulawesi: Rasit Rahmat, age 40, a fisherman and elementary school graduate; Masna Stirman, a fisherwoman/housewife; and Juhria Ratubahe, a fisherman. The plaintiffs and their families were all people who lived on ancestral land around Buyat. The residents' homes had been handed down to them by their parents. They were fishermen, their income was greatly dependent on the fish in Buyat Bay, and as a result of the alleged pollution, they claimed that their incomes had significantly declined. In addition, they had been deprived of their right to clean water because of the pollution of the water they used on a day-to-day basis. They usually sold the fish they caught in other areas and transported them on rented vehicles. They did not have any means of transportation other than their boats.

Prior to the arrival of PT Newmont Minahasa Raya, catching fish had been very easy. Since the arrival of Newmont, however, it had become increasingly difficult to catch fish. In addition, the quality of the fish caught had declined drastically, as shown by the "black liquid that was often present in the fish that were caught."

In the beginning, the plaintiffs were represented by the Health Legal Aid Bureau. During the case, however, the plaintiffs replaced their counsel allegedly because they were disappointed with their performance. The plaintiffs took the view that the Health Legal Aid Bureau had been less than transparent with the plaintiffs in its handling of the case. The plaintiffs then selected the Jakarta Legal Aid Bureau, JATAM (Jaringan Advokasi Tambang), and the PBHI (Indonesian Legal Aid and Human Rights Association[41] to represent them.

Jakarta Legal Aid Bureau is the Jakarta branch office of the Indonesian Legal Aid Foundation, one of the oldest NGOs in Indonesia and founded by the Indonesian

---

[41] See http://www.pbhi.or.id/.

Bar Association (PERADIN).[42] PBHI has aims similar to those of the Indonesian Legal Aid Foundation; in fact, its founders previously worked for the Indonesian Legal Aid Foundation. Typically, the Jakarta Legal Aid Bureau and PBHI do not focus on cases regarding health; instead they work on a broader level, mainly on cases that affect the poor in the context of the structural legal aid movement. The other representative, JATAM, is the network for mining advocacy.[43]

The suit was brought under Articles 359 and 361 of the Criminal Code, together with Articles 8 and 9 of the National Health Law (No. 23 of 1992). In essence, the plaintiffs argued that the government, as the party responsible for exercising the power of the State, was required to strive to improve public health. The defendant's counsel took the view that the plaintiff's claim was misdirected, because it was PT Newmont Minahasa Raya, and not the Minister of Public Health, that had caused the pollution. In addition, counsel for the plaintiffs considered the substance of the claim to be very weak evidentially and to be generally not supported by the facts. They persuasively argued that the claim against the Minister of Health was groundless, and the claim was eventually withdrawn.

No decision was handed down in this case. Thus, the plaintiffs failed to obtain what they had been seeking as the action was withdrawn unconditionally. This only became apparent after counsel from the Health Legal Aid Bureau had been replaced for failing to accommodate the wishes of the plaintiffs, who were primarily interested in obtaining a settlement with PT Newmont Minahasa Raya. They eventually did so, in the case *People of Buyat v. Newmont.*

During the trial, the Minister of Health made several attempts to improve conditions in Buyat Bay, though it is unclear whether these efforts were sincere attempts at improvement or attempts to pacify the plaintiffs in the case. The Minister of Health visited Buyat Bay to see the conditions for himself and to deliver humanitarian assistance. The assistance was symbolic, but the Minister promised that more assistance would be delivered following his visit. Additional aid was to be effected by Republic of Indonesia Minister of Health Decree No. HK.00SJ.IX.2235, which provided for the setting up of a Humanitarian Assistance Team to provide medical aid in Buyat Bay. The Minister of Health continued to deny that his ministry's newfound interest in the welfare of the Buyat people had anything to do with the legal action being brought against him, arguing rather that it was an essential part of the work of the Ministry of Health. A week before the legal action of the citizens of Buyat Bay was dropped, the people of Buyat received free medication from the Ministry of Health. It was alleged that much of the assistance intended for Buyat Bay was later stolen by corrupt officials. The Minister of Health had promised seventy-five packages of medicines for seventy-five families, but only fifty packages were eventually handed out.

Other promises made to the residents of Buyat Bay by the government were to rehabilitate Buyat Bay, relocate the local people, and provide an ambulance for their local health clinic if they agreed to be relocated to a designated location. The government promised that the relocation effort for seventy-one families would

---

[42] See http://www.ylbhi.or.id/.
[43] See http://www.jatam.org.

be completed within three months. The relocation was to be coordinated by two regencies, Bolaang Mongondow and Minahasa Selatan, and a total of 8.6 billion IDR (Indonesian rupiahs) was to be provided to fund the effort. This was realized through Minister of Health Decree No. HK.00SJ.IX.2235. However, the residents refused to be relocated to the place designated by the government, as they claimed it was still contaminated by pollution from PT Newmont Minahasa Raya's tailings. Thus, the relief promised to the residents in the form of the building of new houses and an ambulance never occurred. In the end, the Buyat Bay people relocated on their own to Buminanga, a place they deemed to be safer. The relocation effort was sponsored by Mercy Corps, an international humanitarian aid and development charitable organization, that built simple new homes for the displaced families.[44]

According to the legal advisers of the plaintiffs, both from JATAM and the Jakarta Legal Aid Bureau, no significant policy changes resulted directly from this case.[45] The only limited policy that emerged was a Minister of Health Decree authorizing the provision of medical assistance to the people of Buyat Bay. Still, the Ministry continued to insist that extending this assistance had nothing to do with the lawsuit, but was rather part of the Ministry's duties as the institution primarily responsible for public health in Indonesia.[46]

People of Kebomas v. Director of PLN and the Republic of Indonesia Government (Civil Case, Jakarta); Case No. 35/PDT.G/1994/PN.JKT.PST
This case was brought in 1994 by the people of Kebomas District in Gresik in connection with a government project for the construction of the 500 KV extra-high-tension power transmission lines over their homes in Gresik. According to the local residents, the government had ignored the recommendations of the environmental impact analysis during the construction of the power lines. According to this analysis, the trajectory of the power lines had to avoid all human habitations. If such habitations were not avoided or evacuated, several health risks would be borne by them.

The local residents' fears of the risks appeared to be supported by the Republic of Indonesia Department of Health in its Directive No. 015/DLU/83 on the amendment of PUIL 1977, which stated that extra-high-tension power transmission lines had the potential to affect the electromagnetic field in human beings. However, the government insisted that the residents remain in their homes and refused to accept the possibility that their fears were well founded. In the end, at their own initiative, a number of the residents decided to leave their homes and relocate and sued the government for compensation for their former homes and land.

Represented by the Jakarta Legal Aid Bureau, ninety-two residents agreed to bring a class action suit. The defendants were the director of the state power utility PLN (1st defendant), the Department of Mines and Energy (2nd defendant) and the Governor of East Java Province (3rd defendant). The action was filed in the

---

[44] See www.mercycorps.org.
[45] Interview with Ines Thioren Situmorang (LBH Jakarta) on January 5, 2006, and Jevelina Punuh (JATAM) on December 23, 2005.
[46] Interview with Manik (Legal Bureau of the Ministry of Health) on February 15, 2006.

court with jurisdiction over the place of domicile of the 1st defendant, the Central Jakarta District Court.

In its decision dated August 8, 1996, the Central Jakarta District Court denied the action on the grounds that it would, if allowed, be prejudicial to the public interest, and that the allegations made by the plaintiffs had not been proved. The decision of the Central Jakarta District Court was upheld on appeal by the high court. To date, the case is still pending a final decision by the Supreme Court.

Despite the plaintiffs' loss at the trial court, new policies have since been put in place with regard to high- and extra-high-tension power transmission lines. First, there is PT PLN Board of Directors Resolution No. 031.K/008/DIR/1997 on General PLN Policies on the Construction of High and Extra High Tension Power Transmission Lines. The purpose of issuing this Resolution was to ensure a uniformity of perceptions, actions, and measures on the ground to deal with and to reduce the number of problems that occur. The General Policies state that the question of compensation and rehabilitation shall be decided by referring to the national regulations on land acquisition (Presidential Decree No. 55/93). They also state that where possible, PLN shall strive to avoid compulsorily acquiring land and relocating residents by adopting alternative trajectories. However, should compulsory acquisition and relocation be unavoidable, PLN will strive to ensure that the circumstances of residents are improved, or at the very least remain the same as they were before the construction of the project. Compensation shall be determined based on the market value of the land and the most recent taxable value. PLN shall also provide advice and guidance to the residents, as well as public services and assistance, and set up a complaints procedure and field monitoring system.

Second, the Minister of Mines and Energy Decree No. 975.K/47/MPE/1999 on the amendment of Minister of Mines and Energy Decree No. 01.P/47/MPE/1992 on uninhabited buffer zones in the vicinity of high- and extra-high-tension power transmission lines was enacted. In the preface to this Decree, it is stated that the development of the electricity sector must also have regard for the social, economic, environmental, and public health considerations in the areas where projects are being developed. Further, Article 5, Section 6, of the Decree holds that land and buildings that existed before those that come within the uninhabited buffer zone for high- and extra-high-tension power transmission lines, besides those vacated for the construction of towers, shall receive compensation.

Expansion of Health Services: Provision to Excluded Groups

53 Indonesian citizens acting for all Indonesian citizens v. the Republic of Indonesia Government (Civil Court, Jakarta); Case No. 28/Pdt.G/2003/PN.Jkt.pusat
This case was brought by fifty-three Indonesian citizens against nine agencies of the Indonesian government that were accused of being responsible for the neglect of migrant workers deported from Malaysia. The case followed the introduction in Malaysia of a new immigration act, on May 20, 2002. Section 2(a) of this Act stated that illegal immigrants would be subject to a fine of 10,000 MYR (Malaysian

ringgits) or a maximum prison term of five years, or six strokes of the cane. On August 1, 2002, the new Act came into effect and the Malaysian government mobilized the police, military, and paramilitary forces to hunt down and catch illegal immigrants, whether or not they possessed travel documents. As a result of this action, Indonesian border crossings were flooded by a wave of illegal Indonesians returning home. Among the places affected were Nunukan in East Kalimantan. These returning immigrants and their families suffered from a variety of health problems. In Nunukan, they were housed in substandard accommodations and were given inadequate supplies of food and water. As a result, at least eighty-one illegal immigrants or members of their families died. This caused concern throughout Indonesia. A number of organizations took the initiative of bringing a civil action against the government agencies they considered responsible for the disaster. At the time, there was no law governing the protection of migrant labor that could serve as a legal foundation for the action. In fact, there was not a single organization in Indonesia whose statutes stated that it was devoted to the protection of migrants. As a result of these factors, and also because of financial considerations that prevented representatives of the migrants being taken to Jakarta, it was decided to bring a "citizen lawsuit," roughly equivalent to a civil action. This represented an important new development in Indonesian law.

There were a number of different types of deportees being accommodated in Nunukan: deportees who wished to voluntarily return to their hometowns, deportees who had agreements with their employers to return after their documents had been put in order, deportees who had been expelled, and deportees who intended to return to Malaysia when it became possible to do so. But most of the plaintiffs in this citizen lawsuit were activists of NGOs, their legal advisers, or representatives from the Jakarta Legal Aid Bureau.

Nunukan regency is an island located in the province of East Kalimantan. It has a population of twenty-two thousand, drawn from all corners of Indonesia. Clean water is a serious problem in Nunukan. The local water utility is only capable of supplying half of the population with water from the Bolong River, and if the pump is broken, the supply of water is interrupted. Because of this, the local population greatly relies on rain water as an auxiliary source of fresh water. With regard to electricity supply, power cuts are common because of damaged machinery and more potential customers than installed generating capacity.

Although there is no hospital in Nunukan, minor health problems are treated in the local community health clinic. This, however, has only seven doctors and eight paramedics and can accommodate only ten inpatients.

The substance of the action was based on Article 1365 of the Civil Code on Unlawful Acts. In this case, it was argued that the government, through its agencies that are responsible for public welfare, had failed to respond as it should to a disaster. Among the legal provisions requiring the state to protect citizens were the Preamble to the Constitution, Article 28(I)(1), and Article 28(4) of the Constitution, and the provisions of the 1999 Human Rights Law (No. 39/1999). The action was allowed by the Court on the ground that although the defendants had not been shown to have conducted specific unlawful acts, such negligence was unacceptable. Accordingly, the Court ordered the defendants to immediately take the necessary concrete measures to overcome the disaster. However, the Court rejected the plaintiffs' argument that the government be ordered to enact legislation to protect migrant workers, to ratify a relevant 1990 United Nations convention, and to enter into a bilateral agreement with Malaysia to resolve the illegal immigration problem. According to the Court, these things were beyond the purview of the judiciary.

During the hearing of the case, and after a decision had been handed down by the Court, progress was being made in Nunukan, including increased assistance to the area and the provision of improved facilities, such as tents, sanitation facilities, and better food. In addition, the illegal immigrants also started to be sent back to their hometowns to reduce the numbers trapped in Nunukan. Eventually, the migrants were shipped back directly to Jakarta so as to reduce the number left in Nunukan.

The government allocated 6.7 billion IDR for the provision of assistance to the migrants in Nunukan. The assistance took the form of food parcels, medicine, clothes, the construction of health-care and sanitation facilities, and the provision of tents. The principal impact of this case was to highlight the government's lack of concern for the plight of migrant workers in Indonesia. Another effect of the case was that it attracted attention to the plight of the illegal workers deported from Malaysia, which resulted in an increase of humanitarian assistance.

This case may be seen as one in which the government was sued in order to force it to fulfill the rights of citizens to health care, however, it did not have any direct impact on health-care policy. This case does have crucial import for policy regarding migrant workers. One year after the case was brought to Court, the parliament enacted Law No. 39 of 2004 regarding the Protection of Migrant Workers. Although the Court refused to order the government and the parliament to enact legislation to protect migrant workers on the basis that this was beyond the purview of the judiciary, the case has contributed significantly to the policy advocacy conducted by NGOs working on the rights of the migrant workers.[47] As a result of this case, the government has been making serious efforts to ratify the 1990 United Nations convention on the protection of migrant workers.

This case is also celebrated as a landmark decision for citizen lawsuits. Until this case, Indonesia did not have regulations on citizen lawsuits, and this case is the first Citizen Lawsuit accepted by the Court. Public interest lawyers have since used this case to advocate for the issuance of Supreme Court regulations concerning the procedure of the citizen lawsuit, which would serve as the grounds for future citizen lawsuits.[48]

Analysis

Three out of the seven cases described herein are medical malpractice cases that do not use the language of the right to health. These cases are mostly about

---

[47] Interview with Choirul Anam, Human Rights Working Group, on February 15, 2006. See also Buruh Migran Kini Punya Posisi Tawar, *Kompas Online*, Wednesday, May 14, 2003. http://www.kompas.com/utama/news/0305/14/075027.htm

[48] I. Sugianto, Kasus Nunukan: Hak Gugat Warga Negara (Citizen Law Suit) terhadap Negara, *Dictum Law Review*, 2nd ed.: 33–55.

compensation to patients who have suffered negligent or substandard care. It may seem that this type of case does not affect the public directly. However, the filing of cases of this type can be seen as a signal of the efficacy of the regulatory framework and the judicial system in protecting patients. From 1999 to 2004, according to the Health Legal Aid Bureau, there have been 126 alleged medical malpractice cases. Most of the cases, however, were not brought before the Court. This is principally because hospitals or other related parties are usually willing to cooperate when patients are represented in negotiations.[49]

The other four cases show an interesting trend: All four cases have affected policies although the plaintiffs may not have accrued direct benefits. The people of Kebomas in the extra-high-tension power transmission lines case lost in district court and the appellate court, but the case has forced the government to issue new decrees regulating the setting up of the extra-high-tension power transmission lines. The mapping of the cases in Table 6.2 shows the trend and its relations to the possible factors.

NGO involvement appears to play a significant role in cases that force the government to take actions (seven of the eight cases involved NGOs). The only case that does not involve an NGO is the judicial review case in the Constitutional Court brought by East Java Legislative Council. This particular case had an indirect impact on the public at large. The Constitutional Court's ruling granted local governments the power to establish and operate their own social security systems. Whether or not giving the authority to the local government is beneficial is another question. It is important to note that, at the time of writing, regulations for the reformed social security system that this case created were still not in place.

It is also useful to distinguish among NGOs. Although the Health Legal Aid Bureau focuses on acquiring remedies for the patients, the other NGOs are not limited to benefiting their clients only. JATAM for example, has stated that compensation for the victim is not their only aim, because compensation does not improve places like Buyat in sustainable ways.[50] This philosophy has prompted JATAM, together with other environmental NGOs, to conduct a series of public campaigns in Jakarta. Among their efforts were documentary films on the cases, discussions held in Jakarta, and press statements that were released in a systematic way.

The importance of the decision of Jakarta Legal Aid Bureau to use citizen lawsuits cannot be overstated. As noted earlier, the case is a landmark decision for citizen lawsuits. A public litigant who worked on the case has recently said that the decision itself was made for the purpose of entirely revamping citizen lawsuits in Indonesia.[51]

It is noteworthy that three of the nonmedical malpractice cases in which NGOs played an important role took place in Jakarta, although none of the three cases originated in Jakarta. Buyat Bay is located in North Sulawesi; the extra-high-tension

[49] LBH Kesehatan, Pasien di Indonesia Tak Terlindungi, Tempo Interaktif, Selasa, July 13, 2004, http://www.tempointeraktif.com/hg/jakarta/2004/07/13/brk,20040713–47,id.html (accessed June 20, 2006).

[50] Interview with Siti Maemunah, JATAM Coordinator, January 18, 2006.

[51] Interview with Choirul Anam, February 15, 2006.

Table 6.2. *Cases on health care*

No.	Case Name	Court, Location, Year	Plaintiff's socioeconomic class	NGO involvement	Win?	Impact on policy
Establishing the relative obligations of patients and providers: Medical Malpractice						
1	Opik v. Republic of Indonesia Government	Civil Court, Cibadak, West Java 2005	Lower class	Yes (Health Legal Aid Bureau)	No	No
2	Manteb Mulyono v. Dr. Amir Toyib, Cipto Mangunkusumo Hospital, and the Republic of Indonesia Government	Civil Court, Jakarta 2005	Lower class	Yes (Health Legal Aid Bureau)	No	No
3	Iwan Pahriwan v. Dr. Ottman Nasution, Karya Medika Hospital, and the Republic of Indonesia Government	Civil Court, Bekasi 2005	Lower class	Yes (Health Legal Aid Bureau)	No	No
Regulation: State Regulation of Providers and Insurers						
4	Judicial Review of the National Social Security System Law by East Java Legislative Council	Constitutional Court 2005	Upper Class	No	Yes	Yes
Regulation: State Regulation of Industrial, Commercial, or Governmental Emissions						
5	The People of Buyat v. the Republic of Indonesia Government	Civil Case, Jakarta 2004	Lower Class	Yes (Jakarta Legal Aid Bureau, PBHI, Mining Advocacy Network)	Yes	Yes
6	People of Kebomas v. Director of PLN and the Republic of Indonesia Government	Civil Case, Jakarta 1996	Lower Class	Yes (Jakarta Legal Aid Bureau)	No, but appealed to the Supreme Court	Yes
Expansion of health services: Provision to Excluded Groups						
7	53 Indonesian citizens acting for all Indonesian citizens v. the Republic of Indonesia Government	Civil Court, Jakarta 2003	Lower Class	Yes (Jakarta Legal Aid Bureau)	Yes	Yes (significant)

electricity case occurred in Gresik, East Java; and Nunukan is located in Kalimantan, near the border with Malaysia. With regard to jurisdiction, certainly these cases can be brought before the Jakarta Court because the cases are filed against the Indonesian government. That fact, however, is not the main reason for taking it to the Jakarta Court. Instead, "litigation as a campaign" is the strategy of Jakarta Legal Aid (and the other branches of the Indonesian Legal Aid Foundation).[52] Siti Maemunah, the coordinator of JATAM, stated that for them the Court is merely the place to bring cases to the public. Although one can never be sure about the outcome of a decision given the extreme corruption within the judicial system, going to Court as a means of campaigning is an end unto itself.[53]

The fact that Jakarta is the capital city and that the political situation in Jakarta is more dynamic have positively contributed to the outcomes in these decisions. Because of the career and transfer system of the judges in the centralized model of the Indonesian Court, usually only highly qualified judges can go to the Jakarta District and Appellate Court. In contrast, the more remote the area, usually the less qualified the judges.[54] This is a reality that is being addressed in the reform plan of the Supreme Court, but for the litigating parties, having a case heard in Jakarta is an opportunity. An example of the difficulties outside of Jakarta may be seen in the Buyat Bay pollution case. When JATAM and other environmental NGOs decided to bring the case to the criminal court in North Sulawesi as well, they lost in the district court level in the criminal court, whereas in the appellate court the case is still pending.

THE IMPLEMENTATION OF THE RIGHT TO EDUCATION AND ITS IMPACT ON POLICY

The research has discovered only five cases related to the right to education in Indonesia. Two can be broadly categorized as cases concerning school choice, especially with regard to the expulsion of students and attendance at particular schools. As for the other three cases, they involve judicial review of the National Educational System Law and are related to claims for public financing and provision of education. No cases involving regulation were found.

Choice of Schooling: Expulsion of Students and Attendance at Particular Schools

The Melawai Junior High School Case (Civil Court, Jakarta);
Case No. PTJ.PDT.425.837.2004
This case concerns a state junior high school in Jakarta that had to be moved from its location in a certain area in Jakarta to another location in the outskirts of Jakarta. The move was due largely to the plan of the city council to change the area into a center for shopping and entertainment. The students and the parents

[52] Interview with A. Patra M. Zen, the chair of Indonesian Legal Aid Foundation, January 17, 2006.
[53] Interview with Siti Maemunah, JATAM Coordinator, January 18, 2006.
[54] See Supreme Court of the Republic of Indonesia 2003.

objected to the plan because they would encounter some obstacles and difficulties in attending school in the new location.

This case, however, is only secondarily related to the right to education. First and foremost, this case concerns a land-swap deal involving land on which the junior high school was constructed. In terms of the right to education, the parents of the students filed a complaint to the National Human Rights Commission.[55] Yet, the case involving the right to education has not been brought to the court, whereas the case on the swap-deal is currently in the process of being resolved. The swap-deal case itself was intended to suspend the relocation of the school.

This class action suit was brought by a number of people grouped in the Melawai State Junior High School Committee, consisting of two parents, two teachers, and the Association of Legal Advisors and Human Rights (APHI), who began to take legal action in 2003. As a class action lawsuit, it is not possible to individually describe the socioeconomic circumstances of the plaintiffs. All of the plaintiffs were members of the school committee, consisting of 55 teachers who disagreed with the land-swap deal (out of a total of 63 teachers) and the parents of 353 students.

The main reason for bringing the lawsuit was that the members of the committee refused to accept the transfer of ownership of the land and buildings of the school. Furthermore, students and teachers refused to be transferred to Jalan Jeruk Perut, on the outskirts of Jakarta, primarily because the members of the committee suspected that corruption had played a significant role in the original decision to develop the area.

According to the plaintiffs, the transfer violated Presidential Decree No. 16 of 1994 and Presidential Decree No. 24 of 1995, both of which require that the transfer of state assets in excess of 10 billion IDR must be approved by the president. Such approval had, however, not been sought by the Department of National Education and PT Tata Disantara. In addition, the land in Melawai was only valued at between 2.5 million IDR and 5 million IDR per square meter. In reality, according to the regulations set by the taxation authorities, the land should actually have been valued at 9.65 million IDR per square meter. The plaintiffs also argued that under the 1989 National Education Law, educational considerations should not be subordinate to business considerations.

In its decision, the Court held that the action of the plaintiffs had to be rejected on the grounds that their claim was incomplete and unclear and that the plaintiffs were incapable of representing the rest of their peers in the class. In fact, the ability of the plaintiffs to represent the interests of their peers had been challenged from the outset by the defendants. In response to that earlier claim, the Court had handed down a provisional decision holding that the plaintiffs had sufficient standing to bring their suit.

While the case was still going through the appeal process, the Jakarta Special District government pressed ahead with vacating the junior high school. The Jakarta administration argued it was justified in doing so based on language from

---

[55] Interview with Commissioner Habib Chirzin of the National Human Rights Commission, January 17, 2006.

the Jakarta High Court Ruling: "A land swap arrangement shall be valid under the law until such time as a final and conclusive decision to the contrary is handed down." Thus, they argued, the land-swap agreement with respect to the Melawai State Junior High School Number 56 should be valid and recognized. According to counsel for the plaintiffs, however, the status quo should prevail and the school should be preserved, despite the decision of the Jakarta High Court. In response to these arguments, the plaintiffs then appealed to the Supreme Court. They argued that the status quo should continue to be binding until such time as the Supreme Court hands down a final and conclusive decision. The plaintiffs emphasized their strong disagreement with the reasoning of the Jakarta High Court concerning the status quo. Since that time, there has been no compensation for the plaintiffs because their lawsuits were rejected both at first instance and on appeal to the High Court.

During the court proceedings, many of the students and teachers who remained in the school were subjected to physical and psychological pressure. Students were threatened with not being given student numbers and annual reports. In fact, at one stage they were forced to study in the veranda of a store after their school was forcibly taken over and padlocked by the Jakarta Special District. As a result, many teachers and parents eventually agreed to make the move until only twenty students remained. The Jakarta Education Service eventually agreed to a school bridging program for the students who agreed to move. About twenty students participated in the program, which was designed to bridge the differences in educational attainments that it was said had resulted from the children being educated in an illegal manner. In the end, these students moved to State Junior High School Number 13 after being told they would be excused from school fees until they had graduated. Ibu Nurlela, one of the last teachers to hold out, was eventually fired from the civil service and is currently in the process of bringing proceedings in the Administrative Court arising out of her dismissal.

Though indirectly, this case involved citizens asking the State, in the form of the Jakarta Special District administration, to respect their basic right to easily accessible education. Remedy was given to the students by transferring them to the Melawai State Junior High School Number 13, a school nearby. Nevertheless, the case does not have impact on policy as the central issue in the case is the land swap deal, rather than the right to education itself.

Petition to Nullify Administrative Action of the President of the
University of Indonesia (Administrative Court, Jakarta);
Case No. 21/G.TUN/2001/PTUN-JKT
On February 2, 2001, when the University of Indonesia held a celebration commemorating its fiftieth anniversary, a number of students rallied against the education fund policy applied by the university. As a reaction to this demonstration, the president of the University of Indonesia issued Decree No. 266/SK/R/UI/2000 dated November 16, 2000, suspending the students from the school for one and two semesters according to the level of violation deemed by the officials.

The students, represented by the Jakarta Legal Aid Bureau, filed a petition on February 1, 2001, to the Administrative Court to nullify the decree of the president of the university. Such a petition is legally appropriate because the University of Indonesia is a state university, and the president of the university is considered a state administrative official. The students also asked for the postponement of the execution of the Decree during the trial. The Court upheld the postponement, but the university did not execute the Court's decision until the Court issued an instruction to execute the ruling.

The argument of the petitioners was that their demonstration was an act protected under the freedom of association and expression, as outlined in Article 28 of the Constitution. The defendant, for his part, argued that the petitioners had obstructed the celebration of the fiftieth anniversary of the university. The Court upheld the argument of the petitioners in May 2001, but the decision was appealed. The Court of Appeal then affirmed the decision of the court of the first instance and ruled in favor of the students. This case has no direct policy impact.

Public Financing for Education

Judicial Review of the National Education System Law in the Constitutional Court; Case No. 011/PUU-III/2005
The petitioners challenged the constitutionality of two provisions in the National Education System Law (No. 20 of 2003), namely Article 49, Section 1, and Article 17, Sections 1 and 2. Article 17, Sections 1 and 2 divides education into two stages: basic education and advanced education. It further qualifies which schools are included in each type of education. Whereas the government declared required measures for basic education, these provisions, it was claimed, would violate the Constitutional principle of providing the best education possible to all Indonesian people. This particular challenge to Article 17 was ultimately rejected by the Court.

The petitioners also challenged the constitutionality of the elucidation of Article 49, Section 1, of the National Education System Law, which states that the government must allocate 20 percent of the national budget to the education sector. However, the provision further explains that the allocation may be done gradually.[56] This provision was said to be in contradiction with Article 31, Section (4) of the Constitution, which clearly states the obligations of the government without allowing for it to occur gradually. Under the first interpretation, the government had allocated only 7 percent of the budget to the education sector in the state budget of 2005. It is important to note that the law regulating the 2005 state budget was also challenged by the same petitioners in a different case. That petition was examined in a separate trial by the Constitutional Court, but as will be seen in the next section, the 2005 state budget case has important implications for the current case.

The Constitutional Court took the view that the obligation of the government as required by the Constitution could not be deferred. In other words, the Constitutional Court ruled that the money stipulated for the education budget could not

---

[56] The elucidation of law in Indonesia is considered a part of the law that has the same consequences as a legislative act. Once a customary practice, elucidation was codified in Law No. 10 of 2004 regarding Statutory Drafting.

be given gradually. According to the interpretation of the Court, the Constitution expressly required that a minimum of 20 percent of the national and provincial budgets be devoted to education. Consequently, the elucidation of Article 49, Section 1 created a new norm and, therefore, conflicted with the principles and theories of statutory interpretation that had been generally accepted and codified in the Statutory Drafting Law (No. 10 of 2004). Furthermore, the education sector in Indonesia had long been neglected. As a result, the Court ruled that it was time that education be elevated to a major priority in the development of Indonesia. For this to be realized, the educational sector would need to be a priority in terms of funding.

Previously, the incorporation of Article 49, Section 1 into the National Education System Law had provided a legal justification for both the national and local governments to not comply with the constitutional imperative of allocating 20 percent of their budgets to education. Accordingly, the arguments of the petitioner were well founded, and the Constitutional Court allowed the petition in part by striking down the elucidation as being repugnant to the Constitution.

Fathul Hadi, the lead petitioner in the case, was a director of the SERGAP (Suara Etis Rakyat Menggugat Ambivalensi dan Abnormalisasi Peraturan dan Perundang-undangan), a civil society organization that strives to correct and improve ambiguous laws and regulations. Mr. Hadi is a resident of Banyuwangi, East Java, a rural area. He represented nine other petitioners based on a special power of attorney. These included lecturers, teachers, the principals of junior high schools and high schools, and students. All of them lived in East Java.

Judicial Review of the 2005 State Budget Law; Case No. 012/PUU-III/2005

The petitioners of the National Education System Law filed a similar lawsuit to the one previously discussed at virtually the same time as that case. The National Education Law petitioners also sought to challenge the law regulating the state budget of 2005. Based on the same argument as the previous case, the petitioners requested that the Constitutional Court rule that the 2005 state budget law contravenes the Constitution, as it only allocated 7 percent for education and not the 20 percent that the Constitution requires.

The Constitutional Court upheld that the obligation of the state to provide education arises from the rights of citizens, guaranteed by Article 28C, Section 1, Article 28E, Section 1 and, particularly, Article 31, Section 1 of the Constitution. With the incorporation of these education-focused articles into the Constitution, the Constitutional Court ruled that the state has an obligation to act to fulfill the rights of citizens to receive education. Accordingly, if the Budget Law fails to allocate a minimum of 20 percent for education, then it will be in violation of Article 31, Section 4 of the Constitution.

The Constitutional Court further recognized the good faith of the government and House of Representatives in planning to gradually increase budgetary funding of education over a number of years. However, the Court also reminded the government and the House that the Constitutional Court in Case No. 011/PUU-III/2005, which was filed by the same petitioners, had already held that the elucidation of Article 49, Section 1 of the National Education Law did not carry the force of law and could not serve as justification for allocating less than the required 20 percent. Thus, compliance with Article 31, Section 4 of the Constitution required an allocation to education of at least 20 percent, a figure which could not be effected gradually.

The reasoning of the ruling read:

> From the human rights perspective, the right to education is... included in the economic, social, and cultural rights. The obligation of the state to respect and to fulfill economic, social, and cultural rights is an obligation to achieve, and not an obligation to behave, as is the case for civil and political rights. The obligation of the state in terms of "obligation to achieve" is fulfilled when the state with good faith has utilized the maximum available resources and has performed progressive realization.... However, as article 31 section (4) of the Constitution sets a norm of prioritizing the education budget at a minimum of 20 per cent of the State Budget, then the nature of the "obligation to achieve" in fulfilling the citizens' right to education has been raised to an "obligation to behave." Therefore, if apparently in a Law regarding State Budget the minimum allocation of 20 per cent for education is not fulfilled, then the Law contravenes article 31 section (4) of the Constitution.[57]

By reading the ruling, it is clear that the Court recognized allocation of the state budget as a binding provision. The Court hinted that future cases need to specifically address the issue of allocation.

The Constitutional Court then concluded that as the Budget Law was in violation of the Constitution, the Constitutional Court should declare it null and void. This state of affairs presented difficult legal and logistical problems. If the national budget was to be declared no longer valid, the government would have to reformulate the budget to include a 20 percent allocation for the education sector and consequently, reductions in the allocations for other sectors. If this were to occur, it would lead to chaos and a lack of legal certainty in the budgetary and financial administration of the entire country. Should the Constitutional Court declare the Budget Law repugnant to the Constitution and therefore null and void, under Article 23, Section 3 of the Constitution, the previous year's budget would continue in effect. Then the situation would be exacerbated as the allocation devoted to education that year was, in fact, less than this year's budget (it was 6.6 percent), and even greater damage would be inflicted on the constitutional rights of the petitioners. Based on these considerations, although the Constitutional Court ruled that the 2005 Budget Law contravened the Constitution, it rejected the petition to declare it null and void for the sake of safeguarding economic stability.

Judicial Review of the 2006 State Budget Law, Case No. 026/PUU-III/2006

Although this case occurs outside the period of focus for this study (1995–2005), its importance warrants consideration. This case was filed by different petitioners than in the previous cases, though the basic arguments remained the same. The petitioners of this case included the members of the Association of Teachers, the

---

[57] Constitutional Court Decision No. 012/PUU-III/2005 on the Judicial Review of the Law concerning the State Budget of 2005. Translation by Bivitri Susanti.

Association of Educational Science Graduates, and Nurani Dunia, a foundation working on the enhancement of the quality of education for Indonesian citizens. The petitioners requested that the Constitutional Court rule that the 2006 State Budget Law contravenes the Constitution as it only allocated 8.1 percent for education, and is therefore null and void.

Although this case is similar to previous cases addressing this issue, this case has made more progress in establishing a constitutional obligation to allocate 20 percent of the state budget for education. The petitioners made the argument stronger by adding the fact that the government and the parliament should have been aware of the opinion of the Constitutional Court in the judicial review of the previous year's state budget. Therefore, the government and the parliament did not demonstrate a good-faith effort by failing to comply with the 20 percent allocation obligation.

The Constitutional Court confirmed the interpretation of the plaintiffs and made a stronger ruling in terms of the law, though one that may not be applicable in terms of practice. Based on the additional argument of the petitioners, the Constitutional Court declared that the state budget with the maximum 9.1 percent allocation was to be null and void. The implication was that the state budget as a whole was deemed effective and applicable; but during the midyear adjustment of the state budget, the government and parliament would have to allocate additional expenditures to education should additional income be received from other sources.

In addition, the Constitutional Court's decision effectively provided a guideline for future cases, by ruling that as long as the budget allocation for education has not reached 20 percent, then the state budget is always in violation of the Constitution. However, in examining future cases, the Court would again consider the legal impact of such a ruling. These considerations would likely include a thorough assessment of overall national, as well as global, economic conditions and a consideration of the policies of the current government and the parliament.

The state budget of 2008 included an increase in education spending to 11.8 percent of the budget.[58] This increase allocated for education suggests improvement in the last four years, from 6.6 percent in 2004, 7 percent in 2005, 8.1 percent in 2006, 9.1 percent in 2007, and 11.8 percent in 2008. The slow pace of change is somewhat expected, as the Minister of Finance has stated that only modest improvements are to be expected until at least 2009.[59] Whether it occurs in 2009 or later, the question of when the 20 percent allocation will actually be allocated to education and what is the role of the Court in facilitating this process, remains an important one for public interest lawyers and activists alike.

Analysis

As is the case with health-care complaints in Indonesia, complaints regarding the right to education are rarely litigated. Cases regarding the School Operational

---

[58] *Jakarta Post*, May 2, 2007, No more money for education, government tells court.
[59] *Media Indonesia Daily*, January 27, 2004.

Support Fund, for example, have never been brought before the Court. Another example of the reluctance to use the formal legal system is the case involving the Sang Timur School in Jakarta in 2004, which involves religious discrimination and lack of access to school. This case could have garnered national attention and resulted in important policy changes, but, instead, it was settled through negotiation.

Reluctance to utilize the judicial system for educational rights is common, and it may be because education is still considered low priority for the marginalized in Indonesia. In contrast to substandard health care, the lack of education does not immediately threaten physical well-being or one's livelihood. Hence, if one faces problems related to the right to education (e.g., a high fee for school), one would typically make adjustments without challenging the policy. The effective remedy for cases regarding the right to education can be achieved by lowering one's standards of educational quality. Bringing a right-to-education case to court, for instance, is not seen as a viable option, because it requires more effort and, surely, more money. For cases regarding school fees, for instance, those negatively affected by the fees can simply stop attending school. For cases regarding school choice, the affected students simply move to another school.

The problems faced by the poor in litigating right-to-education cases are apparent by their scarcity: all five of the right-to-education cases reviewed involve middle class plaintiffs. Also, the fact that four of the five cases reviewed (the Melawai Junior High School Case is an exception) have important implications for policy shows that the plaintiffs did not merely desire individual compensation. It suggests, rather, that the desire for more systematic changes may have played a role in the decision to bring these cases to court. These intentions are especially visible in cases involving the allocation of the state budget. See Table 6.3 for a listing of the cases reviewed concerning the right to education.

DOES THE COURT MATTER?

This study shows that the constitutional and regulatory framework for the rights to health care and education are, at least in principle, fundamentally sound. Amendments to the Constitution have brought the language of international norms concerning economic, social, and political rights into Indonesian law and society. These norms were further elaborated in the laws regarding human rights, and in the adoption of the ICESCR as national law.

The fact that Indonesia has major problems in terms of poverty certainly is an important factor contributing to its failure to fulfill these rights. As in many other parts of the world, the lack of resources has always been pointed to as the main reason barring the fulfillment of economic, social, and cultural rights. However, new programs have been undertaken that attempt to combat these barriers and to improve the quality of the services available to Indonesia's poorest citizens. The oil subsidy compensation program for schooling and health care, for example, is in place. The government also provides direct services through regional government in order to serve geographic areas that may be missed by private sector providers.

Table 6.3. *Cases on education*

No.	Case Name	Court, Location, Year	Plaintiff's socioeconomic class	NGO involvement	Win?	Impact on policy
Choice of Schooling						
1	The Melawai Junior High School Case	Civil Court, Jakarta	Middle Class	Yes	No	No
2	Petition to nullify Administrative Action of the President of the University of Indonesia	Administrative Court, Jakarta	Middle Class	Yes	Yes	No
Public Financing For Education						
3	Judicial review of the National Education System Law	Constitutional Court	Middle Class	Yes	Yes	Yes
4	Judicial Review of the 2005 State Budget Law	Constitutional Court	Middle Class	Yes	Yes	Yes
5	Judicial Review of the 2006 State Budget Law	Constitutional Court	Middle Class	Yes	Yes	Yes

It is abundantly clear that the quality of health care and education in Indonesia is not up to the level of Indonesia's constitutional and regulatory framework. Statistics and recent reports show that the quality of education and health services is still poor. The consequence of this, in theory, should be an enforcement of such rights on the part of the Court. That logic, however, works only if the judiciary is utilized by the public and is sufficiently empowered to compel compliance with its rulings.

In spite of the limited number of cases, two distinguishing features are apparent in the cases reviewed.

First, there is clearly a high degree of reluctance from the public to pursue their legal rights. The small number of cases is striking when seen in the context of Indonesia's geographical, social, and political realities. In a large country with more than 240 million people, there were only twelve relevant cases available for examination in the period of 1995 to 2005. It is clear that litigation is not the preferred avenue for people to pursue complaints pertaining to the rights to health care and to education.

Second, in most of the cases reviewed, litigation was used as a campaign strategy. This is evident from the fact that NGOs advocating in each case employed strategies designed to boost the visibility of the case. In the case of the Buyat Bay pollution, for instance, the representatives of the plaintiffs not only sought an effective remedy for the plaintiff, but also sought a broader, judicial remedy.[60]

The Lack of Trust in the Judicial System

The cases studies reveal that a lack of trust in the judicial system contributes significantly to the reluctance on the part of citizens to utilize the Court. Most of the problems in health care and education are resolved by directly lobbying the policy makers or negotiating with the provider of health care or education services, instead of opting for a resolution by the Courts. The preference for informal dispute mechanisms has also been documented in a World Bank study of village justice in Indonesia.[61]

A classic example of the use of the musyawarah principle is the Sukabumi polio case. In that case, a civil litigation against the government regarding the polio vaccine program was withdrawn by the plaintiff, following negotiations between the government and the plaintiff. Commenting on his reasons for withdrawing his civil suit, Opik, the plaintiff, said that for him it was better to accept the offer from the government because it provided him with direct and immediate compensation: "If I go to Court, who can guarantee that I would win the case? I do not have the money to bribe."[62]

Opik's remarks highlight the degree to which corruption in the judiciary discourages civil suits, but they also point to why plaintiffs in these cases were typically from the middle class. Bringing a lawsuit before the Court not only requires trust in and knowledge of the judicial process, but also financial resources. In cases where the plaintiffs are from the lower classes, this has usually only been possible with the involvement of NGOs and activists. Their role in these cases is not only to represent the plaintiffs, but also to educate the community so that the people understand their rights.

Litigation as a Campaign

The litigation of the rights to health care and education on the part of NGOs serves social mobilization and campaigning as much as direct redress. The Nunukan case best exemplifies this conclusion. Choirul Anam, one of the representatives of the plaintiffs, said that the refugees' need for a remedy led the attorneys at the Jakarta Legal Aid Bureau to develop a citizen lawsuit. At that time, it seemed a precarious strategy because a citizen lawsuit had never before been litigated in the courts.

---

[60] See also interview with Siti Maemunah, JATAM Coordinator, January 18, 2006, as quoted in this chapter.
[61] The World Bank 2005. Village justice in Indonesia, p. 1–53.
[62] Interview with Opik, May 5, 2006.

It was chosen significantly because it would also be useful as part of a public campaign to claim economic and social rights.[63]

The Nunukan case was a success story for NGOs, mainly because they were able to raise public awareness and bring attention to the issues of the case. Press statements were released and press conferences and public discussions were held, usually with the sponsorship of the network of NGOs working on the case. In addition, NGOs also submitted requests for hearings in parliament and arranged a series of meetings with relevant government ministries.

A. Patra M. Zen, the Chair of the Indonesian Legal Aid foundation, confirmed this strategy:

> the Indonesian Legal Aid Foundation does not deal with the quality of education, except budget, and does not deal with the quality of health, except for malpractice. We do this because we believe that we need to promote economic, social, and political rights through litigation.[64]

Moreover, Zen argues in one of his articles that the justiciability of economic and social rights should be further developed by encouraging NGOs and advocates to submit their cases to the court even though he expected judicial reluctance at first, given that the practice of class action lawsuits took almost fifteen years to be accepted by the court and legislature.[65]

In sum, the cases reviewed lead to a tentative conclusion: within limits, and notwithstanding the relatively small numbers of cases seen so far, the Indonesian courts can enforce the rights to health care and education. Although it is true that, as a result of deeply rooted corruption, the ordinary Indonesian judicial system is often mistrusted, there remain important possibilities for change. Of the two types of remedies that may be obtained from litigating economic, social, and political rights – the effective, which involves the redress of specific grievances, and the judicial, which involves court-led directives to change policy – the courts in Indonesia may emerge to play an important role in the latter, which then might figure in campaigns to achieve the former.

CONCLUDING REMARKS

If the question is whether or not decisions of the Indonesian courts have an impact on policy on the rights to health care and education, the cases reviewed in the research suggest that the answer is a tentative yes. Out of the twelve cases considered here, the analysis concludes that seven of them have significant implications for policy. This may be an overly simplistic conclusion to reach, however, at this stage

---

[63] Interview with Choirul Anam, February 15, 2006. He said that the idea actually came from Munir, the former director of the Indonesian Legal Aid Foundation, who was poisoned in a plane to the Netherlands in 2004.

[64] Interview with A. Patra M. Zen, the chair of Indonesian Legal Aid Foundation, January 17, 2006.

[65] A. Patra M. Zen 2003. Justisiabilitas Hak-Hak Ekonomi, Sosial, dan Budaya: Menarik Pengalaman Internasional, Mempraktikannya di Indonesia [Justiciability of economic, social, and cultural rights: Observing the international practices and the practice in Indonesia]: 36–47.

of the research cycle. Moreover, the reluctance of Indonesian citizens to bring complaints before the courts limits the judicial impact on policy making. Asked in so many words, most Indonesians would not consider the courts important political actors.

The limitations on legalizing demand for economic and social rights stem from problems of the Indonesian judicial system itself. It is a question of larger judicial reform, as well as of civil society activism necessary for Indonesians to claim their fundamental rights.

BIBLIOGRAPHY

Asia Foundation. 2001. *Citizens' perception of the Indonesian justice sector.* Jakarta: Author.
Assegaf, R. S. 2004. The Indonesian Supreme Court (*Mahkamah Agung*): A portrait. Paper presented at the Conference on Indonesian Legal Institutions, Asian Law Center, University of Washington School of Law, Seattle, April 22–23.
Churchill, G. 1992. *The development of legal information systems in Indonesia: Problems and progress to date.* In Van Vollenhoven Institute for Law and Administration in Non-Western Countries Research Reports 2. Leiden, The Netherlands: Van Vollenhoven Institute.
Cumaraswamy, D. P. 2002. Civil and political rights, including questions of independence of the judiciary, administration of justice. *Report of the Special Rapporteur on the Independence of Judges and Lawyers, Submitted in Accordance with the Commission on Human Rights Resolution 2002/43.* Report on the Mission to Indonesia, July 15–24.
Jayasuriya, K. 1999. Corporatism and judicial independence within statist legal institutions in East Asia. In Kanishka Jayasuriya (ed.), *Law, capitalism and power in Asia* (pp. 173–204). London and New York: Routledge.
Lev, D. S. 2000. Judicial institutions and legal culture. In D. S. Lev, *Legal evolution and political authority in Indonesia, selected essays* (pp. 161–214). The Hague: Martinus Nijhoff.
Nasution, A. B. 1992. *The aspiration for constitutional government in Indonesia: A socio-legal study of the Indonesian Konstituante 1956–1959.* Jakarta, Indonesia: Pustaka Sinar Harapan.
Pincus, J. 2002. The poverty of Indonesian economics. *Van Zorge Report on Indonesia* 4(1). Available at: http://www.vanzorgereport.com.
Pompe, S. 2005. *The Indonesian Supreme Court: A study of institutional collapse.* Ithaca, NY: Cornell University Press.
Supreme Court of Indonesia. 2003. *Blueprint for the reform of the Supreme Court of Indonesia.* Jakarta: An English summary is available at: http://siteresources.worldbank.org/INTINDONESIA/Resources/CGI03/13th-CGI-Dec10-11-03/SupremeCourt.pdf.
———. 2006. *Annual report 2005.*
Tanter, R. 1991. Oil, IGGI, and U.S. hegemony: The global preconditions for Indonesian rentier-militarization. In A. Budiman (ed.), *State and civil society in Indonesia* (pp. 51–93). Clayton, Victoria, Australia: Monash University, Centre of Southeast Asian Studies.
United Nations Development Programme (UNDP). 2005. *Indonesia human development report 2004. The economics of democracy: Financing human development in Indonesia.* Bappenas, Indonesia: BPS Statistics and UNDP.
World Bank 2003. *Combating corruption in Indonesia, enhancing accountability for development.* World Bank East Asia Poverty Reduction and Economic Management Unit, October 20. Available at http://siteresources.worldbank.org/INTINDONESIA/Resources/Publication/03-Publication/Combating+Corruption+in+Indonesia-Oct15.pdf.

————— 2004, February. *Village justice in Indonesia: Case studies on access to justice, village democracy and governance.* Social Development Unit, Indonesia, Working Paper Number 31616.

Zen, A. P. M. 2005. Eksplorasi: Justisiabilitas dan Hak Klaim Masyarakat Korban Industri Pertambangan (Explorations: Justiciability and rights claims regarding communities and the mining industry). In *Tak Ada Hak Asasi Yang Diberi* (pp. 69–72). Jakarta: YLBHI.

—————. 2003. Justisiabilitas Hak-Hak Ekonomi, Sosial, dan Budaya: Menarik Pengalaman Internasional (Justiciability of economic, social, and cultural rights: Drawing from international experience), Mempraktikannya di Indonesia. *Jurnal HAM,* 1(1): 36–47.

7 Transforming Legal Theory in the Light of Practice: The Judicial Application of Social and Economic Rights to Private Orderings

HELEN HERSHKOFF

More than a half century ago the Universal Declaration of Human Rights defined education and physical well-being as human rights to "be protected by the rule of law."[1] Although a significant number of national constitutions now include language that embraces a right to education, to health, or to both,[2] disease and illiteracy remain pervasive throughout the world. Almost a billion individuals, a sixth of the international population, cannot read;[3] similar numbers lack access to

---

[1] Preamble to the Universal Declaration of Human Rights, Adopted and Proclaimed by General Assembly Resolution 217 A (III) of December 10, 1948, available at http://www.un.org/ Overview/rights.html (accessed June 21, 2006).

[2] See Varun Gauri 2005. Social rights and economics: Claims to health care and education in developing countries. In P. Alston and M. Robinson (eds.), *Human rights and development: Towards mutual reinforcement* (pp. 65–66). Oxford: Oxford University Press. (Of 165 countries surveyed, 116 refer to a right to education and 73 refer to a right to health care.) In addition, about one hundred national constitutions guarantee a right to a healthy environment. See Dinah Shelton 2007. Human rights, health and environmental protection. *Hum. Rts. & Int'l Legal Discourse* 1: 9, 56. See also David M. Beatty 2004. *The ultimate rule of law.* Oxford: Oxford University Press: 119 ("Most of the constitutions that were written after the Second World War make some mention of social and economic rights, although they vary greatly both in substance and style").

[3] See Report of the United Nations High Commissioner for Human Rights to the Economic and Social Council, UN Doc. E/1999/96, 2000. In H. J. Steiner and P. Alston (eds.), *International human rights in context: Law, politics, morals.* Oxford: Oxford University Press: 239. Educational deficits reflect a gendered pattern. See V. Muñoz Villalobos 2006. Economic, social and cultural rights: Girls' right to education. In *Commission on Human Rights, Report submitted by the Special Rapporteur on the right to education,* E/CN.4/2006/45: 9 ("According to the most conservative estimates, 55 million girls still do not attend school and at least 23 countries risk failing to achieve universal primary education by the year 2015, as proposed in the Millennium Development Goals").

The author is the Anne and Joel Ehrenkranz Professor of Law and Co-Director of the Arthur Garfield Hays Civil Liberties Program at New York University School of Law. Research assistance from Deepika Bansal, Márcia Bento, Adan Canizales, Patrick P. Garlinger, Faiza S. Issa, Natalie Y. Morris, Alexander Moulter, Sarah Parady, Tali Reisenberger, Elizabeth Seidlin-Bernstein, Joanna L. Shulman, Anisa Aro Susanto, and Megan Thomas is gratefully acknowledged. I thank John Easterbrook for support in preparing the manuscript for publication. Acknowledgment is given to the World Bank Law Library for access to Manupatra, and to Linda Ramsingh and Mirela Roznovski of New York University School of Law for exemplary library assistance. I thank Menaka Guruswamy for discussion and Siddarth Narrain for materials concerning Indian tort law. Finally, appreciation is expressed to Dan Brinks, Varun Gauri, and Stephen Loffredo for comments and encouragement.

health care or to potable water.[4] These deprivations cause physical harm,[5] under-mine a person's sense of autonomy,[6] and subvert democratic possibilities.[7] Against this dismal background, skeptics question not only the conceptual foundation of social and economic rights,[8] but also their strategic value in fostering improvement for the disadvantaged and dispossessed.[9]

The current project examines a specific aspect of this problem: the extent and efficacy of using national courts to enforce constitutionally based claims to health and to education services. Focusing on five nations – Brazil, India, Indonesia, Nigeria, and South Africa – the project offers an ambitious account of institutional practices based on cross-disciplinary, comparative case studies that combine quantitative with qualitative analysis. The countries under discussion have all codified social and economic rights in their national constitutions and in some places have enacted legislation to effectuate these provisions.[10] The preceding chapters do not revisit the wisdom or legitimacy of extending constitutional protection to health or educational services. Instead, the investigation takes for granted the existence of such rights and focuses on whether and to what extent litigation – taking unmet claims to court – helps secure their enforcement in ways that improve individual

---

[4] Susannah Sirkin et al. 1999. The role of health professionals in protecting and promoting human rights: A paradigm for professional responsibility. In Y. Danieli, E. Stamatopoulou, and C. J. Dias (eds.), *The universal declaration of human rights: Fifty years and beyond* (pp. 357–358). New York: Baywood. See also Ramin Pejan 2004. The right to water: The road to justiciability. *Geo. Wash. Int'l L. Rev.* 36: 1181 (Reporting that at least 1.1 billion people lack "access to sufficient and clean drinking water"; citing World Health Organization 2003. *The right to water.* Geneva: World Health Organization, p. 7).

[5] See, e.g., Alicia Ely Yamin 2003. Not just a tragedy: Access to medications as a right under international law. *B.U. Int'l L. J.* 21: 325 (Referring to "Sub-Saharan Africa where an estimated 29.4 million adults and children are living with HIV/AIDS . . . [and] dying simply because they lack access to life-saving sustaining medications").

[6] For an autonomy justification of social rights, see Cécile Fabre 2000. *Social rights under the constitution: Government and the decent life.* Oxford: Clarendon Press.

[7] K. D. Ewing 2003. The case for social rights. In T. Campbell, J. Goldsworthy, and A. Stone (eds.), *Protecting human rights: Instruments and institutions* (pp. 323, 326). Oxford: Oxford University Press (acknowledging social rights as "a precondition of democratic government").

[8] See Dwight G. Newman 2003. Institutional monitoring of social and economic rights: A South African case study and a new research agenda. *S. Afr. J. on Hum. Rts.* 19: 189 (stating that "social and economic rights are still often considered a separate category from civil and political rights").

[9] See, e.g., Parmanand Singh 2006. Social rights and good governance: The Indian perspective. In C. Raj. Kumar and D. K. Srivastava (eds.), *Human rights and development: Law, policy and governance* (p. 437). Hong Kong: LexisNexis (arguing "that social rights, such as the rights to adequate nutrition, health care, housing, education and work cannot be realized just by judicial enunciation of these rights as aspects of human rights, but by a set of public policies, political planning, and participation of civil society to enhance the capabilities of the poor and disadvantaged people"). See also Ran Hirschl, 2004. *Towards juristocracy: The origins and consequences of the new constitutionalism.* Cambridge, MA: Harvard University Press (p. 13, associating constitutional review with the decline in "progressive concepts of distributive justice"). But see Leslie Friedman Goldstein 2004. From democracy to juristocracy. *Law & Society Rev.* 38: 611, 626 (criticizing Hirschl's account of the relation between constitutional entrenchment and socioeconomic redistribution as "unconvincing").

[10] See William F. Felice 2003. *The global new deal: Economic and social human rights in world politics.* New York: Rowman & Littlefield (pp. 7, 51–53, defining economic and social rights).

lives and enhance social conditions. Working from the ground up, the case studies attempt to trace the particular local processes that influence the judicial and extra-judicial implementation of health and education claims, dealing with issues that range from the availability of money damages to compensate for substandard medical care,[11] to the regulation of private school practices affecting student conduct.[12]

From the perspective of a U.S. lawyer, the case studies tell an unexpected and important story – particularly when considered against the usual discussion of the justiciability of social and economic rights. The question of whether federal courts in the United States can and should enforce affirmative constitutional claims tends to focus on the capacity of judges to deal with polycentric, value-laden policy questions in disputes involving the government, and also on the legitimacy of having unelected courts mandate goods and services that are not provided by the democratically elected branches of government.[13] These arguments, wedded to American doctrine, have spilled over to the jurisprudence of other nations and even to transnational analysis.[14] "[W]hatever the logic and moral force of social and economic rights," David M. Beatty states, "their enforcement seems to compromise the democratic character of government and the sovereignty of the people to determine for themselves what the collective, public character of their communities will be."[15] Implicit in this well-trod discussion is a state-centric focus: the assumption that social and economic rights, if justiciable at all, run against the state and the bureaucratic officials who work as its agents, but not against private actors. Moreover, the debate takes a narrow approach to the concept of state duty, so that the government is constitutionally obliged to redress only those deprivations for which it is directly responsible. Although private actors play a vital role in realizing or defeating access to social and economic goods, the conventional account leaves the manufacturer of pharmaceuticals, the manager of a private school, and the doctor who vaccinates a child subject only to the private rules of tort, contract, and property law, and immune from constitutional regulation.[16]

---

[11] Indian Medical Association v. V. P. Shantha and Others (1995) 6 SC 651 (India), available at Manu/SC/0836/1995 (accessed Jan. 3, 2008).

[12] Christian Education South Africa v. Minister of Education 2000 (4) SA 757 (CC), August 18, 2000 (South Africa).

[13] See, e.g., Lawrence G. Sager 2001. Thin constitutions and the good society. *Fordham L. Rev.* 69: 1989–90 (stating that "affirmative rights come wrapped with questions of judgment, strategy, and responsibility that seem well beyond the reach of courts in a democracy").

[14] See, e.g., John Smillie 2006. Who wants juristocracy? *Otago L. Rev.* 11: 183, 183–184 (making the case against constitutional review on the grounds that it is "undemocratic" and that courts are "ill-suited" to decide disputes involving complex policy questions); Marius Pieterse 2004. Coming to terms with judicial enforcement of socio-economic rights. *S. Afr. J. Hum. Rts.* 20: 383, 384 (explaining that many "South African legal scholars . . . mechanically (and almost ritualistically) regurgit[ate]" the legitimacy debate, despite the codification of such rights in the national constitution).

[15] Beatty, *Ultimate rule of law*, 117.

[16] Jonathan M. Mann et al. 1999. Health and human rights. In Jonathan M. Mann et al. (eds.), *Health and human rights: A reader* (p. 10). New York: Routledge ("while human rights law primarily focuses on the relationship between individuals and states, awareness is increasing that other societal institutions and systems, such as transnational business, may strongly influence the capacity for realization of rights, yet they may elude state control").

The prevailing story of social and economic rights does not capture the complexity of judicial developments abroad. Overall, the case studies provide evidence of constitutional rights affecting the shape and content of private market transactions in ways that seem unusual if public law is limited to state action, particularly in the narrow sense of government responsibility only for the direct consequences of its conduct. The majority of health and education lawsuits filed in the national courts under investigation (with the singular exception of Brazil) involve claims against nongovernmental defendants – doctors, private schools, insurance companies, and hospitals – and not against the state. In India, for example, almost half of the cases surveyed involve the obligations of private providers, and only 15 percent concern government provision and financing of health care or educational services.[17] Even in countries where the formal legal regime confines social and economic rights to government actors, courts appear to be treating constitutional norms as fundamental principles to be taken seriously in interpreting common law rules (in cases involving private entities as defendants) or in shaping government regulation (in cases involving the state as defendant). Some of the decisions, recognizing the role of private and private–public arrangements in the production and distribution of social and economic goods, take a flexible approach to the public–private divide in seeking to reshape private power in line with public and not simply market goals.[18] At the same time, the decisions attempt to give appropriate respect to autonomy interests, reasonable expectations, and the demand of separation of powers. The result, as Varun Gauri and Daniel Brinks observe in their introduction to this volume, is a situation in which courts are applying "formal economic and social rights to a much wider set of actors, and in so doing have delineated duties and liberties for which a variety of specific actors, and not (or, in some cases, not only) the state, are legally accountable."[19]

The preceding chapters, thus, deviate from the usual account of whether social and economic rights can be judicially enforced against the state.[20] Instead, the case studies open a window to a topic variously called the privatization of constitutional rights,[21] the constitutionalization of the private sphere,[22] and the horizontal

---

[17] Chapter 4, this volume.

[18] See J. M. Balkin 1995. Populism and progressivism as constitutional categories. *Yale L. J.* 104: 1935, 1968–69 (book review) (calling for a "more flexible" approach to the public/private distinction).

[19] Chapter 1, this volume.

[20] See, e.g., Kristen Boon 2007. The role of courts in enforcing economic and social rights. *Geo. Wash. Int'l L. Rev.* 39: 449, 456. Reviewing R. Gargarella, P. Domino, and T. Roux (eds.), Courts and social transformation in new democracies: An institutional voice for the poor? Aldershot, U.K.: Ashgate (commenting that the editors do not consider "the extent to which courts can intervene to protect [economic and social rights] where traditional government activities have been transferred to the private sector or international financial institutions"). For a discussion of the role of non-state actors in the enforcement of international human rights, see Manisuli Ssenyonjo 2007. Non-state actors and economic, social, and cultural rights. In M. A. Baderin and R. McCorquodale (eds.), *Economic, social and cultural rights in action.* Oxford: Oxford University Press.

[21] Andrew Clapham 1995. The privatisation of human rights. *Eur. Hum. Rts. L. Rev.*: 20.

[22] Murray Hunt 1998. The "horizontal effect" of the Human Rights Act. Public Law: 423–424 (referring to the extent to which "U. K. courts will be required to ensure that all law which they apply accords with the [European] Convention [on Human Rights], and to that extent the law which governs private relations will have been 'constitutionalised' by the passage of the Human Rights Act").

application of constitutional rights[23] – all of which involve the extent to which constitutional rights may be enforced, directly or indirectly, against non-state actors in their relations with individuals. As such, the case studies challenge the mechanistic command-and-control conception of the state, which separates public regulation from private initiative and assigns a monopoly for this purpose to the government.[24] Consistent with theories of the constitutive and expressive power of law, the case studies illuminate the important interpretive role of constitutional norms in reshaping private orderings to encourage the achievement of public goals.[25] Not only do these provisions influence courts in their decision making, but also they produce cognitive effects in individuals. The filing and nature of tort and contract cases suggest that social and economic clauses may motivate individuals to seek judicial protection against mistreatment by private actors whose market behavior blocks access to vital health or education services. From this perspective, the developments set out in the case studies form part of a broader trend involving decentered regulatory processes, the reallocation of authority between administrators and the courts, and interactions between public power and private actors.[26]

I do not wish to overstate the extent of these developments. Cross-country comparisons are notoriously difficult. Legal traditions, political cultures, and judicial practices differ from country to country and affect court behavior.[27] Sample sizes across the case studies vary considerably.[28] The number of lawsuits in some nations is unfortunately small. Courts do not always articulate, or articulate clearly, the basis for their decisions. Nor are legal opinions publicly available in all of the

---

[23] See Stephen Gardbaum 2003–2004. The "horizontal effect" of constitutional rights. *Mich. L. Rev.* 102: 387.

[24] See generally Georg Nolte 2005. European and U.S. constitutionalism: Comparing essential elements. In Georg Nolte (ed.), *European and US constitutionalism* (pp. 3–20). Cambridge: Cambridge University Press.

[25] See Fabrizio Cafaggi and Horatia Muir Watt 2006. The making of European private law: Regulation and governance design. Available at http://ssrn.com/abstract=946284 (accessed May 12, 2008) (emphasizing the public regulatory role of torts and contract law).

[26] For a summary of these developments, see Fabrizio Cafaggi 2006. Rethinking private regulation in the European regulatory space. In F. Cafaggi (ed.), *Reframing self-regulation in European private law* (pp. 3–76). Leiden, The Netherlands: Kluwer Law International.

[27] See generally Barry Friedman 2005. The politics of judicial review. *Tex. L. Rev.* 4: 257, 336 (explaining that "the scope of constitutional remedies, the question of negative and positive rights, and the force of *stare decisis* can all be understood as pragmatic reactions to the political environment of judicial review").

[28] By way of example, consider the number of education and health cases surveyed in each country set out in the following table:

Country	Number of education and health cases surveyed
Brazil	7682
India	315
South Africa	22
Indonesia	12
Nigeria	27

Source: Brinks and Gauri calculations on the basis of data presented in this volume.

countries surveyed.[29] Nevertheless, the case studies provide important insight into how courts actually approach the enforcement of social and economic rights and, thus, are of critical importance to theorists and policy makers interested in whether legalization strategies can affect social improvement.[30]

Commentators known for their skepticism or even outright hostility toward social and economic rights have altered their views in the light of actual judicial practice: Cass Sunstein and Dennis Davis, for example, two internationally recognized scholars, are said to have undergone "profound conversions on the basis of a single case."[31] Whatever their limitations, the case studies raise important questions about the relation between social change and constitutional rights. No longer can analysts confine the influence of social and economic rights to public law cases demanding services from the government; to the contrary, a more abiding influence may flow from their radiating effects in private law cases involving common law rules that reconfigure social relations and destabilize entrenched hierarchy.

This chapter explores the developments described in the case studies in six parts: The first part rehearses the conventional understanding of rights, typical to United States constitutional doctrine, as affording protection only against the government and as playing a very limited role in regulating private actors. Against this background, the second part highlights the critical perspective of the case studies and how their motivating assumptions differ from that of the prevailing thin state-centered approach to constitutional enforcement. The third part considers the different doctrinal avenues through which social and economic rights can be enforced against private actors, drawing on the existing literature concerning the horizontal enforcement of constitutional rights. The fourth part examines selected court decisions from the case studies to illustrate the influence of health and education constitutional clauses in disputes involving private, and not governmental, activity. The decisions fall into two categories. The first is a familiar, although somewhat unusual, category of constitutional cases seeking government regulation of market behavior. The second is a less familiar category of common law cases involving contract and property disputes between private litigants. The fifth part compares the interpretive practices reflected in these cases with existing academic models of horizontal constitutional enforcement. Finding a gap between theory and practice, I offer an alternative model that focuses on social relationships rather than direct (or even indirect) extension of constitutional duties and obligations. The last part concludes by briefly considering the political economy of constitutional privatization in the countries surveyed. I raise some of the potential criticisms of these developments and set down questions for future research. Even if these cases fall short of a trend, they mark an important development that invites further attention.

---

[29] The inaccessibility of legal decisions in Indonesia is discussed in Sebastian Pompe 2005. *Access to court decisions and the problem of lawmaking. The Indonesian Supreme Court: A study of institutional collapse.* Ithaca, NY: Cornell University, Southeast Asia Program Publications, pp. 435–455.

[30] See, e.g., Orly Lobel 2007. The paradox of extralegal activism: Critical legal consciousness and transformative politics. *Harv. L. Rev.* 120: 937, 939 ("An argument that has become increasingly prevalent in legal scholarship states that the law often brings more harm than good to social movements that rely on legal strategies to advance their goals").

[31] Beatty, *Ultimate rule of law*, 126.

CONSTITUTIONAL RIGHTS AND GOVERNMENT ACTION

Commentators typically describe constitutional rights as affording protection against the over reaching actions of government,[32] with "the constitution ... seen as ... delineat[ing] the boundary between the state and the private sphere."[33] Michael J. Perry takes a characteristic view in referring to "the main sort of human rights that national constitutions and the international law of human rights protect" as "human rights against government."[34] In a similar vein, commentators describe constitutional rights as trumps that block the exercise of government power and so protect against official abuse.[35] Illustrated by United States doctrine interpreting the scope of the Fourteenth Amendment to the federal Constitution, the classical understanding sees constitutional rights as affording protection to individuals in their relations with the state as an all-encompassing Leviathan.[36] As Laurence H. Tribe explains, focusing on U.S. law,

> With the exception of the Thirteenth Amendment, the Constitution does not directly concern itself with private actors; its self-executing guarantees of individual rights protect individuals only from conduct by the state. That is, the Constitution controls the deployment of governmental power and defines the rules for how such power may be structured and applied. The Constitution, therefore, is not a body of rules about ordinary private actions, but a collection of rules about the rules and uses of law: in a word, *metalaw.* [37]

A corollary of the state-centric approach is the view that constitutional rights function "as individual protections *against* the aggressive state, not as private entitlements *to* protection by the state."[38] The conception of rights as bulwarks against government action is allied with the conventional, although criticized, distinction between negative and positive rights:

> A positive right is a claim to something – a share of material goods, or some particular good like the attention of a lawyer or a doctor, or perhaps the claim to a result like health or enlightenment – while a negative right is a right that something not be done to one, that some particular imposition be withheld. Positive rights are inevitably asserted to scarce goods, and consequently scarcity implies a limit

---

[32] See Paul Kauper 1962. *Civil liberties and the constitution.* Ann Arbor: University of Michigan Press, p. 129 (stating that "the Constitution is concerned with constitutional liberties in the classic sense of the Western world; i.e. as liberties of the individual to be safeguarded against the power of the state").

[33] Aileen McHarg 2006. The constitutional dimension of self-regulation. In Cafaggi, *Reframing self-regulation in European private law,* 80.

[34] Michael J. Perry 2003. Protecting human rights in a democracy: What role for the courts? *Wake Forest L. Rev.* 38: 635, 644.

[35] Ronald Dworkin 1977. *Taking rights seriously* (pp. 90–94 and 364–368). London: Duckworth (setting forth this view).

[36] See Richard S. Kay 1993. The state action doctrine, the public–private distinction, and the independence of constitutional law. *Const. Commentary* 10: 329, 349–358 (discussing this conception).

[37] Laurence H. Tribe 1985. *Constitutional choices.* Cambridge. MA: Harvard University Press, p. 246.

[38] Cass R. Sunstein 2001. *Designing democracy: What constitutions do.* Oxford: Oxford University Press, p. 222.

to the claim. Negative rights, however, the rights not to be interfered with in forbidden ways, do not appear to have such natural, such inevitable limitation.[39]

The literature generally associates negative rights with civil and political rights, such as the right to speak freely about political issues without government censorship, and positive rights with economic and social rights, such as a right to government-funded education. It is broadly recognized, however, that negative rights require regulatory action that generates considerable budget expense and, conversely, that economic rights require protection against government intrusion.[40] Yet, for a long time, the conceptual fault line between negative and positive rights inhibited even the theoretical possibility of constitutionalizing social welfare norms.[41] "To most American lawyers," Herman Schwartz observed in 1995, "putting economic and social rights in a constitution verges on the unthinkable."[42] Indeed, writing five years later, in 2000, Cécile Fabre went even further, saying that the idea of constitutionalized social rights was not seriously considered by "hardly anyone in mainstream Anglo-American contemporary political philosophy."[43]

Another basic feature of the classical model is that it extends constitutional protection only against government and not nongovernment action, even though the state authorizes and confirms private power and the private use of resources.[44] The emphasis, as F. A. Hayek explains, is that of "constructing a suitable legal framework,"[45] and not the mandating of "particular elements that by themselves appear desirable."[46] United States doctrine, thus, draws a line between voluntary private acts taken by social or market actors and public acts taken by the government.[47] Although acknowledging that the government sets in place the legal infrastructure

---

[39] Charles Fried 1978. *Right and wrong*. Cambridge, MA: Harvard University Press, p. 110.

[40] See John C. P. Goldberg 2005. The constitutional status of tort law: Due process and the right to a law for the redress of wrongs. *Yale L. J.* 115: 524. As John C. P. Goldberg explains:

> The slogan that the [United States] Constitution is exclusively a "charter of negative...liberties" is just that – a slogan. Constitutional rights sometimes do generate duties to act. If a guard is aware that a prisoner is choking to death, his failure to provide aid deprives the prisoner of life without due process.... The point...is not to reason from these cases to a general right of assistance. Rather, it is to establish the falsity of the broad claim that the Constitution never requires government to act for the benefit of an individual.

Id. at 592–593 (citation omitted). See also Cass R. Sunstein 2005. Why does the American Constitution lack social and economic guarantees? *Syracuse L. Rev.* 56: 1, 6 ("most of the so-called negative rights require governmental assistance, not governmental abstinence").

[41] See Helen Hershkoff 1999. Positive rights and state constitutions: The limits of federal rationality review. *Harv. L. Rev.* 112: 1131, 1133 (acknowledging this argument).

[42] Herman Schwartz 1995. Do economic and social rights belong in a constitution? *Am. U. J. Int'l L. & Pol'y* 10: 1233, 1235.

[43] Fabre, *Social rights under the Constitution*, p. 4.

[44] For an overview, see Andrew Clapham 1993. *Human rights in the private sphere*. Oxford: Oxford University Press, pp. 150–162.

[45] F. A. Hayek 1948. *Individualism and economic order*. Chicago: University of Chicago Press, p. 22.

[46] F. A. Hayek 1973. *Law, legislation and liberty*. Chicago: University of Chicago Press, p. 56.

[47] See, e.g., Michael K. Addo 2005. Human rights perspectives of corporate groups. *Conn. L. Rev.* 37: 667, 675 (referring to "the enduring belief in the separation between the private domain [to which economic affairs belong] and the public domain"). See also Jody Freeman 2000. The private role in public governance. *N.Y.U. L. Rev.* 75: 543, 551 ("'private' refers to organizations that we associate with the pursuit of profit, such as firms, or ideological goals, such as environmental organizations").

within which society and commerce are constituted,[48] conduct within those realms is considered to be distinct from that of the state and so immune from constitutional regulation.[49] Private actors do not hold the same duties as government actors and are not held to similar constitutional requirements.[50] As a result, the framework draws a strict distinction between "inequalities for which the state is directly responsible and those that are said to arise from purely private activities."[51] The fact that private law fails to generate socially optimal results at best calls for market correction or political oversight, but does not warrant constitutional modification.[52]

The requirement of state action is subject to some well-known exceptions – famously, the regulation of public utilities, public inns, and aspects of the employment relation.[53] But the application of public norms in private settings is exceptional and requires explanation (for example, the fact that the entities are engaged in a public function or are inextricably intertwined with government action).[54] Overall, federal doctrine in the United States leaves broad areas of private activity constitutionally unregulated; Congress can undertake regulation by enacting statutes or by establishing administrative agencies, but a citizen cannot typically compel the legislature to take such action.[55]

The model, thus, insulates many indirect effects of government conduct from constitutional regulation. For example, an aggrieved individual cannot constitutionally challenge the decision of a publicly funded hospital to transfer him or her to a less-equipped institution.[56] Nor does the federal Constitution provide relief for children receiving unequal educational opportunities because of differentials in state funding processes.[57] And, notoriously, the federal Constitution provides no protection to a child who is brutally assaulted by his father, even where the state arranged, supervised, and permitted the custodial relationship.[58] Indeed,

---

[48] See Jean Braucher 2007. New frontiers in private ordering – An introduction. *Ariz. L. Rev.* 49: 577, 577 ("Contract law itself is a mixture of the public and the private, a means by which the state supports private ordering with remedies for breach of some promises").

[49] See Paul Schiff Berman 2000. Cyberspace and the state action debate: The cultural value of applying constitutional norms to "private" regulation. *U. Colo. L. Rev.* 71: 1263, 1279 (criticizing the state action doctrine on the ground that "[a]ll private actions take place against a background of laws").

[50] See Larry Alexander 1993. The public/private distinction and constitutional limits on private power. *Const. Comment.* 10: 361, 365 (noting that "even if there is always state action, it does not follow that the [private] defendant is a state actor subject to constitutional duties" or "that private choices... are held to the same standards as the Constitution imposes on, say, the state police or welfare department").

[51] Stephen Loffredo 1993. Poverty, democracy and constitutional law. *U. Pa. L. Rev.* 141: 1277, 1361.

[52] This paragraph draws from Viktor J. Vanberg 2005. Market and state: The perspective of constitutional political economy. *J. of Institutional Economics* 1: 23–49.

[53] See Michael Taggart 1997. The province of administrative law. In M. Taggart (ed.), *The province of administrative law* (pp. 1–21). Oxford: Hart.

[54] See, e.g., Jackson v. Metropolitan Edison Co., 419 U. S. (1974): 345 (public function exception); Shelley v. Kraemer, 334 U. S. (1948): 1 (attribution theory).

[55] See, e.g., Smith v. Illinois Bell Tel. Co., 270 U. S. (1926): 587. For an early discussion, see Jerre S. Williams 1963. The twilight of state action. *Texas L. Rev.* 41: 347.

[56] See Blum v. Yaretsky, 457 U. S. (1992): 991.

[57] San Antonio Independent School Dist. v. Rodriguez, 411 U. S. (1973): 1.

[58] DeShaney v. Winnebago Co., 489 U. S. (1989) 189.

American constitutional doctrine takes it as a point of intellectual pride that market and social actors are left "unhampered" – with intervention regarded as an intrusion on individual autonomy and overall efficiency.[59]

Admittedly, a felicitous consequence of the vertical application of constitutional rights is the creation of a broad private space in which individuals can enjoy a reasonable degree of autonomy in their everyday lives untouched by direct government supervision.[60] As Michel Rosenfeld explains, "... in the private sphere, no obligation is owed to anyone unless it has been freely chosen, and, even then, it is only owed to the limited number of individuals to whom the obligor has freely chosen to make a commitment."[61] Indeed, many commentators argue that the extension of constitutional duties into the private sphere would create a normatively unattractive world; enforcing constitutional rights in private spaces like the family or social club would require an Orwellian bureaucracy, pervasive and intrusive, subversive of the very constitutional order that privatization seeks to achieve.[62] Justice Rehnquist, thus, famously pointed to the "'essential dichotomy' between public and private acts,"[63] insisting that "the mere existence" of common law or statutory law did not turn private activity into public action subject to constitutional constraint.

The boundary between the public and the private, although notoriously contested, thus marks, as Paul Starr observes, "pervasive dualities – or perhaps better said, polarities" that significantly affect constitutional enforcement in the United States.[64] Increasingly, however, this binary distinction does not map onto

---

[59] Viktor J. Vanberg 1999. Markets and regulation: On the contrast between free-market liberalism and constitutional liberalism. *Constitutional Political Economy* 10: 219, 220 (quoting Ludwig von Mises' concept of the "unhampered market economy"). For a similar view of British constitutionalism, see Murray Hunt, Constitutionalism and the contractualisation of government in the United Kingdom. In Taggart 1997, *The province of administrative law*, p. 24 (stating "that, for Dicey, the rule of law was nothing short of the encapsulation of his particular Whig conception of societal ordering, according to which the individual's private rights, of property, personal liberty, and freedom of discussion and association ought to be sacrosanct from interference by the state").

[60] On protection of individual autonomy, see Paul Brest 1982. State action and liberal theory: A casenote on Flagg Brothers v. Brooks. *U. Pa. L. Rev.* 130: 1296, 1323 (referring to "our psychological and ideological need to believe that there are essentially private realms, albeit circumscribed by state and society, in which actions are autonomous"). On protection of social institutions, see, Moose Lodge, No. 107 v. Irvis, U. S. 407 (1972): 163, 179–180 (Black, J., dissenting) ("My view of the First Amendment and the related guarantees of the Bill of Rights is that they create a zone of privacy which precludes government from interfering with private clubs or groups.... The individual can be as selective as he desires.").

[61] Michel Rosenfeld 1985. Contract and justice: The relation between classical contract law and social contract theory. *Iowa L. Rev.* 70: 769, 772.

[62] See Boris I. Bittker and Kenneth M. Kaufman 1972. Taxes and civil rights: "Constitutionalizing" the Internal Revenue Code. *Yale L. J.* 82: 51, 86 (arguing that "a governmental program to discover and eradicate ... [invidious discrimination exercised by private fraternal orders] necessarily imposes social costs; a society that tries to punish every instance of man's inhumanity to man may lose its humanity while crusading against the enemy").

[63] Flagg Brothers v. Brooks, 436 U. S. (1978): 149, 165 (quoting Jackson v. Metropolitan Edison Co., 419 U. S. (1974): 345, 349). See Brest, *State action and liberal theory*, p. 1296.

[64] Paul Starr 1988. The meaning of privatization. *Yale L. & Pol'y Rev.* 6: 6, available at http://www.princeton.edu/~starr/meaning.html (accessed Jan. 10, 2008).

governance structures or the reality of power relations.[65] The last thirty years have witnessed important changes in the nature of sovereignty, the contraction of the state, an increasing reliance on market arrangements to provide social services, and the subtle transformation of citizens into purchasers and clients. Martin Shapiro points out that "the very distinction between governmental and non-governmental has been blurred, since the real decision-making process now continually involves, and combines, public and private actors."[66] Similarly, government increasingly depends on private and hybrid public–private arrangements to produce and distribute public goods such as schooling and health services. Alfred C. Aman Jr. explains: "[D]eregulation and . . . various other regulatory reforms . . . have merged the public and the private in various ways, utilizing what were previously primarily private-market means of advancing public-interest goals.[67] Despite the threat that unregulated private power poses to democracy, accountability, and egalitarian goals, American constitutional doctrine for the most part has not developed new forms of public regulation.[68] Jody Freeman observes, "As a practical matter, there appears to be little judicial appetite for eroding the fundamental public/private distinction at the heart of the American constitutional order, which limits the potential for state action doctrine to be a meaningful limit on private power."[69]

THE RESEARCH STRATEGY: CONSTITUTIONALIZING A NETWORK OF ENFORCEMENT

The classical approach to constitutional enforcement, typical to the United States, assumes the autonomy of economic activity, a distinct sphere for the social, and a government that is constitutionally responsible only for the direct effects of its conduct. The assumptions motivating the case studies challenge this model in a number of respects. In their Introduction to this volume, Varun Gauri, an economist, and Daniel Brinks, a lawyer and political scientist, take as their legal subject the "'whole network' of state agencies and social organizations" needed to realize or defeat social and economic claims. The constitutional network that they explore includes not only the state and its bureaucratic and regional arms, but also the full array of social and market actors who control resources and so

---

[65] See Orly Lobel 2004. The renew deal: The fall of regulation and the rise of governance in contemporary legal thought. *Minn. L. Rev.* 89: 342, 344 ("governance signifies the range of activities, functions, and exercise of control by both public and private actors in the promotion of social, political, and economic ends").

[66] Martin Shapiro 2001. Administrative law unbounded: Reflections on government and governance. *Indiana J. of Global Leg. Studies* 8: 369, quoted in Carol Harlow 2005. Deconstructing government? In T. Ginsburg and R. A. Kagan (eds.), *Institutions & public law: Comparative approaches* (p. 141). New York: Pete Lang.

[67] Alfred C. Aman Jr. 2004. *The democracy deficit: Taming globalization through law reform*. New York: New York University Press, p. 93.

[68] See, e.g., Matthew Ellman 2006. *Does privatising public service provision reduce accountability?* Available at http://ssrn. com/abstract=1002830 (accessed Jan. 4, 2008).

[69] Jody Freeman 2000. The private role in public governance. *N.Y.U. L. Rev.* 75: 543, 591.

affect access to health and education services. As Roderick M. Hills, Jr. explains in an analogous context, nongovernmental actors "have the power to influence, or if you prefer a question-begging term, 'coerce' individuals by withholding the resources that they control. Private organizations have power: They fire, expel, boycott, strike, and enforce contracts obtained through threats to do the same."[70] The case studies, therefore, train their attention on private activity as it relates to the provision or production of health and education services. Within this broadened frame of reference, the research strategy seeks to explain how social and economic claims are taken to court, examining "demand channels" – usually but not always litigation strategies – that use public as well as private law. In this part, I excavate the motivating assumptions of the case studies and highlight their critical differences from the classical constitutional account.

First, and most obviously, the case studies assume the binding legal status of health and education norms codified in a national constitution. Despite critics who dismiss such language as simply oxymoronic – social and economic rights cannot possibly assume legal form – the case studies take for granted their legitimacy and enforceability. This is so despite broad differences in constitutional language and emphasis. The Nigeria Constitution, for example, uses the language of "social objectives," mandating that "[t]he State shall direct its policy towards ensuring that . . . there are adequate medical and health facilities for all persons. . . ."[71] The Brazil Constitution casts health care as a duty of government and a right shared by all: "Health is the right of all and the duty of the National Government and shall be guaranteed by social and economic policies aimed at reducing the risk of illness and other maladies and by universal and equal access to all activities and services for its promotion, protection and recovery."[72] The South Africa Constitution uses the language of rights and affirms that "Everyone has the right to have access to . . . health care services, including reproductive health care. . . ."[73] The Indonesia Constitution likewise treats health care in terms of individual rights: "Every person shall have the right to live in physical and spiritual prosperity . . . and shall have the right to obtain medical care."[74] Finally, the India Constitution contains a complex of principles that contemplate "[p]rotection of life and personal liberty"; the development of policy "securing . . . that the health and strength of workers . . . are not abused"; and the "[d]uty of the State . . . to improve public health."[75] Against the classical model that rejects social and economic rights as constitutionally

---

[70] Roderick M. Hills Jr. 2003. The constitutional rights of private governments. *N.Y.U. L. Rev.* 78: 144, 149–150.

[71] Nigeria Constitution, Art 17(3)(d) (1999), in *Constitutions of the countries of the world*, available at http://www.oceanalaw. com/gateway (accessed Dec. 7, 2007).

[72] Constituição Federal [C. F.] [Constitution] Art. 196 (Brazil), in *Constitutions of the countries of the world*, available at http://www.oceanalaw. com/gateway (accessed Dec. 7, 2007).

[73] S. Afr. Const. 1996 § 27(a)(a) (South Africa), in *Constitutions of the countries of the world*, available at http://www.oceanalaw. com/gateway (accessed Dec. 7, 2007).

[74] Undang-Undang Dasar 1945 [Constitution] Art. 28 H (Indonesia), in *Constitutions of the countries of the world*, available at http://www.oceanalaw. com/gateway (accessed Dec. 7, 2007).

[75] India Const. Art. 21; Art. 39(e); Art. 47 (India), in *Constitutions of the countries of the world*, available at http://www.oceanalaw. com/gateway (accessed Dec. 7, 2007).

implausible, the case studies accord them vitality and respect. As Amartya Sen explains in a related context:

> The rhetoric of human rights is sometimes applied to actual legislation inspired by the idea of human rights. There is clearly no great difficulty in seeing the obvious juridical status of these already legalized entitlements. No matter what they are called ("human rights laws" or whatever), they stand shoulder to shoulder with other established legislations. There is nothing particularly complicated about this bit of understanding.[76]

Second, the research strategy builds on the pragmatic insight that social and economic rights call for the provision of various goods and services and that the production and distribution of these goods depend on the interrelated efforts of diverse actors. These actors include the government and state agencies. But they also are recognized to include nongovernmental actors, such as corporations, individuals, and social organizations. Gauri and Brinks, thus, characterize the effectuation of social and economic rights as involving a set of triangulated relations among three categories of public and private entities: first, the state and its agents; second, private entities running the gamut from civil engineers and landlords to pharmaceutical companies and teachers; and third, recipients, citizens whose rights are realized through the delivery of essential goods and services. The authors focus their attention on the kinds of action needed from public and private providers to support the effectuation of economic and social rights. For health rights, Gauri and Brinks identify three broad categories: establishing the relative obligations of patients and providers; state regulation of providers (including private health insurance companies); and the expansion of state-provided health-care services. For education rights, the triangle includes three broad categories: choices in education (including school curricula and policies); state regulation of education providers (including private and independent schools); and the expansion of state-provided education services through increased funding or provision. This triangulated network of activity, whether prescribed by the government, privately agreed to in contracts, or negligently inflicted by indifference, is the space within which enforcement of social and economic rights takes place. Their conceptualization of these networks recognizes that private organizations – the pharmaceutical company that manufactures critical medicines, the physician who provides essential medical care, the construction company that builds infrastructure needed for hospitals[77] – control resources that directly affect the production and distribution of health and educational services and so can defeat or realize important social goals.

---

[76] Amartya Sen 2006. Human rights and the limits of law. *Cardozo L. Rev.* 27: 2913, 2915.

[77] Thomas Pogge offers the example of patent protection:

> [P]atent protections are more problematic, morally, than copyrights, especially when they confer property rights in biological organisms (such as seeds used in food production), in molecules used in medicines, or in pharmaceutical research tools needed in the development of new pharmaceuticals. Patents of these kinds are morally problematic insofar as they, directly or indirectly, impede access by the global poor to basic foodstuffs and essential medicines.

Thomas Pogge 2007. Montréal statement on the human right to essential medicines. *Cambridge Q. of Healthcare Ethics* 16: 97–108.

Third, the research strategy assumes that all branches of government, including the courts, share responsibility for the enforcement of social and economic rights, whether by developing policy frameworks, enacting legislative regulations, bringing criminal prosecutions, carrying out administrative compliance efforts, or interpreting common law rules of tort, contract, and property. Focusing on the court's role, social and economic rights afford judges interpretive authority through which to devise and revise terms of accountability for all network participants using legal tools of constitutional enforcement, statutory interpretation, and common law application.

Finally, the case studies ally themselves with theorists who conceptualize constitutional rights as constitutive of social relations and not simply as protective barriers against the overreaching state. Some of the national constitutions explicitly provide that constitutional clauses bind a nongovernmental entity in its relation with other private individuals. The South Africa Constitution, for example, states: "A provision of the Bill of Rights binds a natural or a juristic person if, and to the extent that, it is applicable, taking into account the nature of the right and the nature of any duty imposed by the right." The Constitution adds that the judiciary "in order to give effect to a right in the Bill, must apply, or if necessary develop, the common law to the extent that legislation does not give effect to that right; and . . . may develop rules of the common law to limit the right."[78] Other constitutions, however, such as that of Nigeria, explicitly limit constitutional obligations to government responsibility: "It shall be the duty and responsibility of all organs of government, and of all authorities and persons, exercising legislative, executive or judicial powers, to conform to, observe and apply the provisions of this Chapter of this Constitution."[79] The research strategy assumes that even if constitutional provisions do not apply – or do not apply tout court – to private activity in all situations, they have radiating effects that shape relationships and consciousness. Gauri and Brinks do not explicitly commit themselves to the horizontal application of social and economic rights. Instead, as the authors explain, "In social life, the legally reviewable duties and liberties that arise from the application of formal rights are always evolving as new technologies interact with new social relationships to create new demands and new rights."[80]

JUDICIALIZING THE NETWORK ENFORCEMENT OF SOCIAL AND ECONOMIC RIGHTS

The preceding chapters approach the question of how social and economic rights are enforced from a perspective that may seem counterintuitive. Constitutional rights are conventionally understood as claims against the state; their enforcement requires state policy making, bureaucratic administration, and government

---

[78] S. Afr. Const. 1996 § 8 (South Africa), in *Constitutions of the countries of the world*, available at http://www.oceanalaw. com/gateway (accessed Dec. 12, 2007).

[79] Nigeria Constitution, Art. 13 (1999), in *Constitutions of the countries of the world*, available at http://www.oceanalaw. com/gateway (accessed Dec. 7, 2007).

[80] Chapter 1, this volume.

funding. Those who study the effectiveness of social and economic rights (or, indeed, of constitutional rights in general), thus, focus on litigation aimed at the government in which the poor or marginalized demand services – such as improved education, available low-cost housing, or needed pharmaceuticals – directly from the state. The research strategy assumes the importance of this demand channel. But it expands the investigation to include the role of market actors in the realization or defeat of social and economic claims. The case studies, thus, assign a place for private law – the rules of contract, tort, and property – in the overall scheme of constitutional enforcement. This is not to say that constitutional rights are assumed to apply completely or in the same way to private actors as they do in the public sphere. Institutional context matters, as do individual autonomy concerns. Indeed, Gauri and Brinks are fastidious in declining to specify the rights and duties that attach to private entities when their actions implicate health and education goods. Instead, they assume an institutional solution in which courts will work out the details of these relationships in collaboration with other legal actors.

The framework that informs the case studies is theoretically allied with the idea of having constitutional rights apply not only vertically, to the relation between the state and the individual, but also horizontally, to the relation between one individual and another. A rich and complicated literature, developed largely outside the United States, currently explores whether and how constitutional rights can influence the shape and content of private activity.[81] As Robert Alexy explains, from the perspective of German constitutionalism,

> The idea that constitutional rights norms affect the relations between citizens, and in this sense have a third party or horizontal effect, is accepted on all sides today. What is controversial is how and to what extent they do this. The question of *how* constitutional norms influence the relations between citizens is a problem of *construction*. The question of the *extent* to which they do this is a question of substance and indeed a problem of *conflict*.[82]

In this part, I explore the various doctrinal avenues that are open to courts to carry out the interpretive practice of integrating constitutional norms into private law rules of obligation and responsibility. Admittedly, normative scholarship tends to avoid discussing doctrine – as Barry Friedman puts it, "Legal realism has made us skeptical of doctrine."[83] But the availability of legal channels through which public law values can be applied in contexts that are conventionally understood to be "private" raises important questions about the role of social and economic rights in facilitating social change. Building on important writing by Robert Alexy, Justice

---

[81] American scholars who have joined the discussion include: Gardbaum, The "horizontal effect" of constitutional rights; Mark Tushnet 2003. The issue of state action/horizontal effect in comparative constitutional law. *Int'l J. Const. L.* 1: 79; Mark Tushnet 2002. Comparative constitutionalism: State action, social welfare rights, and the judicial role: Some comparative observations. *Chi. J. Int'l L.* 3: 435; Helen Hershkoff 2006. The New Jersey Constitution: Positive rights, common law entitlements, and state action. *Alb. L. Rev.* 69: 553.

[82] Robert Alexy 2002. *A theory of constitutional rights*, trans. J. Rivers. New York: Oxford University Press, p. 355.

[83] Cf. Barry Friedman 2001. The counter-majoritarian problem and the pathology of constitutional scholarship. *Nw. U. L. Rev.* 95: 933, 953.

Aharon Barak, and Stephen Clapham (among others)[84] I map out various legal channels through which health and education constitutional clauses can potentially affect common law relations. Although doctrine does not control the results in particular cases, the availability of these legal channels significantly reframes the question whether legalization strategies hold progressive potential.

As the South Africa Court observed in *Du Plessis v. De Klerk,* "there is no universal answer to the problem of vertical or horizontal application of a bill of rights."[85] The existing literature identifies at least four doctrinal channels through which constitutional rights can affect the scope of private activity. The first, or nonapplication model, assumes that constitutional rights apply only to government acts and not at all to private acts. However, this approach does not foreclose the court from relying on constitutional rights in its interpretation of the legal rules that order and arrange private activity. Just as human rights law imposes on state parties the duty to respect, to protect, and to fulfill, arguably a government that has committed itself to health and education rights has an obligation to shape legal rules – both private and public – to achieve the fulfillment of those guarantees.[86] As William F. Felice explains:

> Economic and social rights create obligations for governments to enact policies and measures that create the proper environment for these rights to flourish. The duty of citizens and governments is to support the policies, institutions, and agencies that meet these social needs. These are legal obligations and not simply altruism. Ensuring the economic and social rights found in human rights law requires that states guarantee that all public and private actors respect these norms.[87]

This understanding of the scope of the government's obligation recognizes the critical role of the state in encouraging and facilitating social and economic relations; market orderings do not arise spontaneously but rather in response to the legal

---

[84] This part draws on the literature identified in Notes 21–25, 81–82, and also Daniel Friedmann & Daphne Barak-Erez (eds.). 2001. *Human rights in private law.* Oxford: Hart, especially Aharon Barak, Constitutional human rights and private law, *id.,* 13–42.

[85] Du Plessis v. DeKlerk, 1996 (3) S. A. 850 at 871D-E (Kentridge A. J.), available at http://www. constitutionalcourt.org.za/uhtbin/cgisirsi/ArSEGDOfFM/MAIN/156340014/503/1781 (accessed Jan. 11, 2008). For a discussion of this case, see Anton Fagan 2001. Determining the stakes: Binding and non-binding bills of rights. In Friedman and Barak-Erez (eds.), *Human rights in private law* (p. 73), Oxford: Hart.

[86] See Report on the Right to Food as a Human Right, U.N. ESCOR Comm'n on H.R., 39th Sess. Agenda Item 11, U.S. Doc. E/CN.4/Sub.2/1987/23 (1987); see also Committee on Economic, Social and Cultural Rights, General Comment No. 12, 1999, U.N. Doc. E/C.12/1999/5 (1995).

[87] Felice, The global new deal: Economic and social human rights in world politics, p. 29. Similarly, Cécile Fabre identifies three kinds of duties the state might be under:

1. A duty to provide the resources warranted by social rights;
2. A duty not to deprive people of these resources if they already have them; and
3. A duty to ensure that other people such as employers fulfill their duties to give resources to people, were it to decide not to fulfill all or part of its duty specified in (1) and (2).

Fabre, *Social rights under the Constitution,* p. 57.

arrangements created by government.[88] Focusing on the right to food, András Sajó, thus, equates the state obligation with "a guarantee of a sociolegal environment conducive to having access to food."[89]

In the context of medications, for example, signatory nations to international human rights conventions have an obligation to protect the right to medication through appropriate regulation of private market activities. The United Nations Committee on Economic, Social, and Cultural Rights explains that the obligation to protect may be violated by a state's "failure to regulate the activities of individuals, groups or corporations so as to prevent them from violating the right to health of others."[90] One commentator offers the following example to illustrate a potential violation of this obligation:

> [T]he state is under an obligation to provide anti-competitive remedies against patent abusers so that brand name drug producers are not permitted to price their medications at prices that exponentially exceed generic equivalents. As a general matter, access to lower priced generics would increase the number of previously disadvantaged persons that could access drugs needed to prolong their lives. Strong enforcement of anti-competition rules where patent holders refuse to grant licenses to generic producers and excessively price their products is therefore a measure that can and should be taken "to reduce the inequitable distribution of health facilities, goods and services." . . . Moreover, such enforcement will also "promote . . . [t]he availability in sufficient quantities of pharmaceuticals and medical technologies."[91]

State actors have similar regulatory responsibilities with respect to the right to education. The Committee states: "By way of illustration, a State must . . . protect the accessibility of education by ensuring that third parties, including parents and employers, do not stop girls from going to school. . . ."[92]

The second approach, or direct application model, assumes that constitutional rights apply to private actors as they do to public actors.[93] As Peter Benson explains, "Such rights, just as they are defined and enshrined in basic laws and constitutions, are to be applied directly both to government–individual relations and to relations between private individuals. The definition and vindication of these rights are fully

---

[88] Cf. Cosmo Graham and Tony Prosser 1991. Privatizing public enterprises: Constitutions, the state and regulation in comparative perspective. Oxford: Clarendon Press, p. 2 (on the need for "bringing the state back in" to deal with the privatization process).

[89] András Sajó 2002. Socioeconomic rights and the international economic order. *N.Y.U. J. of International L. & Politics* 35: 221, 232.

[90] General Comment 14: The Right to the Highest Attainable Standard of Health, U. N. Comm. on Econ., Soc. & Cultural Rts., 20th Sess., ¶ 51, U.N. Doc. E/C.12/2000/4 (2000), quoted in Yamin, Not Just a Tragedy, 355 n. 129.

[91] Yamin, Not Just a Tragedy, 355–356.

[92] Committee on Economic, Social and Cultural Rights, General Comment No. 13, 1999, U.N. Doc. E/2000/22, quoted in Klaus Dieter Beiter 2006. *The protection of the right to education by international law.* Leiden, The Netherlands: Martinus Nijhoff, p. 569.

[93] The term is neither accurate nor felicitous, but is used in the literature. See Christian Starck 2001. Human rights and private law in German constitutional development and in the jurisdiction of the Federal Constitutional Court. In Friedmann and Barak-Erez (eds.), *Human rights in private law* (p. 97). Oxford: Hart ("The terms 'direct' and 'indirect' do not describe different types of effects particularly accurately, yet they are commonly used in the literature on third-party effect").

independent of the doctrines and operation of private law."[94] From this perspective, the fact that no right of action exists as a matter of tort or contract law is irrelevant to the court's application of the constitutional norm. Rather, the right affords the court interpretive space to shape and define relations in the light of constitutional provisions. For example, conceivably a court could apply the constitutional right to education directly to a parent who forbids a child from attending school in order to make time for employment; or to a parent who withholds education opportunities from an adopted or out-of-wedlock child. Similarly, the right to health care could be directly applied to an employer who subjects employees to unsafe workplace conditions or exposes members of the surrounding community to toxic pollutants.

A third approach, or indirect application model, assumes that constitutional rights provisions apply to private orderings, but they are enforced through the rules and doctrines of private, and not public, law. As Justice Aharon Barak explains, "In other words, constitutional human rights do not permeate private law 'in and of themselves,' but rather by means of existing or new private law doctrines."[95] In some cases, the application of the constitutional norm may be impeded if the private law does not recognize a private cause of action, although it is open to the court to imply such a right and to interpret it in a way that comports with constitutional norms. And as Roger Brownsword has demonstrated, constitutional norms may comfortably be incorporated into the "good reasons" that courts recognize as a constraint on contractual liberty.[96] So, for example, the existence of a constitutional right to health care could provide the basis for a court's ordering a remedy of damages for pain and suffering, in addition to pecuniary injury, where medical care is withheld or inadequately provided.[97] Similarly, the constitutional right to education could inform a court's determination that a private school fee is excessive if it serves to bar a child from educational opportunities.

The fourth approach, called the *judiciary application model*, builds on the idea that courts, as institutions of government, are equally subject to constitutional requirements and are constrained from enforcing private arrangements that would undermine, violate, or subvert constitutional duties – "a court is barred from enforcing private law claims that are deemed to impair constitutional rights."[98] This model assumes that constitutional rights apply directly only to government but indirectly regulate private activity through, for example, the withdrawal of judicial remedies for private activity that would offend or subvert public values.[99] Thus,

---

[94] Peter Benson 2001. Equality of opportunity and private law. In Friedman and Barak-Erez (eds.), *Human rights in private law* (p. 205). Oxford: Hart.

[95] Daphne Barak-Erez 2001. Constitutional human rights and private laws. In Friedmann and Barak-Erez (eds.), *Human rights in private law* (p. 21). Oxford: Hart.

[96] See Roger Brownsword 2001. Freedom of contract, human rights and human dignity. In Friedmann and Barak-Erez (eds.), *Human rights in private law* (pp. 181–183). Oxford: Hart.

[97] Cf. Barak, Constitutional human rights and private law, p. 24 (referring to Italian case law as an example of courts' interpreting constitutional provisions in ordering private law damage remedies).

[98] Benson, *Equality of opportunity and private law*, p. 205.

[99] See William Wade 2000. Horizons of horizontality. *L.Quarterly Rev.* 116: 217; see also Sudhir Krishnaswamy 2007. Horizontal application of fundamental rights and state action in India. In Raj Kumar & K. Chockalingam (eds.), *Human rights, justice, and constitutional empowerment* (p. 65). Oxford: Oxford University Press.

in *Shelley v. Kraemer,*[100] the United States Supreme Court held that it would be unconstitutional for a state court to enforce a racially restrictive covenant, even though the covenant was itself not unconstitutional, on the ground that "the action of state courts and judicial officers in their official capacities is to be regarded as actions of the State within the meaning of the Fourteenth Amendment."[101] The theory appears to be that the state courts are barred from enforcing even private contractual or property terms that the legislature could not itself enact. However, *Shelley* is virtually unique in United States law; courts not only have limited its holding to the area of racial discrimination, but also have declined to enforce it even within that context.[102] As applied to health or education rights, a hypothetical case would include a court's refusal to enforce a private school's decision to expel a student for nonpayment of fees or a private hospital's decision to terminate care for lack of health insurance.

JUDICIAL APPLICATION OF HEALTH AND EDUCATION RIGHTS TO PRIVATE ORDERINGS

Each of the case studies provides some evidence of the radiating effect of constitutional norms in influencing the shape and scope of private obligations – a development understood in academic and judicial circles to involve the horizontal application of constitutional rights. It bears emphasis that none of the national courts surveyed has articulated a systematic approach to this issue; indeed, in some cases (as, for example, the medical malpractice cases discussed by Bivitri Susanti in the chapter on Indonesia[103]) the court never even refers to the existence of the constitutional right. Arguably, however, the judicial decisions, as well as litigant strategies, acquire greater coherence when viewed within a motivating constitutional framework.[104] This part of the chapter focuses on two categories of decisions: first, those involving state regulation of (or failure to regulate) private industry; and second, those involving judicial interpretation of private law doctrines in the area of contracts and property.

Reshaping the Regulatory Landscape in Light of Constitutional Norms

I focus in this section on judicial activity in Indonesia and India, where – despite broad differences in docket activity, judicial access, and public interest

---

[100] 334 U. S. (1948): 1.
[101] *Id.,* 14.
[102] See Mark D. Rosen 2007. Was Shelley v. Kraemer incorrectly decided? Some new answers. *Cal. L. Rev.* 95: 451, 469 (stating that "Shelley's attribution rationale has not fared well").
[103] Chapter 6, this volume.
[104] An analogy can be drawn to Dean Lawrence Gene Sager's approach to constitutional decisions in the United States that appear to protect a right to minimum welfare, despite the absence of such a right in the written constitution. The assumption of such a right, even if beyond enforcement of a court, seems to influence judicial interpretive practice regarding subsidiary matters such as due process procedural protection. See Lawrence G. Sager 2004. The why of constitutional essentials. *Fordham L. Rev.* 72: 1425–1426 (explaining that certain United States constitutional decisions can be best explained by "the tacit existence of a right to minimum welfare").

culture – litigants have pressed constitutional claims that, in effect, seek to reorder market relations by asking the court to integrate constitutional norms into the legislature's regulatory process. Even in cases in which the courts do not impose direct legal mandates calling for the provision of particular education or health services, the fact that health and education hold a constitutionalized status – whatever that status might be – has influenced the terms of judicial decision making in discrete regulatory contexts.

The Indonesia Constitutional Court and natural resource privatization

Few issues raise so crisply the distinction between the public and the private as that of privatization, yet the term itself lacks precise definition. Paul Starr explains:

> Privatization is a fuzzy concept that evokes sharp political reactions. . . . Yet however varied and at times unclear in its meaning, privatization has unambiguous political origins and objectives. It emerges from the countermovement against the growth of government in the West and represents the most serious conservative effort of our time to formulate a positive alternative.[105]

In many industrializing nations, struggles about privatization relate to ownership and control of natural resources – in particular, oil, gas, and water. Efforts to privatize natural resources in Indonesia have brought forth charges of official corruption, self-dealing, and inappropriate pressure by multinational corporations on government policy.[106] At the same time, the state has been unable to meet legitimate demands for basic services – for example, it is estimated that 70 million Indonesians lack access to electricity.[107] Constitutional litigation has focused on how best to develop natural resources and to make them more broadly available.

Following the Indonesia legislature's enactment of Law No. 22 Year 2001 concerning Oil and Natural Gas, a number of nonprofit groups, including the Indonesian Legal and Human Rights Consultants' Association, the Indonesian Legal Aid and Human Rights Association, and Country and National Solidarity, petitioned the Indonesia Supreme Court to review the statute's constitutionality. Among other allegations, petitioners pointed to the predictable and deleterious effect that the statute would have on health and educational rights, emphasizing that its implementation would "reduce society's opportunity in improving its local capability such as education, training, information access, nation and character building, etc."; and also weaken the country's Human Development Index.[108] The

---

[105] Starr, *The meaning of privatization.*

[106] See Public Citizen's Water for All Program 2003. *Water privatization fiascos: Broken promises and social turmoil.* Available at www.wateractivist.org (accessed Dec. 26, 2007) ("Water privatization in Indonesia is a story of how the interests of global water corporations, corrupt dictatorships and World Bank loans pushing privatization worked together to rob the public resources and assets of Indonesian citizens").

[107] See The World Bank, Energy and Mining Sector Unit, Infrastructure Department, East Asia and Pacific Region 2005. *Energizing the economy: Strategic priorities for the power sector in Indonesia.* Available at http://web.worldbank.org (accessed May 13, 2008) ("Over 70 million Indonesians are estimated to be unconnected to electricity").

[108] Judicial Review of Law of the Republic of Indonesia No. 22 Year 2001 regarding Oil and Natural Gas (Law No. 22 Year 2001), against the 1945 Constitution of the State of the Republic of Indonesia,

specific question focused on the law's compatibility with Article 33 of the 1945 Indonesia Constitution, which provides, in part: "The national economy shall be organized based on economic democracy with the principles of togetherness, efficiency with justice, sustainability and environmental insight, independence and by keeping a balance between progress and unity of the national economy"; and "Land and Water and the natural resources contained therein shall be controlled by the state and shall be used for the greatest prosperity of the people."[109] The Court upheld most of the statute, but invalidated those portions that remitted the pricing structure of oil and gas solely to the market, on the view that the government constitutionally could not cede control of basic resources to private, profit-making corporations.[110] The Court underscored that the pricing of natural resources could not constitutionally be left to the unregulated private market:

> Article 28 Paragraphs (2) and (3) of the *a quo* law prioritizes competition mechanism over the Government's intervention which is limited to specific community groups, and as such it does not guarantee the meaning of the economic democracy principle as regulated in Article 33 Paragraph (4) of the 1945 Constitution in order to prevent the strong from preying on the weak. According to the Court, the prices of domestic Oil Fuel and Natural Gas should be stipulated by the government by paying attention to specific community groups and considering a fair and reasonable business competition mechanism. Therefore the aforementioned Article 28 Paragraph (2) and (3) must be declared *contradictory* to the 1945 Constitution (emphasis in original).[111]

One commentator explains the court's approach by emphasizing the overall impact of the government's withdrawing from market oversight: where regulations affect not only "vital production sectors," but also "the livelihood of many people," the government has an important role – amounting to what must be a "dominant feature" in any regulatory scheme – of determining the price structure.[112]

The next year, the Indonesia Court was asked to review legislation involving the nation's water resources. The Water Resources Law, enacted in 2004, requires the state to "guarantee everyone's right to obtain water for their minimum daily basic needs," while authorizing decentralization of water management and participation by private, profit-making companies."[113] The Court found the law to be "conditionally constitutional, which means that the law is constitutional, on the condition that it is interpreted or applied in a certain way."[114] Jimly Asshiddiqie,

---

Constitutional Court of the Republic of Indonesia, Decision No. 002/PUU-I/2003 of December 15, 2004, available in English translation at http://www.mahkamahkonstitusi.go.id/eng/putusan_sidang.php?pg=6 (accessed Jan. 11, 2008).

[109] Quoted in *id.*

[110] Judicial Review of Law of the Republic of Indonesia No. 22 Year 2001.

[111] Quoted in *id.*

[112] Mohamad Mova Al'Afghani 2007. Safeguarding water contracts in Indonesia. *Law Environment and Development Journal* 3(2): 152, available at http://www.lead-journal.org/content/07148.pdf (accessed Dec. 26, 2007).

[113] Water Resources Law (No. 7/2004), Art. 5 (Indonesia).

[114] Mohamad Mova Al'Afghani 2006. Constitutional Court's review and the future of water law in Indonesia. *Law Environment and Development Journal* 2(1): 1, available at http://www.lead-journal.org/content/06001.pdf (accessed Dec. 26, 2007).

the court's president, explained: "Although the law takes into consideration merely some parts of the Article 33 of the Constitution, it doesn't mean the Law is at odds with the Constitution."[115] The Court articulated various principles expected to inform future regulatory enactments, including that of "guaranteeing access for everyone to the water source to obtain water" and that regional waterworks "shall not be established with a view of only seeking profit, as an enterprise who performs state functions in materializing Article 5 [of the Indonesia Constitution establishing a right to water]."[116] In effect, the court set out a constitutional framework for future action, while not directing the legislature to take any specific steps. The decision left open the possibility of further judicial challenges if, as counsel for the claimants put it, "we find any flaws in the implementation of the law."[117] In both cases, although petitioners did not seek directly to enforce constitutional provisions relating to health or education, these constitutional clauses nevertheless influenced the Court's decision making as guiding principles.

The India Supreme Court and market regulation

The India case study highlights many instances in which the India judiciary, famous for its public interest docket,[118] has intervened to regulate market transactions, including water quality,[119] blood banks,[120] air pollution,[121] and sugar distribution;[122] in its decisions, the India Supreme Court has relied on constitutional norms as fundamental principles and effectively extended constitutional rights in the horizontal position.[123] The India Court's approach to the problem of unlicensed medical practitioners, including faith healers, illustrates the ways in which constitutional

---

[115] Quoted in English in WALHI [Wahana Lingkungan Hidup Indonesia – Friends of the Earth Indonesia], Court rejection makes people's access to water more difficult. *Campaign update* (July 29, 2005), available at http://www.eng.walhi. or.id.kampanye/air/privatisasi/050729_waterpriv_cu/ (accessed Dec. 26, 2007).

[116] Quoted in English in Al'Afghani, Safeguarding water contracts in Indonesia, pp. 152–153.

[117] Statement, available at http://www.vannbevegelsen.no/inter/2005–07-20_court_reject_indonesia.txt (accessed Dec. 26, 2007).

[118] For a summary of social justice cases through 2000, see Atul M. Setalvad 2000. The Supreme Court on human rights and social justice: Changing perspectives. In B. N. Kirpal, A. H. Desai, G. Subramanium, R. Dhvan, and R. Ramachandran (eds.), *Supreme but not infallible: Essays in honour of the Supreme Court of India* (pp. 232–255). Oxford: Oxford University Press.

[119] See, e.g., Prasanta Kumar Rout v. Government of Orissa (Or HC PIL, 1994), Manu/OR/0203/1994, available at www.manupatra.com (accessed April 28, 2006).

[120] Common Cause v. Union of India and Others, SC, 1996, Manu/SC/0362/1997, available at www. manupatra.com (accessed Jan. 3, 2008). See also M. Vijaya v. Chairman and Managing Director, Sinareni Collieries, Co., Manu/ AP/0574/2001, available at www.manupatra.com (accessed April 28, 2006) (holding hospital negligent in tort for violating Article 21 of the India Constitution for failure to test a blood transfusion for HIV).

[121] See Kamlawai v. Kotwala, Manu/UP/0785/2000, available at www.manupatra.com (accessed April 28, 2006) (requiring government to order cessation of pollution by brick kilns).

[122] See R. Ramanujam Chettiar v. The Commissioner and Secretary to the Government of Tamil Nadu, Food and Co-operative Dept. Madras (Mad HC, 1981), Manu/TN/0250/1982, available at www.manupatra.com (accessed Jan. 3, 2008).

[123] For further examples, see Krishnaswamy, Horizontal application of fundamental rights and state action in India, pp. 47–73; Fabre, *Social rights under the constitution*, p. 160 (discussing regulation of rickshaw driver loan and employment contracts in Azad Rickshaw Pullers Union v. Punjab (1981) 1 SCR 366).

norms inform the judiciary's interpretive practice. *Rajesh Kumar Srivastava v. Verma and Others*[124] concerned contempt proceedings following on earlier actions mandating the state "to stop the menace of the unqualified and unregistered medical practitioners proliferating all over the State." As a result of these earlier proceedings, more than twenty thousand criminal prosecutions had been commenced against identified "quacks." In this follow-up miscellaneous application to the High Court of Allahabad, the question focused on whether "faith healers" fell outside this regulation on religious grounds. Although recognizing a guarantee to freedom of conscience under Article 25 of the India Constitution, the court emphasized the importance of the right to health in shaping appropriate relief:

> Supreme Court has by a dynamic interpretation of Article 21 expanded the meaning of right to life, to include right to health. This right to health can be guaranteed only if the State provides for adequate measures for treatment and takes care of its citizens by protecting them from persons practicing or professing unauthorized medical practices.[125]

Thus, as in the Indonesia context, the India judiciary did not directly apply the right to health in its assessment of the government regulation; instead, the right to health served as a guiding principle that shaped the relations at issue.

Reordering Private Contract Relations in Light of Constitutional Norms

The classical constitutional model sees contract doctrine as a set of neutral rules "in which economic actors establish relations in a realm of freedom"; as David M. Trubek and Alvaro Santos explain, the private law of contracts "is contrasted with the sphere of public or 'regulatory' law, which is presented as coercive, and an 'intervention' in an otherwise level playing field."[126] The case studies interrogate this model through judicial decisions that challenge the impartiality of contract doctrine, acknowledge its distributive implications, and try to align contract rules with constitutional goals. Some of these decisions involve the private provision of health and educational services such as insurance coverage or school admission. The case studies indicate a willingness by courts to scrutinize contract terms in the light of constitutional norms; the public policies expressed in the constitutional provisions inform not only the court's interpretation of the contract term, but also, in some cases, its formulation of the governing common law rule. Although the small number of cases does not constitute a trend, the decisions sketch out a judicial practice of seeking to reconcile private contract terms with the broader public interest in securing health and education rights. I discuss a few examples from India, Brazil, and South Africa to illustrate the emergent practice.

In *LIC of India*, the India Supreme Court held that private insurance companies have a public duty to offer "just and fair terms and conditions accessible to all the

---

[124] Manu/UP/0452/2005, available at www.manupatra.com (accessed May 1, 2006).
[125] *Id.*
[126] David M. Trubek and Alvaro Santos 2006. Introduction: The third moment in law and development theory and the emergence of a new critical practice. In D. M. Trubek and A. Santos (eds.), *The new law and economic development: A critical appraisal* (p. 14). Cambridge: Cambridge University Press.

segments of the society" in conformance with various constitutional guarantees, including Article 21 of the Indian Constitution, such that "in issuing a general life insurance policy of any type, public element is inherent in prescription of terms and conditions therein."[127] The specific question involved the insurer's right to limit a special class of coverage to "salaried persons in Government, quasi-Government or reputed commercial firms" on the ground that a private company "is free to incorporate as a part of its business principles, any term of its choice." Looking at recommendations made in 1980 by the Sezhivan Committee Report "to make available policies to wider Sections of the people," the Court framed the controversy as one within the principles of "socio-economic" justice expressed in the Preamble Chapter of Fundamental Rights and Directive Principles of the India Constitution, as well as Article 25 of the Universal Declaration of Human Rights. The Court explained that the Fundamental Rights and Directive Principles of the Constitution deem a right to livelihood to be necessary to "a meaningful life." Just as social security and disability benefits "are integral schemes of socio-economic justice," life insurance, "within the paying capacity and means of the insured to pay premia," is an additional security measure "envisaged under the Constitution to make [the] right to life meaningful, worth living and [the] right to livelihood a means for sustenance."

The Court also acknowledged that the insurance company possesses broad discretion to set the terms and conditions of insurance policies that it offers to the public for purchase. However, that discretion is subject to constitutional principles of socioeconomic justice:

> We make it clear at this juncture that the insurer is free to evolve a policy based on business principles and conditions before floating the policy to the general public offering on insurance of the life of the insured but ... insurance being a social security measure, it should be consistent with the constitutional animation and conscience of socio-economic justice adumbrate[d] in the Constitution[.]

To this the Court added:

> [I]t should be no answer for the ... person whose acts have the insignia of public element to say that their actions are in the field of private law and they are free to prescribe any conditions or limitations in their actions as private citizens, simplicitor, do in the field of private law. ... The distinction between public law remedy and private law field cannot be demarcated with precision. Each case will be examined on its facts and circumstances to find out the nature of the activity, scope and nature of the controversy. The distinction between public law and private law remedy has now become too thin and practicably obliterated.

To similar effect are judicial decisions from the state of Bahia in which Brazilian courts intervene in the relation between individual health insurance contract beneficiaries and their private insurers.[128]

---

[127] LIC of India v. Consumer Education & Research Centre and Others, Manu/SC/0772/1995, available at www.manupatra.com (accessed May 1, 2006).
[128] Chapter 3, this volume.

Other cases concern the contract obligations of private educational bodies that are deemed to be engaged in the "performing of a public duly [*sic*]."[129] On this basis, India courts extend certain constitutional requirements, particularly equality concerns, to the activities of private educational institutions. Thus, the High Court of Punjab and Haryana in *Ravneet Kaur v. Christian Medical College*[130] rejected petitioner's request for school admission on the merits, but emphasized that private entities serving particular public purposes must be held to the same standards as public institutions, particularly if public funding is involved:

> The Constitution cannot be interpreted to mean that there are two sets of rules for the same game. It is only right that every Institution which is charged with a public duty follows the mandate of Article 14 [regarding equal protection of the laws].... [T]here cannot be a dichotomy – a division of the institutions performing public duties into two strongly contrasted classes. The private institutions performing public duties supplement the State's effort. They are partners with the Stale [*sic*]. The private and Governmental institutions are the two sides of the same body. The right side cannot smile when the left side is pinched.

The India courts also have used the principle of "congruence" or "parity" to shape contracts involving private school admission or fees. Recognizing that the state regulates public educational institutions, the courts analogize private institutions to public schools based on their shared educational mission, which then becomes the base on which to extend constitutional norms into the private realm. In these cases, India courts affirm the constitutional right of the private entity to establish a private school, but interpret the right in the light of public purpose. For example, considering the question of school admission policy, the High Court of Andhra Pradesh explained "that private unaided professional colleges have no unbridled power or authority to admit students in their colleges dehors the State law.... They can only do so with regard to certain percentage but the percentage shall have to be determined by the Government having regard to local needs."[131] This principle of equality was applied to create parity in pay scales for teachers in private schools, even where the school received no state aid:

> In view of the long line of decisions of this Court holding that when there is an interest created by the Government in an Institution to impart education, which is a fundamental right of the citizens, the teachers who teach the education... [acquire] an element of public interest in the performance of their duties. As a consequence, the element of public interest requires regulating the conditions of service of those employees on par with Government employees.[132]

In other cases, the right to education has served as a background norm of "proportionality" that informs the court's interpretation of the private entity's

---

[129] Miss Ravneet Kaur v. The Christian Medical College and Another. Manu/PH/0075/1997, available at www.manupatra.com (accessed May 1, 2006).

[130] *Id.*

[131] Vignana Educational Foundation v. NTR University of Health Sciences and Another, Manu/AP/0078/2003, available at www.manupatra.com (accessed May 1, 2006).

[132] K. Krishnamacharyulu and Others v. Sri Venkateswara Hindu College of Engineering and Another, Manu/SC/113/1997, available at www.manupatra.com (accessed May 1, 2006).

contractual obligations.[133] Litigation involving the Hindi Vidya Bhavan Society, an "unaided" private school, that is, one not receiving any state financial support, concerned the level of fees appropriately charged to students. Although the school possessed statutory autonomy to determine student admission and fees, the Court deemed it essential to protect against "profiteering by the institution" while ensuring sufficient funds to ensure academic quality. The Court explained:

> Proportionality... preserves the balance between the societal interest in ensuring the quality of education and the societal interest in protecting parents and their children from the vice of profiteering.... [There must be a] balance... if rights are not to conflict with rights and rights are not to be exercised in a manner that would conflict with duties. Education, like many other sectors of our society, is confronted with serious questions about the [manner in] which the content of a fundamental human right will be shaped by private initiative.[134]

The South Africa case study reveals a similar interpretive approach to contract enforcement (although without success for the claimant). In *Afrox Healthcare Bbp v. Styrdom*,[135] the Supreme Court of Appeal considered whether a private hospital could include in patient contracts an exclusion of liability for damages caused by its nursing staff's negligent conduct. The Pretoria High Court had ruled in favor of the patient, finding, as one commentator explains, "a legitimate expectation that the services to which they have access would be rendered with skill and care by professional and trained health care personnel."[136] The judgment was reversed on appeal and did not decide whether a minimum level of care is required. The agreement at issue had gone into effect in 1995, two years before adoption of the South Africa Constitution and so involved, at least in part, a question of the retrospective and indirect application of constitutional principles to private parties in their private relations. The court considered the parties' "subjective" expectations and determined that although common law rules generally "had to be changed to promote the spirit, purport and object of the Constitution," in this case the exclusion clause, because "standard" and "expected," was deemed to be binding and not subject to invalidation.

Subsequently, in *Barkhuizen v. Napier*,[137] the Constitutional Court made explicit the relation of constitutional principles to contract enforcement in a case involving a time limitation in a short-term insurance policy. Section 34 of the South Africa Constitution provides: "Everyone has the right to have any dispute that can be resolved by the application of law decided in a fair public hearing before a court or, where appropriate, another independent and impartial tribunal or forum." Section

---

[133] Hindi Vidya Bhavan Society and Another v. State of Maharastra and Others, Manu/MH/0530/2005, available at www.manupatra.com (accessed Jan. 3, 2008).

[134] *Id.*

[135] SA 21 (SCA) – 31 May 2002, available at http://products.jutalaw.co.za (accessed Nov. 2, 2007).

[136] Marius Pieterse 2006. Resuscitating socio-economic rights: Constitutional entitlements to health care services. *S. Afr. J. Hum. Rts.* 22: 495 (citing Styrdom v. Afrox Healthcare [2001] 4 All SA 618 (T) 626b–h; 627f–g).

[137] Barkhuizen v. Napier, Unreported Decision of the South African Constitutional Court, Case No. CCT 72/05 (April 4, 2007) (South Africa), available at http://www.constitutionalcourt.org.za/uhtbin/cgisirsi/o0j5uwm5vx/MAIN/156340014/503/4040 (accessed Jan. 3, 2008).

36(1) further provides: "The rights in the Bill of Rights may be limited only in terms of law of general application to the extent that the limitation is reasonable and justifiable" in the light of principles of dignity, equality, and freedom. In this case, the applicant was denied coverage for damage to a motor vehicle on the ground that he "had failed to serve summons within 90 days of being notified of the repudiation of his claim" by the insurer, as required by the contract to which he had freely assented. The Court first set out its methodological approach, recognizing that the dispute involved the question of whether Section 34 "raises the question of horizontality, that is, the direct application of the Bill of Rights to private persons." However, the Court then avoided this issue, treating the question instead as one of indirect application through the requirement of conformance with public policy, explaining:

> [T]he proper approach to the constitutional challenges to contractual terms is to determine whether the term challenged is contrary to public policy as evidenced by the constitutional values, in particular, those found in the Bill of Rights. This approach leaves space for the doctrine of *pacta sunt servanda* to operate, but at the same time allows courts to decline to enforce contractual terms that are in conflict with the constitutional values even though the parties may have consented to them.

Nevertheless, the Court emphasized: "No law is immune from constitutional control. The common law of contract is no exception. And courts have a constitutional obligation to develop common law, including the principles of contract, so as to bring it in line with values that underlie our Constitution." The Court then determined to assess the fairness of the time limitation "by reference to the circumstances of the applicant."[138] The Court considered the time limitation from the applicant's subjective position, taking a fact-specific approach, rather than setting down objective rules for all cases. Faced with a virtually empty record, the Court dismissed the appeal.

Aligning Property Rights with Constitutional Goals

The classical model of constitutional enforcement remits property rights to the private sphere; when invaded – through takings or, occasionally, by other regulatory acts – the property holder is entitled to compensation from the state. As Joseph William Singer explains,

> The classical view of property concentrates on protecting those who have property. . . . The classical view focuses on individual owners and the actions they must take to acquire property rights, which will then be defended by the state. It assumes that the distribution of property is a consequence of the voluntary actions of individuals rather than a decision by the state. Property law does nothing more than protect property rights acquired by individual action. Distributional questions, in this conception, are foreign to property as a system.[139]

---

[138] Excerpts from the court's opinion appear in *id.* at ¶¶ 3, 23, 30, 35, and 94.
[139] William Joseph Singer 1996. No right to exclude: Public accommodations and private property. *Nw. U. L. Rev.* 90: 1283, 1466–1467.

By contrast, critical theory places the distributional aspects of property law front and center, emphasizing the role of property rules in shaping social relations and perpetuating or destabilizing hierarchy.[140] The case studies suggest that in some situations, social and economic rights afford courts interpretive space within which to reconfigure property rights in the light of public aspirations. This is not to say that private property becomes collective or state-owned;[141] rather, in some situations, the inclusion of social and economic rights in a national constitution persuades a court to reconfigure the boundaries of the property right to reflect the significance of interests that in other contexts might be given less weight or not included at all in the balance.

Whether property rights could defeat the South African government's provision of emergency shelter to the indigent came to the forefront in the *Kyalami Ridge* case decided by the Constitutional Court.[142] In this case, petitioners challenged the state's authority to create temporary settlements on public land for indigent people made homeless through flooding caused by heavy rains. Budgetary appropriations had been made to deal with the emergency, and the government chose to site a transit camp on a prison farm using land that the government owned. Nearby residents filed suit to enjoin the siting decision. They argued that the government could not site the camp on the farm because it lacked specific legislative authorization to take such action. They also argued that the siting decision violated requirements of administrative legality because the government had failed to secure consents from ministerial functionaries, had failed to meet environmental standards, and had failed to comply with town planning ordinances. Claimants further challenged the government's decision on the ground that "the choice of the prison farm as the site of the transit camp . . . will affect the character of the neighbourhood and reduce the value of their properties," and that the transit camp "would constitute a nuisance." It bears emphasis that the claimants at no point disputed the constitutional right of the flood victims to be afforded access to temporary shelter.

The Court found that the government's use of its own property was not unreasonable for the intended purpose, and, further, that existing laws neither "excluded nor limited the government's common law power to make its land available to flood victims pursuant to its constitutional duty to provide them with access to housing." In addition, even if claimants were prejudiced because of a reduction in the value of their property or a change in the "character of their neighborhood," they pointed to no "rights or legitimate expectations" that were "affected or threatened," as required to secure relief under the principle of procedural fairness. The Court

---

[140] *Id.* at 1474 ("Property law helps to structure and shape the contours of social relationships. Choices of property rules ineluctably entail choices about the quality and character of human relationships").

[141] Cf. Liam Murphy & Thomas Nagel 2002. *The myth of ownership: Taxes and justice.* Oxford: Oxford University Press, pp. 175–176 (referring to the "conventionality of property," but emphasizing the fact that the "state does not own its citizens, nor do they own each other collectively. But individual citizens don't own anything except through laws that are enacted and enforced by the state").

[142] Minister of Public Works and Others v. Kyalami Ridge Environmental Association and Others, 2001 (7) BCLR 652 (CC) (South Africa), available at http://www.saflii.org/za/cases/ZACC/2001/19.rtf (accessed May 20, 2008).

left open the question whether prospective rights (as, for example, asserted by an applicant for a license) would satisfy the requirement, assuming "that procedural fairness may be required for administrative decisions affecting a material interest short of an enforceable or prospective right." Looking, then, at the competing interests of the adjacent property owners and the homeless flood victims, the Court insisted that one factor not be privileged over the other, but rather that a balance be struck, depending on "the nature of the decision, the 'rights' affected by it, the circumstances in which it is made, and the consequence resulting from it":

> The fact that property values may be affected by low cost housing development on neighbouring land is a factor that is relevant to the housing policies of the government and to the way in which government discharges its duty to provide everyone with access to housing. But it is only a factor and cannot in the circumstances of the present case stand in the way of the constitutional obligation that government has to address the needs of homeless people, and its decision to use its own property for that purpose.

The Court left open whether other legal restraints might be interpreted to limit the government's conduct, emphasizing that the state "cannot ... on the basis of its rights as owner of the land and a constitutional obligation to provide access to housing, claim the power to develop its land contrary to legislation that is binding on it."[143]

Conversely, whether the burden of the state's housing efforts can be imposed on any single property owner came to issue in the *Modderklip Boerdery* litigation,[144] which raised, but elided, the question of the horizontal application of Section 25 of the South Africa Constitution ("No one may be deprived of property except in terms of law of general application, and no law may permit arbitrary deprivation of property"[145]). Over time, the Modderklip farm became the site of informal settlements by residents from an adjacent and overcrowded township in Benoni. In May 2000, four hundred settlers came to live on the farm and resided in fifty dwellings. After discussion with the Benoni City Council, Modderklip tried to evict the settlers, but the head of the local prison requested that the prosecutions not go forward "as the prison would be hard-pressed to find space to accommodate convicted unlawful occupiers should they be sentenced to prison terms." Modderklip continued to try to resolve the matter short of eviction, going so far as offering to sell the occupied portions of the farm to the township. In the meantime, informal settlements continued to develop. By October, eighteen thousand people, in four thousand dwellings, had come to occupy Modderklip's farm; at the time of decision, the number had mounted to forty thousand, collectively organized into the Gabon Informal Settlement. Unable to evict the settlers, Modderklip filed suit in the Pretoria High Court claiming that the continued occupation of the farm constituted an unconstitutional arbitrary taking of property. In their response, the police "contended that the problem was not a police matter but one of land

---

[143] Excerpts from the court's opinion appear in *id.* at ¶¶ 94, 24, 96, 48, 92, 101, 108, and 115.

[144] President of the Republic of South Africa and Another v. Modderklip Boerdery (Pty) Ltd. 2005 (CCT 20/04) [2005] ZACC 5; 2005 (5) SA 3 (CC) (13 May 2005) (South Africa), available at http://www.saflii.org/za/cases/ZACC/toc-P.html (accessed May 20, 2008).

[145] Quoted in *id.*

reform," and asked the court to consider where the settlers would live if they were evicted from the farm. The court ruled largely in favor of Modderklip, finding:

> [T]he state had breached its [constitutional] obligations... to take reasonable steps within its available resources to realise the right of the occupiers to have accesses to adequate housing and land... [and that] this failure by the state effectively amounted to the unlawful expropriation of Modderklip's property and also infringed Modderklip's rights to equality... by requiring it to bear the burden of providing accommodation to the occupiers, a function that should have been undertaken by the state.

The Supreme Court of Appeal generally agreed with the lower court, declaring that Modderklip was entitled to damages for the occupation of the land, but that the settlers "are entitled to occupy the land until alternative land has been made available to them by the State or the provincial or local authority." The appeals court further found that Modderklip's rights to fair treatment under Section 25 of the Constitution had been violated by the settler's occupation of the land.

The Supreme Court declined to address whether Section 25 "has horizontal application and if so, under what circumstances." But it found that "it was unreasonable of the state to stand by and do nothing in circumstances where it was impossible for Modderklip to evict the occupiers because of the sheer magnitude of the invasion and the particular circumstances of the occupiers." In crafting relief, the Court balanced Modderklip's interest in using the farm, with the occupants' interest in safe and stable dwellings. The occupants were recognized to "have formed themselves into a settled community and built homes" and to "have no other option but to remain on Modderklip's property." The Court, thus, held that the occupants' "investment into their own community on Modderklip's farm must be weighed against the financial waste that their eviction would represent," consistent with the overall goal of achieving "the constitutional vision of a caring society based on good neighbourliness and shared concern."[146]

The Supreme Court declined to order eviction of the occupants, pointing to their constitutional right to access to affordable shelter, or to order expropriation of the Modderklip farm, citing separation of powers concerns, despite the owner's willingness to make the sale. Instead, the Court ordered the state to compensate Modderklip for the occupants' use of the farm, even though the government had not authorized the residents to settle there. Rather than approaching the question as one of direct or indirect application of constitutional rights to private actors, the Court instead looked at the specific relations at issue and balanced highly contextual factors in the light of the constitutional commitment both to provide judicial access and to secure access to housing.

RECONCEPTUALIZING CONSTITUTIONAL ENFORCEMENT IN THE LIGHT OF JUDICIAL PRACTICE

The case studies tell a story of constitutional enforcement that plainly does not map on to the classical approach. Courts in the countries surveyed do not adhere,

---

[146] Excerpts from the court's opinion appear in *id.* at ¶¶ 5, 14, 15, 21, 26, 48, 54, and 55.

or at least do not consistently adhere, to a binary distinction between the public and the private. Instead, constitutional norms radiate into the world of common law doctrine and reshape private rules in specific contexts reflecting constitutional aspirations. But these judicial practices likewise do not cleanly trace the alternative horizontal models set out in the academic literature. Courts seem reluctant to decide whether constitutional rights are violated by non-state actors and, conversely, whether non-state actors owe constitutional duties to other private individuals. It is not only that courts avoid what Craig Scott has called the "stark either/or division of the applicability of rights into the categories of 'horizontal' versus 'vertical.'"[147] More than that, courts appear to avoid even the language of rights and duties when analyzing the application of constitutional provisions to non-state actors. Yet, the constitutional provisions clearly are influencing their interpretive practice.

Consider the *Modderklip* litigation. Here, the South Africa Court did not characterize the private farm owner as owing a duty to provide access to shelter to the settlers occupying the land; neither did the Court deem the settlers responsible for a "taking" of the Modderklip farm when they used it to construct an alternative community. The duty – to provide shelter or to compensate for the use of land – at all times remained with the government. But the court also recognized that Modderklip could not simply evict the settlers and leave them to the hazards of homelessness. The Court looked to social and economic norms as reflecting a constitutional vision of solidarity that altered the relation of the property owner to the settlers. The Court did not use the language of rights and duties to describe this influence. Instead, the constitutional provisions afforded the Court interpretive authority to modify powers typically associated with common law entitlements – in this situation, the common law power of a property owner to exclude uninvited guests.[148]

One way to conceptualize the court's approach is to see it as a shift from the language of rights and duties to that of power and liability in discrete relations.[149]

---

[147] Craig Scott 1999. Reaching beyond (without abandoning) the category of "economic, social and cultural rights." *Hum. Rts. Q.* 21: 633, 646.

[148] Joseph William Singer explains:

> If "property is a set of social relations among human beings," the legal definition of those relationships confers – or withholds – power over others. The grant of a property right to one person leaves others vulnerable to the will of the owner. Conversely, the refusal to grant a property right leaves the claimant vulnerable to the will of others, who may with impunity infringe on the interests which have been denied protection.

Singer, Sovereignty and property, p. 41.

[149] According to Peter Jaffey, the formal distinction is as follows:

> Y has a duty to X, which means Y is required to act or refrain from acting in a certain way (for the benefit of X), and X has a correlative right to the performance of the duty.... In a power-liability relation, by acting in the way prescribed for the exercise of the power, X can alter Y's legal relations. X's power is correlated with a liability on the part of Y to the alteration of Y's legal relations.

Peter Jaffey 2004. Hohfeld's power-liability/right-duty distinction in the law of restitution. *Can. J. L. & Juris* 17: 295. See also Walter Wheeler Cook 1919. Hohfeld's contributions to the science of law. *Yale L. J.* 28: 721, 725 (explaining that in "Hohfeld's terminology any human being who

In the classical conception, common law powers can be used in the holder's discretion to maximize self-utility; the egoistic exercise of power is assumed to conduce toward the general welfare. The presence of social welfare norms in a constitution alters this background assumption. From a constitutive theory of law, the powers assigned to individuals must now be interpreted and applied within the orbit of constitutional commitment and not simply within that of self-regarding concern. In some situations, the individual's private power – to extend medical services, to produce pharmaceuticals, to ensure workplace safety – will be channeled so that it is exercised beneficially for claimants who otherwise would be adversely affected in their social position. In this sense, the constitutional norm exercises a radiating effect on a legal relation and in some settings the court must recalibrate the balance of interests guiding the private entity's exercise of power.[150]

The South Africa Court, thus, made clear that Modderklip's power to control access to the farm could not be exercised in a way that would unduly burden the occupants' background right to housing, notwithstanding the fact that the farm owner does not owe a duty of shelter to the settlers. By constraining the exercise of the common law power, the court effectively altered the occupants' legal relation in the sense that they now possessed shelter. But, rather than prescribing rights directly owed from one individual to another, the court instead reshaped a power relationship in a specific context in the light of different facts and circumstances. By declining to set down a hard and fast rule for future claimants, the court's approach may introduce unpredictability into its decision making. However, it also has the benefit of avoiding ossification, a significant attribute when dealing with social welfare norms and other complex areas that raise broad policy questions. The court's approach may be likened to forms of provisional review used by American courts, both state and federal, in structural reform litigation involving social welfare claims.[151]

CONCLUSION: CONSIDERING THE POLITICAL ECONOMY OF CONSTITUTIONAL PRIVATIZATION

"In framing an ideal," Aristotle warned, "we may assume what we wish, but should avoid impossibilities."[152] One criticism of social and economic rights is that they rest on the utopian fantasy of unlimited resources, unimpeded distribution, and unfettered access. Their provision to all comers demands a strong state that is rich in national productivity, strong in administrative capacity, and devoted in its

---

can by his acts produce changes in legal relations has a legal *power* or powers" [emphasis in original]).

[150] Alexy, *A theory of constitutional rights*, p. 352.

[151] See Hershkoff, Positive rights and state constitutions, p. 1158 (developing the argument that state courts in the U.S. approach state constitutional decision making with an eye toward "provisional solutions"); Michael C. Dorf & Charles F. Sabel 1998. A constitution of democratic experimentalism. *Colum. L. Rev.* 98: 267.

[152] Aristotle, 2000, *Politics*, trans. Benjamin Jowett. Mineola, NY: Dover Publications, p. 68.

political will – otherwise constitutional claims will far surpass supply and breed distrust in the law. As Mark Tushnet puts it,

> Protecting private law rights and first- and second-generation constitutional rights is cheap, though not free. Protecting social welfare rights is expensive. Constitutional rights with large fiscal consequences require someone to raise the funds, either through taxation or through the redirection of existing taxes, to ensure that the constitutional rights are effectively realized. But courts lack the power to raise money through taxes. Only legislatures can do that.[153]

Reacting to this criticism, national constitutions that include positive obligations often temper these guarantees with the realism of disclaimers that speak of "available resources" and "progressive realization."[154] In turn, courts, presented with claims for relief, respond by demanding – if demanding anything at all – that the defendant state take only reasonable steps toward realization of the claimed right. In *Soobramoney v. Minister of Health, KwaZulu-Natal*,[155] for example, the South Africa Supreme Court denied the claimant's request for emergency dialysis treatment, expressing concern that "[i]f everyone in the same condition as the appellant were to be admitted the carefully tailored programme would collapse and no one would benefit...." Efforts to bolster this approach typically are found in arguments about institutional competence, separation of powers, and democratic accountability.[156]

Aristotle's warning on avoiding impossibilities could invite an alternative, or at least a complementary, response – as political economists would put it, "not simply to accept constraints on choice, but rather to acknowledge and study these constraints in order to change them in desired directions."[157] At least some of the judicial decisions surveyed in the preceding chapters seem to take this other road. Faced with weak state infrastructure, limited resources, and extensive poverty, courts rely on social and economic rights in ways that allow them to leverage private resources on behalf of public norms. Private law no longer is treated only as an instrument of corrective justice, but rather understood to be relevant to distributive goals consonant with social and economic rights. Against those critics who see private law as upholding status quo distributions of property and social resources, the courts in some cases recalibrate doctrinal rules to take account of unjust background regimes.[158]

---

[153] Mark Tushnet 2004. Social welfare rights and the forms of judicial review. *Tex. L. Rev.* 82: 1895, 1896–1897.

[154] See Eric C. Christiansen 2007. Adjudicating non-justiciable rights: Socio-economic rights and the South African Constitutional Court. *Colum. Hum. Rts. L. Rev.* 38: 321, 341.

[155] 1998 (1) SA 765 (CC), available at http://www.constitutionalcourt.org.za (accessed Dec. 26, 2007).

[156] See, e.g., Albie Sachs 2000. Social and economic rights: Can they be made justiciable? *SMU* 3: 1388–1389.

[157] Ilchman and Uphoff 1998. *The political economy of change*, p. 27. New Brunswick, NJ: Transaction Publishers.

[158] For a discussion of corrective and distributive theories of private law, and in particular of tort law, see Peter Cane 2005. Anatomy of private law theory: A 25th anniversary essay. *Oxford J. Legal Stud.* 25: 203–217.

That rules of contract, tort, and property can be designed to serve distributive goals is a controversial but familiar idea. As to contracts, Anthony T. Kronman explains that once it is agreed that the state can redistribute wealth, then the choice of methods as between taxation and regulation of contracts "ought to be made on the basis of contextual considerations that are likely to vary from one situation to the next."[159] Kevin A. Kordana and David H. Tabachnick, writing from a Rawlsian perspective, add:

> It . . . is not clear why contract and tort law cannot be leveraged to help in meeting the demands of the difference principle. Political and legal institutions have complex and dynamic effects on one another. It thus seems unlikely that an economic scheme that maximizes the position of the least well-off would rely exclusively on tax and transfer for distribution.[160]

This is not to say that the states under investigation are collectivizing private resources, expropriating industry, or treating capital and resources as if they were owned by government and not by individual entrepreneurs. Rather, they are recognizing that the laws that regulate market and social relations must be consonant with constitutional norms, which include provisions, even if weak or aspirational, to health and education services. By reinterpreting contract clauses, recalibrating tort liability, reconfiguring property relations, or otherwise regulating market activity, courts in some cases help progressively realize constitutional goals by aligning the responsibilities of private actors who control access to essential health and educational services with public goals. In India, the courts tried to improve health conditions by reducing air pollution caused by taxis, a process that involved adapting regulatory frameworks.[161] In South Africa, the Constitutional Court upheld the provision of temporary shelter despite arguments that surrounding property values would diminish.[162] In Brazil, the courts in Bahia adapted contract terms, on an individual case-by-case basis, thereby extending insurance coverage to needy patients.[163] Rather than imposing essentially unfunded mandates on governments that are unable – or unwilling – to front the political and budgetary costs, the case studies reveal that courts, in some cases, use constitutional norms to relocate financial obligations onto market actors, relying on individual claimants to monitor enforcement. Jonathan Berger, thus, states in his chapter on South Africa,

---

[159] Anthony T. Kronman 1980. Contract law and distributive justice. *Yale L. J.* 89: 472.

[160] Kevin A. Kordana and David H. Tabachnick 2005. Rawls and contract law. *Geo. Wash. L. Rev.* 73: 598, 652.

[161] See Smoke Affected Residents Forum v. Municipal Corporation of Greater Mumbai and Others (Bom HC 2002), available at Manu/MH/0139/2002 (accessed Jan. 3, 2008); M. C. Mehta v. Union of India and Others (SC, Writ Petition (C) No. 13029 of 1985), available at Manu/SC/0276/1991 (accessed Jan. 3, 2008). In M. C. Mehta, the Supreme Court of India directed the Ministry of Environment to "carry out appropriate experiments" with antipollution devices and to take steps to require appropriate devices in vehicles. *Id.*

[162] See Minister of Public Works and Others v. Kyalami Ridge Environmental Association and Others, 2001 (7) BCLR 652 (CC) (South Africa), available at http://www.constitutionalcourt.org. za/uhtbin/cgisirsi/nyWciuPTgE/MAIN/156340014/503/625 (accessed Jan. 3, 2008). For a discussion of the *Kyalami Ridge* decision, see Richard J. Goldstone 2006. South African perspective on social and economic rights. *Hum. Rts.* 13(2), Brief 4.

[163] See Chapter 2, this volume.

"The interpretation and development of the common and statutory law – insofar as the private sector is concerned – have become the new sites of struggle." At the same time, however, courts are mindful that they cannot simply externalize constitutional enforcement onto the backs of market actors. Concepts of proportionality and reason inform their interpretive practice; so, too, does consideration of reasonable expectation and predictability.

Some commentators criticize legalization strategies as unequivocally supporting hegemonic elites.[164] The case studies question that view, suggesting that positive rights in some contexts exert a force field on the private infrastructure of common law rules. Changing private law rules in the light of constitutional norms will likely produce strong reactions from market players. Sophisticated actors will try to contract around judicial decisions; they will seek new and less risky incentives for investment; they will lobby politicians to rein in the courts. If courts continue on the path identified in this chapter, we might expect new forms of political blockage to emerge that will require different strategic approaches to constitutional enforcement. At the same time, changes in tort and contract rules, as they become publicized and known, will affect individual aspirations and alter political expectations. Looking forward, we cannot predict how constitutional social welfare norms will reshape common law baselines that are so critical in perpetuating historic inequities.

But all of this is getting ahead of the story. Thirty years ago, Morton Horwitz, in a critical review of E. P. Thompson's now-classic history, *Whigs and Hunters: The Origin of the Black Act*, challenged the view that the rule of law is "an unqualified human good." To be sure, Horwitz emphasized, the rule of law "undoubtedly restrains power... but it *promotes* substantive inequality," he added, "by creating a consciousness that radically separates law from politics, means from ends, processes from outcomes.... [W]e should never forget," Horwitz warned, "that a 'legalist' consciousness that excludes 'result-oriented' jurisprudence as contrary to the rule of law also inevitably discourages the pursuit of substantive justice."[165] The case studies challenge us to think that the rule of law can aspire to a vision of substantive justice that includes schooling, health care, and the material conditions of a decent, autonomous life. At a minimum, they raise important questions about the short- and long-term effects of constitutionalizing social and economic rights. By focusing attention on the relation of private law to social justice, the case studies point to exciting issues for future research.

[164] See, e.g., Linda C. McClain and James E. Fleming 2005–2006. Constitutionalism, judicial review, and progressive change. *Tex. L. Rev.* 84: 433–438 (recounting this debate).
[165] Morton Horwitz 1976–1977. The rule of law: An unqualified human good? Yale L. J. 86: 561, 566 (reviewing E. P. Thompson 1975. *Whigs and hunters: The origin of the Black Act.* New York: Pantheon Books).

8   A New Policy Landscape: Legalizing Social and Economic Rights in the Developing World

DANIEL M. BRINKS AND VARUN GAURI

Summarizing the information presented in the preceding country chapters is a daunting task. Although they touch on similar themes and provide an abundance of comparable information, the country chapters are rich and varied, illustrating the diversity of experiences encountered in each country. Even the most cursory review of the chapters, however, leads to an undeniable conclusion: for good or ill – or, more accurately, for good *and* ill, as we will see – the language of rights, the mechanism of courts, the intervention of lawyers, and the cumbersome tools of the law have become a permanent and prominent part of the policy-making landscape. Even in countries in which the courts are weak and social and economic (SE) rights litigation is rare, judicial enforcement is already part of the imaginary of social activists, awaiting only the right conditions to make its presence felt.

That legalization involves a coincidence of good and ill suggests the proverbial glass, either half-filled or half-empty. From the perspective of activists and public intellectuals, for whom the social injustices of their societies are all too evident, the achievements of the courts are bound to be disappointing. Several activists in South Africa, for instance, expressed to us in interviews some frustration at the deference to policy makers that the courts there tend to exhibit. In India, the more common lament was a sense that grandiose judicial rhetoric far exceeds actual achievements – sound and fury signifying little. From a historical perspective on SE rights, however, or one premised on the largely pessimistic United States–based academic literature on the role of courts in social change, the achievements of courts documented in the previous pages appear downright impressive. This divergence in perspective, even on the same country, is evident in the contrast in tone between Justice Goldstone's somewhat optimistic and historically minded Foreword and Jonathan Berger's mixed account of activism and judicial achievement on SE rights since the South African transition. Our perspective in this chapter is more comparative and empirical, with our reference points other countries and academic accounts. As a result, we often strike a different tone than that of the country chapter authors. We are impressed by what courts have been able to achieve, particularly given the low regard in which some of the recent academic literature has held them. We also are able to show, in the pages that follow, that legalizing demand for SE rights might well have averted tens of thousands of deaths in the countries studied in this volume and has likely enriched the lives of millions of others. Although we might note that the courts are, by definition, acting in areas where the other branches have failed, we do not believe it is useful or proper to compare those figures to what the legislative or executive branches have done; courts play a different role, and in and of itself, that is a striking achievement.

A second reason for the more sanguine tone of this conclusion, relative to some of the country chapters, is that our explanatory variable is "legalization," not the courts acting alone. As we described in the introduction, we understand legalization to be the participation of legal actors and the use of legal concepts in policymaking processes. In particular, the concept includes postdecision follow up on the part of plaintiffs and applicants. As a result, although civil society actors and others understandably bemoan the authorities' resistance or foot-dragging following court directives on social and economic rights, as well as the reluctance of courts to enforce their own orders, our more panoramic vantage point notices that litigants can and sometimes do monitor compliance, return to court to obtain new orders, lobby public officials, and organize public campaigns to spur governmental or corporate action. This divergent perspective is visible in assessments of compliance with medications cases in Brazil, where, after litigants and their public defenders apply further pressure on the state, authorities eventually do provide the large majority of drugs that patients demand; and in the right-to-food litigation in India, where, though it has taken several years of civil society campaigning, most state governments are now, in fact, complying with the court-ordered midday meals scheme.[1] The full process of legalization has, by construction, more impact than courts acting alone.

Examined carefully, the legalization phenomenon documented in this volume is also decidedly not a story of judicial activism. In general, across the many countries and policy areas discussed in this book, we see neither judicial activists crafting state policy out of whole cloth nor judges vetoing majoritarian policy innovations, as some of the "judicialization" jeremiads might suggest. Our research reveals courts responding, often but not always, to individual and occasionally collective demands, seeking to bring more or less inchoate statements of general policy to bear on particular circumstances, in ways that can lead either to policy innovation or to stasis. Courts' decisions do not so much stop or hijack the policy debate as inject the language of rights into it and add another forum for debate.

Many countries in the developing world, including the ones we examine here, have drafted laws and constitutions that promise far more than their present institutional capabilities can deliver.[2] We are not here to debate whether this initial "overdraft" was a cynical attempt at window dressing, a laudable but mostly symbolic attempt to set aspirational goals, or a robust effort to entrench enforceable rights to particular goods for the benefit of the disadvantaged. Whatever the framers' intent, these laws and constitutions are far from self-executing; they

---

[1] "By March 2004, fourteen states (including Delhi) were providing cooked midday meals to all primary school children, nine states were implementing the scheme partially and four states were distributing foodgrain" (De, Noronha, and Samson 2005)

[2] Indeed, some have criticized such detailed and rights-laden constitutions, like the Brazilian one, with its many promises, as being too cumbersome and idealistic to survive for long (Rosenn 1990). Others welcome such "thick constitutions" as more democratic and responsive to post-transition democratic realities than more procedurally oriented ones might be (Scheppele 2005).

announce universal rights or entitlements that are, in practice, well beyond the reach of many citizens. To benefit from these universal mandates, individual citizens or groups must find some hook, some demand mechanism, to bring universal principles to bear on their own particular situation. Where they are active and effective, the courts have become one of many such possible mechanisms.

It is true, of course, that using the judicial hook requires a significant investment of resources and might favor the advantaged over the truly destitute. The country chapters offer some evidence of this bias, as we will see later. But claiming the benefits of supposedly universal programs is always costly, whether they are claimed through judicial or other channels. For example, in Latin America the public universities are free and open to all – but parents must be at least moderately well off to pay their daughter's expenses while she goes to the free university in the capital for six years. In many countries, formal sector workers of a certain age are entitled to a pension, but it is surely true in Brazil, Nigeria, and elsewhere that a personal connection may be required in order to ensure that any individual pension is processed timely and correctly. Public services are theoretically open to all citizens, but very often only a clientelistic, exchange-based connection with a patron politician will secure for a few what government is supposed to afford everyone. And, to state the obvious, popular mobilization, lobbying, and the other more reputable tools of representative democratic politics are not free and equally accessible, either. Each of these mechanisms for bringing the universal to bear on one's particular circumstances requires some kind of expenditure – wealth, connections, a greased palm, a surrender of political rights, persistent mobilization and the investment of time and resources, a particular language and expertise.

Is the legal avenue especially suited to universalizing rights for the most remote and destitute populations? The country analyses make it clear that it is far harder to secure and realize a collective than an individual remedy; that courts are more likely to engage in particularizing the universal than in universalizing the particular; and that courts' attention is drawn, logically enough, to the demands of those who have the resources to engage with the legal system. But the chapters also describe how, in the course of bringing rights to bear on one claimant, the courts often trigger the effective extension of this right to other similarly situated individuals. Occasionally, in the course of deciding particular claims, courts modify the normative framework, extend policy-making structures, or alter the practices of providers to the benefit of many who will never set foot in a lawyer's office or a courtroom. As a result, we do see courts occasionally acting as catalysts for change that affects populations far beyond direct judicial influence.

But even this qualified description of the courts' role might suggest more uniformity across countries than is the case. The chapters show that where the courts are relatively hostile to these claims (as in the ordinary courts of Nigeria and Indonesia) SE rights litigation is barely incipient; it seems clear that receptive courts are a prerequisite to the presence of active public interest litigation. Where the courts are not receptive, even a well-developed civil society will take its claims elsewhere; where the courts are an attractive demand mechanism, civil society will develop the structures needed to support litigation. This somewhat contradicts Epp's emphasis on the primacy of civil society organization and his suggestion (2003: 22) that a support structure can do much to generate judicial support. At the same time, even in the countries that show the most legalization in one policy area, there is virtually no activity in other areas that seem to offer equally promising grounds for judicial intervention: clearly, it is more than the characteristics of the national judicial system that determine rates of legalization.

We will explore the underlying causes of this diversity in the pages ahead. In very general terms, however, the experiences of the various countries indicate that the courts are most engaged and most effective when they act in dialogue with political, bureaucratic, and civil society actors.[3] Public interest litigation arises when (a) the existing policy infrastructure fails to provide answers to deeply felt needs and (b) the courts appear as an even minimally viable mechanism for pressing claims. Indeed, at times litigants bring lawsuits with virtually zero probability of success, merely to open negotiations, generate publicity, or highlight governmental failures. Analytically, lawsuits arise on the basis of this litigant calculus, rather than as a result of civil society capacity. Indeed, our findings suggest that, given a minimal level of capacity, which we find in each of our cases, civil society develops the structures it needs for the strategies it decides to pursue.

Public interest litigation thrives and produces broadly significant real-world effects, however, only when a positive balance on the litigant calculus is coupled with positive state, social, and political conditions: (a) a well-developed policy infrastructure with latent capacity (a concept to which we will return), (b) a constituency on the particular issue with substantial legal capacity,[4] and (c) substantial support for the claims being made from politically consequential actors, either governmental or social. Under these conditions, judicial intervention becomes not a substitute for, but a complement to, the democratic process of policy development and service delivery monitoring. In the next few sections, we summarize the findings of the country chapters, explore the implications of these findings for the causes and consequences of the legalization of demands, and then set forth what this implies for the function of courts in a democracy.

VARYING LEVELS OF LEGAL MOBILIZATION ACROSS COUNTRIES

In this and the following section, we compare and explain the levels of legal mobilization in the different countries, policy areas, and classes of cases by looking purely at the number and kind of cases filed. Later in this chapter we go further and

---

[3] This process bears considerable similarity to the process of triadic governance described by Stone Sweet (1999), in which courts, in the course of dispute resolution, cooperate in an iterative process of adjustment to and modification of the existing normative framework.

[4] This constituency may be a demographic group with the legal organizational capacity to press collective, group-identity-based demands – what Epp has labeled the litigation "support structure" – or it may be a less coordinated group with ready access to legal services for pressing individual demands. The latter is what drives the astonishingly high volume of individual claims for particular health goods in Brazil, which arises mostly out of the middle class, though it includes the poor where they have access to state legal services, and shows very little evidence of coordination. Indeed, the threshold appears fairly low, and every country was home to civil society groups that would have the capacity to pursue a legal strategy if they so chose.

discuss the extent and nature of legalization of the policies surrounding the rights to health and education in each country. There we estimate the magnitude of the policy impact legal strategies have had, using informed estimates of the number of people directly or indirectly affected by judicial decisions. We intersperse numerical measures with a more qualitative evaluation of the sorts of issues courts have tackled in each place, and of the importance of their intervention.

What is most striking is the extent of variation both at the cross-national and subnational levels. The countries and subnational units examined in this book vary not only in terms of the number of cases, but also in the relative frequency of collective versus individual cases and in the kinds of cases they emphasize. If we do a quick comparison across countries of the number of cases being filed in these two areas of social and economic rights, one finding stands out. Canvassing only the apex courts in four states and at the federal level in Brazil, and going back only as far as electronic databases would allow, Hoffman and Bentes and their team located nearly eight thousand cases that relied on a right to health or a right to education. After comprehensive searches of electronic databases on all the state high courts and the Supreme Court of India, a country with six times the population of Brazil, Shankar and Mehta located 382 comparable cases. South Africa followed, with fewer than one hundred, and Indonesia and Nigeria (if we count only court actions) were in the low double digits.[5]

On a per capita basis, the imbalance is even more notable. Assuming the states examined are approximately representative, Brazil compiles nearly 125 cases per million of population – the state of Rio Grande do Sul registers a remarkable *893 cases per million*. In South Africa, its nearest competitor, Berger and his colleagues found just more than three cases per 10 million inhabitants, and in India there were two cases for every 10 million inhabitants. Rates in Nigeria and Indonesia, the countries with the lowest level of activity, were 0.6 and 0.3 cases per 10 million, respectively.[6] The volume of litigation in Brazil is simply on a different scale.

In addition, the pattern of litigation differs in each country. Throughout this chapter, we organize the presentation using the tripartite distinction laid out in the introduction. Briefly, we argued that one can usefully classify SE rights cases into those that relate to three sets of duties: *Provision* – imposing a duty on the state to pay for or provide a service directly; *regulation* – modifying the regulatory environment by imposing (or removing) state-enforced duties on providers; and

---

[5] The sampling methods were not identical in all countries. In particular, in an effort to increase the number of cases studied, the Indonesia chapter included medical malpractice cases, and the Nigeria and South Africa chapters included health and education cases even if they did not mention the rights to health or education explicitly. University cases were excluded in Brazil but included in Nigeria and India. If these additional criteria had been incorporated into the Brazil and India samples, the disparities between those two countries and the others would have been even larger. The search criteria for the Brazil and India electronic databases were broadly comparable. Although the India sample went back to 1950, the significant majority of cases were filed after 1980. These small differences in sampling do not, we believe, change the rank ordering of our per capita case counts.

[6] The figure for Nigeria would climb to 1.8 if we include the more than one hundred cases brought to the National Human Rights Commission that also raise health and education rights.

obligation – modifying the provider-recipient relationship by imposing (or removing) a duty on the provider that the recipient herself must enforce.[7] The level of state intervention and investment required never disappears, but it certainly declines as we move from direct provision, to regulation, to private enforcement of horizontal obligations.

In the health rights area, Indonesia and Nigeria record so few cases they hardly merit classification into patterns. In both Brazil and South Africa, on the other hand, litigants do, in fact, demand government provision. In South Africa, litigants also demand government regulation of the activities of private providers, while in Brazil there is a secondary focus on the horizontal relationship between the claimants and private providers (primarily in the area of private health insurance). In India, by contrast, rights bearers use the courts primarily to impose civil accountability directly on the providers of these services and to alter the regulatory environment; in other words, they aim at interventions that impose the least burden on the state. In general then, litigation in South Africa seeks to impose the greatest burden on the state, followed by Brazil, and then India. In Indonesia and Nigeria there is very little litigation, and it is scattered across these categories. These findings on litigation patterns are based on case counts obtained from the country chapter authors. They bear both similarities and marked differences when compared to the cross-national impact of cases on individuals, presented in graphical form later.

In education, in contrast, we see less litigation everywhere. What litigation there is in Brazil and South Africa focuses almost exclusively on regulation and provision of services; in India and Nigeria, it emphasizes the relative duties of educators and students, in addition to regulation and provision. In Indonesia the few cases that have appeared have not yielded judicial remedies for claimants, though they have had significant effects nonetheless, as we will see. To summarize, there were, on average, in all countries studied, twenty-one times more health than education cases, and there were very few cases involving direct claims against the state for more or better primary education (exceptions were one important case in Indonesia, some demands presented by public prosecutors in Brazil, and a few scattered cases on rural schools in India).

There is also striking variation in levels of legal mobilization at the subnational level. In Brazil, for example, there was a litigation explosion in the South but not the Northeast: the courts in Rio Grande do Sul receive 893 health care demands per million of population – seventy-five times more cases than the courts of Bahia. In India, as Shankar and Mehta document, the poorer, so-called BIMARU states represent only a fraction of the activity we see among the non-BIMARU states. There were no recorded cases in the northern state of Kaduna in Nigeria. In general, then, within any given country, richer states saw more litigation than poorer states.

---

[7] As in the introductory chapter, we use the term "provider" to refer not just to the direct providers of health and education services, but to any entity whose activities affect health or education rights, including, for example, industrial plants whose emissions damage air or water quality.

EXPLANATIONS FOR DIFFERENCES IN CASE COUNTS – EXPLORING THE CAUSES OF LEGAL MOBILIZATION

The first question we must answer, then, is what accounts for varying levels of legal mobilization across countries and subnational units? In the introduction we argued that litigants choose to bring their demands to the courts when it appears that the courts will be an effective mechanism for processing them, either because other mechanisms have failed to respond, or, more frequently, in conjunction with demands pressed in other forums. This calculus, and the resulting level of legal mobilization, in turn, is a function of demand-, supply- and response-side factors, all of which are interconnected by the strategic calculations of potential litigants, courts, and respondents. Although the chapters do not, in a strict sense, test the theoretical propositions laid out in the Introduction, they do offer important suggestions about the relative impact of these various factors.

Demand-Side Factors: Who Sues, and Who Doesn't?

As noted in the introduction, before some aspect of the human predicament can become a need – particularly a need to be satisfied by the state – it must appear to reasonable people that the state can satisfy this need. That kind of expectation on the part of the population is not, however, a sufficient condition for litigation, as a quick glance around the developing world might tell us. Moreover, earlier we questioned Epp's hypothesis that mobilizing courts on behalf of social and economic rights requires rights-advocacy organizations – a "support structure" – on the model of the civil rights or women's rights movements in the United States and Canada. We suggested, instead, that legal mobilization imposes a fairly low threshold of civil society organizational development, which is easily met whenever groups decide to pursue legal strategies. Evidence for these propositions is apparent from the case studies in this volume.

Perhaps the strongest evidence that large-scale litigation does not require a classical support structure comes from Brazil, where an undeniable medical rights revolution figures significantly in the public health landscape. Hoffmann and Bentes document that the cost of medicines received directly in response to court orders is an estimated $1 billion reals, or some 1 to 2 percent of public-sector health spending. But the budgetary impact of the legalization of health care in Brazil is undoubtedly higher: Judicial rulings on hospital maintenance, the impact of administrative inquiries on the part of the Ministério Público, and, above all, spending decisions on the part of public authorities made either in reaction to or in anticipation of judicial rulings have been large enough to spark a policy discussion of the economic consequences of judicial activity on health rights. Although less than 1 percent of the Brazilian population benefits from this phenomenon by having access to new products or services first ordered by the courts (calculations are detailed in the following sections), interviews with public health officials suggest that nearly every interaction between an unhappy user of public health services and the bureaucracy now takes place in the shadow of the law. As Scheingold

(2004) or McCann (1994) might have predicted, the effect of these many decisions is most keenly felt in the negotiations and interactions between rights bearers and providers.

This legalization of health care in Brazil has not resulted from the coordinated action of civil rights advocacy organizations – the paradigmatic support structure – but from the accumulation of many individual actions on the part of middle and lower middle class claimants, who have been availing themselves of individual public and private lawyers in an uncoordinated, unorganized way. Presenting thousands of individual claims for particular medications (which can be enforced through short-term individual follow up with particular bureaucrats) requires no more than a well-developed legal profession and a middle class that can access lawyers but not the medical services being sought. The Brazilian "rights revolution" has, therefore, taken place without the presence of the organized support structure Epp found necessary for the development of the civil rights movement in the United States and elsewhere. It appears to have been kicked off by organized civil society groups mobilizing around HIV/AIDS issues, but quickly spread to other areas and other claims. The graphs of case counts in the Brazil chapter show exponential growth, likely resulting from the learning effects and dropping marginal costs of each individual case, as described in the introduction to this volume.

But for other kinds of litigation, a more robust demand structure has appeared necessary. The novel collective claims brought on behalf of South African HIV-positive pregnant women – most of whom were neither middle class nor especially adept at engaging the legal system – seeking medication to prevent viral transmission to their children required compliance by a large number of geographically dispersed local government officials. The eventual effectiveness of the initial Constitutional Court decision rested on the presence of a litigation-oriented civil society organization that could not only bring the initial claim but also initiate follow-up litigation and negotiations in various states across the country. The Treatment Action Campaign (TAC) succeeded in both the judicial and implementation phase because it possessed and exercised its considerable organizational capacity to maintain pressure on public health officials across the country. Another South African case, *Grootboom*, involved another novel collective claim – housing rights of squatters. Although the case did lead to the creation of municipal emergency housing funds across the country and established a precedent that greatly facilitated the defensive use of the right to housing against eviction orders, it had little impact on macro-level housing policy in South Africa.[8] Both Constitutional Court rulings addressed complex socioeconomic rights, and neither involved a direct structural interdict to government. Supervision in the HIV prevention case was left to TAC, which, as Berger notes, though not as aggressive in following up on the case as it could have been, did eventually manage to use its resources to help achieve a significant rollout of prevention of mother-to-child transmission of HIV

---

[8] See the discussion in Kamneshi Pillay, "Implementation of Grootboom: Implications for the enforcement of socio-economic rights, http://www.communitylawcentre.org.za/Projects/Socio-Economic-Rights/research-project/2002-vol-6-law-democracy-and-development/kameshni-pillay-12-march.pdf/.

in South Africa. The Court directed the South Africa Human Rights Commission to supervise the implementation of *Grootboom*. But the Commission lacked the broad-based, independent mobilizing capacity of TAC; consequently, the country saw less court-initiated change in housing policy than in HIV prevention.

The significantly larger number of health than education cases in our sample can also be explained in terms of the demand structure. As we mentioned, to our surprise, we discovered almost no cases on the quality of basic education. The reason for this is likely related to the fact that education is provided in schools, whereas clinical health care typically involves one-on-one encounters with providers. As a result, litigation to improve schools requires demand-side coordination among a larger number of applicants than a claim for a medication or health insurance reimbursement.[9] In sum, for collective and explicitly policy-oriented litigation, which require sustained follow up, further legal mobilization, and coordination among a larger set of actors, a support structure appears important.

Even where one observes a relationship between "support structure" and a litigation campaign, the causal arrow may, in fact, go in the opposite direction – from litigant goals to support structure. Consider the difference between levels of legal mobilization around health and education rights in Brazil. In São Paulo, Brazil, both of the authors of this chapter spoke to civil society groups whose primary focus is access to quality education. Advocates in these groups attend international meetings and are well aware of the discussions surrounding the justiciability of education rights. They have funds, well-equipped offices and computers, networks spanning Brazil and the world, and the capacity to raise further funds to staff potential litigation. At least one organization, Ação Educativa, has even been tracking the actions of the public prosecutor in this area. Staff members indicated that, in light of the success rates in health rights cases, they consider litigation an option and have even hired a lawyer to evaluate the possibilities. But their own review found just a 10 percent success rate for education cases, which indicated to them that the courts were not yet open to these claims. As a result, the organization had thus far focused on traditional lobbying and advocacy tactics and not litigation.[10]

---

[9] There are additional explanations for why we see more health than education claims: (a) judges have been decidedly less enthusiastic about education claims, perhaps because the requisite response to typical health claims – for medications or reimbursement – is more observable to judges and less complex than the response to claims for better education inputs; (b) the middle classes, who have the resources to bring claims, have largely opted out of public primary educational systems, whereas they still use public hospitals in many countries; (c) civil mobilization around AIDS spread to other health issues, whereas no similar mobilization exists in education.

[10] Interviews with Ação Educativa, São Paulo, Brazil: Varun Gauri, May 8, 2005; and Daniel M. Brinks June 23, 2005. An Ação Educativa analysis uncovered eighty-six cases on education brought by the Ministério Público (MP) in the municipality of São Paulo between 1996 and 2003, nearly half of which involved access to preschool education. Most of these cases had been recently litigated, and in only ten cases had decisions been rendered. In all but one of those ten cases, the courts had ruled in favor of the state and against the MP. This probably understates the impact of litigation on education rights because it excludes the impact of administrative inquiries on the part of the MP. Nevertheless, for the calculations of civil society organization such as Ação Educativa, it is the win–loss rate that is relevant, not administrative inquiries, which it cannot initiate on its own.

Interviews in Indonesia and Nigeria also revealed civil society organizations that are steeped in the language of rights and the debates surrounding their enforcement, and that have essentially all the elements needed to support a litigation campaign – access to lawyers, information about what other groups have done, favorable laws and treaties, and the requisite funds – but have concluded that, at this point, the courts' lack of receptiveness makes other demand channels more attractive. Indeed, the Nigerian groups explicitly stated that they were pursuing "rights-based" tactics, training people at the village level in the language of rights, and disseminating information about treaties and constitutional commitments. But they were consciously emphasizing local-level politics and activism over litigation because they believed the courts would not be receptive to their claims.[11] Various activist groups in Indonesia are staffed by lawyers, but have also opted not to file lawsuits, with the few but important exceptions detailed in Susanti's chapter.

The Indian experience similarly confirms civil society's strategic, instrumental view of the courts, but takes it one step further. Shankar and Mehta report that organized civil society groups often choose traditional political approaches over litigation because it is keenly aware that even the most favorable judicial pronouncements often lead nowhere. Although judicial decisions are often favorable and provide ringing endorsements of the claims presented, the frequent failure of implementation renders them a second-best solution to more effective, if less bombastic, intervention by political actors. Indeed, one of the authors of this chapter interviewed a prominent Indian constitutional rights advocate, who indicated that she and her organization were beginning to shift their focus from litigation to political lobbying because of the number of instances in which Indian courts have not followed up on their expansive rulings.[12]

Finally, on a macro-comparative level, variation in levels of legal mobilization does not correlate with variation in the density of rights-advocacy organizations. Here it is important to recognize that the most widely used measure of legal mobilization, case counts, assumes that all court cases are homogeneous and excludes by construction any consideration of the scope and ambition of the cases brought. Using total case counts, as seen in Table 8.1, Nigeria can look as if it has more legal mobilization than South Africa.

But there is more legal mobilization in a society where civil society organizations bring a series of direct, sophisticated challenges to government health policy than in a society where individual plaintiffs bring an equivalent number of uncoordinated cases regarding medical malpractice. Collective cases are more difficult to bring and have broader impact. On this understanding of legal mobilization, we could argue that India's legal mobilization is stronger than South Africa's, let alone Indonesia's or Nigeria's, lagging only behind Brazil. Health and education litigation in India

---

[11] Daniel M. Brinks interviews in Abuja, Nigeria, January, 2006, with Otive Igbuzor of Action Aid; Chibuike Mgbea of the Women's Aid Collective; Fabian Okoye of Global Rights Nigeria; James Shegun of Women's Rights and Advancement Nigeria; and representatives of Education for All, Nigeria. Also interviews in Jakarta, Indonesia, with representatives of Education Legal Aid Foundation; the Legal Aid Foundation, Jakarta, and others.

[12] Varun Gauri interview with Indira Jaisingh, Lawyers Collective, New Delhi, India, February 23, 2006.

Table 8.1. *Number of individual and collective health and education rights cases filed in Brazil, India, South Africa, Indonesia, and Nigeria*

	Health		Education	
	Individual	Collective	Individual	Collective
Brazil	7,248	141	237	56
India	61	91	93	19
South Africa	3	8	2	9
Indonesia	3	4	0	5
Nigeria	9	3	12	3

is more ambitious and typically involves more direct challenges to policy. And yet, despite having more legal mobilization, India is reputed to have relatively weak and uncoordinated rights advocacy organizations – Mehta and Shankar make this claim in this volume, Epp argued that India's "rights revolution" fizzled because of its weak support structure, and interviews with Indian civil society litigators disclosed a lack of coordination among key actors.[13]

Moreover, it is clear that collective actors are not always the primary engines behind legal mobilization. Mehta and Shankar show that NGOs were plaintiffs in just 19 percent and 7 percent of health and education rights cases, respectively; in education rights cases, NGOs were plaintiffs less often than individuals, private institutions, the state, and trade unions. Brazil is, by most accounts, endowed with relatively robust and vibrant rights advocacy organizations, as Hoffmann and Bentes point out. South Africa has several relatively well-endowed rights advocacy organizations that even sometimes coordinate their efforts when launching test cases. Indonesia is considered to have a strong civil society that played an important role in the democratization process. In other words, among the countries studied in this volume, legal mobilization in India is among the most ambitious; yet, its legal support structure is not obviously the strongest.

Summarizing, we can say with some confidence that whereas an appropriate support structure is necessary for initial legal mobilization and is a key factor for explaining the persistence of certain mobilization campaigns, demand-side shortfalls do not seem to be the most significant constraint on legal mobilization. At least at this stage of development of the NGO and activist community, even countries with low per capita GDP, such as India, Indonesia or Nigeria, have civil society groups that could pursue litigation but choose not to. In countries where rights litigation is virtually nonexistent, civil society groups have at least thought about the possibility and have the resources to resort to courts if they

---

[13] Varun Gauri interviews in New Delhi with Anup Srivastava, Human Rights Law Network, January 30, 2006; Indira Jaisingh, Lawyers Collective, February 2, 2006; Usha Ramanathan, Center for the Study of Developing Societies, New Delhi, February 2, 2006. Former Supreme Court Justice Kuldip Singh also indicated that, for several important environmental cases that came to the Court's "Green Bench," the Court identified and appointed well-placed advocates rather than waiting for civil society to bring cases (Varun Gauri interview with Justice Kuldip Singh, New Delhi, January 31, 2006).

felt this was the most effective strategy. And once the courts begin to respond – as in Indonesia after the creation of the Constitutional Court, and its initial positive reactions to education rights – the support structure rises to meet the needs of claimants who wish to litigate. Given a basic level of resources, potential litigants can create the structures they need to pursue the goals and strategies they identify. The more important constraint, then, may be the supply of judicial services appropriate to the task at hand. This brings us to questions regarding the characteristics of the courts and legal environment in each policy area.

Supply-Side Factors: Why Do the Courts Support Some Claims and Not Others?

We identified certain features in the introduction that were likely to have an impact on the decision to pursue a claim through the courts or through some other means. It should be clear already that some of the gross attributes of the legal system, which have often been identified as determinative, do not crucially affect the role courts can play in the political system. Scholars in the past have occasionally argued that, for various reasons, countries that belong to the civil law tradition are highly unlikely to develop an independent, activist, creative judiciary (see, e.g., Rosenn 1987; von Hayek 1960). Merryman's (1985) description of the civil law tradition tends in this direction as well, though it is more equivocal. In our cases, the civil law tradition does not appear as an important factor at all in determining the size and ambition of legal mobilization. We have common law countries at the high (India) and low (Nigeria) end of the spectrum, and civil law countries at the high (Brazil) and low (Indonesia) end of the spectrum. South Africa ranks quite high despite its somewhat ungainly blend of English common law and Dutch civil law features. This result is largely consistent with large-N, quantitative analyses of the effect of legal tradition on institutions (Acemoglu, Johnson, and Robinson 2001; Berkowitz, Pistor, and Richard 2003).

At the same time, it is important to note that the legal tradition does shape the contours of litigation. As we will see when we discuss the impact of legalization, in Brazil we see an astonishing number of cases, each producing a small individual impact, that together add up to something similar to what the courts in South Africa produce with much less effort. This is likely a consequence of its civil law system and traditions, in particular the reluctance to acknowledge the binding effect of prior decisions, which produces large numbers of repetitive cases. As we will discuss more fully in the section on the effects of legalization, this increased reliance on direct over indirect effects in Brazil compared to common law countries is likely to exacerbate whatever regressive bias legal mobilization may have.

Similarly, it is not clear that the centralized, abstract judicial review typical of the civil law tradition is a less conducive institutional framework for robust constitutional development than the diffuse and concrete review of common law systems. Clearly, if standing rules limit claimants to major political actors, then the possibility of accessing the court as a member of civil society is drastically curtailed (see Ginsburg 2003: 36–40, for a discussion of access issues). Similarly, we might expect that locating the court in the national capital will impose significant limitations on who can as a practical matter make use of it. But in our cases, access to constitutional courts is not unduly limited, civil society groups that pursue important collective claims through legislation or litigation are already located in the capital, and compared to the ordinary courts, centralized constitutional courts appear to be equally (in the case of Brazil or India) or more (in the case of South Africa or Indonesia) receptive to these claims.[14] Logistical issues matter a great deal when it comes to individual claims, as we will see in a moment with respect to individual obligations claims. But in the case of large-scale collective claims, they take a back seat to judicial receptiveness, and in this respect, centralized courts seem, if anything, more likely to have an important impact than the others. The answer to the question whether centralized/abstract review is better than diffuse/concrete is that it depends on how receptive their judges are to the claims presented.

The next question then is, of course, what affects how receptive the courts are to particular claims. Clearly, some judges are more supportive than others – the difference between Indian and Nigerian judicial attitudes is dramatic, as exemplified in the drastically restrictive standing doctrine developed by the latter, in comparison to the PIL procedure created by the former. We have seen that the same courts might invite health claims but discourage education claims, or welcome individual claims while rejecting collective ones. But where do judges come by their preferences? A full answer to this question is not presented in the country chapters and is beyond the scope of this project. At the same time, the cross-national variation strongly suggests some answers that mesh with the existing literature on judicial decision making.

The principal observation we can make is that judges are qualified creatures of their political environment. We will describe in a subsequent section how the courts in each country follow a model of rights provision that broadly matches the dominant national pattern. A closer look at the appointment of judges fills in the story behind that correlation. The views of current South African apex court judges were developed, like Justice Goldstone's, in the midst of a struggle to create a more equal South Africa. They were appointed by the first fully democratic president of South Africa, Nelson Mandela, with the consent of the ANC-dominated congress and the input of the Judicial Services Commission, which likewise came about in the immediate aftermath of the struggle against apartheid and which sought to democratize South Africa's judiciary. Given this appointment process, it is no surprise that these judges take a favorable view of social and economic rights and take their mandate seriously enough to challenge the ANC government in terms of particular policies. Similarly, the difference between constitutional court judges and ordinary judges in Indonesia is instructive. The newly appointed justices of the Indonesian Constitutional Court, the first court to be fully staffed in democracy, mark a clear break with the authoritarian past. These judges have exhibited an

---

[14] In Brazil the apex courts in general are, by conventional wisdom, less receptive than the trial courts of states like Rio Grande do Sul, Rio de Janeiro, or São Paulo. But they are more receptive than the courts of Bahia, for example. And the statistical evidence presented in the Hoffmann & Bentes chapter suggests some of this conventional wisdom may be mistaken anyway.

aggressive pro-rights posture, whereas the bulk of the ordinary courts in that country, largely holdovers from the previous regime, are either hostile or ineffectual on these issues.

More generally, what determines the dominant ideological bent on a particular bench is largely the appointment process that populates it. This accounts for differences, for example, between the more adventurous trial court judges (selected in a relatively apolitical manner and insulated from politics) and the more cautious (politically appointed) apex court judges in Brazil; or between the active, largely self-governing Indian Supreme Court (whose members select their own replacements) and the more restrained courts elsewhere. Recruiting judges primarily from among civil servants, as in Nigeria, can produce a judiciary with a straitened view of the judicial role.

Not surprisingly, judicial autonomy is a critical precondition for legal mobilization. Provision claims against the government fade into the background whenever courts are weak relative to political actors, as in the Brazilian state of Bahia or in Nigeria. There are virtually no successful claims against the state in the ordinary courts of Indonesia, which are weak relative to local political actors,[15] whereas the stronger Constitutional Court has begun to issue important challenges to the central government.

Similarly, obligations cases, which do not involve claims against the government and, thus, often do not raise questions of independence from political actors, fade when the legal system is insufficiently autonomous from powerful social actors. Unlike constitutional claims, horizontal disputes between private parties can always be adjudicated locally and are therefore amenable to lower-cost enforcement structures – in nearly every jurisdiction, the logistical supply-side characteristics favor them. As a result, this type of case can be found in both courts and human rights commissions (as in Nigeria's National Human Rights Commission), and in states where the courts are strong (Rio Grande do Sul) or weak (Bahia) in relation to the government. But these cases disappear when the courts are not trustworthy vehicles for imposing national standards on local power relations. This is the case of the ordinary courts, but not the Constitutional Court, in Indonesia; and the courts generally, but not the Human Rights Commission, in Nigeria. Corruption, in these court systems, imposes a local logic over the national logic of legislation and rights.

The same dynamic may limit the usefulness for rights enforcement of the customary and religious courts that dominate remote rural areas in these two countries. Parallel legal systems, whether sharia or customary, work within a local context, with little nationalizing influence. They are populated by local power holders – village elders, religious leaders – and their lack of detailed legal texts means local knowledge and norms dominate decision making. These systems follow a logic that is distinct in many ways from the westernized, internationally informed language of rights on which we have focused our research. We asked the country chapter authors to look into this issue to the extent possible and have

---

[15] Judges, although centrally appointed and administered, are typically dependent on local political officials for their day-to-day operations, to the point of receiving their office space, supplies, and staff from local authorities.

been unable to uncover any significant rights-based activity in the informal court systems. As Odinkalu reports, in Nigeria it is likely that these local customs are inimical to the protection of certain rights, at least for women and at least for now. It is possible, of course, that these courts serve to protect certain groups or individuals, improve accountability of local government officials, and enhance access to health care or education, but when they do, they do not use the language of rights and they do not favor the weakest actors in the local social structure.

Does this focus on politics and judicial attitudes mean that the text of laws and constitutions is irrelevant? We said in the introduction that the legal framework for these claims should matter, even if it is not determinative. And, in fact, we see litigation often tracking specific, objective constitutional language. The 20 percent minimum education-spending requirement in the Indonesian Constitution is one example. On the other side of the coin, in Nigeria the courts have repeatedly used the constitutional non-justiciability language as a rationale for denying SE claims. Meanwhile in Brazil the courts can and do invoke the much less equivocal constitutional language in support of the right to health care. At one level, then, one explanation for the paucity of SE litigation in Nigeria and its prominence in Brazil is that the former courts deny these claims because the rights on which they would be based are non-justiciable by express constitutional design, whereas the latter are simply following the letter of the 1988 Brazilian Constitution.

At another level, this answer is incomplete at best. Working from a constitutional structure that is similar in intention to the Nigerian one, the Indian courts have gone out of their way to incorporate explicitly non-justiciable rights, such as the rights to health and education, into justiciable ones like the right to life. Nigeria, on the other hand, is a signatory to the Africa Charter on Human and People's Rights, which contains all the requisite rights language with no express limitation on justiciability. The Charter has been incorporated into domestic legislation and could easily serve as an independent basis for legal claims. But the Nigerian courts have used the non-justiciability provision in the Constitution to make the Charter non-justiciable, rather than using the Charter as an independent source of justiciable rights. We see the other side of the coin in Indonesia, with extensive protection of SE rights in its Constitution and a weak record rivaled only by Nigeria's. Cross-national differences clearly cannot be traced to constitutional texts, even though judicial decisions always refer back to these texts for justification.

It is also hard to explain intranational differences by reference to the letter of the law. The northeastern states of Brazil show dramatically lower levels of health litigation than the southern states, although they share the same legal framework. Indeed, the high level of activity on behalf of health rights and the low level regarding educational rights runs directly counter to nearly universal formal differences in the legal framework. On a global scale, the number of constitutions guaranteeing the right to education was at 80 percent of its all-time high by 1900, whereas the right to health care is clearly a post–World War II phenomenon.[16] Moreover, the language protecting education rights is typically stronger than that

[16] This observation is based on data graciously supplied by Zachary Elkins, based on his collaborative effort with Tom Ginsburg to record and code provisions in all constitutions and amendments since 1789.

protecting health care. In South Africa, for example, the Constitution says only that "the state must take reasonable legislative and other measures, within its available resources, to achieve the progressive realisation of" the right to health (Constitution of the Republic of South Africa, Art. 27(2)). With regard to the right to education, on the other hand, it is only higher education that is expressly subject to the progressive realization standard, whereas the right to basic education is unconditional.[17] And, yet, we see more consequential health cases than education cases; and within education, we see more higher education and "right to language of choice" (which is similarly subject to reasonableness standards) cases than basic education cases.[18] The language of formal rights is a starting point for the analysis, then, but clearly not the end point. It may condition which claims appear first or the language used to accept or deny the claims; but it will not pose an obstacle to a determined court, as in India, and it will not foster litigation where the courts are untrustworthy, as in Indonesia.

If we direct our gaze a little lower, however, it becomes clear that certain aspects of the law matter a great deal. Litigation seems to follow on infra-constitutional legal developments, or what we have called a well-developed policy infrastructure. Comparing the relative presence of provision cases across jurisdictions, for example, we see that provision cases are most common (in Brazil and, to a slightly lesser extent, South Africa) in the context of a well-developed policy structure (Brazil's comprehensive, multi-tiered universal public health system, or South Africa's more developed bureaucratic state). The *TAC* case in South Africa is a classic example of the close relationship between an existing policy infrastructure and judicial intervention. As Berger notes in his chapter, members of TAC lobbied and agitated through conventional, representative avenues until they had at least a rudimentary policy framework, and then shifted to legal mobilization to tackle particular short-comings in that framework – its absence of effective prevention of mother-to-child transmission, its failure to reach the prison population, and similar shortcomings.

Similarly, when the South African Constitutional Court granted social assistance benefits to non–South African residents, in the landmark *Khosa* case, it relied both for its remedy and legal reasoning (which was based on the prohibition of unfair discrimination) on the existence of a well-developed, decades-old state program of social grants for dependents and disability. In Brazil, the vast majority of the thousands of right-to-health cases litigated are punctual interventions in individual cases in which the available medical treatments are – at least in the eyes of the prescribing doctor – inadequate. This is especially true in the HIV/AIDS arena, in which the courts are the vehicle through which medical innovations, imported from abroad, are incorporated into the regularly offered courses of treatment. In India, when, in orders following the People's Union for Civil Liberties (PUCL) writ

---

[17] "Everyone has the right: (a) to a basic education, including adult basic education; and (b) to further education, which the state, through reasonable measures, must make progressively available and accessible." Constitution of the Republic of South Africa, Art. 29(1).

[18] "Everyone has the right to receive education in the official language or languages of their choice in public educational institutions where that education is reasonably practicable." Constitution of the Republic of South Africa, Art. 29(2).

petition of 2001, the Supreme Court sought for the first time to enforce the right to food, it did not direct the government to establish new policies. Rather, it converted eight preexisting government food distribution schemes into constitutional legal entitlements. Its most expansive order, which directed the state governments to provide universal, free, cooked midday meals with a minimum protein and caloric content, also relied on a preexisting policy and bureaucratic infrastructure: Many states had been providing uncooked, dry midday meals at schools, though unevenly and of varying quality, and at least two of them, Gujarat and Tamil Nadu, had in place relatively well-functioning midday meals programs already. Courts, then, do not typically order the wholesale expansion of policy structures, but rather seek to fill in gaps or address shortcomings in the existing structure. This is the first element in the strategic interaction between litigants, courts, and respondents – litigants sue, and courts back their claims,when there is a response structure present and able to provide an effective remedy.

Indeed, there is a great deal of evidence that latent capacity weighs heavily on the courts' decision to intervene. The courts impose greater burdens on the state in countries that have greater financial capacity to bear them. India's courts, for example, must address provision demands to a state that draws on about half (in purchasing power parity terms) the per capita income of Brazil. Indian courts are extremely visible and active; in many ways, as Shankar and Mehta's chapter illustrates, they may be the boldest courts in our sample, taking on the government on varied and important issues and even arrogating to themselves control over judicial appointments, despite contrary constitutional language (see, e.g., Epp 2003: 80–89). But they are markedly cautious in the remedies they order and noticeably reluctant to impose on the state an open-ended obligation to provide effective care to the hundreds of millions who do not have access to adequate health services in that country. More forthrightly, the courts in South Africa have ex-pressly – to the frustration of litigants – conditioned their remedies on the capacity of the state to provide an effective response with the means at hand. And in the 2005 case involving minimum levels of education spending, the Indonesian Constitutional Court ruled that the existing budget was unconstitutional but did not strike it down completely, even though such an order might have been the logical legal consequence of its ruling. Courts are not, with notable exceptions, inclined to tilt at windmills, if for no other reason than to preserve their credibility – a point Justice Goldstone makes in the Foreword.

All of this – the reluctance to impose impossible burdens or issue unenforceable decisions, the deference to dominant political actors – is evidence that judicial actors craft their decisions with one eye on the case at hand and one looking ahead to the next stage, anticipating the likely response to a given decision, as the strategic model of judicial behavior would suggest. This is not to say, however, that the courts will only issue orders for which compliance is unproblematic. In fact, we observe a continuum of risk taking, with the Indian courts at one end and the Nigerian courts at the other. The *TAC* and *Grootboom* cases in South Africa, the education-funding cases in Indonesia, the public health cases in India, even the abundance of medication cases in Brazil, all pose considerable challenges to the status quo and to the de facto policies of governmental actors. As the number and cost of medications cases continues to mount in Brazil, there is some evidence that a political backlash might be germinating. The entire course of antiretroviral litigation in South Africa is the story of a strong challenge to President Mbeki and his Minister of Health. In fact, our study has unearthed an abundance of cases, including some of the Indian public health cases, that produce limited compliance and sometimes none at all. But although the courts are willing to issue challenging decisions, they will not ordinarily issue doomed ones, no matter what the law might seem to require.

These findings strongly support the conclusion that judges are qualified strategic actors who will take chances when properly motivated, but who do not (knowingly or typically) make futile gestures. Judges come to their task with a particular ideological bent, which, we argued earlier, derives significantly from the recruitment process. Ideological predispositions include a general orientation toward highly political issues, such as those involved in SE rights litigation, and a sense of the proper judicial role, as emphasized in Hoffman and Bentes's discussion of Brazil. Judicial decisions largely shape the law toward the court's dominant ideological bent within the bounds of what appears possible given the political and infrastructural context. However, either out of conviction or miscalculation, these decisions frequently test, and occasionally go well beyond, the limits of what political actors are willing to accept.

Thus, the model of judicial decision making that emerges is a strategic one, akin to what others have observed for the U.S. Supreme Court (Epstein, Knight, and Martin 2001), or the German Constitutional Court (Vanberg 2001), but with more latitude for judicial freedom of action and a greater role for prior judicial preferences than is typically acknowledged by advocates of this model. At the same time, it is precisely when the courts locate themselves farthest from the political mainstream that they have the most difficulty with implementation. As Rosenberg (1991) might have predicted, the strong challenges to dominant policy in South Africa and India, detailed earlier, are the same cases that languish for failure of implementation or that fail to produce indirect effects. This brings us to the response-side factors that condition the likely outcome of litigation strategies.

Response-Side Factors: What Makes the Target of Litigation More Likely to Comply?

One of the most difficult tasks in empirical legal studies is ascertaining exactly what happens once the courts have decided. With varying degrees of success, our country chapter authors have done an admirable job of following up with various litigants and the groups that represent them and of attempting to identify the real-world consequences of court decisions and the factors that influence compliance and effectiveness.

We have already noted the most important response-side factors: the presence of an existing policy infrastructure with latent capacity and a congenial political environment. Courts are more willing to intervene, and compliance is more likely, when remedies can be met out of existing state structures. In contrast, when courts issue orders that do not have a clear point of insertion in existing bureaucratic structures, implementation becomes much more of a problem. Compare, for example, the Indonesian school funding cases or the Indian public health cases with the directive of a Brazilian court to a particular bureaucrat that he or she must purchase and supply a specified medication within forty-five days or face a penalty.

The dominant political orientation of the government plays an important role in the character of the judiciary, as we previously argued, but it is also a determining factor in the response to judicial orders. The expansive compliance seen in Brazil takes place in the context of a left-leaning government that generally supports universal health care and is generally willing to adopt the latest technologies when confronted with shortcomings in existing policy. The formulation and insertion of the right to health in the 1988 Brazilian constitution, as well as the establishment in 1990 of the health-care system intended to realize that right, were largely the work of a social movement, the *movimento sanitarista*, rooted in opposition to the military regime and aiming at the universalization of a health-care system that was previously limited to formal sector workers (Gauri, Beyrer, and Vaillancourt 2007; Weyland 1995). Many activists from that movement and their allies assumed government posts after democratization. Many still remain there, which generates sympathy in many quarters of the government for legally based medications claims (though not an uncomplicated sympathy, as Hoffmann and Bentes describe). In interviews with one of the authors of this chapter, a municipal health official in Rio de Janeiro said that he would, in fact, welcome lawsuits demanding more condom availability and improvements in the overall quality of care, rather than demands for medications only; and solicitors for a state and municipal government said that they were sympathetic to many medications claims because government supply facilities were too often poorly stocked.[19] Some of the principal civil society organizations that bring health and education rights claims in courts, including the leading AIDS NGOs and the association of parents of children with disabilities, actually receive direct funding from sympathetic federal and state governments.

But in cases in which the government is not willing to comply merely because a court has identified a deficiency in a program, the most important factors leading to compliance are not the characteristics of the respondent but those of the initial claimant and of the judicial process leading up to the order. A well-organized and persistent claimant is more likely to prod reluctant officials into action – here Epp's support structures play an important role. Even in Brazil's individual cases, where compliance is not a very great hurdle, when the litigant is represented by the public prosecutor, the bureaucracy is more likely to comply than when the litigant relies on an individual private lawyer with fewer organizational resources. In South Africa, the *Grootboom* case, in which the litigants were represented by individual pro bono lawyers, failed to produce significant effects. The *TAC* case, meanwhile, produced national consequences when the Treatment Action Campaign mobilized resources and filed or threatened follow-up litigation where health officials failed

---

[19] Varun Gauri interviews with Dr. Sérgio Aquino, Department of Sexually Transmitted Diseases and AIDS, Secretariat of Health, Municipality of Rio de Janeiro, May 13, 2005; and Flavio Pupo, Rio de Janeiro, May 12, 2006.

to comply. Similarly, the Right to Food Campaign in India, which consists of many volunteers but which also counts on advice and support from high-profile activists and intellectuals, is monitoring compliance with the court-ordered midday meals program and has supported complex, ongoing litigation on the issue. As a result, the right-to-food case has produced more significant effects on policy than the right-to-education cases, which lack a similarly well-organized claimant.

The judicial process leading to the order is also important. In particular, a dialogical process and a negotiated order are more likely to produce compliance than a unilateral edict. Berger makes an important observation in his chapter that helps us understand the impact of the judicial process on the likelihood of implementation. He notes that courts can become places of negotiation and dialogue that produce new solutions not contemplated by either of the parties at the outset of the litigation and, in fact, quotes the South African Supreme Court of Appeal's understanding of judicial action in the *Kate* case as an effort to create "a kind of dialogue between it and the provincial government." The South Africa chapter – where informed readers might expect to find a muscular court imposing its will on the other branches – is replete with examples of this kind of iterative decision making. The courts (as noted by Berger in his chapter, and by Goldstone in the Foreword) tend to issue general orders under the assumption that the government will, in good faith, attempt to comply and issue more detailed orders out of frustration with the litigation tactics or compliance failures of the government. They become more directive only after the government has repeatedly failed to comply.

Similarly, the Brazilian prosecutors use legal processes, including administrative inquiries, to trigger and motivate serious negotiations on the creation of additional educational spaces and the availability of medicines. The Constitutional Court in Indonesia, when faced with repeated litigation challenging the government's failure to meet the constitutional minimum spending for education, began to engage the executive branch in an attempt to move the government closer to constitutional requirements. In an interview in January 2006, an assistant judge of the Constitutional Court told one of the authors of this chapter that the court would like to begin working with the executive branch earlier in the budget process to make sure the constitutional standard is considered at the time of creating the proposed budget. What the court did not do was rewrite the country's budget law. The Indian courts have created outside bodies to collaborate with executive branch agencies and state governments in a number of cases, including the Environmental Pollution (Prevention and Control) Authority to monitor air quality and work with authorities to examine potential responses and two commissioners to monitor and support the implementation of the right to food in several states. This behavior is quite distant from the idealized judicial model that forms the basis for many discussions of "judicialization": a final "decision made by an impartial judge" who ascertains the facts and the relevant rule to find "the only correct solution" (Tate and Vallinder 1995: 14). In fact, although some judicial behavior approximates this ideal (most notably, in our cases, the individual decision making of the Brazilian courts in medication cases), in the most important cases the process does not look like this at all.

In fact, then, litigants and courts have adapted themselves to a model of the policy-making process that, in the countries studied in this volume, has shifted, at least in part, from command and control to iterative experimentation. Sabel and Simon (2004) chronicle a similar adaptation in U.S.-based public interest litigation, calling this a "destabilization model" of rights enforcement, with the idea that litigation upsets the status quo, creating the context for a joint search for new solutions to ongoing problems.[20] They argue that remedies typically feature stakeholder negotiation, rolling rules that can be updated in response to either party's concerns, and greater transparency and public scrutiny of the target's operations and compliance. Judicial orders are often open ended, specifying goals rather than the procedures for attaining goals. Dixon (2007), on the basis of *Grootboom* and other South African cases, proposes a related dialogical model for public law litigation.

In all the countries we examine, there is a great deal of variation along the command-and-control to dialogical continuum, but when tackling complex and expensive issues, the most effective judicial interventions tend to fall on the dialogical end of the spectrum. The forms of dialogue we see broadly conform to the three ways of revising the terms of accountability that we described in the introduction, where we proposed that legalization can result in (a) proposals to allocate responsibility for the provision or regulation of goods and services, (b) suggestions for standards against which to assess provision or regulation; or (c) penalties and other means for enforcing failures in provision or regulation. Regarding (a), in the most prominent judicially encouraged dialogues on SE rights described in this volume, including those concerning the rights to food and clean air in India, social grants and HIV/AIDS policy in South Africa, the provision of medications at the state level in Brazil, and educational spending in Indonesia, parties have been able to come to terms, for the most part, on the kinds of evidence and information that are relevant to the dialogue and who is responsible for provision and regulation. The South African courts, for instance, have clearly ruled that the national government, not the provinces, is responsible for the provision of social grants and HIV/AIDS policies. The Indian Supreme Court, working within the parameters of the Constitution, has effectively charged and monitored state governments for the regulation of air quality and provision of midday meals in schools. Brazilian courts are something of an exception here and have been reluctant to decide whether municipal, state, or the federal government is primarily responsible for the provision of medications. On the other hand, with regard to (b), although there are a few exceptions in India, courts have been reluctant to propose specific standards against which to assess performance of public and private actors. Only the Indian and South African courts have leaned heavily on specially appointed commissions or experts to provide information on standards. And as we have described earlier, in

---

[20] It is interesting that these authors claim judges apply both a legal and a political prerequisite to judicial intervention. "The prima facie case for public law destabilization has two elements: failure to meet standards and political blockage. The first element is explicit and is the focus of evidence and argument in the liability phase. The second is less discussed but remains an important background premise" (Sabel and Simon 2004: 1064–1067). This second element will reappear in our discussion of the proper function of courts in a democracy, in the final section of this chapter.

complex, expensive cases, courts in all countries have been extremely circumspect in proposing, let alone enforcing, sanctions for identified failures in provision or regulation.

THE IMPACT OF LEGALIZATION – HOW MANY PEOPLE BENEFIT FROM SOCIAL AND ECONOMIC RIGHTS LITIGATION?

In this section we lay out the effect of these legal strategies and judicial interventions on the policy landscape. We start with a brief description of the most salient features of legalization in each country. Then we explain in some detail how we measure the impact or effectiveness of judicial interventions in these policy areas. Finally, we present our systematic measurement of the impact of legalization, based on both quantitative and qualitative measures.

With the exception of the 1981 court decisions preventing the abolition of private schools in Lagos, which shaped the educational alternatives available to more than 2 million school age children, and two decisions requiring adequate medical care for prisoners, the few judicial decisions regarding SE rights in Nigeria do not affect anyone beyond the immediate litigants. Similarly, with the exception of a series of four decisions involving the constitutionally required minimum 20 percent spending on education, the courts in Indonesia have been virtually silent on or hostile to claims that seek to vindicate SE rights. But that single series of decisions has prompted a widespread debate on education spending, and the release of contending reports by government, civil society, and external actors such as the World Bank. It has also, arguably, played some role in prompting the Indonesian government to raise the percentage of the national budget allocated to education from 7 to 11.8 percent – a 60 percent increase in spending for education over the course of four years.[21]

The courts in India, Brazil, and South Africa, on the other hand, have acted more broadly and consistently over a panoply of issues, primarily in health but also in education. It is far more difficult to summarize their interventions than those of the Indonesian and Nigeria courts, and we have alluded to several of the key cases earlier in this chapter, as have, of course, the country chapter authors. Here, therefore, we merely cite the cases, to give the reader a sense of the cases being raised in each country, before moving to a more quantitative accounting of the courts' policy impact in each of these countries.

The South African courts are perhaps the best known for interventions on housing rights (through the renowned *Grootboom* case[22]), the provision of medication

---

[21] On May 2, 2007, *The Jakarta Post* noted the Court's third ruling on the constitutionally required, and legislatively backed, minimum allocation of 20 percent of the state budget on education. The case had been brought by the teacher's association. The government responded that it had increased the allocation to 12 percent and could go no higher that year. *The Jakarta Post* reported on June 17, 2008, that the government believed the 2009 budget would comply with the constitutional requirement if regional development funds were incorporated or if teachers' salaries, now counted as education expenditures and not only civil service expenditures as a result of a 2008 Constitutional Court ruling, were included in the education budget. The first case was Judicial Review of the National Education System Law in the Constitutional Court, Case No. 011/PUU-III/2005.

[22] Government of the Republic of South Africa v. Grootboom, 2001 (1) SA 46 (CC).

to pregnant HIV-positive women to prevent vertical transmission (the *TAC* case[23]), and cases that extended social grants to non-citizen residents.[24] Particularly salient sets of cases in India relating to health have involved the conversion of commercial vehicles in Mumbai[25] and Delhi[26] to cleaner fuels, the decisions that secured the safety of blood banks,[27] and cases that have imposed environmental restrictions on Pepsi, Coca-Cola, and other corporations in the name of health rights.[28] If India is characterized by collective public health solutions that do not imply growing the health services offered by the state, Brazil is marked by thousands of cases in which individuals seek and secure an individual course of treatment at state expense. Courts are willing to order the state to fill or pay for almost any prescribed remedy or medical intervention, whether or not the treatment is currently part of the public health offering or even approved as a safe and effective treatment by regulatory agents.

In almost every country, education cases are much less salient than interventions related to health. Perhaps the most important intervention we have seen in the education area is India's court-sponsored school midday meals program.[29] In Brazil, the courts have intervened on behalf of children with disabilities seeking appropriate educational facilities, monitored state compliance with constitutional minimum spending requirements, and overseen negotiations between public prosecutors and education officials to widen access to preschool. In South Africa, the courts have mostly been involved, with very mixed results, in monitoring compliance with minority-language education rights and government compliance with due process in its education-related decision making.

But these are snippets of information. It is difficult to know how representative they are of the overall experience in each of these countries and even more difficult to use them to draw explicit comparisons across countries. Relying solely on the language of the decisions – the legalistic approach that prevails among jurisprudential analyses – typically overstates the impact of courts on policy. The grandiose language of many decisions vastly overstates their actual impact on health or educational rights on the ground – the chapter on India makes this abundantly clear. Occasionally, however, it may understate the impact: Justice Goldstone gives a perfect example of an apparently narrow decision to require proof of alternative accommodations in eviction proceedings that had a significant impact on prosecutorial policies and ultimately on urban housing segregation in South Africa.

[23] Minister of Health v. Treatment Action Campaign (No. 2), 2002 (5) SA 721 (CC).
[24] Khosa v. Minister of Social Development; Mahlaule v. Minister of Social Development, 2004 (6) BCLR 569 (CC).
[25] Smoke Affected Residents Forum v. Municipal Corporation of Greater Mumbai and Others (Bom HC 2002).
[26] M. C. Mehta v. Union of India and Others (SC, Writ Petition (C) No. 13029 of 1985).
[27] "Common Cause" A Registered Society Through Its Director, Petitioner v. Union of India and Others, Respondents, 1996-(SC2)-GJX-0943-SC (01–05–1996).
[28] See, e.g., Santhosh Mittal v. State of Rajastahan and Others (2004.10.20).
[29] People's Union for Civil Liberties, Petitioner v. Union of India & Others, Respondents, Writ Petition (Civil) No.196 of 2001 Writ Petition (Civil) 196 of 2001, Supreme Court interim orders of November 28, 2001; May 2, 2003; and April 20, 2004.

Alternatively, we could measure levels of legalization simply by counting the number of decisions – a common strategy among more quantitatively oriented political scientists (Ginsburg 2003; Helmke 2002; Iaryczower, Spiller, and Tommasi 2002). But this method can undercount the impact of legalization as often as it overcounts. On the one hand, there are implementation issues that lead many decisions to be a dead letter, and there are vast differences between the impact of individual and collective decisions. On the other hand, there are decisions that are taken up by legislatures and transform the policy landscape, so their indirect effect can be much more than what the number of cases suggests. The difference between the numbers presented in Table 8.1, on legal mobilization, and the numbers we will present next makes this strikingly clear.

In order to compare the impact of legalization across countries and subnational units, therefore, we use a formula that captures, albeit imperfectly, all these dimensions: the extent of implementation, the direct effects on parties to the cases, and the indirect effect of cases in a policy area. The formula we use is $Impact = (N_{ind}{}^* DE_i) + (100N_{col}{}^* DE_c) + (N_{IE}{}^*I)$, where N_{ind} is the number of individual cases, and DE_i is the direct effect of those cases, calculated as the proportion of individual cases that favored the plaintiff and in which the judicial order is implemented. N_{col} is the number of collective cases, which we multiply by 100, an arbitrary number meant to denote the average number of individuals potentially directly affected by each collective case in that policy area.[30] DE_c is the direct effect of these collective cases, calculated as the product of the percentage of collective case decisions that favor the claimants and the estimated proportion of the ordered relief that is actually carried out. N_{IE} is a measure of what we called in the introduction the generalization of judicial remedies – the estimated number of persons potentially reached by the indirect effects of litigation in each area, primarily through legislated changes produced in response to successful (or even unsuccessful) legal strategies. Finally, I (for implementation) is the estimated proportion of those benefits that actually reached the intended beneficiaries.

Some examples may clarify the formula and how it is applied. Two collective claims[31] seeking free antiretroviral treatment in India led to relief in one of the cases – an order to the government to create a new AIDS-treatment program – and a decision against the plaintiffs in the other. In response to the pro-plaintiff decision, a program was, in fact, created that promised free antiretrovirals to roughly one hundred thousand people living with HIV/AIDS. On the basis of Shankar and Mehta's research, however, we conclude that no more than 10 percent

---

[30] We used 100 as an estimate of the relative importance of a collective case because there are too many cases and not enough information to use a less arbitrary number. A coefficient of 100 makes them important but does not allow them to completely overshadow individual cases. Obviously, some collective cases affect far fewer and some far more people (compare, e.g., a lawsuit that greatly affects seventeen secondary school students in Indonesia to a clean air case in India that affects, in a very small way, all the residents of Mumbai). For the heuristic purposes of this exercise, however, this rough estimate will suffice.

[31] Voluntary Health Association of Punjab v. Union of India (Writ Petition Civil, 311/2003) (in the Supreme Court of India); Subodh Sarma and Another v. State of Assam and Others (PIL) (1996–2000) (in the Delhi High Court).

of the benefits promised by that program have actually been implemented. In this example, then, $N_{coll} = 2$, $DE_c = .5$, $N_{IE} = 100,000$, and $I = .10$. The impact value of these two cases is $(100*2*.5) + (100,000*.10) = 10,100$. The number should roughly coincide with the number of people whose health or health care was significantly affected, directly or indirectly, by the decision.[32]

The data on the numbers and types of cases are taken from research conducted by the country study authors in this volume. As noted, the sampling methods used in the five country chapters are not identical (see footnote 5), but whatever biases this might introduce are small; and, because they tend to deflate the estimated impact of obligation cases in Brazil and India, the two countries where impact of obligation cases is already highest, they would not in any case affect our key findings. For Indonesia, Nigeria, and South Africa, the number of cases was small enough that estimates of people affected could be obtained by summing the impact of cases one by one. For India and Brazil, however, this was not possible. For those countries, we first identified, on the basis of interviews and the findings in Shankar and Mehta's chapter, the key policy areas where legalization has been influential, on the (it turns out) well-founded assumption that indirect effects swamp the direct effects of court cases (more on that in the following). Then we investigated the impact of those interventions and attributed some portion of the overall impact to legalization. Our estimates for the impacts of the various interventions that the bureaucracy implemented in response to court decisions were drawn from the secondary policy evaluation and econometric literature. Wherever uncertainty existed, or where there were confidence intervals for impact, we selected estimates at the bottom of the range to make the estimates as conservative as possible.[33]

For certain specific and prominent cases, we do not use all of the parameters in the equation; rather, we rely on counterfactuals drawn from the secondary literature. For instance, a comparison of enrollment rates between regions of India where the midday meals program is available to regions where the former dry grains program still operates finds that the midday meals program is increasing enrollments among girls by 10 percent in the first year of school.[34] Using publicly available numbers for current national enrollments and estimating that the

---

[32] We recognize that this estimate of the effects still treats very different things as if they were the same – it equally values a court order requiring free lunches, one that guarantees antiretrovirals to critically ill AIDS patients, and one that requires commercial vehicles to convert to compressed natural gas. Moreover, as mentioned already in the introduction, this estimate does not capture many other possible indirect effects of SE rights litigation – the discursive and mobilizing effect of defining certain needs as rights, the mobilizing effect of participating in group litigation efforts, etc. We estimate impact only from the time of implementation through 2007, which underestimates the total effects of court decisions in most cases. We focus only on first-order effects, such as access to AIDS treatment, and exclude more subtle effects, such as potential synergies of treatment with HIV prevention or drug resistance. We do not attempt to identify if there is overlap in the identities of beneficiaries among different cases, which is likely to be small. Still, this simplifying approach leads to valuable insights and is therefore worth presenting here.

[33] For more details on the impact calculations, please contact the authors.

[34] Farzana Afridi, 2007, March. *The impact of school meals on school participation: Evidence from rural India.* Syracuse University, http://www.econdse.org/seminar/seminar2.pdf.

judicially ordered program has only had an impact in about half the country, we estimate that about 350,000 Indian girls a year are newly enrolling in school as a result of the indirect effects of the right-to-food litigation.

In order to present on the same graph the widely disparate figures that result, we use a logarithmic transformation.[35] This transformation emphasizes variation at the lower and middle registers, where we find Indonesia, Nigeria, and South Africa, and flattens out the numbers from India and Brazil, which are several orders of magnitude greater. The graphs also use a population-adjusted value of the estimates to compare across jurisdictions of radically different sizes. The estimates are approximate, but we are confident that, at minimum, they preserve the rank order of our cases. We would, in any event, have to be off by an order of magnitude to produce a one point error in our measurement. The graphs utilize our tripartite typology of provision, regulation, and obligation, into which we slotted each of the cases the country chapter authors collected. In short, for all its infirmities, this method graphs all the countries along the same axes, yielding significant benefits in clarity and comparability.

The first thing to notice from these graphs is that in nearly all the jurisdictions, as anticipated earlier by the data on simple case counts, the impact of right-to-health cases dwarfs that of education cases. If we simply add the total direct and indirect policy impact of litigation across all the countries in the study, and exclude as outliers the cases challenging the constitutionality of the education budget in Indonesia, health cases affect nine times more people per million than education cases do.[36] On average, the litigation of health issues directly touches 181 people out of every million in these countries, whereas the litigation of educational issues affects only 22 per million. The only countries in which the courts' involvement in education policy appears to be more important than their involvement in health policy are Nigeria and Indonesia, the two countries with the lowest degrees of legalization overall, and in both cases this is the consequence of isolated and somewhat exceptional cases.

Within these broad policy areas, there are interesting differences arising from the tripartite classification.

---

[35] A base 10 logarithmic scale such as the one we use (similar to the Richter or decibel scales) adds 1 point for every order of magnitude – 1 represents an impact on 10 people/million, 2 represents 100 people/million, 3 represents 1,000 people/million, and so on. The log scale also minimizes measurement error in the jurisdictions where we are least confident of the result. We are much more certain of the values we plug into the formula when the cases are fewer. In Indonesia, Nigeria, and South Africa we know with a relatively high level of certainty the subsequent history of cases that favored the plaintiffs, how much of the purported benefit the plaintiffs actually received, and whether there were any legislated changes that can reasonably be attributed to the case. In India and Brazil, where the cases number in the hundreds or thousands, we are forced to rely on estimates (albeit estimates informed by extensive fieldwork and follow up) of the extent of compliance with judicial orders, and on secondary information on the connection between litigation and subsequent changes to public policy. We use the log transformation for the graphs. The numerical comparisons across countries in the text use the actual numbers.

[36] Again, we have not attempted to attach relative weights to interventions that might extend life (e.g., the South African *TAC* decision) versus those that might improve the quality of life (e.g., the decision compelling the Indonesian government to spend more money on education or the Nigerian decision preserving private educational opportunities).

Provision Cases

Especially when we look at the impact of the cases, it becomes clear that, except in the Brazil health cases and the Indonesia education area, provision – the type of case that serves as the explicit or implicit model for much academic and journalistic writing about the justiciability and judicialization of SE rights – is not the most important form of judicial intervention. When courts do get involved in provision cases, their interventions are most often measured and cautious, with limited impact beyond the parties. They typically order a narrow individual remedy, as in the vast majority of medication cases in Brazil. When they issue a more general order, it is often in the nature of a general requirement and a deadline, leaving the policy makers to design the actual framework for implementation, as in most of the South African HIV/AIDS cases. A classic example here is the South African Constitutional Court ruling in the *TAC* case, giving the government a deadline for beginning to issue nevirapine to HIV-positive pregnant women, but leaving most details (and the hard work of monitoring compliance) to the government and to civil society. India's collective cases on HIV/AIDS treatment are similar: The court ordered the government to prepare and implement a plan, but did not dictate the details of the plan. As described earlier, the decision-making process on remedies in the collective cases follows a more dialogical, rather than a monological command, model.

The triangles in Figure 8.1 illustrate important cross-national differences. In India, Brazil, and South Africa, the health provision decisions do extend previously unavailable health-related resources to significant numbers of people; collectively, they widen, in large and small ways, the range of options the state offers. But the impact of legalization on the effectiveness of the right to health is far less in Nigeria, and virtually nonexistent in Indonesia. In Nigeria the courts have developed a doctrine of standing that, somewhat ironically, allows them to dismiss any claims that might benefit many beyond the immediate claimant. The more likely it is that a favorable decision will extend its benefits to many others, the more likely it is that it will be dismissed without even a consideration on the merits. In Indonesia, meanwhile, it is not so much that claimants lose cases (although they do) as that they simply do not bring many health provision cases before the ordinary courts and have not yet brought important health provision cases to the Constitutional Court.

Meanwhile, in education, the courts have made much more modest, but still significant, efforts to enhance provision. It is important to note that they have validated claims to special schooling on behalf of children with disabilities, and they have served as a mechanism for the public prosecutor in Brazil to pressure state governments to expand access, particularly in preschool. Perhaps the most important intervention, India's cooked midday meals program, is, again, met through existing infrastructure. The Indonesian Constitutional Court's rulings on the constitutional minimum spending on education are perhaps the strongest demands to increase spending, although they have been, as we have discussed, tentative and cautious. The right to education lags far behind the right to health as a subject of litigation, though it has produced some results.

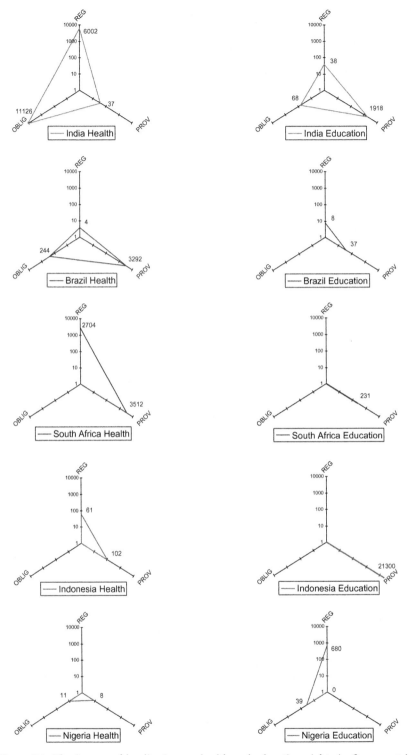

Figure 8.1. The impact of legalization on health and education rights in five countries (persons affected/10 million of population).

Regulation Cases

It is through their impact on the regulatory context that the courts most consistently and dramatically affect health and education policies. Even in Indonesia (where the courts have done little to impose new duties of provision on the state and, as we will see later, have done virtually nothing to improve the standing of recipients vis-à-vis providers) the courts have been willing to examine the effect on health rights of water delivery privatization or high-tension electrical tower placement. In most nations the number of cases is relatively small, but their scope is magnified because they apply to all recipients of services from the providers in question. The potential impact is also more egalitarian because the benefit accrues even to those who do not litigate, and enforcement of the new duties remains with the state rather than being dependent on those with resources to do follow-up litigation.

For the very same reasons, however, implementation and enforcement is much more of a challenge. The many public health cases in India that seek to regulate industrial emissions, for example, often produce very little in the way of actual behavioral change or environmental improvement. Once the decision is rendered, the primary interaction runs between the state and the regulated entity. The effectiveness of the decision then rests on the actions of a possibly reluctant government that is charged with regulating and monitoring the behavior of a recalcitrant provider. The courts in India have, at times, tried to address this problem by establishing oversight and reporting bodies (see the enforcement discussion in Shankar and Mehta's chapter), but, in the end, in these cases effectiveness depends crucially on government cooperation. The court's role, then, is to point out that there is a need the current regulatory framework does not adequately address and then to rely on the government to do what it needs to do to address it.

In the introduction we quoted a scholar who argues that the courts are primarily at the service of neoliberal interests and policies (Hirschl 2004). Quite to the contrary, after reviewing the overall pattern in our countries, we are left with the strong impression that the courts' decisions are marked by a distrust of market mechanisms as a way to guarantee SE rights. Courts often require a state-backed guarantee of access to the relevant public good in the short term, rejecting arguments that market forces will make this same good available more efficiently over the long run. Examples of this distrust are court-imposed restrictions on teacher or doctor strikes;[37] limits on patent protections;[38] authorization of price control schemes[39] and other government interventions into pricing;[40] and the disapproval of privatization schemes that are supposed to enhance the supply of

---

[37] Court on its own Motion v. All India Institute of Medical Sciences (Del HC, 2001–2).

[38] The Hazel Tau decision in South Africa is one example.

[39] See the 2002 Supreme Court decision discussed in Shankar and Mehta's contribution to this volume, p. 178. The Brazilian constitutional court also upheld as constitutional a federal law that capped at the rate of inflation the rate at which private schools could increase tuition (Confederação Nacional dos Estabelecimentos de Ensino – CONFENEN v. Presidente da República e Congresso Nacional, ADIn No. 319–4 (1992)).

[41] For example, *Affordable Medicines Trust* and *New Clicks* cases in South Africa.

goods through market mechanisms.[41] In some cases, the courts stand in the way of a state retreat – the social grant cases in South Africa, for example, have acted as a brake on the attempts to reduce or limit the level of social protection in some provinces. In other cases, they require or permit the state to interfere with market processes. The Nigerian courts are the exception and have been favorably disposed to the private provision of education.

India's courts especially favor this model of SE rights litigation. Setting to one side, for the moment, the indirect effects of regulation cases, even regulation case counts are very high in India, competing with any of the other categories. There are many examples. The Indian courts have acted forcefully and effectively to improve the quality of blood supplies. They have intervened, though with far less success, in water quality cases, attempting to force state and local governments to monitor industrial waste discharge into river waters that serve urban areas.[42] As noted earlier, they have ordered commercial vehicles in Delhi and Mumbai to convert to compressed natural gas, producing a marked improvement in air quality and in the quality of life of all those with respiratory ailments in that city. When one examines the indirect effects of regulation cases, shown in the triangles in Figure 8.1, it is clear that regulation cases in India have far greater impact than direct provision cases. The South African courts have also acted to modify regulations in varied and interesting ways, though these cases have often suffered from a lack of implementation – the government has dragged its feet in drafting new regulations or legislation, as in the South African *PMA* case.[43] The Brazilian courts, by contrast, are conspicuously weak in this area, relying much more often on provision than on regulation to affect the supply of education and health goods.

In sum, in many instances in which the courts are unwilling to impose new duties of provision on the state, they will still respond to demands that a particular policy (or its absence) unduly harms the protected interests of a particular group. At times, the new approach will shift the burden of provision onto private parties; at other times, it will protect or enhance the quality of public goods. Generally speaking, and sometimes with input from specially appointed commissions, courts will require the state to monitor compliance with that directive.

Obligations Cases

In these cases, the effect of the judicial intervention sometimes heightens obligations on the part of providers and puts existing dispute resolution systems at the

---

[41] In Indonesia, the Constitutional Court struck down new water and electricity supply privatization laws, in Judicial Review of the Water Resources Law (No. 7/2004) No. 058–059–060–063/PUU-II/2004 and 008/PUU-III/2005, and Judicial Review of the Electricity Law (No. 20/2002) No. 001–021–022/PUU-I/2003, respectively.

[42] Siromani Mittasala, Chairman, Paryavarana Parirakshaka Parishad v. President, Brindavanam Colony, Welfare Association (AP HC, PIL, 2001); S. K. Garg v. Respondent: State of U.P. and Others (Al HC, PIL, 1998); Dr. K. C. Malhotra v. State of MP and Others (MP HC, PIL, 1992–93); Prasanta Kumar Rout, Orissa Law Reviews v. Respondent: Government of Orissa, represented by Secretary, Urban Development Department and Others (Or HC PIL, 1994); Suo Moto v. State of Rajasthan (Raj HC, 2004).

[43] Pharmaceutical Manufacturers' Association of South Africa v. President of the Republic of South Africa, No. 4183/98, High Court of South Africa (Transvaal Provincial Division).

service of the rights bearers. One of the crucial cases in India sounds trivial, but it has had a profound effect on doctor–patient relations: The courts determined that patients had the right to access consumer protection measures and alternative dispute resolution procedures.[44] Similarly, the story of judicial intervention into education in Nigeria is primarily, as Odinkalu puts it, the establishment and protection of "rights in education" rather than the right to education – the courts have shown solicitude for students' due process rights and for equalizing the relationship between educator and student, even when they have not done much to expand rights of access to education or the quality of the education being offered. In the health area, the Brazilian courts have intervened repeatedly in the relationship between private health insurers and their clients. Indeed, in the state of Bahia, where courts are the least interested in SE rights, this is nearly the only kind of intervention we find. Perhaps the most egregious failure to provide even this minimal level of protection is found in Indonesia. There, this task would fall to the ordinary courts rather than to the constitutional court, and we see a nearly complete judicial failure to protect the rights of patients or students. There, injured patients must resort to negotiation and compromise, under the *musyawarah* practice described by Susanti, to secure what recourse they can.

Legalization Follows Legislation

We can summarize these distinct patterns in the numbers of people affected by legal mobilization by showing that courts are not pursuing idiosyncratic preferences; rather, they are responding to and working within the dominant state model. "Indian socialism" has entailed more state planning and control than direct state provision of welfare goods, especially when considered in light of the vast need and the susceptibility of the state to interest group capture at the local level. Rudra (2007) calls this model of welfare provision a "protective welfare state," characterized by a distrust of markets, protections targeted at a relatively small formal sector labor force, and relatively low levels of welfare provision for the general population. This approach entails a relatively low share of public spending in aggregate health expenditures (Figure 8.2). At the same time, and consonant with this model, Indian court activity has been characterized by regulation, a distrust of markets, direct interventions into the provider–recipient relationship, and a relatively low share of provision cases.

Brazil and South Africa, on the other hand, both have a dominant state welfare model somewhere between Esping-Anderson's (1990) "conservative" and "social-democratic" regimes, in which state benefits are provided on the basis of organizational membership or citizenship, respectively. As the graph demonstrates, these two countries not only spend more on health than India, but spend more government money, as a share of GDP, on health care, indicating the relative importance of state provision. The Brazilian and South African courts, by focusing their

---

[44] Cosmopolitan Hospitals and Another v. Vasantha P. Nair v. V. P. Santha and Others; Dr. A. Indira Narayanan v. Government of India and Others (MANU 1993); Saroj Iyer and Another v. Maharashtra Medical of Indian Medicine, Bombay and Another (MANU 2001); T. T. Thomas v. Eliza (MANU 1986); Gurukutty v. Rajkaran (MANU 1991).

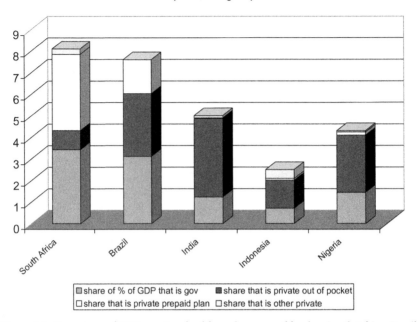

Figure 8.2. Percentage of GDP spent on health, and sources of funds – South Africa, Brazil, India, Indonesia, and Nigeria.

remedies on the direct provision of protected social goods, are enforcing a welfare state model of rights satisfaction. Indonesia and Nigeria do not have well-developed welfare regimes, and public spending on health care is low.[45] Not coincidentally, courts in those countries do not focus on provision or regulation cases. Even in obligation cases the courts at times leave recipients without a forum for effective enforcement of private law to discipline horizontal relationships, though the chapters suggest this is less a choice than a manifestation of judicial weakness. In each case, however, the courts' interventions mirror long-standing patterns of policy delivery, rather than imposing alien judicial preferences. Public interest litigation and the resultant judicial decisions, in short, reflect and work within existing policy models.

UNDERSTANDING THE EFFECTS OF LEGALIZING SOCIAL AND ECONOMIC RIGHTS: WHO BENEFITS?

Recall that legalization is the substantial incorporation of courts as relevant actors, and of legal concepts and logics as relevant arguments, into the policy-making

---

[45] As discussed in the respective chapters, Nigeria is just beginning to implement its 1999 National Health Insurance Scheme Act, whereas Indonesia ranks 106th out of 191 member countries in a WHO ranking of health-care provision.

and implementation process. We have shown that certain policy areas in certain countries have become legalized to a substantial degree, even though, of course, the legislative and executive branches remain leading decision makers in these areas. It is difficult to understand the everyday workings, limitations, and possibilities of the Brazilian universal health-care system, for example, without taking into consideration the role the courts have played in that area. Any discussion of HIV/AIDS policy in South Africa must include a discussion of the role of the courts and the discourse of health rights, even as it must present the point–counterpoint of executive and legislative responses to judicial and civil society initiatives. The question of minority-language rights in education in South Africa is inextricably linked to the – still muddled – jurisprudence of the courts. Although Indian public health care and education are only tangentially affected by the Supreme Court's interpretation of the right to health and the right to life, many questions of environmental quality and policy, as well as food distribution, are defined in terms of their impact on these rights. Even in Indonesia, where courts are either silent or negative on most issues, the Constitutional Court has become an essential part of the annual debate over the budget for public education. In sum, legalization (which may or may not reflect what others have called judicialization) is not a mirage, though it does not happen everywhere, and it does not happen in the way many scholars have imagined, as we have tried to make clear throughout.

But the more important question is, to what end? Who benefits when courts and legal language become necessary aspects of the policy debate, formulation, and implementation process? Is this merely an elite game that only serves to further concentrate resources and government services among the upper reaches of society, leaving less and less for the have-nots?

There are two principal mechanisms through which increased legalization might have a regressive effect on the distribution of public goods. The first is *beneficiary inequality*, in which courts get to determine who benefits from nominally universal programs. If it is true that only the wealthy have access to the courts and, therefore, only they will directly benefit from judicial allocations, then in this scenario the courts would be acting as a rationing device for services that are nominally available to all but in practice accessible only to those who can afford lawyers and litigation. The second is *policy area inequality*, in which the wealthy use the courts as a mechanism to focus the government's attention on issues that are important to the wealthy and to block the government's efforts to focus on issues that are important to the poor majority. In this case, the courts would have the effect of shaping the overall policy offering of the state so that it disproportionately benefits "legally enfranchised" elites.[46]

---

[46] Note that both of these mechanisms rest on the assumption that elites have more privileged access to courts than to the other branches of government, an assumption that may not always be warranted. Marxist critiques of democracy made similar claims about the state and "bourgeois democracy" more generally. And Terry Karl has made the argument that the maldistribution of political power in Latin America has led to policies that disproportionately favor the wealthy: "High [economic] inequalities bias the political rules of the game and mold polities in favor of the wealthy and privileged," producing public policies that disproportionately favor the powerful (Karl 2003: 136, *passim*).

In fact, of course, we do not have conclusive evidence of the *overall* effect of legalization on the distribution of public goods in a society. Dworkin confidently claims that, because of judicial review, "the United States is a more just society than it would have been had its constitutional rights been left to the conscience of majoritarian institutions" (Dworkin 1986: 356). This implies, of course, greater confidence in the judicial conscience than in the representative one, and it is far from a self-evident claim. Just as Dworkin offers no proof to support his claim, it is difficult to support empirically the claim that more (or fewer) people have better access to higher quality health care or education in, say, India because the courts have become a viable demand mechanism than they would have if India had strictly observed parliamentary supremacy over the last fifty years. It is even harder to prove that quality health care and education are more (or less) equitably distributed in India than they would have been without judicial intervention.

We can, however, make a series of more modest claims based on the evidence presented here. It seems likely that some modes of legalization – those which, like Brazil, rely to a greater extent on individual cases and narrow remedies and to a lesser extent on state or other organized litigation support structures – carry greater risk of producing beneficiary inequality, given that litigation is typically concentrated in urban, more affluent regions. But in India and South Africa the vast majority of direct and especially indirect beneficiaries are among the poorest members of society. As to policy area inequality, legalization has produced great benefits for groups that could hardly be considered privileged, such as Indian primary school students at greatest risk of dropping out, or HIV-positive pregnant women in South Africa. And it is clear that the courts have not favored powerful economic interests, at least in the context of these rights-based claims. The Indian and South African courts have repeatedly shifted burdens for rights satisfaction onto large multinational corporations, and the Brazilian courts have imposed ever greater burdens on private health care insurers. Especially in litigation where indirect effects dominate direct effects, the benefits of legalization reach far beyond the more privileged groups in society, crossing demographic and geographic divides.

The Direct Beneficiaries

If we simply look at who sues, it seems quite clear that, with important exceptions, the direct beneficiaries of litigation typically are neither the most disadvantaged nor the wealthiest citizens. On the one hand, the truly wealthy withdraw from public services and rarely use litigation to seek public goods. They benefit primarily when they use courts to block state nationalization of private goods – when the state seeks to close private schools and universities in Nigeria or desegregate minority-language schools in South Africa, for example. There are a few cases that could be seen as attempts to use the language of rights to insulate the wealthy from redistributive policies enacted by representative policy makers – minority-language education cases in South Africa, litigation challenging the quota system for higher education in India, and corporate attempts to use the courts to resist antimarket drug policies in South Africa. But these attempts have met with mixed success at best; they often delay implementation but ultimately fail. There is virtually no evidence that wealthy elites are hijacking courts or the discourse of SE rights to preserve their status.

At the other extreme, there is little evidence of legalization coming from or directly benefiting the deeply marginalized. The destitute, the truly marginal and remote, who have little or no access to public health and public education, also have little access to public legal or judicial services or to organized civil society. The rural population of Nigeria, the remote villagers of Indonesia, the slum and shantytown dwellers in all these countries, and the inhabitants of the rural northeast of Brazil are relatively absent from the roll of litigants. The northern Nigerian state of Kaduna recorded no cases at all seeking to vindicate SE rights. There is, perhaps, only one deeply marginalized and politically powerless group that consistently benefits from judicial protection – the imprisoned. The courts have typically been quite solicitous of their claims, either requiring the state to provide health benefits directly, as in South Africa, or at minimum requiring that they be released to pursue their own private health care (though some of the prisoners released for health reasons in Nigeria were, in fact, influential political elites). But this is the exception that proves the rule. This is a population that is, by definition, in contact with the legal system and, therefore, that has more of an opportunity to present a claim. As to the rest, it is to some extent self-evident that a person who has little or no access to state educational or health services will have limited access to legal and judicial services. Litigation, then, is an unlikely bootstrap for raising oneself from absolute need.

Most of the direct activity, as a result, comes from somewhere in the middle of the social spectrum. Cases of all kinds, in all the countries our collaborators examined, are concentrated in wealthy rather than poor states; this is clearly true in Brazil, India, and Nigeria, as already discussed.[47] Similarly, in India and Brazil, where information was available, cases were concentrated in urban, not rural, areas. Litigants also tended to be middle class. In India provision and obligation cases tended to involve those who had government jobs or private health insurance; in Brazil, a number of litigants were using privately retained attorneys, and many other middle class litigants were using free public legal services under the expansive definition of "indigence" used in many states. Even the difference between levels of litigation in health versus education can be explained this way: The middle and upper middle classes still rely on public health services, especially for tertiary care and certain pharmaceuticals; but education litigation focuses not on basic education, where the middle class is absent, but on higher education, where we still find wealthier students. The primary direct beneficiaries of legalization, then, are likely to be the middle class residents of modernized, urban settings who have at least passing knowledge of legal procedures and access to legal processes. And, for the same reason, there appears to be a tendency to emphasize issues that matter to these groups.

---

[47] In Indonesia and South Africa, the fact that the constitutional courts are centralized means that cases are filed in national capitals, often by national organizations with primary residence in those large urban areas. But this does not necessarily imply that they are being filed on behalf of metropolitan populations, as we see immediately in the following.

There are, however, significant exceptions to this pattern in both health and education policy. In Brazil, public defenders and sometimes public prosecutors undertake medication cases for the direct benefit of the least privileged. Their success rate on behalf of indigent plaintiffs in individual cases, especially at the implementation stage, may be higher than that of the middle class, as Hoffman and Bentes point out. In South Africa, *Grootboom* was brought on behalf of a squatter community; the social grants cases were brought on behalf of the disabled and those with dependents; and the Treatment Action Campaign mounted an important litigation campaign on behalf of all those living with HIV/AIDS, who are, Berger points out, "heavily stigmatized" and "disproportionately poor." The South African, Brazilian, and even Nigerian courts have taken a clear stance in favor of critically ill prison inmates. The Nunukan litigation in Indonesia, although formally unsuccessful, nevertheless produced important benefits for thousands of homeless migrants stranded in a refugee camp on a remote island near Malaysia. All these cases were undertaken with private charitable or public support and benefited some of the most marginalized populations in each country.

We see similarly important exceptions in the education area. In India, one of the critical interventions of the courts in the education area was the expansion of the free midday meals program, whose benefits accrued most importantly to the most needy, and which has drawn disadvantaged children, especially poor girls, into the educational system. In Indonesia, the courts' signature interventions have sought to increase funding for public education, which in principle benefits all school-age children regardless of income and may improve services in the neediest areas. To the extent it fails to produce a more egalitarian public education system, it will not be the fault of the Indonesian courts but of the representative branches who translate the budgetary mandate into actual programs. It is clearly not the case, then, that the direct effects of legalization are limited to the elites or even to the middle class. With support from state legal aid offices or organized civil society, marginalized populations often receive benefits they would otherwise be denied.

The Indirect Beneficiaries

More important, the results of this research fully validate a statement we made in the introduction: Whatever the direct effects of legalization, they are vastly overshadowed by its indirect effects. Those affected by public-policy initiatives triggered in one way or another by litigation vastly outnumber the people who benefit directly from the execution of a targeted judicial remedy. Drawing on data about the impact of legalization, described earlier, in Table 8.2 we divided our estimate of the number of people who benefited indirectly by litigation by the number of people who obtained a direct judicial remedy to get the ratio of indirect to direct beneficiaries. Clearly, the civil law system in Brazil means less generalization of the benefits of legalization. Even there, however, nearly twenty similarly situated people benefit for every one that can bring a claim. The more public-policy, *erga omnes*–oriented jurisdictions like India or South Africa produce

Table 8.2. *Number of people benefited
indirectly for every person benefited directly*

	Health	Education
Brazil	17	1
India	13,195	1,696
Indonesia	201	42,775
South Africa	521	51
Nigeria	8	309

vastly higher levels of generalization and therefore produce benefits for many more who may not have the resources to litigate. The high numbers for Indonesia and Nigeria in education are similarly the product of decisions that affect the entire educational system.

More qualitative evaluations tell a similar story. AIDS litigation in Brazil was spearheaded by the relatively well-off and still originates primarily in more affluent states, but the innovations introduced by the judiciary were quickly incorporated into the public health system and spread to many others who have never brought a legal claim. A prolonged series of private cases regarding more than one hundred medications in Rio de Janeiro eventually led to a successful public class action brought by prosecutors that made the same benefits available to all who have access to the public health system. A similar pattern has recently emerged in the southeastern state of Rio Grande do Sul, where the public prosecutor has entered into an agreement to monitor the implementation of medications policies throughout the state. Litigation prompted the Indian government to create an antiretroviral distribution program to benefit at least ten thousand AIDS patients; and litigation compelled the South African government to roll out its antiretroviral AIDS treatment program much sooner than it would otherwise have done. There is evidence of considerable indirect effects even when legalization is otherwise weak. When a few university students managed to work their way through the legal process in Nigeria to gain due process rights in expulsion proceedings, the ruling prompted that and other universities to adopt similar standards for expulsion proceedings. Although *Grootboom* did not lead to a long-term solution to the housing needs of the Wallacedene community, it led to the establishment of emergency housing funds in many municipalities and was used to protect large numbers of informal settlers from eviction orders.[48] When we examine the effect of legalization, then, we must consider the indirect effects as much as the direct ones.

The key point is that indirect effects are much less tied to the initial endowment of the claimant. As all the examples in the previous paragraph suggest, the results of broad-based patterns of litigation claiming individual remedies, as well as of particular cases asserting collective rights, are often picked up by the other branches

---

[48] See, e.g., the discussion at http://www.escr-net.org/caselaw/caselaw_show.htm?doc_id = 401409.

and converted into public policy through legislation or other modifications to the legal framework. Once the results generalize through the ordinary public-policy mechanisms, of course, they are subject to the same advantages and disadvantages that exist in the public-policy system already. The Brazilian public health system spends more and is stronger in wealthier southern cities than in northeastern rural areas; "leakage" in Indian antipoverty schemes is notorious; and many Nigerian students remain at the mercy of powerful social and political patrons regardless of official university policies on due process. But to the extent these results are unequally distributed, this is a function of the policy structure and policy biases already in place – a function, in other words, of the ordinary politics of the country, rather than a consequence of the nature of litigation.

Are these benefits to the poor the exception or the rule? Can we draw an overall conclusion about the tendency of litigation to produce a more or less egalitarian distribution of health care or education goods? Whereas an enumeration of the sources and subjects of litigation might suggest a clear tendency to favor those who already have access to some level of services, a rough overview of the cases with the greatest impact suggests the poor are at least as likely to benefit. Cases like the Indonesian school-funding cases, the South African nevirapine case, the Indian cooked-midday-meals cases benefit most those who fall far below even a middle class standard of living.

Policy Area Inequality

It is appropriate to mention, however, that some varieties of legalization seem more prone to regressive effects than others. Privately funded individual litigation, of course, poses the highest risk of exacerbating inequality. The high volume of medication litigation in Brazil, for example, operates at times as a rationing device, in which claims are denied to all except those who have the resources to retain a private lawyer or the initiative to engage (and the good fortune to live near) a public lawyer. It is true that some of the benefits of this activity still reach the poor when the medication formularies in the public health system are updated, which happens more regularly for HIV/AIDS than for many other diseases. Still, one cannot help being concerned that the large numbers of private demands tend toward de-universalizing the public health system. Even if we grant the basic premise of this litigation – that the courts are simply requiring public servants to do what they are required by law to do – we must still be concerned that the law will benefit only those who litigate, or at least move them to the front of the queue. Collective claims and indirect effects, on the other hand, by their very nature, tend to spread the benefits beyond the immediate litigants, following the more traditional logic of public policy distribution.

This might suggest that policy makers should encourage institutions that promote collective claims and remedies, and the efficient translation of judicial decisions into legislative or quasi-legislative status – in other words, they should promote the universalization of the particular policies identified by courts. Brazil's *ação civil pública*, India's public interest litigation and broad public-policy remedies, South Africa's binding precedent, and Indonesia's abstract constitutional challenges to legislation are all mechanisms to accomplish precisely that. But this assumes the courts know which issues need to be addressed. And this assumption brings into sharp focus the second potentially regressive effect of legalization, policy area inequality. Is it the case that legalization draws the attention of the policy machinery to the preferred issues of an elite group or a privileged minority? If so, the universalization of judicial decisions is precisely the wrong direction to take. The researchers in this volume have certainly uncovered examples that raise this concern, which we described earlier: a focus on higher rather than lower levels of health care and education, on formal rather than informal sector beneficiaries, on private rather than public school choice of schooling, on equal protection used in a way to promote the interests of Afrikaners and higher castes rather than the excluded, for instance.

On the other hand, we have already mentioned plenty of examples of cases and policies that benefit the marginalized: midday meals in Indian public schools, clean water for the urban poor in Delhi, effective treatment for the millions living with HIV/AIDS in South Africa, a safe blood supply for anyone seeking emergency medical care in India. There have been strong rulings in favor of social assistance rights in South Africa. There have been cases on health services for homeless refugees in Indonesia and education rights for asylum seekers in South Africa. And there have been rulings against child labor, in favor of more teachers in public schools, in favor of price controls, and against stronger patent protections for drug manufacturers in India and South Africa. The courts have been instrumental in all these, and they are far from the pet projects of economic and social elites.

It is hard to calculate the net effect of all these examples, especially when we consider the programs that go unsupported by litigation campaigns: unheralded epidemics of childhood diarrhea and malaria, high rates of health worker and teacher absenteeism in Indian clinics and schools, and the like. At the same time, as we saw earlier, in terms of numbers of people benefited, the "protection of privilege" cases tend to lose, and those that win tend to benefit a mere handful of people. Moreover, the cases that benefit the poor tend to encompass a vast number of beneficiaries. This finding surely calls into question the assumption that the courts, in the social and economic rights area at least, are the instrument of elites, for the conservation of privilege. Rather, it appears that rights and courts, whatever the original intent, have become political resources that can be appropriated by anyone, to contest policies that in one way or another appear to impinge on interests protected by the language of rights. And the most successful claims are those that garner the support of well-organized civil society actors like TAC in South Africa, or large numbers of citizens, like the threatened middle class in Brazil.

We have not addressed the large, looming question of general equilibrium effects and the impacts on long-run growth and poverty. In other words, if the courts, in fact, succeed in increasing expenditures and/or policy focus on health care and education, what is the opportunity cost for, say, infrastructure, which is also important for growth and poverty? Obviously, this touches on the large debate on the impact of welfare spending and social transfers on growth.[49] As to this, we can respond only that the laws, by incorporating certain rights and not others, express a primary commitment not to let certain issues languish even as the country pursues other undeniably important interests. Ultimately, then, the justification when the courts strike down water privatization laws in Indonesia, patent protections in South Africa, or price controls in India, is that they are taking antimarket stances to protect basic rights in the short term, and that other means must be found to promote economic development without imposing unbearable short-term hazards to basic rights protected in constitutions.

ON THE ROLE OF COURTS IN DEMOCRACIES

We do not have the information, nor have we modeled a counterfactual, to determine whether there is more or less inequality, more or less human suffering in the presence of legalization. An example from a country that is not the subject of this research is illustrative of the difficulties inherent in such an enterprise. As we noted in the introduction, in Costa Rica, a single decision by the Constitutional Chamber of the Supreme Court led to an 80 percent reduction in mortality rates among AIDS patients. The other side of the coin, of course, is that the public health system now spends 8 percent of its medication budget to treat 0.012 percent of its patients. What exactly were the opportunity costs of the decision, and did legalization lead to a net improvement in health outcomes or human welfare? All the empirical and theoretical difficulties that attend the utilitarian calculus of the greatest good for the greatest number, including assumptions regarding the quality of life, the displacement of private expenditures, the discount rate, and the private and public value of life, are present here.

Neither the critics nor the advocates of the justiciability of SE rights have persuasively tackled, let alone answered, this question. Instead the debate tends to pit critics who contend that courts do not have the democratic legitimacy to make these substantive allocations against advocates who argue that the courts are merely making effective the rights that the (usually) democratic process of constitution- or law- or rule-making has identified as most basic, most important. Which of these is right is again a question without an easy empirical answer. But our research can answer some questions that lie near the heart of this normative debate even if we cannot resolve the main issue head on. These questions bring us to the role courts play in enforcing social and economic rights in a democracy.

The first of these questions is, are the courts "usurping" or displacing the decision-making function of more representative policy-making bodies or squelching democratic debate about the content and actualization of rights? Vallinder argues that "judicialization" means "the expansion of the province of the courts *at the expense of* the politicians and/or the administrators, that is, *the transfer of decision-making rights from the legislature, the cabinet, or the civil service to the courts*" (Tate and Vallinder 1995: 13; emphasis ours). Similarly, Tushnet argues

---

[49] Peter Lindert (2004) reviews available studies and presents estimations arguing that there is little long-term relationship, negative or positive, between social welfare spending and growth.

that, by definition, when courts find a constitutional violation of SE rights, they "displace legislative judgments about how social policies should be ranked" (Tushnet 2004: 1897 [he will go on to argue that by adopting weak remedies, this displacement can be kept to a minimum]). Waldron makes a similar objection. In his view, enshrining rights in constitutions and giving courts the capacity to enforce them is tantamount to "taking [those] issues away from the people" (Waldron 1993: 50). And Tate's theory of where judicialization is most likely to happen (where judges least share the political orientation of the politicians that surround them) is premised on the same assumption that judges are displacing or substituting for the elected branches (Tate and Vallinder 1995: 34–36 and Table 3.1).

It should be clear by now that this does not accurately describe most of what we observe. What we see and what we have described as "legalization" is not so much the courts closing off debate in more representative venues as it is adding another venue for debate. What we observe is not the courts substituting their own judgment for a legislative one, but rather injecting new concerns into a debate or perhaps foregrounding goals derived from constitutional or legislative concerns. In other cases, we see them appointing commissions to devise plans, then monitoring while legislatures and private parties decide how to integrate these goals and concerns into their decision-making process. Whether their intervention results in the iterative crafting of a remedy, as in South Africa, or in an ongoing annual dialogue between the Constitutional Court and the Indonesian Parliament on the education budget, the courts have become not *the exclusive* but *an additional* place for deliberation and debate. They have become not the last word on issues that affect SE rights, but another interlocutor. And they are most consequential not when they most oppose other branches, but when they work in congress with them. Legalization, when it meets these conditions, is democracy by other means.

Neither is the purported nonnegotiable, nontransferable logic and language of rights preempting discussions about the allocation of resources across competing goods. The courts occasionally adopt language that raises this issue: when they support medications claims, some courts in Brazil expressly renounce any consideration of budgetary trade-offs – if the remedy is due, they argue, the government will simply have to find a way to fund it and everything else too. But the background to this is a profound distrust of government's claimed inability to fund its own legislatively enacted mandate and a reasonable belief that more efficient allocations are possible. And everywhere, to the frustration of claimants and advocates, we see a proliferation of devices for avoiding judicially created financial debacles. In Brazil the courts have avoided ordering large-scale remedies to collective claims, ostensibly fearing the budgetary implications of following the language of rights to its logical conclusion. In South Africa, where collective claims and remedies are most prevalent, the courts have explicitly adopted the progressive realization logic that so frustrates activists. In India, where the need is great and resources few, the courts have emphasized the state's regulatory function over state-funded direct provision of social goods. And in Indonesia, the court refused either to invalidate the budget or to arrogate to itself the decision-making rights on that subject by drafting a new one. As noted in the discussion of compliance issues, remedies often take on an "experimentalist" or dialogical character that allows for the evolution of public policy under the direction of policy makers, but with stakeholder participation and judicial oversight.

A related objection, that SE rights become too costly when courts begin enforcing them, rests on the implicit assumption that courts will order states to undertake ever greater obligations to meet ever greater demands (Tushnet 2004: 1896). But two or three decades after Brazilian and Indian courts began enforcing SE rights and more than one decade after the new South African constitution, courts in all those countries have yet to make any health or education decisions of macroeconomic consequence.[50] Courts have been exceedingly cautious, many would argue excessively cautious, in imposing undue burdens on the state. And what we have seen here is that although the courts often do require the state to do more in terms of health care or education, their more consequential incursions involve regulation, not more state spending. Where they most actively extract expenditures from the state, as in Brazil, they do so with the tacit approval of many state officials, and rarely venture much above an unspecified but well understood budgetary ceiling.

Another necessary piece of many critics' argument is that the courts are unelected and therefore unrepresentative or countermajoritarian actors who should not be making important political decisions. As we have seen throughout, however, the courts are, in very important ways and to differing degrees, responsive to and dependent on both public opinion and the support of the allegedly more representative branches. The lower courts in Brazil are less responsive, the higher courts more so; the courts in India seem to be quite autonomous, whereas the courts in Nigeria are clearly less so. But what we see is that the courts' dependence on political and social actors for enforcement and implementation, not to speak of their very existence, means judges rarely stray too far from the political mainstream. They are seldom unaccountable or countermajoritarian in any strong sense of these words (often, it must be said, to the chagrin of those who care about the enforcement and realization of SE rights). We return to this issue later.

Moreover, even when most autonomous, courts hew quite closely to a legislative script. The courts will occasionally, as in the Indian case, work out extensive implications from vague statements about the "right to life." But for the most part, they much prefer to work from more specific policy frameworks. As Shankar and Mehta point out, the Indian courts have focused more on compliance with the existing legal framework than on crafting a new framework or even addressing its shortcomings. Substantially all the cases of successful legalization follow on, rather than precede, the legislative creation of more or less detailed and comprehensive policy frameworks – litigation follows legislation. The courts then work interstitially on

---

[50] Courts in Brazil, Argentina, Colombia, and Hungary have all made it difficult for governments to roll back social security benefits. These decisions have affected macroeconomic debates. But these are exceptions that prove the rule: Note that in doing so these courts have still relied on previously existing constitutional and legislative texts, and have been preserving existing entitlements, rather than creating new, expensive mandates. See Rios-Figueroa and Taylor (2006), Scheppele (2004), Smulovitz (2005), and Taylor (2008).

those frameworks to ensure that certain overlooked interests are protected, rather than creating policy from scratch.

This is, perhaps, the most important point to glean from this research. When the courts go off on quixotic projects of their own (as they occasionally do in India) or when they respond to narrow sectoral interests (as one could characterize some of the "own language" education cases in South Africa), they are least likely to secure the support they need, and they will have at best individual, direct effects. But when the courts work jointly with the other branches of government and the state, then their decisions are often picked up and amplified by various generalizing devices – legislation; bureaucratic rule changes; voluntary compliance; negotiated, programmatic solutions. The key point is that courts can accomplish very little on their own. For effectiveness, they require partners, whose identity might vary from issue to issue, as we will see later, and who must provide the courts the political weight they require to generate at minimum grudging and at best expansive compliance with judicial directives. Because of this and because courts are strategic actors interested in maintaining or expanding their influence, they largely refuse to undertake politically unrealistic projects. Activists, in turn, are aware of this and decline to press legal claims that have little chance of winning. Legalization, like legislation, is as much a collaborative as an adversarial enterprise.

This conclusion could well prompt critics like Rosenberg (1991: 22–24 and Chap. 2) to argue that, in that case, the courts are really superfluous, and anything they could accomplish can be done more efficiently, more effectively, and with less risk to representative politics by working through the other branches of government. Certainly, as Waldron (1993) points out, it is not the case that courts are *more* representative than the other branches. This brings us to the question of what legalization adds to the democratic process, which we raised in the introduction, and an account of the conditions under which the courts can meaningfully contribute, in the area of social and economic rights, something beyond what the other branches offer.

Some of the conditions for effective representative politics are the same as the conditions for effective judicial politics. There is clear evidence in the various country chapters that substantial modernization is at least a necessary condition for legal mobilization and consequently for legalization – litigation clusters around more developed, more affluent, more urban and modernized areas. There is also evidence that legalization flourishes most in places where democracy is best expressed. Rio de Janeiro and Rio Grande do Sul, by most accounts, have more democratic, more participatory institutions than Bahia. Nigeria, in particular, has struggled to secure democratic politics during the period of this study, with clear consequences for its judicial system. Why, then, do we see the legalization of politics in precisely the more fully democratic polities? Why resort to the courts exactly when representative institutions become more responsive and populations become more capable of participating?

As noted in the introduction, various authors, most of them in the context of the United States Supreme Court, have made different arguments for the function of courts in a democratic political system. Our own analysis of the courts' role in SE law and policy in these five countries demonstrates that the courts, indeed, do add something important and different to the policy-making process, precisely when they are working together with one or more of the other players in that process. Moreover, our comparative analysis suggests that the courts do not have a single role to play but rather several roles, unified, perhaps, by a common logic.

Based primarily on studies of the U.S. and Israeli Supreme Courts, we had expressed a theoretical expectation that courts might solve political roadblocks, becoming more active when political actors were stymied by political fragmentation or unruly coalitions. Sable and Simon (2004) describe and defend the same "immunity to political correction" precondition to judicial intervention, and Dixon describes "inertia" in the legislative process that courts can usefully overcome (2007: 402–403). But we have seen very little evidence of this. In the first place, the courts act most often after a legislative intervention – again, litigation follows legislation. Even in Brazil, where legislative politics is notoriously fractious, the courts play an important role in updating the public-health offerings, but it is not clear that they are solving a lawmaking impasse. Their avoidance of collective remedies and skepticism of collective claims suggests, rather, that the more public-policy-like their intervention would be, the less they like it.

Similarly, it is difficult to account for the activism of the Indian Supreme Court or the South African courts using these arguments. The ANC dominates all levels of politics in South Africa; the country is hardly a case of a fragmented political system. The impasses over HIV/AIDS policy that led to court cases were not the result of an inability of the political system to pass legislation altogether, even in the area of HIV/AIDS. Rather, they resulted from an accountability deficit, a question to which we turn in a moment. Similarly, when the Indian Supreme Court launched its career in SE rights enforcement in the early 1980s, national politics was still characterized by Congress Party majorities (with the exception of the period in the immediate aftermath of the emergency), and there were already a number of laws on the books regarding basic social and economic policies. Again, deadlocked lawmaking was not the obstacle that prompted the courts to respond. In fact, in both the current South Africa and, until the early 1990s, in India, it has been precisely the monopoly power of the dominant parties that many observers blame for the failures of legislative oversight regarding executive branch economic and social policy making. An exception to this generally negative finding on the role of legalization in resolving political roadblocks, and one that may well increase in the future, is the involvement of South African courts on pharmaceutical policy, an area in which globalized markets might be making it too costly, and too politically difficult, for the governments to respond to health demands.

The courts' principal roles seem to involve, rather, what we earlier referred to as fire-alarm monitoring and the resolution of incomplete commitments. In the first case, courts serve an information-generating function that facilitates the accountability of the various parts of the state (or even private providers) to each other, using formal rights and their judicial gloss as yardsticks. When the courts intervene in the state–provider relationship, that function often involves solving agency drift or bringing private providers in line with national requirements. Here the courts are the partner of the national executive and legislature. When they rule in provision cases, they sometimes bring lower-level or state bureaucracies in line with stated national policy (or occasionally empower local officials to widen national policies); in either case, they again claim as partners the policy designers. When they appear to be expanding the program, rather than merely enforcing its provisions, they are most often working out logical extensions, or bringing the program to bear on overlooked but similarly situated beneficiaries. Their partners here are often the bureaucrats themselves, who are struggling to apply a delimited program to a set of ambiguously included beneficiaries. And when they decide on obligations cases, they prevent power inequities in provider–recipient relationships from frustrating the goals of enabling legislation or regulation.

A series of examples will illustrate these points:

- Brazil's medication litigation regularly highlights places where the list of publicly provided or publicly reimbursable drugs falls behind pharmaceutical advances (Hoffman and Bentes, pp. 130, 137, 140). In these cases, courts are monitoring the extent to which executive agencies are updating services, as foreseen in national legislation.
- In South Africa we see courts, particularly in the social grants cases, bringing provincial and lower-level bureaucracies to account by spotlighting officials who are not in compliance with national policies (Berger, p. 50). This is consistent with Shapiro (1981), who long ago suggested that courts are, inter alia, instruments that impose a national, unifying body of law in exchange for intervening in otherwise unequal local relations of power, especially in cases involving local authorities. But courts sometimes prefer local to central governments as partners: the Indonesian Constitutional Court partnered with a locality against the central government in allowing local governments to develop their own social security programs (Susanti, p. 246).
- In a few cases in Brazil, we see them identifying public health facilities whose services fail legislated standards (Hoffman and Bentes, p. 124). In India, they identified health care providers and universities that failed to meet national certification and public service standards (Shankar and Mehta, pp. 158, 172).
- In both India and South Africa, the courts have pointed out places where lax regulation of drug suppliers clashed with an apparent constitutional commitment to accessible health care (Shankar and Mehta, p. 158; Berger, pp. 56–60). In India, the courts directed and empowered pollution boards to enforce environmental standards more strictly (Shankar and Mehta, p. 174).
- A classical role for courts, and one in which they assist national policy makers, is the adjudication of conflicting constitutionally and legislatively enacted liberties. In India, the courts have attempted to reconcile the right to strike on the part of providers with the broader social right to service provision (Shankar and Mehta, pp. 160, 170). And in South Africa, they have balanced the rights of informal settlers to housing against the property rights of landowners (Berger, pp. 48–49).

The other crucial role for courts in democracies is what we referred to in the introduction as the resolution of incomplete commitments. Particularly in developing countries, there exists a dissonance between shared, universalistic discourses supporting constitutional and political aspirations for "social justice" or "human dignity" on the one hand, and the clientelistic and particularistic exchanges used to construct and maintain political order, on the other. Social and political actors are all generally aware of these dissonances; but for any given claim, they may not possess specific knowledge whether the fulfillment of aspirations is economically, politically, and technically feasible. It is often in the interest of political elites, moreover, to hide the true cost of fulfilling universalistic commitments so that public expenditures can continue to be used for narrow partisan or sectarian agendas. Courts provide a forum in which information regarding the feasibility of specific social and economic claims can be investigated. In this scenario, courts ally with the organized public. This form of partnership can be particularly attractive for courts because it enhances their own legitimacy and standing. As a result, when working in this manner, courts tend to be particularly drawn to highly charged and emotional issues. Again, a series of examples will help illustrate this function of the courts.

- South African courts helped adjudicate the government's claim that new AIDS treatments would be too difficult, dangerous, or costly (Berger, pp. 54–55), and brought HIV/AIDS policies in line with a general commitment to public health measures and commonly accepted scientific knowledge.
- In a series of orders on the right to food, the Indian Supreme Court reviewed existing government food distribution schemes, and agreed with the petitioners that inefficiencies, rather than a lack of funds, prevented wider coverage.[51]
- The Indonesian Constitutional Court's findings triggered a recurring national debate on the appropriate level of educational expenditures in light of strong constitutional language mandating minimum spending for that purpose (Susanti, pp. 258–261).
- The Indian Supreme Court, through its cases regarding the potential conversion of commercial vehicles in Delhi to compressed natural gas, developed an impartial authority to assess the technical feasibility of conversion, which was opaque to nonexperts.[52]
- In some cases, the Brazilian courts assess the affordability of medications claims against local governments (Hoffmann and Bentes, p. 121).
- The South African (Berger, pp. 56–60) and Indian cases (Shankar and Mehta, p. 178) related to medicine pricing involved an examination of claims that pharmaceutical producers and distributors were charging excessive prices, even allowing for substantial profits.

In sum, the evidence from the various countries supports the claim that courts can solve accountability deficits between policy makers and those who carry out their policies, whether (public) bureaucracies or (private) regulated industries, by delegating monitoring and enforcement to private litigants. They can also solve

---

[51] See the interim orders on the right to food, available at the Right to Food Campaign Web site: http://www.righttofoodindia.org/orders/interimorders.html
[52] See Ruth Greenspan Bell et al, Clearing the air: How Delhi broke the logjam on air quality reforms, *Environment* 46(3), April 3, 2004, available at http://www.usaid.gov/in/Pdfs/Clearing-the-Air-Environment-Magazine.pdf.

accountability problems between publics and policy makers, when the latter's decision making in one area noticeably clashes with the general principles and sentiments expressed in constitutional or legislative acts, especially strongly felt or emotionally charged ones. And, given that courts need allies if they are to be effective, we should expect them to be most effective in those areas in which the normal democratic divisions of power create the greatest number of potential partners with actual political influence.

SHOULD SOCIAL AND ECONOMIC RIGHTS BE JUSTICIABLE? SOME NORMATIVE CONSIDERATIONS

Whereas this book has primarily analyzed the conditions for, and the impact of, legalizing demand for social and economic rights, the country chapters have touched on several important normative issues. Every one deserves an account, maybe a book, of its own. Here we touch on them very briefly.

Basic legal services remain largely unavailable for the poorest segments of most societies. Increasing access for the poor could help more of their concerns reach the courts and could reduce inequalities in the benefits that follow implementation. Second, because collective claims have a greater likelihood of benefiting a wider swath of society than individual claims, it would likely be equity-promoting to encourage and strengthen civil society actors and autonomous public-sector litigant organizations. Nevertheless, the key bottlenecks in the countries studied in this book appear to involve supply-side obstacles, rather than the litigation support structure. Therefore, third, unlocking procedural obstacles involving standing and petition rules, and/or shifting the burden of proof in certain constitutional cases, as in the Indian PIL or the Costa Rican Constitutional Chamber, would likely lead to a significant increase in SE rights claims that reach the courts. Fourth, although courts have made SE rights decisions involving all three categories – provision, regulation, and obligations – the last area may be the most significant in the future. There is substantially more scope for courts to interpret horizontal tort law and other civil disputes among private parties in light of constitutional social and economic rights. The preceding chapter by Hershkoff explores this issue in some detail. Fifth, laws and constitutional provisions regarding the freedom of information have had a reciprocally important relationship with social and economic rights: Those laws have greatly facilitated legal demands for social and economic rights and have, in turn, been reinterpreted in light of basic social and economic constitutional guarantees. Sixth, a nonpartisan judicial appointment process would promote the emergence of courts with the independence to hold public actors accountable for legislative and constitutional commitments. At the same time, political skill in judges is important because judicial activity in the area of SE rights emerges as a dialogical process in which courts aim primarily to persuade political actors, rather than coerce them. Finally, judicial competence in certain technical areas, such as educational quality and budgetary trade-offs, seems to limit both the emergence of certain kinds of cases and the accountability role of courts in those areas; so changes in judicial training or selection that reflect this likely caseload, or even the development of specialized courts, would be useful.

At this point, some readers will undoubtedly think that the preceding paragraph has skirted the largest question, the real elephant in the room: Should courts be allowed to adjudicate SE rights claims in the first place? As we mentioned at the outset, this has been a long-running and heated question in legal and political circles. For purposes of that controversy, the main lesson from this book is that the desirability of justiciable social and economic rights is not a problem that can be addressed, nor indeed should be posed, generically. Because the characteristics of a country's legal and political landscape interact significantly with the numbers and kinds of claims that arise once social and economic rights are made justiciable, as well as on the impact and distributional benefits of those claims, a general answer is simply not useful.

In some ways, this lesson mirrors developments in other areas of the social sciences. For instance, it was once thought crucial to answer whether it would be desirable for countries to move from presidential to parliamentary systems, or vice versa. But more recently, it has become clear that interactions with other features of the institutional landscape – federalism, the party system, political culture – dominate the direct effects of executive structure on governance. Similarly, the effects of making SE rights justiciable depend crucially on institutional factors beyond the constitutional text, its interpretations, and the forms of remedies that courts choose to adopt. This book has described many of these institutional characteristics, including the overall litigation support structure in a society, the cross-sectoral strengths and weaknesses of civil society advocacy organizations, the procedural and physical accessibility of courts, judicial recruitment and attitudes and probity, prevailing interpretations of certain civil and political rights, national patterns in the provision of basic services, and latent policy capacity. This chapter and the introduction have analyzed some of the patterns of interaction among these institutional characteristics and the outcomes that matter. But, clearly, much more needs to be done, and not least is expanding the analysis to other countries and other rights.

The second principal lesson from this book is that many of the bugaboos thought to be associated with social and economic rights adjudication – imperial judges, runaway deficits, crumbling democratic faith – are just that, bogeymen. Judges depend on the state far too much, not only for resources but for the very outcomes their rulings pursue, for them to tread routinely on the terrain of legislators or executive agencies without a democratic invitation to do so. Whether their forays into this field, which appear to be on the rise in many countries, will be useful and equitable will depend on the broader legal and institutional environment, as we have argued throughout. But the forays are extremely unlikely to be revolutionary, perhaps to the disappointment of advocates.

In fact, social and economic rights adjudication will probably resemble the judicial review of civil and political rights more than it differs from it. Courts in all likelihood will be unable to prevent predatory states from inflicting social and economic misery on the disadvantaged, in the same way that they have been largely unable to keep tyrannical states from eviscerating domestic liberties. The principal restraint that courts can provide is not the restraint against state-led adventurism, but rather the restraint against the innate human tendencies toward self-regard, the narrowing of sympathies, and group divisions. Benjamin Cardozo put it this way:

The restraining power of the judiciary does not manifest its chief worth in the few cases in which the legislature has gone beyond the lines that mark the limits of discretion. Rather shall we find its chief worth in making vocal and audible the ideals that might be otherwise silenced, in giving them continuity of life and expression, in guiding and directing choice within the limits where choice ranges. (Cardozo 1921: 94)

REFERENCES

Acemoglu, D., S. Johnson, and J. A. Robinson 2001. The colonial origins of comparative development: An empirical investigation. *American Economic Review* 91(December):1369–1401.

Berkowitz, D., K. Pistor, and J. F. Richard. 2003. Economic development, legality and the transplant effect. *European Economic Review* 47:165–195.

Cardozo, B. 1921. *The nature of the judicial process.* New Haven, CT: Yale University Press.

De, A., C. Noronha, and M. Samson. 2005. Toward more benefits from Delhi's midday meal scheme. New Delhi: Collaborative Research and Dissemination.

Dixon, R. 2007. Creating dialogue about socio-economic rights: Strong-form versus weak-form judicial review revisited. *International Journal of Constitutional Law* 5 (3):391–418.

Dworkin, R. 1986. *Law's empire.* Cambridge, MA: Belknap Press.

Epp, C. 2003. *The rights revolution.* Chicago: University of Chicago Press.

Epstein, L., J. Knight, and A. Martin. 2001. The Supreme Court as a strategic national policy maker. *Emory Law Journal* 50 (2):583–611.

Esping-Anderson, G. 1990. *The three worlds of welfare capitalism.* Princeton, NJ: Princeton University Press.

Gauri, V., C. Beyrer, and D. Vaillancourt. 2007. From human rights principles to public health practice: HIV/AIDS policy in Brazil. In C. Beyrer and H. F. Pizer (eds.), *Public health and human rights: Evidence-based approaches.* Baltimore: The John Hopkins University Press.

Ginsburg, T. 2003. *Judicial review in new democracies: Constitutional courts in Asian cases.* Cambridge: Cambridge University Press.

Hirschl, R. 2004. *Towards juristocracy – The origins and consequences of the new constitutionalism.* Cambridge, MA: Harvard University Press.

Karl, Terry Lynn. 2003. The Vicious Cycle of Inequality in Latin America. In *What justice? Whose justice? Fighting for fairness in Latin America* S. E. Eckstein and T. Wickham-Crowley, eds. Berkeley: University of California Press.

Lindert, P. 2004. *Growing public: Social spending and economic growth since the eighteenth Century.* Volume 2, Further Evidence. New York: Cambridge University Press.

McCann, M. 1994. *Rights at work: Pay equity reform and the politics of legal mobilization.* Chicago: University of Chicago Press.

Merryman, J. H. 1985. *The civil law tradition: An introduction to the legal systems of Western Europe and Latin America*, 2nd ed. Palo Alto, CA: Stanford University Press.

Rios-Figueroa, J., and M. Taylor. 2006. Institutional determinants of the judicialisation of policy in Brazil and Mexico. *Journal of Latin American Studies* 38:739–766.

Rosenberg, G. N. 1991. *The hollow hope: Can courts bring about social change?* Chicago: University of Chicago Press.

Rosenn, K. S. 1987. The protection of judicial independence in Latin America. *Inter-American Law Review* 19 (1):1–35.

Rosenn, K. S. 1990. Brazil's new constitution: An exercise in transient constitutionalism for a transitional society. *American Journal of Comparative Law* 38 (Fall):773–802.

Rudra, N. 2007. Welfare regimes in developing countries: Unique or universal. *Journal of Politics* 69 (2):378–396.

Sabel, C., and W. Simon. 2004. Destabilization rights: How public law litigation succeeds. *Harvard Law Review* 117:1016.

Scheingold, S. A. 2004. *The politics of rights: Lawyers, public policy and political change.* 2nd ed. Ann Arbor: University of Michigan Press.

Scheppele, K. L. 2004. A realpolitik defense of social rights. *Texas Law Review* 82:1921.

Scheppele, K. L. 2005. Democracy by judiciary (or why courts can be more democratic than parliaments). In A. Czarnota, M. Krygier, and W. Sadurski (eds.), *Rethinking the rule of law after Communism.* Budapest, Hungary: Central European University Press.

Shapiro, M. 1981. *Courts: A comparative and political analysis.* Chicago and London: University of Chicago Press.

Smulovitz, C. 2005. Petitioning and creating rights: Judicialization in Argentina. In R. Sieder, L. Schjolden, and A. Angell (eds.), *The judicialization of politics in Latin America.* New York: Palgrave / Macmillan.

Stone Sweet, A. 1999. Judicialization and the construction of governance. *Comparative Political Studies* 32 (2):147–184.

Tate, C. N., and T. Vallinder, eds. 1995. *The global expansion of judicial power.* New York: New York University Press.

Taylor, M. 2008. *Judging policy: Courts and policy reform in democratic Brazil.* Palo Alto, CA: Stanford University Press.

Tushnet, M. 2004. Social welfare rights and forms of judicial review. *Texas Law Review* 82:1895.

Vanberg, G. 2001. Legislative–judicial relations: A game-theoretic approach to constitutional review. *American Journal of Political Science* 45 (2):346–361.

von Hayek, F. A. 1960. *The constitution of liberty.* Chicago: University of Chicago Press.

Waldron, J. 1993. A rights-based critique of constitutional rghts. *Oxford Journal of Legal Studies* 13 (1 [Spring]):18–51.

Weyland, K. 1995. Social movements and the state: The politics of health reform in Brazil. *World Development* 23:1699–1712.

Index

1979 Constitution. *See* Constitution, Nigeria
1988 Constitution. *See* Constitution, Brazil

ação civil pública (Public class action), 125, 339, 340
Ação Educativa, 311
Access to public goods, rationed by courts, 221
Access to justice
　Brazil, 111, 112, 142, 143
　India, 154
Accountability
　courts as agents of, 33, 323, 346
　Nigeria, 184
Acquired immune deficiency syndrome. *See* HIV/AIDS
Activism, 147
Adewole & Others v. Alhaji Jakande & Others, 203
Adeyinka A. Badejo v. Federal Minister for Education & 2 Others, 205, 222
Advocacy organizations, 313
Affirmative action, 115
Affordable Medicines Trust v. Minister of Health, 58
African Charter on Human and Peoples' Rights, 187, 188, 194, 195, 202, 209, 212, 213, 317
African Charter on the Rights and Welfare of the Child, 187
African Commission on Human and Peoples' Rights, 32, 187, 212, 219, 221
African Court on Human and Peoples' Rights, 194, 195
African National Congress (ANC), 346
Afrox Healthcare case, 46, 53, 60, 61, 69, 293
AIDS. *See* HIV/AIDS
Air and water pollution. *See* Pollution
Alexy, Robert, 282
Alternative dispute resolution procedures, medical malpractice and right to health, 333
ANC (African National Congress), 346

Antiretroviral treatment (ART)
　Brazil, 120, 122, 136, 144
　effects of litigation on access to, 83
　India, 161, 326
　Interim Procurement case, effect on availability, 93
　South Africa, 53, 56, 79, 84, 93
Apartheid, courts' action during, ix
Archbishop Okogie & Others v. Attorney-General of Lagos State, 203, 204, 219, 221
ART or ARV. *See* Antiretroviral treatment (ART)
Asia Foundation, 225, 226, 227
Asshiddiqie, Jimlie, 288
Association of Judges for Democracy, 106
Association of Legal Aid, Indonesian, 248
Asylum seekers, and right to education, 63, 341
Attitudes, judicial, 315
Attitudinal model, 17, 317
Attorneys, private, 310, 337
Autonomous courts, 18

Backlash in Brazil, 136
Barak, Justice Aharon, 283, 285
Bar association, Indonesian, 248
Basil Ukaegbu v. Attorney-General of Imo State, 205
Beatty, David M., 270
Bel Porto School Governing Body v. Premier, Western Cape, 46, 66
Beneficiary inequality, 335
Bentham, Jeremy, 33
Bhagwati, P. N., 149, 153
Bhopal, 159
BIMARU states, 3, 31, 152, 155, 164, 167, 308
Binding precedent
　Brazil, 103, 136
　India, 148
Boehringer Ingelheim, 57, 87, 96
Bonded labor, protection from, 2
Brandeis briefs, need for in South Africa, xii

Lightning Source UK Ltd.
Milton Keynes UK
UKOW06f0224161016

285345UK00018B/1186/P